KU-418-440

THE I.R.A. AND ITS ENEMIES

'Hart writes with sensitivity, sociological insight and, when necessary, controlled · passion . . . an instant classic.'
Roy Foster, *New Statesman* Books of the Year

'Irish historians have written extensively about the "Troubles" of 1916-23, but few have done so as masterfully or with as much originality as Hart . . . an illuminating, often gripping account that students of modern history, politics, and sociology will find immensely useful.'
Gary Owens, *Choice*

' . . . a rigorous and unflagging exploration of the mentalities and fates of those – Republicans, British forces (and the Free State army) and civilians – caught in the triangular violence of Cork . . . He has set a standard of forensic documentary research which other historians, whether those preparing local studies of the Irish revolution, or those rushing to the defence of the good name of Cork Republicanism, may conceivably emulate but surely will not surpass.'
Eunan O'Halpin, *Times Literary Supplement*

' . . . brilliant new study . . . he has mastered the subtle nuances without an understanding of which community and politics in Cork (and Ireland generally) have little meaning.'
Pauric Travers, *Irish Historical Studies*

' . . . a well researched book, an important book, a controversial book.'
 Brian P Murphy, *The Month*

'There are many surprises in Peter Hart's long-awaited historical masterwork . . . This book's exemplary deployment of statistics and testimonies relates the heroism and terrors of revolutionary Ireland in the context of the society which produced them.'
Patrick Maume, *Irish Studies Review*

The I.R.A.
and Its Enemies

Violence and Community in Cork,
1916–1923

PETER HART

CLARENDON PRESS • OXFORD

*This book has been printed digitally and produced in a standard specification
in order to ensure its continuing availability*

OXFORD
UNIVERSITY PRESS

Great Clarendon Street, Oxford OX2 6DP

Oxford University Press is a department of the University of Oxford.
It furthers the University's objective of excellence in research, scholarship,
and education by publishing worldwide in

Oxford New York

Auckland Cape Town Dar es Salaam Hong Kong Karachi
Kuala Lumpur Madrid Melbourne Mexico City Nairobi
New Delhi Shanghai Taipei Toronto
With offices in
Argentina Austria Brazil Chile Czech Republic France Greece
Guatemala Hungary Italy Japan South Korea Poland Portugal
Singapore Switzerland Thailand Turkey Ukraine Vietnam

Oxford is a registered trade mark of Oxford University Press
in the UK and in certain other countries

Published in the United States
by Oxford University Press Inc., New York

© Peter Hart 1998

The moral rights of the author have been asserted

Database right Oxford University Press (maker)

Reprinted 2009

All rights reserved. No part of this publication may be reproduced,
stored in a retrieval system, or transmitted, in any form or by any means,
without the prior permission in writing of Oxford University Press,
or as expressly permitted by law, or under terms agreed with the appropriate
reprographics rights organization. Enquiries concerning reproduction
outside the scope of the above should be sent to the Rights Department,
Oxford University Press, at the address above

You must not circulate this book in any other binding or cover
And you must impose this same condition on any acquirer

ISBN 978-0-19-820806-8

To my grandmother, Mary Hart,
and to the memory
of my grandfather, Stanley Hart

Preface

What was it like to be in the I.R.A., to fight them, or to be at their mercy? What sort of people joined the organization, and why? What forces or motives drove these men—and their Irish and British opponents—to such heights of violence, transforming them into heroes, martyrs, and killers? These, to me, are the most important and fascinating questions of the Irish revolution of 1916–23. Answering them requires looking at the whole revolution, from beginning to end, in terms of its victims as well as its protagonists. It also means exploring the families and communities in which the guerrillas and their enemies—real or imagined—lived.

This, then, is a study of the rise and fall of the revolutionary movement within a single county: Cork, the most violent of all Irish counties in 'the troubles'. Part I charts the course of the struggle and examines the origins and nature of guerrilla war, as well as its consequences. Part II asks who joined the I.R.A. and Part III asks why—and why some members were willing to do anything and risk everything for their cause. Part IV looks at the people who became targets because they were suspected or accused of opposing the revolution, or because they fell outside the boundaries of the I.R.A.'s 'nation'. The focus throughout is on how the revolution was experienced, presented as often as possible in the words of the participants, observers, and victims themselves. The book, and each of its Parts, begins with a chapter devoted to reconstructing a single event or group: one night of murder and reprisal, one ambush, one flying column, one family, one massacre. These stories illuminate the central themes of comradeship, self-sacrifice, revenge, and betrayal in intimate and often tragic detail.

That it is possible, seventy or more years after the fact, to know so much of what people were thinking and doing at Kilmichael, on Broad Lane, or in Ballinadee is a testament to the magnificent sources available to the historian of the Irish revolution. Thousands of pages of I.R.A. records survive for Cork alone, along with hundreds of interviews and memoirs. We are particularly indebted to the great collectors of such material, Siobhan Lankford, Richard Mulcahy, Art O'Brien, Florence O'Donoghue, and Ernie O'Malley. Official records have largely been declassified, and these include hundreds more statements by victims and their relatives. Vast stores of information are contained in census returns and land records and, at a very different level, in daily and weekly newspapers.

Most importantly, I was able to talk with dozens of those who were there, who could tell me what happened and what it was like. As a group, I liked the former revolutionaries I met very much and, in many ways, I admire them. They still possessed a powerful sense of fellowship, duty, honour, and honesty, reflecting the nobility of commitment which took them through the revolution. What I hope this book shows is that, while we must accept the reality of these virtues, it was these same ideals and passions that unlocked their communities' extraordinary potential for violence. For those on the receiving end of the revolution—whom I have also interviewed—the 'spirit of the movement' could look very different indeed.

This book began as a doctoral thesis at Trinity College, Dublin, under the supervision of David Fitzpatrick. His book *Politics and Irish Life 1913–1921* was one of the primary sources of my interest in Irish history and I feel very fortunate to have had him as a teacher as well. This work would not have been possible without his constant advice, criticism, and encouragement. Also at Trinity College, Aidan Clarke, Louis Cullen, and David Dickson were instrumental in making the Department of Modern History a friendly, supportive, and stimulating place to study. The Social Sciences and Humanities Research Council of Canada provided one of their invaluable doctoral fellowships. I owe a great deal to the teaching of Lucien Karchmar, at Queen's University (Canada), who introduced me to the study of revolution and guerrilla war. Paul Kennedy and Jim Scott of Yale University encouraged my interest in combining these subjects with Irish history. At Memorial University of Newfoundland, I must acknowledge the generosity and help of Rosemary Ommer and the Institute of Social and Economic Research which, along with a further postdoctoral SSHRC fellowship, allowed me to continue my research and writing. Thanks also to Roxanne Millan and Eleanor Fitzpatrick. A University Visiting Fellowship at the Department of Politics, Queen's University at Belfast, enabled me to finish the manuscript.

Among my fellow students in Ireland, Joost Augusteijn, Fergus Campbell, Tom Crean, Kevin Herlihy, Jane Leonard, Chris Morash, Brian Murphy, and Martin Staunton provided irreplaceable debate, companionship, and help. Richard English, Tom Garvin, Michael Hopkinson, and Charles Townshend have all given valuable assistance in the course of this project, just as their work has made the subject an exciting and fascinating one. My writing has benefited especially from the advice and critical attention of Anne Hart, who read it from beginning to end, leaving few pages unimproved. David Hart sharpened many of the arguments and statistics presented here. Robin Whitaker has a share in the making of this book as a reader, critic, and problem-solver, and also because she has shared my life while it has been written—for which, much more than thanks.

The staffs of the following libraries and archives were enormously hospitable and helpful in guiding me through their collections, and I am grateful for their permission to quote from the documents in their care: the University College Dublin Departments of Archives and of Irish Folklore, the National Library of Ireland, the National Archives, the Irish Valuation Office, the Trinity College Record Office, the Representative Church Body Library, the Imperial War

Museum, the family of A. E. Percival, the National Army Museum, the Liddell Hart Centre for Military Archives, the House of Lords Record Department, the Public Record Office, the Cork Archives Institute, the Cork County Museum, the Cork City Library, the County Cork Library, the Public Record Office of Northern Ireland, Queen's University Special Collections, the Grand Orange Lodge of Ireland Archives, the Buffs Regimental Museum, the Staffordshire Regiment Museum, the Queen's Lancashire Regiment Museum, the Regional History Department of the National Museums and Galleries on Merseyside, the Tameside Local Studies Library, the Trustees of the Museum of the Manchesters, the Royal Gloucestershire Regiment Archives, and the Boston Public Library. In particular, I would like to acknowledge the help (far beyond the call of duty) of Peter Young and Victor Laing of the Irish Military Archives, Patricia McCarthy of the Cork Archives Institute, Seamus Helferty of the UCD Archives, Kieran Burke of Cork City Library, Peter Liddle at Leeds University, and Gerry Lyne of the National Library.

In Dublin, I owe many thanks to Marion and Jim O'Driscoll for their help and kindness, and for introducing me to Cork. Terry and Eithne Barry, Anita Begley, Dr John Chisholm, Uinseann MacEoin, Kevin Myers, and Sean O'Mahony were generous with their time, assistance, friendship and hospitality. I am most grateful to Eithne Barry as well for allowing me to read Marie O'Donoghue's writings. In Cork, my debts are far too numerous to acknowledge, so the list that follows must unfortunately be partial: Sean Beecher, Michael Burrows, David Catterall, Con and Oriana Conner, John Faris, Ferran Glenfield, Sean Hales, Peter Hanna, Richard Henderson, Jack Lane, Dermot Lucey, Harold Miller, Liam O'Donnchadha, Donal O'Donovan, Patrick O'Flanagan, George O'Mahony, and Pat O'Sullivan. Particular thanks to John Fenning, Richard Moylan, and to Bernadette and Louis Whyte. The many interviewees who remembered the revolution with me made this a wholly different and better work. I cannot thank them by name because so many wished to remain anonymous, but I delighted in meeting them, and I treasure their words. I know that not all of these people will agree with everything I have written but I could not have written without them.

At Oxford University Press, Tony Morris was a most patient and supportive guide in steering this project on its way, Jackie Pritchard saved me from many errors by her superb copy-editing, and Jane Williams brought it happily to its conclusion.

P. H.

Contents

List of Figures

List of Tables

Abbreviations

Adj.	Adjutant
AFIL	All For Ireland League
A/G	Adjutant General
Bde.	Brigade
Bn.	Battalion
CI	County Inspector
Cork 1	1st (Mid-) Cork Brigade
Cork 2	2nd (North) Cork Brigade
Cork 3	3rd (West) Cork Brigade
Cork 4	4th (North-West) Cork Brigade [from July 1921]
Cork 5	5th (South-West) Cork Brigade [from July 1921]
Coy.	Company
C/S	Chief of Staff
D/I	Director of Intelligence
DI	District Inspector
Div.	Division
GHQ	General Headquarters
IG	Inspector General
I/O	Intelligence Officer
I.R.A.	Irish Republican Army
I.R.B.	Irish Republican Brotherhood
O/C	Officer in Command
Org.	Organizer
R.I.C.	Royal Irish Constabulary

ARCHIVES

CAI	Cork Archives Institute
HLRO	House of Lords Records Office
IWM	Imperial War Museum
MA	Military Archives of Ireland
NA	National Archives of Ireland
NLI	National Library of Ireland
PRO	Public Record Office, London
PRONI	Public Record Office of Northern Ireland
TCD	Trinity College Dublin Archives
UCC	University College Cork Archives
UCD	University College Dublin Archives

RECORDS

CO	Colonial Office
CSO	Chief Secretary's Office
DE	Dail Eireann
GPB	General Prisons Board
HO	Home Office
SIC	Special Infantry Corps
WO	War Office

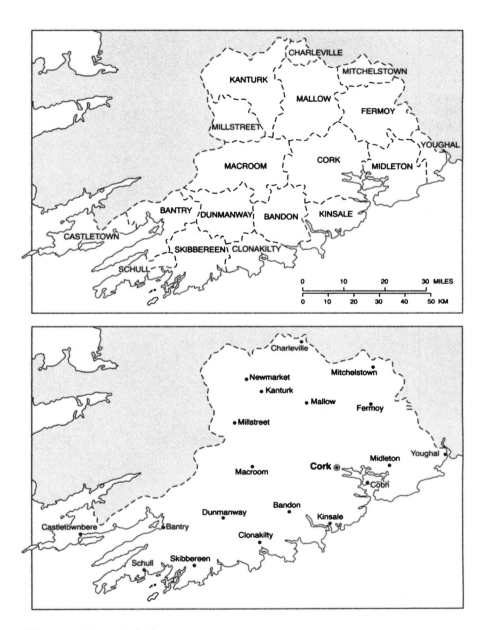

Districts and towns in Cork

Note: The boundaries shown are those of the Rural/Union Districts.

1

Introduction: The Killing of
Sergeant O'Donoghue

Men like my father were dragged out, in those years, and shot down as traitors to their country. Shot for cruel necessity—so be it. Shot to inspire necessary terror—so be it. But they were not traitors. They had their loyalties, and stuck to them.

(Sean O'Faolain, *Vive Moi!*)[1]

James O'Donoghue was born in 1874 into a large farming family near the town of Cahirciveen, in western Kerry. The O'Donoghues were good tenants and good Catholics—exemplars of rural respectability. Their hillside farm was small but land gave them the security to educate their children well despite the economic ups and downs which troubled western Ireland in the 1870s and 1880s. Their ambitions were aided by their older daughters, Mary, Julia, Ellen, and Nora, who emigrated to the United States and sent money home to provide for the training of their younger brothers and sisters. These efforts were repaid by the new generation's rapid advancement up the professional ladder, primarily through service to church and state. One sister entered a convent in America, another became a nurse, and one brother became a doctor. Another, Michael, entered the priesthood, thus fulfilling the dream of many an Irish family ('There was the old tradition of respectability with its three hallmarks—a pump in the yard; a bull for your cows, and a priest in the family'[2]). In 1898, at age 24, James joined the Royal Irish Constabulary, another avenue of social mobility popular among the farming people of Kerry and a further guarantor of the family's rising social status.[3] After serving in several counties, he was transferred to Cork city.[4]

---

[1] Sean O'Faolain, *Vive Moi!* (Boston, 1963), 39. His father was a member of the Royal Irish Constabulary in Cork city.

[2] Peter Somerville-Large, *Cappaghglass* (Dublin, 1984), 325. The social benefits and financial costs of having a son enter the priesthood are vividly portrayed in T. C. Murray's 1912 play *Maurice Harte*, set in West Cork.

[3] Patrick O'Shea, *Voices and the Sound of Drums* (Belfast, 1981) is the memoir of a son of another Kerry policeman (a contemporary of O'Donoghue's) and a valuable insight into their values and attitudes.

[4] This account of the O'Donoghues is based on the R.I.C. General Register (PRO, HO/184/30), on information from Eithne Barry, the granddaughter of James O'Donoghue, and on the Marie O'Donoghue Papers (in Eithne Barry's possession). Marie, James's daughter, kept a detailed diary between October 1968 and April 1970 while searching for her father's killers in Cork city (hereafter referred to as O'Donoghue Diary). This extraordinary document includes interviews with old I.R.A. men, their relatives, and other witnesses.

James married in 1905 and settled with his wife on Tower Street, on the south side of the city. They lived on the edge of an old and densely populated working-class and commercial district centred on nearby Barrack Street. A number of other policemen lived close by so their children grew up together, with much of the families' everyday life revolving around the barracks. Their immediate neighbours were artisans, shopkeepers, and clerks who lived in decent houses, but the other end of the road was considerably rougher, with more labourers and lodgers and fewer family homes.[5]

Whether he knew it or not, James was following in the footsteps of generations of his people, who moved east to Cork from their hill and valley homes. Barrack Street—'Barracka'—the main artery of the area, had traditionally been the city's road to the west, and the neighbourhood had thus been heavily settled by migrants from West Cork and Kerry, several of his comrades among them. Three out of seven constables at O'Donoghue's station were Kerrymen in 1911.[6] Here was one of Cork's 'unacknowledged Irishtowns'.[7] These settlers helped create a distinctive communal identity around such local institutions as St Finbarr's hurling club and the Barrack Street Band with their networks of pubs, rooms, and supporters. As with all such strong neighbourhoods in the city, it was frequently at odds with the others over politics, sports, and everything else.[8]

James O'Donoghue was, in many ways, a typical Irish policeman. Most of his colleagues had similar upbringings on small Catholic farms. When James joined in 1898, the R.I.C. was at the height of its status and popularity as a career, both in Ireland as a whole and in Kerry in particular. 'In Kerry you could hardly go into a house without a son on the police or if they hadn't they had a brother.' Neighbouring boys with the right qualifications often vied for a place on the force.[9]

James did well. He passed his exams and was promoted to sergeant after twenty-one years of service, a good (although not spectacular) record.[10] With luck he could look forward to being made a head constable before his time was

---

[5] This information, and the description of Tower and Barrack streets, came from the manuscript returns for the 1911 census (National Archives (hereafter NA)), and from Sean Beecher, *The Story of Cork* (Cork, 1971), 60, 62–3.

[6] 1911 census return, Tuckey Street barracks.

[7] Sean O'Faolain, *An Irish Journey* (New York, 1943), 81.

[8] See Richard T. Cooke, *Cork's Barrack Street Band: Ireland's Oldest Amateur Musical Institution* (Cork, 1992); Con O'Leary, *Wayfarer in Ireland* (London, 1935), 162; and Anthony Griffin, 'The Origins, Growth and Influence of the G.A.A. in Cork City', BA thesis (University College Cork, 1988), 14–15. For some reflections on the social geography of the city, see William J. Smyth, 'Explorations of Space', in Joseph Lee (ed.), *Ireland: Towards a Sense of Place* (Cork, 1985), 9–12.

[9] John D. Brewer, *The Royal Irish Constabulary: An Oral History* (Belfast, 1990), 66. For the social background of police recruits, see ibid. 33–43, 53–4, and *Appendix to the Report of the Committee of Inquiry into the Royal Irish Constabulary and the Dublin Metropolitan Police* (Cd. 7637, 1914), 18, 31, and 126. See also Brian Griffin's excellent Ph.D. thesis, 'The Irish Police, 1836–1914: A Social History' (Loyola University of Chicago, 1991), 849, 855.

[10] *Committee of Inquiry into the R.I.C. and the D.M.P.*, 11.

up. The sergeant's role was an important one, with substantial prestige and authority. He was in charge of his constables and barracks on a day-to-day basis and was also the symbol of the government in his district. 'A sergeant of the police, they all went to him for everything, nearly, he was the chief advisor and all like—even in 1921 and 1922'; 'the sergeant was the main man in the constabulary, he was the pivot man'.[11] In return for this advancement and authority, O'Donoghue remained steadfastly loyal to the system—not just to the Crown and the constabulary, but also to the traditional way of doing things, with discipline and moderation.

Loyalty to the service was also underlined by the tight-knit camaraderie of the men and their families and by the distance between this world and the rest of Irish society, which increased after the turn of the century. In the decade after O'Donoghue joined the quality and quantity of recruits began to go down, a consequence of government neglect and better opportunities elsewhere. This was accompanied by a rise in hostility towards the force and its officers. County, district, and municipal councils in the south, in the hands of the nationalist Irish Party after the Local Government Act of 1898, discriminated against serving and retired policemen over jobs and housing. Some trade unions followed suit. The increasingly influential Gaelic Athletic Association refused to admit policemen, and these sentiments were echoed by other groups. It was generally felt by such organizations and many of their members that the R.I.C. was anti-nationalist.[12] This may have had little impact on popular attitudes—the sergeant's authority was still intact in many places well into the revolution—but it certainly intensified the sense of isolation within the R.I.C. When a Royal Commission was created in 1914 to investigate the condition of the force, witness after witness told of the anxiety which permeated the constabulary about their place in Irish society and their fears for the future.[13]

It was worse than they could have imagined. The rise of Sinn Fein, an insignificant political force before the Easter Rising of 1916, swept away the old political order and paved the way for confrontation, revolution, and a gradual descent into guerrilla war, with the men of the R.I.C. on the front lines. In 1920 Cork became one of the main battlefields.

Sergeant O'Donoghue was stationed on Tuckey Street in 'the flat of the city' from before the Great War, and became well known and respected there. He had little to do with political policing and by all accounts 'was good to the Sinn Feiners around the city'.[14] The I.R.A. considered him neither an active enemy nor a 'spy' and even his superiors considered him a 'harmless unoffending man'.[15] He and his family stayed on good terms with their neighbours, despite

---

[11] Brewer, *The Royal Irish Constabulary*, 56, 81.

[12] See, however, Griffin, 'The Irish Police', 690–3.

[13] See *Committee of Inquiry into the R.I.C. and D.M.P.*, 25, 75, 83, 102.

[14] Interview with Charlie O'Brien in O'Donoghue Diary, 13 Feb. 1969. See also interview with Elizabeth O'Connor, 6 Feb. 1969, and with two unnamed witnesses to the shooting, 31 Oct. 1968.

[15] Monthly Report of the County Inspector for the East Riding of Co. Cork (hereafter: CI Monthly Report, East Cork), Nov. 1920. (CO 904/113).

the fact that a number of them were sympathizers or members of the republican movement.

O'Donoghue remained committed to his job and the force, but after the summer of 1920 the stolid constabulary to which he had devoted his life began to change rapidly and for the worse. His constables were given rifles, grenades, and machine guns and were put on a war footing to face the aggressive young guerrillas of the Irish Republican Army. Irish recruits dwindled almost to nothing and resignations rose sharply. New British recruits began to pour in, belligerent, badly trained, and ignorant of the country. They were veterans of the Great War ready to fight another.

These men—dubbed 'Black and Tans' because of their motley uniforms—were hard to manage and had little respect for the older officers. The discipline and restraint which were so much a part of O'Donoghue and his force began to disintegrate along with the old order. Police riots and killings became routine. One old Irish policeman said of the new men: 'They weren't as disciplined as the R.I.C., not at all. They were on their own, hurt one and you hurt them all.'[16]

Tuckey Street acquired a bad reputation along with the new arrivals. 'They took over Tuckey Street and the pub beside it.'[17] O'Donoghue himself had to contend with more than one drunken outburst or brawl. On Saturday, 2 October, for example, two drunken Auxiliary cadets (a special police force recruited from ex-military officers) being taunted by a crowd on Patrick Street opened fire on their tormentors and wounded two civilians. In the fracas that followed, one of the Auxiliaries was also wounded, but constables from Tuckey Street, led by O'Donoghue, arrived in time to prevent further trouble.[18] A similar incident involving 'a drunken Tan' took place on 31 October.[19]

October also saw the war move decisively into the city. It was the worst month by far for I.R.A. ambushes. One policeman was killed and three were wounded, along with one soldier killed and two wounded in an ambush on Barrack Street.[20] O'Donoghue nevertheless still felt safe following the usual habits of the neighbourhood policeman, although his wife grew increasingly worried. Many other policemen moved into barracks. He wore his uniform openly, never carried a gun, and continued to live on Tower Street, walking to work every day. Such was his routine on Wednesday, 17 November, as his daughter Marie later recalled:

---

[16]   Brewer, *The Royal Irish Constabulary*, 111.

[17]   Interview with BY, 17 Nov. 1994 (to maintain their anonymity, the people I interviewed are identified with initials only, former I.R.A. and Cumann na mBan members having the first letter 'A', Protestant civilians, the first letter 'B'. See also the note on interviews in the bibliography). See also Maud Mitchell, *The Man with the Long Hair: The Spirit of Freedom in a Woman's Story* (Glenwood, 1993), 41.

[18]   *Cork Examiner* (hereafter referred to as the *Examiner*), 4 Oct. 1920.

[19]   O'Donoghue Diary, 31 Oct. 1968.

[20]   The sources for these figures are detailed in the Appendix.

My father came home from duty about 3.15 p.m. He was in uniform: no coat . . . It was a mild day with a touch of frost later. I asked my father when he was returning to Tuckey Street police station, intending to accompany him—it had been a practice of mine in dangerous times—but my father detested it and only agreed to it because it relieved mother's anxiety. He said he would leave at 5.50.

I went out after tea and spent some time at Timmins' house. The ringing of the Angelus—as I believed—made me rush out and when I reached the house I found that my father had left. 'He is gone only a few minutes.' I was terribly disappointed. I had arranged to call for groceries at Union Quay police station and Kitty Keating was to accompany me. At the gate I heard shots—there seemed to be six. I told my mother and she came out. There were no further reports. I made my way towards Union Quay with Kitty Keating.

I collected the provisions and returned with Keating. I met Nellie O'Connell in Douglas street. She stopped me and told me. There I learned that it was my father who was shot. 'Your father was shot in White Street this evening and your mother is in Tuckey Street.' Mrs. Mary A. Hayes, the wife of Sgt. Mick Hayes, had brought the news. She had heard the shots and rushed out as Sgt. Hayes had just left the house on Eastview Terrace. She kept saying he (my father) was only wounded. I knew he was dead.

I went with my mother to Tuckey Street station to get further information. 'Nothing definite' said Head Constable Brown, being evasive.

There were some Tans present. Someone declared that somebody would pay for the night. My mother begged that no further violence or vengeance should follow.

We returned home sick at heart. I found my brother and we spent the night praying. My mother did not know that my father was dead. Mrs. Timmins brought the news in the morning. My mother was overcome.

We awaited the arrival of Father Michael O'Donoghue and he and my mother went to the Military Hospital to identify my father. We never saw our father again.[21]

James O'Donoghue was shot three times as he walked down White Street on his way back to work—twice in the back and once in the head. Dusk and the gloom of an oncoming storm allowed the killers to fire at very close range. An ambulance and a priest were quickly on the scene but James O'Donoghue was already dead.[22]

His body was brought to the military hospital in Victoria Barracks on the north side of the city. Here his wife and brother identified him and then took his remains to church. No undertaker would handle a policeman's body because of the Sinn Fein boycott so a car had to be rented outside the city to take James's remains to his family plot near Cahirciveen.[23]

Who shot James O'Donoghue? Some of his enraged comrades at Tuckey Street thought they knew. The night of 17 November was an extremely stormy one. Cork was lashed by high winds and heavy gusts of rain.[24] As the Corporation

[21]   Marie O'Donoghue, MS account of the events of 17 Nov. 1920 (Marie O'Donoghue Papers).
[22]   *Examiner*, 18, 24 Nov. 1920; eyewitness accounts in O'Donoghue Diary, 31 Oct. 1968. See also *Cork Constitution* (hereafter *Constitution*), 18 Nov. 1920, which suggests that O'Donoghue fell after the first two shots and was then finished off with a bullet in the back of the head.
[23]   O'Donoghue account.
[24]   See Celia Saunders's Diary, 18 Nov. 1920 (TCD, Frank Gallagher Papers, MS 10, 055).

had retaliated against the military-imposed curfew by shutting off the street lights, the city was in complete darkness—a haven and stalking ground for killers. On this terrible night, six hours after O'Donoghue's death, two armed and disguised men made their way through a dark warren of streets to an old and crowded tenement house in the poorest part of downtown Cork, known as 'the Marsh':

Mrs. Coleman, wife of Stephen Coleman, 2 Broad Street, said she was awakened about 11.45 p.m. by the noise of the front door being broken open. The next thing she heard was the sound of a man running up the stairs, and there and then a crash at the bedroom door. The door was kicked open, it being forced on its hinges, and in rushed a man in police uniform, a policeman's cap, and goggles. He came over towards the bedside, and she saw he had a flash lamp in one hand and a revolver in the other . . . The man merely exclaimed 'Hallo!' and flashing the lamp on the bed, he raised his revolver and fired point blank into the bed. The bullet wounded her husband in the arm. The assailant then turned and walked out of the room, leaving Mrs. Coleman screaming . . .

Mr. John Kenny, who was sleeping upstairs with Mr. Patrick Hanley, stated that Hanley opened the door when he heard a man rushing up the stairs. The man, in police uniform, had just come from Mrs. Coleman's room. Hanley, standing at his bedroom door, said 'Don't shoot! I am an orphan and my mother's chief support!' 'Very well!' replied the man, and, raising his revolver, he fired at Hanley. The bullet missed him, but the man fired a second time, and the bullet struck Hanley just above the heart, killing him instantly . . . The rooms occupied by Mrs. Long and her mother on the same landing as Mr. Coleman were also broken into by the same assailant, but seeing there was nobody there only two women, he went out without discharging any shots. The man in police uniform also rushed into the bedroom of Mr. Collins, who was sleeping with his wife and child in a room adjoining that in which Hanley was killed. 'The man . . . carried a revolver in one hand and a flash lamp in the other. He flashed the light on the bed and fired point blank at us. The bullet grazed my head, and passed through the bedclothes and bed. I found it under the bed the next morning.' Mr. Collins said he remained perfectly still, and by doing so probably saved his life, for his assailant rushed out of the room, leaving him for dead.[25]

As the two masked men left the house, one turned and, in a final gesture of rage, threw a grenade which exploded and wrecked the hall. From Broad Street the pair walked around the corner to No. 17 Broad Lane:

The front door was broken in about midnight, and a man in police uniform with a police-man's cap, and wearing goggles, burst into the hall . . . He rushed straight up the stairs, and [Eugene] O'Connell, who was sleeping with his wife and child in a room on the first floor, came out to the landing to see what all the noise was about. Just before he reached the landing, the man flashed his lamp on O'Connell, and raising his revolver, fired point-blank at him. The bullet struck O'Connell in the wrist. He ran into the bedroom, where his wife and child were in bed, and was followed relentlessly by his assailant, who shot

[25] *Examiner*, 19 Nov. 1920. There is little doubt about the accuracy of these accounts, which were corroborated by witnesses both at the time and at the subsequent inquest, and repeated in the unionist *Constitution*.

him dead in the bedroom in the presence of his wife. The man then came out of the bedroom and ran up another flight of stairs.

Mrs. O'Brien . . . hearing the shots downstairs, came out of her room. She states she was met half-way down the stairs by the man, revolver in hand, rushing up. She called to him that there was no one above only two children, but he paid no attention to her, and when she endeavoured to prevent him from going up, he pushed her roughly aside, and continued towards Charles O'Brien's room. She heard a shot above them, and in a half-fainting condition she saw the policeman hurry downstairs past her. When she got to the room, she found her son Charles, stretched on the floor near the bed, bleeding from the mouth.

Her other son, Michael, a boy of ten years was in bed in the same room. He told her Charles had gone to the landing and was shot there by a man. He managed to crawl in to where he had fallen. He also said the assailant had come over to the bedside and flashing the lamp on him, raised his revolver. The boy exclaimed, 'Don't shoot me. I am too young.' The man then lowered his revolver and hurrying downstairs went out of the house.[26]

Patrick Hanley had been shot in the heart and killed. Eugene O'Connell had been hit three times and killed. Stephen Coleman had been wounded in the arm. Charles O'Brien had been shot in the face and critically wounded. Minutes later, despite continued wild shooting and the presence of police in the area, 'a number of women [from Broad Lane] came screaming and calling for the ambulance to the Grattan Street Fire Station'. O'Brien and O'Connell were taken to the Mercy Hospital. The residents of Broad Street were not so brave, and did not venture into the dark streets for two hours, by which time Hanley was beyond help.

If Mrs O'Brien had waited that long her son would have died as well. However, Charlie O'Brien was lucky and survived, losing an eye and much of his jaw. He took months to recover and was kept hidden in the meantime. When he finally left the hospital he was smuggled out in a laundry basket.[27]

The final act of the night took place at No. 15 North Mall, just across the north channel of the Lee from 'the Marsh', at around four o'clock in the morning. Here James Coleman (no relation to Stephen) and his family were awakened by a loud knocking and shouts of 'Military!' Such raids had become commonplace in Cork as the police and army were constantly searching for arms and wanted men. Mrs Coleman's account follows:

When my husband opened the door a tall man, wearing a policeman's cap and a heavy overcoat, stepped in, and asked 'Are you Coleman?' My husband said 'yes.' This man then fired two shots point blank at my husband, and he fell on the chair beside the door. The man then swung around as if to leave, but he again turned and fired two or three shots more.

I rushed to my husband's assistance, but he never spoke. The man who had murdered him left, and pulled the door quickly after him. Ten minutes later a 'Black and Tan'

---

[26] *Examiner*, 19 Nov. 1920.
[27] Interviews with Elizabeth O'Connor and Charlie O'Brien (O'Donoghue Diary).

whom I know by appearance came to the door and the maid who had come down to me, opened it for him. He had a revolver in his hand, and when he came inside the door, I said to him: 'There is enough done.' The maid, who knows him, said: 'He is alright; he will do nothing.' I then said to him: 'Why did ye kill him?' He answered: 'We didn't do it.' I said: 'Ye did it: I saw it being done' and he replied 'Perhaps it was Sinn Feiners dressed in our uniforms.' I repeated that I knew who did it, and asked what would I do. He felt my husband's pulse and said he was dead.[28]

No one was ever brought to trial for the killings on White Street, Broad Street, Broad Lane, or the North Mall. The police made perfunctory inquiries about the civilian deaths, but they were refused admittance to No. 2 Broad Lane. Hannah O'Brien, the mother of Charlie and mother-in-law of Eugene O'Connell, also refused to testify at the inquest.

At James O'Donoghue's funeral Father Michael was told by another policeman that 'We got one of the men who killed your brother Wednesday night.'[29] He was right. Three men had shot the sergeant. Charlie O'Brien was one of them. The other two were his older brother William, and their neighbour (and future brother-in-law) Justin O'Connor. The police knew that the O'Brien brothers were 'deep in the movement'.[30] In fact the whole family was.

William (Willie Joe), a hairdresser, 21, was a junior officer in the local I.R.A. unit (G Company, 1st Battalion). He had been arrested and imprisoned twice before and had taken part in hunger strikes. He was now on the run from a third arrest, sleeping away from home, and was thus not there on the night of the 17th. William was the main target of the police reprisals—the one that got away. Charlie, an apprentice mechanic aged 17, was officially a member of the Fianna Eireann, the republican boy scouts. More importantly, both he and William were part of the small, informal 'active squad' of gunmen who took most of the risks and did most of the dirty work.[31] These men and boys formed the cutting edge of the guerrilla campaign.

Tom O'Brien, 29, Charlie and William's older brother, was an official of the Seamen's and Firemen's Union. He was not a fighter like the other two. In any case he was too important a part of the Cork Brigades' arms pipeline from Liverpool and Germany to be risked in gunplay. Going by the name of Fitzgerald, and living away from Broad Lane, he managed to evade police notice.

Hannah O'Brien, 53, was a native of the 'Marsh'. Her husband had died while working on a Cork Steampacket Company ship torpedoed during the war,

---

[28]   *Examiner*, 19 Nov. 1920. See also the report of the inquest on 26 November for a slightly different account.

[29]   Quoted in 'Private Investigations into Murder', a MS account by Marie O'Donoghue's brother of his own researches (Marie O'Donoghue Papers).

[30]   Interview with Elizabeth O'Connor (O'Donoghue Diary). The following biographical information comes from these interviews with Elizabeth O'Connor and Charlie O'Brien, manuscript census returns, and an I.R.A. register of Civil War prisoners in the Irish Military Archives (MA, A/1135).

[31]   Interview with Charlie O'Brien (O'Donoghue Diary).

but she had been the effective head of the family for many years before that. Hannah was the great political influence in her children's lives. She was a long-time friend of Liz Walsh, a committed Gaelic Leaguer and republican who married Tomas MacCurtain, the Sinn Fein Lord Mayor of Cork and commander of its I.R.A. brigade until he was murdered by policemen in March 1920. Mrs MacCurtain was Charlie's godmother and Hannah named her only daughter after her.

Mrs O'Brien was a determined and active rebel who brought her children up to be as ardently republican as she. She carried arms and messages for the I.R.A. (wearing a long fur coat to cover the bandoliers of bullets) and encouraged her sons in their fight. When they went to prison she brought them food and clean clothes every day. Inevitably her family was marked down by the British—and later the Free State—authorities and her house became a frequent target for raids. Hannah's defiance of the enemy, whether English or Irish, was uncompromising. On the night of 17 November she was the only person to stand up to the intruders and she refused to cooperate in any way with the police or the inquest.

Elizabeth (Lizzie) O'Brien, her daughter of 25, shared the family politics and helped her brothers as best she could. In 1919 she married Eugene O'Connell, who was to fall victim to the shootings in Broad Lane a year later. Eugene was a veteran of the Royal Munster Fusiliers, whose family belonged to a very different tradition of service in the British army. Eugene's father, two uncles, and two of his brothers had all served in the ranks, and he himself had been wounded in the war. He and Elizabeth now lived with their baby girl in the flat below the O'Briens.[32]

For the O'Briens, family and politics were inextricably linked and Eugene was swiftly drawn into his in-laws' circle. 'He did not join the I.R.A., but drilled them in the use of guns, manœuvres etc., and helped them whenever necessary.'[33] Ex-soldiers were generally considered enemies by the I.R.A. and were rarely allowed to join. Once the organization became embroiled in a shooting war in 1920, however, activists like the O'Briens sought out veterans to help them with weapons and training. Nevertheless, considerable suspicion of these men remained, and O'Connell's ambiguous status may reflect this. After Eugene O'Connell's death Elizabeth married Justin O'Connor, the third member of the party that shot O'Donoghue. Once again marriage and the cause went hand in hand.

The other fatal victim in the 'Marsh' that night was Patrick Hanley, a manual labourer and a close friend of Charlie O'Brien. They were the same age and had joined the Fianna together. Patrick was no O'Brien, however, being neither militant nor bright. 'Hanley's mother and sister were simple. He had a want, but not quite as bad as they. He never handled a gun. He would run from one. The Fianna movement made him happy.' He joined to belong and to be with friends—'it would not have mattered to what party he belonged.'[34]

---

[32] *Examiner*, 19, 24 Nov. 1920.
[33] Interview with Elizabeth O'Connor (O'Donoghue Diary).   [34] Ibid.

Hanley and O'Connell were targets by association. Whatever information the police received about the O'Briens presumably also linked them with Hanley and O'Connell, who was thought by some neighbours to be in the I.R.A. Stephen Coleman and Mr Collins had no connection with the O'Briens, as far as can be discovered. They were both ex-Munster Fusiliers like Eugene O'Connell and simply had the misfortune to live at No. 2 Broad Street with Patrick Hanley and his family. They became targets by proximity.

James Coleman was a different case altogether. A highly successful and progressive businessman at 43, he owned a mineral water factory and several pubs, and was the treasurer of the Cork Industrial Development Association and a prominent member of the Chamber of Commerce, one of many active new members who joined during the prosperous war years.[35] Coleman had had several confrontations with the new English policemen over the previous months. He had refused to serve them in one of his pubs when they got rowdy, and complained to the military authorities about their behaviour. He had been threatened several times on this account but he was no Sinn Feiner. His clashes with the Tans and Auxies were probably enough to mark him out as being 'disloyal' and an enemy, and perhaps the drunken killer also wanted personal revenge for his slights.

It is unclear whether James Coleman's killer was one of the men who shot up Broad Street and Broad Lane. Certainly all of those involved were policemen and probably Black and Tans. One witness reported hearing English accents. Such reprisals were growing increasingly common as the R.I.C. became more and more beleaguered and frustrated. In October, soldiers and policemen had shot five people, bombed a home and a shop, and set fire to the City Hall. In the first two weeks of November Christy Lucey, an active I.R.A. officer, was gunned down in the street and two more civilians were shot. The dark hours after curfew were dangerous ones.

These murders were also becoming more organized. There is considerable evidence that, as republicans asserted then and ever since, some sort of death squads had emerged within the R.I.C. by late 1920. There may well have been a regular group of men in Cork, the counterpart of the I.R.A.'s 'active squad', who carried out extrajudicial killings. Whether coordinated or not, the killings were usually carried out under a common cover name: the Anti-Sinn Fein Society. Threatening letters were issued under the same title. This mysterious body was presented as a widespread secret society, but the disguise fooled no one.

These government vigilantes had little reason to fear getting caught. Their superiors usually turned a blind eye or even encouraged them to take the law into their own hands. Although the killers probably acted on their own initiative, the shootings of 17 and 18 November were at least tacitly approved of by the

---

[35] See the 1919 Annual Report of the Cork Industrial Development Association (CAI, U141) and Thomas Linehan, 'The Development of Cork's Economy and Business Attitudes, 1910–1939', MA thesis (University College Cork, 1985), 41.

local district inspector. It was he who told Father Michael O'Donoghue that 'we got one of the men' who shot the sergeant.[36]

Such groups and their activities were an outgrowth of the siege mentality and accompanying sense of desperate comradeship that prevailed in police barracks, especially among the British newcomers. They had to put their faith in their friends and fellows alone, in the face of a hostile population and a judicial system and political leadership which had completely failed to stop the guerrillas. Even when dangerous men like William O'Brien were caught, they were soon let go to serve popular opinion and the vagaries of British policy. Policemen could not help feeling betrayed and afraid for their lives, and it is not surprising that they reacted so violently when attacked. 'Hurt one and you hurt them all.'

Some, like Sergeant O'Donoghue, tried to keep a low profile and maintain the old routines. 'In County Cork you just fluffed your way through the streets as well as you could without drawing any attention.'[37] Others, like those who avenged O'Donoghue's death, hit back—against suspected guerrillas, their sympathizers, and the Irish as a whole. One survivor recalled: 'you were at war, you had to try and make the best of it, and if you didn't kill someone, someone was going to kill you.'[38]

Broad Lane was run-down, very poor, and very crowded, a dense little world held together by families and a common workplace. Like other streets and lanes in the city it had been colonized by a particular occupational group—in this case, dock labourers and seamen. Most of the men of Broad Lane worked on ships or quays, including Hannah O'Brien's husband and her son Tom.[39]

The Lane was a jumble of ancient, once grand, tenement houses and tiny shops, the inhabitants of which lived three to a room on average. Illiteracy and infant mortality were both high. Two of Hannah O'Brien's own children had not survived childhood. Working on the docks sometimes paid well but it was hard labour with little job security. The army and navy offered one way out of unemployment and distress and it is not surprising that the Munster Fusiliers gained so many recruits like Eugene O'Connell from these streets.[40] This was a 'rough', overwhelmingly Catholic neighbourhood inhabited by the oft-reviled 'laneys' and 'shawlies', looked down on by more respectable working-class and middle-class

---

[36]   O'Donoghue Diary, 6, 13 Feb. 1969.
[37]   Brewer, *The Royal Irish Constabulary*, 89–90.
[38]   Ibid. 103.
[39]   Census returns for Broad Lane, 1901 and 1911.
[40]   See Martin Staunton, 'The Royal Munster Fusiliers in the Great War, 1914–1919' (MA thesis, UCD, 1986), 22–3, 82. The description of Broad Lane is based on manuscript census returns for 1901 and 1911, the *Examiner*, 18, 19 Nov. 1920, and Beecher, *The Story of Cork*, 70. See also Michael Verdon, *Shawlies, Echo Boys, the Marsh and the Lanes* (Dublin, 1993), 33–43, 64–75. A lengthy portrait of tenement life in 'the Marsh' can be found in Frank O'Connor's novel *The Saint and Mary Kate* (London, 1932).

areas located above the flat of the city (such as the one in which the O'Donoghues lived). It did not have a GAA club or a band to follow but it did produce strong loyalties, at least among the women. This solidarity was demonstrated by those who helped Hannah O'Brien and Lizzie O'Connell on the night of 17 November, and who paid their respects to Eugene O'Connell and Patrick Hanley at the mortuary and the funeral.[41]

Having lived in Broad Lane for over twenty years, the O'Briens were very much a part of this community—but they were moving up and, eventually, out. Even in 'the Marsh' there were many degrees of poverty and Hannah's family was rising steadily through the ranks. In the decade after 1901 the O'Briens moved from living nine to a room in No. 8 to five rooms for seven people in No. 7. This represented a great leap forward in their standard of living and made them much better off than most of their neighbours. By 1920 they had even more space and no longer needed to take in a lodger.[42] Due in large part to Hannah, the O'Brien children all had secondary educations, a signal achievement in the slums of Edwardian Cork. Tom, Willie, and Charlie were all upwardly mobile and learning trades or, in Tom's case, moving from manual labour to office work and union organizing.

In their youth and social and family background, the O'Brien brothers were typical of many of their fellow I.R.A. activists. Drawn almost entirely from the working and lower middle classes but disproportionately literate, skilled, and employed—more so than their fathers or neighbours—the guerrillas tended to be young men getting ahead in the world: the 'finest young men in the country'.[43] The way in which kinship and politics were intertwined in the O'Brien household was also very common, as the I.R.A. usually ran in families. Nor was Hannah's matriarchal role at all unusual. At least a quarter of the Army's membership had absent fathers, and mothers were very often the main political force in their families.

Therefore, while James O'Donoghue's son denounced his father's killers as 'punks, *canaille* from the back lanes,'[44] this reveals more about his—and general—attitudes to the poor than it does about the O'Briens, who were hardworking, religious, and no doubt entirely 'respectable' in their own eyes. Their patriotism and familial spirit of loyalty, self-improvement, and self-sacrifice testifies to this.[45] Indeed, their republicanism reflected these determinedly middle-class virtues. Just as the O'Donoghues of Cahirciveen gained prestige by having a priest and a policeman in the family so the O'Briens used their fight for Ireland as a badge of respectability. The two families seem to have shared many

---

[41] *Examiner*, 19, 22 Nov. 1920. See also Lil Conlon, *Cumann na mBan and the Women of Ireland, 1913–25* (Kilkenny, 1969), 138.

[42] These changes can be seen by comparing the census returns for 1901 and 1911 with the descriptions of the O'Briens given in the *Examiner*, 19, 24 Nov. 1920.

[43] TCD, Erskine Childers Papers, MS 7808/29, 8.

[44] Undated, undelivered letter to Charlie O'Brien (Marie O'Donoghue Papers).

[45] The quotation is from an undated letter in the O'Donoghue papers.

of the same values, virtues, and ambitions. If the O'Brien brothers had been born twenty years earlier, they too might have aspired to positions in the church or the constabulary, while James O'Donoghue might well have joined the I.R.A. if he had been born twenty years later. The divisions between them had as much to do with generation and circumstance as with ideology or personality.

So why did they shoot O'Donoghue, who was unarmed and known for being 'too good to the boys'? This question is particularly interesting in light of the fact that the Cork I.R.A. officially apologized in writing to his family a week after the shooting and stated that the killing had nothing to do with them. People in the White Street neighbourhood thought the same thing and attributed it to the Tans, because of their run-ins with their no-nonsense sergeant. Another explanation was that the O'Briens and O'Connor had panicked and shot O'Donoghue because Desmond's Yard on White Street was an important arms dump. Against this it must be pointed out that O'Donoghue walked to and from Tuckey Street every day and that he must have passed the Yard scores of times before.

Fifty years later, Charlie O'Brien accounted for his actions as follows:

The reason for that shooting dates back to a funeral in Macroom in 1918. Macroom was a town that was hanging back in the movement, showing no interest. At this particular funeral it was decided that six officers of Cork City No. 1 Battalion should attend in full uniform, carrying rifles. O'Donoghue attended that funeral. Within a few weeks, every one of the six officers was arrested.[46] O'Donoghue was good to the Sinn Feiners round the city, but he had those officers arrested . . .

It was a dark, cold, wet November evening. The three were standing in Desmond's small gateway . . . They were 'on a job', meaning waiting for someone whom they were to kill. It was getting on for 5.30 and the man had not turned up. They were thinking of going away, but O'Donoghue came along, and they decided to get him then. It sounds horrible, awful, but we did not think so at the time. It was just part of the day's job. We gave as much as we got, or even more. The people to be pitied were those who had no defence. We hit back.[47]

This seems a rather meagre (and dated) reason to kill someone, perhaps cobbled together afterwards by the gunmen to defend their action to their superiors. Another I.R.A. man told O'Donoghue's son that he had identified an army deserter in Watergrasshill in 1920 but O'Brien made no mention of this.

The real reason may lie in his phrase 'we hit back'. Terence MacSwiney, MacCurtain's successor as mayor and I.R.A. commander, had died on 25 October after a seventy-three-day hunger strike. His highly public death and funeral, which took place only three days before the shootings, had convulsed

---

[46] I can find no record of these events in newspapers, police records or I.R.A. documents or memoirs. In fact, the Macroom I.R.A. was quite active. See Charlie Browne, *The Story of the 7th* (Macroom, n.d.).

[47] Interview with Charlie O'Brien (O'Donoghue Diary).

Cork but the young militants' plans for revenge attacks had been forbidden.[48] On top of this, the arrival of large numbers of young and trigger-happy British ex-soldiers added a new edge to the violence as vandalism, beatings, and shootings became increasingly common, especially during the curfew. Known guerrillas were in great danger and could expect terrible consequences if caught, as demonstrated by the killing of Christy Lucey only a week before O'Donoghue's death. Willie, and later Charlie, O'Brien were forced to go on the run and their house became a target for frequent raids. In this atmosphere of fear and anger, every policeman and soldier was an enemy, and on 17 November O'Donoghue was a suddenly opportune target with an old mark against him. He died because he was in the wrong place at the wrong time.

Whatever the reason, the assassins acted on their own initiative, to the fury of their superiors. The I.R.A. issued an apology and the O'Briens and O'Connor were court-martialled 'but they managed to bully the officers in charge and get out of it'.[49] The O'Briens and their comrades did what they liked and got away with it, convinced that they were the vanguard of the revolution. This rebellious mixture of initiative and independence grew out of the subculture to which the O'Briens belonged—not just republican but also young, male, and tough. Theirs was a world in which cliques and friendships, charged with a youthful intensity, merged with political loyalties and helped sustain a passionate devotion to the cause. These were the true believers who kept on fighting the government even after it became Irish. The O'Briens were staunchly opposed to the Anglo-Irish Treaty of December 1921 and resumed their underground activities in opposition to the new Irish Free State in 1922. Broad Lane became the site of a bomb factory,[50] the brothers went on the run when troops landed in August, and Willie and Charlie went to prison (and on hunger strike) again shortly thereafter.[51] Hannah and Elizabeth also remained committed to the wearying struggle. 'Oh God, how we have suffered,' exclaimed Elizabeth, looking back over her family's history. 'The Tans came to kill us, the Free State came to torture us. For months [in the Civil War] my brothers were in . . . prison in Cork, when meals and laundry etc. had to be brought to them every day.'[52] Charlie O'Brien, on the other hand, looked back more in anger than in sorrow, his youthful convictions undimmed after fifty years: 'My one regret was that more was not done.'[53]

There remains one question. Who informed on the O'Briens? The police knew who shot O'Donoghue within hours of the event and also apparently knew of their connection with Patrick Hanley and Eugene O'Connell. This suggests that the information, no doubt exaggerated or distorted as such intelligence

---

[48]   P. S. O'Hegarty, *The Victory of Sinn Fein* (Dublin, 1924), 46–7.
[49]   Interview with Charlie O'Brien (O'Donoghue Diary).
[50]   *Examiner*, 14 July 1922.
[51]   William O'Brien appears in an I.R.A. register of Cork prisoners (MA, A/1135).
[52]   Interview with Elizabeth O'Connor (O'Donoghue Papers). For the similar experiences of a near neighbour, see Mitchell, *The Man with the Long Hair*.
[53]   Interview with Charlie O'Brien (O'Donoghue Diary).

usually was by rumour and personal enmities, came from a friend or neighbour who had some inside knowledge of the I.R.A. The O'Briens were thinking along the same lines and suspicion soon fell on 'Din-Din' O'Riordan. O'Riordan was a gunman and a comrade of the O'Briens but also apparently a heavy drinker and a relative newcomer to the city from Kerry. He was seized and held while his alibi was checked. This proved to be false. Frank Busteed, an I.R.A. officer from Blarney with relatives who lived near the O'Briens, recounted what happened next:

They bundled Din-Din into a car and again drove him out to the Viaduct. It was a cold drizzly night, and Din-Din was shivering, but not from cold . . . When they got to the Viaduct Jim Grey stopped the car.

'All right Din-Din, get out,' [Dick] Murphy ordered. 'You are a proven informer, in fact you are worse than an informer, you are a traitor. You are on our side, and you are with them at the same time. The O'Briens[54] were killed by the Auxies the night before you cashed the ten pound note in Mrs. Riordan's [a local pub]. Who gave it to you?'

Din-Din remained silent. 'You know why we're here. But we will give you a chance. If you will tell us who gave it to you we will book your passage to England and give you fifty pounds.'

Din-Din talked. He got the money from Mr. Nicholson of Woodford Bournes, the wine and spirit merchants. He had been recruited a month before by another I.R.A. man who told him there was easy money to be earned. He was desperate for drink at the time and took it. He gave the name of the other I.R.A. man.

They shot him and buried him at the Viaduct. Next night they shot the other I.R.A. contact.[55]

Elizabeth O'Connor remembered the events somewhat differently, with a greater role being played by the O'Briens. O'Riordan was 'very courageous in a tight corner, but they began to suspect him, set a trap for him, and found he was selling information. They finished his career in the Lee fields.'[56]

Also suspected of spying was a member of the Hawkins family of No. 6A Broad Street, long-time neighbours of the O'Briens. On the evening of 20 May 1921 Daniel Hawkins, a chairmaker, and his son Edward, a labourer in the military barracks, had just left their house when:

Two civilians came upon them and called out 'halt there; put your hands up' at the same time placing revolvers to their breasts. The armed men then said 'come along' and marched them to Mardyke. Opposite St. Joseph's School three more men joined them and the whole party proceeded to the quarry at Mountdesert. Witness and his son were

---

[54] Busteed clearly misremembered the exact circumstances of the killings and just recalled the involvement of the O'Briens.

[55] Sean O'Callaghan, *Execution* (London, 1974), 59–60. Despite its bad reputation among Cork I.R.A. veterans, much of this book appears to be substantially accurate, although marred by the egotism of O'Callaghan's chief informant, Frank Busteed.

[56] Interview with Elizabeth O'Connor (O'Donoghue Diary). There is no police or newspaper report of O'Riordan's killing. The only evidence he was killed comes from Frank Busteed and Elizabeth O'Connor. Like other victims, he was alone in the city and simply disappeared.

ordered to sit down and two of the armed civilians remained on guard over them while the other three went round the corner of the quarry returning in about two minutes. On coming back they searched a man who had been in the quarry with several others when witness arrived there. When [Edward] saw them searching this man he tore up all the papers in his possession, including a barrack permit and army discharge papers . . . After this the witness, his son and the man who had been searched were forced to sit in a row with about a foot between each man. The deceased said 'Spare my father.' Three of the armed civilians then fired on them from a distance of a few feet each man firing four times. Witness was wounded in right elbow and left ear and fell forward. He remained down without moving and distinctly heard one of the murderers say 'Skeet now.' When they had gone he got up and saw that his son was dying. He at once ran to the Lee Road and attempted to swim the river but finding himself too weak he asked a man with a horse and cart to drive him to the institution. Arriving there he requested them to telephone for an ambulance.[57]

When the ambulance arrived Edward was dead. The third man, who also died, was John Sherlock, another ex-soldier from the tenements of Devonshire Lane, a few streets to the north of Broad Lane. Sherlock worked as a driver in the barracks.[58]

Unlike O'Riordan, who was tricked but who may well have been guilty, the Hawkinses and Sherlock were not interrogated or 'tried' as official I.R.A. policy demanded.[59] They were condemned by suspicion alone, because they were ex-soldiers and (in the case of Edward and John) military employees—and perhaps because of their politics. Many ex-soldiers in Cork remained loyal to the Crown, if only passively so, and many who regarded themselves as nationalists were still anti-Sinn Fein.

Such men had a hard time in the new Ireland dominated by the republicans. They had gone to war as heroes in 1914 and returned in 1919 as traitors. The Home Rule party that they had believed in and voted for (most soldiers' votes in Cork went to the Irish Party in 1918[60]) had been swept away. Jobs were scarce and local councils and trade unions were hostile, just as they were to policemen. Many turned to drink and crime. Scores of ex-soldiers passed through the Cork police court for fighting, neglecting or abusing their families, or theft. Veterans did try to organize themselves politically but they made little headway in the midst of civil war. For this reason, ex-soldiers in Cork prized those jobs given

[57]   Military Inquiry in lieu of an inquest (CO 904/189).

[58]   Information on the victims comes from their 1901 and 1911 census returns, and from the *Examiner*, 21 May 1921.

[59]   It is possible that none of these men was guilty. Busteed later shot at least one other innocent man, and his account of the interrogation of O'Riordan may not be too reliable. Marie O'Donoghue remembered seeing officers questioning a boy at Tuckey Street station after her father's death. Perhaps he was a witness to the shooting.

[60]   One indication of this is the sample (the only one available, and presumably more or less random) of accidentally spoiled soldiers' and sailors' ballots in the Cork city district. Out of sixty-six such ballots, only six first-place votes went to Sinn Fein candidates. Fifty-six of these men cast both their votes for Irish Party candidates. *Examiner*, 31 Dec. 1918.

by the government and the army and they often hung on to old friends and loyalties. Men like Edward Hawkins and John Sherlock would have naturally gravitated to the company of servicemen and old comrades and thereby damned themselves by association in the eyes of republicans like the O'Briens.

Many veterans like Eugene O'Connell and his family or Mr Collins of Broad Street quietly reimmersed themselves in civilian life and managed to escape persecution. A great many others who were unwilling to give up their old political or social ties or who fell under suspicion were shot, beaten up, or driven out of the city. A very few were actual informers. Most were innocent victims. The three men shot on 20 May were considered enemies of the republic and informers not because of what they did but because of who they were. This seems particularly true of Daniel Hawkins who, according to Elizabeth O'Connor, was not personally suspected of informing and was not connected to the army. He was probably shot because he was Edward's father just as Eugene O'Connell was shot by the police for being the O'Briens' brother-in-law.

If the murders of Hawkins and Sherlock demonstrate the plight of war veterans in Cork, they also confirm the importance of the war itself in shaping the lives of all the actors in these events. Most of the victims—Edward Hawkins, John Sherlock, Eugene O'Connell, Stephen Coleman, and Mr Collins—were ex-soldiers. The British policemen who terrorized 'the Marsh' had fought in the same army, against a common foe. Mr O'Brien, Charlie's and Willie's father, had died in a German submarine attack. All of these people and their families had been touched and scarred by war long before the I.R.A. took up arms.

This story unites two families at opposite political poles—the O'Briens and the O'Donoghues—in tragedy. As statistics, symbols, or members of organizations, the deaths of O'Donoghue, Hanley, Coleman, O'Riordan, Hawkins, and Sherlock, and the maiming of O'Brien, make some kind of sense, but on an individual level they do not. O'Donoghue did not even carry a gun and was liked and respected by republicans. Why was he shot and his family's lives shattered? Why Hanley and O'Connell, who probably had no idea why they were singled out and gunned down? Coleman's death was equally senseless. O'Brien, definitely, and O'Riordan, very likely, were 'guilty' as suspected but the Hawkinses and Sherlock may have been guilty only of being loyal ex-soldiers living in a republican neighbourhood.

Ultimately, individual identities were irrelevant in the face of politically imposed labels and the ever-widening division between 'us' and 'them'. Violence was directed not at people so much as categories. Coleman, Hanley, and O'Connell were 'Shinners' and 'rebels' along with O'Brien. Sherlock and the Hawkinses were 'spies' and 'informers' like O'Riordan. O'Donoghue was just another uniform.

This little cycle of killings reveals the runaway tit-for-tat logic of the guerrilla war in Cork, driven by fear and the overwhelming need to respond. 'Hurt one and you hurt them all.' 'If you didn't kill someone, someone was going to kill you.' 'We gave as much as we got, or even more.' 'We hit back.' All of the victims were unarmed and helpless when shot and all were killed or kidnapped near home. The revolution produced many skirmishes and casualties by combat, but many more people died without a gun in their hands, at their doors, in quarries or empty fields, shot in the back by masked men. Murder was more common than battle.

This dirty war was waged largely by small bands of gunmen, young, tough, and barely under the control of their superiors. The 'active squads' on both sides did what they liked, undeterred by orders or discipline from further up the organization. Although the I.R.A., the R.I.C., and the army numbered in the hundreds and thousands in Cork, most of the killing was done by a few hard men like the O'Briens or the anonymous Black and Tans who shot up Broad Lane, Broad Street, and the North Mall. It was these men who forced the pace and, in a sense, the revolution came down to a confrontation between these groups, even if its victims were often innocents or outsiders.

It was an intimate war, played out within homes and neighbourhoods, often between people who knew one another. The O'Briens were acquainted with everyone they shot. James O'Donoghue was the local sergeant. Din-Din O'Riordan was a fellow I.R.A. man. Edward and Daniel Hawkins and John Sherlock were neighbours.

It was a civil war, fought not just between Irish people, but between rival visions of Ireland. James O'Donoghue loved and served his country. He was a good Catholic and a good Irishman. The same can be said of the O'Briens. The sergeant's death represented a clash between the old loyalties of the policeman and the new certainties embraced by the gunmen.

We know about the events of 17 November because Marie O'Donoghue wanted to find out who shot her father and found the O'Briens.[61] However, asking who shot whom and why leads inevitably to broader questions of motive and identity. How did the killing begin and why did it escalate? Who joined the I.R.A. and why? How did they think of themselves and how did they justify their actions to themselves and to others? Who were their victims and enemies?

The following chapters will explore these questions in detail but I will also attempt to put a human face on my analysis of violence and revolution and give the participants and victims as much of a voice as possible. Individuals were often obscured, and sometimes blotted out, by other people's fears and myths. It is the purpose of this book to elucidate the mythologies and understand the fear, but also to identify and understand those who fought and suffered and died in obscurity.

---

[61]   See n. 4.

PART I

Revolution, 1916–1923

2

The Kilmichael Ambush

Then here's to the boys of Kilmichael
Who feared not the might of the foe,
The day they marched into battle
And laid all the Black and Tans low.
('The Boys of Kilmichael')[1]

Does any man say that Barry is a murderer? If he is, he is a very good one.
(Gearoid O'Sullivan, Sept. 1921)[2]

On 28 November 1920, the flying column of the West Cork Brigade ambushed a police patrol near the village of Kilmichael, just south of Macroom. Three Volunteers and seventeen Auxiliary cadets, members of an elite anti-I.R.A. force, were killed. Only one Auxiliary survived, crippled and comatose.

The Kilmichael ambush delivered a profound shock to the British system, coming only a week after the 'Bloody Sunday' assassination of a dozen army officers in Dublin, and days after a large section of the Liverpool docklands was burned down. Dublin and Liverpool revealed British vulnerabilities, but Kilmichael showed that the I.R.A. could beat British officers in the field. The guerrillas were not just a 'murder gang', they were also a military threat. On 1 December the cabinet decided, in view of 'the recent outrage near Cork, which partook of a more definitely military character than its predecessors', that martial law would be introduced wherever it was considered necessary. County Cork headed the list.[3]

In West Cork, and in Ireland as a whole, Kilmichael became the most celebrated victory of rebel arms, the archetypal ambush. Tom Barry, the column commander, became a folk hero and a revolutionary celebrity.[4] Barry's, and

[1] This song was written shortly after the ambush and became hugely popular in Cork and throughout Ireland. Its author is unknown, although it may have been a local teacher, Jeremiah O'Mahony (see Flor Crowley, *In West Cork Long Ago* (Cork, 1979), 18–19). Several slightly different versions exist—the one quoted here is the one I have heard sung most often, which is printed in Ewan Butler, *Barry's Flying Column* (London, 1971), 173–4.

[2] *Cork Co. Eagle*, 1 Oct. 1921. The police reported a near-identical speech given by Sean Hayes, TD, in October. R.I.C. Report, n.d. (CO 904/152).

[3] Cabinet minute quoted in Charles Townshend, *The British Campaign in Ireland, 1919–1921* (Oxford, 1975), 133. On 29 November (after the arson attacks in Liverpool but before news of Kilmichael had reached London) Sir Henry Wilson asked Winston Churchill if the government was going to declare martial law: 'He replied no.' The next day they were discussing its implementation: 'They now want to try it in Cork and Cork city.' Wilson Diary excerpts in Martin Gilbert (ed.), *Winston S. Churchill*, companion volume iv, part 2 (Boston, 1978), 1256–7.

[4] See, for example, *Examiner*, 25 Aug. 1921 and *Southern Star* (hereafter *Star*), 14 Jan. 1922.

Kilmichael's, fame even reached beyond the borders of Ireland, at least in the vivid imaginations of West Cork. It 'jerked the people of India to a new appraisal of their position. Egypt stood amazed. It ultimately pervaded darkest Africa.' The German army studied the ambush in the Second World War and Barry's memoirs became 'required reading at military academies', including Sandhurst and Westpoint. Most impressive of all, it has been reported that when the Japanese army captured Singapore, they marched in singing 'The Boys of Kilmichael'.[5]

The classic account of Kilmichael appeared in Tom Barry's memoirs, *Guerilla Days in Ireland* (first published in 1949), a version of events which he repeated on numerous occasions thereafter, in print and on radio and television. The following succinct version is taken from one of his last interviews:

The Auxiliaries first arrived in Cork late in the summer of 1920 and from that day on they spent their time driving into villages and terrorizing everybody. They'd beat people and strip them and shoot the place up, and then go back to their barracks drunk on stuff they'd looted. We knew we had to stop them, and that was what the fight at Kilmichael was all about.

We nearly had to call it off before it happened. I'd selected a spot near Macroom—the only spot we were sure they'd pass—and we had a long march there all night through the rain. We didn't know when they'd come, and we had to wait lying low in the ditches all day without food. By four o'clock . . . it was getting dark, and I nearly called it off then. But then we heard two lorries of them coming.

There was a bend in the road there, and we had to make sure they'd slow up. So I had an I.R.A. officer's tunic, and the idea was that when they came along the road they'd see an officer standing in the ditch facing them, they'd see this man in a trench coat and leggings and they'd slow down to see who it was. They might even think it one of them-selves . . . And that's what they did, they slowed down about fifty yards away and kept coming, very slow, until they got to about fifty yards away and a Mills bomb was thrown from our side. It landed right in the driver's seat and killed him. Fire was opened up then and it became a hand-to-hand fight. It was so close that one of our fellows caught a spurt of blood full in the mouth from a severed artery of one of the Auxies. We had the better of them there because they were screaming and yelling and our fellows just kept quiet and wiped them all out. There were nine of them dead on the road and all our men were still alive.

In the meantime the second lorry had come along, and another section of our men was up the road giving battle to them. So I went along the side of the road with some of the men from the command post and as we got up behind them—they didn't see us—they threw away their rifles and we heard them shouting, 'We surrender! We surrender!' Three of our men stood up then from their positions to take the surrender, but the minute they did the others opened fire on them and killed two of them. So we continued up

---

    [5] The first quotation comes from an oration by Father O'Brien at the ambush site, *Examiner*, 11 July 1966; the story about the German army studying Kilmichael is printed on the back of the paperback edition of Ewan Butler's book; the report of the military academies, *Sunday Independent*, 7 Mar. 1976; the Singapore story, P. J. Twohig, *Green Tears for Hecuba* (Dublin, 1979), 59. Variations on all of these can still be heard in West Cork.

behind them and I gave the order to keep firing until I said to stop, and then after we killed a couple more of them and they saw they were sandwiched in between two lines of fire they started shouting 'We surrender!' again. But having seen the false surrender I told the men to keep firing and we did until the last of them was dead. I blame myself of course for our own losses, because I should have seen through the false surrender trick.

Afterwards some of our men were shaken by the whole thing and I had to drill them in the road, march them up and down, to preserve discipline . . . it was a strange sight, with the lorries burning in the night and these men marching along, back and forth between the blood and the corpses . . . But if they didn't keep their discipline we might lose everything. Discipline was all we had.[6]

The key episode here is clearly the 'false surrender', which caused the deaths of the three I.R.A. men and doomed the remaining Auxiliaries to annihilation. The official British report, 'prepared by a senior officer of police in the Cork neighbourhood from evidence available', gave a completely different story:

District Inspector Crake took out a patrol in the ordinary course of duty. They were going in search of a man wanted in the Dunmanway direction, and had been previously working in cooperation with the Essex Regiment at Dunmanway. When dusk was falling, at about 5 p.m., the patrol was proceeding along the Macroom–Dunmanway road and reached a point where the road curves. Low stone walls flank the road and there are narrow strips of tussocky bogland, rising to boulder-covered slopes of high ground on either side.

It is surmised from an examination of the site and from inquiries that the attackers, who were all clad in khaki and trench coats, and wore steel helmets, had drawn their motor lorry across the road and were mistaken by the first car of cadets for military. The first car halted, and the cadets, unsuspecting, got out and approached the motor lorry . . . shooting began, and three were killed instantaneously. Others began to run back to the first car. The cadets in the second car ran along the road to the help of their comrades. Then from a depression in the hillside behind the second car came a devastating fire at close range. The cadets were shot down by concealed men from the walls, and all around a direct fire from the ambushers' lorry also swept down the road. After firing had continued for some time, and many men were wounded, overwhelming forces of the ambushers came out and forcibly disarmed the survivors.

There followed a brutal massacre, the policy of the murder gang being apparently to allow no survivor to disclose their methods. The dead and wounded were hacked about the head with axes, shot guns were fired into their bodies, and they were savagely mutilated. The one survivor, who was wounded, was hit about the head and left for dead. He had also two bullet wounds . . . terrible treachery on the part of local inhabitants is indicated by the fact that, although many people attending Mass on Sunday morning were diverted from their route by the murder gang, no word was sent to the police, and the ambush sat there until dusk.[7]

Here the treachery is Irish. British uniforms were falsely worn (an act punishable by death under international legal conventions) and wounded and disarmed

[6] Kenneth Griffith and Timothy O'Grady, *Curious Journey: An Oral History of Ireland's Unfinished Revolution* (London, 1982), 181–2.   [7] *The Times*, 2 Dec. 1920.

men were butchered: 'every law of civilized warfare was thrown to the winds.'[8] The martial law proclamation itself, issued by the Lord Lieutenant on 11 December, gave the character of the attack as its main rationale:

Because of attacks on Crown forces culminating in an ambush, massacre, and mutilation with axes of sixteen cadets, by a large body of men wearing trench helmets and disguised in the uniform of British soldiers, and who are still at large, now I do declare Martial Law proclaimed.

In his memoirs, Barry dismissed these charges as a pack of lies, a typical example of 'atrocity' propaganda.[9] And, indeed, it is his account which has come to be accepted as authoritative and has been retold as such by other authors.[10] It is now more or less the 'official' Irish history of the event, as commemorated every year at the ambush site.

The British story should not be so completely dismissed, however. Even at first glance we can see that some of its details agree with Barry's story. The men of the column were not disguised as soldiers, but some of them were wearing steel helmets and Barry was wearing something very like an officer's uniform. Both accounts agree that it was this ruse which enabled the I.R.A. to catch the Auxiliaries by surprise. The British investigators were also right about the ambushers being in position from early morning and ordering churchgoers to return home.[11] Clearly, intelligence officers had been able to piece together some of what happened from local witnesses or rumours, from the wounded survivor, and possibly even from lower-echelon I.R.A. informants. They were certainly able quickly to identify many of the participants.[12] If police officials got this much right, can we dismiss the rest of their account?

There is also the evidence of Dr Kelleher, the Macroom coroner. His examination found that most of the cadets had been riddled with bullets. Three had been shot at point-blank range (probably by guns held to their heads), several had been shot after death, and another had his head smashed open, apparently with a club or axe.[13] The lone survivor had been both shot and hit in the head—the doctors were amazed that he was still living.[14] In other words, while the medical evidence does not support the accusations of mutilation, it does raise further questions about Barry's story.

---

[8]   Gen. Sir Nevil Macready, *Annals of an Active Life* (London, 1924), ii. 17.

[9]   Tom Barry, *Guerilla Days in Ireland* (Dublin, 1949, 1981), 50–1.

[10]   See, for example, Butler, *Barry's Flying Column*, 66–71 and John McCann, *War by the Irish* (Tralee, 1946), 128–9.

[11]   Interviews with AA, 3 Apr. 1988 and AE, 19 Nov. 1989.

[12]   See 'Raymond' [Flor Crowley], 'Black and Tan Diary', *Star*, 23 Oct.–27 Nov. 1971.

[13]   *Examiner* and *Irish Times*, 12 Jan. 1921. See also *Eagle*, 4 Dec. 1920 and the Report of the Military Court of Inquiry (WO 35/152).

[14]   See *Examiner*, 18 Jan. 1921 and James Gleeson, *Bloody Sunday* (London, 1962), 73–4. This book includes the invaluable reminiscences of Bill Munro, an Auxiliary cadet stationed in Macroom at the time. It is to his account that I shall be referring in the following pages. Gleeson, incidentally, also accepts Barry's story as the correct one.

Since the police very likely got some of their information from people living in the neighbourhood, it is interesting to see what local oral tradition has made of the ambush. Two accounts were collected by the Folklore Commission in the 1930s. The first is from Dunmanway:

> In the year 1916 the old I.R.A. ambushed the 'Black and Tans' at Kilmichael. They sent a false letter to Dublin telling them that a certain man from Coppeen wanted them. The British had to pass Kilmichael to go to Coppeen. The I.R.A. made preparations. They set a bomb under a bridge there.
>
> When the 'Tans' came the bomb exploded and a lorry of them was blown up. They were all shocked. Then the I.R.A. attacked them with their guns. Three of the I.R.A. were shot.[15]

The second comes from Deshure:

> They had mines laid on the road which blew up the last lorry. The Republicans fired on the survivors and there was a counter-attack. The whole thing lasted about half an hour but the shots could be heard miles away.

Much has been changed in the telling but the details are intriguing. The first version does contain an element of trickery, although not the I.R.A. in disguise. It also states that the patrol was searching for a wanted man near Dunmanway, just as the police said. The mines mentioned are presumably references to the Mills bomb that Barry threw, although they also featured in early news reports.[16] Most importantly, these storytellers make no mention of a false surrender, despite Tom Barry's later claim that 'there was hardly a Volunteer in West Cork who did not know' of it.[17]

To further muddy the waters, Barry wrote earlier descriptions of the ambush which seem to undermine his later claims. To begin with, there is his original after-action report written for his superiors:

> The column paraded at 3.15 a.m. on Sunday morning. It comprised 32 men armed with rifles, bayonets, five revolvers, and 100 rounds of ammunition per man. We marched for four hours, and reached a position on the Macroom–Dunmanway road . . . We camped in that position until 4.15 p.m., and then decided that as the enemy searches were completed, that it would be safe to return to our camp. Accordingly, we started the return journey. About five minutes after the start we sighted two enemy lorries moving at a distance of about 1,900 yards from us. The country in that particular district is of a hilly and rocky nature, and, although suitable to fighting, it is not at all suitable to retiring without being seen. I decided to attack the lorries . . . The action was carried out success-fully. Sixteen of the enemy who were belonging to the Auxiliary Police from Macroom Castle being killed, one wounded and escaped, and is now missing . . .
>
> P.S.:—I attribute our casualties to the fact that those three men were too anxious to get into close quarters with the enemy. They were our best men, and did not know danger

[15] UCD, Dept. of Irish Folklore, Schools MS 307, p. 53, 339, p. 60.

[16] *Eagle*, 4 Dec. 1920.

[17] Tom Barry, *The Reality of the Anglo-Irish War 1920–21 in West Cork: Refutations, Corrections and Comments on Liam Deasy's Towards Ireland Free* (Dublin, 1974), 17.

in this or any previous actions. They discarded their cover, and it was not until the finish of the action that P. Deasy was killed by a revolver bullet from one of the enemy whom he thought dead.[18]

Barry provides remarkably little information about the engagement (in contrast to his later accounts), but he still manages to contradict his later description in several places. No false surrender occurred by this account; the Irish deaths are attributed to their own carelessness. Curiously, he also suggests that the column was not seeking action but evading it, and that the ambush was an unavoidable last-minute affair.

Barry wrote another account of Kilmichael in 1932. After bombing the first lorry:

[the] I.R.A. and Auxiliaries were engaged in a death struggle. After eight or ten minutes of terrific fighting the first lorry of the enemy was overcome and a party of three men . . . advanced up the road to help their second section. They were firing as they advanced to the relief of their sorely pressed comrades, three of whom had already fallen. The end was at hand and in a short time the remainder of the Auxiliaries fighting the second section were dead. They like the I.R.A. had fought to a finish.[19]

Again, no trick surrender. The three I.R.A. casualties had already been hit by the time Barry and his party ran to help and the Auxiliaries then manfully 'fought to a finish'—a direct contradiction, in substance and tone, of what he wrote in 1949.

What makes these accounts doubly interesting is Barry's reaction to Paddy O'Brien's recollections of Kilmichael, published in Liam Deasy's memoirs, *Towards Ireland Free*, in 1974. O'Brien describes the battle around the second lorry as follows:

The Auxies had jumped out . . . We then opened fire from their rear and when they realised that they were caught between two fires they knew that they were doomed. It was then realised that three of our men had been killed.[20]

Barry was infuriated at this 'fantastic' story which he felt 'depicted me as a bloody-minded commander who exterminated the Auxiliaries without reason'. It was, he insisted, 'the false surrender after which I.R.A. freedom fighters were

---

[18] General Staff 6th Division, *The Irish Rebellion in the 6th Divisional Area from after 1916 Rebellion to December 1921* (IWM, General Sir Peter Strickland Papers, P.362), 63–4 (hereafter referred to as *6th Division History*). That this is an authentic captured document seems unquestionable. It contains details such as the division of the column into three sections and their deployment, the length of the march to Kilmichael, the time the ambush took place, and the fact that two of the three I.R.A. casualties died of wounds, which could hardly be known by the British military. Moreover, this report was only printed in an unpublished and confidential history to demonstrate its falsehood. If it had been forged for propaganda reasons it would presumably have reflected the official story and would have been publicly released. In fact, there are no known cases of I.R.A. documents being forged.

[19] Tom Barry, 'The Story of the Kilmichael Ambush', *Irish Press*, 26 Nov. 1932.

[20] Liam Deasy, *Towards Ireland Free* (Cork, 1973), 172.

treacherously killed' which 'ensured the extermination of the Auxiliaries concerned'.[21]

These wild denunciations are not very convincing, but they are revealing. O'Brien's account does not paint Barry as 'bloodthirsty', it merely describes a 'short but grim fight' in which (as in Barry's 1932 article) the I.R.A. and police 'fought to a finish'. It is Barry who introduces the issue of 'extermination' and who clearly feels very defensive about it. Why? Because in the interview quoted above (and in his memoirs) he says that, after the bogus surrender, several Cadets shouted 'we surrender' a second time, but that the guerrillas kept on firing until all had been killed. So, if there was no trick, the Auxiliaries were gunned down 'for no reason'. Yet we know that Barry himself made no mention of a false surrender in 1920 or 1932. What really happened at Kilmichael?

The eighteen ambushed Auxiliary cadets belonged to 'C' Company, stationed at Macroom Castle. These men were ex-army and R.A.F. officers, discharged veterans of the Great War. Most of the patrol were young junior officers (their average age was 27), one had been a major in the Indian Army (OBE) and their commander had been a lieutenant colonel in the Bedford Regiment. All of them had been decorated in wartime: three had Military Crosses, one held the Distinguished Flying Cross.[22]

They came from all over Britain in the summer of 1920 in response to advertisements offering £1 a day and the rank of sergeant to join an elite police corps. Most had jumped at the chance. The job offered very good money and potential excitement, an escape from the chronic unemployment and boredom of post-war Britain. Perhaps best of all, it meant a return to the fellowship of active service.[23]

'C' Company was one of the first to be raised. Its personnel (who numbered 115 in late November) were recruited in July and August and sent to the Curragh for a hasty six-week training course in police methods.[24] By the middle of September they were in Macroom.

The Auxiliaries' ill-defined task was to hunt the I.R.A. in the areas where it was most active. In Macroom they found themselves in a district whose police chief declared it to be 'practically in a state of war'.[25] The town was under

---

[21] Barry, *The Reality of the Anglo-Irish War*, 15–18. It should be noted that Stephen O'Neill was the first Kilmichael veteran to mention the false surrender in 'The Ambush at Kilmichael', *Kerryman Christmas Number* (Dec. 1937). The first writer to do so, however, was F. P. Crozier in *Ireland for Ever* (London, 1932), 128. O'Neill's and Barry's subsequent accounts may in part have been prompted by Crozier. However, as Crozier demonstrates, and interviews confirm, the 'false surrender' story was circulating within the I.R.A. as early as 1921.

[22] Personal details of the ambushees can be found in the Dublin Castle Press Statement (CO 904/168), the Report of the Military Court of Inquiry (WO 35/152), and in *Irish Times*, 12 Jan. 1921.

[23] These circumstances and motives are described by Bill Munro in Gleeson, *Bloody Sunday*, 56–9. See also Townshend, *British Campaign*, 110–12 and A. D. Harvey, 'Who Were the Auxiliaries?', *Historical Journal* (Sept. 1992).

[24] For company strength see Townshend, *British Campaign*, 210.

[25] CI Monthly Report, West Cork, Aug. 1920 (CO 904/112).

curfew and all fairs and meetings had been banned. Almost all the outlying police barracks had been evacuated and burned down, along with local court-houses.

The army had stepped in in May to try and restore order and found itself embroiled in a vicious little war in the Muskerry hill country west of the town. After trading lethal ambushes and counter-ambushes with the Ballyvourney I.R.A., the rural infantry detachments—two platoons of the Manchester Regiment—were withdrawn in early October. The Manchesters lost three dead (including two officers) and six wounded, the I.R.A. lost one. The Macroom detachment simply stopped patrolling the western portion of the battalion area. The townspeople themselves could also be hostile: one patrol was stoned in August, leaving two men badly injured.[26] When the new force of cadets arrived, the R.I.C. garrison had 'ceased to function' and control of the countryside had been ceded to the rebels.[27] One Macroom I.R.A. officer described it as 'a hinter-land unpoliced and unwatched'.[28]

The Auxiliaries' presence transformed the situation. They raided constantly and aggressively. Where previously rural Volunteers might not have seen a policeman for weeks or months at a time, now there were no safe havens. An Auxiliary patrol might appear at any time, day or night. They were fast, well armed, and strong in numbers. There were no small bicycle patrols to provide easy targets. Micheal O'Suilleabhain remembered them as:

A tough crowd. I knew them well. I had seen them jump walls with their rifles in their hands, hampered by their revolvers and other equipment. They travelled by night and day on bye roads, and came from totally unexpected directions. I had plenty experience of their physical fitness when I had to run from them on several occasions, and when, were it not for darkness, they would have had me.[29]

Tom Barry has vividly described their activities as a 'terror campaign'.[30] This label may well apply to other units or to the record of the Auxiliary Division as a whole, but it does not fit 'C' Company. Its commanders were responsible men who kept their cadets under control and prevented serious mischief or drink-ing.[31] The people of Macroom were understandably very nervous of this 'new force of Tans', whose arrival came as a complete surprise, but they 'made dili-gent efforts to make a good impression . . . and took pains to let it be known that

---

[26] Twohig, *Green Tears*, 22–30; Browne, *The Story of the 7th*, 17–25 and Micheal O'Suilleabhain, *Where Mountainy Men Have Sown* (Tralee, 1965), 70–87 give the Irish side of this struggle. For the British side, see the very detailed Record of Service of the 1st Battalion, Manchester Regiment (Tameside Local Studies Library, Manchester Regiment Archives, MR1/1/2/4). For one notorious incident, see H., D. F., 'A Side Show in Southern Ireland, 1920' (IWM, k.37957). Further useful detail can be found in the Preacher's Books for the Church of Ireland parishes of Ballyvourney and Macroom (Representative Church Body Library, P131/8/1; P137/8/4).

[27] CI Monthly Report, West Cork, July 1920 (CO 904/112).

[28] Browne, *The Story of the 7th*, 18.

[29] O'Suilleabhain, *Mountainy Men*, 90.

[30] Barry, *Guerilla Days*, 36–7.

[31] Crozier, *Ireland for Ever*, 198.

they did not come for trouble and did not want it'.[32] Liam Deasy, a senior West Cork officer, remembered Lieutenant Colonel Crake—who died in the ambush—for his 'soldierly humanity'. Other I.R.A. men recalled their decency and restraint.[33] The caretaker at Macroom Castle, who was adamantly opposed to their presence, nevertheless reportedly found them to be 'very nice boys indeed'.[34]

Their first and only victim before Kilmichael was James Lehane, a married labourer from Ballymakeera, shot and killed on 17 October. Like the previous two men killed by the army in that neighbourhood, he was not a Volunteer. Bill Munro, a member of 'C' Company, wrote: 'This incident depressed us, especially as it was a stupid and unnecessary death and it had, so to speak, opened war, which we had not wanted.'[35]

The real war was yet to come, however. In fact, the Auxiliaries had cowed the Macroom and Ballyvourney Volunteers and not a single ambush was mounted against the force until the end of November. I.R.A. activity in the area stopped almost completely.[36] The county inspector for Cork's West Riding was delighted. His end-of-the-month report for October declared Macroom to be 'now about the quietest part of the County'. His November report, written just before hearing of the disaster at Kilmichael and heavy with unintended irony, crowed that 'C' Company had had 'a most beneficial effect' and that 'the I.R.A. has also appreciated their presence and doubtless will do so more later on'.[37]

The Auxiliaries themselves did not feel quite so sanguine. They spent all their time either on patrol or in their barracks, isolated in an unknown, unfriendly landscape. The farmers and townspeople who saw them as an indomitable force were seen in turn as hostile and unfathomable. Their intelligence was usually weak so they could only grope in the dark against their foes, who refused to show themselves. They made few arrests.[38]

The I.R.A. drew first blood in early November. Two Auxiliary intelligence officers disappeared while travelling from Macroom to Cork. They had been kidnapped, interrogated, and executed, their bodies secretly buried.[39] The police never found out what happened.

[32]   Unnamed newspaper reports from Sept. 1920 (the *Star*?), quoted in Barry O'Brien, *A History of the Macroom G.A.A. Club, 1886–1987* (n.d.), 90.

[33]   Charlie Browne, interview (O'Malley Papers, P17b/112) and *The Story of the 7th*, 26–7; Deasy, *Towards Ireland Free*, 167; O'Suilleabhain, *Mountainy Men*, 91–2. Neither the *Examiner*—usually reliable in reporting police excesses—nor other newspapers in this period have any record of a 'reign of terror'.

[34]   Katherine Everett, *Bricks and Flowers* (London, 1949), 153 and Twohig, *Green Tears*, 61.

[35]   Gleeson, *Bloody Sunday*, 70. There are several different accounts of this incident—see Twohig, *Green Tears*, 30; *Examiner*, 18 Oct. 1920.

[36]   Twohig (*Green Tears*, 34) claims that this cessation of hostilities was ordered by Brigade Headquarters.

[37]   CI Monthly Reports, West Cork, Oct.– Nov. 1920 (CO 904/112).

[38]   Gleeson, *Bloody Sunday*, 62–9. Their poor arrest record can be deduced from newspaper reports and from the Manchester Regiment Record of Service.

[39]   I/O Cork Command to D/I, 9 July 1923 (MA, A/0909); Browne, *The Story of the 7th*, 34; Gleeson, *Bloody Sunday*, 69; *Examiner*, 5 Nov. 1921.

As winter approached, patrols became colder, wetter, and more perfunctory. The Auxiliaries had no real protection from the weather. They had been equipped as hastily as they were trained, did not have proper overcoats (one Volunteer at Kilmichael was astonished at how poorly dressed they were), and still travelled in open-topped lorries:

our patrols were no longer looked forward to, indeed they were becoming unpleasant. We finished each patrol soaked to the skin despite our mackintoshes. This discomfort I think may have been responsible for our disinclination to deviate from known roads. We would take patrols which we knew would only last so long; then we would be back to the dubious comfort of the Castle. However it came about, it is certain that each section officer got into the habit of doing the same patrol each time he was on duty. So much so was this the case that, knowing which one was on duty on any particular day, we knew where his patrol was going.[40]

So did the I.R.A. When the eighteen men of No. 2 section left the Castle on the bleak Sunday afternoon of 28 November, the West Cork flying column was waiting. The hunters had become the hunted.

The object of that day's patrol was a night-time search for a suspect to the south, near Dunmanway, in cooperation with troops of the Essex Regiment. The day had been a frosty one and now threatened rain, the storm clouds adding to the gloom of dusk. Dulled and overconfident after months of inaction, huddled together against the cold, the cadets looked ahead to one more routine mission. They had no reason or inclination to suspect a trap. When the first lorry rounded a corner and the driver and District Inspector Crake ('not a quick thinker although sound enough'[41]) saw what appeared to be a British officer ahead waving them down, no suspicions were aroused. The man in the uniform was Tom Barry.

Thomas Bernardine Barry was, in many ways, an unlikely revolutionary. The third son of a policeman turned publican, he had grown up in a large, prosperous, and loyal household in two loyalist towns, Rosscarbery and Bandon. Despite his later identification with the 'plain people' of West Cork, he had been well educated and well provided for. 'Bernard'—or 'Bernie', as he was often known before the troubles—spent a year in Mungret College in Limerick as an apostolic student but became a shop assistant rather than a priest.[42]

When war came in 1914, Barry was as carried away with excitement and patriotism as any other young man of Bandon. He joined up in June 1915, lying about his age in order to get in. His enthusiasm, family connections, and respectable background soon earned him the offer of a commission in the Munster Fusiliers, but he turned it down to remain an artilleryman. He saw

[40] Gleeson, *Bloody Sunday*, 70.   [41] Ibid. 71.
[42] *Mungret Annual* (1911–12), 48, 82.

action in France and was gassed at Ypres. By Easter 1916 Bombardier (later Sergeant) T. B. Barry was in Mesopotamia, the pride of patriotic West Cork:[43]

> And what of Gunner Barry,
> A fearless son is he;
> We hope he will return
> With the shining bronze V.C.

Sergeant Barry returned home in early 1919. Like his fellow veterans who ended up in the Auxiliary Division, Barry did not adjust easily to civilian life. Contemporaries describe him as a restless man looking for somewhere to fit in. He 'palled around' with other ex-soldiers but also sought out Volunteers and eventually tried several times to join the Bandon I.R.A. This and other units refused to have him, however, mistrusting his military service, associations, family—and intentions. He disliked, and was disliked by, one of the most important I.R.A. families in the district. It was even rumoured that he was a spy (although the same was said of many blameless ex-soldiers). The first public act for which he is remembered was his raising of the Union Jack on Armistice Day 1919.[44]

Barry has said that his nationalism was first awakened by the 1916 rising, deepened by his reading of Irish history, and aroused by the 'terrible arrogance' of the British forces.[45] This may well be true but local Volunteers felt that he 'could have gone either way' and that his turn towards republicanism was occasioned by a break with the veterans' association in Bandon. Apparently he felt slighted over his pension.[46]

Local prejudice kept him out of the movement until the late summer of 1920, by which time he was enrolled at a commercial college in Cork city. Times were changing, though, and the onset of outright guerrilla warfare was making new demands on the West (3rd) Cork Brigade. Men were needed who could shoot a rifle and teach others to do the same. Barry was approached, this time by the brigade staff rather than local battalion or company commanders, and he was

---

[43] The song was published as 'Fighting Men of Skib' (n.d.), a copy of which is in the Centenary File of the Abbeystrewrey Parish Union. This biographical information comes from a variety of sources, but primarily from the Barry family's manuscript census return for 1911 (NA) and from interviews with several I.R.A. comrades and Bandon contemporaries, especially with AE, AD, 28 Apr. 1989, and AC, 6 Apr. 1990. The file on Barry compiled by Dublin Castle—which describes him as suffering from a 'swollen head'—includes references to his service record (WO 35/206). See also Fionntan O Leathlobhair, 'Tom Barry', in *The Spirit of Freedom* (Dublin: 1983), 60–3 and Meda Ryan, *The Tom Barry Story* (Cork, 1982), 12–15. For admiring reports of his military career, see *Examiner*, 10 Nov. 1915 and *Eagle*, 22 Jan. 1916. I am grateful to Martin Staunton for the former reference.

[44] Interviews with AD and AB, 2 Apr. 1988; Ted O'Sullivan (O'Malley Papers, P17b/108). It should be noted that O'Sullivan's testimony, like that of some other West Cork veterans, was coloured by considerable personal animosity. However, see also Ryan, *Tom Barry Story*, and O Leathlobhair, 'Tom Barry'.

[45] Griffith and O'Grady, *Curious Journey*, 86–7, 125 and Barry, *Guerilla Days*, 2–3.

[46] Interviews with AE and AD.

finally given the post of brigade training officer (and later, flying column leader). It was also probably no coincidence that Barry was suddenly recruited immediately after Tom Hales, the founding commandant of the West Cork Brigade, was captured and replaced by Charlie Hurley, who had not previously known him.[47]

In the end, though, it might have been his family connections which got him in. Barry had several cousins in the movement who vouched for him, although none of his brothers joined and his parents' conservative politics apparently remained unchanged. For him, as for many others, the rebellion against Britain may also have served as a rebellion against his father.[48]

Barry's personality—vain, angry, and ruthless—dominated events at Kilmichael just as his version of those events has dominated their history. He was a harsh disciplinarian and a tough commander. He imposed his rule by force of personality, which could be withering. Some who served under him became fiercely loyal and remained so for the rest of their lives. Others disliked him. Everyone respected his fighting abilities. To Tom Barry, revolution meant combat and killing, and he used this yardstick to judge everyone else.[49] He was a hard man obsessed with his own hardness.

This ruthlessness was well demonstrated in his planning for Kilmichael.[50] The terrain at the ambush site was rocky and barren and the column was placed very close to the road, allowing only for attack and not retreat. Everything was staked on achieving surprise: if the Auxiliaries were alert and gained the upper hand, the column would be trapped. Barry was intent on total victory. He gave an order to fix bayonets and posted men to prevent any Auxiliaries escaping. It was to be a fight to the finish, he declared.

Barry did not tell his men the plan (or his choice of target) until the last minute and he did not tell his superiors at all:[51] They might well have stopped him if they had known (and this may account for his claim in the 1920 report that the encounter was unplanned). Kilmichael was not only risky, it was also outside brigade boundaries, in the 1st Cork Brigade area. This was a matter of great sensitivity where I.R.A. units, and particularly Cork 1, were concerned. The Macroom and Ballyvourney Battalions had in fact been planning their own assault on Macroom Castle, which had to be cancelled after Kilmichael to their considerable annoyance.[52]

[47]   Michael Crowley statement (NLI, Crowley family papers, Acc. 4767).

[48]   Barry has not once publicly referred to his parents or siblings in connection with his revolutionary career. I was told several times by contemporaries that Barry and his father did not get along and that this was part of the reason he ran away to join the army in 1914.

[49]   See Barry, *The Reality of the Anglo-Irish War*, 14, 58–9; C. S. Andrews, *Dublin Made Me* (Dublin, 1979), 280.

[50]   It is clear that, contrary to Barry's initial report, the ambush *was* planned: the positions had been previously reconnoitred, scouts were called up from a nearby company, and the column itself was in position, waiting, all day.   [51]   Barry, *Guerilla Days*, 38.

[52]   Mick O'Sullivan (O'Malley Papers, P17b/111); Browne, *The Story of the 7th*, 32. The former is the same Micheal O'Suilleabhain who wrote *Where Mountainy Men Have Sown*, and the latter is the name used in this book.

Barry 'made his name out of Kilmichael' and this was probably one of his aims from the outset.[53] He had a lot to prove. He was still under suspicion and was 'watched day and night whilst he was helping at training'.[54] His first attempted ambush at Fanlobus did not come off, although part of the column did score a success at Newcestown in his absence on 9 October. The second ambush in which he participated, at Toureen on 24 October, found its mark but Barry was not the planner and only commanded a section. Each of these actions had followed a training camp. The third camp did not even try an ambush. Barry also attempted two assassinations with the brigade O/C, Charlie Hurley, but neither came off.[55]

Kilmichael, then, represented Barry's first independent command (a fact he ensured by keeping it a secret) and his main chance to prove himself. Hence, perhaps, the risk-taking and ruthlessness. To his men, on the morning of the ambush, his intentions were clear. There could be no retreat for either side.[56]

As the first lorry slowed to a halt, Barry threw a grenade into the window of the cab and gave the signal to begin firing. The grenade exploded on top of the driver and District Inspector Crake. Both men were killed or badly wounded and the tender lurched off the road and into the ditch. The remaining passengers were caught completely by surprise. Some of these seven Auxiliaries were too shocked or did not have enough time to return fire before being mown down. The lorry itself offered no protection. Several tried to run up a nearby lane but did not get very far. All were shot at very close range, in some cases, face to face. One at least was bayoneted to death according to Tom Barry, who was in the thick of the action.[57]

Within a few minutes all of the first lorry's occupants were dead or incapacitated. Events happened so fast that no coherent account can be assembled. The dominant impressions that remain are the Auxiliaries' panic and the furious shooting of the guerrillas.

[53] Interview with AD.   [54] Ted O'Sullivan (O'Malley Papers, P17b/108).

[55] Barry, *Guerilla Days*, 24–35; Deasy, *Towards Ireland Free*, 141–7, 154–60; Con Crowley, 'West Cork Column Taught the Essex a Lesson at Toureen', in *Rebel Cork's Fighting Story* (Tralee, n.d.), 102–3.

[56] The following reconstruction is based on six detailed interviews carried out with Kilmichael veterans, three of them conducted by Dr John Chisholm, two by myself (interviews with AA, 3 Apr., 25 June 1988; AF, 19 Nov. 1989), and one held by the Ballineen/Enniskeane Area Heritage Group. In addition, the latter have a detailed statement written by one of the ambush party. I was also fortunate enough to be given a tour of the ambush site by one of my interviewees. Dr Chisholm recorded extensive interviews in the late 1960s while researching and editing Liam Deasy's memoirs (hereafter referred to as 'Chisholm interviews'), and the Ballineen/Enniskeane Group have also collected a unique set of material on the ambush in the 1990s. I am very grateful to both for giving me access to their research. Names have been withheld to protect confidentiality: several interviewees were extremely nervous about discussing Kilmichael in detail. A good map of the ambush site can be found in the Ballineen/Enniskeane Group's *The Wild Heather Glen: The Kilmichael Story of Grief and Glory* (Ballineen/Enniskeane, 1995), along with a reproduction of a police map, 37, 148–9. Photographs of the site can be found in 'A Report on the Intelligence Branch of the Chief of Police, Dublin Castle, from May 1920 to July 1921', 7 (WO 35/214).

[57] Barry, *Guerilla Days*, 44.

The second lorry was about a hundred yards behind the first when the ambush began. The driver reacted immediately and tried to turn around. The road was narrow, however, and he reversed into a bog and became stuck. At this point the second section of guerrillas began firing but they were some distance from their targets and did not have quite the same advantage of surprise as Barry's section. Consequently, most of the Auxiliaries survived the first volley and were able to get out and down on the road or under the lorry. These men proved difficult to suppress and were able to return fire. Two Volunteers, Jim O'Sullivan and Michael McCarthy, were hit in the head and killed where they lay.[58] The cadets had little cover, however, and most were quickly put out of action. Soon only three were left fighting.

Accounts of what happened next around the second lorry are coloured by the confusion and noise of battle, the speed with which the action took place, and the difficulty of seeing in the growing darkness. Because of this, no one person saw everything and different witnesses describe events somewhat differently. Nevertheless, certain facts are agreed upon by several independently interviewed witnesses. At least two Auxiliaries stood with their hands up and surrendered:

There was a Tan under the lorry—I came up behind him. He was firing down the road. I fired at him, told him to put his hands up. He came out and laid down his arms and said 'what am I going to do?' I told him to go down the road to the others and they'll tell you . . . I saw [an I.R.A. man] with another surrendered Tan.[59]

Two were left—I don't believe they were ever wounded. They got up with their hands in the air and approached [Michael] McCarthy's section.

One of these men was shot in the head. The other was clubbed down and then shot several times.[60]

Another Auxiliary ran away towards the only visible farmhouse: 'Some began to surrender. The driver of the lorry tried to run. I ran after him. He could have shot me as well as I could have shot him . . . [he was] shot down with his hands up.'

At about the same time Pat Deasy was shot in the stomach and mortally wounded. It is not clear whether this occurred before or after the surrenders. Two witnesses saw him get up from his position but no one remembers seeing him get shot. The Auxiliaries were spread out and it is reasonable to suppose that, while the others were giving up, another wounded Cadet (whom Deasy

---

[58] All of the men interviewed agree on this point: McCarthy and O'Sullivan did not stand up and did not die because of a fake surrender. Two of these veterans considered Barry's account to be an insult to the memory of these men.

[59] This and the following four quotes are from Chisholm interviews.

[60] Meda Ryan (*Tom Barry Story*, 35) states that: 'one Volunteer told me that he had come behind a man and ordered him to drop his gun which he did. He was walking him up the road as a prisoner when a shot dropped him at his feet.' This may have been the encounter described in the first quotation above.

thought was dead) did not see or care, and fired at Deasy when he approached (as Barry reported in 1920).[61]

Possibly even before this took place, Volunteers at the first lorry had begun finishing off wounded Auxiliaries. One man pulled from the lorry pleaded, 'Don't shoot me, I'm a Catholic' but was immediately 'shot off'. All were given the same treatment. One guerrilla observed, 'I saw the first lorry below and men shooting Tans' (and added 'I suppose I shouldn't be saying that now').

After Barry came up to the second lorry and the surrendered Englishmen had been executed, the same procedure was followed. One I.R.A. man came upon a wounded Auxiliary 'crying after me', and told Barry. He said, 'finish him', placed his revolver to the man's head and pulled the trigger.[62] 'Barry made us,' said another. 'He shot one, then we shot one.' Eventually each man was shot in the head. Some of the Volunteers apparently refused to take part and several 'were getting hysterical' from the shock of so much death on both sides. 'One man got sick on the road and he had to be taken away.' To regain discipline and control, Barry then drilled his men amid the bodies and past the burning lorries.

Cadet H. F. Forde survived being clubbed and shot in the head, but remained paralysed with brain damage for the remainder of his life. He was fortunate in a sense that his condition so approximated death. If he were more obviously alive he would undoubtedly have been shot again. Another Auxiliary, Cecil Guthrie, actually managed to escape. He was the driver who had run and been 'shot down'. This was in fact an error as the man who had done the shooting forgot to check the body. Guthrie survived and slipped away in the darkness towards Macroom. He got to within 2 miles of town before being spotted and recaptured by two local Volunteers pretending to be armed. Guthrie was executed two days later and buried secretly in Annahala Bog, south of town.[63]

Finally, one more death should probably be added to the Kilmichael list, that

---

[61] In *Guerilla Days*, Barry tells this story as having happened to him. One witness (AF—a scout rather than a rifleman, and therefore further away from the ambush site than the other interviewees) saw several Auxiliaries surrender *after* the three Volunteers were hit, but then heard further firing, some of which he believed came from the Englishmen. Because of this, he says there was a sort of false surrender, but that no I.R.A. men died as a result. To confuse things further, Meda Ryan (*Tom Barry Story*, 34) concluded from her investigation that Deasy died *before* any Auxiliaries surrendered, falsely or otherwise (although it should be mentioned that Ryan is a firm believer in the 'false surrender' story).

[62] This and the following two quotations are from the interview with AF. Barry, in one of his many about-faces, seems to have admitted what happened to Meda Ryan (*Tom Barry Story*, 35): 'At this stage Barry didn't want prisoners—especially men who used deceptive tactics . . . Barry himself said he accepted full responsibility for shooting them outright. "Soldiers who had cheated in war deserved to die." '

[63] See the correspondence between the Guthrie family and others contained in the Dept. of Justice file H16/6 (NA). As a result of these inquiries, Guthrie's body was discovered, exhumed, and buried in the Inchigeela Church of Ireland graveyard in 1926. See also I/O Cork Command to D/I, 9 July 1923; Browne, *The Story of the 7th*, 34. Barry claimed (presumably knowing the truth) that 'after he had been shot, he crawled to the bog hole near the side of the road, where he died and his body sank out of sight'. *Guerilla Days*, 51.

of the commander of 'C' Company, ex-Colonel Buxton Smith. Shortly after his unit was disbanded in January 1922 he committed suicide in London. It was said at the inquest that he had been constantly depressed over the deaths of his men, for which he held himself responsible.[64] A week after Kilmichael, Buxton Smith told a visitor:[65]

When I first came here I little knew what I was in for. I can trust no one. Already I have lost twenty-five of my men, and they are getting hard to hold. I can't give them any exercise—can't even allow them to knock a ball about in the park, lest they are sniped at from over the wall. They can't walk a yard or go into a shop without danger, and they are savage for revenge.

Buxton Smith did manage to hold them: 'he kept his own men in order which was something.'[66] Only a few half-hearted reprisals against houses and haysheds were carried out around Macroom, belying their reputation as terrorists.[67] They even protected their prisoners from revenge attacks. When policemen from other barracks came to interrogate Con Crowley, a Kilbrittain I.R.A. man arrested before the ambush, he was warned and sent to Cork Hospital to keep him from harm.[68]

The company was too badly mauled to continue effectively. Within a month they were moved to Dublin, where they ceased to act as an independent unit.[69]

The account which emerges from detailed interviews with survivors supports much of the official British story. The Auxiliaries were decoyed by what appeared to be a British officer and attacked by men wearing steel helmets and carrying service rifles with fixed bayonets. Helpless wounded men and prisoners were killed after the battle was over. Axes and shotguns were not used but bayonets and revolvers at point-blank range were. In retrospect, British information seems to have been remarkably accurate. Barry's 'history' of Kilmichael, on the other hand, is riddled with lies and evasions. There was no false surrender as he described it. The surviving Auxiliaries were simply 'exterminated'.

The question remains: why? It may well be that the deaths of O'Sullivan, McCarthy, and Deasy enraged some of their comrades enough to seek revenge. This was how one of them remembered it: 'they died, to my mind, a cruel death, because the men that were in with Mick McCarthy, where he was shot, they knew their two men were shot and they came out and they shot them and I think a bayonet was used on one or maybe two of them.'[70] General Crozier, after resigning and becoming a vocal critic of the Auxiliary Division and British policy in Ireland, asserted that:

[64] *Star*, 11 Feb. 1922. See also Crozier's (largely inaccurate) account in *Ireland for Ever*, 196.
[65] Everett, *Bricks and Flowers*, 154.   [66] Crozier, *Ireland for Ever*, 196.
[67] See *Memories of Dromleigh, a Country School: 1840–1990* (1990), 72–4, which suggests that British troops killed a man in Kilmichael in reprisal for the ambush. No other source supports this story.   [68] Michael Crowley statement.
[69] Gleeson, *Bloody Sunday*, 75–6.
[70] Taped interview in the possession of the Ballineen/Enniskeane Heritage Group.

It was perfectly true that the wounded had been put to death after the ambush, but the reason for this barbarous inhumanity became understandable although inexcusable . . . Arms were supposed to have been surrendered, but a wounded Auxiliary whipped out a revolver while lying on the ground and shot a 'Shinner' with the result that all his comrades were put to death with him, the rebels 'seeing red', a condition akin to going mad.[71]

Perhaps Deasy *was* shot after the other policemen surrendered and this was perceived as a trick. On the other hand, why execute all the wounded men and Cadet Guthrie? Presumably 'to allow no survivor to disclose their methods' (or identities) as British investigators suggested. There is also a strong possibility that Barry intended to wipe the Auxiliaries out from the very beginning to ensure total victory and to impress both the British and his detractors. It was he who ordered the wounded to be killed and made sure it was done. Taken together with the shooting of prisoners and the original order to let no one escape, the killings appear to be part of a premeditated plan. It certainly seems significant that in previous attacks where Barry was not the only brigade officer present—such as at Toureen—enemy prisoners were treated decently, but at Kilmichael and subsequent actions they were liable to be summarily executed.[72]

Kilmichael is important not just because of its effect on the course of the revolution in Cork but also because it has helped define the revolution in military and moral terms. This is how Barry and other I.R.A. chroniclers wanted it to be seen, as a 'formal engagement', the centrepiece of a heroic military campaign.[73] The I.R.A. fought fairly and won a brilliant victory. The Auxiliaries were terrorists. They acted treacherously and deserved to be annihilated.

Kilmichael was a brave, daring, and even brilliant ambush but it turned into a massacre. In the end, it belonged to the same world of 'disappearances' and revenge killings as the shootings on White Street and Broad Lane (which happened only a week before). Such events shared a common language, used by all sides: the victim is always a 'terrorist' or 'spy', he is often killed 'attempting

---

[71] Crozier, *Ireland for Ever*, 128. Crozier stated that 'I journeyed to Cork to find out the truth about this carnage, and as I was in mufti and unknown, learned a great deal, not only about the ambush.' That a senior British police officer could have infiltrated the West Cork I.R.A. to such an extent is simply incredible. It is clear that Crozier picked up this information—which certainly does not have an authentic ring to it—*after* he had resigned and after he had become *persona grata* to republican leaders such as Michael Collins (see 219–24). Much of the material in his book clearly came from this source.

[72] For example, two of three captured British soldiers were shot in Bandon on 22 Feb. 1921 in revenge for previous British killings (Cork 3 Column Report No. 4: Mulcahy Papers, P7/A/38). The famous attack on Rosscarbery barracks on 23 March 1921 is another interesting case, with a parallel claim of a police 'false surrender'. Compare the account in *Guerilla Days* with his initial report (Column Report, 6 Apr. 1921: Mulcahy Papers, P7/A/38) and Ted O'Sullivan (O'Malley Papers, P17b/108).

[73] Tom Barry's foreword to Butler, *Barry's Flying Column*.

to escape' or after a false surrender. Or he is simply 'the enemy' and must be killed to avenge a past killing or deter a future one: 'If we didn't wipe them out, they'd wipe us out.'[74]

The reality of Kilmichael shows how difficult it is to categorize acts of violence or give them moral and military coherence. It also raises important questions about the nature and dynamics of the guerrilla war in Cork, which is the subject of the following chapters.

[74] I.R.A. 'survivor', quoted in the *Star*, 16 Jan. 1971.

3

Rebel Cork

There is a high political spirit down there, and they are a very divided race.
(Head Constable William Butler, Cork city, 1914)[1]

Cork . . . is a modern Bagdad for romantic and astonishing happenings.
(*Daily Mail*, Feb. 1917)[2]

Cork is the first county of twentieth-century Ireland by area and the second by population (392,000 in 1911), including its third largest city (77,000).[3] It is certainly the most various in its geography, bordered on the north and east by the plains and rolling hills of Tipperary, Limerick, and Waterford, on the west by the Kerry mountains, and on the south by a long, often rugged coastline of many harbours and islands. These elements are to some extent drawn together by three major rivers running west to east, the Blackwater, the Lee and the Bandon.

The economy of turn-of-the-century Cork was correspondingly diverse, although many of its sectors were united in long-running decline. Cork had once been the most populous county in Ireland, with extensive industries; nowhere had nineteenth-century changes been more costly. Woollen mills, breweries, and distilleries were still important employers in the city and surrounding towns before the Great War, but many had closed in previous decades, and Cork businesses had lost ground to competitors in Dublin and Belfast (although Murphy's and Beamish and Crawford's were holding their own against Guinness in local beer markets). Business was booming for flour mills throughout the county but, while investment was growing, the number of mills and workers was declining. Shipbuilding had almost disappeared apart from the repair work done at the naval dockyards in Cork Harbour.[4] The brightest spot was the city's new Ford tractor and car factory, which started production in 1919 and employed nearly 2,000 men.[5]

---

[1] *Appendix to the Report of the Committee of Inquiry into the R.I.C and D.M.P.*, 103.

[2] Quoted in *Examiner*, 27 Feb. 1917.

[3] The city total for 1911 does not include the suburbs of Douglas and Blackrock. Dublin city and county together had a larger population in 1911 but, cities apart, Cork had the largest rural and small town population in the country.

[4] Andy Bielenberg, *Cork's Industrial Revolution 1780–1880: Development or Decline?* (Cork, 1991); Maura Cronin, 'Work and Workers in Cork City and County 1800–1900', in Patrick O'Flanagan and Cornelius G. Buttimer (eds.), *Cork: History and Society* (Dublin, 1993), 721–54; Linehan, 'Cork's Economy and Business Attitudes'; D. J. Coakley (ed.), *Cork: Its Trade and Commerce. Official Handbook of the Cork Inc. Chamber of Commerce and Shipping* (Cork, 1919).

[5] *Ford in Ireland: The First Sixty Years, 1917–1977* (Dublin, 1977), 12–16; D. S. Jacobson, 'The Political Economy of Industrial Location: The Ford Motor Company at Cork, 1912–26', *Irish Economic and Social History* (1977).

A single imported plant, even with all of its opportunities for skilled workers, could not reverse the steady shrinkage of most native traditional trades, from coopers to shoemakers.[6] However, this negative trend and accompanying poverty[7] (by no means confined to Cork) was accompanied by another product of post-famine modernization and economic growth: modern services and their associated industries and professions. Railways (five altogether in the county), electric power, the Post Office, telephones and telegraphs, motor cars, branch banking, general and department stores, schools and colleges, general hospitals, surgeries and dispensaries, even a small but active stock market, all created jobs where none had existed before. And much of this new economy required literacy, numeracy, secondary or university education: the foundation for a new middle class.

It was agriculture that supported much of this industry and most of Cork's communities. Most crops and livestock were raised on family farms, but their circumstances and output varied with their size and the quality of the land. Western Cork, with its hills and bogs, was dominated by small mixed farms and sheep pastures. To the north and east, the soil was better, the ground more level, urban markets closer, and farms much larger. Here in lowland 'cow country', dairying and cattle-raising predominated, entailing as well a substantial agricultural labour force.[8] 'Big houses' and their demesnes, built by landlords in the eighteenth and nineteenth centuries, still held a prominent place in many of these communities but their land—and with it their remaining power—was rapidly and massively being transferred to their former tenants under the 1903 and 1909 Land Acts.[9] In fact, the farmers of Cork led the country in the extent of their purchases.

The landed gentry were typically Protestant, as were many of the city's leading businessmen, but most of their co-religionists were farmers, shopkeepers, or workers. Together they formed a sizeable minority in the city and suburbs, and in the south-western towns and parishes of Somerville and Ross's 'Mr. Knox's Country'. The great majority were members of the Church of Ireland but the city had active Presbyterian and Baptist churches as well, and there were also Methodist congregations of long standing around the county, as well as a persistent non-sectarian tradition of household worship.[10] This large rural Protestant

---

[6] Maura Cronin, *County, Class or Craft? The Politicisation of the Skilled Artisan in Nineteenth-Century Cork* (Cork, 1994), 1–58, and (as Maura Murphy) 'The Economic and Social Structure of Nineteenth Century Cork', in David Harkness and Mary O'Dowd (eds.), *The Town in Ireland* (Belfast, 1981).

[7] A. M. MacSweeney, *Poverty in Cork* (Cork, 1917).

[8] See James S. Donnelly, Jr., *The Land and People of Nineteenth Century Cork* (London, 1975). Also useful for their detailed analysis of farm life are M. Murphy, 'Financial Results on Mixed Dairy Farms in 1937–'38' (in West Cork) and 'Financial Results on Sixty-One West Cork Farms in 1940–'41', *Journal of the Statistical Society of Ireland* (1938–9, 1941–2).

[9] The story of one 'big house' is brilliantly told in Elizabeth Bowen, *Bowen's Court* (London, 1942).

[10] See Ian D'Alton, 'Southern Irish Unionism: A Study of Cork Unionists, 1884–1914', *Transactions of the Royal Historical Society* (1973); id., 'Keeping Faith: An Evocation of the Cork Protestant Character, 1820–1920', in O'Flanagan and Buttimer (eds.), *Cork: History and Society,*

population, which set Cork apart from its even more Catholic neighbours, was itself in part a residue of sixteenth- and seventeenth-century plantations. These people and their past—by no means forgotten—lent a distinct and sometimes sectarian cast to local society. The town of Bandon, for example, was known as 'Orange Bandon' and 'the Derry of the South'. Finally, and not insignificantly, the city also contained a compact and vital Jewish community—'Jewtown'— recently transposed from several Baltic villages.[11]

These deeply rooted regional differences—physical, economic, social, religious, and cultural—inevitably produced distinct local identities, with their own accents, vocabularies, senses of place, and loyalties towards people, parties, or teams. In 1918 the local government inspector for Cork reported that:

You meet parties everywhere whose outlook, on most aspects of life, is altered by a Parish boundary. In dealing with Parochial matters many of them display striking originality, but their intensity of feeling on these minor subjects, combined with their bitter intolerance of opposition and their multifarious petty jealousies, seems to completely consume their intellectual brilliance . . . They follow, with unquestioning obedience, on any matter not strictly local, the view of their leader for the time being.[12]

In West Cork (roughly, west of Bandon and south of Macroom), resentment of the city was accompanied by equally fierce internecine quarrels, ably chronicled and fuelled by its own Skibbereen-based newspapers, the *Southern Star* and the *Eagle* (which had famously warned the Tsar that it had its eye on him). Both papers had devoted followers who spurned the other, the *Eagle* having a less 'national' and more 'Protestant' reputation. As with other recognizably bounded areas, West Cork was marked out by names, such as O'Sullivan or Kingston, and the long-tailed territories and families that embodied them.[13]

Another self-conscious region lay north of Macroom and west of Mallow, in the north-western baronies of west Muskerry and Duhallow. This place, roughly corresponding to the Gaelic heartland *Sliabh Luacra*, was home to the largest concentration of Irish-speakers in the county and, partly as a result, had a particularly rich oral and verse culture.[14]

Cork city (usually simply 'Cork') itself stood out perhaps most of all in terms

755–92; and his more detailed 'Southern Irish Unionism: A Study of Cork City and County Unionists, 1885–1914', MA thesis (Cork, 1972). Also illuminating, in very different ways, are George Bennett, *The History of Bandon and the Principal Towns in the West Riding of County Cork* (Cork, 1869) and Lennox and Tom Robinson, and Nora Dorman, *Three Homes* (London, 1938).

[11] Louis Hyman, *The Jews of Ireland from Earliest Times to the Year 1910* (Shannon, 1972), 218–33; John Crowley, 'Cork's Jewish Community', BA thesis (Cork, 1987); Cecil Hurwitz, *From Synagogue to Church* (Cork, 1991).

[12] LGB Inspector, Cork, to Sir Henry Robinson, 28 May 1918 (IWM, Lord French Papers).

[13] Jeremiah O'Mahony, *West Cork and its Story* (Cork, 1961, 1975); Crowley, *In West Cork Long Ago*; William J. Smyth, 'The Personality of West Cork', *Chimera* (1989–90); *Southern Star Centenary Supplement 1889–1989* (Skibbereen, 1989).

[14] Brendan Clifford, *Duhallow: Notes toward a History* (Cork, 1986); Brendan Clifford and Jack Lane (eds.), *A North Cork Miscellany* (Cork, 1987) and *Ned Buckley's Poems* (1987).

of its self-regard and self-absorption, its steep hills and island core adding to its insularity. Its industrial stagnation added to the occasionally passionate resentment of Dublin. This urban Cork was dense with its own particular accent, slang, characters, nicknames, dynasties, and local knowledge, fed from outside by arrivals from the country and criss-crossed by neighbourhood allegiances and rivalries. It too possessed a divided audience for its daily newspapers, the nationalist *Examiner* and the unionist *Constitution*.[15]

Despite these separate and sometimes antagonistic regions, there did exist an overarching sense of identity, of Corkness.[16] However stereotyped, this provoked strong characterization from outsiders and Corkmen and women alike. Among the adjectives applied: provincial, proud, boastful, sly, secretive, dark, clever, clannish, grasping, brash, vain, domineering. John Barry Arnold, an inspector for the Ministry of Pensions in Cork during and after the war, found that, 'like the peoples of the east the inhabitants . . . thrive on brokerage' and 'if there was Government money going a begging it was to be raked in at every opportunity'. 'The mentality of the Cork man', he added, 'provided me with considerable amusement. He is as clever as they make them and suavity personified.'[17] For Ernie O'Malley, an I.R.A. organizer from Dublin, 'there was a bumptiousness in the Cork temperament. They resembled the Gascons; quick and volatile, but they seemed too conscious of their qualities; as if they were surprised at possessing them.'[18]

For outsiders in the revolutionary movement and elsewhere, Corkness often seemed to manifest itself in clever and ambitious young men on the make, Michael Collins (from West Cork) being the outstanding example. An earlier generation of such men had already made their mark on Irish nationalist politics, led by William O'Brien and Tim Healy. Both men became national leaders within the Irish Party, and attracted ardent followers, but they were also natural dissidents. When O'Brien's (and Healy's) enemies in the party notoriously ordered that no one with a 'Cork accent' would be allowed on the platform at the 1909 'baton' convention, dissent and outraged pride crystallized into a new party, the All For Ireland League.[19]

[15] O'Faolain, *An Irish Journey*, 75–93; Sean Beecher, *A Dictionary of Cork Slang* (Cork, 1983) and *The Story of Cork*; Smyth, 'Explorations of Space'; Verdon, *Shawlies, Echo Boys, the Marsh and the Lanes*. See also Frank O'Connor's comments in Hew Wheldon (ed.), *Monitor: An Anthology* (London, 1962); John O'Brien, 'Population, Politics and Society in Cork, 1780–1900' and A. M. Fahy, 'Place and Class in Cork', in O'Flanagan and Buttimer (eds.), *Cork: History and Society*, 699–720, 793–812.

[16] John A. Murphy, 'Cork: Anatomy and Essence', in O'Flanagan and Buttimer (eds.), *Cork: History and Society*, 1–14; Sean Dunne (ed.), *The Cork Anthology* (Cork, 1993).

[17] John Barry Arnold recollections, 127–9 (Peter Liddle Collection, Leeds University).

[18] Ernie O'Malley, *On Another Man's Wound* (London, 1936), 198.

[19] Joseph V. O'Brien, *William O'Brien and the Course of Irish Politics 1881–1918* (Berkeley, Calif., 1976), 185–211; Paul Bew, *Conflict and Conciliation in Ireland 1890–1910: Parnellites and Radical Agrarians* (Oxford, 1987), 185–9. Two memoirs of Cork politics are Cpt. D. D. Sheehan, *Ireland since Parnell* (London, 1921) and John J. Horgan, *Parnell to Pearse: Some Recollections and Reflections* (Dublin, 1948).

From the start, this organization was effectively confined to Cork. Its newspaper, an O'Brienite rival to the *Examiner*, began life as the defiantly titled *Cork Accent*, although it was soon renamed the *Cork Free Press*.[20] After the second election of 1910, all of its MPs sat for Cork constituencies—and every Cork member but one was an AFIL supporter. John Redmond's Home Rule party and its affiliates, the United Irish League and the Ancient Order of Hibernians, remained a vital force, however, which fought back successfully in by-elections and in the city- and county-wide struggle for control of local government.[21] Thus, after 1909, politics in Cork was uniquely divided between competing nationalist parties, and the battle between O'Brienites and Redmondites— between 'All Fors' and 'Mollies'—often followed the twists and turns of neighbourhood and faction. As Frank O'Connor depicted it:

I don't profess to remember what we inhabitants of Blarney Lane were patriotic about: all I remember is that we were very patriotic, that our main principles were something called 'Conciliation and Consent,' and that our great national leader, William O'Brien, once referred to us as 'The Old Guard.' Myself and other kids of the Old Guard used to parade the street with tin cans and toy trumpets, singing 'We'll hang Johnnie Redmond on a sour apple tree.'

Unfortunately, our neighbourhood was bounded to the south by a long ugly street leading uphill to the cathedral, and the lanes off it were infested with the most wretched specimens of humanity who took the Redmondite side for whatever could be got from it in the way of drink . . . It always saddened me, coming through this street on my way from school, and seeing the poor misguided children, barefoot and in rags, parading with tin cans and toy trumpets and singing 'We'll hang William O'Brien on a sour apple tree.' It left me with very little hope for Ireland.[22]

Few areas of Cork's public life were left undivided by the struggle, including organized labour. This had its own political traditions. The Trade and Labour Council was able to maintain a steady presence on the corporation, but it did little to change the complexion of debate due to its conservatism: the *fin de siècle* Irish Republican Socialist Party had not survived clerical and trade union hostility. The prospect of a more radical working-class politics appeared with the enlistment of unskilled labourers by James Larkin's new Irish Transport and General Workers' Union in 1908 and 1909. It lost its struggle for control of the city docks to rivals and the emergent Employers' Federation but it was not this which defeated labour in the 1911 and 1914 municipal elections. The Trade and Labour Council, caught up in the all-embracing party

[20] Brendan Clifford (ed.), *Reprints from the 'Cork Free Press': An Account of Ireland's Only Democratic Anti-Partition Movement* (Cork, 1984).

[21] For parliamentary seats, see Brian M. Walker, *Parliamentary Election Results in Ireland, 1801–1922* (Dublin, 1978); for local elections, see *Constitution*, 17 Jan., 6 June 1914; *Cork Free Press*, 6–8 June 1914.

[22] Frank O'Connor, 'The Cornet Player Who Betrayed Ireland', *Collected Stories* (1982), 686–7. See also his memoir, *An Only Child* (London, 1961), 6.

conflict, backed William O'Brien and the AFIL, while a breakaway group turned to the UIL.[23] So too did the Land and Labour Associations—farm labourers' unions—split. Independent labour candidates were simply squeezed out of the running.

The mysteries of Conciliation and Home Rule did not entirely exhaust the political sentiments of Cork. Unionism existed in the organized form of the Irish Unionist Alliance and a few unionist clubs and Orange lodges, in the pages of the *Constitution*, and as the preference of most Protestants. For most, though, this was a passive, unexpressed allegiance as they joined no organizations and had no unionist candidates to vote for.[24]

At the other end of the ideological spectrum, there was also a constellation of small clubs, leagues, and societies in the city and some towns decrying party politics in favour of national regeneration. The largest of these was the Gaelic League, which sought to revive the Irish language, and which was officially apolitical. The activists within the League tended to be active outside it as well, as cultural or republican nationalists under the rubric of Sinn Fein.[25] Some of these attached themselves as a separatist fringe to the AFIL, partly out of a mutual opposition to the Home Rule party machine. This generally youthful counter-culture was notable for the participation of women—usually barred from mainstream political life—and the consequent strain of feminism found therein. It also found literary expression in journals and in a home-grown theatre movement which included T. C. Murray, Daniel Corkery, and Lennox Robinson.[26]

The most militant men of this radical clubland led a double life as members of the underground Irish Republican Brotherhood (I.R.B.), known to initiates simply as 'the organization'. This revolutionary secret society had existed in Cork since the 1860s, and had once thrived among its shopworkers and tradesmen.[27] By 1910 it was moribund, a home for old Fenians. In the years before the war, it underwent a modest revival, particularly in Cork and Dublin, brought

---

[23]   Stephen McQuay Reddick, 'Political and Industrial Labour in Cork 1899–1914', MA thesis (Cork, 1984); Emmet Larkin, *James Larkin: Irish Labour Leader 1876–1947* (London, 1965), 65–72.

[24]   Ian D'Alton, 'Cork Unionism: Its Role in Parliamentary and Local Elections, 1885–1914', *Studia Hibernica* (1975); Peter Hart, 'The Protestant Experience of Revolution in Southern Ireland, 1911–1926', in Richard English and Graham Walker (eds.), *Unionism in Modern Ireland: New Perspectives on Politics and Culture* (London, 1996).

[25]   Examination of Mrs Margaret Buckley (NA, Sinn Fein Funds Case, 2B/82/118).

[26]   The most detailed guide to this little world is Liam de Roiste's memoirs, serialized in the *Evening Echo* beginning on 19 Aug. 1954. These were based on de Roiste's voluminous diaries, which can be found in the de Roiste Papers (CAI, U271). See also Roibeard Langford statement (Langford Papers, CAI, U155); Liam Ruiseal, *Liam Ruiseal Remembers* (Cork, 1978), 9–20; Moiron Chavasse, *Terence MacSwiney* (Dublin, 1961), 22–34; Florence O'Donoghue, *Tomas MacCurtain: Soldier and Patriot* (Tralee, 1971), 15–25; and Patrick Maume, *'Life That is Exile': Daniel Corkery and the Search for Irish Ireland* (Belfast, 1993), 9–52.

[27]   Maura J. B. Murphy, 'The Role of Organized Labour in the Political and Economic Life of Cork City, 1820–1899', Ph.D. thesis (Leicester, 1979), 209–56.

about by an influx of fervent Irish-Irelanders. The Cork circle was led by Sean O'Hegarty and Tomas MacCurtain.[28]

The prospect of Home Rule did little to alter this state of affairs but it did galvanize a third political force into existence: the Irish Volunteers. The founding of the Volunteers in Cork proceeded town by town and parish by parish. The first public meeting was held in the city hall on 14 December 1913, three weeks after the movement was inaugurated in Dublin as a nationalist response to the unionist Ulster Volunteer Force. As in Dublin, Cork's provisional committee was dominated by cultural activists and—behind the scenes—by the Irish Republican Brotherhood.[29] Unlike in Dublin, however, the southern organization had a contentious birth as the local Ancient Order of Hibernians (Board of Erin) objected to the involvement of the schismatic AOH (American Alliance). When this provocation was compounded by Eoin MacNeill's speech apparently praising Edward Carson, the assembled 'Mollies' rushed the stage and knocked the chairman unconscious. Despite this inauspicious beginning over 400 men were enrolled that night, and the first drill class took place the following week.[30]

Outside the city, and independent of it, small groups of men were simultaneously starting their own branches. Anyone with initiative could form a local committee and assume the title of Volunteers. Nevertheless, few local pioneers presented themselves and those that did were dismissed as young 'nobodies'.[31] Both main parties held aloof so membership and the number of branches remained small for the first six months. Even the R.I.C. barely noticed their existence amidst the furore of local elections.

All this changed dramatically in May 1914, as crisis loomed in the north. In West Cork, where the movement previously had the smallest of footholds, 'it sprang into existence with startling suddenness'.[32] In the East Riding during the same month, the county inspector noted that branches had been formed in every district except Newmarket and Kanturk.[33] This sudden progress finally attracted

---

[28] Diarmuid Lynch, 'The IRB. Some Recollections and Comments' (NLI, Diarmuid Lynch Papers, MS 11, 128); obituary of Sean O'Hegarty (O'Donoghue Papers, MS 31, 334).

[29] For the birth of the movement in Dublin, see F. X. Martin, 'MacNeill and the Foundation of the Irish Volunteers', in F. X. Martin and F. J. Byrne (eds.), *The Scholar Revolutionary: Eoin MacNeill, 1867–1945, and the Making of a New Ireland* (Dublin, 1973), 99–181 and F. X. Martin (ed.), *The Irish Volunteers 1913–1915: Recollections and Documents* (Dublin, 1963), 3–116. For counties other than Cork, see Oliver Coogan, *Politics and War in Meath 1913–23* (Dublin, 1983), 1–31 and especially David Fitzpatrick, *Politics and Irish Life 1913–1921* (Dublin, 1977), 101–10.

[30] The main sources for this and the following paragraphs on the origins and early development of the Cork Volunteers are: Florence O'Donoghue, 'History of the Irish Volunteers' (O'Donoghue Papers, MS 31, 437), 'The Irish Volunteers in Cork 1913–1916', *Journal of the Cork Historical and Archaeological Society* (Jan.–Dec. 1966), 41–8, and *Tomas MacCurtain*, 29–40; J. J. Walsh, *Recollections of a Rebel* (Tralee, 1949), 22–28; Roibeard Langford Statement (CAI, Langford Papers, U155); Douglas Community School, 'The Rank and File Response: Cork City Corps, Irish Volunteers, 14 Dec. 1913–30 Aug. 1914' (unpublished essay, 1988).

[31] See CI Monthly Report, East Cork, Dec. 1913 (CO 904/91).

[32] CI Monthly Report, West Cork, May 1914 (CO 904/93).

[33] CI Monthly Report, East Cork, May 1914.

the predatory interest of the Irish Party, which demanded, and got, control of the executive committees in Dublin and Cork, and whose followers rushed to join and form their own branches. Respectability followed closely in their wake. By the end of June the constabulary inspector for West Cork reported that 'the Catholic Clergy, Professional men, and public representatives . . . are now openly patronising the movement'.[34]

Redmondites and respectability transformed the organization into a mass movement in a matter of weeks. In West Cork, in July, the number of branches rose from five to twenty-five and the number of recruits from 400 to over 2,000. In August, five more companies and 1,000 more members appeared. This growth peaked in September with thirty-three branches and 2,996 members.[35] In the city 700 men joined in one week alone.[36]

Then came the Great War. Cork, like the rest of Britain and Ireland, was at once possessed by a spirit of patriotic endeavour. Hundreds of army reservists were called up, followed by thousands of eager volunteers, nationalist and unionist, Protestant and Catholic alike.[37] Both Redmond and O'Brien declared their full support for the British war effort. The Kaiser was denounced in pubs and on street corners. A thrill of suspicion gripped the coast, and German spies were discovered everywhere. One unfortunate 'mysterious stranger' on a sketching holiday was arrested three times in two days and finally 'forwarded, under heavy escort, to the General commanding the forces in Cork'.[38] Only republicans and other dissident nationalists voiced their opposition.

The Great War divided the Volunteers and decimated their membership. The original founders parted ways with the Redmondite majority in September over the issue of British army recruitment. The former retained the title of Irish Volunteers but few members; the latter renamed themselves the Irish National Volunteers.

The new and reorganized Irish Volunteer companies which emerged after the split were both anti-Party and anti-British. As such, they were the main beneficiaries of nationalist disillusionment with their parliamentary leadership and the growing apprehension over conscription. Their fortunes improved as those of the National Volunteers fell. In February 1915 the West Cork National Volunteers were said by the police to exist 'only on paper'.[39] By August they had 'practically ceased to exist' in the east.[40] In the meantime the dissidents had

[34] CI Monthly Report, West Cork, June 1914 (CO 904/93). For the development of one such company, see the Minute Book of the Lord Carbery Branch, Irish National Volunteers, Clonakilty (West Cork Regional Museum).

[35] CI Monthly Reports, West Cork, July–September (CO 904/94). See also the National Volunteer company returns in the Maurice Moore Papers (NLI, MS 10, 544; 10, 547 (6)).

[36] Douglas Community School, 'The Rank and File Response', 6. This surge followed the Howth gun-running and the Bachelors' Walk shootings.

[37] Staunton, 'Royal Munster Fusiliers'; David Fitzpatrick, 'The Logic of Collective Sacrifice: Ireland and the British Army, 1914–1918', *Historical Journal* (1995), 1017–30; Dermot J. Lucey, 'Cork Public Opinion and the First World War', MA thesis (Cork, 1972).

[38] *Eagle*, 15 Aug. 1914.   [39] CI Monthly Report, West Cork, Feb. 1915 (CO 904/96).

[40] CI Monthly Report, Aug. 1915 (CO 904/97).

established a small but 'very active' presence in the city and in a dozen parishes around the county, including such future revolutionary strongholds as Macroom, Ballinadee, Kilbrittain, and Mourneabbey.[41] At the end of 1915 there were forty-six Volunteer companies in Cork of varying degrees of efficiency and activity.[42] Together they mustered something over a thousand members.

In theory the Volunteer organization, as originally laid out, had both civil and military components. Companies were formed and run by committees whose military responsibilities were devolved to a captain and his officers. On paper, each unit contained an elaborate structure of half-companies, sections, and non-commissioned officers.[43] In practice, the committees quickly faded into the background and the military and civil hierarchies were merged in the persons of a captain, secretary, and treasurer.[44] The county became a brigade and its executive committee and military council gave way to a military staff, with Tomas MacCurtain as commandant. He in turn was responsible to General Headquarters in Dublin. Terence MacSwiney was appointed as the county organizer in August 1915.

In the autumn of 1915 most companies were grouped into battalions in the city and around Bandon, Macroom, Millstreet, and between Mourneabbey and Donoughmore. The main exception to this scheme was the Mitchelstown area which formed part of the independent Galtee Regiment headquartered across the border in Limerick. It was in this guise that the Cork Volunteers entered the year 1916.

Violence was a familiar feature of the pre-war political landscape. Faction fights were a constant of party disputes: eleven people were shot in riots or ambushes in the election years 1910 and 1914, two of them fatally.[45] Among policemen, Cork ranked with Belfast for its troublesomeness.[46] Curiously, the Irish Volunteers, for all their guns, and martial airs and intentions, and in spite of frequent Redmondite provocations, were the least belligerent of organizations. Brawling in the streets was for the old parties, not for the new Ireland they represented: so thought the idealists among them.

At this stage, the Volunteers as a body were neither republican nor revolutionary. Many of their officers and organizers were both, however. These I.R.B. men and their accomplices were participants in an insurrectionary conspiracy to be realized on Easter Sunday 1916. When the appointed day arrived, however, the plans collapsed. The authorities in Dublin Castle were warned, the promised

[41] CI Monthly Report, East Cork, July 1915.

[42] O'Donoghue, 'History of the Irish Volunteers', 70.

[43] See Martin (ed.), *The Irish Volunteers*, 127–8.

[44] See the Constitution and Organization of the Cork Corps, Irish Volunteers, and the Cork Company Returns, 17 Mar.–9 Apr. 1916 (MacSwiney Papers, L233).

[45] CI Monthly Reports, East and West Cork (CO 904/80–94).

[46] See the comments of Head Constable William Butler at the head of this chapter and in the *Appendix to the Report of the Committee of Inquiry into the R.I.C. and D.M.P.*, 103.

German guns were sunk in Cork Harbour, and a muddle of contradictory orders issued from Volunteer headquarters, where a faction opposed to rebellion was attempting to ward it off. The southern leaders were paralysed, first by confusion, then by indecision, coupled with an inveterate distrust of outsiders, especially Dubliners. 'Is a fine body of men like the Irish Volunteers to be dragged at the tail of a rabble like the Citizen Army?' asked Mary MacSwiney (sister of Terence) with characteristic venom, writing later to the United States that 'it seemed to us here that Dublin had made a criminal mistake.'[47]

The MacSwineys, Tomas MacCurtain, Sean O'Hegarty, and their fellow conspirators spent the week anxiously huddled in their homes and club rooms, restraining their men, and negotiating with the Catholic bishop and British military authorities. When Maud Griffith encountered them, 'they had not slept for nights, and now gaunt and unshaven, the desperate position they knew themselves to be in was imprinted on them'.[48] At the end of the week, they gave up their arms and were arrested without firing a shot. Their inaction haunted them for the rest of their lives.[49]

In the end, the Easter Rising in Cork was limited to one family, the Kents of Bawnard, near Fermoy. Even here, the 'blood sacrifice' was the result of tragedy, not calculation. The Kent brothers were large farmers, three of whom—Thomas, David, and Richard—were stalwarts of the movement well known to the local constabulary. When the government moved to round up suspected rebels, theirs was one of the first homes to be visited.

The police arrived at four in the morning with bayonets fixed and magazines loaded. As David testified at his subsequent court martial: 'I was wakened up by the knocking at the door that morning. My brother Richard got very excited and shouted out, "We will all be shot". He rushed from the room. I heard the call of the police outside.' Richard was highly strung, perhaps mentally unbalanced, certainly paranoid. He slept with a loaded gun. When William, the fourth brother (who was 'always opposed to his brothers' activities'), got up he met Richard 'with a shot gun in his hand. I said "In the name of God, what do you want the gun in your hand for?" He said, "The police are below . . . Don't you attempt to go down or it will be worse for yourself."' As Head Constable Rowe

---

[47] Langford statement; unsigned letter from Mary MacSwiney, June 1916, *Documents Relative to the Sinn Fein Movement* (Cmd. 1108, 1921), 17–18. On the latter, see Desmond Ryan, *The Rising: The Complete Story of Easter Week* (Dublin, 1949), 233–4. See also Langford's comments on O'Donoghue, *Tomas MacCurtain* (O'Donoghue Papers, MS 31, 434); Annie MacSwiney's memoir of Mary (UCD, P48 A/462); Chavasse, *Terence MacSwiney*, 83.

[48] Padraic Colum, *Arthur Griffith* (Dublin, 1959), 152.

[49] For the rising in Cork (in addition to the previously listed sources), see the Tomas MacCurtain and Terence MacSwiney Diaries (Cork Co. Museum, MacCurtain Papers, L330; MacSwiney Papers); Major Wallace Dickie correspondence (Mary MacSwiney Papers, P48c/128–30); unpublished (and unexpurgated) Cork 1916 Committee Statement (O'Donoghue Papers, MS 31, 434); and the accounts in O'Donoghue, *Tomas MacCurtain*, Chavasse, *Terence MacSwiney*, and Francis J. Costello, *Enduring the Most: The Life and Death of Terence MacSwiney* (Dingle, 1995).

dutifully read the Riot Act, Richard shot him from a bedroom window, shouting 'we will never surrender; we will leave some of you dead'. Rowe was killed instantly, 'the top of his head was blown off and brain matter was lying around him'. His enraged constables immediately returned fire. David was shot through the kitchen door as he tried to get out, and lay wounded as Richard and Thomas fought for an hour until military reinforcements arrived. The police shot Richard dead as he tried to run away. Thomas was put in front of a firing squad. These men became Cork's Easter martyrs.[50]

What direction would politics take in the aftermath of the rising? A by-election, held in West Cork in December, was conducted in the usual manner by the usual parties and was won by the Redmondite candidate. This occasioned the inevitable and expected fight between 'All Fors' and 'Mollies' in Bantry.[51] By this time, however, it was clear to most observers that there had been a sea change in Irish nationalist sentiment and that the old factions were suddenly obsolete:

Old landmarks in the form of names such as 'Mollies', 'Redmondites', 'All For Irelanders', so much in evidence before the war, are almost now obliterated. One seldom hears them now. An excursion, for instance, which before would be called either a 'Molly' or 'All-for-Ireland' excursion, is now a 'Sinn Fein' one, or else not known by any political name at all.[52]

There were rumours of a second rising within weeks of the first,[53] and a constable was shot at in Charleville, but early manifestations of the new 'Sinn Fein' movement took encouragingly conventional forms. In June 1916 Sinn Feiners broke up a meeting in the city and prevented William O'Brien from speaking. In July there were marches and fights with opponents and police in the city and Charleville. City council sessions were disrupted by rowdy youths. The offices of the *Cork Examiner* were attacked on several occasions.

Such events were a customary part of normal political proceedings; attacking council meetings and the Redmondite *Examiner* were practically local traditions.[54] Flag-waving, singing, fighting, and even gunfire and rioting were hardly revolutionary acts by Cork standards, whatever alarmist English journalists might think. When Harold Ashton, a *Daily Mail* correspondent, visited in February:

[50] The quotes are taken from the transcript of David Kent's court-martial trial, 14–15 June 1916, and attached statements (WO 35/68). See also Patrick J. Power, 'The Kents of Bawnard, Castlelyons', in *Rebel Cork's Fighting Story*, 33–8.

[51] *Examiner*, 5 Jan. 1917.

[52] CI Monthly Report, West Cork, Aug. 1916 (CO 904/100).

[53] CI Monthly Report, West Cork, May 1916.

[54] See *Examiner*, 13, 20, 22 July, 5 Aug. 1916; CI Report, East Cork, June 1916; Muriel Murphy to Tomas MacCurtain, 27 June 1916 (Cork County Museum, L330)—who complained that the *Examiner* was too well protected to damage effectively.

The city was in a jumpy mood. Dublin may be the capital of Ireland, but Cork is the chief city of Sinn Fein and its many ramifications . . . Sinn Feiners were out in platoons roving the streets in a spirit of high bravado. Explosions like revolver shots sent the crowd skipping and the girls screaming, and for an hour or so the warm night was very lively with detonations, explosions, and alarms, but the tall, quiet-eyed men of the R.I.C., moving always in couples among the press, cleverly broke up the demonstrators and never allowed any massed formation.[55]

In fact, to considerable local derision, the report actually described Patrick Street on a Saturday night, after a football match between the Presentation and Christian Brothers colleges.[56]

By June 1917 the county inspector for West Cork concluded that 'this Sinn Feinism is of a very undefined sort. It is anti-British, anti-recruiting, and above all, anti-Redmondite: it is a voting, a shouting, a marching Sinn Feinism, but it is not a fighting one.'[57] Political life would, he hoped, settle back into its old grooves with only the names of the parties and excursions changed.

This assessment was at least partly correct with regard to electoral politics. Sinn Fein won and guarded its new political turf with the obligatory minimum of street-fighting and gunplay. However, in the course of the revolution the familiar exuberance of party competition turned into killing on an unprecedented, unimagined scale. The political arena was transformed into a nightmare world of anonymous killers and victims, of disappearances, massacres, midnight executions, bullets in the back of the head, bodies dumped in fields or ditches. Over 700 people died in Cork in revolutionary or counter-revolutionary shootings or bombings between 1917 and 1923, 400 of them at the hands of the Irish Volunteers—soon rechristened the Irish Republican Army. One hundred and ninety-two Volunteers were themselves killed, although 27 of these deaths were self-inflicted, by accident or hunger strike. More than a third of the dead were civilians, neither soldiers, policemen, nor guerrillas. Nearly 900 others were seriously wounded, for a total revolutionary casualty list of well over 1,600 victims.[58] Measured against the county's 1911 population, this amounted to one victim for every 240 people, making Cork by far the most violent county of Ireland.[59]

[55] Quoted in *Examiner*, 27 Feb. 1917.

[56] *Examiner*, 27 Feb., 2, 3 Mar. 1917; *Christians: The First Hundred Years. A Celebration of 100 Years of Christian Brothers College Cork* (Cork, 1989), 179.

[57] CI Report, West Cork, June 1917 (CO 904/103).

[58] For the sources of these figures, see the Appendix. For interesting statistical analysis of another Irish revolution, see Michael McKeown, *Two Seven Six Three: An Analysis of Fatalities Attributable to Civil Disturbances in Northern Ireland in the Twenty Years between July 13, 1969 and July 12, 1989* (Lucan, 1989) and Malcolm Sutton, *An Index of Deaths from the Conflict in Ireland 1969–1993* (Belfast, 1994).

[59] Only Belfast had more casualties per capita over the whole revolutionary period—although the I.R.A. was not responsible for most of them. To draw a contemporary comparison, between 1969 and 1975, Northern Ireland experienced one 'political' death for every 1,100 people. Between 1917 and 1923, Cork experienced one for every 530 people. W. D. Flackes, *Northern Ireland: A Political Directory* (London, 1983).

TABLE 1. Victims of the revolution in Cork, 1917–1923

R.I.C.		British Army		National Army		I.R.A.		Civilians		Total	
K	W	K	W	K	W	K	W	K	W	K	W
108	145	93	155	70	175	195	113	281	289	747	877

Notes: K = killed; W = wounded. For the sources of these figures, see the Appendix. The numbers are categorized by those responsible, and do not include shootings with agrarian motives or as a result of labour disputes or robberies that were not obviously 'political'. Nor do they include people shot by Cork gunmen more than a few miles beyond the county borders, or those killed or wounded fighting in Limerick or Tipperary in the Civil War.

TABLE 2. Destruction of property in Cork, 1917–1923

Buildings by			Bridges by I.R.A.
I.R.A.	Crown forces	Unknown	
301	237	8	211

Notes: For sources and definitions, see the Appendix. The National Army did not destroy any houses in Cork during the Civil War.

The numbers of dead and wounded were only the most visible and terrible aspect of the new politics of violence created by guns and gunmen. Submerged beneath the assassinations and ambushes, recognized but largely unreported, was a vast everyday traffic in terror and destruction. Beatings, raids, kidnappings, torture, arson, robbery, and vandalism left few families or communities untouched. Hundreds of people fled or were driven out of their homes to become refugees and exiles. Hundreds of homes were burned. Many lives were destroyed other than by bullets.

Tables 1 and 2 in fact describe only a fraction of the revolution's violence. Table 1 is restricted to those confirmed killed or else seriously wounded by bullets or bombs.[60] I have limited the figures for the wounded in this way because it marks a threshold, below which it is often impossible to tell how badly someone was hurt. The casualty list could be considerably extended if it included those who were injured in other ways, in beatings, fires, or riots. Scores of I.R.A. men suffered terrible injuries after being arrested or imprisoned, and dozens of people received bayonet wounds or broken bones from R.I.C. or military riot squads. The Volunteers administered their own punishments to their enemies, uniformed or otherwise. Two R.I.C. constables kidnapped near Macroom in February 1922 were flogged nearly to death with wire whips, for example.[61] However, while one

[60] 'Serious' wounds are defined by excluding those described as 'light', 'slight', or 'not serious', or those which apparently did not require hospitalization.

[61] *Examiner*, 11 Feb. 1922.

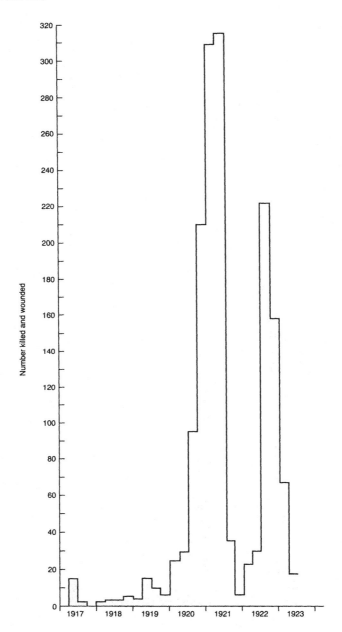

FIG. 1. Victims of the revolution in Cork, 1917–1923

Note: Each number represents the total number of killed and wounded (as defined in Table 1) for a three-month period, beginning in January 1917 and ending in June 1923.

death or one serious gunshot wound can be assumed to be essentially the same as any other, the same is not true for other sorts of assaults. Nor do these statistics even include all the killings that took place. In some cases, people disappeared without a trace, or with only the word of a single unverified witness to suggest another buried body here or there. The numbers presented here can only weigh the known and the confirmable acts and victims. The others lie below the visible (or documented) surface of the revolution.

The cautious optimism of the Cork police in early 1917 that local politics was resuming its normal bumptious course—that Sinn Fein would shout, march, and vote but not fight—was quick to fade. Certainly the movement itself showed no signs of faltering in the two years that followed, beginning with the early release of nearly all the Volunteer deportees at Christmas, and culminating in a sweep of Cork seats in the December 1918 general election.

Sinn Fein and the Volunteers were transformed by the rebellion and the subsequent wave of popular enthusiasm. Both grew into mass organizations, with thousands of members by mid-1918. The reorganized Volunteers had nearly 200 companies in Cork by this point (140 outside the city). As these units began to function as quasi-military formations, the office of secretary gradually fell into disuse in favour of the more strictly martial arrangement of a captain, adjutant, and first and second lieutenants. Quartermasters and intelligence officers were later added, although these were often little more than honorary positions. The companies were now grouped into eighteen battalions: the 1st and 2nd Battalions in the city and the rest formed around towns or key districts.[62]

The Cork Brigade and its staff was re-established in 1917 (again under Tomas MacCurtain), eventually including the previously separatist Mitchelstown section. An extra layer of authority was introduced the following year in the form of brigade and battalion councils—comprised of their staffs plus subordinate units' commanders—but these only met occasionally and were abandoned when they went underground.

Organizational tinkering, a hallmark of the new I.R.A., continued in 1919. With only four full-time brigade staff to run the whole county, it was decided that Cork would be subdivided into 1st, 2nd, and 3rd Brigades: Mid-Cork (including the city), North Cork, and West Cork. Meetings were held to elect commandants and staffs in January 1919. Liam Lynch was chosen in the north, Tomas MacCurtain in the city, and Tom Hales in the west. These were the men who would put the army on a war footing.[63]

The aggressive rise of republicanism and the government's apparently equivocal responses left the officers and men of the R.I.C. feeling uncertain and insecure.

[62] A full order of battle, dated 6 Sept. 1918, can be found in the O'Donoghue Papers, MS 31, 180.

[63] For Cork 1, 2, and 3, see O'Donoghue, *Tomas MacCurtain*, 151–2 and *No Other Law* (Dublin, 1986), 35–6; Deasy, *Towards Ireland Free*, 57–8.

TABLE 3. Riots in Cork, 1915–1919

1915	1916	1917	1918	1919
2	7	24	16	23

Notes: Most of the riots in 1916 occurred in the second half of the year. The statistical definition of 'riots' can be found in the Appendix. These figures do not include reprisals carried out by crowds of soldiers or policemen.

Words like 'uneasiness', 'anxiety', 'unrest', and 'unsettled' began to appear in inspectors' reports with growing frequency, reflecting the state of the constables as well as the country.[64] Nationalist hostility was directed less and less towards rival factions. More and more, it was focused on the R.I.C. themselves. Violence followed in its wake.

For the first time since the 1880s, violence, or the threat of violence, became a constant feature of regular police work. Every arrest or patrol carried the risk of a fight, every brush with the young men and women of Sinn Fein meant trouble. No longer could constables walk their districts without fear of challenge. The spread of rioting across the county, as detailed in Table 3, provides a gauge of political feeling.

The experience of Mallow in the tension-filled summer of 1917 illustrates how such riots began. Sparring between the movement and the R.I.C. began in May when Volunteers illegally put up republican flags around the town. Whenever the police tore one down, a crowd would gather, scuffles would break out, and a new one would immediately appear.[65] In town, their steps were dogged by jeering youths who took to marching after them banging tin cans.[66] Feelings came to a head during a Sinn Fein demonstration on 22 May. Shouts of 'Up the rebels', cat-calls, and the appearance of a tricolour led to a baton charge and brawl. By most accounts, the constables were out for revenge and showed no mercy.[67] They claimed they were provoked but to locals it was straightforward police brutality:[68]

> There was Kennedy the brute
> He used his baton and his boot,
> Sinn Feiners he would like to shoot
> For flying flags in Mallow.

When another patrol tried to stop the youthful tin-can drummers two weeks later, a crowd drove them into their barracks, where they remained until rein-

---

[64] See CI Monthly Reports, West Cork, Jan. 1917, Apr. 1918 (CO 904/102, 105); East Cork, Jan., Feb. 1918 (CO 904/105).

[65] *Examiner*, 8, 26 May 1917; Bartholomew Walsh, *My Memoirs*, 1–3 (County Cork Library); Siobhan Lankford, *The Hope and the Sadness* (Cork, 1980), 97–8.

[66] *Examiner*, 19 May, 4 June 1917.

[67] Ibid. 13 July 1917; Lankford, *The Hope and the Sadness*, 98.

[68] A commemorative song quoted by Lankford, *The Hope and the Sadness*, 99.

forcements arrived the next day.[69] The barracks' humiliation was completed in court where they were condemned by lawyers and magistrates alike.[70] Their frustration was revealed in an incident in November when a farmer refused to shake hands with a constable in a pub. The policeman, later summoned for assault, tried to force him, exclaiming, 'I'm just as good an Irishman as you.'[71]

The inspector general of the R.I.C. reported in July that 'where some of the smaller fry have been prosecuted for drilling or unlawful assembly, the attitude of Sinn Feiners towards the police is distinctly hostile, and they will hardly speak to a policeman'.[72] In north Tipperary, Volunteers were 'distinctly insolent and menacing. Men of principle are getting afraid.'[73]

Confrontations followed one upon another in a growing number of hot spots. The most routine police work could provoke hostility:

The Sinn Feiners entertain a bitter hostility towards the police. On Sunday night, at Newmarket, a police patrol, while holding up two men for not having a light on a donkey-cart, were attacked. The two men shouted for the Sinn Feiners to come and assist them. A big crowd gathered round and the police had to draw their batons, which they used with effect in dispersing their assailants. This, though small in itself, shows the spirit and the power that the police have to contend with.[74]

The government responded to incidents such as these with military orders banning drilling, wearing uniforms, or carrying weapons (including hurleys).[75] Almost any overt act, including singing nationalist songs and waving flags, might now be considered disorderly. In the wake of the rising all such displays had acquired revolutionary significance, in the eyes of the authorities at any rate. Even 'voting, marching, and shouting' were not to be tolerated. In this atmosphere every move made by one side was considered provocative by their opponents.

Arrests soon followed. All of the remaining rebellion prisoners and a few more recent deportees had been released in June as part of a general amnesty but prisons soon began filling up again with recalcitrant Volunteers who refused to recognize the courts. Irish prison authorities, unlike those in England, refused to treat them as political prisoners. One group of Volunteers in Dublin's Mountjoy prison went on hunger strike in protest, presumably inspired by pre-war suffragists. Their leader, Thomas Ashe, the head of the rejuvenated I.R.B., was force-fed. The procedure went awry, and he died in September. After this, the Irish government backed down and granted their demands.[76]

---

[69] *Examiner*, 4 June 1917. [70] Ibid. 26 May, 13 June 1917.
[71] Ibid. 16 Nov. 1917. [72] IG Monthly Report, July 1917 (CO 904/103).
[73] CI Monthly Report, North Tipperary, July 1917 (CO 904/103).
[74] DI Report, Newmarket, 20 Nov. 1917 (CO 904/122).
[75] *Irish Times*, 30 July 1917.
[76] Ibid. 19 Nov. 1917. The best account of these prison battles is found in J. Anthony Gaughan, *Austin Stack: Portrait of a Separatist* (Mount Merrion, 1977), 75–82. See also Fionan Lynch, 'Recollections of Jail Riots and Hunger Strikes—Grim Times in Mountjoy, Dundalk and Belfast Jails', in *Sworn to be Free: The Complete Book of I.R.A. Jailbreaks 1918–1921* (Tralee, 1971), 63–76.

The continued influx of convicts and officials' attempts to reassert their authority kept the prison wars raging through October and November. Each new hunger strike sent Dublin Castle scrambling to placate public opinion but the strikers remained obdurate. The deputy governor of Cork gaol plaintively reported that 'I tried to reason with them and practically asked them what treatment they wanted . . . they are difficult to deal with'.[77] Max Green, the chairman of the Prisons Board, echoed his protest at the beginning of November: 'the practice of granting concessions piecemeal as the pressure by the prisoners increases . . . is calculated to undermine not only the discipline of the prisoners but also that of the prison staff.'[78]

The constabulary were equally dismayed when the administration finally capitulated two weeks later and released all of the prisoners, tried and untried, well over one hundred in all. At least seventy were Corkmen. They returned home to victory celebrations, demonstrations, and, inevitably, riots.[79] The June amnesty had produced disturbances in Cork city but these were worse. The police had endured threats, abuse, and assaults to arrest these men and now they were back as heroes, carrying on exactly as they had done before. Of the 148 people tried by courts martial in 1917, 24 per cent were released after hunger strikes and 61 per cent had their sentences remitted. Only one in ten served out their sentences.[80] Further arrests and rearrests were followed in the new year by more hunger strikes, which were almost automatically rewarded by early release.[81] To the demoralized police, the same futile cycle was simply being repeated again and again.

After one group of prisoners—arrested only weeks before— returned home to Newmarket, the district inspector observed that 'the quick release of these Sinn Feiners has given them a false conception of the strength of their cause, while the law-abiding are becoming despondent and say there is no protection for themselves or their property'.[82] Inspectors throughout Munster and Connaught held the same glum opinions:

the fact that men whom the police have had great difficulty and danger in arresting and bringing to justice should be a few days afterward released and enabled to defy and sneer at them has had a most discouraging effect on the force.[83]

The army's intelligence officer for Munster sympathized. 'It is really very little use arresting them.'[84]

---

[77] Deputy Gov., Cork Prison to Chairman, General Prisons Board, 31 Oct. 1917 (NA, GPB Papers, Carton 7).

[78] Chairman, GPB to Under-Secretary, 2 Nov. 1917 (GPB Papers, Carton 7).

[79] *Irish Times*, 19 Nov. 1917; *Examiner*, 1, 13, 20 Nov. 1917.

[80] Register of Civilians Tried by Courts-Martial for Breaches of the Defence of the Realm Regulations (WO 35/132).   [81] See *Examiner*, 11 Feb., 2, 9 Mar. 1918.

[82] DI Report, Newmarket, 20 Nov. 1917.

[83] CI Monthly Report, Kerry, Feb. 1918 (CO 904/105).

[84] Quoted in Townshend, *British Campaign*, 5. See also CI Monthly Report, Clare, Nov. 1917 (CO 904/104) and IG Monthly Report, Feb. 1918 (CO 904/105).

In many cases, however, even arrests and convictions were problematic as the paralysis of the prison system was compounded by a wavering judiciary and undependable jurors. As early as January 1916 the R.I.C. had pointed out that magistrates and juries could not be depended upon to enforce the Defence of the Realm Act, the main legal weapon against the republican movement.[85]

The first signs of this breakdown appeared in Clare, where the Petty Sessions had become 'useless and more or less of a farce' by July 1917. The same symptoms quickly spread throughout the Munster circuit.[86] Cork courts reached the same point a few months later. A typical case was that of Pat Harnedy, a Drimoleague I.R.A. officer arrested for bombing the local barracks in February 1918. He went on hunger strike and was discharged by a sympathetic jury.[87] In March a member of Cumann na mBan who refused to answer questions in a Bandon court was discharged to cheers from the gallery.[88] After this no convictions were forthcoming there until a Special Court was established in September.[89] At the Cork city assizes that summer, carefully picked juries still failed to convict on what the county inspector felt were 'clear cases'.[90]

The Attorney-General removed all but one case from the Grand Jury's jurisdiction in Kerry in anticipation of the same problem.[91] In Tuam, Galway, two resident magistrates were heckled by justices of the peace as they sentenced a group of Volunteers.[92] The most notorious case of all was that against some Volunteers accused of killing a man during an arms raid in Silvermines, Tipperary. The government brought them to trial three times, but no Irish jury would convict and they eventually had to be released.[93] Increasingly, courts were simply a stage for nationalist rhetoric and abuse of the police. The judicial and penal systems had become political battlegrounds and Sinn Fein was winning.

As convictions grew harder to obtain, fewer cases were brought to trial. The main problem was evidence. Out of fear, prudence, or patriotism, few witnesses were willing to testify against republican defendants. In Ireland in 1917, 'in *all* cases of violent outrages, no one has been arrested as witnesses refuse to come forward'.[94] Mr Justice Moore, speaking at the Cork County Assizes the following summer, remarked: 'when one reads the police reports of all these matters . . . one could not but be struck with the statement in nearly every case: "The police have been unable to procure sufficient evidence to bring the perpetrators to justice."' [95] In August the county inspector for West Cork bemoaned the fact that all 'ordinary sources of information are closed'.[96] A typical example of unsolved

[85] *Report of the Royal Commission on the Rebellion in Ireland* [Cd. 8311], HC 1916, 10.
[86] CI Monthly Report, Clare, July 1917 (CO 904/103).
[87] *Eagle*, 23 Feb., 9 Mar. 1918.   [88] Ibid. 16 Mar. 1918.
[89] CI Monthly Report, Sept. 1918 (CO 904/107).
[90] CI Monthly Report, East Cork, July 1918 (CO 904/106).
[91] *Irish Times*, 13 July 1918.   [92] *Notes from Ireland*, Aug. 1918.
[93] IG Monthly Report, July 1918 (CO 904/106); *6th Division History*, 9 (Strickland Papers).
[94] IG Monthly Report, Dec. 1917 (CO 904/104).   [95] *Notes from Ireland*, Aug. 1918.
[96] CI Report, West Cork, Aug. 1918 (CO 904/107).

TABLE 4. Indictable offences in Cork, 1915–1919

	1915	1916	1917	1918	1919
1. Reported offences	498	413	392	562	676
2. Persons proceeded against	476	357	324	351	306
3. Ratio of (2) to (1)	96	86	83	62	45
4. Percentage of (2) convicted	66	56	60	48	63

Source: Judicial Statistics, Ireland, 1917/18 (Cd. 8636); 1918 (Cd. 9066); 1919 (Cd. 43, 438); 1921 (Cd. 1431).

crime was the savage beating of two naval seamen in a Bantry pub in September 1918. When the local police went to investigate, 'no one in the place would give the slightest information about the occurrence.'[97]

Thus, as crime rose, the arrest rate for the Cork R.I.C. (line 3 in Table 4) fell precipitously after 1917. And, although the conviction rate (line 4) rebounded to its 1917 level in 1919, the number of actual convictions remained about the same due to the decline in indictments.[98]

Police anger over government vacillation and lack of support merged with a long list of other grievances: low pay, poor conditions, and lack of promotion. The Treasury even refused to install telephones in the barracks or in the home of the city inspector. Chief among the officers' problems was the sheer lack of men. Not only were the police not reinforced, their numbers were actually falling across Ireland. The Cork constabulary was 15 per cent below its established strength.[99] With their foes gaining the upper hand, neglect seemed to border on betrayal.

For those arrested, the early success of the hunger strikes did represent a clear victory and inspired an easy contempt for the law. 'Mere boys now commonly defy the Police, and when charged in Court declare themselves citizens of the Irish Republic, or soldiers of the I.R.A., and refuse to acknowledge jurisdiction.'[100] J. W. Reid, a Cobh Volunteer, wrote home from Belfast that 'I never spent such a good Hallows Eve as I did this time in jail . . . Tell Leahy he is losing the time of his life.'[101] A Clare Volunteer expressed the views of many of his fellows when he referred to his sentence as 'a holiday at the expense of the crown'.[102]

[97] *Examiner*, 5 Feb. 1919.
[98] The ratio of arrests to crimes by county in 1917 is one of the best predictors of the geography of subsequent I.R.A. violence: Peter Hart, 'The Geography of Revolution in Ireland, 1917–1923', *Past and Present* (May 1997), 193. See also Fitzpatrick, *Politics and Irish Life*, 13, and 'The Geography of Irish Nationalism 1910–1921', *Past and Present* (Feb. 1978), 121–2.
[99] Return of Sergeants and Constables, Jan. 1917 (NA, Chief Secretary's Office (CSO) misc. papers). For conditions within the R.I.C., see Richard Hawkins, 'Dublin Castle and the R.I.C. (1916–1922)', in T. Desmond Williams (ed.), *The Irish Struggle 1916–1926* (London, 1966), 167–82 and Fitzpatrick, *Politics and Irish Life*, 4–16.
[100] IG Monthly Report, Mar. 1918 (CO 904/105).
[101] J. W. Reid to Miss Hawkins, 1 Nov. 1917 (GPB Papers, Carton 7).
[102] *Irish Times*, 5 Mar. 1918.

However, militant high spirits were coupled with the constant threat of arrest and suppression. Prison victories were often short-lived. Each prison had to be conquered separately and gains made were frequently withdrawn, so the same battles had to be fought over again. Hunger strikers released under the Temporary Discharges Act (the 'Cat and Mouse Act') could be rearrested at any time. In fact, by the end of April 1918 many of the heroes of the previous autumn were back inside to complete their terms.[103] By this point the same cadre of activists had been arrested up to three or four times since the rising.

On the outside, most public activities were now illegal without express police permission so most of the movement's leaders were liable for prosecution.[104] Activists experienced these years as a never-ending confrontation with policemen and warders for what they saw as their basic rights to expression, association, and political status. And behind it all was a sense of imminent danger. The memory of the 1916 executions haunted many republicans and the prospect of conscription loomed larger as the war in Europe dragged on. Michael Collins (who himself had left London to avoid being called up) wrote to a colleague in the summer of 1918 that 'there is no knowing what they may do after all'.[105]

While republicans were afraid of a 1916-style crackdown, Dublin Castle's policy shifts arose from their fear of provoking a second rising.[106] The events of 1916 cast a long shadow over the Irish administration. Rumours and predictions of renewed rebellion came thick and fast in 1917 and 1918 and were taken seriously. Troops were hurriedly deployed to Munster in November 1917 in the belief that the Sinn Fein Ard-Fheis signalled an uprising[107] and the 'German Plot' arrests of the following May were based on reports indicating another attempt at German-sponsored rebellion would be made in June.[108]

The British cabinet's sudden decision in April that conscription would be extended to Ireland intensified these fears. Both the Irish Command and R.I.C. headquarters continued to expect a 'spectacular revolution' along Dublin lines well into 1919.[109] Still, few, if any, officials or soldiers saw the

---

[103] See CI Monthly Report, Clare, Feb. 1918; *Examiner*, 4, 5, 10 Apr. 1918.

[104] By June 1918 a meeting was illegal if marching took place, if 'seditious emblems' were displayed, if disloyal language was used, or if police were refused admittance. IG Circular, 5 July 1918 (NLI, MS 10, 472). Under these conditions any Sinn Fein or Volunteer gathering could be suppressed.

[105] Michael Collins to Joseph McDonagh, May 1918 (GPB Papers, Carton 7).

[106] For differing analyses of British policy, see D. G. Boyce and Cameron Hazlehurst, 'The Unknown Chief Secretary: H. E. Duke and Ireland, 1916–18' and Eunan O'Halpin, 'H. E. Duke and the Irish Administration, 1916–18', *Irish Historical Studies* (Mar. 1977), 286–311 and (Sept. 1981), 362–76.   [107] *Irish Times*, 3, 5 Nov. 1917.

[108] See Eunan O'Halpin, *The Decline of the Union: British Government in Ireland 1892–1920* (Dublin, 1987), 159–61.

[109] IG Monthly Report, May 1918 (CO 904/109). See also the report for Jan. 1919 (CO 904/108); Irish Command Weekly Intelligence Summaries, 21 Aug., 11 Oct., 6 Nov. 1918 (IWM, Lord Loch Papers, 71/12/9).

seeds of a guerrilla campaign in the raids and riots now becoming a constant feature of provincial police reports, despite the warnings being sounded by some local unionists.

Faced with the prospect of being overwhelmed by 'superior force' or 'sheer numbers' while trying to enforce conscription, the commanders of the Munster R.I.C. panicked.[110] In north Tipperary 'Police can do nothing and they are practically always confined to their barracks fearing an attack.' The stations in the South Riding of that county were equally paralysed with apprehension. Limerick was 'seething with hatred for the government'.[111]

West Cork was also seething. Malcolm Bickle, the newly arrived (English) pensions officer in Castletownbere, witnessed the changes wrought by the crisis. The tone was set by Sinn Fein-dominated anti-conscription meetings and paramilitary rallies, complete with pledges of resistance and pointed denunciations of the watching police. When Mary MacSwiney arrived to administer the women's pledge:

it was quite a scene . . . first the band. Then a selection of ladies wearing green military hats. Then the rank and file—bare headed girls wearing green yellow and white sashes and carrying honey suckle . . . After them came a group of young men then women sympathizers . . . There were two banners, one with I.R. on it the national colours of course one green with a white motto 'we will not have our men conscripted . . .' Altogether one was left with an Alice in Wonderland feeling.

MacSwiney—with the priest behind her—declared 'the police were worms—no decent girl would walk on the same side of the road with one of 'em. The police who had been listening with approval up to this point got a severe shock at this.' That night, 'the band went out and halted outside the barracks. The people howled and screamed and some one shouted "To hell with England" and "Up the Kaiser". There was more excitement in the air than I've before seen.'[112] Such scenes were repeated in every village on the Beara peninsula.

Everywhere Bickle travelled on his pensions route, the first topic of conversation was conscription, discussed either with foreboding or defiance. Half the shops in his district posted anti-conscription pledges in the window. This communal opposition overrode the dislike many felt for the republican movement: 'coming into the village staying til 10 o'clock on Sunday nights singing and rowing. They get about a bottle or so of stout and think they're nation builders.'

The county inspector for West Cork, now fifty men short of his 'fixed strength' of 250 men, felt no confidence in his ability to keep control:

---

[110] Both phrases were used by the Irish Chief Secretary in cabinet meetings; see Boyce and Hazlehurst, 'The Unknown Chief Secretary', 300 and O'Halpin, 'H. E. Duke', 370.

[111] CI Monthly Reports, North and South Tipperary, Limerick, Apr. 1918 (CO 904/105). See also *6th Division History*, 21 (Strickland Papers).

[112] Malcolm Bickle Diary, n.d. (Peter Liddle Collection, University of Leeds).

As a result of the general unrest, the rancour versus the police, the probability of attacks on them and their barracks, the raids for arms, it has been found necessary to concentrate the police, and with this objective in view eight permanent stations, protection posts and one coast-watching post have been discontinued.[113]

This withdrawal tipped the moral balance even further against the beleaguered force. Three constables in Bandon resigned rather than carry out an arrest order and two others were similarly dismissed in Castletownbere.[114] In one evacuated district a local republican exulted that 'there are no policemen in Drinagh nor in Ballygurteen, they were afraid of the Sinn Feiners and the priest too for he said to put a mark on anyone they saw talking and telling stories to any one that would side with conscription'.[115]

Where before policemen had felt isolated, now they were systematically ostracized. 'A movement to boycott the police seems to be in general contemplation throughout the Riding [West Cork],'[116] often spearheaded by priests like Father O'Keefe of Drinagh or Father Dennehy of Eyeries. The latter told his flock that 'any Catholic policeman . . . who assisted in conscription would be excommunicated and cursed . . . that the curse of God would follow them in every land'.[117] In material terms, the boycott manifested itself in a general refusal to drive the R.I.C. (who did not have their own cars) or supply their barracks. Those that did were themselves boycotted or attacked. A number of barrack servants were also forced to leave.[118]

Public antipathy did not diminish even after the threat of conscription receded. In August, the Bandon headquarters wrote of 'the strong and bitter feeling which prevails generally'.[119] In September, 'ill feeling towards the police still continues almost everywhere'; 'The attitude of the people varies from complete indifference to active hostility.'[120] Malcolm Bickle, on his rounds, visited a family whose son had lost his wife: 'I enquired what the son was and they were very embarrassed. The terrible truth came out at last—the son was in the R.I.C. They were thoroughly ashamed of themselves at having to say such a thing—a nice comment on the state of the country.'[121]

Police anger ensured frequent skirmishes. On St Patrick's Day, 1919, for example, Bickle wrote:

[113] CI Monthly Report, Apr. 1918 (CO 904/105). For R.I.C. strength in West Cork, see CI West Cork to IG, 7 Oct. 1918 (CO 904/169/3).   [114] *Examiner*, 16, 20 May 1918.

[115] Letter from Co. Cork, 20 May 1918 (Censorship Summaries and Précis, CO 904/164).

[116] CI Monthly Report, West Cork, Apr. 1918.

[117] Quoted in A. W. Samuels to Lloyd George, Apr. 1918 (IWM, Sir John French Papers, 75/46/12). See also Philip Bagenal, 'The Royal Irish Constabulary and Sinn Fein', *Nineteenth Century and After* (July 1922), 122.

[118] See the report from West Cork in the Weekly Intelligence Survey, 6 Nov. 1918 (Loch Papers).   [119] CI Monthly Report, Aug. 1918 (CO 904/107).

[120] CI Monthly Report, West Cork, Sept. 1918 (CO 904/107); CI West Cork to IG, 26 Sept. 1918 (CO 904/169/3).   [121] Bickle Diary, n.d.

I heard a few shouts of 'Up the Rebels' and a bit of scuffling and running about. It was a baton charge. At the other end of the town was a bayonet charge. It all arose out of the hostility between the police and the local people . . . Next morning I was downtown I heard an excited click click of tongues . . . and I saw a youth go through the pantomime of hitting with a baton. It carried a stir up locally apparently.

The police finally caught up with their most aggravating adversaries on New Year's Eve, 1919. As the band marched downtown playing 'Oh Come All Ye Faithful', they were ambushed by the forces of law and order and their drum was captured and smashed. 'We had very little time to think about the New Year coming in', Bickle dolefully recorded.

Hostility was accompanied by direct armed action, as police barracks and patrols came under attack. In March 1918, raiders seized four rifles from the Eyeries barracks. In July, Ballyvourney Volunteers ambushed two armed constables, shooting one and beating the other senseless ('an attack calculated to shake to its foundations all sense of public security'). In August, men of the Eyeries station were again attacked and beaten. In September, a two-man patrol in Bantry was disarmed and so badly mauled that both men were hospitalized and forced to retire. Ballyvourney police were again assaulted on patrol in October. In November, the first police death in West Cork was recorded when a constable pretending to be a raider as a practical joke was shot by one of his barracks-mates.

These attacks continued into the new year—accompanied by numerous minor assaults—and culminated in May 1919 with yet another ambush by the hyperactive Eyeries Volunteers, who wounded three constables. When the district inspector from Bandon arrived to investigate, he reported that 'as far as I can ascertain no one in Castletownbere denounced the recent outrage either in public or private, on the contrary . . . a great number regretted that they were not shot dead'.[122] Along the rugged western fringes of the county, unrest was taking on the semblance of guerrilla war.

Declining morale was stopped short of free fall in West Cork by the arrival of a battalion of troops in mid-May 1918. Detachments of cyclists were stationed throughout the riding. This garrison was reinforced by two more battalions when the riding was declared a Special Military Area in September, in response to the second Ballyvourney ambush. Cork was not alone. Other battalions had been sent to Special Military Areas in Clare and Kerry in February and June.

Military intervention restored a sense of stability and allowed the police to carry out a new wave of raids and arrests.[123] Court-martial convictions rose, and the convicts were much more likely to stay in prison. In 1917, nearly 90 per cent of the 148 men tried were let out early. In 1918, none of the 199 military cases

---

[122] DI Bandon Report, 13 May 1919 (CO 904/169). The report concluded that 'the police have been attacked, boycotted and impeded in every possible manner'.
[123] CI Monthly Report, July 1918 (CO 904/106).

was released on hunger strike, and only a quarter had sentences remitted.[124] After the initial impact had been absorbed, however, little seemed to have changed. The army entered the fray with reluctance and soon found itself with the same problems and complaints as the R.I.C. One senior officer who toured the military areas in August reported that the people were 'sullenly resentful and were only keeping quiet because they are obliged to'. Soldiers were being jeered at and harassed. He himself had his tyres slashed.[125] A General Staff memo drafted in October remarked upon:

the bitter feeling there is amongst the soldiers for the Irish. Many of them are being taunted by young Irishmen and are getting in such a state that they may take the law into their own hands. The situation would be perfectly simple to deal with if the Government only had a policy and stuck to that Policy, but where there is no Policy or at least a Policy that changes like a weather cock with every breath of air, it is quite impossible to form any military plans.[126]

In Castletownbere (dubbed 'Castleterrible' by the British troops), even Bickle was dismayed by the raids, the 'soldiers knocking about with fixed bayonets', and the 'shockingly mismanaged' show trial of Volunteer leader Charlie Hurley: 'the town was in a bad way' under the military regime. Moreover, rebel Eyeries carried on 'as Sinn Feiney as usual': 'I didn't find the people very harassed by martial law, in fact they all seemed inclined towards laughter and excitement and the little shops seemed to have new stock in to sell to the soldiers.'[127]

The military presence may have had an immediate calming effect but violence was reduced for a short time rather than halted for good, and public opinion was not reversed. Moreover, the army itself became a target. In September 1918 two officers were beaten up in Bantry and two soldiers were held up in Castletownbere. Such attacks became commonplace in 1919.

Soldiers' frustrations with this situation could not be contained indefinitely. After an attack on a church party in Fermoy in September 1919—and the subsequent refusal by the coroner's jury to bring a verdict of murder—their enraged comrades rioted and wrecked many of the town's shops. A week later, off-duty members of the same regiment were fighting in the streets of Cork city. Both Fermoy and the city saw further riots and reprisals that year, but most ominous of all was the arrival of the Essex Regiment (soon to become notorious in West Cork) in Kinsale in October. On the day they arrived, parties of Essex soldiers paraded the town, intimidating the residents and smashing windows. Their colonel reluctantly apologized but defended his men by saying they had been provoked.[128] Such official permissiveness and appeals to the logic of reprisal would be heard more and more in the coming months.

[124]　Register of Civilians Tried by Courts-Martial (WO 35/132).
[125]　Lt. Col. G. S., Report on Special Military Areas in Clare and Tralee, Aug. 1918 (Loch Papers).　　　　　　　　　　　　　　[126] General Staff Memo, Oct. 1918 (Loch Papers).
[127]　Bickle Diary entries, Aug. 1918, 24 Apr. 1919.
[128]　*Examiner*, 23 Oct., 5 Nov. 1919.

The army had little faith either in the Irish administration or in the long-term efficacy of the Special Military Areas.[129] Officers and men alike were eager to have done with their new duties. However, the R.I.C. in Cork and elsewhere were now dependent on military aid to do their jobs. These detachments were seen as the only barrier between them and a complete breakdown in law and order. 'It is due to the activity of the military cyclists . . . that things are not a good deal worse'; 'without them the police could do nothing'.[130] When troops were temporarily withdrawn from outlying posts in late 1918 (over strenuous police objections) the denuded district inspectors predicted disaster.[131] Once again they had been abandoned. If the force was to continue to operate, declared Bantry's district inspector, emergency measures were required 'clearly indicating to the rank and file . . . that the Government view attacks on them as a very serious matter'.[132]

Military withdrawal and post-war demobilization drew the same reactions in February 1919. To make matters worse, when the 'German Plot' deportees were released later that spring, many other political sentences were also remitted in an apparent replay of the disastrous amnesties of 1917.[133] Police requests for military assistance continued unabated.[134] West Cork's military regime, lifted in February, was reimposed in April after further ambushes had taken place.[135] In June the inspector general admitted that popular feeling against the R.I.C. was so strong that the army's help was needed in every political case.[136] The last of the original army detachments in West Cork, in Kilbrittain, did not leave until August.[137]

The Cork constabulary on their own were no match for the moral and physical campaign being waged against them. They were undermanned and poorly paid, inadequately trained and armed, isolated, immobile, and spread thinly across the countryside. The traditional emergency apparatus of Crimes Acts, Special Courts, and resident magistrates was useless without information or witnesses—or effective prison sentences. Barracks were issued with army surplus towards the end of 1919—sandbags, barbed wire, steel shutters, rifles, and grenades—but these defensive measures did nothing to offset their occupants' sense of helplessness.[138]

---

[129]   Brig. Gen. J. Brind, Note on the Present Situation in Ireland, 28 Apr. 1919 (French Papers).

[130]   CI Monthly Reports, West Cork, Aug., Dec. 1918 (CO 904/107).

[131]   See Draft Memo from GOC Irish Command to Lord Lt., Feb. 1919 (Loch Papers).

[132]   DI Report, Bantry, 24 Sept. 1918 (CO 904/169/3). See also, in the same file (and the same vein): DI Macroom to IG, 25 Sept. 1918; DI Millstreet to IG, 24 Sept. 1918; CI West Cork to IG, 26 Sept. 1918.

[133]   See the files on DORA prisoners in the GPB Papers, Cartons 4–6.

[134]   The Irish Command's Weekly Intelligence Surveys between 30 May 1918 and 5 Mar. 1919 show that police requests for military assistance remained roughly constant.

[135]   CI West Cork to IG, 10 Apr. 1919 (CO 904/169/3).

[136]   IG Monthly Report, June 1919 (CO 904/109).

[137]   CI Monthly Report, West Cork, Aug. 1919 (CO 904/109).

[138]   *Irish Times*, 19 July, 25 Sept. 1919.

The ambush of two constables in the village of Berrings (near Blarney) made plain these dilemmas. On Sunday morning, 28 September 1919, Constables Sweeney and Walsh were jumped by a group of Volunteers as they left church.[139] Walsh gave up his gun without a fight, crying, 'don't shoot me'.[140] Sweeney resisted and was wrestled to the ground by several attackers. He called out for help but Walsh told him to 'give it up Michael'.[141] Sweeney continued to struggle and was shot twice before being disarmed.

Initial police investigations revealed little. Nobody would publicly admit to knowing the attackers. The county inspector for East Cork, who took personal charge of the case, was told by 'several respectable nationalists' that 'the people are in a state of terror from the Sinn Feiners and afraid to speak to, or have any communication with, the police'.[142]

Nevertheless, someone must have secretly informed. Two days after the attack six men were arrested in Donoughmore (6 miles north of Berrings), members of a militant Volunteer company already well known to the police. By the authority of the local resident magistrate they were remanded in custody for eight days. The police actually missed the two men suspected of shooting Sweeney as they had already gone on the run. One was found a week later. Sweeney, still recovering in hospital, was unable to recognize any of the men. Walsh identified only one, to the disgust of his superiors who believed he was afraid to name the others.[143]

The resident magistrate renewed the suspects' detention for several eight-day periods but no more evidence was forthcoming. The county inspector gloomily reported that 'the people are in such an abject state of terrorism that I believe they would rather go to prison than identify any of the gang'.[144] The prisoners were finally discharged on 23 October.[145] The missing man, whom the police believed to be the organizer of the raid, had still not been found and the inspector doubted if a Special Crimes Inquiry (which had the power to compel attendance) would do any good.[146]

The resident magistrate disagreed. On 5 January 1920, over three months after the shooting, he issued a Certificate for Preliminary Inquiry under the 1887 Crimes Act. Twenty-three local witnesses were summoned to appear before him. Their statements provide a good illustration of the state of public opinion in Cork on the verge of guerrilla war.

---

[139] See *Examiner*, 29, 30 Sept. 1919. The following account of the ambush and subsequent investigation is based on the complete police and judicial files on the incident (CO 904/177). The 'statements' quoted below are those of witnesses called before the criminal inquiry in 1920. These documents are doubly valuable as very few records of individual investigations and prosecutions have survived. Because of this they allow an almost unique insight into the workings of the Irish criminal justice system. See also Tim Sheehan, *Lady Hostage (Mrs. Lindsay)* (Dripsey, 1990), 47–8; P. J. Feeney, *Glory O, Glory O, Ye Bold Fenian Men: A History of the Sixth Battalion Cork First Brigade 1913–1921* (Dripsey, 1996), 77–8.   [140] Statement of John Collins.
[141] CI Report, 6 Oct. 1919.   [142] CI Report, 1 Oct. 1919.
[143] CI Reports, 30 Sept., 6 Oct. 1919.   [144] CI Report, 23 Oct. 1919.
[145] *Examiner*, 24 Oct. 1919.   [146] CI Reports, 20 Oct., 3 Nov. 1919.

As usual on a Sunday morning, the young people of Berrings had quickly retreated to crossroads, dances, coursing meets, and hurling games while the older churchgoers from the village and nearby farms had stayed to talk or discuss business in the churchyard or the pub across the road. There were thus about fifty people present when Sweeney and Walsh were ambushed. The attackers, who 'looked hardy young men' all wore 'caps and brown suits', no doubt their own Sunday best.[147]

When the fight commenced 'the crowd closed in' to watch. 'There were a good many people looking on.' Some called out to 'mind the other policeman' when Walsh appeared. One man, Michael Sullivan, told the Volunteers that it was 'a shame to harm the man'. Others hurried away to avoid trouble. 'I went away as I never like to see rows going on, and I would rather have nothing to do with them'; 'I turned my back when I saw that and faced the hill to my own house.' 'Come out of this place, there's some desperate work going on,' said one man to another.[148]

Among the crowd were John Concannon, a failed R.I.C. candidate (whose father had served in the British army), Patrick Dilworth, a retired policeman, and Michael Mullane, a recently demobilized soldier. All three watched but none of them helped the constables in any way. Mullane explained why:[149]

A. [Mullane] Well of course through being a demobilized soldier I didn't want to interfere.
Q. That is the reason you should interfere.
A. Maybe I might get shot.

The rest of the onlookers watched passively until the two shots were fired. They then scattered and ran: 'The women and children were screeching and the people running hither and thither.' Several men carried Sweeney to the pub but one, John Collins, 'heard a voice that I had no right to remove him. I was nervous and got away as soon as I could.' As the Volunteers marched away down the Millstreet road at an even pace, one onlooker cried, 'Oh look at the boys who done the damage'—although whether in admiration or just amazement is unclear.[150] Not one of these witnesses was willing to identify any of the hardy young men in brown suits and the inquiry was soon closed with no charges laid.

In Berrings and a hundred other villages in Cork most people were keeping quiet and out of trouble. Uneasy ambivalence seems to have been the dominant feeling of most communities. If support for Volunteers' operations was far from universal, fear provided a more than adequate motive for acquiescence and silence. Michael Mullane, already suspect because of his war service, was afraid of getting shot. All around him people like John Collins feared the anonymous voices who could label him a traitor if he stepped out of line.

[147] Statement of John Collins.
[148] Statements of Jeremiah McCarthy, John Concannon, John Collins, Michael Sullivan, Maurice Murphy, and Patrick Dilworth.   [149] Statement of Michael Mullane.
[150] Statements of William Regan, John Collins, and John Herlihy.

Police and judicial inquiries merely succeeded in laying bare the dangers faced by small and isolated barracks, the demoralization personified by Constable Walsh, and the inefficiency and futility of the legal system. The end-of-year report from the West Cork R.I.C. reflected this sense of frustration and foreboding:

A system of universal terrorism exists, and this prevents the law-abiding section of the community from asserting itself. The principal efforts of Sinn Fein and the Irish Volunteers are directed against the R.I.C., whom they regard as the chief obstacle in their path, and who are now working under a strain which is almost unbearable. Their numbers are too small to deal with the existing state of things, and everything possible is being done to break their spirit. The ordinary processes of the law are useless now. The people in general will not give evidence in criminal cases, fearing attack . . . and police inquiries are met with a refusal to answer any questions or make any statements. Under these circumstances the police are fighting with their hands tied and can achieve very little in spite of much hard work. No hope of any improvement under present conditions is anticipated.[151]

The Berrings attack was typical not just for the public response and the legal outcome but also for the motives which inspired it. The Donoughmore Volunteers were not out to shoot policemen but to seize their arms. Sweeney was shot only because he resisted. Nearly every I.R.A. operation in 1918 and 1919 had the same objective.

Raids for arms were not uncommon in 1917. In February 1917 the Special Branch of the R.I.C. estimated that, in the whole of Cork, the Volunteers had 19 modern magazine rifles, 68 obsolescent rifles, and several hundred shotguns and hand guns.[152] After a year this was supplemented by several dozen purchased or stolen Lee-Enfields, although the main source for these was cut off in January 1918 when soldiers were forbidden to bring their personal weapons home with them.[153]

The I.R.A.'s drive to acquire weapons gained sudden urgency with the threat of conscription in April 1918. May brought a new regime in Dublin Castle under Lord French and a new round of arrests, deportations, and restrictions, including an unprecedented programme of raids and searches.[154] Previous R.I.C. raids had been limited in number and purpose. From the spring of 1918 onwards, Crown forces were engaged in a more or less constant search for fugitives, arms, or incriminating evidence. Private homes and rooms were repeatedly invaded and searched. For a large number of Volunteer activists, whose families were increasingly subject to police harassment, the only option was to go on the run.

These budding guerrillas soon felt almost as beleaguered and isolated as their opponents cooped up in their barracks. Popular support seemed as elusive for

[151] 'I.O.' [C. J. C. Street], *The Administration of Ireland 1920* (London, 1921), 66.
[152] Return of arms in Cork, 28 Feb. 1917 (CO 904/29/2).
[153] Townshend, *British Campaign*, 7.
[154] For contemporary republican perceptions and statistics, see *Irish Bulletin*, 18 Oct. 1920.

one as the other. The same householders who wanted nothing to do with the police usually had no time for the disorderly young rebels either. Frank Busteed of Blarney received such a hostile reception from the country people he visited that he returned home a few weeks after going on the run and later grumbled that 'there were few people to depend on'.[155] Sean Moylan of Newmarket, perpetually in prison or on the run after the conscription crisis, wrote that 'we organizers depended on a narrow circle of faithful to support us'.[156] He, like many others, fell ill from exhaustion and exposure. 'The hardships incurred . . . were very great,' remembered Liam Deasy of Bandon: 'Life "on the run" was considered very difficult and trying by many of my comrades.'[157] Armed and wanted men were almost universally unwelcome. One of the most wanted, Dan Breen of south Tipperary, bitterly recalled that 'our former friends shunned us . . . even from the Irish Volunteers we got no support . . . many whom we thought we could trust would not let us sleep even in their cattle-byres'.[158]

Militant Volunteers responded by arming themselves by any means possible. The main targets of Volunteer raids were farmers, whose shotguns were rounded up by the score. The Ballinadee Company, for example, seized about thirty guns while the Grenagh Company's arsenal went from six to fifteen weapons in one night.[159]

All of these operations were undertaken on local initiative: necessarily so, since both the Dublin and Cork headquarters forbade most of these activities. In March 1918 the Volunteer executive and the Cork Brigade declared that 'raiding of police, soldiers and private houses for arms must not be allowed'.[160] These general orders were widely ignored, just as had been earlier orders to desist from rioting.[161]

Policemen and soldiers were attacked whenever the opportunity presented itself. In most cases the victims were quickly overpowered and disarmed without any shooting (although many were badly beaten). Indeed, most ordinary Volunteers were very reluctant to open fire. Almost all the veterans I interviewed remember their first enemy casualties with regret. 'Nobody wanted to kill anybody.'[162] Mick Leahy of Cobh declared that 'any time we went into a scrap we wanted to get arms first, but we did not want to kill anyone, only to save our own men'.[163] When shots were fired, it was sometimes by accident. At the Coolea ambush near Ballyvourney in July 1918, the two constables were not holding their carbines but one was shot anyway. 'Just a reflex action of a nervous kind,' one of the ambushers later ruefully admitted.[164]

[155] Frank Busteed (O'Malley Papers, P17b/112).   [156] Sean Moylan memoir, 20.

[157] Deasy, *Towards Ireland Free*, 22, 78.

[158] Dan Breen, *My Fight for Irish Freedom* (Tralee, 1964), 40–1.

[159] Cornelius Flynn, 'My Part in Irish Independence', *Bandon Historical Journal* (1988), 57; John J. Duggan, *Grenagh and Courtbrack during the Struggle for Independence 1914–1924* (Cork, 1973), 33.   [160] *Irish Times*, 26 Mar. 1918.

[161] See Ch. 11.   [162] Interview with AI, 27 Apr. 1989.

[163] Mick Leahy (O'Malley Papers, P17b/108).   [164] Twohig, *Green Tears*, 14.

In fact this sort of accident harmed more Volunteers than policemen, as most had never handled guns or explosives before. Denis Quinlan, the captain of the Inchigeela Company, shot himself in May 1918; in December Joseph Reed and William Murphy killed themselves, in Cobh and Clogheen respectively. In April 1919 a secret I.R.B. bomb factory in the city blew up (the first of many), killing two Volunteers and injuring three others. In the famous Fermoy ambush of September 1919, the only I.R.A. casualty—Liam Lynch, the commander—was shot by his own side.[165]

Newly acquired arms were used to resist arrest (two city policemen were shot in this way in 1918 and 1919) and to seize more arms. Beyond these immediate goals lay that of defeating conscription and the ultimate ideal of 'the next rising'.[166] Like the county inspectors and Dublin Castle, most Volunteer leaders in Cork thought of future rebellion in terms of 1916. According to a number of plans drawn up by brigade and battalion officers and captured by the police, in the event of conscription, 'the whole force would be called out on active service'.[167] Upon mobilization, each unit would seize public buildings, block or destroy roads, bridges, and rail lines, and attack police barracks. Loyalists would be confined to their homes or, if necessary, shot.[168] Similar orders were issued throughout Ireland.[169]

The vision of a second rising persisted well beyond the end of the Great War. Tomas MacCurtain of the 1st Cork Brigade and Michael Brennan in east Clare both planned sudden, all-out assaults on police barracks in their areas before being restrained by a nervous Dublin headquarters.[170] MacCurtain himself later vetoed a like plan proposed by the Ballyvourney Battalion.[171] Terence MacSwiney continued to think in the same vein, to the dismay of more cautious leaders in Dublin. According to Richard Mulcahy, the chief of staff, MacSwiney claimed 'they could last for a fortnight and in six weeks time the same could happen in Galway . . . I said to him you can't have a travelling rising like that.'[172] He revived this idea after he succeeded MacCurtain at the head of Cork 1 in 1920 but was again countermanded. He was arrested and went on hunger strike shortly thereafter and the plan died with him.[173]

---

[165] Jim Gosse (O'Malley Papers, P17b/123).

[166] These were the words of a raider in Galway. *Notes from Ireland*, Feb. 1918.

[167] O'Donoghue, *No Other Law*, 23.

[168] For the Beara Battalion's plans, see *Examiner*, 19 Dec. 1918; for Mallow see *Examiner*, 14 Mar. 1919.

[169] For rising plans in north Dublin see *Irish Times*, 2 Jan., 2 Apr. 1919. For Galway see the same paper, 20 Oct. 1919. For the Baltinglass Battalion in Carlow, see the Weekly Intelligence Survey, 6 Nov. 1918 (Loch Papers).

[170] O'Donoghue, *Tomas MacCurtain*, 156–7; Michael Brennan, *The War in Clare 1911–1921: Personal Memoirs of the War of Independence* (Dublin, 1980), 38.

[171] Twohig, *Green Tears*, 18.

[172] Notes of Conversations with Joe Sweeney (Mulcahy Papers, P7D/43). MacSwiney may well have suggested this scheme as an alternative to the uncontrolled violence he saw sprouting up all around him. He had little contact with the gunmen and never participated in any operations; he thought of violence primarily in romantic terms, as gesture and self-sacrifice.

[173] See O'Hegarty, *The Victory of Sinn Fein*, 46–7; Chavasse, *Terence MacSwiney*, 139, 213.

As nationalist violence accelerated in 1918 and 1919 it began to encompass the I.R.A.'s perceived enemies within their own communities. Under the threat of conscription a 'dead set' was made against suspected or declared loyalists, and thus Protestants in general.[174] Many of the raids for arms were directed against 'local loyalist families', as much to intimidate and disarm them as to arm the Volunteers.[175] Anyone stubborn enough not to sign the anti-conscription pledge or donate to their local anti-conscription fund could be singled out for abuse, boycott, or attack. One group of anti-republican farmers in Lisheen, Skibbereen, were humiliated, bombed, and shot at in 1919 for refusing the pledge.[176] Another man was wounded in Newmarket that December after he refused to pay money to Sinn Fein collectors.[177] Others were shot for resisting arms raids. Nationalist unity and resistance implied coercion: 'they are making the Protestants join in now, or if not they will be boycotted or go to England's war.'[178]

The year 1919 ended with the first assassination of a policeman in Cork (other such killings had already taken place in Tipperary and Dublin). On Sunday, 14 December, Constable Edward Bolger was shot dead as he walked from his home to the barracks in the village of Kilbrittain. The two killers made sure of the job by shooting him several times after he had fallen. He was unarmed. His comrades replied by firing blindly in the direction of the assassins but did not venture out to help Bolger until his daughter came knocking at the barracks door.[179]

Bolger was shot because of his zeal in 'suppressing' the republican movement in his district, one of the most militant in the county.[180] He had gained a reputation as a 'political' and a brutal officer: a declared enemy of the Volunteers. Most recently he had arrested seven Volunteers in October and he had been the principal witness at their trial in November, the occasion for a serious riot at the courthouse.[181] Significantly, the men he had arrested were released on the Friday before the shooting.

This unauthorized killing infuriated Cathal Brugha, the Dail's Minister of Defence, who demanded that those responsible be punished. Tom Hales, the West Cork Brigade commander, replied that it had been an accident—'a brush'—but that it had fortuitously succeeded in cowing the previously aggressive barracks.[182] Jack Fitzgerald, one of the men Bolger had arrested and beaten

---

[174]   CI Monthly Report, West Cork, May 1918 (CO 904/106).
[175]   Duggan, *Grenagh and Courtbrack*, 33. See also George Power's statement (NLI, O'Donoghue Papers, MS 31, 335).   [176] *Examiner*, 16 Aug., 30 Oct. 1919.
[177]   Ibid. 6 Dec. 1919.
[178]   Letter from Co. Cork, 20 May 1918 (Censorship Summaries and Précis, CO 904/164).
[179]   *Irish Times*, 16 Dec. 1919.
[180]   CI Monthly Report, West Cork, Dec. 1919 (CO 904/110).
[181]   *Examiner*, 14 Oct., 6 Nov. 1919.
[182]   Liam Deasy, 'Notes on the "Innishannon" Recollection', 16 Jan. 1963 (Mulcahy Papers, P7/D/45).

TABLE 5. Victims of the revolution in Cork, 1917–1919

R.I.C.		Army		I.R.A.		Civilians						Total	
						By I.R.A.		By Crown forces		Unknown			
K	W	K	W	K	W	K	W	K	W	K	W	K	W
2	11	1	6	6	7	4		1	11		5	10	44

Notes: K = killed; W = wounded. For the sources and construction of these statistics, see the Appendix. The 'Unknown' category refers to shootings which cannot be definitely attributed to any organization—including those people inadvertently caught in crossfire or an explosion.

up, remembers that the killing was deliberate and based on the policy that 'we would only be allowed to shoot *bad* R.I.C. men'. But he also acknowledged an ominous element of revenge: 'in practice, however, the ones shot were ones people didn't like.'[183]

In three years, fifty-four people had been shot or blown up although only ten had died. Fifteen of these casualties occurred during riots, the majority in one night in the city in July 1917. Crowd violence fluctuated in response to public events but (as Table 3 shows) remained fairly constant from late 1916 onwards, reflecting the rise of republicanism as a mass movement and the growth of public antipathy toward the post-rising regime.

Armed violence followed a different curve, rising from less than one shooting a month in the winter of 1918–19 to two a month in the remainder of 1919. By the end of the year, every brigade had its coterie of blooded gunmen. Nearly half the total casualties were soldiers or policemen but these did not occur in battle: there had been little opportunity for them to shoot back. More rebels were killed or wounded in accidents than by their enemies.

By the end of 1919 all the ingredients of guerrilla war were in place. The civil law had broken down and the overextended and demoralized police force had lost much of their legitimacy and authority. The revolutionaries, forced underground, were rapidly arming themselves and now posed a threat to every small post or patrol. Neither side's leaders had a coherent policy or any real control over the drift of events. In this vacuum the direction of events devolved to those who were willing to act ruthlessly, the emerging players of the new politics of violence. In their hands, the shooting war began to acquire its own momentum.

[183]   Jack Fitzgerald (O'Malley Papers, P17b/112). See also Jim Bromagh (P17b/123).

4

Dying for Ireland

Cheer up boy! You are dying for Ireland!

(Elizabeth to Tomas MacCurtain, 20 Mar. 1920)[1]

You probably can imagine, but very few all-English people can, with what a burning hatred for the unutterableness of these beasts one is absolutely consumed. I'd do anything to get a chance to kill them and destroy their country, in fact I would not leave one stone upon another from end to end of it.

(Lt. E. N. Evelegh to his mother, 1921)[2]

January 1920 marked a turning point for both government and guerrillas. The headquarters staff of the I.R.A. bowed to provincial realities and—partly in order to suppress even wilder schemes—authorized open attacks on Crown forces. This decision loosed a wave of assaults on police barracks all over the country. In the first three months of the year ten R.I.C. stations were attacked in Cork alone. Only two, in Carrigtwohill and Castlemartyr, were captured, but one policeman was killed and six others were wounded.

The constabulary, still hobbled by inadequate manpower, responded by closing down most of the smaller barracks in both the city and the county, leaving many areas entirely unpoliced.[3] The I.R.A. took advantage of the withdrawal to cap their campaign with a county- and nationwide arson spree on the night of 5 April, the anniversary of the Easter Rising. Twenty-eight government buildings were destroyed that night in Cork alone.

Anyone in uniform was now a potential target. Police and military patrols were regularly ambushed, often with great daring and little or no bloodshed. These successes, on top of the raids of the previous year, transformed the fighting power of the more active I.R.A. units. As of June 1920, for example, the Bandon Battalion had acquired 29 rifles, 44 revolvers, and 146 shotguns: almost as many weapons as the whole of Cork at the beginning of 1917.[4]

As the pace of violence began to accelerate, however, it also began to change direction. Increasingly, I.R.A. squads set out not just to disarm but to kill. Some

---

[1] *Inquest on Late Alderman Thomas MacCurtain, Lord Mayor of Cork* (CO 904/47), 19.

[2] Undated letter (National Army Museum, Lt. Col. E. N. Evelegh Papers, Acc. 7807–58).

[3] The Cork R.I.C. was still under establishment as of January 1920, although less so than in 1917 (by 8% rather than by 15%): Nominal Return of Men Serving on Jan. 1, 1920 (HO 184/61).

[4] Arms Roll, 1st Bn., Cork 3, 4 June 1920, in 'Sinn Fein and the Irish Volunteers', a British army pamphlet printed in Oct. 1920 (Strickland Papers).

of their victims were specially targeted and warned before being assassinated. Sergeant Mulhern, a Special Branch officer in Bandon, received several threatening letters in early 1920 as a result of his intelligence work. The first attempt on his life in March failed; the second, in July, succeeded.[5] The same procedure was followed when three army officers were shot in Cork city in May.[6]

In other cases the victims had no discernible mark against them, apart from wearing a uniform. Such was the case when Michael McCarthy, a constable of the unarmed Dublin Metropolitan Police, was killed in April in Clonakilty. He was home on leave. McCarthy was shot six times, 'then they asked him if he had had enough'.[7] Three days later in Innishannon, two policemen on patrol were shot down without warning. Their attackers used shotguns at point-blank range to terrible effect.[8] On 13 June a Constable King was ambushed on the road to Glengarrif. Caught alone and unawares, he was wounded but still managed to escape. King ran to a nearby farmhouse, shouting 'Hide me! hide me! They are after shooting me.' The family hid him but he was found, dragged to the yard, forced to his knees, and shot in the back of the head.[9]

The I.R.A.'s aggressiveness raised casualty levels to new heights. As many policemen were shot in the first three months of 1920 as in the preceding three years, and more were dying: three between January and March, ten between April and June.

In the eyes of the police, the events of these months unfolded in a familiar way. The winter offensive against R.I.C. barracks was greeted with the usual complaints and appeals for help:

The police and military forces are too small to cope . . . Our men are practically tied down to guarding against surprise attacks on their own barracks at night and the small forces of military at Bandon, Bantry and Macroom can afford little assistance.[10]

The crisis in the rural constabulary set the scene for renewed military intervention. This time, with a much smaller force at their disposal because of demobilization, the Irish Command could not place detachments in the troubled areas. Instead, local Competent Military Authorities were granted extraordinary legal powers and the permission to use them in a counter-offensive against the rebels. In the first hint of a British counter-insurgency strategy, a plan was drawn up to systematically deport and intern 'dangerous persons'. I.R.A. officers and known militants—the 'murder gang'—would be the main targets.[11]

---

[5] *Examiner*, 13 Mar., 26 July 1920.   [6] Ibid. 12 May 1920.
[7] Ibid. 23 Apr. 1920.   [8] Ibid. 26 Apr. 1920.
[9] Ibid. 14 June 1920. King was the first 'Black and Tan' to be killed in Cork—a fact which may help account for the mercilessness of the killers.
[10] CI Monthly Report, West Cork, Jan. 1920 (CO 904/111).
[11] *Record of the Rebellion in Ireland in 1920–21, and the Part Played by the Army in Dealing with it*, i (Operations). 5–7 (IWM, Sir Hugh Jeudwine Papers); *6th Division History*, 26–7 (Strickland Papers). See also Townshend, *British Campaign*, 47–59 and Colm Campbell, *Emergency Law in Ireland 1918–1925* (Oxford, 1994), 19–26.

These new rules were put into operation on the night of 30 January by new units. Beginning in November 1919, the Southern Command had been reorganized and replaced by the 6th Division, headquartered in Victoria barracks in Cork city and commanded by General Peter Strickland. This in turn was divided into three brigades: the 16th in Fermoy, the 17th in Cork, and the 18th in Limerick. A fourth (Kerry) Brigade was later created and headquartered in Buttevant.[12]

The military offensive was an immediate success. Searches uncovered a large volume of documents (although few arms) and picked up key activists all over the county, men such as Liam O'Dwyer and Sean O'Sullivan in Castletownbere, Tadg Manley in Midleton, Ralph Keyes in Bantry, and Con Neenan in the city.[13] A steady stream of arrests continued in the weeks that followed. In one sweep of the Bandon district in March, police and soldiers managed to capture most of the officers from the crucial Kilbrittain, Mount Pleasant, and Newcestown companies. Liam Deasy, now the West Cork Brigade adjutant, called it 'the black month': 'The arrest and imprisonment of so many of the most militant officers and men was a serious blow, and caused major difficulties in our plans.'[14] *An tOglach*, the I.R.A.'s in-house journal, concurred: 'it is only fair to remember that many districts have been hit hard through capture of their best officers.'[15]

Even before the army's plan was put into effect, however, it was blunted by Dublin Castle's insistence on following cumbersome legal procedures. Deportation warrants, the key to the whole scheme, were often refused for lack of evidence.[16] In the meantime, the slowly accumulating 'dangerous persons' were being held without charge or trial and those who were deported once again found themselves without 'political' status in British prisons. These conditions prompted yet another energetic amnesty campaign and another round of hard-fought protests, ending in a mass hunger strike among I.R.A. prisoners in England and Ireland.

The result was a complete republican victory. The government backed down on 14 April and released not just the untried prisoners being held in Cork and Dublin but all the hunger strikers, including those convicted and deported— hundreds in all, up to a hundred men from Cork alone.[17] Even those opportunists who only joined the strike after the first releases were set free.[18] The strike had gripped the attention of nationalist Ireland (in Timoleague, for example, 'the

---

[12]   *6th Division History*, appendix 2; Townshend, *British Campaign*, 44.

[13]   Complete lists of deported prisoners can be found in the Art O'Brien Papers (NLI, MSS 8443–4).

[14]   Deasy, *Towards Ireland Free*, 99. For similar comments about the South Tipperary Brigade, see the captured letter from Sean Treacy to Michael Collins, Mar. 1920, as printed in the *Irish Times*, 19 May 1921 (under the false impression that it was written in 1921—see *Irish Times*, 9 June 1921).

[15]   *An tOglach*, 1 May 1920.

[16]   *Record of the Rebellion*, i. 7–8; William Wylie Memoir, 48–9 (PRO, 30/89/2).

[17]   According to Irish Command lists, 224 men were released from Irish prisons, 22 of whom had Cork addresses (WO 35/111).   [18]   *Examiner*, 15, 16, 28, 29 Apr., 5, 8 May 1920.

newsagent's shop was congested from an early hour, and scores of country peasants trudged into the village eager for one word of information concerning the prisoners'[19]) so the releases were an enormous coup for the republican movement.

The hunger strike revealed the complete inability of Dublin Castle to cope with the mounting crisis. Indeed, Irish government seems to have reached an almost surreal plane of disorganization and unreality at this point. The Lord Lieutenant, Sir John French, justified his decision to release the prisoners on the grounds that he was merely granting them parole, and he expected them to keep their word.[20] His assistant under-secretary, John Taylor—one of the architects of the new security policy—resigned in frustration, thereby paving the way for a wholesale purge of the Irish administration. The Chief Crown Solicitor, William Wylie, thought French 'a dear old man . . . but I often wondered how the first British Expeditionary Force [commanded by French] ever got back from Mons.'[21]

'RIC in bad way,' noted General Strickland on 6 May.[22] For the constabulary, the strike was inevitably a disaster for morale. It was the end of another futile cycle of apparent progress followed once again by an executive reversal undoing all their efforts, just as in 1917 and 1919. After three months of dangerous activity they were even further behind and facing the same opponents they had arrested only a short time before. An enormous amount of careful intelligence work was set at naught. And, to complete the evisceration of the counter-insurgency policy, most of the army's new powers were withdrawn again in early May to promote a new programme of conciliation.

In West Cork, the British state was gradually ceasing to exist: physically as its barracks, offices, and coastguard stations were burned, politically as the authority of its servants dwindled away. When the Castletownbere custom house was burned down in May, Malcolm Bickle—still carrying out his duties as pensions officer—accompanied the excise officer to the police barracks:

Its the first time I've been in. You knock at the door. A gruff voice says who's there and then the door is opened a little on a chain. Seeing we were safe they let us in and we went upstairs to where Oates the District Inspector was. Curley was with him. They greeted us with a great laugh. Oates said every government official would be there before they'd done.[23]

In June, he met an army officer stationed in Bantry:

he seemed to think the police are getting pretty demoralised . . . He also described how they went to some houses. In one, the brother of a suspected murderer was in bed. The officer heard a huge row upstairs and went up to find the police having a fine fight some raining blows down on the bed and one policeman wanting to shoot another.[24]

[19]   Ibid. 19 Apr. 1920.
[20]   French to Andrew Bonar Law, 16 Apr., 18 May 1920 (French Papers, 75/46/12).
[21]   Wylie Memoir, 49. See also O'Halpin, *Decline of the Union*, 180–213.
[22]   Strickland Diary, 6 May 1920 (Strickland Papers). See also *6th Division History*, 29 and *Record of the Rebellion*, i. 11.   [23]   Bickle Diary, 1 June 1920 (Peter Liddle Collection).
[24]   Ibid. 24 June 1920.

When the local priest spoke of doing something about the burnings, 'he said he thought he could bring the matter before a Sinn Fein court—which I thought a rather curious idea'. They later disagreed over a pensions case, whereupon he told Bickle 'I'd better do justice or I might get shot.' As popular hostility became focused on him, 'I felt rather acutely that I was a stranger in a strange land.' By the summer of 1920, power was in the hands of the gunmen.

At the end of July, the county inspector for West Cork reported that his men had reached the breaking point. 'They may be considered to have ceased to function . . . the men consider that they are merely pawns in a political game.'[25] Those police officers responsible for arrests and intelligence gathering had to be transferred for their own safety.[26] Many others applied or threatened to resign.[27] In north Tipperary they were being 'treated as social outcasts'.[28] In west Galway 'their condition of life in barracks with light and air shut out by sand bags, shell boxes and steel shutters is very irksome and disagreeable'; The police 'have to take the necessities of life by force. Their wives are miserable and their children suffer in the schools *and nobody cares.*'[29]

The horror and humiliation of their situation, and the rage it produced, is captured in two reports from small garrisons in Tipperary. On 4 April, an agitated Sergeant Anthony Foody, stationed in Monroe, discovered upon entering the local chapel that:

the pew and form which the late Colonel Trant gave to the Sergeant and men at Dovea some six years ago had been removed. We were forced to kneel on the floor to-day; occasionally I could see persons looking in our direction and laughing . . . My wife and children had gone to Divine Service before us. At the Church gate four men . . . followed them from the gate and got between them and the Church door; [William] Small said 'Let them clear off to hell they wont get into our Chapel'. [William] Lowry said 'We wont have their breath amongst us'.[30]

Five days later, on 9 April, a three-man cycle patrol was ambushed near Newport:

we found the late Constable Finn lying on his back on the centre of the road quite dead—both eyes blown away and the lower part of his forehead—brain matter scattered on the road and a large pool of blood. About five yards in advance, on the left hand side of the road, we found the late Constable McCarthy in a sitting posture against the wall of the road and a bullet wound in his neck.[31]

[25]   CI Monthly Report, West Cork, July 1920 (CO 904/112).
[26]   *6th Division History*, 29.
[27]   See Cpt. John Regan to John Kerr, 18 July 1961 (PRONI, D2022/1/35). For police resignations (many of which were withdrawn) see the R.I.C. Weekly Summaries for 1920–1 (CO 904/148–50) and Fitzpatrick, *Politics and Irish Life*, 37.
[28]   CI Monthly Report, North Tipperary, June 1920 (CO 904/112).
[29]   CI Monthly Reports, West Galway, June, Aug. 1920.
[30]   The sergeant's report of 4 Apr. 1920 is in CO 904/148.
[31]   DI Report, Newport, 9 Apr. 1920 (CO 904/148).

The wounded survivor had been refused water at a neighbouring house. When reinforcements arrived, suspect young men were dragged from their homes and the nearby creamery, beaten, and 'made to kneel down in the blood of our murdered comrades and kiss the road and say "The Lord have mercy on the souls of the men we murdered this morning." '

While some policemen contemplated resignation, others were thinking of revenge:

There is a feeling among the [West Cork] police which is becoming prevalent in places where murders of police have been committed that the only way to stop these murders is by way of reprisals or retaliation . . . It is becoming difficult to restrain men's passions aroused at the sight of their murdered comrades and when they have the means of executing vengeance it is likely that they will use them when driven to desperation.[32]

Undermanned and under siege behind iron shutters and locked and chained doors, the men of the city force had long been left to shift for themselves. There were few reinforcements or replacements, even for the chronic 10 per cent absent due to illness. New blood was scarce. As of March 1920, the average Cork policeman had served for twenty-four years, nine years in the city. In an emergency, headquarters on Union Quay had little more than a dozen men and three cars to respond. Most other stations had half that many men. Military support from the regiments in Victoria barracks was confined to arresting suspects. A plain clothes squad had been formed for 'special duty . . . of a very private nature' but they numbered only six constables and two sergeants, and only worked in the daytime. At night, regular patrols had been suspended completely and most of the force was more or less confined to barracks. Rather than the previous two-man, two-hour duties, each station now contributed to two large patrols for either the north or south side of the city. On the north side, the men on duty simply guarded King Street barracks.[33] In other words, the I.R.A. could more or less do as they liked after dark.

The anger building up inside these barracks boiled over on 10 March, when District Inspector McDonagh was shot and wounded while guarding ballot boxes in a municipal by-election. That night, after the news had spread, policemen throughout the city left their stations with their rifles to smash windows and look for Sinn Feiners. Club rooms and homes were raided and wrecked, families were threatened, and one man was pulled from his car and pistol-whipped before head constables and inspectors could restore order.[34] The sister of Sinn Fein alderman Jack Sullivan was told, 'we will shoot him this night'. 'The days for knocking are over,' one constable declared. Another said they were 'out for

---

[32] CI Report, West Cork, June 1920 (CO 904/112).

[33] This description has been assembled from the testimony of policemen to the uniquely detailed *Inquest on MacCurtain*, esp. 113, 160, 188, 231, 236, 256–7, 286. The figures for length of service were based on a sample of eighteen such policemen.

[34] *Examiner*, 11 Mar. 1920.

anything and everything now'.[35] No arrests were made and no disciplinary action was taken. A line had been crossed and a precedent established.

On 18 March, another Sinn Fein alderman, Professor W. P. Stockley, was attacked—possibly because his colleague had eluded the police a week earlier. The attack was ineffectual, but on the following evening a policeman was gunned down on Pope's Quay. Constable Murtagh of Sunday's Well was unarmed and on leave; like Sergeant O'Donoghue and most of the force, he was a veteran officer with no political record. He was shot seven times.[36]

Several hours later, in the early morning of 20 March, a group of anonymous men appeared at the Blackpool home of Tomas MacCurtain, the Lord Mayor of Cork and commandant of the 1st Cork Brigade. After they began to smash the door, his wife Elizabeth went downstairs to let them in. When she opened the door, 'a man rushed in with a black face and eyes shining like a demon', followed by several others, all disguised, all armed. One caught Elizabeth and two more rushed upstairs to where Tomas was still in bed. She called after them that 'you have a mother and I am a mother—for God's sakes let me bring down the baby'. They stopped at the bedroom door and shouted 'come out, Curtain'. As he did, they shot him three times in the chest and ran out of the house. Elizabeth's brother and sisters raised a cry of 'murder' and called out the windows for help, but they were fired on from the street. Tomas lay where he fell. 'It was then I saw the terrible change that had come over him,' said David Walsh, his brother-in-law. 'I saw that he was dying.'[37] He died minutes afterwards. All this took place within sight of the nearby Blackpool police barracks.

The police were immediately blamed for this assassination and, in a lengthy and highly publicized coroner's inquest, it emerged that a considerable number of masked or disguised men with rifles had been seen holding up traffic in the vicinity of MacCurtain's house. The police did not attempt to investigate the crime, while government lawyers concentrated on defending the police and Dublin Castle blamed rogue I.R.A. gunmen. After hearing of the killing, one constable commented, 'that should stop the shooting: one for one—that will be the way for the future.'[38]

The events of March gave birth to a spirit of murderous self-reliance within the city police, screened by a wall of silent colleagues and superiors. The inquest also revealed the isolation which prompted it—from the government in Dublin (which had no control over the police or the coroner and had almost no presence in Cork), the army (uncommitted to the fight), local government (in the hands of their enemies), and judges, juries, coroners, and lawyers (untrustworthy or antagonistic). When questioned at the inquest about official policy, a constable of thirty-three years' standing replied: 'I am not responsible for the action of my

[35] *Inquest on MacCurtain*, 290–4.   [36] *Examiner*, 20 Mar. 1920.
[37] Accounts by Elizabeth MacCurtain, David Walsh, and other members of the household: *Inquest on MacCurtain*, 16–42.   [38] Ibid. 307.

Authorities.'[39] They could neither protect themselves nor depend on the legal system. Typically, the inquest itself was a political disaster for the reputation of the R.I.C. and for the government as a whole, but the police had no way to respond and the government was incapable of doing it effectively. The revolution retained the initiative.

Nor was the killing over. The coroner's jury concluded that 'the murder was organised and carried out by the Royal Irish Constabulary, officially directed by the British Government' and returned a verdict of wilful murder against Prime Minister Lloyd George and most of the senior officers of the Cork police. Among those named was District Inspector Swanzy, in whose area of command MacCurtain had lived. In fact, Swanzy had dogged MacCurtain's footsteps for years and was well known to city republicans.[40] He, like many other marked men at the time, was transferred out of the county. The I.R.A. found him, months later, in Lisburn, County Antrim, just as he had feared. The city battalions insisted on sending a team of Corkmen to do the job. They shot Swanzy in the back on 22 August as he came out of church, and escaped to Belfast.[41] Some local unionists, assuming it to be the work of local men, attacked and burned Catholic homes and shops. The riot raged out of control for twenty-four hours, leaving at least one person dead, hundreds homeless, and over sixty buildings destroyed.[42]

It is certain that MacCurtain did not approve of Murtagh's death. He had been trying to curb the wild men of the I.R.B. and various 'active squads' for months and he had publicly commiserated with Constable Murtagh's family that very night. It is also very unlikely that Murtagh had anything to do with the attack on Stockley.[43] The case against Swanzy personally (as opposed to the police in general) was, at best, unproven. Murtagh died because he was a policeman and an easy target. MacCurtain and Swanzy died because they were prominent and nominally in control. All of the victims were helpless and unarmed when shot.

This tit-for-tat cycle of violence would be repeated many times over, with many variations but the same basic themes: the overriding motive of revenge, the ability of the anonymous gunmen on either side to do what they liked, the frequently random or mistaken choice of victims, and their helplessness.

Such murderous exchanges were still relatively rare in the spring of 1920. The next incident of this type in Cork did not occur until June when a Bantry Volunteer was shot in his bed after an ambush.[44] Less rare, however, were

---

[39] Ibid. 180.

[40] See O'Donoghue, *Tomas MacCurtain*, 166–93 and the Wylie Memoir, 43–6. It is clear that both the jury and evidence were manipulated by the I.R.A. Florence O'Donoghue's own retrospective doubts about Swanzy's guilt are given in an interview with Ernie O'Malley (O'Malley Papers, P17b/96). But see also his letter to the *Sunday Press*, 2 Oct. 1955.

[41] See the accounts by Roger MacCorley (O'Donoghue Papers, MS 31, 313) and Sean Culhane (O'Malley Papers, P17b/108). [42] *Belfast News-letter, 23 July–6 Aug. 1920.*

[43] On MacCurtain, see O'Donoghue, *Tomas MacCurtain*, 171 and Ch. 11 below.

[44] *Examiner*, 26 June 1920. As in the case of Charlie O'Brien, the gunmen were looking for the victim's older brother.

reprisals against property. Spontaneous outbreaks of rioting and vandalism by policemen or soldiers gradually gave way to a more deliberate and habitual use of arson. An I.R.A. family's barn and dairy was burnt down in Ballinadee in May and another barn was destroyed outside Fermoy in June, as were several shops in Bantry. July and August saw burnings all over West Cork, while September brought the beginning of a persistent arson campaign in the city— which peaked in December with the destruction of the City Hall and a large portion of Patrick Street, the main shopping thoroughfare.

Reprisals mushroomed as the guerrilla war escalated through the summer of 1920. Crown force losses tripled, rising from 17 between April and June to 52 between July and September. I.R.A. losses went from 3 to 17 over the same period. The guerrillas were also shifting their sights from police barracks (now less numerous and better defended) to the roads, where R.I.C. patrols and military lorries became the most frequent targets. This shift was accompanied by an ongoing republican arson campaign against courthouses, customs and excise offices, coastguard stations, and evacuated barracks.

With escalation came a vast increase in casual violence. The ceaseless round of searches, patrols, and arrests went hand in hand with intimidation, beatings, and petty theft. Any young Irishman unlucky enough to be suspected of rebel sympathies (as most of them were) could expect rough treatment. A typical case was that of Peter Henchion of Coachford:

The Sergeant in charge repeatedly struck me and knocked out a front tooth. He also kicked me about the legs, which are marked still. He struck me several times with the butt end of his rifle on the back and shoulders. He also gave me several thrusts with the point of his rifle. He repeatedly struck me with his closed fist on [my] head . . . I was unable to get any sleep for more than a week as I was not able to lie on my back.[45]

Assaults like this one became an everyday occurrence in the autumn of 1920.

Republican fears and violence followed the same trajectory. Getting caught could easily mean torture or worse. Going on the run meant putting one's family at risk. For many of the I.R.A. veterans I talked to, their worst memories were of their families' suffering. Homes were wrecked, fathers and brothers were beaten up, arrested, or shot. One 87-year-old man grew enraged all over again as he recounted how his father had been used by Auxiliaries as a hostage.[46] Frank Busteed's mother was thrown down a flight of stairs by a military search party.[47] Incidents such as these bred an urgent desire to respond in kind.

In this environment information and popular support now became a matter of life or death. Informers and opponents of the movement had to be deterred or punished. Opposition or even neutrality could no longer be tolerated. Only

---

[45] Peter Henchion statement (UCD, Desmond Fitzgerald Papers, P80/135). The Fitzgerald Papers contain scores of similar internees' statements. See also the testimony from Cork in *Evidence on Conditions in Ireland Presented before the American Commission on Conditions in Ireland* (Washington, 1921), 740–57.   [46] Interview with AA.

[47] O'Callaghan, *Execution*, 181–2.

TABLE 6. Armed robberies of businesses in Cork, 1917–1921

1917	1918	1919	1920	1921 (to 11 July)
—	2	7	47	41

people 'in the movement' could be trusted; 'Those who were not for us at the time were against us.'[48]

One large class of instant enemies were those who refused to pay I.R.A. levies. One such was Con O'Driscoll, one of a number of similar victims in the Skibbereen area punished for resisting the republic in December 1920:

A party of eight or nine men said that they wanted the anti-Sinn Feiner . . . All the raiders were masked, some having bandages over their faces. There were arms in every man's hand and at least one of them had a gun. [O'Driscoll] was sitting by the fireside and the raiders caught him and dragged him out, and said that he was their prisoner. They took him . . . to a labourer's cottage, where they put a revolver to his face and said that he was keeping all his neighbours from subscribing to the Arms Fund. The men then tied his hands behind his back, blindfolded him, and proceeded to cut off his whiskers with a sort of clipping machine, used by barbers, and then tortured him by using an old razor. While cutting off his beard they put a revolver muzzle into his ear.[49]

Men on both sides turned to armed robbery, on a large—but largely hidden—scale. I.R.A. and Crown forces raiders often used their operations to steal. Postmen and post offices, for example, often had money orders or stamps stolen along with the mail.[50] It is impossible to know just how many robberies took place or who was responsible but, if we count those armed robberies of money from shops, banks, and post offices mentioned in newspapers or police reports, we can get some idea of the shape of the revolutionary crime wave (see Table 6). These figures represent only the tip of the iceberg (raids on private homes and highway robbery were far more frequent) but they do indicate the speed with which a crime which was practically non-existent in Cork before 1918 became commonplace in the last half of 1920.

The reprisal movement within the R.I.C., and much of the casual violence that went with it, was largely a creation of non-Irish recruits: the Black and Tans. These British ex-soldiers began arriving at the constabulary depot in Gormanstown in January 1920, and this trickle became a flood in the summer. With the army once again in the background, it was up to them to provide the R.I.C. with the manpower as well as the military muscle and combativeness to fight this new kind of war. In September they were joined by the first ex-officers

---

[48] Report by Vice O/C 2 Bn., Cork 3, n.d. [1922] (MA, A/0659).

[49] *Eagle*, 29 Jan. 1921. O'Driscoll also had his windows broken and his horse stolen.

[50] For police robberies, see Crozier, *Ireland for Ever*, 110, 120. For the court martial of two Auxiliaries in Dunmanway for a bank robbery, see *Irish Times*, 8 Feb. 1921.

of the Auxiliary Division. As West Cork's police chief noted, 'the character of the force is changing a good deal on this account'.[51]

The new recruits shared none of the R.I.C.'s traditional sense of discipline, restraint, or Irishness. They had little in common with the old force and often kept apart by mutual consent. 'We didn't really know them. We just didn't approve of their methods . . . they were never popular with the regular force'; 'We didn't like them, we would have no place for them, we didn't like them coming along and mixing with us'; 'The Black and Tans were all English and Scotch people see, and they were . . . very rough, f-ing and blinding and boozing and all.'[52]

Their training was perfunctory and did nothing to alter their view that they were soldiers in enemy territory rather than policemen in their own country.[53] Their brutality was a direct consequence of their alienation and wartime experience, and their arrival frequently acted as a catalyst for violence ('from the minute that the Black and Tans came on the scene, all the shutters went up on the windows and things like that'[54]).

Alienation also created a fierce solidarity and protectiveness among these otherwise friendless men: 'They were on their own, hurt one and you hurt them all.'

There was a comradeship there that you wouldn't get anywhere else . . . We were all ex-servicemen except three or four old R.I.C. men . . . It was the same ribaldry and the same give and take as in the trenches . . . You had no real contact with the community at all . . . We were all young men, you see, and I suppose in a sense it was quite natural when somebody starts ambushing you, the rest reply.[55]

The Tans' ethnic hostility was shared by the English soldiery, who usually began to lump all Irishmen together as dirty and treacherous soon after their arrival. The resulting distaste and hatred are deeply etched in nearly every regimental journal, letter, or memoir from this period of service. From the East Lancashire Regiment in North Cork, the '59ths Alphabet':[56]

> B is for Buttevant; you know it quite well,
> When asked if we like it, we say 'Go to ——!'
>
> L is the longing we have to be over,
> And settle ourselves in the barracks at Dover.

[51] CI Monthly Report, West Cork, Sept. 1920 (CO 904/113).

[52] Interviews with R.I.C. veterans quoted in Brewer, *The Royal Irish Constabulary*, 111, 112, 113, 116.

[53] See Douglas V. Duff, *Sword for Hire* (London, 1934), 57–60, 73.

[54] Brewer, *The Royal Irish Constabulary*, 103. The role of these men in the escalation of violence is underlined by the character of the earlier British counter-offensive between February and April. Although the R.I.C. and the army were raiding constantly, there were comparatively few complaints about looting, reprisals, or brutality. These became numerous only after the Black and Tans arrived *en masse*.

[55] Brewer, *The Royal Irish Constabulary*, 111, 107–10.

[56] *Lilywhites' Gazette* (Dec. 1921), 36.

An officer of the Oxford and Buckinghamshire Regiment, after service in Cork and other Munster counties: 'I don't like the Irish, I don't like their soft Irish accent, their soft Irish faces, their soft Irish habits or anything soft or Irish about them.'[57]

British anger also occasionally expressed itself in sectarian terms. Anti-Catholic songs were heard sung during reprisals, threatening notices and letters from the so-called 'Anti-Sinn Fein Societies' often used Orange imagery, priests were sometimes singled out for revenge, and rioting soldiers sometimes declared themselves out to get 'the Catholics'. This does not seem to have been a major factor in Crown forces violence, however.[58]

The same process took place among Irish republicans. The old image of the 'peelers'—distrusted or despised perhaps, but familiar—was replaced by that of an occupying army. The label 'Black and Tans' connoted lawless foreign invaders: 'terrorists' with drunken and criminal habits.

The politics of revenge also took an unexpected direction as nationalism veered towards sectarianism in late 1920 and guerrilla war became, in some places, a kind of tribal war. As the war escalated, Cork's Protestant minority increasingly came to be seen by the I.R.A. as 'the enemy within'. As 1920 progressed, they became prime targets for robbery, extortion, dispossession, and murder.[59]

There was a much lower threshold of violence along these growing ethnic divides. The British, soldiers and ex-soldiers alike, arrived with the standard mental baggage of Irish stereotypes which were rapidly inflamed by the constant insecurity and isolation of barracks life. For the Black and Tans and Auxiliaries, their nationality and background separated them as much from the old R.I.C. as from the general population. Like their Irish comrades, however, they felt betrayed by government indecision and indifference and, with only each other to support them, reacted savagely to any attack on themselves or their comrades. And, since almost any Irishman was automatically deemed a 'Shinner' and an enemy (just as native Protestants were so often defined as 'loyalists' and enemies by the I.R.A.), casual violence became routine. Alienation generated violence and vice versa.

Further shifts in British policy followed in the course of the year, but these merely fuelled the accelerating cycle of terror and counter-terror. As in 1918, military detachments were sent back to some troubled districts in May but to little effect. They were hamstrung by a lack of both men and legal authority and were easy targets for local I.R.A. units, now armed with captured rifles and carbines. Between Ballyvourney and Macroom, for example, the Manchester Regiment's bicycle patrols and lorries were successfully ambushed three times

---

[57]   *Oxford and Buckinghamshire Light Infantry Chronicle, 1922* (London, 1923), 155.
[58]   Crozier, *Ireland for Ever*, 114–15; *Irish Times*, 1 Dec. 1920; *Examiner*, 25 Sept. 1921.
[59]   See Part IV.

within a month, losing nine men killed and wounded, four vehicles, and over a dozen rifles. Their own ambushes and searches failed to find their targets, and after October the Duhallow I.R.A. were left in possession of the battlefield.

By the time the platoons in Ballyvourney were withdrawn, however, the problem of legal authority had been addressed by the Restoration of Order in Ireland Act, which placed a large number of crimes under the jurisdiction of military courts at divisional or brigade level. The newly appointed and empowered court-martial officers produced convictions with dispatch, up to sixty a week in Ireland as a whole.[60] These were secured on the evidence of arms and documents found in searches carried out under the new legal regime accompanied by a policy of aggressive raiding. The army was once again gradually going on the offensive. In the week between 'Bloody Sunday' and the Kilmichael ambush, for example, there were over 450 police and military raids in Cork (and over 50 arrests) in five days.[61] Considering its traumatic effect on these households, whether republican or not, this massive assault on the privacy and property of Irish communities had an immense and inflammatory impact.

One of the first to be convicted under the Act was Terence MacSwiney, MacCurtain's successor as Lord Mayor and brigade commander. A breakdown in I.R.A. security produced a stunning British coup on 12 August, when the army swooped on a clandestine meeting in the City Hall to capture MacSwiney and his brigade staff, several key battalion commanders, and Liam Lynch, the O/C of the North Cork Brigade. This was exactly the sort of result the Act was designed to achieve. Sustained success was to prove as elusive as always in 1920, however. Military intelligence had no idea who they had arrested, apart from the well-known mayor, and apparently did not consult the police. So when the prisoners joined a hunger strike already in progress in Cork gaol (aimed in part at the illegitimacy of military courts), all but MacSwiney were freed. Twenty other adult strikers went with them, along with those classed as 'juveniles'. After this, however, protests from Irish Command and Dublin Castle led to a firming up of government resolve: no more releases, no more concessions, and increasingly tough rhetoric from the British cabinet.[62]

If Lloyd George and his ministers were unwilling to bend, they had met their match in Terry MacSwiney—now lodged in Brixton gaol—and the small band of strikers remaining in Cork. On taking office in the wake of the MacCurtain murder, he had declared that 'we see in their regime a thing of evil incarnate.

---

[60] *Record of the Rebellion*, i. 22.

[61] *Irish Bulletin*, 27 Nov. 1920; *Examiner*, 23–30 Nov. 1920.

[62] The raid is described in Con Harrington, 'Arrest and Martyrdom of Terence MacSwiney', in *Rebel Cork's Fighting Story*. For its circumstances, see the 1921 I.R.B. 'Enquiry relative to allegations of negligence against former County Sub-Centre for Cork' (NLI, Maire Nic Shiubhlaigh Papers, MS 22,567); O'Donoghue, *No Other Law*, 87–94. For the hunger strikes, see the *Examiner*, 12, 13, 17, 20 Aug. 1920; Stuart Mews, 'The Hunger-Strike of the Lord Mayor of Cork, 1920: Irish, English and Vatican Attitudes', in W. J. Shiels and Diana Wood (eds.), *The Churches, Ireland and the Irish* (Oxford, 1989); Chavasse, *Terence MacSwiney*; Costello, *Enduring the Most*.

With it there can be no parley any more than there can be truce with the powers of hell. We ask no mercy and we will accept no compromise.' This republican faith—and an equally powerful desire to prove himself through sacrifice—sustained him through a remarkable seventy-four-day ordeal, lasting until 25 October. His death was followed by those of Mick Fitzgerald, O/C of the Fermoy Battalion, and Joe Murphy, a city Volunteer, before the strike was finally called off from Dublin after ninety-four days.[63]

MacSwiney's slow progress towards martyrdom became an international event and the focus of rapt nationwide attention and anger in Ireland. The authorities braced themselves for what they thought would be the inevitable violent backlash. Plans for a bloody revenge were laid in both Cork and Dublin and gunmen from both cities travelled to London to assassinate Lloyd George and others.[64] The hysteria passed, however, and the movement's political common sense reasserted itself. MacSwiney's funerals in London and Cork were marked by impressive, disciplined dignity and mass grief and were not marred by republican violence despite the presence of hundreds of I.R.A. men on the streets. The government may have blunted the hunger weapon and buoyed the morale of its men in Ireland, but it had achieved nothing in military terms and had produced only despair and enmity among the population at large.

This last, greatest, strike signalled the end of tactical retreats under political pressure, and the beginning of the last stand of the old regime. From here the path led only towards martial law and civil war. In Cork, the funeral also marked a shift within the I.R.A. itself. MacSwiney was the last of the gentlemen. His passing meant the elevation of Sean O'Hegarty, the *éminence grise* of the urban guerrillas and, ironically, one of the key players the British had arrested and then released in August. O'Hegarty had run his own I.R.B. campaign against the police—and against the wishes of MacCurtain and many others in Sinn Fein and the Volunteers. Where MacSwiney saw self-sacrifice and the maintenance of honour at the heart of the struggle, O'Hegarty saw guns and bombs and enemy targets. The events of August removed a militarily ineffective leader, turned him into a national symbol of resistance, and replaced him with a ruthless operator.[65]

Rising police numbers and arrests, and the increased likelihood of conviction and of imprisonment with little prospect of early release, did force many activists to go on the run, as they had been doing sporadically since 1916. I.R.A. fugitives travelled the same circuits of safe houses and neighbourhoods, and had naturally banded together for company, in a spirit of underground camaraderie. The guerrillas had likewise tended to work together with the same small circles of activist acquaintances. In the late summer and autumn of 1920, under

---

[63] On Fitzgerald, see Tomas O'Riordan, *The Price of Freedom* (Cork, 1971) and Ch. 11.

[64] See Pa Murray (O'Malley Papers, P17b/88), William Aherne (P17b/99), Denis Brennan, Frank Thornton, and Liam Tobin (P17b/100).

[65] On O'Hegarty's activities, see Ch. 11. His British military intelligence file is interesting, if only for how little they were able to find out about him (WO 35/207).

renewed British pressure, these groups were fused and formalized into flying columns and active service units. Going 'on the run' meant, for many, being 'on the column'.

These were full-time units, typically made up of a nucleus of permanent members who could draw upon the larger pool of fighters in their area to carry out operations. Columns typically fielded a dozen or so riflemen but could reach a hundred or more, as at the famous battle of Crossbarry in March 1921. They were first officially launched by the three brigades, and by the end of the year both Cork 1 and 2 had two such units apiece. These brigade columns rapidly attracted an enormous—although furtive—popular reputation, especially those commanded by Tom Barry in West Cork and Sean Moylan in North Cork. A certain rivalry even built up between 'Barry's flying column' and 'Moylan's Black and Tans' with their distinctive operating styles. Informal and *ad hoc* formations remained throughout the county, however, including the 'active squad' in the city and the 'foreign legion' or 'three musketeers' in North Cork, much to the annoyance of their superior officers.[66]

The government's continual tinkering with the police and legal system was designed in large part to avoid the politically embarrassing introduction of martial law. The flying columns and the Kilmichael ambush—themselves products of the new regulations and paramilitary forces—ensured its ultimate imposition. Martial law was declared in Cork and three adjoining counties on 11 December.

The new British measures did produce results. More Volunteers were being shot: I.R.A. losses peaked at 82 between January and March. Twelve Corkmen were officially executed in 1921. More Volunteers were being arrested: the rate of reported arrests in Cork more than doubled after July 1920, with the months of November and December accounting for over a third of total arrests in 1920. This rose again by a quarter in 1921.[67] At least 165 Corkmen were convicted, and at least another 350 were interned in 1921. At the time of the Truce there were over 1,100 men in the Cork archipelago of prisons and detention camps.[68]

Still, police and military casualties kept on rising, from an average of 17 a month in the late summer of 1920 to 44 a month in the spring of 1921. Neither

---

[66] For the 'official versions' of the formation of the West and North Cork flying columns, see Deasy, *Towards Ireland Free*, 158–9 and O'Donoghue, *No Other Law*, 97–8. For the Ballyvourney Battalion, see O'Suilleabhain, *Mountainy Men*, 93–4. See also *6th Division History*, 54–5. For the development of columns in general, see the pamphlet issued by GHQ Ireland in June 1921, 'The Irish Republican Army' (Strickland Papers); *Record of the Rebellion*, i. 4; Charles Townshend, 'The Irish Republican Army and the Development of Guerrilla Warfare, 1916–1921', *English Historical Review* (Apr. 1979), 330; Fitzpatrick, *Politics and Irish Life*, 217–19; and Joost Augusteijn, *From Public Defiance to Guerrilla Warfare: The Experience of Ordinary Volunteers in the Irish War of Independence, 1916–1921* (Dublin, 1996), 124–44.

[67] As reported in the *Examiner*, 1920–1. Unfortunately, reporting was incomplete and grew more so as the revolution progressed: these figures are indicative of trends but inexact.

[68] Register of Prisoners in Military Prisons (WO 35/143); martial law area Internees Register 1921 (WO 35/144); weekly Return of Prisoners and Internees in martial law area (WO 35/138).

TABLE 7. Victims of the revolution in Cork, 1920–1921

Combatants						Civilians						Total	
R.I.C.		Army		I.R.A.		By I.R.A.		By Crown forces		Unknown			
K	W	K	W	K	W	K	W	K	W	K	W	K	W
105	131	85	136	135	57	114	35	53	85	31	69	523	513

Notes: K = killed; W = wounded. These figures include the R.I.C. victims of two ambushes carried out by Cork I.R.A. men in 1921 just across the border in Kerry.

TABLE 8. Percentage of casualties due to combat in Cork, 1920–1921

	I.R.A. victims		Crown forces victims		All victims
	Crown forces	All	I.R.A.	All	
1920					
Jan.–June	76	54	29	25	48
July–Dec.	74	67	30	15	56
1921					
Jan.–July	49	36	49	30	34

Notes: These figures do not include the twelve I.R.A. men who were officially executed or those who died because of hunger strikes or accident. Where circumstances are doubtful I have considered casualties to have occurred in combat. In cases where an ambush led to a massacre, as at Kilmichael or Clonmult, all victims are included under 'combat'. Consequently, Table 8 represents a conservative estimate of the numbers killed other than in combat.

the Restoration of Order Act nor martial law—nor Tans and Auxiliaries—succeeded in curbing the I.R.A. or violence in general. So not only did the government's problem not get better after the introduction of martial law—it was getting progressively worse (see Fig. 1).

The complete casualty toll of the guerrilla war is shown in Table 7. The combination of higher casualties, martial law, and flying columns suggests an increasingly militarized conflict, a war of movement between patrols and guerrillas. This is indeed how the struggle has generally been portrayed by the participants—as a succession of ambushes and round-ups—but the figures in Table 8 tell a different story. Table 8 divides casualties in 1920–1 according to whether or not they occurred in combat: i.e. whether the victims were part of an armed and active group or unit when attacked or else alone or unable to fight back. The resulting statistics show that in 1921 only one-third of 566 casualties—less than half of police and military casualties, and only a third of all I.R.A. shootings—occurred in combat. Crown force shootings followed the same pattern. After June 1920 more than half of all casualties (and 45 per cent of all victims in 1920–1) were civilians. Clearly, in these terms the violence was becoming less rather than more 'military'.

These statistics are underlined by another, equally significant. Only one in ten

TABLE 9. I.R.A. combat performance in Cork, 1920–1921

	Number of successful[a] attacks	Crown forces casualties per attack
1920		
Jan.–Mar.	12	0.8
Apr.–June	9	1.4
July–Sept.	18	2.2
Oct.–Dec.	21	4.2
1921		
Jan.–Mar.	20	4.4
Apr.–June	19	2.4

[a] By 'successful' I mean attacks which inflicted at least one enemy casualty or led to the seizure of arms.

of Crown forces losses in 1920–1, and less than one in five of the I.R.A.'s, occurred in engagements where the other side also suffered losses. In this whole period there were only nine such encounters (including Kilmichael). In other words, even when combat took place the attacker almost always had an overwhelming advantage. Guerrilla war favoured the hunters, who more and more preyed on the most vulnerable.

The image of 'hunters' calls to mind the legendary ambushes and escapes of the Cork I.R.A.: Upton, Toureengarriffe, Clonbannin, Crossbarry, Coolavokig, Rathcoole, and, of course, Kilmichael.[69] These battles were certainly closer to conventional skirmishes than the nocturnal attacks on barracks and bicyclists of 1919 and early 1920. But were they typical of I.R.A. operations? Table 9 shows the guerrilla campaign in a different and less flattering light. The brigade flying columns (or 'active service units') did pack a heavier punch, judging by the increase in casualties per attack after September 1920. However, while successful I.R.A. attacks grew more destructive in the autumn and winter of 1920–1, they did not grow more frequent. In any case the increase in enemy losses was modest—and temporary.

Flying columns also made easier targets and exposed the I.R.A. to counter-ambushes. Major T. A. Lowe of the Essex Regiment wrote that 'it was these . . . which gave back the initiative to the Crown Forces'.[70] British casualties may have risen after September 1920 but I.R.A. losses in combat rose even faster, from seven between October and December to forty-four between January and March. Several guerrilla bands were surprised and either captured or wiped out in these months, at Dripsey, Clonmult, Clogheen, and White's Cross. Other units, such as the West Cork column at Crossbarry or North Cork columns at

[69] For these engagements and others, see the contemporary I.R.A. reports in the Mulcahy Papers (P7/A/17–9; 38) and the later accounts collected in *Rebel Cork's Fighting Story*.

[70] Brevet Major T. A. Lowe, 'Some Reflections of a Junior Commander upon "The Campaign" in Ireland 1920 and 1921', *Army Quarterly* (Oct. 1922), 53.

Mourneabbey and Nadd, barely escaped the same fate (although not without loss). Consequently, Volunteers were the only category of victim *more* likely to be shot in combat in 1921. Recognition of this danger was one of the principal reasons why the brigade columns were broken up or fell apart that spring, to be replaced by battalion-level units or the ubiquitous unofficial 'squads'. Operational effectiveness was reduced, but so were the risks.

The reality behind the myths of battle was that most planned ambushes never made contact with the enemy and most operations were aimed at one or two 'enemies' (civilian or uniformed) and had little to do with combat. I.R.A. units spent most of their time avoiding the enemy or waiting, often fruitlessly, for an opportune target.

The following weekly report from the Castletownroche Battalion provides a good description of life 'on the column' in the winter of 1921:

The Battalion A[ctive] S[ervice] S[ection] moved into g. Company area on 15-1-21 to watch a police patrol from Doneraile. We got into a place on Monday [but] they only went out a short distance from the town that day on a road it would be impossible to attack them in. We were out again on Tuesday morning at dark. The police did not go out at all that day. We were out again on Wednesday at dark and got into position on a road we had good reason to suspect they would patrol, but they went out on a different road that day. The road they patrolled was too far from our position for us to get there and intercept them. On Wednesday night we took up positions to defend the men falling the bridge leading from Ballyvonaire [army] Camp. We were prepared that night to attack any troops or patrols that would be going to Doneraile, but nothing turned up. We watched the police patrol again on Thursday in the same position as the previous days, but they again went out on a different road . . . They went out again but they were very much on the alert . . . We had the same bad luck Saturday . . . we could not stay any longer with the Company as too many people noticed us. We hope to chance it again in the near future. It was our bad luck on the men as they had to stay in a position from dark to dark. One family refused to take in our men, the door was locked on them when they called one evening very late. We only spent a couple of nights there. They also tried to keep other people from taking our men in. What should be done with these people?[71]

The column's local foes, Captain R. A. Pinkey and two platoons of the Buffs Regiment, faced many of the same frustrations.[72] When they first arrived in Castletownroche in September 1920 they could only search suspect homes and set up road blocks in the hope of catching I.R.A. men red-handed. These efforts proved fruitless. Intelligence was nearly non-existent, composed of outdated R.I.C. tips and vague anonymous letters. The I.R.A. had stripped the countryside of guns and hid them well. Incessant raids on prominent I.R.A. families, notably

---

[71] A copy, dated 22 Jan. 1921, can be found in the CI Monthly Report, East Cork (Mallow), Jan. 1921 (CO 904/114).

[72] For the strength of the detachment, see Compositions and Dispositions of the 6th Division, 29 Oct. 1921 (MA, A/0627).

the Shinnicks and O'Sullivans, turned up nothing except, rather embarrassingly, their own stolen correspondence.[73]

Pinkey's men made no recorded arrests until the 'Bloody Sunday' shootings in Dublin on 21 November. The next day they were ordered to arrest all I.R.A. officers on sight. With surprise on their side for once they were able to capture a third of their suspects. The rest went on the run—and on the column.[74]

After this sudden shift in gear, and especially after the introduction of martial law, the flow of information improved. The detachment's log for 1921 is peppered with notations of rumours and 'information received'. As with their opposite numbers in the Active Service Section, however, most of this came to nothing. Almost invariably the raiding party would arrive at the suspect pub, house, or ambush site to discover that the 'boys' (if they were ever there in the first place) were gone. The detachment's one encounter with the enemy came by chance on 21 April; two guerrillas were caught wrecking a bridge and two more were wounded in a subsequent raid on an I.R.A. safe house.[75]

Apart from this, Pinkey's men experienced the war as an unceasing series of patrols, searches, and ambushes which yielded only scattered arrests. Their elusive enemies made their presence felt through occasional long-distance sniping attacks and by stealing bicycles, attacking supposed loyalists, blocking roads, blowing up bridges and railway tracks, and chopping down telegraph poles.[76]

No reinforcement or relief was possible due to the constant demands of empire. The battalion, headquartered in Fermoy, lost 154 men to Mesopotamia in January and 52 more in February, receiving only 63 new recruits in return. One hundred and eighty-five more men were discharged on 31 March as their two years' service was up. The result was that battalion manpower fell from 947 in June 1920 to 816 in February and 681 in March. 'The depreciation in numbers was greatly felt.'[77] Just as important, they lost half of their experienced officers and men and had constantly to retrain men in Irish conditions. Even Captain Pinkey had to be transferred to other duties between December and April, leaving the detachment in the hands of a single lieutenant.[78] In a war which depended on the leadership of junior officers, this was a serious loss.

When an English reporter visited nearby Buttevant he found a garrison that was physically and mentally in a state of siege.

We careened at 35 miles an hour through the country, wide stretches of gorse and heather falling rapidly behind, and a white ribbon of road diminishing in front. Every two or three miles the officer pointed to patches of loose road-material where a trench had been filled

[73] See Castletownroche Detachment Log, 9 Sept.–17 Nov. 1920 (Buffs Regimental Museum, Canterbury).   [74] Castletownroche Detach. Log, 22–3 Nov. 1920.

[75] Castletownroche Detach. Log, 21 Apr. 1921; *Examiner*, 22, 23 Apr. 1921.

[76] See Castletownroche Detach. Log, 25 Dec. 1920, 10 Feb., 1, 15 Mar., 9, 10, 22, 30 Apr., 12, 13, 27 May, 22 June 1921.

[77] 1st Bn., the Buffs, Historical Records from Discontinuance of the War Diaries to 31 March 1922 (Buffs Museum). See also Townshend, *British Campaign*, 217.

[78] Castletownroche Detach. Log, 7 Dec. 1920, 28 Apr. 1921.

in or where no long while before an ambush had taken place. When we came to corners he grasped his revolver more tightly and every now and then looked back to see whether the lorry and its armed load were keeping its distance. Once or twice we met parties of civilians, and when this happened the rifles were raised to the 'ready'.

Later he spoke to a staff officer:

People in England . . . don't seem to realize what things are like out here—or else they don't care . . . You've seen yourself the conditions we get about under. We can't go outside barracks without the risk of being shot in the back . . . Only the other day an officer went over to a place five miles away on a motor-bike, and has never been heard of since.[79]

The problems encountered by Pinkey and the Buffs were common to all regiments stationed in Cork. The first of these was manpower. There were eight infantry battalions and one cavalry regiment stationed in the county in August 1920, along with four artillery and machine gun units. The 17th Lancers and the Machine Gun Corps subsequently departed, and one battalion was transferred to Kerry, to be replaced by three new infantry battalions in December, January, and March. Four further regiments—two of infantry, two of mounted artillery—arrived in the last weeks before the Truce, too late to have any immediate impact.[80] From September on, British brigade and divisional commanders also had a number of Auxiliary companies nominally under their control, located in Macroom, Millstreet, Dunmanway, and (briefly) the city.

However, while unit numbers remained essentially stable, the numbers of officers and men did not. Almost all these battalions were still preoccupied with demobilization and reorganization in 1919 and 1920. Most were below strength when martial law was declared, and—like the Buffs—continued to lose men through the critical winter and spring months. The hard-pressed Manchesters in Ballincollig sent 112 other ranks to India in December and gave up their own quota of 135 short-service men on 31 March, representing nearly a third of the men available the previous summer. Thirty recruits were sent from their depot in July in slight recompense.[81] The King's Liverpool Regiment arrived in Bantry in July 1920 with 621 soldiers, half of whom were sent to Egypt over the following year, and a further 89 of whom were discharged when their time expired. They were replaced by 195 new men from home, most in the last month of the campaign. Even with these last-minute drafts, by July the battalion was only two-thirds the size it had been the year before.[82] The Essex Regiment arrived in West Cork in December 1919 with 400 other ranks to demobilize and 300 recruits to train: 'at this time . . . the situation was so

[79]   'Life in Mallow: An English Officer's Impressions', *The Times*, 19 May 1921.

[80]   *6th Division History*, appendix 2.

[81]   1st Bn., The Manchester Regiment Record of Service from July 1919 (MR1/1/2/4).

[82]   1st Bn., The King's Regiment Digest of Service, 1919–1922 (Regional History Dept., National Museums and Galleries on Merseyside).

extremely difficult that Colonel Moffit and his staff had to "think in individual men".' 'Though largely composed of young soldiers', and despite formidable conditions and high losses (38 killed and wounded), they still had to find 200 men to send abroad in 1921. 'Month after month the men enjoyed but three nights in bed a week.'[83]

Not all units were so badly off. The South Staffordshires, stationed in the city, had to send only 42 men to Singapore.[84] The East Lancashires in Buttevant managed to put off sending their large draft to Jamaica until August.[85] Nevertheless, the pattern throughout the Irish Command was for infantry battalions to lose one- to two-thirds of their trained and experienced men, in exchange for a much smaller number of raw recruits.

There was a similarly rapid turnover among regimental officers. The King's Regiment gained nine and lost six in 1920. The Manchester Regiment gained three and lost four in 1921, not including those killed and wounded. To plug the resulting gaps and to carry out the proliferating extra duties required in Ireland, scores of air force, artillery, and education officers were seconded to the Cork battalions. The East Lancashires received eight, the Manchesters eleven (and another from the Lancashire Fusiliers), the South Staffordshires six—and eight more from the Rifle Brigade.

Each regiment was made responsible for a specified district. The Manchesters, for example, had No. 3 Area, which encompassed 240 square miles along the Lee valley, between Blarney and Waterfall, Ballincollig and Millstreet. The Gloucestershire Regiment later took over part of this zone when they established themselves at Kanturk, to cover Duhallow: about 300 square miles of previously unknown territory.[86] With dwindling resources, troops had to be found to man detachments and perform guard and convoy duties, including for prisoners and prison camps and gaols in the city, Kilworth, and on Spike and Bere Islands. In cities and towns there was the curfew and other punitive regulations to be enforced. Training also had to be carried on somehow in order to turn recruits into soldiers. The South Staffordshires, who were lodged in a proper city barracks ('a miniature fortress'[87]) and who suffered least from overseas drafts, found that:

when all necessary Garrison and Regimental employments had been filled . . . the total number of duty n.c.o.s and men was less than 200, which meant, owing to the numbers of duties to be found, that no dutyman got more than two consecutive nights, and sometimes only one night, in bed.[88]

[83] *The Essex Regiment Gazette*, July 1921, Oct. 1922. See also John William Burrows, *Essex Units in the War, 1914–1919*, i (Southend-on-Sea, 1923), 269–77.

[84] 2nd Bn., The South Staffordshire Regiment Digest of Service, 1919–21 (Staffordshire Regiment Museum).

[85] 2nd Bn., The East Lancashire Regiment Digest of Service, 1919–22 (Queen's Lancashire Regiment, Fulwood Barracks).

[86] R. M. Grazebrook Diary, 18 (Royal Gloucestershire Regiment Archives).

[87] Lt. Col. M. B. Savage, 'Looking Back—the Story of My Life' (Staffordshire Regiment Museum), 124.   [88] South Staffordshire Regiment Digest of Service.

Given these conditions, the military challenge facing these section, platoon, and company commanders was to find, then catch—or kill—their elusive enemy. The first requirement was accurate intelligence. Collecting it was the job of the newly appointed battalion and brigade intelligence officers, in collaboration (and sometimes in competition) with their colleagues in the police. That they were generally successful in improving the quantity and quality of information by early 1921 was not due to organization, training, or doctrine as these barely existed before the Truce. Nor did it have anything to do with 'secret service' work, as there were no spies or agents as such in Cork. It was, rather, due to the efforts of these 'young, keen and energetic' officers in getting to know their districts, liaising with the often reluctant constabulary, interrogating prisoners, examining captured documents, and building up contacts and a who's who of the local I.R.A.[89] They were essentially on their own: the divisional and GHQ staffs did little useful to help. The nature of their work exposed them to terrible danger. Many died or disappeared, picked off by the I.R.A. as they travelled about by road or train.

Success came quickly once martial law was introduced. Previously secure columns, safe houses, and arms dumps were all suddenly liable to betrayal in the early months of the new year. January alone saw major arms finds in Clogheen, Fermoy, Glanworth, Ballymore, and on old Ballincollig Road in the city.[90] The guerrillas were equally quick to adapt, however. Columns were broken up, arms were moved and more carefully stored, dugouts were built as hiding places. Suspected informers or scapegoats were driven out or shot down in ever greater numbers. The early intelligence coups were rarer after March, but information gradually continued to accumulate. By the time of the Truce, most battalions and Auxiliary companies had a very accurate picture of the organization and men they were fighting.[91]

Tactically useful intelligence was always rare, though. To keep information flowing, to collect the necessary documents and prisoners to examine, to 'show the flag' and maintain the desired 'offensive spirit', a constant pulse of military activity was required regardless. To do otherwise was contrary to the whole professional ethos of the British army and its regiments. Thus, every battalion and detachment followed a more or less regular routine of patrols, and of more or less random searches:[92]

> His not to care two pins
> His but to harry Shins
> Into the Crossley went
> He and six others.

[89] *6th Division History*, 22; General Staff, Irish Command, *Record of the Rebellion*, ii (Intelligence). 6–9.   [90] *Examiner*, 14, 18, 20, 25 Jan. 1921.

[91] See Sean Moylan Memoir, 244; Dunmanway Auxiliary Company Intelligence Diary, Dec. 1920–Mar. 1921 reproduced in 'Raymond', 'Black and Tan Diary', *Southern Star*, 23 Oct.–27 Nov. 1971 hereafter referred to as *Star*.

[92] 'The 43rd in Ireland', *Oxfordshire and Buckinghamshire Light Infantry Chronicle 1921*, ed. J. F. C. Fuller (London, 1922), 64.

The Manchesters sent out motor patrols four times a week on average between November and January. 'A run like this through unknown country in two rickety lorries, always liable to break down, was no joy ride and often a great strain.'[93] Foot patrols were much rarer until May: less than one a week. Unless themselves ambushed or simply fortunate, these labour-intensive, frustrating, and boring operations almost never encountered their targets.

Perhaps inevitably, brigade and division staffs contrived brigade- and division-sized solutions to this problem. These took the form of 'drives', 'sweeps', and 'round-ups': searches of large tracts of country by several units at once, sometimes taking days and hundreds of men. Equivalent operations were mounted in the city through chosen neighbourhoods.[94] Their ostensible objectives were usually flying columns or I.R.A. brigade or divisional headquarters. The greatest of these efforts—known subsequently to the I.R.A. as 'the big round-up'—came in early June, in north-west Cork and Kerry. Its aim, defined in language with more than a whiff of Flanders châteaux, was that of 'seeking out the I.R.A. columns, bringing them to action and annihilating them'.[95] The searchers did sometimes come close, as at Crossbarry where converging forces killed the West Cork Brigade commander, Charlie Hurley, and nearly trapped the column.[96] More often, the results were meagre and the effort expended disproportionate. The operations were hard to coordinate and covered too much ground, the guerrillas had too much warning, and arrested men were difficult to identify on the march.[97]

Staff officers persisted in planning 'drives' up to the 11 July Truce (and continued to do so thereafter) but did not otherwise attempt to impose any uniform doctrine. Left to themselves, individual regiments grappled with their problems in a variety of ways. Enterprising officers—perhaps harking back to their schooldays—experimented with buried explosives, traps, and lures, but technological advantage proved difficult to exploit. Motor vehicles were noisy and decreasingly mobile once roads and bridges were wrecked; once armoured, their passengers were safer—until the I.R.A. began to construct workable mines. Bicycles were quieter but their riders were much more vulnerable. Machine guns and armoured cars provided life-saving firepower in ambushes, but the latter were otherwise difficult to employ. 'They weren't allowed to do this on account of the springs and they weren't allowed to do that on account of the tyres.'[98]

[93] Grazebrook Diary, 7.   [94] *Examiner*, 21 Jan. 1921.
[95] Quoted in O'Donoghue, *No Other Law*, 171. See also O'Suilleabhain, *Mountainy Men*, 128–38; Patrick J. Twohig, *Green Tears for Hecuba* (Cork, rev. edn., 1994), 270–333.
[96] For accounts, see Lowe, 'Some Reflections of a Junior Commander'; Deasy, *Towards Ireland Free*, 231–54.
[97] For a variety of opinions on 'sweeps', see F. A. S. Clarke, 'The Memoirs of a Professional Soldier in Peace and War' (Liddell Hart Centre), 1–4; *6th Division History*, 99–113; O'Donoghue, *No Other Law*, 170–2; Townshend, *British Campaign*, 176–7, 182–9. For a contemporary I.R.A. view: Report on Enemy Round-Up, 4 Bn., Cork 2, 27 June 1921 (Mulcahy Papers, P7/A/20).
[98] Grazebrook Diary, 26. See also Ronald Lewin, *Man of Armour: A Study of Lieut-General Vyvyan Pope* (London, 1976), 48–51: Pope commanded an armoured company in Cork.

Bloodhounds were introduced in a few areas (and suffered casualties) but the hunted rarely obliged with suitable scents to pursue. Only Niger, 'a witty, sagacious brute' attached to the Essex headquarters in Kinsale, succeeded in making an impression on both soldiers and locals.[99] Aircraft proved a failure at reconnaissance because there was nothing to see.

With better intelligence and knowledge of the countryside, but fewer and fewer men, most battalions eventually tried to come to grips with their foes with their own squads and columns. These were still sometimes awkwardly large, like the multi-platoon mobile columns devised by Major Percival of the Essex Regiment.[100] 'This Essex column was not so very mobile', Dorothy Stopford recalled, 'as we always knew at least half an hour before they appeared.' Jack Buttimer also scoffed at Percival's 'mule column'.[101] Similar long-range foot patrols with fewer men seem to have had more effect in North Cork.[102] Smaller, more secretive squads—often operating undercover and often at night—were deadlier still, and could play the game as well as their I.R.A. rivals. Most units had an official or unofficial 'raids' or 'stunts' officer to organize such groups and their expeditions; in some cases they were entirely composed of officers. In the Gloucestershire Regiment this special force was known as the 'Battalion Scouts':

It was realized in the Battalion in general and to the Intelligence Officer in particular the advantages that would occur in training a small body of picked men for intelligence duties. Available at all times for this work only and excused all guards and fatigues . . . They were at various times called upon to undertake risky and unusual jobs, some of which I own I should not have liked to do myself.

Some of the regimental officers also 'used to come down with me in mufti after mess and prowl around in the dusk just before curfew'.[103]

These hunters frequently adopted a policy of 'shoot to kill' and, when good intelligence came in or a reprisal seemed called for, this was increasingly the result. According to one soldier of the East Lancashires:

We were on several skirmishes with intelligence officers in charge. And they were after certain persons, and if they didn't find them persons, they'd come back with somebody or, should I say, take somebody out and put 'em in the back van, in the back lorry . . . But the intelligence officer gave instructions that he be put in the back of the Crossley and then let he to escape and when he were escaped, he were shot in the road and left there. I was on that patrol meself.[104]

[99] Burrows, *Essex Units in the War*, 276; Clarke, 'Memoirs', 4–5.

[100] Major A. E. Percival, 'Guerrilla Warfare—Ireland 1920–21', part 2 (Percival Papers).

[101] Dorothy [Stopford] Price, 'Kilbrittain' (NLI, Dorothy Price Papers, MS 15, 343[2]); Jack Buttimer (O'Malley Papers, P17b/111). Charlie Browne of Macroom, on the other hand, remembered 'they moved fast when they did move' (P17b/112).

[102] See Patrol Report around Clogheen, 4–7 June 1921, in *6th Division History*, 118–19; O'Donoghue, *No Other Law*, 166–7.   [103] Grazebrook Diary, 14–15, 47.

[104] Interview with soldier of 2nd Bn., East Lancashire Regt., Aug. 1986 (courtesy of Adrian Lewis).

On 27 June, the Manchester intelligence officer in Ballincollig, Lt. Vining, found out that some much-wanted I.R.A. men had gathered at a pub in Waterfall. The response was rapid and decisive, as recorded in the battalion's record of service:

Lt. Colonel W. K. Evans and Lt. Vining proceeded across country to Innishcarra Bridge at 2000 hours, picked up four officers from Cork in two Ford motor cars. Proceeded to Kilumney, no sign of rebels; went on to Waterfall. At Donovan's Publichouse Leo Murphy rushed out and was shot dead of Lt. Col. Evans. The remainder of occupants were held up, 39 in all. Twenty three of these were kept and proved to be the most active members of 3rd Battalion I.R.A. Amongst them was Charles Daly wanted for the murder of L/C. Hadnett, the Hampshire Regt., in Cork. Leo Murphy was known to have been one of Captain Thompson's [the previous Manchester intelligence officer] murderers.

Walter Leo Murphy, known locally as 'a very bad boy', was shot in the back and, according to one version of events, dragged back to barracks behind one of the cars.[105] Charlie Daly was also a marked man, as an I.R.A. officer, an ex-hunger striker on the run and a named suspect in the death of a soldier. A British raiding party had told his sister: 'Your brother is not far away, we will get him in the fields here and shoot him.' The day after his capture he was handed over to the Hampshires, who exacted their promised revenge: 'Daly attempted to escape from his escort proceeding from Victoria Barracks, Cork to Cork Gaol, and was shot dead.'[106]

We can see the same themes emerging on each side: the elusive enemy, poor information, and incessant, wearying activity. Also a sense of isolation, shared by Irish guerrillas and English infantrymen alike. The 'boys' were resented as troublemakers and they in turn did not trust the locals not to betray them. Life on the column was one of constant movement and nagging discomfort. Their official reports were filled with complaints and requests for fresh clothing ('be sure you make no mistake about the socks') as well as rifles.[107] To the men of the Buffs and sister regiments the Irish landscape was suffused with danger, with every turn in the road a potential ambush site and every countryman a suspected rebel.

Guerrilla war in Cork in 1921 was not primarily an affair of ambushes and round-ups. It was terror and counter-terror, murder after murder, death squad against death squad, fed by both sides' desire for revenge. Each new atrocity demanded a reply and so set off another round of reprisals. 'We suggest that for

[105] Manchester Regiment Record of Service. See also *6th Division History*, 123–4; *Examiner*, 29 June, 4 July 1921; Register of Courts of Inquiry on Civilians, June 1921–June 1922 (WO 35/163); interview with BG, 18 Apr. 1993.

[106] Manchester Regiment Record of Service. Catherine Daly's testimony is included in a collection of witness statements which contradict the official version of Daly's death (O'Donoghue papers, MS 31, 178).

[107] Adj., 3 Bn. ASS, Cork 2, 22 Jan. 1921 in CI Monthly Report, East Cork, Jan. 1921.

each prisoner shot in future we shoot one local loyalist';[108] 'if you didn't kill someone, someone was going to kill you';[109] 'I ordered them shot as a preventative against their shooting any more unarmed prisoners';[110] 'it was a case of who got the first shot in.'[111]

This pattern was repeated all over the county. What at first appears as an indistinguishable welter of shootings, bombings, and house-burnings can in many cases be broken down into sequences of interlocking reprisals. For example, in 1920 the Macroom and Ballyvourney Battalions mounted a series of successful ambushes against military and police patrols while losing only one man in combat and another to an army trap. They also assassinated one policeman, wounded another, and shot an army recruit.

The arrival of the Auxiliaries in Macroom changed the course of the war there. Only once did the Muskerry Volunteers take on the Auxiliaries in battle, as part of the Cork 1 column, at Coolavokig on 3 February. Three cadets died and five were wounded in that ambush. In other operations between September 1920 and July 1921, three cadets were wounded by a bomb while playing billiards and two ambulance drivers were shot and their vehicle (containing patients) burned. Nine soldiers and policemen, and two suspected informers, were executed in the same period, seven of whom 'disappeared' into unknown bogs. The Crown forces in Macroom responded by shooting four Volunteers and three civilians who either 'failed to halt' or 'attempted to escape'. One other killing took place whose perpetrators and motives remain unknown.

Midleton, at the other end of the county, experienced one of the most punishing exchanges of reprisals in Cork in 1921. The year 1920 was one of triumph for the 4th Battalion of the 1st Cork Brigade (covering Midleton, Cobh, and Youghal) due to the bold leadership of Diarmuid Hurley. A string of victories— including three captured R.I.C. barracks—culminated in December with the local column's daring breakout from a surrounded house in Cloyne, followed by a successful ambush in the town of Midleton itself.[112]

The spree came to an end on 20 February 1921, when the intelligence officer of the Hampshire Regiment tracked the column to an abandoned farmhouse near the village of Clonmult. Like the Macroom Auxiliaries three months before, the men of the 4th Battalion had become overconfident and had fallen into a traceable routine.

What ensued can be described as Kilmichael in reverse. The column was attacked and besieged by a combined force of soldiers and police, and both sides suffered losses in the firefight. According to the official British

---

[108] O/C 1st South. Div. to C/S, 4 May 1921 (Mulcahy Papers, P7/A/19).

[109] Brewer, *The Royal Irish Constabulary*, 103.

[110] Column Report No. 4, Cork 3, 22 Feb. 1921 (Mulcahy Papers, P7/A/38).

[111] Brewer, *The Royal Irish Constabulary*, 105.

[112] See Seamus Fitzgerald, 'East Cork Activities—1920', *Capuchin Annual* (1970) and Padraig O Ciosain, 'Operations in East Cork', in *Rebel Cork's Fighting Story*.

communiqué, several guerrillas came running out with their hands up but others continued to fire. A number of Black and Tans were shot as they went to accept this 'false surrender'.[113] Out of twenty Volunteers, twelve were dead and four were wounded before army officers got the enraged policemen under control. The Irish survivors testified convincingly that there was no treachery on their part. They surrendered in good faith and were gunned down as they emerged or else stood against a wall and executed. 'The whole scene was hellish and indescribable, some dead, others dying and moaning in pain, their blood flowing in all directions while those of us who survived were left lying on the bloodstained ground.'[114]

After Clonmult every suspected informer and every man in uniform (including coastguards and Marines) became a legitimate target to be 'shot on sight' in the I.R.A.'s quest for vengeance.[115] 'Things went to hell then in the battalion . . . they had terrorised the people.'[116] Where no one had previously been shot as a spy, six were killed in rapid succession in Midleton and neighbouring villages. Several of these were accused of leading the enemy to Clonmult. Worst hit was the village of Carrigtwohill, described by Mick Leahy, the vice O/C of the brigade, as 'a bloody pile of spies'. Leahy described one such 'job':

I sent Dathai O'Brien to pick up [Michael] O'Keefe there for we had the goods on him. I told him to go down and get this man. O'Brien arrived back in an old Ford car . . . 'He's in Patsy Connors' he said. 'But I told you to bring him back here'. 'I know that' O'Brien said, 'He's on the sidewalk outside and we couldn't bring him back because he's dead. We went down to his house and when we were passing up the street at Patsy Connors I turned round and let him have it for he jumped out of the car'. 'You had no authority', I said, 'to shoot him'. It was casual enough this shooting of O'Keefe but they didn't worry about it.

After three retaliatory massacres of unarmed policemen and Marines in early May it was once again the army's turn for revenge. And once again Carrigtwohill was the scene for kidnappings and drive-by shootings, this time carried out by British soldiers, who used the same excuse as Dathai O'Brien, that their victims had tried to escape. Similar reprisals took place in Ballycotton in July after a lorry ran over a mine.

Nowhere did these underground vendettas follow a more tangled course than in Cork city—'the city of spies'[117]—where 'active squads' hunted their victims and each other through a labyrinth of suspicion and betrayal. In some cases the motives for a shooting are so indecipherable that it is impossible to say who was

[113]   *Irish Times*, 17 May 1921; Report of the Military Court of Inquiry (WO 35/155A).

[114]   Survivor's statement, Mulcahy Papers, P7/A/12. For different accounts of the battle, see the I.R.A. report in the Mulcahy Papers (P7/A/13); O Ciosain, 'Operations in East Cork', 190–5; Report of the Military Court of Inquiry (WO 35/155A); *Hampshire Regimental Journal* (Mar. 1921), 37 and (May 1921), 80–2.

[115]   CI Monthly Report, East Cork, May 1921 (CO 904/115); O Ciosain, 'Operations in East Cork', 197.   [116]   Mick Leahy (O'Malley Papers, P17b/108).

[117]   'Life in Cork: An English Officer's Impressions', *The Times*, 18 May 1921.

responsible. Here the war proceeded murder by murder, disappearance by disappearance, with almost every night producing another body. In the months following the shootings of James O'Donoghue and Charlie O'Brien, the city I.R.A. carried out 8 successful attacks on patrols or barracks—and fully 131 shootings of helpless victims. Both sides had their black lists: 'Mick [Murphy] would blow smoke out of his mouth and say "Just you shoot them . . . and you shoot them also", and as the names went on he'd let out a puff of smoke.'[118]

Any acceleration of this steady pace was quickly reciprocated. After an Auxiliary section was badly shot up at Dillon's Cross on 11 December, their comrades burned Patrick Street and the City Hall, murdered two I.R.A. men in their beds, and shot five other people. On 28 February, the day that six Volunteers were executed in the city barracks, twelve unarmed soldiers were shot in the streets by I.R.A. squads. British intelligence blamed most of these shootings on what they called 'the Blarney Street murder gang'.[119] When six of these men were tracked to a barn in Clogheen they were wiped out in a hail of bullets, reportedly trying to escape:

the officer who found them, told them that he would give them a sporting chance, there was a hedge on the side of the hill, and he told them that his men would open fire when they got there. 4 of them were killed, the 5th got away, but ran into another of our pickets, and they shot him, this saved the time and trouble of a Court Martial.[120]

Tit for tat.

The city's atmosphere of fear and menacing uncertainty was caught by a visitor in April 1921:[121]

To be a stray Englishman . . . was to be almost invariably mistaken for a Government agent . . . plain clothes visitors to the barracks are objects of peculiar interest to the various groups of young men who lounge at street-corners in that vicinity . . .

There was a calm spring evening when I made my way out to Blackrock . . . Near to the city, at an open ground where children play, high commotion prevailed. Mothers, fathers, children and strangers were all jabbering together in a crowd, pointing in the direction of the town. Somebody's child, it appeared, had been kidnapped by a mysterious individual in a motor-car.

Which side was the mysterious individual on, if any? What was his motive? The area was a favourite hunting ground for the I.R.A., who abducted and executed several young teenagers about this time, but we shall never know for sure what happened.

These incidents were linked by more than the chain of reprisals and counter-reprisals. Guerrilla war was a game with few players and most of the killings

[118] Con Neenan (O'Malley Papers, P17b/112).

[119] See 'Some Types of the Sinn Fein' compiled by the Intelligence Branch, 6th Division (Strickland Papers).

[120] Savage, 'Looking Back', 126. See also Adj., Cork 1 to A/G, 4 Apr. 1921 (Mulcahy Papers, P7/A/38).   [121] 'Life in Cork', *The Times*, 18 May 1921.

were carried out by the same cliques of 'hard men', the O'Briens, Busteeds, Barrys, and their still anonymous British counterparts. Frank Busteed's career is a good example of this. Besides the shooting of Din-Din O'Riordan, he was involved in that of Mrs Lindsay and her chauffeur in Coachford, the twelve off-duty soldiers mentioned above, and three British officers in Macroom in 1922. He also led his battalion column in 1920 and 1921 and participated in an unknown number of other attacks up to (and perhaps beyond) the end of the Civil War.[122]

We have less evidence from inside the R.I.C. but there were clearly informal police death squads as well, often masquerading under titles such as 'the Anti-Sinn Fein Society'. One constable stationed in Bandon (an area which saw a large number of I.R.A. deaths) said of the Black and Tans:[123]

if they were ambushed and had a lot of them shot, well then they retaliated. One man, a Head Constable, he took charge of a squad, he was always in plainclothes, never wore a uniform, and they had a big price on his head . . . But they never got him . . . Well he was on a special squad; he had his men with him, four or five of them all dressed like old farmers, they gathered the information. Oh there was quite a lot of undercover work.

Another policeman in Cork was said to have had thirty-seven 'kills' to his credit before being transferred.[124]

These executioners were frequently self-appointed. The O'Briens on White Street, Tom Barry at Kilmichael, and Dathai O'Brien at Carrigtwohill all carried out unauthorized operations and got away with it just as did the assassins of Tomas MacCurtain and of the victims at Clogheen and Clonmult.

As time went by, these political serial killers and their methods became virtually indistinguishable, their 'stunts', 'jobs', and 'operations' a blur of masked men in trench coats, 'attempted escapes', and disfigured bodies. 'A shot was fired, and he fell to the ground. The civilians then fired at his head four or five times as he lay on the ground and then ran'; 'the assailants took him, stood him in the gutter and shot him. They all fired at him as he was lying on the ground and then ran away'; 'between three and four o'clock this morning armed and disguised men suddenly appeared'; 'one of the intruders said "Are you Patrick Sheehan?" He replied "yes" and the next instant he was shot dead, bullets passing through his heart and neck.'[125]

Another weapon of retaliation and terror used by both sides was arson. British reprisals against property began in the summer of 1920 and quickly

---

[122] See Frank Busteed (O'Malley Papers, P17b/112); O'Callaghan, *Execution*; D/I Report on Busteed, 30 May 1924 (MA, A/0825).

[123] Brewer, *The Royal Irish Constabulary*, 115.

[124] Commander J. E. P. Brass, 'Diary of a War Cadet 1914–1921', 234 (IWM, 76/116/1). See also Richard Bennett, 'Portrait of a Killer', *New Statesman* (24 Mar. 1961), 471–2; Hervey de Montmorency, *Sword and Stirrup* (London, 1936), 354–5; Crozier, *Ireland for Ever*, 147, 159; Townshend, *British Campaign*, 97, 100–1, 116.

[125] *Examiner*, 17 Apr., 30 Mar. 1921; *Irish Times*, 16 May, 24 Mar. 1921. The first two quotations describe I.R.A. killings, the last two British reprisals.

TABLE 10. The destruction of buildings in Cork, 1920–1921

	By I.R.A.	By Crown forces	Unknown	Total
1920				
Jan.–June	74	3	8	85
July–Dec.	42	146	2	190
1921				
Jan.–July	93	67	5	165
Total	209	216	15	440

Note: The prominence of the July–Dec. 1920 period for Crown force arson is due to the 'burning of Cork' on 11 Dec. 1920. In the first half of 1920 most buildings destroyed by the I.R.A. were R.I.C. barracks. Thereafter they concentrated on private houses.

became routine, though not officially sanctioned until January 1921. Sometimes the houses and shops destroyed belonged to republican families. More often they did not. The I.R.A. began to burn Protestant homes in reply that winter. By the spring of 1921 the combatants had become locked into an arson competition which became part of the cycle of reprisals. A killing would be answered by another killing, but also provoked beatings and attacks on suspect homes. As in the shooting war, it was the non-combatants who were caught in the middle. The resulting spiral of destruction is shown in Table 10.

Arsonists shared the revenge mentality of the gunmen. Then-Major Bernard Montgomery admitted that 'it never bothered me a bit how many houses were burnt'.[126] Liam Lynch echoed this sentiment: 'The Enemy seems inclined to burn out every house and we may as well have our share.'[127] Arsonists, like assassins, acted much the same no matter which side they were on, as the following account demonstrates:

A great burning took place in this district in the month of June in the year one thousand, nine hundred and twenty one. Two dwelling houses the property of Samuel Daly at Lisheencreagh, Ballydehob were burned to ruins.

One of the houses was an outside farm, which Daly had bought about a year before that, and this was burned to ruins on the twenty second of June. The burning was performed by a party called the Flying Column, as they suspected the Daly family of being informers to the British forces.

On the eve of the twenty ninth of June the party again visited Daly's house. They accused his sister of being an informer, and they cut the hair from her head. Later that night they again came. The Dalys were in bed and they were ordered to leave, as the house was to be destroyed. Daly's mother, who was an aged woman, was reluctant to leave the house, and she was treated roughly, and taken out by force.

The soldiers then put the house on fire. Into the flames they cast harness and all other things they could lay hands on. All next day the fire continued and in the evening nothing remained but the black walls.

[126] Major B. L. Montgomery to Major Percival, 14 Oct. 1923 (IWM, A. E. Percival Papers).
[127] O/C 1st South. Div. to C/S, 20 May 1921 (Mulcahy Papers, P7/A/21).

The farm animals, which numbered about fifteen cows, some heifers, calves and horses were carried off by the destroyers. One calf, which remained behind, had to be killed through scarcity of milk. The Dalys then lived in a stable.[128]

These attacks originated in Samuel Daly's refusal to give money to the I.R.A. arms fund. His family was both Protestant and loyal—two of his brothers were policemen and another was a soldier. They were boycotted from late 1920 on so that no labourer or neighbour would work on his farm, no one would help put out the fire, and no doctor would come to treat his mother who was paralysed from shock. After the police and army withdrew in the winter of 1922, the I.R.A. renewed their demands. This time Daly paid.[129]

This story concerns an I.R.A. 'operation' but with a few changes of names it could easily have been about a British reprisal. It is told very much in a traditional mode, even beginning with the formulaic 'a great burning took place' but in this case the language was inverted and turned against the conventional folk heroes. Instead of the 'soldiers' and 'destroyers'—the brutal outsiders—being Black and Tans, they are 'a party called the flying column'. The storyteller probably saw little difference between the two.[130]

The dynamic of escalation acted not only to raise the casualty rate but also to broaden enormously the arena of violence. Guerrilla war in Cork was a kind of total war in miniature, with fewer and fewer barriers to violence and the burden of suffering falling increasingly on civilians. The spread of violence shattered normalcy and disrupted the lives and commerce of every community in Cork.

From 1918 on, Britain's coercion policies depended on punishing the general population for I.R.A. actions. To suppress the rebellion the army made itself a suffocating presence, blanketing daily life with curfews, restrictions on trade and movement, arbitrary detentions, and other forms of harassment.[131] Mass raids and searches were used to trawl whole neighbourhoods and parishes for suspects and arms. Reprisals were frequently directed against communal targets such as creameries and town halls. The mere prospect of one was enough to cause families and whole districts to leave their homes at night and go on the run *en masse*.

The people of Cork also had to negotiate the new rules laid down by 'the republic'. The Belfast boycott, which often effectively included British goods and Protestant firms, was enforced with threats, guns, and kerosene. The I.R.A.

[128]   Dept. of Irish Folklore, SMS 288, 361–2.

[129]   Samuel Daly statement (Irish Grants Committee Papers, CO 762/192); *Star*, 25 June 1921. His marriage plans were also destroyed, according to Catherine Kingston's statement (CO 904/184). Neither Samuel nor his sister were listed as suspected spies by local I.R.A. intelligence officers in late 1921 (MA, A/0897).

[130]   As with all the schools manuscripts, this story was collected by a student from an elder (in this case unknown).

[131]   The martial law authorities did attempt forcibly to enrol civilians as civil guards but this failed due to non-cooperation. For the Drimoleague civil guards, see *Irish Times*, 15 Feb. 1921; for Liscarroll and Ballincollig, *Examiner*, 25 Feb. 1921.

TABLE 11. Attacks on communications in Cork, 1920–1921

	Bridges destroyed	Raids on mails
1920		
Jan.–June	—	15
July–Dec.	—	65
1921		
Jan.–July	110	147

also threw its weight behind the railways strike of 1920. Both sides tried to suppress hostile newspapers. The *Southern Star* was closed down by the police in 1919; the other three local newspapers, the *Examiner*, the *Cork Constitution*, and the Skibbereen *Eagle*, all had their employees and premises attacked and their papers seized and burned by the rebels.

Worst of all was the I.R.A.'s assault on roads, bridges, railway, telegraph and telephone lines, and the mails. These attacks were carried out in every parish of the county from the winter of 1920 onward, paralysing travel and communications. Roads were trenched or blocked with trees (usually by conscripted civilians), railway tracks were broken or blown up, telephone wires were cut and poles were chopped down (and repairmen were threatened or held up) so often and so repetitively that the incidents defy enumeration. Paddy O'Brien, a guerrilla leader in North Cork, recalled that 'there was scarcely a day that they [the British] would not be out trying to put the roads in order and we would block them again at night'.[132] Reliable data can be assembled for raids on mails and destroyed bridges (see Table 11).

These acts of sabotage began as part of individual Volunteer attacks, to prevent or delay reinforcements. In 1921, partly as a result of central direction and partly by force of imitation, this destruction became an end in itself. As a campaign to immobilize government forces it was a clear success. Major Percival in Bandon concluded that 'it is really impossible . . . to keep the road communications open if the enemy are determined'.[133] When Colonel Hugh Elles toured Ireland in June he found that travel was 'laborious and difficult'. 'To go from Dublin to Cork one may fly, one may go by T.B.D[estroyer] and be met by escort at the docks, or one may go—very slowly—by armed train.'[134] Captain Pinkey and his men in Castletownroche were so isolated they heard about the Truce by aeroplane and pigeon.[135]

Road-wrecking and mail interception were also weapons of intimidation, to be used against antagonistic households or communities. A trenched road could not only block an exit from a farm but also divert traffic across private land and

---

[132] Paddy O'Brien (O'Malley Papers, P17b/108).
[133] Percival, 'Guerrilla Warfare', lecture 1.
[134] Col. Hugh Elles, 'The Military Situation in Ireland', 24 June 1921 (PRO, CAB 24/125, CP 3075).   [135] Castletownroche Detach. Log, 9 July 1921.

attract the attention of the police. Catherine Murphy (whose father was an ex-policeman) experienced this near Banteer:

On the eve of the 16 of June, my Father Brother and two Aunts, including myself were in the house having some tea . . . when all of a sudden a Captain of the I.R.A. not living far from here rushed in the door and made a roar at my brother to get out: put him at once to cut down a tree right opposite the door, never said there was an ambush to take place . . . While my brother and another boy was felling the tree, The Captain drew what carts were in the yard and threw them on the road . . . then the Captain and 5 other boys whom we know well took their departure, never telling us what to say when the military would arrive.[136]

The army blamed the Murphys, as 'the boys' knew they would, and Catherine's brother was beaten up and arrested the next day.

The only type of violence to decrease in 1920 and 1921 was that of crowds. The number of riots subsided from twenty-three in 1919 to thirteen in 1920, and to zero in 1921 (up to the Truce). True to their rich factional heritage, it was the street fighters of Cork city's north side who persisted the longest. This decline reflects the increased danger of such activity but it also indicates the end of republicanism as a mass movement and the dampening of popular enthusiasm for 'the cause'. By 1921 the revolution had hardened into a contest between gunmen.

In retrospect, participants on both sides claimed the upper hand in the months approaching the Truce. Among British officers at all levels of command, this was a belief universally expressed and genuinely felt. 'This d——d effort at peace much more arduous than the other thing,' growled Strickland to his diary on 11 July, a sentiment he amplified upon leaving Ireland a year later:

And so this is the end of two and a half years toil. A year ago we had a perfect organization, and had 'them' beat. A short time more would have completed it thoroughly. 'They' knew this and got the ——— Politicians to negotiate . . . It almost makes one wish one had never been concerned in the show.

When Winston Churchill's military secretary talked to staffs around the country, 'they all, without exception, said that the rebels were beaten, and that if, instead of agreeing to an armistice, the Government had stuck it out for another fortnight, they would have been glad to surrender'. 'C' Company of the East Lancashires were convinced they were winning 'our old game of worrying the wily Shin . . . and we doubt not that one or two enemy leaders are rubbing their eyes and thinking hard thoughts'. Then-Lieutenant Frederick Clarke of the Essex Regiment complained that 'the British politicians had arranged an armistice *just when we could have quelled the rebellion*'. According to his superior, Major Percival, 'we had conclusive evidence that, at the time of the Truce in

---

[136] Catherine Murphy to Min. of Defence, 30 Nov. 1921 (MA, A/0668).

July, our tactics of rapid movement and surprise had such a demoralising effect on their nerves that in another few weeks the back of the Rebellion would have been broken'.[137]

A similar chorus of frustration issued from I.R.A. men opposed to the Anglo-Irish Treaty after 7 December. Sean Moylan, a TD for North Cork as well as its brigade leader, argued furiously in the Dail that 'we have driven the British garrison into the sea'. Florence O'Donoghue, a city staff officer, maintained that 'the whole armed effort was gathering a powerful momentum' and that the south Munster brigades 'held the initiative and felt confident of being able to retain it'. For Liam Deasy, commander of the West Cork Brigade at the time of the truce, 'it seemed to me that our struggle had brought us to a position of strength which warranted high expectations'. Tom Barry felt that the I.R.A. 'was capable, not alone of fighting back but of actually threatening to smash their military power in Ireland in the not too distant future'.[138]

Was either side winning? The 6th Division's historian asserted that 'the initiative had passed definitely to the Army' in April. The city's police chief began making this claim in March, and reported that conditions had 'somewhat improved' by June. The county inspector in Mallow recorded an 'outburst' in May but sensed the following month that 'enemy morale is distinctly weakening'. The view from Bandon was not so rosy. Not only could the R.I.C. commander there detect 'no signs of improvement' in the western half of the county in May, Crown forces were actually losing ground and 'touching only at the fringe of things'. In July, affairs were 'worse than ever' although he briskly added the familiar refrain 'that the I.R.A. were in a bad way, and that several months of intensive action on the part of the Crown Forces would have beaten them out of the field'.[139]

'Initiative' and 'momentum' are matters of perspective, but they can also be measured. Volunteers were certainly being arrested, interned, and convicted at a faster rate after March: arrests in the Manchester Regiment's district doubled between April and July, and convictions tripled in the 6th Division as a whole.[140] On the other hand, I.R.A. casualties were falling almost as rapidly—by more than half over the same period—while Crown force losses rose by 11 per cent. For the first time, as well, the majority of victims were soldiers, not policemen. Arson attacks and robberies were also up, and the guerrillas showed no sign of slowing down in any area in July. The fabled columns may have dwindled but their firepower had been replaced by the growing threat of mines. Indeed, the

[137] Strickland Diary, 11 July 1921, 17 May 1922; Gen. Sir Alexander Godley, *Life of an Irish Soldier* (London, 1939), 275; *Lilywhites' Gazette* (Sept. 1921), 6; Clarke, 'Memoirs', 10; Percival, 'Guerrilla Warfare', part 2.

[138] O'Donoghue, *No Other Law*, 176–7; Deasy, *Towards Ireland Free*, 312; Barry, *Guerilla Days*, 224.

[139] *6th Division History*, 99; CI Monthly Reports, Mar.–July 1921 (CO 904/114–16).

[140] Manchester Regiment Record of Arrests in Ireland 1921 (Manchester Regt. Archives Collection, MR 1/11/2); Register of Prisoners in Military Prisons (WO 35/143).

TABLE 12. I.R.A. brigade performance in Cork, 1917–1921

	Crown forces casualties		I.R.A. casualties	
	Total	Per 10,000 people	Total	Per 10,000 people
Cork 1	236	12	68	3.4
Cork 1 (rural units)	149	13	49	4.3
Cork 2	99	11	40	5.0
Cork 3	142	14	52	4.5

Note: I.R.A. casualties do not include accidents, executions, or hunger strikes.

worst single ambush of the whole Irish campaign occurred on 30 May, when a bomb hidden in a culvert blew up the Hampshire regimental band near Youghal, causing twenty-nine casualties.[141]

And, contrary to the apparent geographical divide in R.I.C. reports, guerrilla activity was increasing fastest in the eastern half of the county: that is, in the optimists' police districts, not the pessimists'. Despite numerous local claims about which unit or region won the war, there was, as Table 12 shows, little to choose between the brigades in terms of aggression or endurance. The North Cork Brigade suffered the highest losses and did the least damage in proportion to its base population, but its record was only slightly less successful than that of the other units.

Each brigade had its strong and weak areas. Bandon district was by far the most violent in 1920 and 1921, followed by Youghal, Midleton, and the city itself. Least active were Schull and Kinsale. The battalions in the county's four poorest districts in the south-west, from Beara to Skibbereen, stood out for their poor performance; those at the eastern—and more prosperous—end of the coast-line were notably successful. Otherwise, the strengths and weaknesses form no obvious geographical pattern.

The Cork brigades may have been running neck and neck, but they were far ahead of the rest of Ireland. In this sense, the proud boast that 'the boys who beat the Black and Tans were the boys from the county Cork' was justified. Cork was notoriously the 'storm centre' of the rebellion and by far the most violent county in the Tan War (and in the revolution as a whole).[142] As such, it formed part of an activist region in the province of Munster (with the exception of Waterford). It was these southern brigades, along with Dublin and Longford, which bore the brunt of the fighting. This pattern was not a static one, however. The western counties of Galway, Mayo, and Sligo, in particular, were requiring more British attention as the summer approached, as was Kilkenny in the

---

[141] *Examiner*, 1 June 1921; *Hampshire Regimental Journal*, June 1921.

[142] Major General Douglas Wimberly, 'Scottish Soldier' (IWM, PP/MCR/182), 146; *6th Division History*, 4. For further discussion of these questions, see Hart, 'The Geography of Revolution in Ireland'. The geography of the revolution in Cork is analysed in much greater detail in my 1992 Trinity College Ph.D. thesis.

south-east. In the country as a whole, police and military losses had increased by 17 per cent between April and June and, as in Cork, seemed set to continue at that rate or worse through July. The campaign had also been extended to mainland Britain, whose police forces had difficulty coping with armed guerrillas.

Whether or not British optimism was justified can therefore only be conjectured, and may well be doubted. It is worth noting that this was not the first time the authorities declared the initiative won, only to see it slip away again. As recently as December 1920, with the advent of martial law, the inspector for East Cork felt that 'the turning point is at hand', only to report two months later that 'the state of the city is grave'. In West Cork, the outlook for the new year was 'hopeful . . . crown forces are getting the situation in hand', a view confirmed in January by 'signs of a return to safe politics'. In February, however, 'the Riding could hardly be in a worse state than it is at the present time'.[143]

The high hopes of June and July appear equally premature. The rebels had fought their way through a bad winter, and had raised their game in the face of the British offensive. Setbacks, as at Clonmult, Clogheen, Dripsey, or Mourneabbey, had been met with heightened ferocity. Perhaps most importantly, they had kept—in some ways tightened—their grip on the political life of the county.

The guerrillas' own claims of imminent victory were just as far-fetched. The Dublin GHQ's visions of military progress were embodied in their creation of the 1st Southern Division in late April. This new formation brought together the Cork, Kerry, Waterford, and West Limerick Brigades under the command of Liam Lynch with the intention of improving staff work and coordination.[144] Paper plans—and paperwork—did nothing to alter local realities. The 'boys' commanded considerable stretches of countryside but their war of attrition was doing nothing to affect the military balance of power in Cork or Ireland. Arms and ammunition had to be carefully husbanded, as captures were now rare and the Cork smuggling networks moved at a cautious pace. A few Thompson guns had begun to arrive but a long-promised cargo of Italian guns had not materialized. By the end of June, one city battalion reported having fewer than ten bullets apiece for its seventy revolvers.[145]

Nevertheless, victory could not be defined in the same way for both sides. Winning, for the forces of the Crown, entailed crushing the I.R.A. and smothering its campaign within a matter of months. The guerrillas had only to

---

[143] CI Monthly Reports, Dec. 1920–Feb. 1921 (CO 904/113–14).

[144] For the formation of the division, see O'Donoghue, *No Other Law*, 146–61; O'Malley, *On Another Man's Wound*, 291–306; Deasy, *Towards Ireland Free*, 266–8; Barry, *Guerilla Days*, 142–52.

[145] O/C 1 Bn. to Adj., Cork 1, n.d. [June 1921] (Mulcahy Papers, P7/A/23). For arms smuggling, see Peter Hart, 'The Thompson Submachine Gun in Ireland, Revisited', *Irish Sword* (Summer 1995).

survive and carry on. Violence, driven by a reciprocal siege mentality and desire for revenge, had become self-sustaining, and could well have continued for a long time to come as both sides turned increasingly to murder and execution. For either side to impose its will on the other was a very distant prospect.

5

The Cork Republic

If Mick Collins went to hell in the morning, would you follow him there?
(Cries of 'Yes' and 'No')
(Mary MacSwiney in the Dail, 21 Dec. 1921)[1]

We have no shining gaiters or no sam browne belts to show
We're ready to defend ourselves wherever we may go,
We're up for a republic and to hell with a free state
No surrender is the war cry of the First Cork Brigade.
('The First Cork Brigade')

In the twenty-four hours before the Truce came into effect, the I.R.A. ambushed two military parties in North Cork, killed a policeman in Skibbereen and a 'convicted spy' in Rochestown, and burned a coastguard station near Midleton and a house near Mallow. Another suspected informer and a police recruit were gunned down on the streets of the city, and four unarmed and off-duty soldiers were kidnapped, taken to a field, and shot in the back of the head. At noon on 11 July, the fighting stopped. For the next five months Cork remained an armed camp. The I.R.A., police, and army were each ready—and expected—to resume hostilities on an even larger scale than before.

The guerrillas—now able to attend to their affairs unmolested—paraded, drilled, recruited new members, and held training camps. Their 'arms funds' were augmented by more or less compulsory levies: Liam Lynch, O/C of the 1st Southern Division, reported in October that his units were spending six times more than they had been before the ceasefire.[2] Gun runners stepped up their traffic, although principally to the benefit of eastern brigades. In Cork, the Truce also brought immediate reorganization. The North (2nd) and West (3rd) Brigades were each divided in half, to create separate North-West (4th) and South-West (5th) units under Sean Moylan and Gibbs Ross. This merely recognized the *de facto* assumption of local control by the neglected and aggrieved westerners. A similar proposal for the 1st Cork Brigade could not overcome commandant Sean O'Hegarty's territorial imperative. Several battalions were also subdivided, for much the same reasons.[3] Some sense of countervailing unity was provided by Liam Lynch and his divisional staff, who were finally able to establish a measure of authority over their fast multiplying formations.

---

[1] *Official Report: Debate on the Treaty between Great Britain and Ireland* (Dublin, n.d.), 114.
[2] O/C 1st South. Div., 27 Oct. 1921 (Mulcahy Papers, P7/A/28).
[3] For more on the origin of these splits, see Ch. 10.

I.R.A. plans called for an even more rigorous reign of terror. In essence, anyone connected by sentiment or employment—or by accusation or supposition—to the old regime was to be attacked. As Michael Collins put it, 'my chief desire is not to single out any particular Institution, but to get at them all'.[4] Protestant hostages would, it was hoped, hold mass executions in check. 'If there is a war of extermination on us', declared Sean Moylan, 'by God, no loyalist in North Cork will see its finish.'[5] In Britain, sabotage would be accompanied by a long-stayed programme of political assassinations.

British official thinking moved along parallel lines. Martial law would be extended and the laws of treason would be invoked. Identified rebels would be arrested wholesale; if armed, executed. The I.R.A. would be subjected to an all-out offensive by the security forces. These measures would be applied by the now-seasoned veterans of the last campaign, crucially reinforced by new battalions. Four of these were assigned to County Cork. General Macready's draft plan urged that:

Time being all important, operations are to be carried out by day and night with the greatest energy, subject only to the limitation imposed by consideration for the health of the troops. The initiative has hitherto, owing to lack of troops, been with the rebels. It must now pass to us.[6]

Macready's officers certainly looked forward to being given a 'free hand', but were less sure that the manpower problem had been solved.[7] A few regiments were withdrawn from Ireland soon after the Truce and the others were still obliged to fill overseas drafts. General Boyd of the Dublin District complained that these were 'largely composed of men thoroughly trained to work in a big city under active service conditions, and cannot be replaced . . . With the troops now available, I have no hope of dealing the rebels in Dublin the swift and heavy blow I had planned.'[8] In Cork, the South Staffordshires gained 64 men over the summer months but their good fortune was rare. The previously spared Gloucestershire and East Lancashire Regiments lost 150 and 185 other ranks in July and August respectively. The Manchesters had to give up another 135 of their men in late July, and a further 94 in early December. The Buffs were ordered to ready 133 men for Aden in September. The King's Regiment were ordered to supply 200 soldiers for duty in Hong Kong in October 'but owing to the weak strength of the Battalion 74 other ranks were all that were available'. They ultimately sent 96 men, but these were largely replaced by new recruits so that overall numbers did not slip by too much.[9]

---

[4] Collins to de Valera, 27 June 1921 (NA, DE 2/296).

[5] *Debate on the Treaty*, 146.

[6] Macready to Sec. of State for War, 13 Sept. 1921 (WO 35/180B).

[7] Grazebrook Diary, 71 (Royal Gloucestershire Regiment Archives).

[8] Gen. Boyd to Macready, 8 Oct. 1921.

[9] 1st Bn., King's Regiment Digest of Service, 1919–22; 2nd Bn., South Staffordshire Regiment Digest of Service, 1919–21; Grazebrook Diary, 63; 2nd Bn., East Lancashire Regiment Digest of Service, 1919–22; 1st Bn., Manchester Regiment Record of Service from July 1919; 1st Bn., Buffs Historical Records.

British commanders were also increasingly concerned about another problem: that of the so-called 'loyalists' whom the I.R.A. had so clearly set its sights on. These ex-soldiers and Protestants could neither defend themselves nor be counted upon to help in the coming struggle. But they had to be protected. After some debate, it was decided to establish refugee centres in each battalion, which would be cleared of 'known rebel sympathizers' and defended by Crown forces. Where possible, the refugees themselves would be armed.[10] Such a scheme would have diverted a great many troops from the proposed offensive, and civilian vigilantes would have only stoked the fires of civil war.

Fortunately, these rival plans were never tested. In their absence, the Volunteers and their opponents waged a constant battle for authority, arresting and kidnapping one another, seizing cars, bicycles, horses, and guns, and exchanging threats, blows, and occasionally gunfire.[11] The atmosphere of this behind-the-scenes war of nerves is evoked by an encounter which took place in Macroom when the O'Suilleabhain brothers of Ballyvourney met an Auxiliary patrol led by an officer nicknamed 'Hollywood'—'a great gunman and guns strapped on to his legs':

I was in the car with a trench coat on me. I had two guns in the slit pockets and I was standing by when 'Hollywood' came along. He walked round and round the car—a big tall pompous man. 'That's our car', he said. 'Is that so?' said I. 'It was', I said, 'but it isn't yours now'. 'Well quite possibly we might own it again'. 'Well we want it at the moment'. 'We'll see about that' he said. 'Well', I said, 'you mean you want it back; you're welcome to it if you can take it back'. I put my hands in my two pockets and if he moved I'd have let him have it.[12]

The stand-off continued in the same vein until the Auxiliaries backed down, presenting a vivid picture of the gangsterish culture of violence inhabited by the gunmen on both sides: the eager toughs in their matching trench coats, revolvers, and Ford cars.

The Truce may have put an end to the war but local vendettas lived on. I.R.A. gunmen secretly executed and disposed of at least two suspected spies in July and August (and wounded another in September) and continued to harass presumed enemies. Some were kidnapped, like James Fehilly and Denis Donovan of Dunmanway. Some were beaten and humiliated like George Mannix of Kanturk. Others were fined, harassed, or boycotted.[13]

The Truce also brought renewed prison battles, hunger strikes, and escapes. Behind the walls of the Cork city gaol and the Spike Island military prison,

---

[10] Irish Command GHQ circular, 5 Oct. 1921 (WO 35/180B). See also Grazebrook Diary, 66–70.

[11] Most of this went unreported by local newspapers but was recorded in detail in the CI Monthly Reports for Cork, July–Sept. 1921 (CO 904/115–16) and R.I.C. Breach of Truce Reports (CO 904/152). See also the correspondence in the Liaison Papers (MA, LE/3/2, LE/4/7A).

[12] Mick O'Sullivan (O'Malley Papers, P17b/108).

[13] See DI Timoleague Report, 14 Aug. 1921 and Liaison Officer, I.R.A. to CI, Mallow, 30 Nov. 1921 (Breach of Truce Reports, CO 904/152).

hundreds of Volunteers mutinied and fought ferocious battles against their captors. In an era of epic prison riots, Spike Island's was the worst. In October, accumulated friction, frustration, and a growing assertiveness exploded into a wild affray: 'One thing led to another and we have destroyed the place.'[14] Some of the prisoners from other counties suspected the uprising was a Cork plot, perhaps cooked up 'by underhand means' by Sean O'Hegarty himself. 'We outnumbered the Cork prisoners. Still, whatever the Cork division said was law for us.'[15]

Whoever was in charge, the awed commander of the Spike Island camp told his superiors in Dublin that 'I am not dealing at all with human beings. I am dealing with madmen.' 'I think they will get the best of us.'[16] They did not quite, although they managed to wreak massive damage before they were subdued. To add insult to injury, seven leading guerrillas, including key Cork officers Moss Twomey, Dick Barrett, and Tom Crofts, escaped a few weeks later.[17]

Despite such aggressive posturing and outbreaks of ill-will, and a host of minor confrontations, the Truce held until the signing of the Anglo-Irish Treaty on 6 December. Most army and police detachments were withdrawn by the end of January 1922, their barracks grudgingly handed over to local I.R.A. units. Captain Pinkey and his two platoons were gone from Castletownroche in mid-December; the Macroom Auxiliaries left a month later. A few regiments remained along with the 6th Division headquarters, concentrated in Victoria and Ballincollig barracks to maintain a British presence while the Free State was established. These were finally abandoned in May. The garrison left Cork city with a mixture of relief and resentment: rather than simply take the Union Jack down, they cut down the flagstaff.[18] After this, only the naval bases at Bere and Spike Islands were left, irrelevant to the coming civil war.

The Treaty ended the jockeying for position and left the I.R.A. in sole possession of the field. It was not the victory most members had anticipated, however. Popular acclaim during the Truce, the losses and sacrifices of the year before, the sense of momentum within the movement, had made any compromise with the republican ideal unacceptable to the majority of fighting men throughout the county. The staffs of the 1st Southern Division and all five Cork brigades unanimously declared their rejection of the deal, urged or ordered local TDs to vote against it, and attempted to silence their opponents.[19] Sean O'Hegarty and Cork

[14] Rioter quoted in Report of Superintendent, Internment Camps and Prisons, 29 Oct. 1921. See also Report of Michael Staines, Chief Liaison Officer to Bere and Spike Islands, 25 Oct. 1921 (Mulcahy Papers, P7/A/26); *The Times*, 19, 20, 26 Oct. 1921. For events at Cork gaol, see *The Times*, 18, 22 Oct. 1921.

[15] P. J. O'Neill [of the 1st Kerry Bde.] to Tadg Brosnan, n.d.: O'Neill accused 'the Cork crowd' of manipulating events 'by underhand means' (Mulcahy Papers, P7/A/30).

[16] Intercepted telegrams, 18 Oct. 1921 (O'Donoghue Papers, MS 31, 230 (1)). For similar riots in Galway, see Duff, *Sword for Hire*, 86–7; *The Times*, 24, 28 Nov. 1921.

[17] Florence O'Donoghue, 'Second Escape from Spike Island', in *Sworn to be Free*, 179–83.

[18] *Examiner*, 19, 20 May 1922.

[19] 1st South. Div. resolution, 10 Dec. 1921; O/C Cork 1 to all TDs in Cork 1 Area, n.d. (Mulcahy Papers, P7/A/32).

1 adopted the most belligerent course of action, breaking up public meetings, harassing local newspapers, and suppressing pro-Treaty publications. When a *Times* correspondent in southern Ireland reported that many members of the Cork city I.R.A. actually supported the Treaty, in line with public opinion, O'Hegarty sent his gunmen to Dublin to kidnap him and force him to write a retraction.[20] In all this, he was backed up by his nominal superior, Liam Lynch, who told the irate (pro-Treaty) chief of staff, Richard Mulcahy: 'I cannot carry out any order against I.R.A. principles.'[21]

This declaration of independence, echoed across Munster, was formalized by an illegal Army Convention held in March, which elected an executive to rival the rump Free State GHQ run by Mulcahy and Michael Collins. Corkmen were well to the fore in this new body, numbering six among sixteen. Lynch became the chief of staff of the whole anti-Treaty I.R.A. Liam Deasy, the former head of the West Cork Brigade, replaced him as O/C of the 1st Southern Division. Most of the rebels were committed to army unity and worked hard to avoid outright confrontation—Tom Barry being an outspoken exception in this regard.[22] In February he led sixty of his men to Limerick to help seize the city for the anti-Treaty side. When the plan miscarried, and the matter was settled by negotiation, getting them out again proved difficult: 'We had an awful job with Barry . . . Eventually they marched off singing and carrying their guns. We had to try and impress on Barry that there would be fighting at some time.'[23] To slake his disappointment, he later urged both a unilateral attack on the British army and the forcible prevention of the June general election.

Although most Cork guerrillas opposed the settlement they were its immediate beneficiaries. For the first seven months of 1922 they constituted the sole real authority in the county and were, by default, the effective rulers of what came to be known (half-jokingly) as the 'Cork republic'. This simulacrum of statehood possessed a police force, tax collectors, censors, and even postage stamps but commanded little loyalty and less legitimacy.[24]

Whatever their claims of statehood, the republicans had become just one party among many, and not a very successful one at that. Cork's 'high political spirit', largely suppressed by the enforced unities of war and revolution, was revived by the Treaty debate and the June general election. Bands, tar barrels, and faction fights returned to the welcoming streets of Cork. The guerrillas

---

[20] Court of Inquiry on A. B. Kay, 5 Jan. 1922; O/C Cork 1 to O/C 1st South. Div., 6 Jan. 1922 (Mulcahy Papers P7/A/32); F. W. Memory, *'Memory's': Being the Adventures of a Newspaperman* (London, 1932), 112–19; *The Times*, 28 Dec. 1921, 6, 7 Jan. 1922.

[21] O/C 1st South. Div. to C/S, 6 Jan. 1922 (Mulcahy Papers P7/A/32).

[22] O'Donoghue, *No Other Law*, 208–46. For an authoritative account of Ireland as a whole, see Michael Hopkinson, *Green against Green: A History of the Irish Civil War* (Dublin, 1988), 34–76.

[23] Oscar Traynor, anti-Treaty O/C of the Dublin Bde., quoted in Hopkinson, *Green against Green*, 65.

[24] The republican propagandists included Daniel Corkery, Sean O'Faolain, Frank O'Connor, and Erskine Childers: see O'Connor, *An Only Child*, 211–14; Sean Hendrick (O'Malley Papers P17b/111).

tampered extensively with the vote but, like guns and sticks, the attempted theft of seats was a traditional part of a game which had many expert players. Outside the county, die-hard republicanism may have seemed to speak with a 'Cork accent' but, in the city and in West Cork, the mantle of William O' passed to Mick Collins—whose electoral coat-tails, it turned out, were almost as long. The Labour Party reaped the rewards of a decade of unionization, while an antagonistic Farmers' Party fought to defend their own wartime gains. Anti-Treaty candidates only did well in Mid- and North Cork, and now it was Mary MacSwiney's turn to be hanged in song 'from a sour apple tree'.[25]

For many guerrillas, of course, the republic had nothing to do with politics. Having power meant one thing: settling old scores and ridding the country of their enemies. And, in the sudden absence of government or armed opposition, a profusion of grievances and feuds sprang back to life. Once again, anonymous shootings, disappearances, and nocturnal raids became commonplace.

The dominant theme of the violence, as in 1921, was revenge. Eight serving or discharged policemen were shot, most in their own homes. Many others were threatened, boycotted, and attacked, and forced to join the growing number of refugees in Britain. In one case in Macroom, two constables against whom a year-old grudge was held were kidnapped and flogged with strands of wire until near death.[26] Similar attacks were carried out all over Ireland in the early months of 1922. In March, for example, two invalided R.I.C. veterans in Galway were killed and another wounded.[27] On 6 April, six were shot in one day in Clare and Kerry.[28] For these men, as for the guerrillas, the revolution was far from over. The long arm of the Cork city I.R.A. even extended to London and New York—as it had done previously against its enemies in Lisburn and Dublin—where gunmen were sent to hunt down escaped informers.[29] One, Patrick 'Cruxy' Connors, was found and shot in Manhattan in April.[30]

In much the same spirit, partisans of the republic resumed their war on the British army. Soldiers were shot in Ballincollig, Carrigtwohill, Castletownbere, Bantry, and the city. Others were beaten up, and more kidnapped. Intelligence officers, still plying their dangerous trade—although the government denied it—were especial targets. One, Lt. Genochio, was shot in February 'attempting to escape' from his captors at the city asylum.[31] When three others were abducted in Macroom in April, a long list of accusations were ready at hand to justify

---

[25] Peter Golden, *Impressions of Ireland* (New York, 1923), 17—and for the new political connotations of the 'Cork accent', p. 31. For election results, *Examiner*, 7–26 June 1922.

[26] *Examiner*, 11 Feb. 1922; Bandon Liaison Office Report, 10 Feb. 1922 (MA, LE/4/7A); intercepted British army telegram, 17 Feb. 1922 (O'Donoghue Papers, MS 31, 230 (6)).

[27] *Irish Times*, 17 Mar. 1922; Duff, *Sword for Hire*, 90.

[28] *Irish Times*, 7 Apr. 1922.

[29] See Mick Murphy, Con Neenan (O'Malley Papers, P17b/112), Pa Murray (P17b/88, 89).

[30] *New York Times*, 14, 15, 17 Apr. 1922.

[31] *Examiner*, 19 Feb. 1922; Cork Liaison Office Report, 15 Feb. 1922 (MA, LE/4/7A).

their deaths. They were killed and their bodies hidden. Their driver was also shot to keep the secret from the ensuing manhunt.[32]

Ex-servicemen encountered the same hostility. One case among many was that of ex-Sergeant Denis Joseph Roche, who returned to Conna to live with his boycotted father in March 1922:

We had just retired to bed, when the front door was battered in and a band of disguised ruffians rushed in and shouted for the 'dog that did England's dirty work'. My father was right behind me and interfered, only to be struck with a rifle and pushed into the parlour. I was surrounded, pushed half naked into the street and put up against the wall with four or five rifles up to my head. Others of the party proceeded upstairs and I next saw them hand bundles of clothing to each other. Then the leader asked me to hand over my revolver as I would need it no more after that night. One fellow said 'We will shoot him here' . . . I was now put on my knees to be shot and was saying my prayers when one suggested that it was too near the priest's house to fire the shots . . .

When I got back, my father was trying to extinguish the fire which they had lit upstairs. All the windows, five in number, the front door and panels were smashed in. I . . . hid next day and slept in various places till I managed to get some clothes. I left the place then and never returned till the death of my poor father who never recovered from his experiences on that night.[33]

In Cork city organized groups of ex-soldiers and the I.R.A. clashed repeatedly, just as they had before the Truce. Two Volunteers and three veterans were shot in brawls between December and March. The Protestant community also came under renewed attack. If anything, sectarian violence worsened after the British left Cork. The worst wave of killings came in April in West Cork after the death of an I.R.A. officer near Bandon. Fourteen Protestant men were shot in revenge and dozens of others were threatened, sparking a mass exodus. In this massacre, as in other incidents, the gunmen were probably acting on their own just as they had done in the Tan War.[34] Most of these killings were disavowed and condemned by their superiors—just as police reprisals had been.[35] And, just as under the previous regime, such condemnations were futile where control could not be exercised.

Very little of this violence was directed at rival I.R.A. factions or other supporters of the Treaty (soon labelled 'Free Staters'). Some pro-Treaty candidates and election agents were attacked and imprisoned but even during the June general election there was far less trouble than Cork had been accustomed to

---

[32] Interview with BG, 19 Apr. 1993; Florence O'Donoghue, Charlie Browne (O'Malley Papers, P17b/96, 112); Col. C. N. French to Macready, 6, 7 July 1922, and related documents (WO 35/180C). See also Twohig, *Green Tears* (rev. edn.), 337–43; O'Callaghan, *Execution*, 189–92; Nigel Hamilton, *Monty: The Making of a General 1887–1942* (London, 1981), 153–4; Eoin Neeson, *The Civil War 1922–23* (Swords, 1989), 101–2.

[33] Denis Joseph Roche statement (CO 762/192).

[34] See Ch. 12 for a full reconstruction of this massacre.

[35] When investigating the killing of three officers in Macroom in April 1922, British authorities were told by the 1st Cork Brigade headquarters that 'it was done by some of the I.R.A. at Macroom who had temporarily seceded from control'. Hamilton, *Monty*, 154.

TABLE 13. Victims of the revolution in Cork, 11 July 1921–1 July 1922

R.I.C.		Army		I.R.A.		Civilians				Total	
						By I.R.A.		Unknown			
K	W	K	W	K	W	K	W	K	W	K	W
1	3	6	3	3	4	21	8	3	7	34	25

Note: K = killed; W = wounded.

before the Great War. Where pro-Treaty Volunteers could muster enough strength and animus—in Skibbereen and Midleton—there were some brief but harmless skirmishes. One man was shot in Mallow on his way to join the new National Army. Apart from these incidents, the guerrillas in Cork remained preoccupied with old enemies. None of the casualties listed in Table 13 occurred in combat.

The outbreak of fighting in Dublin on 28 June found the anti-Treaty I.R.A. far better equipped and financed than a year before. The Bandon Battalion, which had 29 rifles in June 1920, had 55 rifles and a Lewis gun in September 1922.[36] The Ballyvourney Battalion had more than doubled their stock of rifles, from 40 to 100.[37] Continued smuggling and arms raiding accounted for this new armoury, which included a number of the picturesque but overrated Thompson guns. It was paid for, in part, by a series of lucrative bank robberies. The most brilliant operational coup of the period was pulled off for free in April, when Cork 1 captured the British arms ship the *Upnor* on the high seas after it had left the Haulbowline dockyards. This elaborate enterprise, involving scores of men and lorries, netted some 400 rifles, 700 revolvers, 30 machine guns, and 25,000 rounds of ammunition.[38] The Royal Navy did win the next round, however, when it intercepted the *Seattle Spirit*, a US ship carrying forty barrels of 'stuff' to Cork city.[39]

Most veteran guerrillas were still committed to the cause. Of those that refused to fight, many—including Sean O'Hegarty—remained neutral rather than go Free State.[40] The result was that the army of the republic actually had more guns than men willing to use them, and a shortage of foes willing to fight within the county itself. The war did not come to Cork, so Corkmen went to find the fighting.[41] In this, they had curiously bad luck. Sean Moylan took a force of

[36] Inspector of Org. to O/C Org. 1st South. Div., 7 Sept. 1922 (MA, A/0991/2); O/C 1st South. Div. Report, 5 Sept. 1922 (MA, IRA/2).
[37] Pat O'Sullivan (O'Malley Papers, P17b/111).
[38] *Examiner*, 5, 6 Apr. 1922; Dan Donovan, Tom Crofts (O'Malley Papers, P17b/95, 108).
[39] O/C 1st South. Div. to Div. I/O, 4 June 1922 (O'Donoghue Papers, MS 31, 253).
[40] For a detailed examination of the choices made by guerrillas in 1922, see Ch. 11.
[41] See Liam Deasy, *Brother against Brother* (Cork, 1982), 48–75; O'Donoghue, *No Other Law*, 255–69; Hopkinson, *Green against Green*, 142–55.

several hundred men by train to Wexford. Finding nothing to do, and little welcome, they soon returned. Another band of Cork fighters later went to Waterford city to help with its defence and they too, feeling overmatched and unappreciated, departed without firing a shot.

The largest contingent, including men from all parts of the county, helped lay siege once again to the Free State garrison in Limerick. This round also ended in a truce negotiated by Liam Lynch, over the table-pounding objections of most of the other Cork commanders. 'I appealed to Lynch and said we'll get the piss kicked out of us,' recalled Dan 'Sandow' Donovan of the city I.R.A., and he was right.[42] Limerick proved to be a decisive defeat for republican forces, as the delay allowed the National Army command to reinforce their troops and dislodge the rebels with ease. The Irregulars (as their opponents now referred to the dissident Volunteers) retreated into the countryside, their will to fight ebbing away. 'Men who had good jobs in Fords of Cork had thrown up their jobs to come to Limerick to fight, and of course they were disgusted.'[43] As for Donovan, 'Deasy wanted me to go to Mitchelstown, but I just went to bed and slept for twenty four hours.'

The Cork columns finally found a semblance of battle along the receding front lines in Limerick and Tipperary. Firefights were frequent and promiscuous. 'We ran out of ammo', Donovan complained: 'five thousand .303 a day and I couldn't stop men firing.'[44] These July skirmishes cost three Corkmen—and more from other counties—their lives, but these were light casualties even compared to the ambushes of a year before. Exhaustion and declining morale played a part: 'fellows were asleep leaning up against ditches tired after their withdrawal from Limerick.'[45] So did the mutual reluctance to shoot one another. Sean Hendrick and his comrades were ordered to 'Fire in the air boys! Don't kill your own.'[46] The often farcical tone of the Munster no man's land was frequently mentioned by observers (especially if they were English), and by some participants, including Frank O'Connor, a courier for Liam Deasy:

At Charleville I checked with the local commandant. He was still in bed but he assured me that there wasn't an enemy soldier within miles. What he failed to remember was that it was a Sunday, and on Sunday the whole Irish race is unanimously moved to go to Mass, so that at that very moment our whole nine-mile front, pickets, machine-gun posts, fortresses and all, had simply melted away, and there wasn't as much as a fallen tree between me and the enemy. In itself that mightn't have been too bad because it might also be assumed that there wouldn't be any enemy pickets either; but a considerable number of the enemy facing us were from the neighbourhood of Charleville, and after his longing for Mass, an Irishman's strongest characteristic is his longing for home and Mother, and anyone who knew his Ireland would have guessed that on that fine summer

[42] Dan Donovan (O'Malley Papers, P17b/95).
[43] Jamie Minihan (O'Malley Papers, P17b/112).
[44] Dan Donovan (O'Malley Papers, P17b/95).
[45] Mick Leahy (O'Malley Papers, P17b/108).
[46] Sean Hendrick (O'Malley Papers, P17b/111).

morning our whole front was being pierced in a dozen places by nostalgic enemy soldiers, alone or in force, all pining to embrace their mothers and find out if the cow had calved.[47]

As civil war approached, the Cork I.R.A. assumed the role of an occupying army, following closely in their predecessors' footsteps. The Black and Tans had impressed Cork people as 'black-berried bullies [in] loud lorries racing along country roads' who 'commandeered without payment food and drink'.[48] The I.R.A. were condemned in nearly identical terms in the summer of 1922. 'The most striking and ridiculous aspect of their movements . . . was the way in which squads of the fellows went tearing from one point to another without absolutely any discipline'; 'During the occupation of the town every available motor vehicle was seized . . . while large quantities of foodstuffs were commandeered.'[49]

In August, Charleville suffered exactly the same treatment at the hands of the Irregulars as had Mallow, Fermoy, and many other towns from vengeful Englishmen the year before:

On Thursday night week [11 August] some Irregulars returned to the town in motors and after partaking of liquor in a local public house, proceeded to complete the work of destruction in the Commercial Club and Courthouse.

About 11.30 pm the townspeople were terrified by the firing of rifle shots through the streets, which increased as time wore on. Knocks were heard at the doors of houses, and several parties called out by name. Some of the local young men who were sought by the Irregulars escaped by the rear of their houses and sought refuge in the fields for the night. The Irregulars getting no reply to their repeated demands for admission, then fired into the houses.[50]

Once again fearful townspeople and farmers were sleeping in the fields at night or going on the run.

The Cork republic crumbled on contact as Free State forces advanced. As the columns along the northern border fell back on their home county, National Army troops landed unopposed in the south-east, at Passage West on 9 August. Then, 'it was all panic'.[51] A thin I.R.A. firing line was assembled to block their route into the city. The two forces met in the suburban hills around Rochestown and Douglas, and some sharp fighting ensued. Both sides appear to have shot prisoners in the heat of battle, making it a bloodier affair than it might have been.[52] The rebels managed to capture quite a number of unwary soldiers but they were outnumbered, outgunned, and exhausted. Olga Pyne Clarke watched

[47]   O'Connor, *An Only Child*, 217–18. See also Deasy, *Brother against Brother*, 70–1.
[48]   Crowley, *In West Cork Long Ago*, 24; Barry, *Guerilla Days*, 37.
[49]   *Freeman's Journal*, 1, 21 Aug. 1922. See also *Irish Independent*, 12 Aug. 1922.
[50]   *Freeman's Journal*, 21 Aug. 1922.
[51]   Jamie Minihan (O'Malley Papers, P17b/111).
[52]   Emmet Dalton to Michael Collins, 12 Aug. 1922; 'Liam' [Tobin?] to Collins, 10 Aug. 1922 (Mulcahy Papers, P7/B/20); Dalton to Min. of Defence, 11 Aug. 1922 (Mulcahy Papers, P7/A/50); Olga Pyne Clarke, *She Came of Decent People* (London, 1985), 57.

as they went into battle ('ragged, dispirited . . . but really tough and brave in their own way') and later, as they began their long retreat:

They were very tired, marching raggedly, no military precision about them. They probably had not been properly fed and had slept rough. Their trench coats were dirty and muddy, their faces hollow-eyed had a starved savage look in them . . . At six pm they came from all directions . . . they were a rabble and they knew it.[53]

The victors entered the city on 11 August, on the heels of the fleeing guerrillas. Other National Army units had landed in Union Hall, near Skibbereen, and in Youghal and were simultaneously advancing against token opposition. ' "We got there without firing a shot" is the remark that one hears every day now with mechanical monotony along all the Cork fronts,' reported the *Freeman's Journal* on 21 August. The only gesture of resistance in most cases was sabotage. As the I.R.A. retreated they left behind dozens of burned buildings, blown railway lines, and wrecked bridges. Within two weeks of the landings almost all of the county's towns had been occupied and the Cork republic had shrunk to a few mountainy redoubts in Duhallow, along the Kerry border.

The war was not over, however. The Free State commander reported on 22 August that 'The Irregulars in Cork and Kerry are still more or less intact. Our forces have captured towns, but they have not captured Irregulars and arms on anything like a large scale.'[54] This point was driven home the same day by the ambush and death of Michael Collins in West Cork. A hard core of Tan War veterans remained, tired and demoralized but still committed to their revolution. They simply returned to their cellars, barns, and safe houses and to their old routine of roadside ambushes, drive-by shootings, nocturnal raids, and sabotage. The first sneak attacks on Free State troops began within a week of the city's capture.

From the outset the Civil War followed a different trajectory. The fact that the revived columns were less numerous but far better armed had little influence on tactics or the number of casualties. Apart from a few frontal assaults, such as on Bantry on 30 August or Ballymakeera on 4 December, the rebels tended to be more cautious than in the last war. There were no do-or-die ambushes as at Kilmichael. Ambushing parties kept a safe distance; there were fewer firefights and more sniping attacks. The I.R.A. also relied much more heavily on mines (as they had done in the last months of the Tan War), the least risky form of operation. As a result (and as Table 14 reveals), attacks were more frequent, but less effective, in 1922 than in 1920–1.

As the number and intensity of attacks declined so did violence as a whole. Unlike the earlier conflict there was no massive turn to terrorism and 'soft' targets. Far fewer civilians were killed (15 per cent of I.R.A. victims in 1922–3 were civilians as opposed to 24 per cent in 1920–1) and a considerably higher

[53] Ibid., *She Came of Decent People*, 55.
[54] Quoted in Hopkinson, *Green against Green*, 164–5.

TABLE 14. I.R.A. combat performance in Cork, 1922–1923

	Number of successful attacks	National Army casualties per attack
1922		
July–Sept.	37	2.5
Oct.–Dec.	29	2.3
1923		
Jan.–Mar.	13	1.5
Apr.–June	2	1.5

TABLE 15. Percentage of casualties due to combat in Cork, 1922–1923

	I.R.A. victims		National Army victims		All victims
	National Army	All	I.R.A.	All	
1922					
July–Sept.	94	81	72	72	68
Oct.–Dec.	94	79	44	29	53
1923					
Jan.–Mar.	72	60	11	11	38
Apr.–June	75	50	71	56	44

proportion of casualties came in combat. As Table 15 shows, in the most intense period of the war, from August to December, nearly 95 per cent of National Army casualties derived from armed engagements. Over the whole of the Civil War, only 9 per cent of Free State casualties (as opposed to 40 per cent of Crown force losses in the Tan War), and 20 per cent of all I.R.A. shootings (that is, including civilians), occurred other than in combat. Despite many opportunities to do so, the I.R.A. in Cork rarely attacked off-duty or unarmed soldiers.

The National Army's record was altogether less gentlemanly than the I.R.A.'s, but more so than their British predecessors'. Fifty-two per cent of I.R.A. casualties were due to combat in the Civil War, compared to 43 per cent in the Tan War. While British forces shot 116 civilians in 1920–1, the National Army shot only 10. Thus, 25 per cent of British victims and 45 per cent of National Army victims came in combat.

Table 15 does show a relative increase in non-combat shootings by both sides after October 1922, and particularly in 1923, but this must be understood in the context of the swift overall decline in violence. Whereas National Army casualties fell from 204 in 1922 to 33 in 1923, civilian casualties inflicted by the I.R.A. only fell from 23 to 11. Similarly, I.R.A. losses in 1923 were less than half the number incurred in 1922. The shift to non-combat shootings was due more to the collapse of the republican military campaign than to any turn

TABLE 16. Victims of the revolution in Cork, 1922–1923

British Army		National Army		I.R.A.		Civilians						Total	
						By I.R.A.		By National Army		Unknown			
K	W	K	W	K	W	K	W	K	W	K	W	K	W
1	10	70	175	51	45	21	11	7	3	30	51	180	295

Notes: K = killed; W = wounded. This table does not include the Cork I.R.A. men killed or wounded outside the county.

towards terrorism. In other words, the dynamics of violence in Cork had been reversed. Rather than exploding, as in 1920, the revolution was imploding.

Another way to look at the changing character of violence and I.R.A. performance is by comparing the numbers of killed with the numbers wounded. In 1920–1, 51 per cent of all casualties, and 42 per cent of those in the Crown forces, were fatal. In 1922–3 the numbers fell to 37 per cent and 28 per cent for National Army casualties. The I.R.A. also suffered proportionately far fewer deaths. In fact, the Civil War accounted for less than a quarter of all revolutionary deaths in Cork.

The key factor in this rapid de-escalation of violence was the absence of reprisals. The Civil War in Cork did not develop a revenge dynamic comparable to that of the Tan War and thus rarely descended into cycles of terror and counter-terror. Revenge killings were not unknown, but they were relatively uncommon. Even when the I.R.A. did carry out reprisals they usually targeted the remnants of their earlier black lists. These kidnappings, shootings, and burnings were less a response to the new round of violence than a stubborn clinging to old vendettas.

Nor did the National Army rely on communal punishments to deter or subdue the rebels. Ambushes were not routinely followed by reprisals—although these did sometimes occur—and civilians were not made to suffer for I.R.A. operations. Despite frequent complaints about indiscipline there was less reported official intimidation and brutality.[55] In the whole of the war the army destroyed not one house in Cork and rarely damaged private property. Only four Corkmen were executed by court martial, as compared to twelve in 1921 (although it must be noted that seventy-three other Irishmen were subject to death sentences in 1922–3).

This official restraint may be attributed to the fact that Cork natives made up the majority of the Free State forces in the county.[56] These men often served in their home districts and actively resisted any extreme measures or death squad

---

[55] For a description of one such episode, see O'Connor, *An Only Child*, 242–4.

[56] A survey of 1093 men of the Cork Command in October 1922 revealed that 55% were natives (usually serving in or near their home districts), although the proportion of officers and NCOs was lower (MA, Army Census, L/S/1).

tactics on their own turf. When these methods were used it was usually the widely hated Dublin 'Guard' and 'Squad' or other outsiders who were responsible. A key confrontation between Dubliners and locals took place in September 1922. An I.R.A. prisoner was murdered after a bloody ambush near Macroom. One of the local commanders reported that:

The shooting . . . has caused considerable contempt among the Garrison here. They have paraded before me and gave me to understand they would not go out on the hills anymore. Therefore you will want to tell these officers from Dublin that they will want to stop that kind of work or they will corrupt the Army . . . the situation here is at present very critical, I may tell you, among the men.[57]

His superior, General Emmet Dalton, then wrote to Dublin:

The shooting was the work of the Squad. Now I personally approve of the action but the men I have in my Command are of such a temperament that they can look at seven of their companions being blown to atoms by a murderous trick without feeling annoyed— but when an enemy is found with a rifle and ammunition they will mutiny if he is shot. On this account I think it would be better if you kept the 'Squad' out of my area.[58]

It is interesting to note how quickly Dalton and other Free State officers absorbed the mentality and language of their British predecessors. Where these triumphed and the 'Squad' stayed, as in Dublin and Kerry, the war was far more savage.

This restraint worked both ways. The local I.R.A. were far less willing to attack not just fellow Irishmen but people from their own neighbourhoods. A strong strain of sectarian violence persisted but the pervasive ethnic friction which so exacerbated the war against the British was largely absent from the Civil War.

This time around it was the I.R.A. who set out to punish the general population for turning against them. According to Paddy O'Brien, O/C of the 4th Cork Brigade, 'in the Civil War we were in the same position that the Brits had been in the first period. They fought the people and then we fought the people.'[59] Their main target was the railway system, its personnel, rolling stock, tracks, stations, and telegraph lines.[60] These attacks began in mid-August 1922 and worked immediately to bring most rail traffic to a halt, a situation that continued well into the new year. By September only a few branch lines of the Cork and Muskerry and Great Southwestern railways were still in operation. Twelve hundred men were out of work in Cork alone.[61] A partial tally of I.R.A. sabotage

    [57] O/C No. 2 Column, Southern Area, Macroom Report, 18 Sept. 1922 (Mulcahy Papers, P7/B/82).
    [58] Dalton to C-in-C, 19 Sept. 1922 (Mulcahy Papers, P7/B/82).
    [59] Paddy O'Brien (O'Malley Papers, P17b/124).
    [60] Most of this sabotage does not show up in the figures in Table 17.
    [61] Report on Cork City and County Railway Situation on the 11th September 1922; C-in-C to Emmet Dalton, 20 Sept. 1922 (Mulcahy Papers, P7/B/66). For a fascinating memoir of the period, see Dr George Hadden, 'The War on the Railways in Wexford 1922–23', *Journal of the Irish Railway Record Society* (Autumn 1953), 117–49.

TABLE 17. Attacks on property and communications in Cork, 1922–1923

Buildings destroyed		Bridges destroyed	Raids on mails
By I.R.A.	Unknown		
81	4	99	111

is given in Table 17. Armed robberies of businesses, which had apparently decreased somewhat between the wars (thirty-one in 1921–2, although this drop may be attributable to poor reporting), shot up again after guerrilla war was renewed, rising to 141 in the Civil War.

In late 1922 the guerrillas began an unprecedented campaign against grocery and bread vans. At least forty-three were held up and burned between December and April 1923. The aim of this policy is unclear but may have been summed up by one reported remark by a Volunteer that 'they were going to starve the country and not fight the Free State troops again'.[62]

I.R.A. operations reports from the winter of 1922–3 reveal the outcome of this attitude: week after week of minor vandalism and nuisance attacks. In a three-week period in December, for example, the Mallow Battalion was active on 11 out of 21 days. On one occasion a bridge was wrecked, on another a mine was laid which never went off. On the other ten days National Army posts and patrols were sniped at, with no result.[63] The weekly reports for the same unit from February to the end of April show the battalion settling into a regular routine. Every week the road from Mallow to Dromahane was blocked, cleared, and blocked again. Every week the telephone and telegraph wires going west were cut, repaired, and cut again. Every week one or two enemy posts were fired at with no perceptible results.[64]

The same minimalist pattern was adopted throughout the county. From the formerly vigorous Bandon Battalion comes this weekly report of 13 January 1923:

Saturday night: Upton railway station burned including signal cabin goods store etc. No rails were removed owing to men not being able to get the necessary tools. Gaggin railway station burned, including goods stores, signal cabin, etc. Telephone wires and two poles cut. No rails were removed as tools for same could not be got.

Sunday night: Sherlock, Solicitor, Bandon, kidnapped and his house burned by men from E. Company.[65]

Serious violence was now confined to weekends and to non-military targets: two railway stations and a lawyer.

---

[62] Cork Command Intelligence Report, 28 Dec. 1922 (MA, CW/OPS/14/F).
[63] Mallow Bn. Summary of Operations, 29 Dec. 1922 (CAI, Siobhan Lankford Papers, U169).
[64] Mallow Bn. Weekly Summaries of Ops. (Lankford Papers).
[65] MA, A/1164.

Free State success had nothing to do with tactical innovation. In fact, the National Army adopted British methods wholesale—minus reprisals—so that military operations were a familiar mix of sweeps, patrols, raids, and counter-ambushes. They even seem to have followed the same learning curve, particularly in the matter of replacing lorries with foot patrols. 'At the end the Free State would move around on foot chiefly. They'd start out late at night guided by the local fellows in the army who would know the district inside out.'[66]

Still, the Irish soldiers did have enormous advantages over their British counterparts. Their commanders had clear goals, unity of command, and little political interference or indecision to deal with. If anything, senior officers and government ministers took a more extreme view of the conflict than the front-line soldiers. The army also had the absolute authority of martial law from the beginning and never had to worry about evidence, juries, magistrates, or amnesties. Hunger strikers could be safely ignored, as 435 prisoners who tried it in Cork gaol found out in September 1922.[67] Nor did they have to engage in crowd control: not one anti-Free State riot took place, a telling statistic for 'rebel' Cork.

The Free State's most important military asset, however, was superb intelligence. The former Volunteers and other locals who joined the National Army all over Cork knew exactly who their opponents were and, often, where they could be found. 'Informers' were easy to find. As soon as the I.R.A. left the city, according to Peter Golden, 'They spread all over town acting as spotters. Suspicious houses are pointed out and suspicious people. The former will be raided soon. The latter subjected to a strict surveillance.'[68] A few weeks later, once the Free State military regime was established, surveillance seemed as omnipresent as it had to English officers and journalists a year before:

Perhaps the most reprehensible thing one meets with here is what is known as 'Intelligence'. One never knows to whom he is speaking. One never knows who is or who is not an 'Intelligence Officer' . . . all eyes seem to gaze and all tongues to whisper in suspicion and doubt wherever one happens to go.[69]

I.R.A. ranks, already diminished because of the Treaty split, were gutted by arrests in the first months of the war. After three weeks of Free State occupation the city battalions had been driven deep underground: 'unless a man asks for immediate arrest he dare not go out on the streets.'[70] Practically every active member of the 2nd (south side) Battalion had been captured—including nearly all the officers—along with many key people from the 1st Battalion. The brigade O/C was, perhaps wisely, 'still confined to bed and will be unable to

---

[66]   Jack Buttimer (O'Malley Papers, P17b/111).
[67]   *Freeman's Journal*, 27, 28 Sept. 1922.   [68]   Golden, *Impressions of Ireland*, 46.
[69]   Ibid. 82.
[70]   O/C City to Adj., 1st South. Div., 6 Sept. 1922 (O'Malley Papers, P17a/97).

resume for some time yet'.[71] Organizers sent out to investigate the state of the movement found the same story in every brigade.

By the end of February the Cork guerrillas knew they had lost. At a divisional conference held on 26 February the brigade commanders were unanimous: 'We are absolutely on the rocks.' The O/C of the 1st Cork Brigade reported that 'active men were very few also the people were very hostile. The only work his brigade could do was very small jobs.' The O/C of the 3rd Brigade said he would soon have no men left. 'It was only a matter of time as to how long we are going to last.' Tom Crofts, the new commander of the 1st Southern Division, concluded that 'We are flattened out . . . if five men were arrested in each area, we are finished. The men are suffering great privations and their morale is going. These men have been continually going for years back.'[72]

Most of those guerrillas still at large turned into survivalists, living literally underground in dugouts or in remote mountain hideouts. According to George Power of Fermoy, 'it was a question of evading arrest and keeping the organization going . . . We could only carry out annoyances, which were very minor.'[73] Another veteran recalled that 'we lived almost back with the foxes in the end and you got as wise as foxes too'. Another: 'We were just like crows going through the country.'[74]

Sean Moylan was sent on a mission abroad in December. Liam Deasy was captured in January and agreed to issue an appeal to his former comrades to surrender. Liam Lynch, intransigent to the last, was shot while running from a Free State patrol, and died on 10 April. His death set the stage for the I.R.A.'s unilateral nationwide ceasefire of 30 April.

The end of the Civil War in Cork itself was symbolized by the 'fall' of the last I.R.A. strongholds in the west around Ballymakeera and Ballyvourney. Since August 1922 these districts had been 'like a border line of an independent state with our [National Army] troops sallying occasionally into the enemy area but never able to reach the most important centres'.[75] The Free State finally came to stay in a week-long operation in the first week in May.

By this time, the vast majority of the Cork I.R.A. was in prison. Violence slowly petered out but never quite ended. The Free State forces continued to hunt down fugitives and shot several in the process. A few stubborn groups of rebels remained at large and active, shooting suspected informers and British soldiers, holding up mailmen, robbing post offices, and harassing Protestant farmers. For those in camps and gaols, the struggle ended with a mass hunger strike in October and November 1923. The last to give up were the Corkmen,

[71] Adj., Cork 1 to Adj., 1st South. Div., 5 Sept. 1922 (O'Malley Papers, P17a/88).

[72] O/C 1st South. Div. to Deputy C/S, 2 Mar. 1923 (O'Malley Papers, P17a/90).

[73] George Power (O'Malley Papers, P17b/100).

[74] Paddy Donagh Owen O'Sullivan; Jamie Minihan (O'Malley Papers, P17b/57, 111).

[75] C/S General Situation Report, 26 Sept. 1923 (MA, A/0875).

heirs to Terry MacSwiney and Mick Fitzgerald. The sister of one, Maud O'Neill of Kilbrittain, wrote: 'Nobody can doubt now the sincerity of the men or the cause of the Republic though what we will do with a Republic when all our lads are dead is doubtful.'[76] Two died, Denis Barry of the city and Andy Sullivan of Mallow, but the government made no concessions.[77] The strike ended. The revolution was over.

[76] Maud O'Neill to Dorothy Price, n.d. (Price Papers, MS 15, 341 (2)).
[77] O'Connor, *An Only Child*, 258–71; Hopkinson, *Green against Green*, 268–71.

PART II

Rebels

6

The Boys of Kilmichael

Forget not the boys of Kilmichael,
Those gallant lads stalwart and true,
Who fought 'neath the green flag of Erin
And who conquered the Red, White and Blue.
                        ('The Boys of Kilmichael')

Kilmichael immediately became a symbol of rebellion and transformed the victors into heroes. The song 'The Boys of Kilmichael' was already a popular favourite by the time of the Truce. That summer the ambush site was visited by crowds of admiring visitors from all over the county.[1] Sporting events were held there in hopes of attracting a larger audience.[2] Tom Barry, now 'well known throughout West Cork', was fêted wherever he went, and his marriage to Leslie Price in August was the social event of a season marked by republican festivities.[3] In Dunmanway, the new year was ushered in by 'a torchlight procession of juveniles, who sang lustily of Kilmichael'.[4] For the people of West Cork, 'our own boys, our neighbours' sons and grandsons' had become 'names to conjure with'.[5] Who were the boys of Kilmichael? What kind of men were they? What sort of Ireland did they represent?

Their opponents, the Auxiliaries, were eager to identify the guerrillas but, as for what sort of men they were, they had little doubt. When 'K' Company moved from Cork city to the Dunmanway workhouse in December, they were quickly able to get names and descriptions of many of the ambushers—some in extraordinary detail. Paddy O'Brien of Girlough 'has sometimes slept at his home. Height 5'-6", inclined to be stout, short, square, not bad-looking. Very thick dark hair, round face, long lines around eyes, blue eyes, wears a cap, twice in raids, his house said to be burned by "unknown men" 6/2/1921.'[6] Known men became wanted men, marked down by the 'K' Company intelligence officer as

---

[1]   *Star*, 27 Aug. 1921.
[2]   'Don't miss the sports at famous Kilmichael!': ibid. 8 Oct. 1921.
[3]   See ibid. 16, 23 July, 27 Aug., 3 Sept. 1921.   [4] Ibid. 7 Jan. 1922.
[5]   The former quotation is from Crowley, *In West Cork Long Ago*, 19, the latter from Dorothy Price, 'Kilbrittain' (NLI, Price Papers, MS 15, 343[2]).
[6]   'Raymond' [Flor Crowley], 'Black and Tan Diary', *Southern Star*, 30 Oct. 1971. This invaluable series of articles reproduces the complete text (minus the names of informers) of the Dunmanway Auxiliary Company's Intelligence Diary from December 1920 to March 1921. It includes an accurate list of local I.R.A. men, along with the sort of descriptions quoted here. See also Gleeson, *Bloody Sunday*, 73–5 and Everett, *Bricks and Flowers*, 154.

'Kilmichael man, for immediate arrest'.[7] Their families became easy targets for the 'unknown men' who burned down O'Brien's house and attacked his father.

The English policemen considered the Kilmichael men to be 'dirty', 'brutish', and 'a thoroughly bad lot', and despised them for what they believed to have been an act of savage butchery.[8] 'The boys' were equally sure of themselves. To them it was the Auxies who were the 'terrorists', 'killers without mercy', and 'prison scum'.[9] Who they were was best represented by Michael McCarthy, one of those killed at the ambush: 'as fine a type of clean, dashing, enthusiastic young Irish man as was to be met with inside or outside the ranks of the Volunteers . . . a most exemplary citizen, a true chum, and a trusted and loyal comrade.'[10]

One Kilmichael veteran told me his comrades were 'a lot of hard men . . . a fine bunch of fellas. They wouldn't let you down.' To Tom Barry, they were 'a fine body of the best type of Volunteers'; 'a tough bunch of men, and above all, decent men'.[11] In September 1921, Gearoid O'Sullivan took public issue with the British charges: 'I say these young men were the bravest of the bravest. I say they took all the risks. They were no cowards or murderers.'[12] Others spoke of the column's 'inbred West Cork courage' and of them as 'a fine lot of good, decent Irish men' and 'West Cork men all, loyal and staunch comrades'.[13] With varying degrees of modesty, then, they accepted their local fame as 'gallant lads stalwart and true'.

The guerrillas were indeed 'West Cork men all'. Their names—five O'Donovans, five O'Sullivans, four McCarthys, as well as Crowleys, Hourihans, O'Briens, O'Driscolls, and O'Neills—echo those of generations of local ancestors and innumerable relatives and neighbours, and evoke an almost tribal identity.

The column was drawn from towns, villages, and farms throughout the West Cork Brigade area. By far the largest contingent of fighting men—half—came from the Bandon Battalion.[14] This was the heartland of rebel West Cork and of its rebellion. At the battle of Crossbarry in March 1921, nearly 60 per cent of the column were from the Bandon area.[15] The other members were scattered around

---

[7] 'Black and Tan Diary', 30 Oct. 1971.   [8] Ibid.

[9] The first two terms are from Barry, *Guerilla Days*, 41; the last is from another song of the period, 'Barry's Flying Column'.   [10] *Star*, 3 Sept. 1921.

[11] Barry, *Guerilla Days*, 38; interview with Barry broadcast on RTE Radio on the occasion of his death in 1980 (tape in the possession of Donal O'Donovan).

[12] *Star*, 1 Oct. 1921. As the numerous references to this paper demonstrate, Kilmichael—and Barry—were rarely out of the news in the second half of 1921.

[13] Interview with AA; *Star*, 16 Jan. 1971; Tim O'Donoghue, 'Destruction of Rosscarbery R.I.C. Barrack', in *Rebel Cork's Fighting Story*, 163; interview with Mr Buckley (RTE Archives, A2792).

[14] A list of the column members and where they came from can be found in the Florence O'Donoghue Papers (MS 31, 301), and in the Ballineen/Enniskeane Area Heritage Group's *The Wild Heather Glen*.

[15] The names and units of the men at Crossbarry can be found in Deasy, *Towards Ireland Free*, 351–5.

the fringes of this core. The Schull Battalion could only muster one Volunteer for the ambush and the nine men sent from the Beara Battalion arrived too late.[16] The unusually large Dunmanway contingent was due to their proximity to the ambush, as the column called on local men to act as scouts. Only 6 per cent of the men at Crossbarry came from the Dunmanway Battalion.

A third of the men at Kilmichael worked on their fathers' farms, which ranged in size from a substantial 174 acres to a comparatively meagre 19 acres (and in value from £11 to £46).[17] Most of these were the eldest sons in their families: potential inheritors. Another third practised, or were apprenticed to, trades such as coopering or harness- or bootmaking, often working for their fathers as well. There were also a number of shop assistants (who had generally grown up on family farms), a publican's son, a couple of labourers, and a scattering of other professions. One had been a policeman and another (the son of a retired policeman) had served with distinction in the Great War. Only one was self-employed. The 'boys' ranged in age from 16 to 35 years old, the average being 24. All (of those for whom the facts could be checked) were literate, unmarried, and practising Catholics. Most had lived with their families until they went on the run, to prison, and to war. They formed, in other words, a fair cross-section of West Cork society, where most men performed some sort of manual labour. As a group, though, they were more likely to have jobs, trades, and an education than was typical of their peers.[18]

Asking who and what 'the boys' were raises another question of identity. The song equates the boys of Kilmichael with 'the boys of the column', but there were ten scouts present besides the thirty-seven men in the ambush party proper. These were the local men, the 'small fry', the ones without guns whose names are rarely mentioned in the chronicles. Kilmichael was their territory—they and their neighbours would probably be blamed by the police—but it was the gunmen who were in charge. What was the column and what did it mean to belong?

In the autumn of 1920, the West Cork flying column consisted of whatever men came together to train and fight, for about a week at a time. It existed episodically, with a series of temporary headquarters and an uncertain and fluctuating membership: whoever could turn up. The same rule applied at ambushes: anyone with a gun was usually welcome. Kilmichael was a secret, and thus more

---

[16] See Liam O'Dwyer, *Beara in Irish History* (New York, 1977), 120–1. For more on the geography of columns, see Ch. 10.

[17] This description of the column at Kilmichael is based on a variety of sources (see the Appendix). Documentary traces of these men, their histories, and families can be found in newspaper and police reports, prison records, I.R.A. reports and rolls, and in the manuscript 1911 census returns in the National Archives and the land records in the Land Valuation Office. *The Wild Heather Glen* also includes a profile of every man at the ambush, with many valuable biographical details.

[18] According to the 1926 census, 54% of the occupied men of the West Riding of Cork were farmers or farmers' sons, and 18% were farm labourers.

carefully controlled, but Paddy O'Brien still seems to have brought in a few willing acquaintances as last-minute reinforcements.[19]

For most of the Kilmichael men, this was their first time 'on the column' under Barry but they were not strangers and they had a great deal in common. Most had joined the movement in 1917 (some even earlier), when many were still teenagers. Almost all were officers in their respective companies and battalions, veterans of many lesser operations. They were wanted men even before the ambush, forced out of their homes and jobs, and on the run for months or even years. A good number had arrest records and had spent time in gaol. Nine—fully one-quarter— had taken part in the great hunger strike in Wormwood Scrubs prison that spring.

Jack Hennessy became a full-time guerrilla in July 1920 after an Essex Regiment raid:

I was taken from my bed and made walk about 400 yards to the south of the town [Ballineen], passing over Ballineen Water Bridge. I was questioned . . . and a revolver muzzle forced into my mouth and the hammer clicked. I was struck on the jaw with the butt of a revolver. They then beat me with their fists and rifle butts. I was ordered to move off and I jumped over a fence as they fired shots over my head. My house was burned and I had to go 'on the run'. We got what arms we could together for our own protection and decided we would fight back against the Essex.[20]

Hennessy was one of the Auxiliaries' marked men after Kilmichael:

Late servant of Doctor Fehilly, about 27 years of age. 5' 6" strong build, full face, eyes showing a lot of white. Surly, hang-dog expression. Wears a slouch hat and leggings. Should have trace of bullet wound somewhere about his head, received at Kilmichael.[21]

These were not quite the 'new men' depicted by Tom Barry: 'mostly quite untrained but many appeared to be splendid natural fighters.'[22] They were, rather, experienced local leaders and activists—'hard men'—with years of organizing and conflict behind them, and many battles ahead of them. Two had been wounded in previous fights. Another died and seven more were interned in 1921. Five were still with the column at Crossbarry four months later.

It was Barry who was the new man, the outsider. Most of the others were already plugged into the heart of the movement they had helped found. In most cases, friends, brothers, sisters, and cousins had also joined. A good number of these relatives were also arrested in the course of the struggle and some were killed. Several emigrated after the Truce, a few went Free State; most remained true to the republican cause. Their farms, villages, and towns remained strongholds of the revolution right through the Civil War. At least one may have been involved in the massacre of Protestants in West Cork in April 1922.[23] Several

---

[19]   Liam Deasy, *Towards Ireland Free*, 169–70. Tom Barry angrily denied this in *The Reality of the Anglo-Irish War*, 14, because it suggested he was not in total control of the proceedings.

[20]   Jack Hennessy statement (Ballineen/Enniskeane Area Heritage Group).

[21]   'Black and Tan Diary', 6 Nov. 1971.   [22]   Barry, *Guerilla Days*, 38.

[23]   See Ch. 12.

were present at the fatal ambush of Michael Collins at Bealnablath in 1922.[24] Two were killed and one was wounded in the months that followed. By 1923 nearly every man present at Kilmichael had been wounded, imprisoned, or killed.

The events of 28 November may have made them heroes of songs, but it did not make them revolutionaries. Tom Barry may have made them victors and killers, but years of hardship and struggle brought them together, armed and determined. What distinguished the riflemen from the scouts at Kilmichael was not just guns and territory, but experience and a mingled sense of purpose and belonging.

What the ambush did produce was 'Barry's flying column' (also the title of a well-known song), which should not be confused with either the West Cork column in general, or the boys of Kilmichael in particular. 'Barry's column' contained only those who were loyal to him personally, who went anti-Treaty 'to a man', stuck with him afterwards (as in Limerick in 1922), and who agreed with his version of history.[25] These were Barry's men, just as other 'big fellas' in West Cork and elsewhere had their followers. Those who were not part of this group, like Paddy O'Brien, were not part of *the* column, according to Barry himself:

I have searched in vain for proof of O'Brien's presence at any fight, except Kilmichael, where any of the enemy were even hurt, but failed to find it, even though he was at some attempted fights and has surely marched more than anyone else in the whole Brigade.[26]

Thus, depending on the definition, 'the boys' assume a variety of distinct identities, built around the formal organization of companies and columns, but also around their actions, neighbourhoods, families, shared experiences, and personalities. They were not just Volunteers, but fighting men; not just warriors but exemplary citizens. Or, from the Tans' point of view, not just rebels and criminals, but degraded killers. They were identified as much by the pervasive imagery of dirt and decency as by names, ranks, and occupations.

Part I of this book examined violence primarily in terms of experiences and outcomes, as a function of death and destruction. While violence was a revolutionary force in itself and did develop its own logic, its continuities were shaped and embodied by individual and group decisions, fears, loyalties, and identities. Violence also resided in language and social relationships. How did the revolution transform some neighbours and strangers into comrades, to kill and die for, and others into enemies, to be hated and hunted? To understand how the Cork of 1913 became the Cork of 1921, and how the Volunteers of 1916 became the Irregulars of 1922, we must examine the lives of its revolutionaries. Part III of this book explores how and why men became Volunteers and guerrillas. The following chapters will examine the kind of men who joined the I.R.A., and the social structure and attitudes of the army they created.

[24]   See Meda Ryan, *The Day Michael Collins Was Shot* (Swords, 1989).
[25]   Interview with AA.
[26]   Barry, *The Reality of the Anglo-Irish War*, 14.

7

Volunteers

This was a war between the British Army and the Irish people.

(Tom Barry, *Guerilla Days in Ireland*)

Surely, what we chiefly do when we speak of the People is to make an historic reference to certain more or less defined loyalties, and to those who fought for them whether under Collins, Redmond, Davitt, O'Connell, or Wolfe Tone. It is a term, that is, which frankly excludes and frankly sets a boundary.

(Sean O'Faolain, 'The Plain People of Ireland')[1]

An enormous amount has been written about the I.R.A., and the name conjures up powerful images and symbols, but we still know very little about what sort of people joined and why. The question goes to the heart of political myths both new and old. Were the Volunteers a nation in arms or a 'murder gang' composed of thugs and corner boys?

Most official British commentators echoed the Dunmanway Auxiliaries' caustic appraisal of the I.R.A. as being 'a thoroughly bad lot' recruited from the lowest classes. Within the Royal Irish Constabulary, initial reactions to the emergent movement ranged from the inspector general's lofty declaration that the Volunteers were 'half educated shop assistants and excitable young rustics'[2] to the local sergeants' easygoing identification of them as 'insignificant' men of 'good character'.[3] A few policemen in places such as Mallow, Firmount, and Cork city were even willing to testify in court that their local Volunteers were 'respectable young men', 'well conducted boys', or 'of respectable family'.[4]

The advent of guerrilla warfare and widespread killing changed this attitude of half-amused condescension into one of bitter loathing, shared by both policemen and soldiers stationed in Cork. However, it did little to alter the basic official contempt for the revolutionaries. 'They looked rather a pallid, unwashed crowd who endeavoured to look important';'young bolshevists who had no stake in the country and who delight in seeing the "stay-at-homes" ruined'.[5] The notorious

---

[1] Sean O'Faolain, 'The Plain People of Ireland', *Bell* (Oct. 1943), 1.

[2] Monthly Report of the Inspector General, Jan. 1918 (CO 904/105).

[3] Reports on illegal drilling in Charleville, 18 Nov. 1917 and Rockchapel, 24 Nov. 1917 (CO 904/122).   [4] See *Examiner*, 26 May, 22 Nov. 1917, 14 Nov. 1918, 14 Aug. 1919.

[5] Clarke, 'The Memoirs of a Professional Soldier in Peace and War', 11 (Liddell Hart Centre); extract from a report by the Col-Comdt. of the Kerry Brigade (whose area covered part of North Cork) included in a letter from Gen. Macready to Frances Stevenson, 20 June 1921 (HLRO, Lloyd George Papers, F/36/2/19).

Major A. E. Percival, stationed in Bandon with the Essex Regiment, dismissed his local foes as: 'Farmers' sons and corner boys who had no stake in the country and preferred earning a living by plunder and murder than by doing an honest day's work . . . they nearly all had an exaggerated idea of their own importance.'[6]

Once Free State troops began to wage their own war against the Cork I.R.A. in late 1922, they began to think in remarkably similar terms. Republicans and their supporters came from the 'poorer classes' and 'backward areas', lacked education, and were little more than thieves.[7] Michael Collins himself was quoted as saying: 'These men . . . are not the men with whom I fought; they are the rebble and rough-necks from all quarters.'[8] National Army officers from outside the county who found themselves fighting in the wilder and more isolated parts of northern and western Cork were especially prone to these attitudes.

This disdainful tone was widely adopted outside the republican movement. One R.I.C. sergeant reported in 1917 that 'the well-to-do inhabitants of Charleville' considered the Volunteers to be 'an insignificant crowd who have no real stake in the country . . . a large majority of the people in Charleville treat these Sinn Feiners with contempt.'[9] The Skibbereen *Eagle* referred to participants in one Volunteer parade in 1918 as 'young rustics, bored by the vacuity of country life, and Skibbereen "sparks" wishful of a change from billiards'.[10] In Bantry the I.R.A. were referred to, rather politely, as 'young men of no means'.[11] In Youghal they were called 'the loafers of the town', in Timoleague, 'ignorant country boys', in Macroom, 'idle, no account fellows', in Castletownbere, 'raw country bogcutters', and in Lissard, 'scum, who didn't own a wheel-barrow of their own'.[12] Above all, they were typically, and endlessly, referred to as 'those corner boys'.[13] These opinions came from shopkeepers, farmers, a businessman, a newspaper editor and reporters, a poor law guardian, and a retired military officer—people with some property and authority who saw the I.R.A. as social upstarts.

[6] Percival, 'Guerrilla Warfare', part 1 (Percival Papers).

[7] General Weekly Return (Irregular), 9 June 1923 (MA, CW/OPS/14); General Report on Cork, 1 Apr. 1924 (MA, A/0825); see also Weekly [Cork] Command Situation Report, 15 Mar. 1923 (CW/OPS/13), Report on Land Seizures to Min. of Agriculture, 19 Apr. 1923 (MA, DOD A/0875), and General Situation Report to Min. of Defence, 20 Sept. 1923 (A/0875).

[8] *Plain People*, 23 Apr. 1922.

[9] Report on illegal drilling in Charleville, 18 Nov. 1917.

[10] *Eagle*, 20 July 1918.

[11] *Irish Times*, 14 Apr. 1920.

[12] Michael Gleeson statement (CO 762/26); letter from Elizabeth O'Donovan, 28 Oct. 1921 (Mulcahy Papers, P7/A/30); *Freeman's Journal*, 21 Aug. 1922; intercepted letter in O/C 1st South. Div. to O/C Cork 5, 13 Sept. 1922 (MA, A/0991/4); a neighbour's comment noted in Edith Somerville Diary, 12 May 1922 (Queen's University Special Collections, Somerville and Ross Papers).

[13] The anonymous author of 'Through an Ulsterman's Eyes: The Birth of the Irish Free State' (*Atlantic Monthly* (Oct. 1922), 545) called those he met in Cork city 'furtive corner boys'. See also 'Sassenach', *Arms and the Irishman* (London, 1932), 77.

Dirt was a constant theme of these descriptions (and of those offered by British soldiers as well). The Volunteers were 'dirty', 'ragged', and even 'verminous': 'a scrubby-looking lot of corner boys'.[14] Protestant families who had guerrillas take over their houses in 1921 and 1922 often complained of their roughness and dirtiness.[15] What did Katherine Everett remember of her encounter with an I.R.A. officer in Macroom? 'A seedy-looking young man in a stained yellow mackintosh.'[16]

We can trace the evolution of one Cork observer's attitudes towards the Volunteers in the diaries, letters, and writings of Edith Somerville, an acute but nevertheless caste-bound observer. Somerville, a lifelong resident of Castletownshend, felt herself to be a countrywoman first and foremost and regarded Irish towns with scorn. Here resided the troublemaking 'Irish intelligentsia [and] their disgusting class—the lower middle drawer!',[17] along with assorted 'counter-jumpers', 'flappers', and 'town blackguards' (a favourite phrase). Against these pernicious townspeople she set the men and women whom she thought formed the moral and social backbone of Ireland, the 'sane and solid' farmers and their wives.[18] To her, Skibbereen was the root of all political evil.

In the early years of the war, and even after the 1916 rising, Somerville saw Sinn Fein and the Irish Volunteers as being more or less a continuation of the old Home Rule agitation—the same 'town blackguards' under another name, harbouring the same fantasies about the coming Irish millennium.[19] In 1914 she gathered that Home Rule meant 'Yees will be we'es, and We'es will be Yees!' while in 1917 the republic was defined to her as 'No polis and no taxes'.[20]

At this stage she still thought of the Volunteers as part of that quaint lower-class Catholic world she imagined, whose foibles and antics she loved to catalogue. In 1918 some tolerance could still be extended (along with considerable mockery) to 'Ourselves Alone', to the 'green-capped boys and fury flappers' otherwise referred to as 'idle, contentious youths' and 'sentimentally seditious shopgirls'.[21] The local company of Volunteers were 'two dozen tom-fools' and the young republican leader she met was misled but meant well.[22] 'There is

[14]   C. H. Bretherton, describing Tom Barry and his men: 'Irish Backgrounds', *Atlantic Monthly* (Dec. 1922), 698.
[15]   The files of the Irish Grants Committee are full of such accounts, from all over the county. See, for example, the statements of Bartholemew Purdon (CO 762/106), Harry Kingston (/150), John Beamish (/177), George Daunt (/180), Samuel Jennings (/183), William Hingston (/192), Samuel Kingston (/193), and Sarah Trinder (/194).   [16]   Everett, *Bricks and Flowers*, 155.
[17]   Somerville to Ethel Smyth, 27 Oct. 1921 (Somerville and Ross Papers, Lot 878).
[18]   Edith Somerville, 'Ourselves Alone', MS article, n.d. [1918] (Somerville and Ross Papers, Lot 899).
[19]   For references to 'town blackguards' and politics, see E. Somerville to Col. John Somerville, 2 Dec. 1913, 2 Apr., 21 May 1914 (Somerville and Ross Papers, Lot 877), and Edith Somerville Diary, 5 Feb. 1919.
[20]   E. Somerville to John Somerville, 21 May 1914; note in 1917 volume of her diary (Somerville and Ross Papers).   [21]   Somerville, 'Ourselves Alone'.
[22]   E. Somerville to Col. J. Somerville, 24 Nov. 1917.

pathos in his eager intelligence, his genuine enthusiasm.'[23] She still hoped that the traditional figures of authority, the priests and established farmers, would exert their influence to curb such enthusiasts.

This benevolent tone quickly evaporated in the face of open rebellion with its attendant killings and vandalism. The eager boys and tom-fools became 'half-educated cads and upstarts' and 'a Thieves' gang'. When she meets an I.R.A. leader he is now described as 'a dirty youth'. By May 1922, 'the scum and the dregs of this wretched country are now in power, and we—the unfortunate middle strata—gentry, farmers, shop people—are helpless'.[24] Even in 1921 and 1922, however, Somerville clung to the idea that the country boys—the sons of the farmers she respected and hunted with—were innocents, coerced or misled by those eternal culprits, the outside agitators: 'paid outside [and doubtless town-bred] Bolshevists'.[25]

Somerville's faith that the peasantry were fundamentally sound, albeit easily cowed, was not necessarily widely shared. Her local ally, P. J. Sheehy, the staunchly anti-republican editor of the Skibbereen *Eagle*, preferred to blame any trouble on 'the lusty young men of the country'. The town's Sinn Feiners were few in number and 'only of Skibbereen in the sense that they reside there at the moment'. 'Why', he lamented, 'don't the young men coming into Skibbereen take as a pattern their compatriots of the town?', the latter being both orderly and loyal.[26]

Sheehy and many others did, however, share Somerville's belief in a silent majority opposed to the revolution. Again and again, hostile observers commented on the division between the revolutionaries and the farmers and shopkeepers—the 'stake-in-the-country men'—and frequently lamented the latter's silence or 'moral cowardice'.[27] Sir Henry Robinson, the president of the Local Government Board, wrote from Cork in May 1919 about local reactions to a riot he had witnessed:

I spoke with a number of persons of the small shopkeeper class about the matter and they all said, in effect, very much the same thing—that they hoped the police would '*give it to them*' and that 'these men who had nothing to lose would have the place under martial law before they were done.' But I noticed that they were more guarded in expressing opinions when speaking to one another.[28]

In the opinion of one judge at the Munster Assizes, 'They have allowed themselves to be cowed, intimidated and down-trodden by a comparatively small number of wicked men.' In 1921, one British commander in Cork concluded

[23] Somerville, 'Ourselves Alone'.
[24] E. Somerville to E. Smyth, 22 Apr. 1922; Somerville Diary, 17 May 1922; E. Somerville to E. Smyth, 2 May 1922.   [25] E. Somerville to E. Smyth, 10 Mar. 1921.
[26] *Eagle*, 13 Jan. 1917, 9 Mar. 1918.
[27] See CI Monthly Report, West Cork, June 1919 (CO 904/109).
[28] Robinson to Vice-President, Local Government Board, 13 May 1919 (French Papers, 75/46/12).

that 'the farmer class as a whole are governed by the gunmen'. In 1923 the National Army's Cork Command was still decrying 'the general rottenness of the moral fibre of the people'.[29]

This depiction of the I.R.A. as 'idle and reckless men' of the lower classes was endorsed by commentators, official and otherwise, throughout Ireland.[30] As in Cork, the most common initial reaction to the Volunteer movement was one of mild disdain. In Drogheda in 1917 they were deemed by the police to be 'persons of no consequence'. In Tyrone they were 'primarily confined to the lower classes'. In Kerry the movement 'embraces the rowdy part of the community'. In Galway, it consisted of 'young rough men and young priests and for the most part bullies', in Kilkenny, 'rowdies and persons of no standing in the locality', and in King's County, the 'hooligan class' predominated.[31] The Local Government Board inspector for Donegal, Derry, and Fermanagh reported in May 1918 that 'they are really just the mischievous characters of the various localities and if there was no Sinn Fein they would probably find some other excuse to behave as they do'.[32] Still writing in the same vein in 1919, Lord French, the Lord Lieutenant, dismissed the Volunteers as mere 'village ruffians'.[33]

Volunteer leaders were not much better and, in fact, were 'barely men in the ordinary sense at all' according to a typical police report from Fermanagh in 1918.[34] In Clare and Mayo local officers were 'of no importance' and had 'practically no influence'.[35] One policeman summed up the prevailing attitude in his characterization of a Tipperary captain: 'He is a man of good character but is not looked upon as being of much importance in the locality.'[36]

Later descriptions dripped with venom. The guerrillas of 1920 and 1921 were 'a horde of proletarians, grocers' curates, farm labourers, porters, stable boys, car-conductors and what not', 'scum', or 'corner boys'.[37] Their 'officers' 'are to be found among the farm hands all over the country, and the shop assistants in the villages and towns'.[38] One Kerry businessman felt that 'those who have to

[29] *Examiner*, 3 Dec. 1919; extract from report of Area Commander in Macready to Stevenson, 20 June 1921 (Lloyd George Papers); Cork Command General Weekly Survey, 12 Apr. 1923 (CW/OPS/14).

[30] CI Report, Galway (West Riding), Feb. 1918 (CO 904/105).

[31] Report on illegal drilling in Drogheda, 30 Dec. 1917 (CO 904/122/3); CI Monthly Reports, Tyrone, Sept. 1917; Kerry, Nov. 1917; Galway (West Riding), June 1918; Kilkenny, July 1918; King's, July 1918 (CO 904/102–7).

[32] Report to Sir Henry Robinson, 29 May 1918 (French Papers, 75/46/12).

[33] Report on the State of Ireland, 15 May 1919 (French Papers, 75/46/12).

[34] CI Monthly Report, Fermanagh, Mar. 1918 (CO 904/105).

[35] Reports on illegal drilling in Bohola, Co. Mayo, 16 Dec. 1917 and Kilrush, Co. Clare, 10 Dec. 1917 (CO 904/122).

[36] Report on illegal drilling in Donaskeigh, 9 Dec. 1917 (CO 904/122).

[37] C. H. Bretherton (the Irish correspondent for the *Morning Post*), *The Real Ireland* (London, 1925), 80. This book was withdrawn soon after publication because of threatened lawsuits, but see also Bretherton, 'Irish Backgrounds', 692–3, which contains further social analysis of the I.R.A.

[38] Memo by Maj. Charles Foulkes, 16 May 1921 (Liddell Hart Centre, Foulkes Papers, File 1).

leave the town [to go on the run] are all corner boys and are a good riddance'.[39] And finally, the R.I.C. Commissioner for Munster No. 1 Division, the formidable General Cyril Prescott-Decie, on the character of his opponents: 'all the corner boys, the criminals and the murderers. This population is one of the worst in the world—cruel, cowardly, idle, and inefficient, corrupt, and born intriguers.'[40]

According to most of these descriptions, in Cork and elsewhere, Volunteers (or 'Sinn Feiners', a blanket term) fell into two main occupational categories: 'shop assistants and town labourers'.[41] In Sir James O'Connor's unfriendly view, 'the "war" was the work of two thousand men and boys, nearly all of them of a low grade of society—farm hands, shop hands and the like'.[42] In County Down, the republicans were 'young shop boys, clerks etc.'; in Tullamore, 'shop assistants and labourers for the most part'; in Longford, 'mostly shopboys'; in Kilkenny, 'shop assistants and persons of that class'.[43] Everywhere it was agreed that this 'couple of thousand Irish peasants and shopboys' were opposed by the 'farmer-policeman-priest class' but that the latter were intimidated into silence.[44] Or, as General Prescott-Decie put it, they were 'wanting in moral and physical courage and easily coerced'.[45]

These opinions were, in many cases, an outgrowth of deep-rooted prejudices: those of the English against the Irish, Protestants against Catholics, the propertied against those without, townspeople against countrymen and vice versa, and so on down through the many layers of Irish society. If, for example, some Protestant farmers in Cork found I.R.A. squatters dirty and untrustworthy, and English soldiers thought the same of those they searched and arrested, they were simply applying the usual stereotypes of the Catholic Irish as a whole.

And indeed, many British soldiers and policemen (and a few native unionists) barely distinguished between the insurgents and the general population. Major Bernard Montgomery, a staff officer in Cork city, admitted he 'regarded all civilians as "Shinners"'. One battalion commander operating in East Cork in 1921 reported that 'the troops gradually learned to hate the Irish and have been inclined to brand them as a nation of murderers'.[46] Here as well, the Irish army followed in their predecessors' footsteps. In January 1923 the Cork Command's

[39] Intercepted letter, Nov. 1921 (Mulcahy Papers, P7/A/31).

[40] Memo by Gen. Prescott-Decie, n.d. (PRONI, D989/A/8/23).

[41] W. Alison Phillips, *The Revolution in Ireland* (London, 1923), 176–7.

[42] Sir James O'Connor, *A History of Ireland 1798–1924*, ii (London, 1925), 296.

[43] CI Monthly Reports, Down, Jan. 1917; King's, Mar. 1917; Longford, Nov. 1917; Kilkenny, May 1918 (CO 904/102–5).

[44] O'Connor, *History of Ireland*, ii. 315; Bretherton, *The Real Ireland*, 80. See also the CI Monthly Reports, King's, Mar. 1918 (CO 904/105) and Co. Dublin, May 1918 (CO 904/106); Report on the Clare and Tralee Special Military Areas, 1918 (Loch Papers, 71/12/9) and the 18th [Limerick] Bde. Weekly Intelligence Summary, 20 Aug. 1921 (O'Malley Papers, P17a/9).

[45] Memo by Gen. Prescott-Decie.

[46] Montgomery to Percival, 14 Oct. 1923 (Percival Papers); Anon., 'Appreciation of the Situation in Ireland', May 1921 (NLI, G. A. Cockerill Papers, MS 10, 606).

Weekly Survey complained that 'some members of the Army consider all inhabitants of Cork County as irregular'.[47]

A few British commanders and intelligence officers did cut through the folklore and stereotypes to achieve a more balanced, even respectful, view of their enemies. Notable among them was General Nevil Macready, the commander-in-chief in Ireland. He began his tenure in 1919 sharing the official view of the I.R.A. as a contemptible murder gang, but by February 1921 he was telling Sir Henry Wilson, the chief of the Imperial General Staff, that they were:

faced with a considerable proportion of the manhood in Ireland under the age of 25 to 30 . . . In country districts these men may be partially educated countrymen and labouring class, but in the towns and cities they are well educated young men, and all are imbued with what, for want of a better term, I would call 'fanatical patriotism'.[48]

The Irish Command's own history of the revolution spoke authoritatively of 'moral degenerates' and the 'underlying cruelty in the nature of many Irishmen' but went on to describe most revolutionaries as 'honest and earnest visionaries', sober and incorruptible.[49] And the 6th Division's final intelligence summary concluded: 'it must be remembered that members of the I.R.A. are drawn from the civil population of every station in life.'[50]

The Irish Command historian's (and Macready's) belief that the republican movement did contain some true patriots was shared by some Irish unionists. They differentiated the decent idealists in Sinn Fein and the Volunteers both from their corrupt rivals in the Irish Party and also from the thugs within their own ranks. One unionist wrote from Cork in March 1917 that 'the active Sinn Feiners are all young and intelligent men, generally teetotallers: unlike the ordinary political fellows they do not patronise public-houses.' J. M. Wilson, an Ulster Unionist organizer, also reported that 'the Sinn Fein movement . . . in Cork elicits sympathy from the better educated class and is not at all confined to the corner-boy element'.[51]

By 1919, with the eclipse of the Redmondites and the rise of the I.R.A., this distinction between 'good' Sinn Feiners and the Party machine was replaced by one between 'good' Sinn Feiners and the 'murder gang':

These methods to which Sinn Feinism has of late shown a tendency to degenerate are entirely contrary to the policy and interests of the Sinn Fein leaders. In their absence Sinn Feinism is getting out of hand and is being locally controlled by the irresponsible hooligan

---

[47]   Cork Command Weekly Survey, 24 Jan. 1923 (CW/OPS/14).

[48]   Macready to Chief of the Imperial General Staff, 18 Feb. 1921 (French Papers, 75/46/12).

[49]   *Record of the Rebellion*, ii. 32 (IWM, Sir Hugh Jeudwine Papers).

[50]   'Notes on the Organisation and Methods of Sinn Fein in the Sixth Divisional Area', 7 July 1921 (Strickland Papers).

[51]   Letter from Cork, 5 Mar. 1917 (PRONI, D989/A/8/7). In September Wilson interviewed a unionist city councillor who was 'full of detestation of the Redmondites and would prefer to deal with a Sinn Feiner "any day" . . . One thing he admired about the Sinn Feiners is their determination to wipe out that pestilent body, the A.O.H., and Molly Maguires.' This was a typical attitude among Cork unionists. J. M. Wilson, notes of tour, 27–8 Mar., Sept. 1917 (D989/A/9/7).

minority, who are in the movement for what they can get out of it and as an outlet for their criminal instincts . . . the town hooligans and the sons of labourers and those who care nothing of Sinn Fein ideals.[52]

At the same time, the London *Daily News* was wondering: 'Will the eminently respectable group of idealists at the top be submerged by an eruption of the men and women at the bottom?'[53] In both cases, political differences entailed class differences.

The I.R.A. did manage to impress some southern unionists, and others, in their role as policemen in the summer of 1920. 'These boys had seemed to me to take very real pride and pleasure in doing the decent thing which appealed to their sense of chivalry.'[54] The polite young men in their Sunday best who kept order at fairs and races, protected property, and kept tinkers and beggars away looked especially good compared with the universally hated Black and Tans who drove them back underground.

Nevertheless, such views seem to have been exceptional, and grew even more so as violence escalated. The general consensus among soldiers, policemen, unionists, and the I.R.A.'s other enemies was that most rebels were unruly and unskilled youths with little social status and too much time on their hands. So pervasive was this image that 'the usual I.R.A. type' became a common description of suspects in military and police reports, even those of the National Army.[55] Major Percival asserted that 'after a little practice one becomes able to select a few likely "types"'.[56] The 6th Division circulated a photograph album entitled 'Some Types of the Sinn Fein'.[57] General Prescott-Decie was able to reduce 'I.R.A. types' to two: 'the one the burly ruffian type; the other a moral and physical degenerate . . . these were the men with whom the Black and Tans had to deal.'[58]

Prescott-Decie's opinions were extreme even by the standards of the Black and Tans, but his belief that he could tell I.R.A. men at a glance was commonplace. To many in the Crown forces, 'Irish' and 'rebel' were synonymous. Attitudes such as these were the despair of British intelligence officers, who tried to point out to their colleagues that 'it is a mistake to imagine that rebels can be recognised through their uncouth state, or by peculiarities of their dress'.[59]

---

[52] Sir Henry Robinson to Sec., Lord Lt., 6 Jan. 1919 (French Papers, 75/46/12).

[53] Quoted in the *Examiner*, 15 Feb. 1919.

[54] E[mily] H[orsley] Ussher, 'The True Story of a Revolution', 40 (Representative Church Body Library, MS 70).

[55] An example of the use of the term 'the usual I.R.A. type' can be found in the (British) 6th Division Circular, 28 Oct. 1920 (MA, A/0413); See also Operational Report, West Cork and South Kerry, 8 May 1923 (CW/OPS/13).   [56] Percival, 'Guerrilla Warfare', part 2.

[57] 'Some Types of the Sinn Fein' (Strickland Papers).

[58] 'How well I know both types! The police photograph books of Irish revolutionaries are full of similar faces.' Prescott-Decie, quoted in *The Times*, 18 July 1922.

[59] 'Notes on the Organisation and Methods of Sinn Fein in the Sixth Divisional Area', 7 July 1921 (Strickland Papers).

Not surprisingly, Cork Volunteers vehemently rejected the charges of being shiftless hoodlums. In their view, the 'terrorists', 'scum', and 'dregs' were in the ranks of the Black and Tans and the British and Free State armies, not the I.R.A. Labels aside, however, they usually placed themselves within much the same modest social categories. They were indeed 'plain people' but they represented the hard-working and respectable heart of the nation.[60] Republican contempt was reserved for the gentry, 'shoneens', and gombeen men above them, and the 'tinkers', corner boys, and 'gutties' below. In the midst of the 1918 general election, Liam de Roiste (subsequently elected as a Sinn Fein MP) produced the following catalogue of opponents:

Some ex-servicemen, their followers and 'women' (our canvassers being hunted out of a brothel quarter in the city); policemen; ex-policemen and their wives; the ignorant 'old ladies' of unionist persuasion; anti-democratic shopkeepers and middle-class people; timid people who fear 'revolutions'.[61]

Theirs was a revolution of 'plain men' and 'ordinary fellas'.[62] Not the sort of committee men, politicians, and hangers-on who infested 'the Party' (and all parties), but rather, in one veteran's words, men 'brought up like myself out of a little farm, [who] had grown up with a highly patriotic sort of background. Those sort of men meant business.'[63]

Wealth, property, and pretension were felt to be inimical to true patriotism. Sean Moylan remembered being looked down upon as 'an ill-advised and *sans-culottes* party'.[64] 'Well-to-do people in towns and big farmers didn't want nothing to do with it,' recalls one Kanturk Volunteer, while in Dunmanway, 'business people and bigger people—they were never part of it'.[65] 'Friends among the business community of Bandon . . . were very few', according to Liam Deasy, and in Kanturk J. J. Walsh scolded those young men not in the movement for being 'too classy to take their place with the people'.[66] One I.R.A. observer, writing after the 1921 Truce, characterized their main opponents as:

wealthy, shoneen people with less than average intelligence or education—who form a certain deadweight of interest in the enemy's favour. These people, who merely seek to curry favour, are in the main devoid of much moral or physical courage.[67]

Florence O'Donoghue wrote of one such antagonistic shopkeeper that 'it is a high time to realise what a nuisance this type of *polished* Irishman is'.[68]

---

[60]   Interview with AB. Padraig O Ciosain, for example, declared that the guerrillas of East Cork were drawn from 'the plain people of Ireland': 'The Heroic Fight at Clonmult', in *Rebel Cork's Fighting Story*, 190.   [61]   Liam de Roiste Diary, 8 Dec. 1918 (de Roiste Papers).

[62]   Rory O'Connor quoted in the *Examiner*, 15 Apr. 1922; interview with AJ, 9 May 1989.

[63]   'Liam Hegarty' (a West Cork veteran) in Somerville-Large, *Cappaghglass*, 88.

[64]   Eileen Magner, 'Sean Moylan: Some Aspects of his Parliamentary Career 1937–1948', MA Thesis (Cork, 1982), 4.   [65]   Interviews with AI, 27 Apr. 1989, and AE.

[66]   Deasy, *Towards Ireland Free*, 11; IG Report on de Valera's Tour of Cork, 18 Dec. 1917 (CO 904/122).   [67]   Anon. memo, n.d. [1921] (Mulcahy Papers, P7/A/32).

[68]   Adj., 1st South. Div. to A/G, 1 Nov. 1921 (Mulcahy Papers, P7/A/31).

Equally 'polished' (a favourite republican term of abuse) and anti-national were the middle-class salariat, derided by Daniel Corkery as 'all the bank clerks, Government officials and tennis players in the land whose spiritual home is the Strand'.[69] Bank clerks, socially influential but widely resented, were singled out as especially suspect, and George Power's comment that Fermoy's 'commercial element . . . lacked any sort of National outlook' was echoed by Volunteers throughout the county.[70]

In the countryside, it was farmers—and large farmers in particular—who held aloof from the struggle or, at best, were only fair-weather republicans. 'The big farmers didn't want us at all.'[71] I.R.A. hostility was strongest in North and East Cork—'cow country'—where agricultural prosperity was most pronounced. These cattle farmers were the *nouveaux riches* of rural Cork, having profited immensely from wartime livestock prices.

Ned Murphy, for example, thought that farmers around Mallow only joined the movement to 'save their skins' from conscription. 'The farmers' sons there never joined up the Volunteers, but the labourers were Volunteers in this area.'[72] In Whitechurch, 'the Volunteer movement was ridiculed by farmers' sons in this area. The movement was good enough for the labouring class but beneath them.'[73] One I.R.A. captain in Ballineen was even more blunt: 'God blast yeer souls ye pack of farmers whatever we are you are not much anyway.'[74]

The Farmers' Union, widely seen as a vehicle for strong farmers, aroused much republican ire, mostly within the 1st Cork Brigade. Sean O'Hegarty, the brigade O/C, called the leaders of the Union 'the reactionary pro-English type, opposed to the republic and an utterly useless class'.[75] At about the same time (late 1921) one of his staff reported that:

Practically every member of the Farmers' Union, with one or two honourable exceptions, are NOT even members of the political side of our movement and unless we act very carefully they will attempt to drive wedges into our Organization in this district.[76]

Volunteers and Union members' sons even brawled occasionally at meetings and dances, each side accusing the other of being un-Irish. The most famous of these fights occurred in January 1920 at the Grenagh 'Farmers' Union Ball':[77]

---

[69] Daniel Corkery, 'Of Visions National and International', *Irish Statesman*, 2 Mar. 1924.

[70] George Power to Florence O'Donoghue, 1 Dec. 1953 (O'Donoghue Papers, MS 31, 421). For the position of bank clerks in Mallow society, see Lankford, *The Hope and the Sadness*, 76–7 and, more generally, George Birmingham, *Irishmen All* (London, 1913), 216, and *An Irishman Looks at his World* (London, 1919), 293–4.　　　　　[71] Dan Browne (O'Malley Papers, P17b/112).

[72] Ned Murphy (O'Malley Papers, P17b/123).

[73] O/C 5th Bn. to O/C Cork 1, 29 Oct. 1921 (Mulcahy Papers, P7/A/37).

[74] Statement by John O'Mahoney, n.d. [1922] (NA, Dail Eireann Courts (Winding Up) Commission, DE 11/220). For other comments on farmers, see Dan Browne (O'Malley Papers, P17b/112), and Vice O/C to O/C Cork 1, 18 Nov. 1921 (Mulcahy Papers, P7/A/27).

[75] O/C Cork 1 to O/C 1st South. Div., 31 Dec. 1921 (Mulcahy Papers, P7/A/32).

[76] Vice O/C to O/C Cork 1, 18 Nov. 1921 (Mulcahy Papers, P7/A/27).

[77] John Murphy, 'The Farmers' Union Ball' (UCD, Dept. of Irish Folklore, SMS 388, 187–93). For a newspaper account, see the *Examiner*, 6 Jan. 1920.

What foolish glowing shadows now
pierced the swelling brain
of them that donned false colours in
the nightmare of Sinn Fein.
They wanted sport and money but
no other should have fun
Now to stop our merrymaking
they robbed the postman's gun.
They didn't face the Saxon; they
might get wounded sore,
They'd rather buff their neighbours
who were living quiet next door.
With masks and blackened faces
dressed in a cowhouse stall
They made straight for the schoolhouse
for the Farmers' Union Ball.

This song mocks the Volunteers but it also asserts the farmers' national creden-
tials: they wore Irish clothing ('for we had no jazzers then'), danced to music 'in
the good old Irish style', and drank Ireland's health. It was the Sinn Feiners who
wore the 'false colours' of patriotism. The Farmers' Union was the genuine
article.

Sinn Fein's ban on hunting illustrates this antagonism well. The all-Ireland
ban originated in early 1919 as a protest against the continued imprisonment of
republican leaders, and was ostensibly aimed at the 'Ascendancy' who
controlled most local hunts. However, it soon pitted Sinn Fein and the
Volunteers—who had to enforce the measure—against the traders and farmers
who, in reality, made up the bulk of the huntsmen.

Cork's hunt clubs—the Muskerry, United, Carbery, Duhallow, Galtees, and
others—were all of a distinct political hue, uniquely combining the rising world
of cattle and 'trade' with that of garrison and gentry. Here, nationalism and
unionism reached a relatively easy accommodation, and many members' sons
had gone briskly to war in 1914.[78]

The hunt committees and their members, Protestants and Catholics alike,
objected vigorously to the ban. Keen sportsmen, they carried on regardless,
provoking confrontations reminiscent of the Land War. Both hounds and huntsmen were sporadically ambushed right up until the end of 1922 (although the
only fatalities were suffered by the hounds).[79] Hunt members saw the campaign

---

[78] See *Examiner*, 5, 8 Feb. 1919 and Edith Somerville to Col. John Somerville, 14 Jan., 24 Feb.
1914, 22 Nov. 1916 (Somerville and Ross Papers, Lot 877). It should be noted that, while hunts were
no longer segregated, they were still stratified. Most farmers rode at the back of the field, behind the
officers and gentry.

[79] On 5 Nov. 1922, the United Hunt Club was held up and its horses stolen. *Examiner*, 6 Nov.
1922. See also Cpt. Eamon O'Mahony to Chief Liaison Officer, 10 Jan. 1922 (MA, Liaison Papers,
LE/4/7A).

against them as an attack from below aimed at farmers and gentry alone. Why else was hunting singled out, and coursing not included in the ban? 'Why should the sport of one class and not another be stopped?'[80] Edith Somerville, master of the Carbery Hunt, reported 'fierce indignation with "the counter-jumpers of Skibbereen"' among local farmers when the ban was announced.[81]

To most republicans, the hunts were 'enemy institutions': nests of British officers, loyalists, and Redmondites, symbols of Anglicization and privilege. Farmers' protests that they were good patriots and certainly not members of the 'Ascendancy' got short shrift. Hunts acted as recruiting agents and refused to employ Sinn Feiners. Hunt members had taken no part in the nationalist movement. They were products of the 'Castle garrison' and 'it is about time they were stopped'.[82] The visceral hostility felt towards the huntsmen was revealed by the fact that Volunteers were still disrupting meets long after the 'German Plot' prisoners had been released in the spring of 1919. Riding horses were also frequently seized in 1921 and 1922. This general harassment followed much the same pattern as that of the Farmers' Union.

The contrast with coursing is a significant one. Coursing was seen as a properly Irish sport, carried on by working men who objected to 'polished boots' sports and gave their dogs names such as 'Irish Volunteer' and 'Sinn Fein Boy'.[83] Volunteers often belonged to coursing clubs. Few, if any, rode to hounds.

The campaign against fox hunting underlined the erosion of deference and of the authority of traditional elites that accompanied the I.R.A. uprising. The defeat of the Irish Party in national and local elections in 1918 and 1920 also signalled the eclipse of the old power brokers, the 'big men' so despised by the 'plain men' of the I.R.A.

The decline of the old order proved fleeting, however. The Treaty with Britain, as the Volunteers saw it, triggered the re-emergence of the old bosses and committee men in the guise of Free Staters. Many of these men joined the new Farmers and Commercial parties in 1922. The guerrillas blamed these men of property, intent on 'preserving the old ranks and grades in society', for the betrayal of the republic and the Civil War.[84] One intelligence officer from North Cork summed up the local Free Staters as 'the Farmers' Union and the Businessmen, Middle-men, Landlord and Capitalist class'. In West Cork they were 'what are termed "respectable law-abiding citizens"'.[85] Seamus Fitzgerald, the Cobh Volunteer officer and TD, stated that 'the only supporters of the Treaty

---

[80] A comment made at a farmers' meeting in Midleton. See *Examiner*, 3 Feb. 1919.

[81] Somerville Diary, 5 Feb. 1919.

[82] A comment made at a farmers' meeting in the Muskerry Hunt district. *Examiner*, 13 Feb. 1919.

[83] Letter from W. O'Sullivan, *Examiner*, 10 Feb. 1919, and *Star*, 10 Nov. 1917.

[84] Letter from W.N., 13 May 1922 (Lankford Papers, U169b).

[85] Cork 4 intelligence memo, n.d. [1923] (CAI, Lankford Papers, U169); I/O Cork 3 to 1st South. Div., 13 Feb. 1923 (O'Malley Papers, P17a/92).

he found in his constituency were the people who had been consistently anti-republican, the well-to-do', acting out of 'purely material and sordid interests'.[86] Sean Moylan spoke for many I.R.A. men in the spring of 1922 when he said: 'It was the plain fighting men that won the war and they would win again. There were some people who did not stand by us the last time and they would not be forgotten.'[87]

The natural corollary of such views was that, as Ted O'Sullivan, a staff officer of the West Cork Brigade, put it, 'all the mountain and the poor areas were good', and that small farmers and 'ordinary working people' were the backbone of the rebellion.[88] Many in the I.R.A shared this belief. In the Macroom Battalion, 'perhaps the most important factor was the sympathy and co-operation of the civilian population, particularly in the poorer and more mountainous districts, where small farmers fed and housed the Columns'. Tom Barry agreed: 'poor people were practically 100 per cent backing the fight for freedom'.[89] Peadar O'Donnell called the republican movement 'a rich mixture of wage earners, small farmers and the almost landless men of the West'. Ernie O'Malley wrote that 'at the beginning it was the poor who stood by us in the country . . . the small farmers and labourers were our main support'.[90]

This sense of plebeian identity produced very little in the way of organizational class-consciousness. Many Volunteers were also officers or members of trade unions (for example, Mick Fitzgerald, the commandant of the Fermoy Battalion in 1920, was also secretary of the local ITGWU branch), and many participated in land disputes and strikes as individuals, but the two loyalties were kept strictly separate. If the I.R.A. officially intervened in a strike, it was almost always to protect property or urban food supplies: 'If it were not for the action of the Volunteers you would not have a crop of any kind saved in East Cork.'[91]

The young activists of the Irish Transport and General Workers' Union were assumed to be allies, but only in so far as they directed their efforts toward the struggle for independence. Militant union organizers were considered a nuisance by leaders such as Sean Moylan and Liam Lynch. Lynch, while commander of the 1st Southern Division, declared that 'my experience is that certain organizers try to put Labour above Freedom, this may go on for some time, but not even their own individual members may stick this'.[92] This disregard for unions within the movement was common enough to spark a lament by the *Voice of Labour* that 'many young men in Ireland who are in the Volunteers think there is no need for a Labour Union'.[93]

[86]   Peadar O'Donnell, *Not Yet Emmet* (Dublin, n.d.), 13; *Debate on the Treaty*, 238.
[87]   *Examiner*, 3 Apr. 1922.
[88]   Ted O'Sullivan (O'Malley Papers, P17b/108); interview with AJ.
[89]   *Record of Activities: 7th Battalion, Cork No. 1 Brigade* (Macroom, n.d.), 8; O'Mahony interview.
[90]   O'Donnell, *Not Yet Emmett*, 1; O'Malley, *On Another Man's Wound*, 123, 144.
[91]   Vice O/C to O/C Cork 1, 10 Nov. 1921 (Mulcahy Papers, P7/A/30).
[92]   O/C 1st South. Div. to C/S, 13 Oct. 1921 (Mulcahy Papers, P7/A/34).
[93]   *Voice of Labour*, 10 Dec. 1921.

These tensions came to a head in late 1921 and 1922 when strikes in Whitechurch, Doneraile, Midleton, and other parts of North and East Cork triggered I.R.A. responses which were immediately attacked as anti-union. In Bartlemy (near Fermoy), 'the entire working class membership of the I.R.A., with the exception of a couple of scabs, refused to obey . . . and broke away from the I.R.A. temporarily'.[94]

Embittered labourers were vociferous in their complaints. 'Many of the farmers' sons are in certain organizations for their own benefit, and to use such against the workers'; 'Most of those who are republicans are such for a sinister motive'; 'terrorist methods [are] now being adopted by the employing element in the local Volunteers.'[95] Despite these grievances, however, union members never mutinied or seriously tried to manipulate the army themselves. Some, like the besieged labourers of Bartlemy, refused to join either side in the Civil War, but this was as much an act of exhaustion as an assertion of independence.

A similar pattern and degree of class conflict existed in Volunteer units elsewhere in the south. In Wexford and Waterford, strikes by farm labourers strained I.R.A. unity and depleted its ranks, at least temporarily. As in Cork, commanders reacted cautiously, but usually intervened to protect farmers.[96] Elsewhere as well, ITGWU organizers were viewed with suspicion as being insufficiently patriotic.[97]

The revolution did sometimes breed a certain primitive Jacobinism among the guerrillas, as when land and cattle belonging to 'enemies of the republic' were seized and redistributed in West Cork in 1921 and 1922. 'We had in effect been the first practical socialists in the country', declared Tom Barry.[98] In many cases, though, these seizures were little more than the usual family and factional gambits to gain more land.[99]

Whatever the levelling inclinations of some, Cork republicans as a group were no sans-culottes. If the social boundaries of 'the republic' skirted around big farms and affluent suburbs, they also generally stopped short of the back lanes, cabins, and workhouses inhabited by the unemployed, idle, or itinerant. Poverty was only a political virtue when it was respectable.

Cork Volunteers thought of themselves not just as 'plain men' but also as respectable and 'above all, decent men'. Their comrades were 'the best kind of

[94] Maurice O'Regan, 'When the I.R.A. Split on Class Issues', *Labour News*, 21 Aug. 1937.

[95] *Voice of Labour*, 10, 24 Dec. 1921. See also Adj. Cork 2 to Adj. 1st South. Div., 30 Sept. 1921 (Mulcahy Papers, P7/A/34); O/C 5th Bn. to O/C Cork 1, 29 Oct. 1921 (P7/A/37); *Irish Farmer*, 10 Dec. 1921, and Dan Bradley, *Farm Labourers: Irish Struggle 1900–1976* (Belfast, 1988), 60–3.

[96] Tom Foran to Min. of Labour, 15 Sept. 1921 (Mulcahy Papers, P7/A/27); South Wexford Bde. Monthly Report, Dec. 1921 (P7/A/32); Dublin District Weekly Intelligence Summaries, 4 and 11 Dec. 1921 (WO/35/93); Ussher, 'True Story', 97–101.

[97] Mid-Limerick Bde. Monthly Intelligence Report, Sept. 1921 (Mulcahy Papers, P7/A/8).

[98] O'Mahony interview. See also 'General Barry on the Causes of Failure', *Irish Independent*, 8 Dec. 1970.

[99] See the letters and reports on land seizures contained in MA, DOD A/613, A/8506, and Special Infantry Corps Papers, SIC/2.

fellas', 'a fine lot of good, decent Irish men', 'all very respectable', 'all a fine bunch of fellas. You feel good when you think of the fellas you knew.'[100] The most frequently used images were those of cleanliness: they were 'strong, healthy, clean-living boys', 'honest, noble, clean', 'brave and clean men', 'sober, clean-living, self-respecting'.[101] These key themes and phrases were enshrined in I.R.A. obituaries, which described men who 'bore the highest character' and who were uniformly 'respectable', 'respected', 'held in high esteem', 'gentle', and 'clean-living'.[102]

Respectability was crucial to the guerrillas' sense of themselves: hard-edged, often puritanical, excluding those who were not 'our type', 'our class', or 'one of us'. 'We had only the best kind of men', 'there were no roughs in it', 'you get a bad kind of man if you have to go into pubs to recruit him'.[103] The 'rough crowd' and 'bad characters' were as much outsiders to the movement as the 'big men' at the other end of the social scale.

'The corner boy, the tramp, the tinker, the drunken militiaman' lived a social world away from the shops, offices, and farms which produced most of the Volunteers, 'outside the pale of decency and respectability'.[104] 'It was impossible not to be struck by the unbridgeable, inscrutable gulf which the mere turn of a corner could evidently create.'[105] The Volunteers defined themselves in large measure against this culture of poverty, with its squalor, drunkenness, prostitution, and idleness (both real and reputed). Good I.R.A. men were hard-working, self-improving, clean-living, and sober.[106]

This was as much a political as a social distinction, as the loyalties of 'the lanes' were felt to be rabidly anti-republican. It was assumed that recruits for the British and Free State armies were almost entirely drawn from the ranks of the undeserving poor ('all the scruff and corner boys'[107]), and ex-soldiers returning from the Great War were tarred with the same brush.[108] These men, along with

[100]   Interview with AJ; interview with Mr Buckley (RTE Archives, A2792); interview with AA; interview with AI.

[101]   O Ciosain, 'Heroic Fight at Clonmult', 191; de Roiste Diary, 5 Mar. 1922; B. Whelan to John Ahearn, 28 Feb. 1923 (NLI, MS 15, 993); Erskine Childers, 'The Irish Revolution', 8 (TCD, Childers Papers, MS 7808/29).

[102]   *Examiner*, 17 May 1917, 17 Aug., 9 Nov. 1920, 8 Jan., 25 Feb., 23, 30 Mar. 1921.

[103]   Interview with AJ; interview with AI; O'Mahony interview with Tom Barry. Some of Frank O'Connor's short stories illustrate these attitudes very well. See especially 'Jumbo's Wife', 'Jo', and 'Alec', in *Guests of the Nation* (London, 1931).

[104]   T. C. Murray, *Spring Horizon* (London, 1937), 81.

[105]   George O'Brien, *Village of Longing* (London, 1990), 130. See also Conrad Arensberg and Solon Kimball, *Family and Community in Ireland* (Cambridge, Mass., 1940, 1968), 324–7.

[106]   Those who were not—especially those who were caught drunk—were liable to be court-martialled. See, for example, the Reports of the 3rd Bn. Council, Cork 1, 5, 8 Aug. 1919 (MA, A/0341).

[107]   These were the words of a Kilrush (Co. Clare) farmer who assaulted a soldier. Staunton, 'Royal Munster Fusiliers', 10.

[108]   Portraits of this enduring class and stereotype can be found in Lankford, *The Hope and the Sadness*, 74–5, 84 and, briefly but evocatively, in John McGahern, *The Barracks* (London, 1963), 78.

their wives and mothers—'shawlies' and 'separation women'—were classed as drunken rabble, and subjected to withering republican scorn. 'They are very ignorant, they understand only violence and force, they have few ideas, and they are easily set on to rows.'[109] This contempt and suspicion would harden into fear and violence as the armed struggle escalated in 1920.

Free State soldiers were believed to belong to the same underclass and to share all these vices. One North Cork Volunteer remembered them as 'fellas not working around and hangers-on who'd been through the 14–18 war'.[110] In West Cork:

The majority of these ex-soldiers, who were the corner boys and loafers of the towns a few months ago, have brought their corner-boy propensities with them into the Free State Army and drunkenness and indiscipline are the order of the day.[111]

In Mallow, 'they have now got the worst type of ex-soldier in the Free State Army', while on the Kerry border, the I.R.A.'s foes were 'the Drunkard, the Traitor, the wife deserter, the wife beater, the Tramp, the tinker and the brute'.[112] The following republican song, entitled 'The National Army', comes from the Kiskeam area:[113]

> There was Sweeney the tinker and Danieleen Kit
> White and some more of the lewdering clique,
> Bound up with gold cursed England to lick–
> The recruits of the National Army.
>
> There were others there too, and they spoke very free
> They talked of my mother and what she used to be!
> Saying 'twas many a basin of milk she gave me
> Before joining the National Army.

What happened when these social worlds collided was demonstrated when Dan Shields, an ex-soldier and 'tinker', was brought into a North Cork flying column—over the passionate objections of his local company. 'He had bad antecedents'; 'We never trusted or liked him and he was aware of it'; 'he came from a very low family . . . the Shields were cheap and low-living . . . he was low and we'll leave it at that.'[114] Simply put, 'he had no right' to be in the column and did not last more than one ambush.[115] When Shields turned informer it confirmed everyone's suspicions, but it is likely that his treatment by his erstwhile comrades was one of the principal causes.[116]

---

[109] De Roiste Diary, 17 Jan. 1919. [110] Interview with AI.

[111] Intell. Report, n.d. [1922] (O'Malley Papers, P17a/34).

[112] I/O Cork 4 to I/O 1st South. Div., 8 Sept. 1922 (MA, A/0991/4); Whelan to Ahearn, 28 Feb. 1923 (NLI, MS 15, 993). This widely held view of the National Army was contradicted by M. J. Costello in a letter to Florence O'Donoghue, 13 Sept. 1953 (O'Donoghue Papers, MS 31, 423/4), with the significant exception of Cork city.

[113] The author was Paddy James Dennehy. John J. O'Riordan, *Kiskeam and That Way Back* (Limerick, 1969), 86–7.

[114] Ned Murphy (O'Malley Papers, P17b/123); interview with AI.

[115] Dan Browne (O'Malley Papers, P17b/112).

[116] As admitted in my interview with AI. See also Grazebrook Diary, 27–8 (Royal Gloucestershire Regiment Archives), which states that Shields was 'conscripted' by the I.R.A.

The I.R.A.'s stringent concern for respectability and its contempt for those who did not fit in or measure up were amply demonstrated in the summer of 1920, when the Volunteers assumed a new role as policemen. Backed by newly elected Sinn Fein majorities on local councils, and in the absence of the R.I.C. from much of the countryside, I.R.A. units in Cork set out to clean up their towns and parishes. Suspected thieves, wife-beaters, prostitutes, and other undesirables were warned, arrested, tried, and sometimes expelled, with considerable support from the community. Pub closing hours were keenly enforced, as was the ban on gambling at GAA meets.

The first and most obvious targets, however, were 'tramps' and 'tinkers'. Although familiar tramps were often welcome in farms and villages, itinerant strangers were usually viewed with alarm and suspicion, especially those who travelled or congregated in groups. Bands, or 'tribes' of tinkers were considered particularly unruly or dangerous, and their presence in Munster towns was almost always resented.[117] This problem was exacerbated after the end of the war, when demobilized and unemployed soldiers flooded the country. Many became tramps and beggars in their search for work. As these poor and dirty unknowns began to collect in their streets and workhouses, town and district councils turned to the R.I.C. for help with the 'tramp nuisance' and the 'tinker pest'.[118] Without draconian legal powers and with a revolution to attend to, Cork's head constables and district inspectors could do little.

The battalion and brigade officers of the I.R.A. zealously took up the slack. Unencumbered by legal niceties, Volunteers began driving 'tramps' out of one town after another. In July 1920, the *Cork Examiner* reported that 'Midleton has become practically free already from what used to be known as "the tramp nuisance"'. 'Undesirable visitors to Midleton this while past who were showing any offensive conduct on the streets were duly rounded up and quickly banished from the town and district.'[119] Further north, in August, 'the Volunteers have done some good work in Fermoy in the way of not allowing members of the tramp class to congregate in town'.[120] The Mallow I.R.A. and others followed suit, as did units in Kerry, Clare, Tipperary, and Kilkenny.[121]

---

[117] Arensberg and Kimball referred to them as 'an outcast lowest class' (*Family and Community in Ireland*, 272). The most comprehensive guide to these attitudes (as recorded in the 1930s) can be found in the Schools Manuscripts in the UCD Dept. of Folklore Archives. See SMS 281, p. 45; 283, p. 384; 285, pp. 92–3, 233; 289, p. 257; 294, p. 67; 346, pp. 58–9; 347, pp. 441–3; 352, p. 104; 353, p. 355; 383, p. 119; 395, p. 275.

[118] *Examiner*, 9 July, 26 Nov. 1918, 13 July 1920.

[119] 'the Midleton guardians . . . expressed themselves well pleased at the very reduced number of casuals of late seeking refuge for the night in the workhouse.'

[120] *Examiner*, 15 Aug. 1920.

[121] Lankford, *The Hope and the Sadness*, 183; *Examiner*, 18 June 1920; O/C 2nd South. Div. to C/S, 7 Apr. 1921 (Mulcahy Papers, P7/A/21) and Dir. of Intell. to C/S, 26 July 1921 and the comments of the Asst. C/S thereon (P7/A/22); James J. Comerford, *My Kilkenny I.R.A. Days 1916–22* (Kilkenny, 1978), 150. See also O/C Cork 2 to A/G, 24 June 1920 and the A/G's reply of 25 June (MA, A/0799).

Those tramps who remained in the Munster war zone were liable to be shot as spies or informers.[122]

When the guerrillas thought of these various enemies and 'undesirables', high and low, they thought of towns. Here were concentrated police and military barracks, loyalists and politicians, bank clerks and corner boys, and all their assorted 'hangers-on'. 'We talk of how the village gave the British army its recruits; gave the police their touts; gave the Imperialists their audiences.'[123] Rural rebels generally viewed towns and villages as 'the organizing centres of evil' and would have heartily endorsed one GHQ inspector's opinion that 'the population of all towns is bad. A little terrorism might have a good effect.'[124]

Almost every town in Cork was felt by local militants to be lacking in national fibre. Skibbereen's inhabitants 'were a race apart from the sturdy people of West Cork. They were different and with a few exceptions were spineless', Midleton was 'a shoneen town', Fermoy 'essentially a loyalist town', and so on.[125] These complaints continued through the Civil War. In Mallow the I.R.A. was faced with 'the awful shoneenism that permeates its walls'. In Dunmanway 'people were very strongly against us in the town'. The 4th (North-West) Cork Brigade even issued an order that 'all men should get strict instructions to avoid hanging around villages'.[126]

Similar sentiments were expressed throughout the I.R.A. Ernie O'Malley, as O/C of the 2nd Southern Division, admitted in August 1921 that 'the army has been steadily losing its grip of the towns and villages' and that 'the men in the towns may not be up to the requisite standard'. 'Towns we could not count on', he later admitted.[127] In Clare it was said that 'the people in the towns did absolutely nil in the war and it is only right that they be asked to do their bit'.[128]

Urban spinelessness and shoneenism was usually contrasted with the natural purity and patriotism of the common people of the countryside. 'The country always was ahead of the towns'; 'You hadn't the same feeling amongst the population of the towns as you had in the country, for there you had the whole population.'[129] In the early days of the Civil War it was reported that 'whole districts' in West Cork 'are solidly republican and the Free Staters have to

---

[122]   See Ch. 13.

[123]   'Are Villages Less National Than Country Districts?', *An Phoblacht*, 31 Dec. 1926. See also 'Bad Influence in our Townland', 7 Jan. 1927.

[124]   'Are Villages Less National'; GHQ Inspector's Report on Roscommon and Leitrim, 17 Oct. 1921 (MA, A/0747).

[125]   Barry, *Guerilla Days*, 89; Edmund Donegan (O'Malley Papers, P17b/112) and George Power (P17b\132).

[126]   Andy O'Sullivan to Brother Miceal, 7 Nov. 1923; Jack Buttimer (O'Malley Papers, P17b/111); O/C Cork 4 to Bn. O/Cs, 14 Sept. 1922 (Lankford Papers).

[127]   O/C 2nd South. Div. to Bde. O/Cs, 5, 26 Aug. 1921 (NLI, MS 17, 880); O'Malley, *On Another Man's Wound*, 144. It is worth comparing the former with comments made by the local R.I.C. divisional commissioner about the same time; his diary is in the O'Malley Papers (P17a/9).

[128]   O/C Mid-Clare Bde. to Sec., Dail Eireann, 17 Sept. 1921 (Mulcahy Papers, P7/A/24).

[129]   Con Leddy (O'Malley Papers, P17b/123); Con Meaney (P17b/112).

depend on their hangers-on in the towns'. It was 'the country fellows who believed in freedom for its own sake' who stayed the course, according to Mossy Donegan, a veteran Bantry guerrilla. 'It was well these men could not discuss documents but they knew what freedom was.'[130]

Town life was Anglicized and degraded, its nationalism 'shallow and rootless'. The Volunteers 'were predominantly a product of the country, having deeper roots in old traditions'.[131] The further away from towns, and from the rich cattle farms of the valleys and plains, the better. Ted O'Sullivan, for example, equated 'good land' with 'bad people' and 'bad land' with 'good people'.[132] Best of all were the small farmers of the mountains—the 'mountainy men'—who were 'as sound as spring water'.[133]

The republican faith in the instinctive nationalism of the countryside drew on the romanticization of rural life within the Irish-Ireland movement, and within Irish nationalism in general. Writers from Charles Kickham to Daniel Corkery had extolled the virtues of 'the people on the land, the people themselves', and their influence can be seen in statements such as Mossy Donegan's.[134] More concretely, and probably more importantly, distrust of towns also reflected the enduring everyday divide between town and country—already encountered in the opposing views of Edith Somerville and P. J. Sheehy.[135] This cut both ways, as it was just as common for townspeople to sneer at the 'country crowd' as vice versa.[136] Farmers were 'regarded with a sort of contempt. A farmer was a fellow who was hunted off the street on fair days because his cows had fouled the curbstone.' 'The farming people were tolerated in the towns, but there was a bit of class distinction, all right.'[137] In George O'Brien's Lismore 'we despised the country and all belonging to it, and felt ourselves immeasurably superior to everything it stood for . . . They, in turn, thought us weaklings, cissies, Mammies' boys, half-men.'[138]

Moreover, farmers and townsmen regularly accused each other of being antinational and un-Irish over all sorts of issues. Throughout the Great War, for example, there was a running battle in Cork newspapers over which class were the worse profiteers, shopkeepers or farmers. And, sooner or later, the debate always came around to the question of who had won the Land War. It was an

---

[130]   Report to I/O 1st South. Div., n.d. [1922] (O'Malley Papers, P17a/34); Mossy Donegan (P17b/108).   [131]   O'Donoghue, *Tomas MacCurtain*, 59.

[132]   Ted O'Sullivan (O'Malley Papers, P17b/108).

[133]   Ernie O'Malley, 'Sean Connolly' (O'Malley Papers, P17b/153), 71.

[134]   Daniel Corkery's foreword to *Tomas MacCurtain*, 11. See also Tom Garvin, *Nationalist Revolutionaries in Ireland, 1858–1928* (Oxford, 1987).

[135]   See Conrad Arensberg, *The Irish Countryman* (Garden City, NY, 1968), 136: 'In many ways the town is an alien world, even a hostile one, to the countryman. He feels its scorn of his rusticity and distrusts its urbane ways.' See also Crowley, *In West Cork Long Ago*, 47–50.

[136]   John Jackson, *Report on Skibbereen Social Survey* (Dublin, 1967), 29.

[137]   Somerville-Large, *Cappaghglass*, 71, 101.

[138]   *Village of Longing*, 130. See also P. D. Mehigan, 'When I was Young', *Carbery's Annual* (1945–6), 125–7.

article of faith among the county's townspeople that they had 'rid the country of the landlords' while the farmers had reaped all the rewards. 'Was there ever a farmer's band seen at a national meeting?' asked one speaker in Skibbereen to scornful laughter.[139]

Such attitudes could be found within the I.R.A. as well. Volunteer officers from Cork or other cities often looked down on the yokels in rural units. Surveying his brigade area, Terence MacSwiney concluded that:

The general body of Volunteers in the City area have the soldier's outlook, and look at things from the soldier's standpoint. They also observe discipline in general in a very satisfactory way . . . In the Country areas it is quite otherwise . . . in general Volunteers in the country districts look at things more from a civilian than a soldier point of view.[140]

One emissary from Dublin pronounced the north Tipperary organization inadequate because of 'the low cultural standard of the area'.[141] The countrymen responded by mocking the city men, playing tricks on them, or simply ignoring them. When Ernie O'Malley arrived in the North Cork Brigade in mid-1920, he was made fun of for his manner and disliked for his arrogance. 'He didn't like our fellows at all, like he was a step above us.'[142] The countrymen of the 1st Cork Brigade, who had previously shunned O'Malley, were equally cool to the attentions of Cork city officers, complaining that 'city men think they know too much'.[143]

The political idealization of 'mountainy men' may be similarly related to the generally perceived differences between the egalitarian culture of poor areas and the snobbishness of strong farmers. In the uplands of Cork, small farmers and labourers worked side by side and ate at the same table without distinction. When these men went to work 'down the country'—in the 'lower country' to the north and east—they often entered a different world, in which they lived and worked apart from their employers.[144] The I.R.A. in these districts probably inherited some of their pride and resentment.

Such prejudices ran deep within the I.R.A., as in their communities, but they were almost always expressed against outsiders. Volunteers thought of their own organization in terms of brotherhood and camaraderie, never class. All of the I.R.A. veterans I interviewed insisted on this point and on the absence of class tension in their ranks. 'No one took any notice of that kind of thing'; 'We were all about the same class'; 'We had all types'; 'we were all just ordinary fellas'.[145]

---

[139] *Eagle*, 4 May, 23 Feb. 1918; See also *Examiner*, 15, 20 Feb., 14 Mar. 1917, 15 Apr. 1919.

[140] MacSwiney to C/S, 21 May 1920 (CAI, Terence MacSwiney Papers, PR4/4).

[141] GHQ Organizer's Report to O/C 3rd South. Div., 6 Sept. 1921 (MA, A/0670). See also J. J. O'Connell to Michael Collins, 5 Sept. 1919 (A/0354) and Training Report for South Connemara, 5 Jan. 1922 (A/0680).   [142] Interview with AI.

[143] Mick O'Sullivan (O'Malley Papers, P17b/111).

[144] UCD, Dept. of Irish Folklore, MS 1828, 1523. See also 'Working for Farmers', *Sliabh Luacra* (June 1987), 49–52.

[145] Interviews with AI; AK, 6 Nov. 1988; AB; AA, 3 Apr. 1988.

The only exception to this was an occasional grumble about 'big fellas pushing their weight about' who had joined the Volunteers when it seemed convenient, but who were not committed to the fight.[146] Militants within the movement sometimes lamented that local officers had been chosen because of their social standing rather than their efficiency. When it came to fighting, however, the gunmen grew impatient with traditional social hierarchies:

The chap generally elected company commander or brigade commandant was the man who was the biggest farmer or biggest shopkeeper's son in the district. Great men to parade with a flag who lent their prestige and their money to the fight, but they didn't fight, and those who didn't vamoose had to be shifted out of the way when the fighting started.[147]

Tipperary activists had the same experience:

Many of the elected officers were elected during the great surge of feeling in 1918 on the conscription issue. At this stage the Volunteers were highly respectable; Parish Priests presided at meetings and a lot of people were elected to posts who were better adapted to peacetime politics than to a fighting organization . . . it was not until these were got rid of and replaced by more determined and active and more truly patriotic men that anything was done.[148]

Hardened guerrillas saw their flying columns as classless societies, united by patriotism. Florence O'Donoghue wrote from the headquarters of the 1st Southern Division that 'it is a wonderful comradeship this, of men drawn from every walk of life, from the Professor to the simple labourer, all united and contented in a noble service'. Tim O'Donoghue remembered the West Cork column as including 'men from all grades—farmers, students, tradesmen, labourers'.[149] This self-image applied to the officers as well as the rank and file. As Ernie O'Malley wryly observed in 1919: 'Often a man—a non-Volunteer—will point with pride and awe to the local President of the Sinn Fein Club; he would not dream of doing so where the local Volunteer Captain is concerned.'[150]

These opposing images of the I.R.A.—its own and that of its enemies—parallel one another in some interesting respects. Policemen, soldiers, and guerrillas all agreed that the Volunteers were mostly men with little or no stake in the country because they were too young or too poor, and that the propertied population lacked the 'moral courage' to either join or oppose them. Each side looked on the other as a mob of armed hoodlums, and themselves as the upholders of

---

[146]   Interview with AA.

[147]   O'Mahony interview with Tom Barry. See also the comments of M. J. Costello in a letter to Florence O'Donoghue, 11 Dec. 1951 (O'Donoghue Papers, MS 31, 423).

[148]   M. J. Costello to Florence O'Donoghue, 11 Dec. 1951 (NLI, O'Donoghue Papers, MS 31, 423). See also O'Malley, *On Another Man's Wound*, 129.

[149]   O'Donoghue to 'Dhilis', n.d. [1921] (O'Donoghue Papers, MS 31, 176); Tim O'Donoghue, 'Destruction of Rosscarbery R.I.C. Barrack', in *Rebel Cork's Fighting Story*, 163.

[150]   Ernie O'Malley to George Plunkett, 5 Dec. 1919 (MA, A/0747).

TABLE 18. Occupations of Volunteers in County Cork

	Officers			Men			Census	
	1917–19	1920–1	1922–3	1917–19	1920–1	1922–3	1911	1926
Sample	139	205	99	255	878	460		
Farmer/son (%)	28	27	29	29	31	18	45	41
Farm labourer (%)	4	6	8	12	12	21	25	18
Un/semi-skilled (%)	6	9	7	15	19	27		14
Skilled (%)	23	24	24	21	18	21		8
Shop asst./clerk (%)	20	13	18	9	9	7		6
Merchant/son (%)	12	12	5	7	5	3		5
Professional (%)	5	4	4	1	2	1		2
Student (%)	1	1	—	2	1	1		0.4
Other (%)	2	3	4	2	2	2		5

TABLE 19. Occupations of Volunteers' fathers in County Cork

	Officers			Men			Census	
	1917–19	1920–1	1922–3	1917–19	1920–1	1922–3	1911	1926
Sample	112	155	62	292	661	174		
Farmer (%)	54	56	52	64	61	40	45	41
Farm labourer (%)	7	5	5	8	10	10	25	18
Un/semi-skilled (%)	3	4	3	4	6	9		14
Skilled (%)	18	17	23	14	14	26		8
Shop asst./clerk (%)	—	1	2	1	0.3	1		6
Merchant (%)	15	14	10	7	7	11		5
Professional (%)	—	1	2	1	0.2	1		2
Other (%)	3	2	5	1	2	3		5

decency. Both saw the 'rabble' and corner boys as being on the other side. Everyone appealed to more or less the same labels and categories to place the I.R.A. and mark its social boundaries.

Tables 18–21 offer a statistical comparison with the perceptions examined above.[151] The rebels came from a broad range of backgrounds, and from most sectors of the Cork economy. The organization had particular success among the building trades, motor drivers, and especially drapers' assistants. Shoe- and boot-makers, living up to their international reputation for radicalism, were also prominent. Other occupations, such as fishing, were almost completely unrepresented.[152]

Artisans and tradesmen provided a solid core of support for the movement throughout the revolution, just as they had for the Fenians fifty years before.[153] In

[151] For the sources and construction of these data, see Appendix.
[152] See the National Land Bank Report on the West Carbery Co-op Fishing Society, 9 Oct. 1920 (NA, DE 2/52).
[153] See Murphy, 'The Role of Organised Labour in the Political and Economic Life of Cork City 1820–1899', 213–43.

TABLE 20. Occupations of Volunteers in Cork city

	Officers			Men			Census 1926
	1917–19	1920–1	1922–3	1917–19	1920–1	1922–3	
Sample	34	49	35	43	195	272	
Un/semi-skilled (%)	—	2	14	21	30	42	39
Skilled (%)	33	39	41	45	37	34	25
Shop asst./clerk (%)	32	35	28	20	23	15	13
Professional (%)	20	16	14	—	1	1	3
Merchant (%)	2	2	—	3	2	3	6
Student (%)	—	—	—	12	5	1	2
Other	11	6	3	—	3	4	11

TABLE 21. Occupations of Volunteers' fathers in Cork city

	Officers			Men			Census 1926
	1917–19	1920–1	1922–3	1917–19	1920–1	1922–3	
Sample	7	8	15	18	54	74	
Un/semi-skilled (%)	—	13	20	11	28	28	39
Skilled (%)	14	13	47	61	26	45	25
Shop asst./clerk (%)	14	—	13	11	13	4	13
Professional (%)	43	25	7	—	—	3	3
Merchant (%)	14	25	7	11	24	15	6
Other	14	25	7	6	9	5	11

the city, the Volunteers recruited at least a third of their members from among the skilled trades, men like Charlie and William O'Brien of Broad Lane—apprentice mechanic and hairdresser respectively—or Dan 'Sandow' Donovan and Mick Murphy, both carpenters and leading city officers. Outside the city, tradesmen were even more over-represented, consistently making up one-fifth of country units despite being less than 10 per cent of the male workforce. The influence of this radical tradition is also indicated by the fact that nearly half of the men who remained in the city I.R.A. for the Civil War had tradesmen for fathers.

Another key group of Volunteers came from the white-collar world of shops and offices. Here, the artisan's cloth cap and apron gave way to the collar and tie of the shop boy, the draper's assistant, and the junior clerk. Their employers, the shopkeepers and merchants who ruled Irish towns, rarely joined the movement, but their sons (who often worked as apprentices or assistants for their fathers) frequently did, in both the city and county.

This was a growing new class of workers, especially in country towns: very few fathers of Volunteers had held such jobs. Assistants and clerks tended to be educated, ambitious, and highly status conscious—habitual joiners of clubs, leagues, and, latterly, trade unions. Such men tended to prize their respectability as well as their political ideals, thus helping to set the social and moral tone of organized republicanism.[154] Significantly, a survey of the 1911 census returns from two towns, Bandon and Bantry, found that 53 per cent of occupied men under 30 who knew Irish were shop assistants or office clerks. Only 18 per cent were tradesmen and 9 per cent were labourers. In other words, those groups which contributed disproportionately to the leadership and ranks of the I.R.A. were also the foot soldiers of the Irish revival.

Upper middle- or upper-class people almost never joined the I.R.A. Most of the 'professionals' in the I.R.A. were teachers, and assistant or part-time teachers at that, and so were at the lower end of the middle class. There were a few ardent republicans among the Cork bourgeoisie, such as the Gallagher and Kennedy families and their circle, but there were not many others who held memberships in both the I.R.A. and tennis clubs.[155] Similarly, nearly all skilled workers in the movement were apprentices or journeymen. Only a very few, such as Sean Moylan, were masters with their own shops. Those with merchant backgrounds were generally small shopkeepers and publicans or their sons.

These upper social limits were matched by lower ones. Few I.R.A. men appear to have been unemployed or indigent, although some did lose their jobs in the depression of 1921 and after. Nor were many casual labourers to be found in their ranks. Most of those described in the tables as un- or semi-skilled had regular jobs as drivers, hotel, railway or shop porters, factory or mill workers. The new Ford's factory in Cork city was a hotbed of militant republicanism, for example, but there were very few dock workers in the Volunteers. The same was true in Cobh. While the shipyard apprentice boys, led by Mick Leahy and Seamus Fitzgerald, were notable for their radical politics, they had few comrades-in-arms among their unskilled co-workers.[156]

The chronically underemployed general labourers visible in the streets of every Cork town—the corner boys—may have voiced support for the I.R.A. and joined in on riots, but they remained outsiders to the movement.

Farming families provided more than their share of sons to the Volunteers, at least until the Civil War. As the data show, however, only half of these actually worked on their parents' land, the rest having migrated to towns to take jobs as shop assistants or clerks. As an occupation, farming was significantly and consistently under-represented in the I.R.A. This was not necessarily a reflection of the popularity of the cause as Irish farms had also been a barren recruiting ground for the British army in the Great War.[157] Farmers' sons simply avoided

---

[154] For an example of the importance of respectability to these men, see the letters regarding the Clonakilty Shop Assistants' Association in the *Eagle*, 28 Nov., 5 Dec. 1914.

[155] See Celia Saunders's Diary for 1920 (TCD, Frank Gallagher Papers, MS 10, 055).

[156] For Ford's, see the occupational entries in MA, Prisoners: Records of Charges [Cork prison]. For Cobh, see 'Sinn Feiners Employed at Haulbowline' [1918] (CO 904/23).

[157] Police reports all agree in this regard. See CI reports, East Cork, Mar. 1915 (CO 904/96); West Cork, Apr. 1915, Jan. 1916 (CO 904/99); IG report, Apr. 1915.

TABLE 22. Values of Volunteers' family farms in County Cork

(a)

	Sample	Value (%)						
		Up to £10	£11–20	£21–30	£31–40	£41–50	£51–100	£100+
Officers								
1917–19	44	16	11	23	16	18	11	5
1920–1	78	15	26	24	15	10	5	4
1922–3	17	18	24	35	6	18	—	—
Men								
1917–19	210	21	25	21	17	10	4	1
1920–1	356	26	23	18	13	9	9	1
1922–3	72	19	21	21	13	13	13	1
Census		43	20	11	7	5	9	5

(b) Median value (£)

Officers			Men			Census 1911
1917–19	1920–1	1922–3	1917–19	1920–1	1922–3	
31	24	23	22	20	25	14

TABLE 23. Average size of Volunteers' family farms in County Cork (median acreage)

Officers			Men			Census 1911
1917–19	1920–1	1922–3	1917–19	1920–1	1922–3	
57	59	48	50	57	49	34

Source: The information for this table was collected from manuscript census returns.

joining anything—unless they took up other work. Those who became shop assistants and the like remained notably reluctant to fight for Britain but became markedly more eager to fight for Ireland. This lack of enthusiasm seems to have prevailed throughout rural Cork, as farm labourers and their sons were as reticent as their employers. Of course, considering the wave of unionization and strikes which coincided with the guerrilla war, many of them might have had another sort of revolution in mind.

Tables 22 and 23 show where Volunteers were situated within the farming community.[158] Data on both the size and value of I.R.A. members' family farms have been calculated because, while the acreage of a farm did contribute to its owner's social standing, his or her income depended more on the quality of the land.

[158] Landholding data were determined from manuscript census returns for 1911 and from the records of the Irish Valuation Office. The census figures for Cork in Table 23 were derived from the *Report of the Royal Commission on Congestion in Ireland*, appendix 2 (Cd. 3786), HC 1907. Those in Table 24 were derived from the *General Report* of the 1911 census, 358–67. Average figures are expressed as medians rather than means because of the distorting effect of a small number of very large farms and estates.

TABLE 24. Position of Volunteers in farming families, County Cork

	Officers			Men		
	1917–19	1920–1	1922–3	1917–19	1920–1	1922–3
Sample	66	82	21	167	369	46
Eldest son (%)	56	51	48	35	41	39

I.R.A. family farms were well above the Cork average in value, and significantly above average in size, so that they would probably have been seen as better off than most of their neighbours. Volunteer families tended to be neither poor nor wealthy—although there were some of both—but rather were somewhere in between, with a decent house, some cattle, and the ability to educate their children.

A Volunteer's social position depended as much on his position within his household as on the size or income of the family farm. Eldest sons were most likely to inherit the whole property, and prospective heirs often had a special status.[159] Table 24 shows that over one-third of the rank and file, and around half of the officers, were the eldest resident sons in their families. The great majority of the households surveyed contained more than one male child in 1911, and most had more than two, large families being the norm in rural Ireland. And, of course, the passage of time between 1911 and the years of the revolution would reduce the number of brothers living at home, presumably increasing the chances of inheritance for the I.R.A. men described here.[160] Therefore we can reasonably conclude that ordinary Volunteers had at least an average chance of inheriting land, while officers' chances were distinctly better than average.

The most striking result shown by these figures as a whole is the extent to which Volunteers had non-agricultural occupations, and lived and worked in urban rather than rural settings. Most people in Cork (60–70 per cent) outside the city lived or worked on farms, but significantly less than half the Volunteers did (around 40 per cent of the rank and file and fewer officers). It might be argued that these figures, which are biased toward those rebels who came to official attention, may reflect the better policing of towns, in both the Tan and Civil Wars. On the other hand, if this were the case, the number of countrymen in the sample should have gone down after 1919, when the R.I.C. were withdrawn from most of their rural barracks and posts.

It would be wrong to draw too sharp a line between the town and the countryside. Kinship and commerce linked them closely together, and many shop

[159] Although this was far from always being the case. See Donna Birdwell-Pheasant, 'The Early Twentieth-Century Irish Stem Family: A Case Study from County Kerry', in Marilyn Silverman and P. H. Gulliver (eds.), *Approaching the Past: Historical Anthropology through Irish Case Studies* (New York, 1992).

[160] Although the wartime stoppage of emigration may have disrupted many individual and family plans.

assistants and general labourers were farmers' sons. Also, one did not have to be a farmer to live away from towns. Teachers, doctors, blacksmiths, carpenters, and tailors could all be found in rural areas. Even with these qualifications, however, it is clear that the Cork I.R.A.'s membership outside the city was predominantly drawn from the non-agricultural population, and that this was a consistent feature throughout the revolutionary period. And, if the very active city battalions are included, the organization's urban orientation becomes even more pronounced.

The basic occupational characteristics of the I.R.A. were shared by both officers and men, but there were also important differences. By and large, officers and their families tended to be of higher social status: somewhat more urban and better educated, white-collar workers or professionals rather than manual labourers, farmers' sons rather than farm servants, heirs to property rather than junior siblings.

The most significant distinction was that between farmers and their sons on one hand, and their employees on the other. Agricultural workers rarely became officers (although their chances increased slightly as time went on), especially in East Cork, which was the main arena of rural class conflict.[161] The farmers had a decisive edge in this respect, but did not dominate the I.R.A. as a whole. This helps account for its general neutrality during agricultural strikes, and for the fact that it usually moved against strikers only when food supplies to urban markets were threatened.

The data do not reveal any dramatic changes in the social structure of the I.R.A between 1917 and 1921. The onset of guerrilla warfare after 1919 did winnow out some officers from larger farms, and also some who were eldest sons (possibly the same people), but this did not represent a major shift in the character of the movement. During 1922 and 1923, as membership and the prospect of victory rapidly receded, farmers and white-collar workers among the rank and file dropped out in large numbers, as did many city officers who worked in shops or offices. Some manual labourers also left the movement, but a greater proportion stayed: as a result, the army became more proletarian. The size and value of officers' family farms also declined.

The greatest contrast is with the county Volunteers of 1916. Out of a sample of 171 pre-rising members, 63 per cent were farmers or farmers' sons, while a survey of 59 post-rising internees outside the city showed they were 47 per cent family farmers. Both figures are higher than for the general population, and about double the rural contribution to the I.R.A. of subsequent years. This suggests that the organization and circumstances of 1917 were far more attractive to the men of the trades and the towns: it was a new movement in its social profile as well as its politics. The city membership, on the other hand, showed

---

[161] In the Civil War, agricultural labourers made up 2% of officers in the East Riding, but 18% in the West Riding. For more detail, see my Ph.D. thesis (Trinity College, 1992).

TABLE 25. Value of family farms: the Volunteers of Behagh Company

	Up to £10	£11–20	£21–30	£31–40	£41–50	£51–100	£100+
1917–19	6	32	29	10	3	3	3
1920–1	7	27	33	13	7	3	3
1922–3	—	13	50	25	—	13	—
District average	30	30	21	10	3	3	3

Notes: This table is based on a sample of 44 company members, from a unit roll in Thomas O'Donovan, 'Behagh Company I.R.A.' (O'Donoghue Papers, MS 31, 332). Their land holdings were determined from manuscript census returns for 1911 (NA) and the records of the Irish Valuation Office. The district average is that of Manch. For a detailed study of Behagh Company, see Ch. 10.

little change, being as dominated by skilled and shop and office workers before the rising as afterwards.

Cork's physical and social geography ranged from inner city slums to mountainside sheep farms, and from the affluent farmers of its northern cattle country to the poverty-stricken fishermen of the Beara peninsula. Consequently, the Cork brigades formed a patchwork of different occupations and communities, with each company and battalion following the social contours of its area. Urban companies were dominated by tradesmen and clerks, while rural ones had mostly farmers' sons and labourers as members. A few units were dominated by a particular occupation or workplace but none were consciously divided along class lines. This did occur in Limerick, but not in Cork. Large and small farmers' sons, labourers, and others all coexisted in the same companies, as did porters, drivers, clerks, tradesmen of all kinds, and shopkeepers' sons.

A study of Behagh Company, just east of Dunmanway, illustrates this point. Located in an area of average wealth for West Cork, this was an entirely rural unit, three-quarters of whose members were farmers' sons, along with a few labourers and artisans. Table 25 shows the value of their families' land. The Behagh Volunteers followed the general Cork pattern by being, on average, slightly better off than their neighbours and by largely excluding the worst off among them. The officers (none of whom were labourers), whose farms were valued at £19, £32, £34, and £74, were, again typically, a notch above their men. Still, there was considerable variation within the unit and its members were fairly representative of the community as a whole.

Regional differences within the organization were not as sharp as might be expected, and not nearly as great as in the general population. The I.R.A. in the more rural west was only marginally more farm-based than in the east (although the gap widened in the Civil War), and had roughly the same proportion of clerks, shop assistants, and teachers—and sometimes more. This solid core of support among tradesmen and white-collar workers in West Cork, despite their relatively minor presence in the economy, underlines the importance of these classes to the movement. On the other hand, western units appear to have been

TABLE 26. Occupations of Volunteers in provincial Ireland

	Officers			Men			Census	
	1917–19	1920–1	1922–3	1917–19	1920–1	1922–3	1911	1926
Sample	680	462	150	1,437	1,984	1,089		
Farmer/son (%)	27	22	21	40	29	13	36	49
Farm labourer (%)	5	4	8	11	12	19	22	17
Un/semi-skilled (%)	4	5	9	9	15	27		10
Skilled (%)	23	26	28	16	19	23		9
Shop asst./clerk (%)	19	22	19	12	14	11		4
Professional (%)	9	7	7	1	4	2		2
Merchant/son (%)	10	11	4	7	5	2		4
Student (%)	1	0.3	—	1	1	1		1
Other (%)	3	4	3	2	2	3		4

Note: These figures cover the whole of Ireland except for the Dublin urban area.

somewhat more egalitarian, particularly in rural areas, perhaps reflecting the much lower level of class conflict and stratification there.

How did the Cork Volunteers compare with those of the rest of Ireland? Table 26 confirms the I.R.A.'s urban bias, as well as the persistent gap between farmers' sons and their employees. Skilled and white-collar workers formed a large part of the membership everywhere, especially among the officers. The only exception to this was the Dublin Brigade (not included in the table), which did have a strong labouring component at all levels. Interestingly, the highly rural province of Connaught resembles West Cork in its dependence on teachers and townsmen for leadership.[162]

Using different methods, and looking only at the organization in parts of four counties as of July 1921, Joost Augusteijn has also concluded that the I.R.A. recruited widely, but not from the highest or lowest ranks of society, and that 'active members . . . had a predominantly urban background'. His further suggestion that 'farmers . . . formed the bulk of I.R.A. members in all provincial areas' conflicts with the data presented here, but this may partly be explained by the rural bias in his samples and the activist bias in mine.[163] The only other intensive analysis of the social composition of the Volunteers comes from David Fitzpatrick's study of Clare. His findings show a parallel, although slighter, gap between officers and men in occupation and status, but reveal an overwhelmingly rural and farm-based rank and file, unsurprising in such an intensely rural county. He also detects the emergence of a more proletarian, less affluent group of fighters, with fewer eldest sons from smaller farms, during the guerrilla campaign of 1920–1.[164] Such a shift cannot be detected in Cork until 1922.

[162] See Peter Hart, 'The Social Structure of the Irish Republican Army, 1916–1923', *Historical Journal* (March 1999).

[163] Augusteijn, *From Public Defiance to Guerrilla Warfare*, 353.

[164] Fitzpatrick, *Politics and Irish Life*, 202–4, 222–4.

TABLE 27. Occupations of National Army recruits in Cork

	County		City	
	All ranks 1922–3	Census 1926	All Ranks 1922–3	Census 1926
Sample	1,361		910	
Farmer/son (%)	4	41	—	—
Farm labourer (%)	37	18	—	—
Un/semi-skilled (%)	33	14	57	39
Skilled (%)	16	8	28	25
Shop asst./clerk (%)	5	6	11	13
Merchant/son (%)	1	5	1	6
Professional (%)	0.3	2	0.2	3
Student (%)	1	0.4	0.5	2
Other (%)	3	5	3	11

Note: These samples include every person from Cork with a specified occupation who enlisted in the army before May 1923 (MA, Enlistment and Discharge Register, vols. 1–31). They do not include those pro-Treaty I.R.A. members who joined informally.

How did the Volunteers of the I.R.A. compare with the men of the National Army? Table 27 shows the social backgrounds of Free State soldiers from Cork. The men of the National Army in Cork (the majority of whom were also recruited in the county[165]) were mostly urban and unskilled. Most local recruits came from Cork city and the East Riding. Almost none described themselves as farmers' sons: the farming community shunned the Civil War as much as it had the Great War. Thus, compared with the British and Irish armies, the I.R.A. actually held an extraordinary attraction for the young men of the farms. The main difference being, perhaps, that one could join the I.R.A. and remain at home, where a son's labour might make the difference between a good year and a bad year.

These statistics show the Volunteers to have been more or less correct in their self-assessment. They were neither very poor nor very well off, but came from the central stratum of 'plain people' in between. The egalitarian image was only partly true, as few unskilled workers became officers, but the organization as a whole was predominantly lower class.

Countrymen may well have been correct in viewing towns as the centres of resistance, but they were wrong in thinking that townsmen did not also contribute to the guerrilla war. Towns produced strong factions of rebels, home rulers, and loyalists, as the early street fights between Sinn Feiners and 'Mollies' showed. This polarization within towns may well have helped mobilize and radicalize the Volunteers, while the presence of hostile civilians, as well as police and military garrisons, may have forced them to go on the run earlier and in greater numbers than their rural comrades.

[165] See the Army Census of Nov. 1922 (MA) which details the personnel of each post and their origins.

TABLE 28. Urban and rural companies in North Cork, 1921

	Reliable (%)	In gaol	On the run	Active
Urban	52	30	12	16
Rural	63	11	5	10

Source: Cork 2 Coy. returns, Feb.–June 1921 (O'Donoghue Papers, MS 31, 223).

We can test this notion in the case of the North Cork Brigade in the Tan War. Company returns from four battalions in the spring of 1921 are assembled in Table 28, giving figures for the 'reliability' and activity of urban and rural units. Urban volunteers were less reliable, just as countrymen suspected, but they also faced greater risks. Consequently, those who were deemed reliable were far more likely to be on active service, on the run, or in gaol than their rural comrades.

I.R.A. fighters were partly right in seeing the farming class as reluctant republicans, but the mantle of rebellion did not thereby fall upon their employees. Agricultural labourers were even less prominent than farmers until the Civil War. Opposing stereotypes, on the other hand, barely survive statistical comparisons. Policemen and other observers were correct in identifying shop assistants as a major republican constituency, but the constant references to 'town labourers' were greatly exaggerated. The I.R.A. did not enrol corner boys. The organization was not nearly as 'proletarian' as was often imagined, nor were its members usually 'idle'. We must, by and large, take them at their own estimation: as plain, respectable, ordinary men.

There is, however, an element of truth in others' estimation of the Volunteers' social worth. The widespread belief that these were 'persons of no consequence' was based not just on class, but on age as well. They were not just 'upstarts' but 'young upstarts'. Nor did I.R.A. men think of themselves only (or even mainly) in terms of their occupations. They joined as shop assistants, carpenters, and farmers' sons—but also as young men, brothers, friends, and schoolmates. It is to these questions of youth, family, and rebellion that we next turn.

8

Youth and Rebellion

At six, when the deserted city was handed over, the masquerade began. Hundreds of boys and girls, escaping from dreary homes, put on their best clothes, their best manner. For a few hours at least they were subject to no authority, audacious, successful, invincible . . . It was their compensation for a dull day in shop or office, the dreary homes, the brutal parents, and the more hopeless these, the fiercer was their appetite for sensation, for masquerade.

(Frank O'Connor, *Dutch Interior*)

My fight for Irish freedom was of the same order as my fight for other sorts of freedom . . . If it was nothing else, it was a brief escape from tedium and frustration to go out the country roads on summer evenings, slouching along in knee breeches and gaiters, hands in the pockets of one's trench-coat and hat pulled over one's right eye.

(Frank O'Connor, *An Only Child*)

'Youth is asserting itself in this Ireland of ours as it never did within living memory of the oldest inhabitant,' observed Mrs William O'Brien from her vantage point in Mallow. 'The young have it all their own way in Ireland.'[1] To her, the most novel feature of the rise of republicanism was the emergence of a new generation and a new man: 'the type of youth we have got to know of late, determined, steady, with a drilled uprightness of bearing . . . a Crusader of modern days.'[2]

This praise echoed the Sinn Fein rhetoric of regeneration and the promise of a new politics sweeping away the old corruption. According to the *Southern Star* (of Skibbereen), 'the moral and intellectual tone of the generation just growing into manhood is noticeably superior to that of the preceding generation'.[3] Erskine Childers called the Irish Volunteers 'the soul of a new Ireland, taken as a whole the finest young men in the country, possessed with an almost religious enthusiasm for their cause, sober, clean-living, self-respecting'.[4]

The enemies of the I.R.A. were also struck by the extreme youth of its volunteers. These observers, however, saw not the Baden-Powellesque vision of sober and clean-limbed youth so dear to republican hearts, but rather an irresponsible

---

[1] Mrs William [Sophie] O'Brien, *In Mallow* (London, 1920), 5.   [2] Ibid. 65, 68.
[3] *Star*, 26 Apr. 1919.
[4] Childers, 'The Irish Revolution', 8 (Childers Papers, MS 7808/29).

and immoral subversion of proper order and authority. Many—policemen and others—thought that this rebellion of 'mere boys' was directed as much against parents and elders as against British rule.[5]

This idea first became a common theme of police and press reports during the by-election campaigns of 1917, beginning with North Roscommon in February.[6] Dubbed a 'women and childrens' election', Count Plunkett's victory as an abstentionist candidate was widely attributed to the activities of those too young to vote.[7] Here as well the nefarious influence of the radical 'young curates' was detected pitted against that of their parish priests, just as it had been seen behind the 1916 rebels.[8] Roscommon also produced the first stories that 'young members of the farmers' families used stringent intimidation on their elders'.[9]

The generational divide had apparently widened even further by May, when the next contest was held in South Longford. One local newspaper warned Irish Party voters beforehand that 'some of the young members of your household may put obstacles in your way'[10] while the *Irish Times* reported that:

the enthusiasm of the young element has reached such a point as to cause family friction in many households. Some refuse to help their fathers on the land unless they exact a promise to support Mr. McGuinness [the Sinn Fein candidate], while daughters decline to pursue their domestic duties without laying similar toll.[11]

These reports of the intimidation of fathers by their children continued unabated through to the general election of December 1918. As for the latter event (when, for the first time, 'boys' could vote alongside their parents), one breathless account had it that: 'the young people (egged on by the curates!) ran it and actually, in many cases locked the old people into their homes so that they might not be able to attend the booths.'[12]

However exaggerated, such claims reflected a widely shared perception of Sinn Fein—and especially the Volunteers—as a youth movement, and an almost equally widely shared apprehension of what this meant. As early as June 1917, the inspector general of the R.I.C. felt able to conclude that 'the movement appears to have captured all the young Nationalists'. A chorus of county inspectors agreed

[5]   IG Monthly Report, Mar. 1918 (CO 904/105).

[6]   The November 1916 election in West Cork, although it involved some republicans, was not apparently notable for its youth involvement.

[7]   Miceal O'Callaghan, *For Ireland and Freedom: Roscommon's Contribution to the Fight for Independence* (Boyle, n.d.), 11.

[8]   Ibid. 8; *Report of the Royal Commission on the Rebellion*, 30. See also IG Monthly Report, May 1917 (CO 904/103).

[9]   J. M. Wilson, notes of tour, 27–8 Mar. 1917 (D989/A/9/7).

[10]   Quoted in *Irish Times*, 7 May 1917.

[11]   8 May, 1917. See also CI Monthly Report, Longford, May 1917 (CO 904/103) and J. M. Wilson report, n.d. (D989/A/9/7).

[12]   Ussher, 'True Story', 25 (Representative Church Body Library). See also *Irish Times*, 19 Dec. 1918 and CI Monthly Report, Mayo, Nov. 1918 (CO 904/107).

with him. Republicanism was 'on the rise among the younger population' in Fermanagh and 'advancing among the mass of young people' in King's County as well as among 'the younger sections of the people' in Kilkenny. Elsewhere, Volunteers were seen as the 'younger and more irresponsible classes' or 'the young bloods in the country'. South Tipperary was 'pervaded with young men who show hostility to any form of control'.[13]

The fear of losing control was uppermost in the minds of many in Cork as well, and was the keynote of quite a number of warnings issued at this time. Few remained as sanguine as Mr O'Brien of the Youghal Rural District Council, who breezily advised: 'Let the young hot-heads run their course, which he didn't believe would be a very long one.' In September 1917, for example, the chairman of the Fermoy United Irish League 'appealed to the delegates, lest their sons and daughters may be engulfed in the whirlpool of Sinn Feinism'. 'A Troubled Parent' wrote a letter to the *Cork Examiner* in January 1918 to say that 'our younger folk . . . are growing uncontrollable'.[14] Later that year Edith Somerville wrote about the decline of youthful deference (no more doffing or touching of caps) and sounded an ominous note:

In this far western parish 'ourselves' [the Volunteers] have begun to feel important . . . Not only have the Government and the Police been derided and defied by meetings and drillings but the parish priest has been set at naught: and this, in a primitive part of Ireland, is a matter neither to be lightly dismissed or desired. It is easy to smile at the green caps and the flappers, but the future is in their hands.[15]

Elsewhere in Munster, in the garrison town of 'Karrigeen':

For the old it began to be a queer time . . . Houses began to be divided against themselves. The Sinn Fein club came into being. In time there was drilling. There was enough to make fathers uneasy: they complained to one another. The elders of Karrigeen were troubled because their day was ending.[16]

By 1920 the situation had been transformed into one of complete domination by the young militants, 'the youth of the country', who held 'in contempt the constituted law' and were 'largely imbued with revolutionary ideas'. 'The old people do not count.'[17] An English visitor to Cork in 1921 was 'repeatedly assured . . . that militant Sinn Fein was a young man's movement exclusively— that the parents disapproved, indeed begged their sons not to participate in political activity'.[18] Some priests tried to tell the fathers of their parishes to curb their

[13] CI Monthly Reports, Fermanagh, May 1917; King's, May 1917; Kilkenny, May 1917; Donegal, June 1918; Kerry, Aug. 1918; Tipperary (South Riding), Jan. 1919 (CO 904/103–7).
[14] *Examiner*, 9 June, 20 Sept. 1917, 24 Jan. 1918.
[15] Edith Somerville, 'Ourselves Alone' (Somerville and Ross Papers).
[16] Neil Kevin, *I Remember Karrigeen* (London, 1944), 42–3. Both the author's and the town's names are pseudonyms—for Don Boyne and Templemore (Tipperary), respectively.
[17] CI Monthly Reports, East Cork, Oct. 1920 and West Cork, Jan. 1920 (CO 904/113, 111).
[18] 'Life in Cork—An English Officer's Impressions', *The Times*, 18 May 1921.

sons, but to little effect.[19] Surveying his district in 1921, a Skibbereen judge concluded that:

The farmers themselves are anxious to settle down and want peace, but their sons won't let them, and the sooner they get rid of their sons the better for themselves, because the country is going to ruin by the actions of irresponsible boys.[20]

Similar things were being said all over Ireland. Everywhere, it seemed, 'the younger generation have taken everything into their own hands'.[21]

British soldiers and policemen brought in to put down the rebellion were of much the same opinion, and were surprised to find themselves fighting 'just youths'.[22] They thought of their opponents as 'young green and inexperienced', 'callow youths who do not really realise what they are doing', and 'f——ing schoolboys'.[23] A battalion commander in East Cork sounded the familiar refrain: 'the youth of Ireland is out of hand and the priests have lost much of their power.'[24]

Farmers and other employers found that their labourers, assistants, and apprentices took time off to parade, train, or fight and still demanded their pay. Sons deserted their fathers' fields and shops. Merchants had to keep them supplied. Householders had to give them food and lodging. Ned Buckley, the poet of Knocknagree, summed up the feelings of many of his generation when he wrote of the social impact of the revolution:[25]

> Then parent and priest may as well be dumb,
> Their precepts were all ignored;
> And who can tell when the time will come
> That their prestige will be restored;
> Then scant was the work of the plough or spade,
> And employers kept silent beaks,
> For the boy was boss and the Mistress maid
> In the time of the ten-foot pikes.

This perceived sense of restlessness among the young was frequently attributed to the stoppage of emigration after 1914, and to the frustration felt by would-be migrants. 'The young men who in the ordinary course would have emigrated . . . have had to remain home and are the source of all the trouble. With emigration re-opened and facilitated, a good deal of the trouble would disappear': so believed the county inspector for West Cork.[26]

---

[19] See *Eagle*, 26 Mar. 1921; Edith Somerville to Ethel Smyth, 3 Oct. 1922 (Somerville and Ross Papers, Lot 878).   [20] *Eagle*, 5 Feb. 1921.

[21] CI Monthly Report, Cavan, Sept. 1921 (CO 904/116).

[22] Pte. J. Swindlehurst Diary, 28 Feb. 1921 (IWM, P36).

[23] Duff, *Sword for Hire*, 85; F. [a staff officer in Cork City], 'Notes on Ireland 1920' (Cockerill Papers, MS 10, 606); Auxiliary cadet quoted by Mick O'Sullivan (O'Malley Papers, P17b/108).

[24] Anon., 'Appreciation of the Situation in Ireland' (Cockerill Papers, MS 10, 606).

[25] Ned Buckley, 'The Time of the Ten Foot Pikes', n.d., in Clifford and Lane (eds.), *Ned Buckley's Poems*, 45–6.

[26] CI Monthly Report, West Cork, Dec. 1918 (CO 904/107).

There were a few isolated cases where thwarted emigrants turned to the Volunteers in anger[27] but there is no documentary or statistical evidence to support this idea. While larger numbers of young men might have facilitated I.R.A. recruitment (and compounded intrafamily resentment), the British armed forces had absorbed most of this 'excess' population. Nor did counties with higher emigration rates before the war produce more active rebel units. And when restrictions were removed and normal traffic was resumed in 1920–1, violence continued unabated.[28] Committed revolutionaries in Cork usually remained committed through the Tan and Civil Wars. Very few active guerrillas left the county until after the 1923 ceasefire.[29]

I.R.A. members were highly conscious of their youth. Being part of 'the younger generation as they called themselves' was central to their sense of identity and with youth came nobility and purity: 'all that was brave and virile, all that was chivalrous, unselfish and highspirited in the best of the young manhood of the nation.'[30]

It was young people who embraced 'the Cause' and 'the older crowd' who opposed them.[31] As one Bandon veteran told me, it was 'the old fellas—the farmers' who were the main obstacle to the movement in his area. A Bantry I.R.A. man recalled that 'our fathers and mothers were more or less against us at the time, but we all joined up, all the neighbours, all the young fellas'. In the Clonakilty area, 'people at home told us we were foolish when we joined the I.R.A. That feeling pervaded among the older generation.'[32] Such was the domination of the movement by the young that one organizer in Charleville felt it necessary to appeal to the middle-aged to join Sinn Fein clubs.[33]

Volunteers in neighbouring counties had the same experience. In the East Limerick Brigade, for example, 'all the older people and the Fenians even remained loyal to the Irish Party; and all their children went into the Irish Volunteers.'[34] Ernie O'Malley found this to be a recurring problem in his organizing work. 'The elder people thought I was mad, as they had very little sympathy

[27] See CI Monthly Report, West Cork, Mar. 1916 (CO 904/99); *Report of the Royal Commission on the Rebellion*, 77 (in reference to a case in Galway).

[28] There is some evidence in any case that the sort of men who usually emigrated were not the sort of people who usually joined the Volunteers. In 1914, for example, 68% of male emigrants described themselves as labourers, as opposed to 7% who were farmers and 4% clerks and accountants. *Emigration Statistics (Ireland) 1914* (Cd. 7883), 12–13.

[29] For other counties, see letter from Dan Breen (in Chicago), 3 Feb. 1922 (DE 2/416); Michael Collins to Eamon de Valera, 29 June 1921 (DE 2/446); US Military Attaché to A/G, 28 Nov. 1924 and Mil. Att. to A/G, 16 Feb. 1925, with a report that the entire East Waterford flying column had emigrated together (O'Malley Papers, P17a/53).

[30] *Irish Times*, 9 Mar. 1918; obituary of Liam Hoare, captain of Gurtroe Company [Cork 1] (O'Donoghue Papers, MS 31, 444).   [31] Interview with AI.

[32] Interview with AE, 19 Nov. 1989; interviews with Mr O'Driscoll and John L. O'Sullivan (RTE Archives, A2790). See also Daniel O'Leary, *Kilmeen and Castleventry Parish Co. Cork* (Jerry Beechinor, 1975), 86.   [33] *Examiner*, 13 May 1919.

[34] Bill Carty (O'Malley Papers, P17b/129).

with us . . . At times the elders of the family, through the sons, insisted on my removal.'[35] As late as November 1921, the adjutant of the 2nd Southern Division was appealing to Sinn Fein 'to strengthen the moral right of the I.R.A., by counteracting the general opinion that we are schoolboys out for a holiday'.[36]

The Treaty split brought out the same attitudes and language on all sides, although in a more muted form. Ted O'Sullivan described Treaty supporters in West Cork as 'older Volunteers and members of Sinn Fein who were not fighting men'.[37] Michael Collins dismissed his erstwhile comrades as 'these young irresponsibles' while in his home constituency in Cork, according to one supporter, 'highly placed officers of the [anti-Treaty] I.R.A. have informed me that they will not permit their fathers etc. to vote in the coming election'.[38] In Castletownshend, Edith Somerville and her friends continued to blame the troubles on youthful anarchy: 'The present generation, boys and girls alike, are poisoned and poisonous. Even the priests have to acknowledge themselves helpless and beaten by these brutalised, depraved boys of the so-called "Army." ' It was still 'the older people' against 'the young ones'.[39]

The Volunteers' response to their elders' opposition was summed up by one Cobh veteran who said simply, and with great good humour: 'we didn't consult them.'[40] This man's cheerful disregard for his parents' opinion was typical of the ex-I.R.A. men I talked to. Nearly all took undisguised pleasure in remembering their defiance of their fathers (and clerical and political father-figures). In one well-known tale from North Cork (related to me twice), a Volunteer turned in his father to make him prove his patriotism. The rebels clearly revelled in their newfound power and freedom; 'eventually one's people had not the slightest say in matters nor did they attempt it.'[41] At the Slippery Rock ambush near Ballyvourney, for instance, 'An ould lad came out to scold his son for not helping in saving hay' but was quickly sent packing by 'the boys' when the shooting started.[42]

This story illustrates how the revolution had turned these men's social world upside down. For once 'the boys' were in charge. To many at the time this radicalization and rise to power of previously unknown young men represented the real revolution, with the battle lines being drawn between generations rather than classes, communities, or parties. 'It was the battle of youth and the New

---

[35]   Cormac K. H. O'Malley (ed.), 'Ernie O'Malley Autobiographical Letter', *Cathair na Mart*, 9/1 (1989), 7. I am grateful to Joost Augusteijn for this reference.

[36]   Adj., 2nd South. Div. to A/G, 17 Nov. 1921 (O'Malley Papers, P17a/101).

[37]   Ted O'Sullivan (O'Malley Papers, P17b/108).

[38]   *Examiner*, 14 Mar. 1922; J. J. Crowley to Collins, 27 Jan. 1922 (NA, DE2/486). He received a similar report from western Ireland: Sean Cawley to Collins, n.d. (MA, A/0971).

[39]   Somerville to Ethel Smyth, 2 May, 20 Apr. 1922 (Somerville and Ross Papers, Lot 878).

[40]   Interview with AJ.

[41]   'Ernie O'Malley Autobiographical Letter', 7.

[42]   Jamie Minihan (O'Malley Papers, P17b/111). Another version of this story is told in O'Suilleabhain, *Mountainy Men*, 84. See also Uinseann MacEoin, *Survivors* (Dublin, 1980), 217.

TABLE 29. Ages of Volunteers in Cork

	Officers			Men		
	1917–19	1920–1	1922–3	1917–19	1920–1	1922–3
Sample	225	306	147	571	1,298	435
Under 20 (%)	20	10	3	29	25	20
20–9 (%)	59	60	69	55	58	64
30–9 (%)	16	25	22	13	14	13
40–9 (%)	2	4	4	2	2	2
50–9 (%)	3	1	1	1	—	—
Mean age	25	28	29	23	25	26

Note: These figures include both the city and the county. For the sources of this data, see Appendix.

Ireland versus the old men and the old servitude . . . it was a fine thing to be young during the years that followed.'[43]

Table 29 confirms the youthfulness of the I.R.A.'s membership. The new men of 1917 and 1918 were a few years younger than the rebels-in-waiting of 1916, whose mean age was 27.[44] The movement aged gradually thereafter, with its membership concentrated in the early and mid-twenties. A Volunteer over 30 was generally considered an 'old man'.[45] Officers were a few years older than their men on average, losing their adolescent fringe by the onset of the Civil War. This was due to the fact that almost all new officers were drawn from the active rank and file, rather than from outside (Tom Barry being a rare exception). The typical Volunteer also aged over the course of the struggle, although not quite so rapidly. The rank and file did retain a significant—albeit declining—proportion of teenagers, suggesting a fairly constant intake of new recruits. Many of these were graduates of the Fianna, the republican boy scouts. Members in their fifties also grew scarcer. These were probably old I.R.B. men who had joined the Volunteers before the war and who hung on after the 1916 rising before retiring or being shunted aside into Sinn Fein. Statistics for Ireland as a whole, presented in Table 30, confirm the Cork pattern.

The guerrillas of the 1920s were, for the most part, the children of the 1890s. They were the beneficiaries of many years of peaceful prosperity before the Great War changed the political and social landscape, preventing emigration and threatening conscription. Theirs was a martial generation all over Europe. Millions of their contemporaries—tens of thousands of their friends and neighbours—died fighting for their countries.

The vast majority of Volunteers in the 1917–23 period were unmarried. Being single was hardly unusual in young Irish men, but I.R.A. members were

[43]   Patrick Kavanagh, *The Green Fool* (Harmondsworth, 1975), 105, 108.
[44]   Based on a sample of 147 members.
[45]   Interviews with AA, AC, AE, and AI.

TABLE 30. Ages of Volunteers in Ireland

	Officers			Men		
	1917–19	1920–1	1922–3	1917–19	1920–1	1922–3
Sample	675	561	335	2,052	2,722	1,409
Under 20 (%)	14	11	3	23	20	17
20–9 (%)	65	68	73	59	68	75
30–9 (%)	20	19	20	14	9	7
40–9 (%)	2	2	3	3	2	1
50–9 (%)	1	1	—	1	0.1	0.1
Median age	25	25	26	23	24	24

Note: Sources are listed in the Appendix. Ages were calculated as of 1918, 1920, and 1922.

unusually celibate (at least in the demographic sense) even by Irish standards. Twenty per cent of occupied men aged 25–9 in the Irish Free State were married in 1926.[46] Out of a sample of 572 I.R.A. prisoners in 1923 whose marital status is known, 27—less than 5 per cent—were married.[47] And, since a higher proportion of the population was married in urban areas (32 per cent), where most active Volunteers lived, the actual celibacy gap between them and their peers was probably even greater. A few older officers, such as Terence MacSwiney, Tomas MacCurtain, Sean O'Hegarty, Dan Corkery, and Sean Moylan, did have their own families and the percentage of married men grew slightly after the Truce as I.R.A. weddings were a fairly common occurrence in the summer of 1921 (Tom Barry's being the most prominent). On the other hand, some older married men probably dropped out after 1916, and again after 1918. So the proportion of Volunteers who were married in 1920 and 1921 must have been close to nil. Being young and single meant having fewer responsibilities and less to risk—and perhaps it also meant having more to rebel against. In some cases, of course, celibacy was a consequence of activism as well as a possible contributing factor.

Free State army recruits from Cork were more or less contemporary with their foes although, as Table 31 shows, they did attract a greater percentage of the very youthful.

The generational conflict embedded within the revolution was a major force in shaping the social perceptions of the I.R.A. It is notable how often the standard labels applied to the Volunteers—'rustic', 'half-educated', 'rough'—had 'young' attached to them, just as the republicans' self-image of cleanliness and decency was bound up with their own sense of youthfulness. The corrupt or spineless opponents of rebellion were not just farmers, shopkeepers, or politicians, they were also 'the old fellas'. And if the I.R.A. was seen by their enemies

[46] Robert E. Kennedy, *The Irish: Emigration, Marriage, and Fertility* (Berkeley, Calif., 1973), 169.
[47] I.R.A. prison and internment camp rolls, 1923 (MA, A/1135, 1137, 1138).

TABLE 31. Ages of National Army recruits in Cork

	All ranks 1922–3
Sample	2,107
Under 20 (%)	25
20–9 (%)	56
30–9 (%)	13
40–9 (%)	5
50–9 (%)	0.1
Mean age	25

Note: This sample includes every recruit from Cork who enlisted before May 1923 (MA, National Army Enlistment and Discharge Register, vols. 1–31).

as 'insignificant' upstarts with no stake in the country, this was as much a product of their age as of their class.[48] One's social status depended as much on one as the other.

The place of young men in early twentieth-century Cork society was one of strict subordination to fathers, employers, and priests. The sons of farmers, shopkeepers, and tradesmen usually worked without pay and owned no property. They had little or no control over their labour nor any say in work or family affairs. 'It goes without saying that the father exercises his control over the whole activity of "the boy".'[49] One such apprentice described his life as follows:

I served my time four years learning the trade of shop assistant to my father, and I don't think I ever qualified in his eyes, for he was that discerning. The slightest fault would mean a good thumping, and you were expected to be twenty-four hours on your feet and always smiling. I learnt a bit about everything and was master of nothing.[50]

Farms or businesses generally passed from father to son when the parents died or decided to retire, and by that time the son would often be well advanced in years. The other main badge of adulthood, marriage, generally followed this inheritance so that 'boy'hood was as much a matter of estate as of age: 'you can be a boy here forever as long as the old fellow is still alive.'[51] Unmarried, unpropertied Volunteers might be deemed 'boys' well into their twenties or even their thirties. Ernie O'Malley retained a vivid impression of the rural families he encountered:

[48] The leading rebel in the Castlehaven parish, for example, was known interchangeably as 'the I.R.A. Pup' and 'Captain Boots' (note in 1922 volume of Edith Somerville Diary (Somerville and Ross Papers)). [49] Arensberg and Kimball, *Family and Community*, 55.
[50] Somerville-Large, *Cappaghglass*, 50. [51] Arensberg, *The Irish Countryman*, 66.

Home life was terribly strict. The men worked like mules and the women like slaves. The boys got an odd sixpence or shilling the day they went to market . . . At the beginning great courage was needed to enable a man to leave home for some hours in the busy season, to leave it for a day was wonderful and, at any time one chose, nothing short of marvellous. I think great credit should be given to the young lads who risked parental displeasure and loss of inheritance by leaving home despite their parents.[52]

For shop assistants, 'the authority of the shopkeeper is not unlike that which he experienced under the supervision of his father'; 'the older people didn't trust the young to do anything right . . . we were only the young fellows, and I'd say that was the general rule'.[53] Many of Siobhan Lankford's schoolmates 'settled into business in Cork and Mallow in drapery and grocery houses. The apprenticeship to business in these firms was hard, and many years elapsed before the workers got the conditions and wages their work entitled them to.'[54] Few shop apprentices received a salary. Even when they became accredited or qualified, and perhaps moved into their own 'digs', their pay remained low or non-existent and they were kept under strict discipline.[55]

Other apprentices led similar lives. When Donncadh MacCurtain was apprenticed at 19 to a Duhallow carpenter, he shared a bed with two other boys in the master's house for three and a half years. They got no pay apart from a half-crown at Christmas so 'we had no money for pubs, pictures or dances'. Farm labourers' employers sometimes 'treated you like a dog more or less'.[56]

Nor were these young men of no property allowed to vote until the expansion of the franchise in 1918. Hence 'the boys', particularly those in their teens and early twenties, formed a sort of underclass without power or authority. As one Dunmanway veteran put it, remembering his early years, 'the young crowd didn't count for anything'.[57]

Fathers generally exercised their near total authority from a great emotional and social distance. Close bonds between fathers and sons were rare, even when they worked together. The two generations inhabited quite separate social worlds. Sean O'Faolain said of his father: 'I never knew him as a person, only as a type.'[58] Children were reared almost solely by their mothers, in a domestic

[52] 'Ernie O'Malley Autobiographical Letter', 9.

[53] Arensberg and Kimball, *Family and Community*, 349; Somerville-Large, *Cappaghglass*, 50.

[54] Lankford, *The Hope and the Sadness*, 69.

[55] Arensberg and Kimball, *Family and Community*, 355–6. See also *Examiner*, 31 July 1917, 22 Oct. 1918, 29 May 1919 for details of shop assistants' lives.

[56] *Seanchas Duthalla* (1986), 98; Somerville-Large, *Cappaghglass*, 245. See also Arensberg and Kimball, *Family and Community*, 246–8; Michael O'Connell, 'The Craft of the Cooper in Clonakilty', *Seanchas Chairbre* (Dec. 1982); 'Working for Farmers', *Sliabh Luacra* (June 1987) and Seamus Murphy, *Stone Mad* (London, 1966) for the life of a young stone-carver.

[57] Interview with AE.

[58] Interview with Sean O'Faolain (RTE Archives, B1179).

culture in which the fathers rarely participated.[59] In so far as children learned their nationalism at home, it was most likely to be their mothers who taught it to them.

It is probably for this reason that so many I.R.A. men have specified their mothers, or their mothers' families, as their primary domestic influence. When asked where he got his patriotism, Tom Kelleher of the West Cork Brigade replied: 'I definitely got it from my mother.'[60] Some 'hard men' had even harder mothers. When Billy Pilkington went to trial in Sligo in April 1919, 'the defendant's mother entered the court, and addressing the figure in the dock, asked "Did you give bail?" The defendant replied "no." "Good" said the mother, "If you did I would not let you into the house again." '[61]

Mothers provided more than just inspiration, however. Many became active revolutionaries in support of their sons, running messages, guns, and safe houses. Hannah O'Brien of Broad Lane was one. 'She wore a long fur coat underneath which she wore the bandoliers with bullets etc. from the boat to the dumping place.' Con Neenan's mother, from the south side of the city, was another:

My mother was wonderful. She was outstanding. My mother was so good that in the Tan War—we had an aunt living in Blackpool on the other side of Cork City; her husband had died, so it was a safe place for putting things. My mother would take a rifle under her shawl and cross the whole city, which was quite a job . . . She was outstanding; a fighting type.[62]

Fathers, on the other hand, were often political as well as emotional outsiders. Apart from a very few Sinn Fein leaders, such as George Power senior in Fermoy, they were almost never involved. It is noticeable, for instance, that Con Neenan's aunt's house was safe *because* his uncle was no longer there. Similarly, when Liam Deasy was on the run and penniless, it was his mother rather than his father who slipped him half a crown. In Frank O'Connor's family, his joining the I.R.A. was 'all too much for poor Father . . . Mother's sympathies were entirely with the revolution, and he would have been more furious still if he had known that not long after she was doing odd errands herself, carrying revolvers and despatches.'[63] And when Mitchelstown's unfortunate stationmaster was arrested in December 1920 because of his family's activities, he vainly protested that 'he could not be responsible for his wife and daughters'.[64]

---

[59] Arensberg and Kimball, *Family and Community*, 53–63, 229–30; Patrick McNabb, 'Social Structure', in Jeremiah Newman (ed.), *The Limerick Rural Survey 1958–1964* (Tipperary, 1964), iv. 229–30; Thomas M. Wilson, 'Culture and Class among the "Large" Farmers of Eastern Ireland', *American Ethnologist* (Nov. 1988), 683. Both Frank O'Connor and Sean O'Faolain give a very similar picture of growing up in Cork city: see O'Connor, *An Only Child* and O'Faolain, *Vive Moi!* The I.R.A. veterans whom I asked about their parents almost all described their relationships in much the same way.

[60] Quoted in MacEoin, *Survivors*, 216. Again, most of my interviewees gave the same answer.

[61] *Irish Times*, 8 Apr. 1919.

[62] Marie O'Donoghue Diary (for more on Hannah O'Brien, see the Introduction); MacEoin, *Survivors*, 236.   [63] O'Connor, *An Only Child*, 202–3.

[64] Mitchelstown Detachment War Diary, 31 Jan. 1921 (Buffs Regimental Museum, Canterbury).

Interestingly enough, a study of 524 Cork Volunteers reveals that, according to their 1911 census returns, 23 per cent had mothers at the head of their households (as compared to 19 per cent in Cork as a whole).[65] This heavy incidence of absent fathers in I.R.A. members' backgrounds (presumably even higher by 1917) also points to the role of parental authority in shaping political involvement.

As adolescents emerged from the domestic sphere of influence and became workers and young adults, they did not immediately enter the older men's social and political circles. 'The subordination of the sons does not gradually come to an end. It is a constant.'[66] The informal village or town 'parliaments' which led public opinion and dominated the political arena were the exclusive province of the established males:

When groups form in pubs, in one another's houses on evening visits, before and after mass in the churchyard, the enthralling game of presenting argument, choosing sides, directing the flow of talk, belongs to the older men . . . At such times the important news of the countryside disseminates itself. Political judgements are formed, and the ephemeral decisions of daily life are made. In all this the boys are silent listeners. It is a bold young man who enters an opinion of his own.[67]

Kept outside the adult world, young men formed their own, somewhat marginal, subculture with its own 'complex norms, valuations and conducts':[68]

The young people recognise themselves as forming a distinct group with interests and sentiments of its own, opposed in the scheme of rural life to the elders. They use the word 'we' and oppose it to 'them' for the old. They recognise places, pursuits and forms of activity as their own . . . [and] greet the suggestion that they should take their place in the gathering of old men in something of the tone of derision which they reserve for women.[69]

This youth subculture was a collective one, formed around long-lived groupings of brothers, cousins, neighbours, schoolmates, and the like who played, and often worked, together. The character of these gangs or 'crowds' varied with the area and individuals involved, but most seem to have had a loose natural leadership made up of the oldest boys, the quickest wits, or the best sportsmen or organizers.[70] In towns especially, these might also follow class lines. In Barrackton, on the north side of Cork city:

---

[65]   The Cork data are based on a survey of the 1911 census returns of 1233 families in 8 District Electoral Divisions and 1 urban district with at least one parent and one resident child. An approximately comparable figure for 'Britain' (which does not include Ireland) is 14% for 'typical' 15-year-old children in 1906. Michael Anderson, 'The Social Implications of Demographic Change', in F. M. L. Thompson (ed.), *The Cambridge Social History of Britain 1750–1950* (Cambridge, 1990), ii. 49.   [66]   Arensberg and Kimball, *Family and Community*, 55.

[67]   Ibid. 171. See also Arensberg, *The Irish Countryman*, 125–42. John L. O'Sullivan discussed rural 'parliaments' in West Cork in an interview on RTE Radio, 15 Feb. 1989.

[68]   Arensberg and Kimball, *Family and Community*, 190.   [69]   Ibid. 168.

[70]   O'Connor, *An Only Child*, 116.

The shop-fronts and gas-lamps were quite as exclusive as city clubs . . . The boys from our neighbourhood usually gathered outside Miss Murphy's shop at the foot of the [Harrington's] Square while the respectable boys of the Ballyhooly Road—the children of policemen, minor officials, and small shopkeepers—gathered outside Miss Long's by the Quarry.

Such groups were exclusively male, close-knit, and assembled frequently, often every day or night. In many communities there was, in any case, an absence of alternative groups or activities. 'The boys' would gather at a house or crossroads to play cards or talk. They went to dances together, followed the local band, played on the same football or hurling teams:

Football was very important to the young lads . . . They also formed a social group, as those same team members would go to the fairs together . . . they were a strong faction agent. It was the most important group to those lads, closer than the relatives. They would all be at church on Sunday, outside and in. They grew up together.[71]

These informal but stable cliques generated both rivalries between groups— often on a territorial basis, between neighbourhoods, parishes, or townlands—and conformity within them. 'They all sort of kept an eye on each other. It ended up so that rarely could a fellow go wrong because even if he was given to bad habits, he would end up getting a hammering from his own gang. So everybody was kept under control.' One study, conducted in an area bordering Cork, concluded that 'the very essence of expression in this community [was] the inability to step outside accustomed behaviour without the support of the group'.[72]

The friendship group functioned both to include and exclude, and the pressure to belong in a small community could be very great. 'A young man's status in the community depends to a great extent on being accepted by this group and by his full participation in its activities.'[73] Such cliques, and their territory, bands, and teams, were a very powerful focus for individual and collective identities and loyalties.

Although essentially marginal and deferential, this youth culture did contain the seeds of rebellion. At one level this mostly consisted of what might be termed passive resistance, i.e. concealing one's activities from one's father or talking behind his back rather than openly challenging him. 'Members of a family are often involved in a conspiracy to keep the father ignorant of their affairs [like Frank O'Connor and his mother].'[74] As Neil Kevin recalled:

---

[71] Interview with a Munster farmer quoted in Mark Shutes, 'Production and Social Change in a Rural Irish Parish', *Social Studies* (1987), 22. This man was also discussing the *meitheal* (neighbourhood cooperative labour) group, another bond between these young men. See also Damian Hannan, 'Kinship, Neighbourhood and Social Change in Irish Rural Communities', *Economic and Social Review* (Jan. 1972), 172.

[72] Shutes, 'Production and Social Change', 22; McNabb, 'Social Structure', 233. See also Eileen Kane, 'Man and Kin in Donegal', *Ethnology* (1968), 252–3.

[73] McNabb, 'Social Structure', 219.   [74] Ibid. 229.

We, who have grown up in the streets of small towns, have short memories if we do not realise the sense of power over the peace and standing orders of a place which is the quite ordinary feeling of these lads, when they roam the town free from the restraints of home and school. How easily a plot was made to raid an orchard; how you locked it up in yourself at home, while you were being youthful and docile about brushing your hair or running a message; how you gave external assent and saved appearance with your father, while you were, in real life, under the jurisdiction of your street leader who was known to have stolen a goose and who would think nothing of burning down a school.[75]

Irish folk culture also contained an accepted element of ritualized rebellion which allowed for a temporary and largely symbolic reversal of roles.[76] On festival days such as St Stephen's Day, St Brigid's Day (or Eve), Shrove Tuesday, or wedding days, young men had a customary right to wear masks or otherwise disguise and decorate themselves, march about in military fashion, and demand food, money, or entrance to houses. On Skellig Night (Shrove Tuesday), gangs also commonly kidnapped and ridiculed unmarried older men and women. If householders refused their demands, the gang would frequently exact a violent revenge ('if they would not get money or drink they would be very cross and if anyone would go out, they would hunt them').[77]

These events were often the occasion for rowdiness, anonymous intimidation, the settling of old scores, and confrontations with rivals or the police. To symbolize this overturning of the normal code of deference, clothes were often worn inside out or else women's clothes were put on. Disguises were invariably worn. Faces were masked, veiled, blackened, or rouged ('these men nearly always had their legs bound with hay or straw, their faces blackened or masked and their coats turned inside out'[78]). Anonymity was vital and fiercely protected. Sticks and hurleys were usually carried. These gangs, or 'batches', made up of a dozen or so young bachelors and led by a 'captain'—the normal friendship group in a different guise—were known as Wren Boys, Biddy Boys, Straw Boys, or just 'the boys'. The following is a description of 'Biddy Boys' or 'Brideogs' from Watergrasshill:

A number of young men disguised themselves and dressed up a figure which they called 'Breeda'. It was the custom to call to every house in the neighbourhood. On entering a house they demanded money for 'Breeda', and generally danced for a few minutes with the girls of the house. In a house in which the owner took the whole thing as a joke they

---

[75]   Kevin, *Karrigeen*, 30–1.

[76]   My discussion is largely based on the 126 volumes of Schools MSS for Co. Cork, containing systematic information on these practices, in UCD, Dept. of Irish Folklore. See especially, SMS 283, p. 422; 288, p. 422; 291, p. 375; 347, pp. 428–30; 350, p. 96; 351, pp. 174, 19; 352, p. 126; 362, pp. 196–7; 373, p. 206; 374, pp. 61–2; 380, pp. 72–3. For Cork city, see P. S. O'Hegarty, 'The Wren Boys', *Bealoideas* (1943–4), 275–6; *Journal of the Cork Historical and Archaeological Society* (1894), 22–3 and O'Connor, *An Only Child*, 135–6. An extended and sensitive account of a 'strawing' appears in John O'Donoghue, *In Kerry Long Ago* (London, 1960), 42–64. See also Alan Gailey, *Irish Folk Drama* (Cork, 1969) and Henry Glassie, *All Silver and No Brass* (Dublin, 1975).

[77]   SMS 394, p. 270 (Cloyne).   [78]   SMS 383, p. 89.

departed quietly, but when they were taken roughly they generally took all the bread they could find in the house away with them. On entering a Public House they took whatever drinks were on the counter. This often caused a row with the people who had paid for the drinks, but as the 'Brideogs' were always in considerable numbers they generally came out best. When two bunches of 'Brideogs' met there was some excitement as the strongest party always relieved the other of whatever money they had collected.[79]

The role of these groups within the community was an ambiguous one. They offered an opportunity for young men to swagger and force people to notice them and meet their demands. They also offered an opportunity for intense bonding: 'They seemed to be all one together, understanding each other, sharing something intimate and happy.'[80] Women had no part in these visitations.[81]

Straw Boys were disorderly, disrespectful, and mocked the established order, to the displeasure of the older and more respectable sections of society, yet they presented no real threat. On the contrary, part of the function of these groups seems to have been to enforce conformity within the community in much the same way as the youth groups controlled themselves. Maura Laverty wrote of the local 'go-boys' that 'they preyed particularly on those who were thoughtless enough to act in any way unbecoming to their age or station in life . . . the fear of attracting their attention kept many of us from committing foolishness'.[82] Skellig Night's attack on bachelors and old maids was a good example of this: 'they used to duck them in the water and frighten them so much that they used be married the next time.'[83] Other victims of charivari included adulterers, troublesome drunks, wife-beaters, and widows who remarried too soon.

These rituals belonged to a political subculture quite apart from the formal political arena which concerned itself with elections, parties, and patronage. The Straw Boys shared their symbols and methods with factions in land, labour, or other disputes, and with agrarian rebels from the Rightboys to the Land League. In such cases the landlord or the land-grabber replaced the adulterer or old maid as the object of attack. In fact, festive occasions sometimes became part of these struggles, as in Mayo in March 1922, when one party in a land feud between families 'strawed' another and two people died in the ensuing fight.[84]

The threads of violence (real or implicit), anonymity, and coerced conformity to group demands or norms ran through all these different scenarios. The threatening letter or notice and the Skellig list existed on the same symbolic continuum, as did the 'captains' of the Wren or Straw Boys and the innumerable 'Captain Moonlights' and 'Captain Rocks' who appeared during agrarian

---

[79] SMS 382, pp. 79–80. [80] O'Donoghue, *In Kerry Long Ago*, 64.

[81] In a few parishes, girls were known to go from door to door collecting money on St Brigid's Day or Eve, but this seems to have been a pale and highly localized imitation of the male version. See SMS 383, p. 91; 393, p. 37; 394, p. 176.

[82] Maura Laverty, *Never No More* (London, 1942), 232–3. Laverty was writing about her village near the Bog of Allen.

[83] Dept. of Irish Folklore, SMS 383, p. 91 (Glounthane).

[84] *Irish Times*, 4 Apr. 1922.

disputes. What they all had in common was the appeal to an ideal of popular unity, or at least uniformity: the demand for support, acquiescence, or silence. The use of masks, the role-playing of the 'captains' and 'boys', and the symbols of higher authority—the wren or the 'Breeda'—served to legitimize these demands and to assert the claim to be acting as the voice of the people rather than as individuals. The masks of 'the boys' became, symbolically, the mask of community.

When this mask was assumed by the Straw Boys and their ilk, it was, in most senses, playful and the symbols were rendered routine and drained of meaning. As they moved along the continuum however, these symbols and rituals acquired overt political content and became radicalized by confrontation. They became meaningful. In these new contexts they had the power to either mobilize or marginalize the people against whom they were directed.

I.R.A. units were a natural extension of this youth subculture and its body of unspoken assumptions and bonds. Usually benign events and practices became vehicles for political mobilization, and customs such as 'strawing' became part of the political struggle. The family resemblance between the majority of I.R.A. 'operations' and the actions of the Straw Boys is close and clear: the same use of masks or blackened and painted faces, often the same 'queer clothes', the same-sized gangs of young bachelors acting anonymously under a 'captain', the same pseudo-military posturing, and the same nocturnal raiding and petty intimidation.

The Volunteers also displayed the same kind of bonding and bravado. Most 'military' activities, such as drilling, robbing postmen, or raiding for arms, involved little risk or serious violence and contained an element of playfulness not far removed from the Straw Boy model. This was especially true of the 1917–19 period, before the organization was committed to insurrection. Even after this, though, I.R.A. activities were generally small in scale and reminiscent of 'strawing'. The following account of a raid on a loyalist household in Tipperary, for example, could as easily be concerned with St Stephen's Day or Skellig Night:

I was up at the old school house at Carrig, where an Irish class was held. I met the defendant, William Herbert, who gave me a message to do something the next day. Other boys in the class got the same message. Herbert told us all to be down at Anna Minnitt's gate . . . At Minnitt's gate we were all in a crowd together, and turned our coats inside out, put handkerchiefs on our faces and went up towards the house in a body and in the door.

Another such example comes from the Ballagh, in Wexford:

[We] remained at Stamp's gate for Pat Breen . . . When Breen arrived we started across the fields . . . The three of us proceeded as far as Ballymacanogue lane. When about twenty yards up the lane we went into a field . . . and dressed or masked ourselves. There were nine more persons in the field when we arrived . . . Bill Murray seemed to be the leader. He said—'Lads, come on'.

When this group burst into the home of the Morris family, they looked enough like Wren Boys that Mrs Morris, 'believing that they were local men playing a joke, said—"Don't be going on with your nonsense!"' She was shot immediately thereafter.[85]

Examples abound of Volunteers borrowing wholesale from Straw Boy rituals. In February 1918 a gang of masked young men dressed in straw costumes mounted a series of raids for arms on Protestant houses in Glanmire. Some people resisted and fighting ensued. On 8 April 1920, in Ballinahalisk, a loyalist ex-officer was shot by men wearing veils. In January of the following year, William Sweetnam of Caheragh was beaten and kidnapped by local Volunteers disguised with rouged faces. In April, in Ballinphellic, republican police with blackened faces, reddened lips, and shotguns gave local drunks and 'troublemakers' sixteen hours to leave the parish.[86] In Cork city, the withdrawal of Crown forces in early 1922 brought an epidemic of Straw Boy-like behaviour into the streets. According to one 'worried woman', her neighbourhood was terrorized in the daytime by boys with hurleys while after dark:

bands of boys, ranging from 12 to 17 or 18 years, go round at night with masks on their faces and bang at the shop and other doors, while a new pest is added, several batches going round nightly with cigarettes and cigar boxes collecting for bogus hurling clubs, threatening respectable inhabitants who can't give them money.[87]

Often the resemblance was so close that one sort of event was confused with the other, and more than one I.R.A. raiding party was met with the question 'Is it Wren Boys?'[88]

Similar incidents occurred all over Ireland. In Dublin a man was shot dead during a raid on his home by 'boys' dressed in scout (presumably Fianna) uniforms, masks, and 'loose clothing like skirts'. In Leitrim three young men dressed in women's clothes and with window blinds over their faces gagged and tarred a girl. In King's County a man was attacked by twenty men with blackened faces, some of whom wore women's clothes. In Limerick, a group of arms raiders wore women's hats and men's hats turned inside out. In Kerry, police captured one suspect wearing female attire, while in Clare another was arrested carrying a Volunteer haversack and a woman's hat decorated with ribbons for 'strawing'. Another was arrested in Tipperary wearing a woman's pink hat with the hat-band pulled down over his face.[89] On one telling occasion in Clare, an I.R.A. officer entered a captured barracks singing 'The wren, the wren, the king of all birds'.[90]

It is impossible to know how many Volunteers participated in these festival

---

[85] *Examiner*, 17 Nov. 1919, 16 Feb. 1920.
[86] Ibid. 27 Feb. 1918, 9 Apr. 1920; *Eagle*, 29 Jan. 1921; *Examiner*, 23 Apr. 1921.
[87] Letter to the *Examiner*, 31 Mar. 1922.
[88] See 'Sassenach', *Arms and the Irishman*, 98.
[89] *Irish Times*, 14 Mar., 6 Sept. 1919, 5, 20 Apr., 21 June 1920, 15 Feb., 9 Mar. 1921.
[90] Paddy MacDonnell (O'Malley Papers, P17b/130).

customs but it is certain that a great many did, and that all would at least have been familiar with them. Nearly every townland had its 'boys'. On occasion, Volunteer activities were even combined with such customs, as in Ballinspittal and Kilbrittain (strongly republican areas) on St Stephen's Day in 1916, when the local 'boys' were arrested for drilling, singing seditious songs, and assaulting the police during the celebrations.[91] On the same night in 1920, Wren Boys who came into Rosscarbery from the country attacked the house of a prominent loyalist.[92] Another St Stephen's Day episode occurred in Dunmanway when a 'batch' of Volunteers stole uniforms and ceremonial weapons from a retired British officer and subsequently wore them as part of their Wren Boy costumes.[93]

Local groups of Volunteers adopted names like 'the Galty Boys' and 'the Hardy Boys' (just as agrarian agitators had called themselves 'the Committee Boys' and the like in the 1880s[94]), while some Wren Boy 'crowds' assumed titles like 'the Green Volunteers' and took to carrying a green flag rather than a wren or other effigy.[95] Perhaps the most significant—and natural—convergence of names lay in the fact that local I.R.A. members were also usually referred to as 'the boys'.

The most important symbolic links were those used to give legitimacy to the I.R.A.'s actions. Where the Wren Boys acted in the name of 'the Wran' (the king) and the Biddy Boys in the name of St Brigid, and agrarian factions acted in the name of 'evicted tenants' or 'the committee', the Volunteers acted in the name of 'the republic' or referred to mysterious 'orders'. These various claims carried very different weight—no one was ever killed in the name of 'the Wran'—but had the same function. Here again we see the appeal to unity and the demand for conformity and silence, the common use of the mask of community.

The Volunteers evoked the same range of responses as the Straw Boys. Some people welcomed them, others only grudgingly complied with their demands, and a few refused them. They were looked down upon and feared as disorderly, disrespectful, and of lower class.[96] 'The boys' could be a term of condescension as well as camaraderie. Townspeople who saw 'strawing' and 'following the wran' as invasions by 'lusty young men of the country' saw Volunteer events in the same way.[97] As with Straw Boys, lack of cooperation undermined the necessary fiction of communal unity and was met by acts of intimidation and revenge.

[91]   *Star*, 13 Jan. 1917.
[92]   Police Report on Malicious Injury Claim (CAI, CS/LA/C/MI/69). The house was later seized by the I.R.A.
[93]   Interview with AE. For another example of Wren Boys turned 'rebels', see Kavanagh, *The Green Fool*, 143–7.   [94] Dept. of Irish Folklore, SMS 350, p. 191.
[95]   See the Mitchelstown detachment War Diary, 31 Jan. 1921 (Buffs Regimental Museum); M. Jesse Hoare, *The Road to Glenanore* (London, 1975), 54; Dept. of Irish Folklore, MS 434, pp. 135–6.
[96]   Dept. of Irish Folklore, SMS 347, pp. 428–30; *Journal of the Cork Historical and Archaeological Society* (1894), 22; O'Brien, *Village of Longing*, 45–6.
[97]   *Eagle*, 13 Jan. 1917.

The revolution turned the reversal of roles implicit in the festival rituals into a political reality. In part, the Volunteer movement did express youthful resentment, generational friction and a desire for status and authority. For once 'the boys' *were* in charge.

However, while this strongly rebellious aspect of the I.R.A. should be recognized, it must also be remembered that the subculture inhabited by these young men was an integral part of the larger community, and that its themes of rebellion and role-reversal existed in a largely deferential and conformist context. The Volunteers may have broken many of the conventional rules, but in other respects they were zealous in defence of their perception of the proper moral order. Adulterers, wife-beaters, drunkards, tinkers, tramps, prostitutes, and other troublemakers generally got short shrift with the I.R.A. just as they did with 'the boys'. I.R.A. men valued their respectability. Like the Straw Boys, they ended up reinforcing communal standards as much as they challenged them.

Indeed, if anything, the Volunteers acted out of a heightened sense of community and saw themselves as embodying 'the people' or 'the nation'. They believed in their imagined united community, and directed their violence towards outsiders or deviants, variously defined. If they had truly sought to attack social norms, instead of just departing from them—for instance, if they had sought to run their households—then their use of communal symbols would have been fruitless and meaningless.

If we return to the 'boys of Kilmichael' we can see that these young tradesmen, shop assistants, and farmers' sons were quite typical of their guerrilla comrades. They were the heirs of respectable, successful households from main streets and decent farms rather than back lanes and bogs. This, in the main, was the I.R.A.: broadly democratic within their self-imposed boundaries of respectability. They were, however, still 'the boys', youths of no property and little consequence until war made them heroes. Nevertheless, respectability and social position cannot explain why these particular men—these particular O'Donovans, O'Sullivans, and McCarthys—ended up at Kilmichael. To go further we must examine the ideals, ambitions, fears, and loyalties which put them on the path to revolution.

PART III

The Path to Revolution

9

The Rise and Fall of a Revolutionary Family

And the Shins in the land
Rent the air with their wails
When they heard of the death
Of their friend John Hales.
('Who killed John Hales?')[1]

On 22 August 1922 Michael Collins set out on a tour of his native West Cork, newly occupied by Free State forces. His last stop was Bandon. There he met with Sean Hales, the officer responsible for driving the I.R.A. out of the towns he had just visited. An hour later Collins was dead, killed in an I.R.A. ambush on the road home. The commander of the ambush was Tom Hales.[2]

The two brothers' involvement in this critical episode was no coincidence. The Hales family had been at the eye of the revolutionary storm in West Cork since the 1916 rising, and their personal histories were closely intertwined with that of the Volunteer movement. A study of one illuminates the other and raises fascinating questions about the choices and forces that transformed these West Cork 'boys' into guerrillas, killers, and martyrs. We therefore begin our exploration of these issues by tracing one family's path through the Irish revolution.

All his life Robert Hales was a pioneer. Born in the shadow of the great famine in 1849, by the turn of the century he stood out as a successful entrepreneur, even among the prosperous farmers of his home district of Ballinadee (several miles south of Bandon). His reputation was that of an 'enlightened and progressive' farmer, one of the first to buy a threshing machine, the symbol of progress in rural Ireland.[3] By 1911 he owned five machines and a steam tractor which his sons worked as contractors; 'this alone would have made them an

[1] This is the chorus of a song written in 1920 by soldiers of the Essex Regiment in Bandon (the title was wishful thinking as they never managed to catch Sean Hales): Percival Papers (IWM). I will use the Gaelicized version of his name—'Sean'—as he and his comrades did.

[2] See Ryan, *The Day Michael Collins Was Shot*; Tim Pat Coogan, *Michael Collins* (London, 1990), 402–12; Edward O'Mahony, 'The Death of Michael Collins', *Magill* (May 1989); and P. J. Twohig, *The Dark Secret of Bealnablath* (Cork, 1991).

[3] Interview with Tom Kelleher by George O'Mahony, 1968 (tape in the possession of Mr O'Mahony). The Haleses' ages and other family details are given in their manuscript returns for the 1901 and 1911 census (NA). See also Kathleen Keyes McDonnell, *There is a Bridge at Bandon* (Cork, 1972), 21 and Mary MacSwiney's testimony in *Evidence on Conditions in Ireland*, 784.

unusual family'.[4] He was a leading horse and cattle breeder—he owned one of the few County Premium bulls—and a major local employer.[5]

Robert Hales was also a political entrepreneur. Active in the Land War and the Plan of Campaign (and a reputed Fenian), he was a lifelong radical and follower of William O'Brien.[6] When O'Brien formed the All For Ireland League in 1910 to oppose the Irish Party, Hales was among the first to join and was elected as an O'Brienite to Bandon's Rural District Council and Poor Law Board.[7]

Hales's children inherited much of his energy as well as his anti-landlord and anti-British politics. His eldest sons, Sean, Bob, and Tom, were GAA pioneers and champion athletes.[8] Staunch O'Brienites, they also learned Irish (as did all the Haleses) and joined Sinn Fein and the clandestine Irish Republican Brotherhood.[9] Like many other AFIL members, however, they initially held aloof from the Volunteer movement in 1914, considering it a Redmondite front. In this, as in business and sports, the other young men of Ballinadee followed their lead.[10]

After the Volunteers split and the dissident minority reorganized itself in early 1915, however, the Haleses became enthusiastic converts. Robert had already taken a public stand against supporting the British war effort.[11] Sean wrote to Terence MacSwiney in April promising that he could raise a hundred men for a Volunteer company, nearly all over 6 feet tall.[12] MacSwiney was amused, then impressed, as the Ballinadee company rapidly grew to be the largest and most active in West Cork.

The Hales delivered the young men of Ballinadee *en bloc* by recruiting friends, neighbours, cousins, work- and teammates. At the centre of this network were the four Hales brothers, Sean, Robert, Tom, and Bill, and their neighbours, the five O'Donoghue brothers (who were also extensive farmers). The women were equally fervent rebels: the local police described Mrs O'Donoghue and her daughter as 'holding most extreme views' and as 'having a great influence in their neighbourhood'.[13] They and Madge and Hannah Hales—the boys' sisters—led the local branch of the Cumann na mBan, the women's counterpart to the Volunteers. Together these two families made up almost a third of the founding

[4]   Kelleher interview; Ernest Blythe, 'Kerry Better Than Cork in 1915', *An tOglach* (Christmas 1962). The latter is an exceptionally valuable memoir by a key Volunteer and I.R.B. organizer.

[5]   The Haleses' stallion Royal Irish Jupiter is described in a newspaper advertisement kept in the Percival Papers; the list of premium bulls is found in the *Report of the Royal Commission on Congestion in Ireland* [Cd. 3839], HC 1908, 374.

[6]   See Pat Canniffe, 'The Eviction at Knocknacurra', *Bandon Historical Journal* (1989), 25–7.

[7]   See *Cork Free Press*, 18, 20 June 1910; *Eagle*, 22 Aug. 1914.

[8]   *Evidence on Conditions in Ireland*, 780; Coogan, *Michael Collins*, 51; McDonnell, *There is a Bridge*, 35.   [9]   Kelleher interview.

[10]   McDonnell, *There is a Bridge*, 21: 'in matters of common concern it [Ballinadee] had but one voice.'   [11]   *Eagle*, 22 Aug. 1914.

[12]   McDonnell, *There is a Bridge*, 35.

[13]   DI Bandon report, 19 Oct. 1916 (Chief Secretary's Office Registered Papers) 16628 1916).

members of the company, which grew from about thirty men in May 1915 to sixty in June, and sixty-eight in July.[14] By April 1916 they numbered 110, despite the fact that some members in neighbouring districts—notably Kilbrittain—had left to form their own units.[15] The county inspector for West Cork singled out Ballinadee for special attention and reported that 'they are almost entirely composed of farmers' sons of military age, who, before the war, were followers of Mr. O'Brien, M.P., but who are now in opposition to his [pro-]war policy'.[16] The ever-vigilant Skibbereen *Eagle* soon made 'the Army' the butt of weekly gibes and satiric verse, complete with farcical reports from 'H.Q., General Staff, Ballinadee'.[17]

Although Sean, aged 35, did much of the organizing work, it was Tom, 25, who became the Captain. Bill, the youngest, was made secretary. When the Ballinadee Company and its satellites were grouped into a battalion in 1916, Tom was appointed its commander and Sean replaced him as captain. Under their leadership the company drilled three or four times a week and conducted a route march every Sunday in order to disrupt recruiting meetings and attract their own recruits.[18] Sean was also able to acquire twelve much-prized Mauser rifles, thereby making Ballinadee the best armed unit in Cork outside the city.[19]

The Easter Rising found the Hales (who, as I.R.B. members in close contact with the leading conspirators in the city, were among the few Volunteers in the county to know about the plan in advance[20]) and their men ready and eager to take part, pikes and all. They were correspondingly disappointed when the original marching orders were countermanded on Easter Sunday. Tom argued strenuously that they should seize the moment and attack regardless, but he was overruled by the brigade commanders, MacSwiney and Tomas MacCurtain.[21] The week that followed was a troubled one. As rumours and reports of the fighting in Dublin were received, Tom grew increasingly eager to enter the fray. He planned an attack on the R.I.C. barracks in Macroom, and was only dissuaded by his I.R.B. superior, Sean O'Hegarty.[22] The frustrated Ballinadee Volunteers

[14] See the CI Monthly Reports, West Cork, May–July 1915 (CO 904/97) and O'Donoghue, 'History of the Irish Volunteers', 72–3. The Ballinadee Company membership roll for 1916 can be found in the West Cork Regional Museum, Clonakilty. See also Kelleher interview and Flynn, 'My Part in Irish Independence'.

[15] Company return, Apr. 1916 (Cork County Museum, Terence MacSwiney Papers, L233).

[16] CI Monthly Report, West Cork, Sept. 1915 (CO 904/98).

[17] *Eagle*, 6, 13, 20 Nov. 1915, 19 Feb., 25 Mar. 1916.

[18] CI Monthly Report, West Cork, June 1915; O'Donoghue, 'History of the Irish Volunteers', 73; Anon. history of the republican movement in the Bandon area (Price Papers, MS 15, 344) (hereafter referred to as 'Bandon History').

[19] Flynn, 'My Part in Irish Independence', 55.

[20] O'Donoghue, *Tomas MacCurtain*, 89; 'Comments on Florence O'Donoghue's Life of *Tomas MacCurtain* by the Cork 1916 Men's Association' (Boston Public Library), 8. The most detailed account of Ballinadee's role in the rising is William Hales's own memoir of the event (in the possession of Sean Hales).

[21] William Hales's Memoir and O'Donoghue, *Tomas MacCurtain*, 101.

[22] O'Donoghue, *Tomas MacCurtain*, 112; McDonnell, *There is a Bridge*, 57.

harassed the local police, ordered the local police sergeant out of the district, and declared their own independence: 'they refused to recognize the British government any longer, that they had their own laws and would exercize their rights.'[23]

The Hales home seethed with schemes and activity. 'I did not quite understand the attitude of the people of the house,' confessed Liam de Roiste, who spent a crowded night there while acting as a courier. 'Though drawing on to 12 o'clock, some of the men began manufacturing "bombs" in the kitchen.'[24] The company tried to smuggle more rifles out of the city but they were forestalled when the Cork Brigade reached an agreement with the British authorities to hand over its arms in return for an amnesty.[25] MacSwiney went to Ballinadee on 3 May to relay these conditions and was met by Bob Hales:

good and free and easy simple careless Bob. His way of acting guide was to go off in his own swinging way—letting us to tumble after him as best we could . . . to our shouts he only returned an occasional surprised response, and inviting us to come on. Picture all that journey in the dark of a pretty dark night, over fields, ditches, then the road for a spell, down the valley, across the slob, over the river, again the road and fields to Hales' house.[26]

When MacSwiney finally arrived at the Hales home in Knocknacurra in the early hours of the morning, he discovered that this rural fastness had been turned into an armed and angry camp centred around the Hales and O'Donoghue houses.[27] The men of Ballinadee were determined at first to put up a fight. 'I was able to calm the boys and advise them and keep them quiet. If I were not there there might have been trouble.'[28]

Tom refused to give up his arms or cooperate with the authorities, ordered his men to follow his example, and promptly went on the run. Several hours later, at dawn, Ballinadee was invaded by a large detachment of the Connaught Rangers and twenty policemen led by County Inspector Tweedy. Bob and Bill Hales, Con and Dan O'Donoghue, and MacSwiney were all arrested. Not entirely without a fight, however. Upon their return to Bandon, 'a large number of men who were at the cattle fair congregated near the police barracks. A man attacked Mr. Tweedy and struck him. Mr. Tweedy replied with a right to the jaw and his assailant bit the dust.'[29]

Sean Hales and Pat O'Donoghue escaped but were captured a few days later and joined the others in the Frongoch internment camp in Wales.[30] Tom continued

[23]   Chief Secretary's Office Registered Papers 5626 1916 (NA).
[24]   Liam de Roiste Diary, 25 Apr. 1916 (CAI, U271).
[25]   'Bandon History'; CI Monthly Report, West Cork, Apr. 1916 (CO 904/99); O'Donoghue, *Tomas MacCurtain*, 113.
[26]   MacSwiney Diary, 25–6 May (MacSwiney Papers, L233).
[27]   The O'Donoghues lived in the townland of Rathdrought. For Volunteer preparations, see William Hales's Memoir.
[28]   MacSwiney Diary; see also Flynn, 'My Part in Irish Independence', 56–7.
[29]   *Eagle*, 6 May 1916.
[30]   Ibid. 56–7; O'Donoghue, *Tomas MacCurtain*, 121 and O'Donoghue, 'History of the Irish Volunteers', appendix 5.

to evade arrest until his brothers were released in December, prompting repeated raids and searches of the family farm and neighbourhood by armed patrols.[31] Much of the unit's arsenal of ammunition and explosives was discovered and seized. To make matters worse, 'in the absence of the officers . . . Ballinadee company became disorganized' and some of the men voluntarily gave up their arms, including eight of the precious Mausers.[32]

The experiences of 1916—the long build-up to the rising followed by the frustration of inactivity, the arrests, raids, and police harassment, the loss of arms, and the fellowship and hardships of life in prison or on the run—radicalized the Haleses and the other Ballinadee activists and welded them and their fellow prisoners into a nationwide movement. In Frongoch they met rebels from all over Ireland and Britain. Sean became friends with Michael Collins and his I.R.B. clique, many of whom were also natives of West Cork.[33]

The brothers returned as heroes and militants, determined to struggle and organize on every possible front. There was a new spirit of resistance in the air and battle was joined almost immediately. Only days after the rebel prisoners had come home, the local sergeant received a threatening letter and a police patrol in Ballinadee village encountered 'defiant hostility' in the form of marching, drilling, and stone-throwing.[34] Still, 'it would be useless, even were the evidence stronger than it is, to bring such a case before a local bench', such was 'the strong feeling against the police since the rebellion'.[35] The patrols were armed and reinforced, and the army was called in to keep the peace on New Year's Eve. One Frongoch veteran observed:

The bold Tom and Donny [O'Donoghue?] gave them a good run for it . . . and I think that they wouldn't hardly meddle with them now. The country changed a whole lot since the rebellion, as they are all Sinn Feiners now with a few West Britons among them.[36]

The Hales threw their energies into a myriad of organizations and activities, always trying to push 'the movement' forward. When Count Plunkett, father of an executed rebel conspirator, formed his short-lived Liberty League he was immediately barraged with letters from Knocknacurra. Robert wrote, with typical Hales exuberance (and local pride), that 'the men of Ballinadee are heart and soul with the movement' but generously added that 'as for the adjoining localities [they] possess plenty good material'.[37] Sean declared that 'we will leave no stone unturned to bring the rest of the surrounding districts within the movement' in

[31] CI Monthly Reports, West Cork, July, Aug. 1916 (CO 904/100); 'Bandon History'.

[32] Flynn, 'My Part in Irish Independence', 57; return of arms in possession of the Irish Volunteers, 28 Feb. 1917 (CO 904/29/2).

[33] Griffith and O'Grady, *Curious Journey*, 95.

[34] DI Report, n.d. [1917] (WO 35/95); CI Monthly Report, West Cork, Dec. 1916 (CO 904/101).   [35] DI Report (WO 35/95).

[36] Letter from a released prisoner in Bandon, 19 Feb. 1917 (CO 904/164).

[37] Robert Hales to Count Plunkett, 4 May 1917 (NLI, Count Plunkett Collection, MS 11, 383).

order to 'fight against corruption and the venality of those who want to make Ireland a Crown Colony'.[38]

A Liberty club was formed. Sean Hales and Pat O'Donoghue were on the executive and Robert was their delegate to Count Plunkett's convention, one of the few from West Cork.[39] And when the League merged with Sinn Fein, the club simply changed its name. Bill became secretary and Tom was made a member of the party's constituency executive.[40] Both followed their father onto the local district council.[41] As republicans did not have to face a contested election in West Cork until 1922, Sean went to work in other campaigns in Waterford, South Armagh, and Donegal, taking contingents of Ballinadee Volunteers with him.[42]

The brothers also continued their father's fight on behalf of evicted tenants by leading their men to intervene in several local land disputes. Other organizations in which they were involved included the Bandon People's Food Committee and the Unpurchased Tenants' Association, the former anti-British (and somewhat anti-shopkeeper) and the latter anti-landlord.[43] Sean helped in the Sinn Fein takeover of the *Southern Star* newspaper and was a member of the new board of directors.[44] In all the welter of political activity that marked 1917 and 1918, the Hales and their Ballinadee cohorts were ubiquitous—and unfailingly prominent. When J. J. Walsh returned to Bandon from prison in June 1917 Tom was in charge of the platform committee while Sean led the parade in uniform and mounted on a white horse.[45] The brothers were again at the head of the de Valera reception in December.[46]

Above all, however, Tom and Sean wanted to ensure that this time 'the movement' would be committed to revolution. The achievement of this goal—and the family's fate—would rest, not on their indefatigable public organizing, but on their underground activities with the I.R.B. and the revived Volunteers, which they were already calling the Irish Republican Army.

The former was the key to the latter. The previously tiny I.R.B. (or 'the organization', as it was anonymously known to its members) expanded rapidly in 1917 as Tom began to swear in those Volunteers he trusted.[47] In Ballinadee it was a brotherhood in fact as well as in name as the Hales and O'Donoghue clans made up more than half the circle.[48] At the same time he moved to purge the

---

[38]   Sean Hales to Plunkett, 9 May 1917 (MS 11, 383).

[39]   See William Hales to Plunkett, 31 May 1917; list of Convention Delegates (MS 11, 383).

[40]   A complete list of Sinn Fein officers for 1921 can be found in the Military Archives (A/1147). The South East Cork executive is named in the *Star*, 9 Feb. 1918.

[41]   Bandon RDC minutes, 7 May 1921 (NA, DELG 6/2).

[42]   Jack Fitzgerald, Sean Breen (O'Malley Papers, P17b/112, 124); Flynn, 'My Part in Irish Independence', 58–9.   [43]   *Eagle*, 16 Mar. 1918; *Star*, 8 Apr. 1922.

[44]   *Southern Star Centenary Supplement*, 62.

[45]   *Eagle*, 30 June 1917; Walsh, *Recollections of a Rebel*, 26.

[46]   R.I.C. Report on Bandon meeting, 12 Dec. 1917 (CO 904/122).

[47]   See, for example, Deasy, *Towards Ireland Free*, 15; Flynn, 'My Part in Irish Independence', 60.   [48]   Flynn, 'My Part in Irish Independence', 60.

battalion of those who had given up their arms or had proven unreliable in 1916, and appointed I.R.B. men in their place. Both Sean and Tom also openly criticized the city leadership, particularly MacCurtain and MacSwiney, for the same reason.[49]

These manœuvres were widely resented and perceived in West Cork as a personal and factional coup; the 'big fellas' throwing their weight around. The battalion split into rival camps and many members who opposed the Haleses and the I.R.B. left altogether. Their anger was such that 'not even during the Black and Tan regime did all these men return to the ranks'.[50] Nevertheless, after a bitter struggle for power, Tom Hales was confirmed in early 1918 as the battalion O/C, Sean was once again captain of the Ballinadee Company, and most of their fellow officers were 'organization' men, sworn to fight for a republic. 'It was the sixty men that I inaugurated outside Ballinadee', Tom declared, 'that made the Third Cork Brigade.'[51]

There would be no more surrenders. When a party of police arrived in Knocknacurra in May 1918 with warrants for several of the brothers, they met with such fierce resistance from the assembled 'boys' that Sean managed to escape and two constables resigned on the spot. The incident soon became famous and raised I.R.A. morale throughout West Cork.[52] The confidence and determination of those days is captured in a June letter from Madge (as republican as her brothers) to Donal, another brother living in Genoa:

You can see the fun has begun. We had a complete victory here this morning. At about five o'clock we were awakened by police asking for permission to come in to look for arms (these toys do not be left inside now for play things). Well, we left them wait outside until it was our getting up time. Mother was the first to get up and in they came, but when in it was not arms they asked for but for John (who was unfortunately the only member of the family inside, except Bob, who is not very prominent).[53]

The police went to Sean's bedroom but he refused to be taken: 'He is a giant you know.' They were reluctant to use force as the memory of the last encounter lingered and the barracks had since received several anonymous letters promising dire reprisals. 'You know a life taken means several more to be paid for it.' 'After some time we got sick of them and went for our gallant soldiers.' Madge lured the police into a room and the Volunteers held the door shut while Sean once again made his escape. 'The poor police were dumbfounded and did not know what to do.'

This humiliating episode gained additional notoriety when the *Southern Star*

---

[49] Roibeard Langford statement (CAI, Langford Papers, U156).

[50] See 'Bandon History' for a detailed discussion of these events.

[51] Testimony before the Referee and Advisory Committee on military pensions, 10 June 1941 (Dept. of Taoiseach, S9243).

[52] *Examiner*, 20 May 1918; 'Bandon History'.

[53] Madge Hales to Donal Hales, 18 June 1918 (CAI, Donal Hales Papers, U53).

was closed down for reporting it. Attention again centred on the family in July when Tom and Bill barely escaped a hail of bullets during a military raid in Innishannon.[54] Both raids and resistance continued that year and the next, with the Haleses maintaining the upper hand.

All the brothers were now on the run. Their position at the vanguard of the struggle was confirmed in January 1919 when Michael Collins placed Tom in command of the newly formed (3rd) West Cork Brigade. At about the same time he was also appointed as the I.R.B. centre for the whole county, and later for South Munster, again with Collins's approval. Sean took Tom's place as Bandon battalion commander (Con O'Donoghue replacing him as company captain) while Bill became head of the Ballinadee I.R.B.[55]

The family was also at the forefront of the burgeoning guerrilla campaign, often exceeding or ignoring GHQ instructions in their zeal. The Bandon Volunteers launched a series of raids and attacks in 1918 and 1919, culminating in February 1920 with simultaneous assaults on R.I.C. barracks in Timoleague and Mount Pleasant, led respectively by Sean and Tom. Sean led the brigade flying column in the Brinny and Newcestown ambushes in the autumn and Bill was also active in several operations that winter. Sean, Bill, and Bob were all present at the battle of Crossbarry in March 1921, Bob participated in the subsequent capture of the Rosscarbery barracks, and Sean organized kidnappings and reprisals against suspected loyalists in June.[56]

These activities followed a very clear geographical pattern. Timoleague, Mount Pleasant, Brinny, Newcestown, Crossbarry, and nearly every other encounter in which the Hales brothers took part (with the exception of Bob at Rosscarbery) were in the Bandon battalion area. When fights took place beyond these borders, such as at Kilmichael, they were usually absent.

The rest of the family was equally dedicated to 'the cause' without being so tied to their home territory. Donal was made the republican consul in Genoa and became part of Michael Collins's I.R.B.-based arms smuggling network. He even managed to negotiate a deal with several Italian nationalist groups to ship arms to West Cork but this fell apart in 1921.[57] Madge acted as Collins's courier

---

[54] *Examiner*, 7 July 1918; Deasy, *Towards Ireland Free*, 22.

[55] See Sean O'Muirthvile to Florence O'Donoghue, 14 Mar. 1921 and Roll of I.R.B. Officers, Nov. 1921 (O'Donoghue Papers, MS 31, 237); Statements re: [I.R.B.] Enquiry relative to Allegations of Negligence against Former County Sub-Centre for Cork (NLI, Maire Nic Shiubhlaigh Papers, MS 22, 567).

[56] For descriptions of most of these actions, see Deasy, *Towards Ireland Free*, 92–315. For Bob's actions at Rosscarbery, see the interview with Tom Kelleher in MacEoin, *Survivors*, 229; for Sean's kidnapping of Lord Bandon, see Coogan, *Michael Collins*, 178. For Ballinadee men in general, see William Hales, 'History Notes from "Ballinadee and the Brigade's War of Independence" ' (in the possession of Sean Hales).

[57] Various accounts of this plan exist. See especially the statement by Michael Leahy in the O'Donoghue Papers (MS 31, 421 (8)). For Donal's voluminous correspondence with Collins and with Art O'Brien, another key I.R.B. figure in London, see the Hales Papers (CAI, U53) and the Art O'Brien Papers (NLI, MSS 8426–30).

in this and other matters and became part of his personal clandestine network, thereby being identified as a 'spy' by British intelligence.[58]

The family's reputation as patriots and leaders, already established before the Great War, rose with each exploit. However, while some Volunteers became loyal followers (to John L. O'Sullivan, Sean Hales was 'a truly great man . . . Next to Collins . . . the best organizer I ever met'[59]) others thought their heroic status far outstripped their abilities. 'They had made a name for themselves and that name stuck to them,' remarked one Bandon veteran. Ernie O'Malley echoed the views of many younger guerrillas outside the Haleses' circle when he wrote:

[Sean] Hales would swear and flounder but he was only a lot of noise. Neither of the brothers were fit to take charge of a Brigade or even of a Battalion. They were the kind of men the movement threw up earlier and whom it was later found had to be put out of their jobs. They were hurlers or something in the G.A.A. and . . . they were fond of themselves and of publicity and decent men at the bottom.[60]

One place their 'name' was definitely secure was in the ranks of the police and the British army.[61] The officers and men of the Essex Regiment stationed in Bandon considered Tom and Sean Hales their arch-foes. One raid on Knocknacurra in March 1920 did turn up an iron cylinder full of ammunition hidden in a hayrick but the police declined to charge Robert—who was too old—or Bill—who was too ill and 'not known to be a Volunteer'—while Sean, Tom, and Bob could not be found.[62] When an R.I.C. patrol was ambushed in May 1920 at Butlerstown, near Timoleague, it was the Haleses who suffered the consequences, losing both their barn and dairy to police arsonists.[63] They even had songs composed about them, like the one quoted at the beginning of this chapter (written in the belief that Sean Hales was 'the rebel leader over most of county Cork'[64]). Another had as its chorus:[65]

[58] See Sean Hales's military intelligence file (WO 35/207); Ryan, *The Day Michael Collins Was Shot*, 10, 171.

[59] Quoted in Griffith and O'Grady, *Curious Journey*, 289.

[60] The former statement is by Flor Begley, the latter by Ernie O'Malley; both can be found in Flor Begley (O'Malley Papers, P17b/111). I encountered similar opinions among most of my West Cork interviewees: interviews with AA and AD.

[61] See Sean Hales's military intelligence file, updated to August 1921 (WO 35/207)—which also reports the same sort of impressions and gossip Ernie O'Malley heard.

[62] DI to HQ 6 Div., 3 Mar. 1920 (WO 35/110).

[63] *Examiner*, 11, 12 May 1920.

[64] Clarke, 'The Memoirs of a Professional Soldier', 10–11 (Clarke Papers), describes this young Essex officer's encounter with Sean Hales. See also the report on the family by the district inspector for Bandon, 23 Mar. 1920 (WO 35/110): 'there is no person in the 3rd (Cork) Bde so far as the police are aware at all equal in importance to John Hales.'

[65] Percival Papers. Major Percival himself was clearly obsessed with the Haleses judging by the number of references to them which occur in his lectures on guerrilla war and by the songs, photographs, and other mementoes which are in his papers.

When Irish eyes are smiling
At the boys they love the best
And the Irish Shins are sighing
For their pals who've all gone West
When the ghosts of Hales and Hurley
Are wailing through the night
Then the lilt of Essex laughter
Will re-echo with delight.

On 27 July the song-writers finally got one of their men, just when revenge was uppermost on their minds. On the night of 25 July the energetic and notorious Sergeant Mulhern of the R.I.C. was killed in a Bandon church. The next day an Essex private was shot dead while hunting his killers. On the following night Tom Hales and Pat Harte, the West Cork Brigade Quartermaster, were flushed from their hiding place near town by British intelligence officers.[66]

The two men were stripped, tied up, and savagely beaten and pistol-whipped. Tom later described the ordeal in a statement published around the world:

I was nearly blind, as blood was running down my face from the injuries I had received. We were taken to Bandon into the Military Barracks yard, and were lined up to be shot. The soldiers were howling for our death and were anxious to shoot us . . . We were still tied with our hands behind our backs, and the soldiers hit us with their fists . . . they punched us and pummelled us the whole way across the yard.[67]

Harte was knocked senseless when his nose was smashed by a rifle butt. That night Hales was interrogated and tortured by the officers who captured him. They beat him again with canes and crushed most of his teeth with pliers but he gave away nothing. Both men spent weeks in hospital.

Eventually, Hales and Harte were tried and sentenced to two years' penal servitude. Defiant to the last, Hales refused to recognize the court or defend himself. Pat Harte proved less resilient. Once in Pentonville prison in England, he initially refused food, was fed artificially, and then began to complain that 'people could read his thoughts' and that 'his thoughts were repeated'. These and other 'incipient signs of a mental breakdown' led ultimately to his incarceration in an asylum, where he died a few years later.[68]

Tom spent the next year and a half in Dartmoor prison, suffering badly from his wounds. Madge visited him in January 1921 and reported that 'his mouth is destroyed . . . He cannot speak as his tongue catches in the broken teeth.'[69]

---

[66] See witness statements by Cpt. C. J. Kelly, Flt. Lt. G. A. Richardson, and Lt. A. R. Koe (WO 35/110). Percival's account can be found in 'Guerrilla Warfare', part 2 (Percival Papers). On Mulhern and the capture, see Hales, 'History Notes'.

[67] *Evidence on Conditions in Ireland*, 780–3. Other, slightly different versions of Hales's statement were printed elsewhere. The unconvincing British denial of these accusations can be found in 'Thomas Hales, Fiction and Fact', Oct. 1920 (CO 904/168) and *Irish Times*, 23 Sept. 1920.

[68] For details of their medical history, see the Cork RAMC reports and Medical Officer, Pentonville, to Governor, 13 Sept. 1920 (WO 35/110).

[69] Madge Hales to Donal Hales, 25 Feb. 1921 (Hales Papers).

Where once letters from Ballinadee had been triumphant, now they were filled with gloom: 'I have missed many a poor boy whom I knew, more than I thought were missing.'[70] The house was robbed and raided, the workmen threatened. 'Father is not well. The black and tans treat him very roughly . . . He is worrying all day long about his dear sons and where are they that they do not come to see him.' In March came the worst blow yet, the burning of the beloved family home:

Instead of the happy girl I was when I wrote to you last, I am now a homeless and almost a fatherless girl . . . Oh dear father what you have seen in your last days the home you made has been burned to the ground and oh how heart piercing to think he was turned out with nothing to keep his poor body from cold and rain and with nothing even on his feet. I never will forget his petition to those heartless masked men. He said he was a dying man and asked for time to crawl downstairs with my mother's maid girl's and my help. The answer he got was we do not care what you are only clear out quickly, five minutes we got to clear out with our lives. I had to drag poor father to the workman's house in the cold and rain with terror in my heart fearing when they got no one inside they would again follow us. We were not out when the house they had sprinkled with petrol was bombed and immediately set on fire the first bomb went off in the parlour as we were just passed . . . Out of all my father's and mother's life long gathering, nothing is saved but what I took with me in my arms.[71]

The house and all of its contents, laboriously built up over the preceding decades, were destroyed: 'nothing of my dear and lovely home is now standing but the four walls.' In June, one of the workmen, John Murphy (also a member of the I.R.A.), was shot and killed in his home by Crown forces.[72] Robert survived, bedridden and near death.[73]

With the July Truce came local adulation and an exhilarating sense of imminent victory. Sean's public speeches—made to standing ovations—stressed the need for vigilance and expressed a warrior's contempt for politics: 'when work is to be done talking should cease.'[74] He looked back on the war as 'that wonderful struggle, or at least the first part of it, for it is too much to think that it is finished. No matter, on, on. Our dead did not die for anything short of Freedom.'[75]

Sean's conception of freedom, it turned out, differed considerably from his brothers'. Although former comrades claim he was against the Treaty when it was first announced, his friendship with Michael Collins—and perhaps the fact that Tom was still in prison—ensured that he voted for it in the Dail.[76] 'I have

[70] Ibid.

[71] Madge Hales to Donal Hales, 8 Mar. 1921 (Hales Papers). See also *Examiner*, 7 Mar. 1921.

[72] *Examiner*, 29 June 1921. See also O/C Cork 3 to O/C 1st South. Div., 8 July 1921 (Mulcahy Papers, P7/A/20). Murphy was arrested on Hales's farm and later found shot and bayoneted to death several miles away.

[73] Madge Hales to W. Cosgrave, 4 Aug. 1923 (Dept. of Taoiseach, S7602).

[74] *Eagle*, 24 Sept. 1921.

[75] Sean Hales to Donal Hales, 3 Oct. 1921 (Hales Papers).

[76] Jack Fitzgerald (O'Malley Papers, P17b/112); Coogan, *Michael Collins*, 39.

travelled down this stormy road since 1916 and it is conviction that leads me to vote for this Treaty.'[77] The only member of the family to support him was Madge, also influenced by Collins. Tom, Bob, and Bill remained adamantly opposed and Donal remained at his post as consul of an increasingly illusory republic.

As the only prominent Cork guerrilla leader to side with Collins, Sean became a key—and very public—player in the ensuing political struggle.[78] Many of his former comrades-in-arms (some of whom were already rivals dating back to the I.R.B. split of 1917) opposed him, as did his brother Tom, who was released in January 1922. When Sean ventured to speak in Bandon in March his platform was set on fire and the meeting was broken up by republican Volunteers.[79] He nevertheless was placed a comfortable third in the June pact election, his victory ensured by Michael Collins's surplus votes.[80] Despite his professed hatred of speeches and 'talk', Sean also showed a politician's gift for taking care of his own. Jobs were arranged, money was solicited for a local industrial school (they 'did everything they possibly could for me . . . and we must not forget them'[81]), 'evicted tenants' or their relatives were reinstated by force.[82] He was still intent on correcting the injustices of the previous century.

Tom and he never openly criticized one another. Tom would only say that 'if my brother stuck to the principles he held always he would be on our side today'.[83] Both worked for army unity and against the extremists in their own camps, but they remained on opposite sides as the divide widened. Tom was elected to the anti-Treaty I.R.A. executive in March, although he came last of the sixteen and got fewer votes than the other five Corkmen. He resigned in June over a proposal to prevent a general election.[84] Faced with a choice between the two brothers, the rank and file of the Ballinadee Company resigned *en masse* and played no further part in the revolution.[85] Only the O'Donoghues soldiered on. Their home in Rathdrought continued as a republican safe house throughout the subsequent fighting.

The opening days of the Civil War found both brothers in West Cork. Tom was in Skibbereen laying siege to the last Free State garrison in the county and Sean was on the run and agitating for a countervailing 'coup'.[86] When National Army troops landed in Union Hall, it was Sean who took command and pushed

[77] *Debate on the Treaty*, 324–5. Hales's speech in private session is quoted in Coogan, *Michael Collins*, 300.

[78] One observer who took note of Hales was Mark Sturgis, who remarked that his 'fine appearance . . . in Stephen's Green in uniform, is somewhat marred by the Homburg hat above it'. Sturgis Diary, 21 Dec. 1921 (PRO 30/59).   [79] *Star*, 25 Mar. 1922.

[80] *Examiner*, 24 June 1922.

[81] Sean Hales to W. Cosgrave, 23 Jan. 1922 (DELG 6/44).

[82] See Sec., Cork Co. Council to Min. Local Govt., 13 Mar. 1922 (DELG 6/44); Dept. of Justice files H5/864 and 1260.   [83] *Star*, 8 Apr. 1922.

[84] O'Donoghue, *No Other Law*, 335, 244. See also *Irish Times*, 2, 9 June 1922.

[85] See Inspector of Org. to O/C Org. 1st South. Div., 7 Sept. 1922 (MA, A/0991/2).

[86] Intelligence Report from M. Connell, 19 July 1922 (Mulcahy Papers, P7/A/50).

the I.R.A. out of Skibbereen, Clonakilty, and Bandon.[87] True to their factional instincts, he and others of Collins's clique of West Corkmen moved swiftly to rebuild their networks and reward their loyalists in and around Bandon. These networks survived both Collins and Hales, as one staff officer discovered on a tour of the district in 1923:

Everywhere in the area one finds 'Commandants', 'Captains' and 'Brigadiers' . . . who say they were appointed by the late Commander-in-Chief; by the late General Hales or by the Adjutant General [Gearoid O'Sullivan], and they seem to think that, regardless of their suitability to hold their offices, that they have a fixity of tenure in the Army.[88]

Then came the ambush at Bealnablath and the death of Collins, a death mourned equally by both brothers. Tom was once more on the run, and was apparently 'deposed' as brigade O/C soon afterwards.[89]

The war—and the revolution—ended for the Hales family in December 1922. On the 7th Sean was assassinated in Dublin in retaliation for an emergency powers bill he had not voted for. His killers were never caught. Tom was captured and interned in the same week. He helped lead the prisoners' hunger strike in Harepark Camp the following year.[90] Hannah died a month later and Bob, still hunted by the new authorities (and apparently rejected by the I.R.A.), became increasingly erratic and troublesome.[91] Robert was moved to a nursing home, despite the family's worsening financial difficulties. Bill was arrested and then released. He ran as an independent candidate in the 1923 election, coming a distant last in a field of fifteen candidates with only 510 votes.[92] Only Madge and her mother Margaret remained at Knocknacurra throughout. Donal continued acting as republican consul, but the position was purely symbolic. Madge's letters to him were now composed largely of memories of the dead, crippled, and imprisoned. 'Oh what bright hopes they had.'[93]

Tom and Sean Hales proved to be successful entrepreneurs like their father. Between them they helped create the republican movement in West Cork and led—or pushed—it down the untried and uncertain path to revolution. By doing so they made history and they made themselves players in Ireland's new politics.

The Hales family embraced revolution and suffered accordingly. They were

---

[87] See Griffith and O'Grady, *Curious Journey*, 288–90; Ryan, *The Day Michael Collins Was Shot*, 27, 90.

[88] Report on Cork Command, 18 Jan. 1923 (Mulcahy Papers, P7/B/67).

[89] Liam Deasy (O'Malley Papers, P17b/86). For an interesting report of the brothers' reactions, see *Freeman's Journal*, 25 Aug. 1922.

[90] Thomas Cotter statement (CAI, Seamus Fitzgerald Papers, PR/6/32).

[91] For Tom, see *Weekly Examiner*, 2 Dec. 1922; for Bob, see Madge to Donal Hales, 9 June 1923, Cork Command Intelligence Report, 13 Nov. 1922 (MA, CW/OPS/14F) and O/C 7 Bn., Cork 1 to O/C 1 South. Div., 25 Sept. 1922 (MA, A/0991/5).

[92] See *Freeman's Journal*, 18 Sept. 1922; *Examiner*, 20, 31 Aug. 1923.

[93] Madge Hales to Donal Hales, 6 June 1923 (Hales Papers).

engulfed by the politics of violence they espoused and, like the O'Briens of Broad Lane, they became the helpless objects of reprisal. Their farm and then their house was burned at night by masked men. Their workman was killed in his own home. Tom was brutally tortured and Sean was shot down in a Dublin street. As usual, none of these victims had any chance to defend himself.

Throughout these events the Haleses, particularly Tom and Sean, displayed an extraordinary devotion to their cause and to their country. Nevertheless, the ideas behind these convictions remain vague: a bedrock hatred of landlords, the Irish Party, and British rule articulated through prevailing clichés ('we must fight against corruption and . . . venality' (1917); 'our dead did not die for anything short of Freedom' (1921); 'I agree with Mick' (1922)[94]). The Haleses acted where others talked, but their basic attitudes were not markedly different from those of a great many other Irish nationalists.

If we are to understand how these ideals became embodied in the Volunteer movement and how they were translated into action and violence, we must also understand their social context. Radicalism ran in the Hales family. It was family pride and loyalty which provided the fundamental basis for political action.[95] The father, sisters, brothers, and cousins were all active in the republican movement.

Closely bound up with this kinship network was the Haleses' strong sense of neighbourhood. Ballinadee produced a trusted cadre of friendly and supportive families and was both a refuge and a power base. The Haleses defined themselves politically in terms of this community: 'there would not be a parliament in Dublin but for the Ballinadee crowd.'[96] It was their leadership of the 'Ballinadee crowd'—the declared ability to recruit 100 men over 6 feet tall—that made them regional leaders in West Cork and it may well be that the company's collapse in 1922 paved the way for Tom Hales to be 'deposed' as commandant. Guerrilla war revealed the outer limits of these networks as the brothers very rarely moved beyond their home territory around Bandon.

The power of cliques and territory was also revealed by Sean's decision to vote for the Treaty. While still at home he had apparently been against it, but the Dail debates brought him into the orbit of Collins and his expatriate West Cork cronies. From then on Sean seems to have spent as much time in Dublin as he did in Cork. In a sense, he switched factions. Madge's loyalty to Collins also influenced her support. In both cases, political decisions were channelled by factional or personal loyalties.

Why did people join the Volunteers and how did some Volunteers become

---

[94]   Sean Hales, quoted in Coogan, *Michael Collins*, 339.

[95]   For the perceived importance of family tradition, see Ryan, *Tom Barry Story*, 17–18 and the national memorial to Sean Hales in Bandon.

[96]   Tom Hales before the military pensions referee and advisory committee, 10 June 1941 (S9243). See also Hales, 'History Notes', on the exceptional nationalism, purity, and physique of the people of Ballinadee.

guerrillas? Patriotism and idealism were certainly part of the answer for the Haleses and others, but not all patriots and idealists joined the I.R.A. and not all members became or stayed activists. In Bandon, many Volunteers dropped or were pushed out of the movement. Even in the stronghold of Ballinadee, less than half the company paraded to fight on Easter Sunday 1916 and almost the entire membership resigned in 1922. To answer these questions, then, we must look beyond the inner drives of nationalism and idealism to examine the social networks through which they were expressed. This is the subject of the next chapter.

10

Volunteering

When 1916 came it had a great impact . . . to quote the late Seamus Murphy
quoting Yeats: 'A Terrible Beauty was born'.

(Con Neenan)[1]

I never joined nothing.
(Non-Volunteer (who wishes to remain anonymous))[2]

Who were the Irish Volunteers? I have discussed what sort of people joined the
I.R.A. but this does not tell us why particular individuals joined or why only a
fraction of these men went on to become active guerrillas. Most shop assistants,
apprentices, and farmers' sons did not get involved and many of those who did,
did little or nothing. To understand these choices and their consequences we
must first explore the experiences, networks, and loyalties that shaped them.

The Volunteer organization which emerged in 1917 had little in common with
its namesake of the year before. The new Volunteer companies were far more
numerous, larger, more dynamic, and part of a wider political movement. They
also had an almost entirely different and younger membership. Fewer than 900
Corkmen had paraded on Easter Sunday 1916 (about 60 per cent of the total force)
even before they knew that a rising was planned.[3] In the wake of the rebellion and
martial law many of these companies collapsed.[4] Most Volunteers surrendered
their arms.[5] Many dropped out and did not return. Others were rapidly pushed out
by the newcomers. Only a greatly reduced nucleus remained.[6] The Volunteers of
1917 and 1918 were not just joining, they were creating a new movement.

---

[1] MacEoin, *Survivors*, 236.

[2] Interview with a contemporary of the Irish Volunteers, 26 Apr. 1989.

[3] A detailed breakdown of the company rolls and turnout on Easter Sunday can be found in the
Florence O'Donoghue Papers (MS 31, 439). See also O'Donoghue, 'The Irish Volunteers in Cork',
41.

[4] By January 1917, when new companies were already starting to be formed, only seventeen of
the original thirty-nine rural companies in the Cork Brigade were functioning and nearly all had lost
members: on average, these units were 22% smaller, which probably reflects an even greater loss of
old members since some new ones had probably already joined. These figures result from a comparison between the brigade rolls as of Easter Sunday 1916 (O'Donoghue Papers, MS 31, 439) and an
equivalent document seized from Sean Nolan by the R.I.C. on 22 Feb. 1917: Michael Buckley to S.
Nolan, 15 Jan. 1917 (CO 904/29/2).

[5] Among the seventeen reactivated companies in January 1917 mentioned in n. 4, for example,
twenty-eight of fifty rifles held in 1916 (or 56%) had been surrendered.

[6] In Dunmanway, for example, one veteran told me that about half of the pre-rising Volunteers
left in 1916. Interview with AA.

The question of personal motivation is oddly absent from most memoirs and memories of the period. Volunteers seem to have regarded their political commitment as completely natural and their motives as self-evident, requiring little reflection. 'It was the thing to do'; 'sure, everybody was joining'; 'I never thought much about it.'[7] Individual decision-making—the act of joining—was lost in an emotional haze of romantic patriotism and youthful camaraderie, all bathed in the reflected glory of the Easter Rising.[8] Veterans are rarely able to recall exactly when and how they joined but they remember vividly how it felt to belong: 'There was a spirit in the air alright';[9] 'I did like it at the time.' ''Twas very adventurous. Since I was a young fellow I was longing for it.'[10] In the early 1970s Liam Deasy wrote that:

Even now, after a lapse of more than fifty years, I can recall the thrill of those early parades—the feeling of high adventure, the sense of dedicated service to the cause of Irish freedom, the secret rendezvous, and the gay comradeship—all were to me and my companions like signs of the return of the Golden Age of Ireland's ancient chivalry.[11]

Sean O'Faolain echoed these sentiments almost to the letter:

Never will I forget the first day I stood in a field . . . with a score of other raw recruits, being given my first drill . . . before we were dismissed our Captain . . . spoke to us about what we were, and were there for, about the coming fight, about secrecy and loyalty . . . this gaiety, this liberation of the spirit, was to stay with us all through the exciting years to come.[12]

With this excitement came a heady sense of transformation. 'What a change you would see to what it was six years ago,' one Volunteer wrote in 1918, 'the free and easy lads of Cahalane's Cross are quite the opposite now. They are soldiers.' 'We have grown different men to what we used to be,' declared another.[13] When Sean O'Faolain joined at University College Cork, 'Straightaway my whole life changed. The university became a conspiracy. I was now both student and revolutionary.'[14] Another new convert in Dublin remembered equally the pleasure of belonging: 'We were young and there was a

---

[7] Interviews with AA, AB, and AI.

[8] Frank Gallagher (a Cork republican) wrote: 'How it was I came to join "K" Company, of the Third Battalion of the Dublin Brigade, I cannot now remember' but 'I think nothing while we live will take from us the thrill of those early days of the Volunteer reorganisation.' David Hogan [pseud.], *The Four Glorious Years* (Dublin, 1953), 228–9.

[9] Interview with AE.

[10] Chisholm interview (tape in the possession of Dr John Chisholm).

[11] Deasy, *Towards Ireland Free*, 8.

[12] *Vive Moi!*, 172–3. See also Frank O'Connor's story 'The Patriarch', *Guests of the Nation*, 155.

[13] Letters from Cork, 17 July 1918 and Cahirciveen, 9 Jan. 1917 (Censorship Summaries and Précis, CO 904/164).

[14] O'Faolain, *Vive Moi!*, 172. Ernie O'Malley: 'The University [University College Dublin] was changed now for me—new associations, new affiliations . . . we smiled knowingly at each other, for we kept a secret that nobody else was aware of.' *On Another Man's Wound*, 46–7.

lot of the boy scout spirit amongst us. We also had the universally satisfying feeling that comes from belonging to an exclusive club or to any group of conspirators.'[15] The 'boys' had become 'soldiers', friendships became 'conspiracies', fields and crossroads became 'secret rendezvous', and sheds and abandoned houses became 'the barracks' or 'Liberty Hall' (in this case, in Ballyvourney): 'headquarters, clubhouse, meeting place, tea rooms, rest-house, according to the occasion and the point of view, its meagre few cubic feet of airspace vibrated and hummed with sedition.'[16]

O'Faolain is one of many Volunteers who described their commitment to the new movement in almost mystical terms, as a conversion experience.[17] 'A revolution had begun in Ireland', his friend Frank O'Connor recalled, 'but it was nothing to the revolution that had begun in me.'[18] The 1916 rising and the executions which followed were frequently a catalyst for politicization, often in an explicitly religious context. Many rebels-to-be were forged during the intense requiem masses celebrated on behalf of the Easter martyrs. These went on all that summer, with emotions kept at fever pitch by the trial and hanging of Sir Roger Casement. 'It became something of an adventure . . . the door swinging to behind us and shutting us into the warm, dim, smelly church . . . where a young priest said Mass for twenty or so other adventurers like ourselves.'[19] Charles Dalton, later a member of the Dublin Brigade (and of Michael Collins's 'Squad'), walked for hours amongst the ruins of the late rebellion 'with a feeling of sadness, and at the same time of holiness and exultation'.[20] Several weeks after this he attended his first patriot mass: 'That was a day of great happiness for me. I had a wonderful, proud feeling, walking in the procession . . . these Masses were held frequently and enabled me to become one of the crowd who attended them.'[21]

Such born-again republicans saw their commitment not just as a political act but as a way of life. For some the movement became a calling, the embodiment of virtue. It was these 'new men' who set the puritanical tone for the movement. Liam Lynch is a case in point. Up to April 1916 he was, with his brothers, an active member of the Ancient Order of Hibernians and the National Volunteers. 'Liam was a terrible Redmond man and he hated the Irish Volunteers.'[22] His then more radical godmother, Hanna Clery Condon, remembers his frequent attempts to convert her 'and the tears ran down his face when I couldn't change':

---

[15] C. S. Andrews, *Dublin Made Me* (Dublin, 1979), 98.
[16] Twohig, *Green Tears*, 21. Practically every company had its own 'barracks': see, for example, Ned Murphy and 'Congo' Condon (O'Malley Papers, P17b/123).
[17] O'Faolain, *Vive Moi!*, 130, 172–3.
[18] O'Connor, *An Only Child*, 155.
[19] Frank O'Connor, 'The Patriarch', *Guests of the Nation*, 154.
[20] Charles Dalton, *With the Dublin Brigade (1917–1921)* (London, 1929), 41–2.
[21] Ibid. 42–3. Ernie O'Malley was at the same mass.
[22] Tom Crawford (O'Malley Papers, P17b/129).

He was a Nationalist until the day the British attacked the Kents of Bawnard [in May 1916] and he saw Thomas Kent being brought in bleeding through the town of Fermoy, and his poor mother dragging along after them . . . He said that when he saw the Kents going through Fermoy it was like a sword going through his heart.[23]

From that point on he was a changed man:

Lynch's associates in Fermoy were either colleagues in the business where he worked or other members of the commercial element in the town. Most of them lacked any sort of National outlook. Immediately he joined the Volunteers [in July 1917] Lynch broke away from this element completely, and associated only with comrades in the movement. From the very start when he joined the Sinn Fein club and Volunteers in Fermoy he attended every meeting and parade and after business hours he invariably went to the Sinn Fein club.[24]

Lynch was possessed by a sense of mission and by revolutionary ardour and remained so until his death in 1923. Many I.R.A. men described him as being 'like a priest' in his attitudes and manner.[25] He was an exceedingly shy man and 'it must have cost him a big effort at the start appearing in public'.[26] However, Lynch's utter commitment drove him to take the lead in organizing the Fermoy area. When he died he was chief of staff of the entire I.R.A. Lynch made himself a leader out of the force of his own convictions.

For all the intensity and impact of these experiences, it was these, and the act of joining itself, which separated the mass of Volunteers from the rest of their generation rather than any prior political, ideological, or personal differences. Liam Lynch, the archetypal evangelical republican, had been almost as ardent in his previous attachment to the Irish Party. Most young men had no 'politics' (in the party sense) at all. William O'Brien's All For Ireland League did have a scattered fringe of youthful radicals (primarily in Bantry, Ballinadee, and the city) but most of these departed after O'Brien declared his support for the war effort in 1914.[27] O'Brienites were seen as natural allies by Sinn Fein in the common fight against the 'Mollies', and as natural supporters during the Tan War by the I.R.A., but there is no evidence that the Volunteers drew proportionately more members from O'Brienite families or districts.[28] The Haleses were an exception in this respect.

[23] Hanna Clery Condon (O'Malley Papers, P17b/132).

[24] George Power to F. O'Donoghue, 21 Dec. 1953 (O'Donoghue Papers, MS 31, 421).

[25] Interview with AI. See also O'Donoghue, *No Other Law*, 10.

[26] Power to O'Donoghue, 21 Dec. 1953.

[27] See David Hogan, *The Four Glorious Years* (Dublin, 1953), 224–8; O'Donoghue, 'History of the Irish Volunteers', 11, 23; Ted O'Sullivan (O'Malley Papers, P17b/108).

[28] Most of the veterans I interviewed did not identify the I.R.A. with either party in any way (one was even offended by the question) but thought that O'Brienites had been friendlier and had played an important role in breaking the Irish Party's hold on local politics. Several had O'Brienite parents but others either had Redmondite families or could not remember. The Ernie O'Malley interviews record essentially the same opinions: see Ted O'Sullivan (P17b/108); Barney O'Driscoll (P17b/95); Paddy Coughlan, Seamus Fitzgerald, and Dan Corkery (P17b/111).

A detailed evaluation of the links between the AFIL, Sinn Fein, and the I.R.A. is impossible at this point as very little is known about O'Brienite membership or support. However, to say, as

Nor did most Volunteers have any previous contact with organized cultural revivalism. Before the rising, the Gaelic League and Sinn Fein existed largely in the form of diminutive urban clubs and isolated enthusiasts, many of whom were older than the average Volunteer. Some of them had played a crucial role in the revival of the I.R.B. and in the formation of the Irish Volunteers. This was where Tomas MacCurtain, Terence MacSwiney, Sean O'Hegarty, Liam de Roiste, and many other early leaders began their activist careers, and their cultural commitment gave the movement much of its ideological fervour. While influential, though, they themselves were rarely fighting men, and their leagues and clubs were too small and introverted to be nurseries for gunmen.[29]

The Gaelic Athletic Association was a different matter (dealt with below) but it too had only a very limited hold on the political imaginations of the 'younger generation'. The great majority of young men joined Sinn Fein, the Gaelic League, and the GAA at about the same time they became Volunteers, in a frenzy of collective joining. All of these organizations expanded suddenly and enormously in this period, in one big rush.[30] Gaelicizing one's name, going to Irish classes, and buying a hurley were all part of belonging to the movement. 'One can still almost date that generation by its Liams, Seans and Peadars.'[31]

As with the Volunteers it was the joining which was important. Just how deep this enthusiasm ran among the new members was open to question. One Gaelic League veteran referred in February 1918 to 'the thousands of young men in this City by the Lee who do nothing beyond wearing badges'.[32] Sean Moylan later spoke with disdain of the 'part-time' or 'shoneen' Gaelic League; 'I am afraid there are a good many of that class of Gaelic Leaguer in North Cork.'[33]

Brendan Clifford does, that 'the A.F.I.L. strongholds were the areas where the war of independence was chiefly fought' is clearly untrue (Clifford (ed.), *Reprints From the 'Cork Free Press'*, 51). In the general elections of 1910 and the subsequent by-elections, the safest O'Brienite seats were in North-East and North-West Cork, while the safest Redmondite seat was East Cork. In general, the guerrillas were more active in the east than the north. We can test this further by correlating I.R.A. violence with the percentage of votes obtained by Redmondite candidates in rural district council elections in 1914 (returns published in *Cork Examiner*, *Cork Free Press*, and *Eagle*, 6–8 June 1914). This reveals no significant district-by-district relationship between the two, except for a strong correlation of .60 between UIL votes and I.R.A. violence in 1917–19. By this—admittedly inconclusive—measure, early I.R.A. activists tended to come from areas where the AFIL had been weaker.

[29] Correlating Gaelic League membership as of January 1917 with I.R.A. violence in each county of Ireland produces a modestly significant coefficient of .41 for 1917–19 but an insignificant .19 for 1920–1, and .23 for the whole period, 1917–23: Hart, 'The Geography of Revolution in Ireland', 197, 202.

[30] See, for example, the annual report of the O'Growney branch of the Gaelic League in Cork city in the *Star*, 9 Feb. 1918 or the 'Notes from Kilbrittain' in the 16 Feb. 1918 issue of the same paper. See also Lankford, *The Hope and the Sadness*, 255 and the 'Bandon History' (Price Papers).

[31] O'Connor, *An Only Child*, 186.

[32] Michael Ua Cuill in the *Star*, 23 Feb. 1918. League organizers also frequently complained of poor attendance at Irish classes: see Notes from Ballinhassig and from Timoleague in the *Star*, 16 Feb. 1918, 5 Apr. 1919. I must also add, however, that one of the veterans I interviewed, AJ, has remained dedicated to the language all his life after first being exposed to it as a Volunteer. There was undoubtedly a small but significant minority like him.   [33] *Examiner*, 19 Sept. 1921.

For the most part, people did not join the Volunteers because they were radical. They became radicalized because they joined the Volunteers. Apart from their Gaelic gloss, the political beliefs of the early Volunteers were not significantly different from those of their peers. Opposition to martial law, military recruitment, and conscription, as well as dissatisfaction with John Redmond's Irish Party, were near-universal in Cork after 1916, as was the retrospective acclamation of the heroes of the Easter Rising. The rapid growth of this patriotic cult depended not only on commemorative masses but also on the flood of rebel memorabilia, of postcards, mass cards, song sheets, pamphlets, flags, badges, pictures, photograph albums, calendars, and a host of other mass-produced icons.[34] Indeed, souvenirs and prayers often went together. As Frank O'Connor remembers, 'In the early mornings Mother and I went into town to the Franciscan or Augustinian church where mass was said for the dead rebels, and on the way back we bought picture postcards of them.'[35] At the same time, in Dublin, Charles Dalton 'began at once to collect souvenirs and papers . . . whenever I could get a photograph of one of the dead leaders I treasured it with a kind of sacred interest'.[36] In Liam Ruiseal's Cork city bookstore, the hurriedly reprinted works of the rebel leaders 'sold like hot cakes. Pictures of the leaders, song books, national songs, etc., made a complete change in the people's attitude.'[37] Irish nationalism was as much consumed as practised.

This new iconography was probably more influential than revolutionary ideas or texts. As A. T. Culloty wrote of the Volunteers of Ballydesmond parish, 'their knowledge of the wider national ideas was vague, and at times, confused', a confusion exemplified by the fact that when de Valera came to speak nearby, no one knew how to pronounce his name.[38] None of the I.R.A. veterans I interviewed had read *Sinn Fein* or any other products of the radical 'mosquito press'. Of far greater importance was John Mitchel's *Jail Journal*. The only other nationalist writer who came close was A. M. Sullivan, who wrote *The Story of Ireland* and helped edit *Speeches from the Dock*. The young men of 1917 and 1918 read these works with passion and imbued them with revolutionary meaning but they were nevertheless a familiar part of mainstream Irish literature, read equally by large numbers of non-Volunteers. Those men who did not join the

---

[34] See, for example, the advertisement for photographs in the *Examiner*, 13 Oct. 1916 or the collection of memorabilia in R.I.C. files (CO 904/166). The importance and ubiquity of these items is also demonstrated by Dublin District Raid Reports from 1920–1. Most suspect houses contained photographs, calendars, songbooks, and the like, all of which were seized and itemized, thus providing a sort of political shopping catalogue (WO 35/70–9). Perhaps the most striking aspect of the cult of martyrs was the circulation of political relics, locks of Terence MacSwiney's hair being one example.

[35] O'Connor, *An Only Child*, 156. In 'The Patriarch' he wrote that 'The boys and girls about me buzzed with it [the rebellion]; instead of stamps or birds' eggs they collected prints of the dead leaders or rebel ballads.' *Guests of the Nation*, 152.

[36] Dalton, *With the Dublin Brigade*, 41.

[37] Ruiseal, *Liam Ruiseal Remembers*, 22.

[38] A. T. Culloty, *Ballydesmond: A Rural Parish in its Historical Setting* (Dublin, 1986), 237.

I.R.A. believed themselves to be just as good nationalists as the Volunteers, whether they were serving or discharged soldiers ('they were as good Irishman as any Sinn Feiner'[39]), policemen ('I'm just as good an Irishman as you'[40]), or anyone else, such as the man quoted at the beginning of this chapter who proudly declared that he 'never joined nothing' and added that 'they were no better than the rest of us'.

The question, then, is not: why did certain men become nationalists? It is, rather: why did certain nationalists become Volunteers? These men shared very real convictions and ideals, but it seems clear that, for the majority of Volunteers, the decision to join was a collective rather than an individual one, rooted more in local communities and networks than in ideology or formal political loyalties. Young men tended to join the organization together with, or following, members of their families and friendship groups. The 'boys' who 'strawed', played, worked, and grew up together became the 'boys' who drilled, marched, and raided together.

The most important bonds holding Volunteers together were those of family and neighbourhood. Indeed, I.R.A. companies were very often founded upon such networks; 'the raw Volunteers were primarily friends and neighbours'.[41] The Gurteen Company was formed by the Crowley brothers around their neighbours at Tinker's Cross (a former battleground in the Land War). Mallow's first Volunteers all lived on Beecher Street. In Ballinhassig the pioneers were the Hyde family, especially the brothers Paddy and Mick. Mick and Eugene Walsh recruited the Clogagh Company from among their neighbours in Gaggin. The Nadd Company was begun by Liam and Aodh O'Brien.[42] Micheal O'Suilleabhain's company in Ballyvourney was led by his uncle and brother. In Dick Barrett's parish near Bandon:

Initially the Irish Volunteer movement did not attract many adherents and the limited numbers who joined were confined to a small area in and around the village of Kilpatrick in the north-west of the parish. Early in the year 1918 units of the Irish Volunteers were organized in Innishannon and Knockavilla as separate companies, the latter being named the Crosspound Company for the probable reason that the leading officers and bulk of the members resided around the road junction three miles north of Upton Station.[43]

Similarly, G Company of the 2nd Battalion in Cork city was known as the 'Phairs Cross' Company because this was 'the heart of the centre from which the company drew its strength'.[44]

---

[39]   *Irish Times*, 10 Nov. 1917. This declaration was made at an informal meeting of Munster Fusiliers.   [40]   *Examiner*, 16 Nov. 1916.
[41]   J. J. O'Connell, 'History of the Irish Volunteers', ch. 1, 3 (NLI, Bulmer Hobson Papers, MS 13,168).   [42]   O'Donoghue, 'History of the Irish Volunteers', 28, 29, 30, 74, 83.
[43]   Joe Walsh, *The Story of Dick Barrett* (Cork, 1972).
[44]   The crossroads was at the juncture of Barrack Street and St Finbarr's Road. The quotation is from a collective obituary for company members, probably written by Florence O'Donoghue (O'Donoghue Papers, MS 31, 444—the newspaper is unknown).

The Kilbrittain Company, one of the most active in the county, was built around a clutch of militant neighbours, the O'Neills, Crowleys, Fitzgeralds, O'Briens, Mannings, and others. The unit started as an extension of the Ballinadee Company, which was also linked by kinship as the Haleses and the Fitzgeralds were cousins. 'Were it not for families like the O'Neills [five of whose sons were in the I.R.A. and with equally active daughters] and others', declared Liam Deasy, 'our Volunteer army could never have continued the fight.'[45]

An analysis of I.R.A. unit rolls bears out this impression of clannishness. Of the members of the Macroom Battalion who can be traced in the census, fully 50 per cent were brothers, as were 58 per cent of the Lisgoold Company, 49 per cent of the Mourneabbey Company, 39 per cent of the Grenagh Company, and 37 per cent of the Kiskeam Company.[46] And, almost certainly, considerably more of these Volunteers were cousins. Most of the I.R.A. veterans I interviewed joined with, or following, an older brother.

The same pattern can be observed all over Ireland. Clare had its leading I.R.A. clans, the Brennans and the Barretts, Donegal had the Sweeneys and the O'Donnells, and so on. In north Kerry, Mike Quill's company were 'all neighbours from the same parish'[47] and the prominent Carnacross Company in Meath 'was almost a family affair with seven Farrelly brothers, five Dunne brothers, another family of four Dunnes, the Lynchs, the Dalys, and two Tevlins making up most of the company'.[48]

Groups of co-workers often volunteered together, like the apprentices at the Haulbowline shipyards—'a little nursery of Republicanism'—led by Mick Leahy and Seamus Fitzgerald.[49] The strength of the organization in the yards was such that, when it became the subject of government concern in 1918, the Admiralty concluded 'the proportion of the workmen employed in the Dockyard who are attached to the Sinn Fein movement is so considerable that to make such attachment a disqualification for employment' would shut it

---

[45] Liam Deasy, 'Sidelights on Ireland's Fight for Freedom' (Mulcahy Papers, P7/D/45): 'Local knowledge, local tradition (in many cases, going back in certain families, through Fenian stock, to '98 and even earlier), local comradeship between men who knew each other intimately from schooldays—all these were potent factors in the development of a determined fighting force.' See also Deasy, 'The Brave Men of Kilbrittain', *Star*, 10 Apr. 1971 and O'Donoghue, 'History of the Irish Volunteers', 75.

[46] These unit rolls can be found in: Browne, *The Story of the 7th*; Tomas O'Riordan, *Where the Owenacurra Flows: A History of the Parish of Lisgoold* (Cork, n.d.); Tom O'Regan, 'Rural Ireland at Easter 1916' (Lankford Papers, U169); Duggan (ed.), *Grenagh and Courtbrack*; J. J. O'Riordan, *Kiskeam Versus the Empire* (Tralee, 1985). All of these rolls except that of the Mourneabbey Company refer to nominal memberships as of 1921. The figures given are percentages of those members identified through manuscript census returns.

[47] Shirley Quill, *Mike Quill—Himself: A Memoir* (Greenwich, 1985), 19.

[48] Coogan, *Politics and War in Meath*, 191.

[49] The quotation is from an obituary of Mick Leahy, probably written by Florence O'Donoghue (O'Donoghue Papers, MS 31, 444—the newspaper is unknown).

down.[50] Other politically significant workforces included those at the Clondulane mills led by Moss Twomey and Mick Fitzgerald,[51] the Blarney woollen mills (including Frank Busteed,)[52] and the Passage dockyards.[53] The recently opened Ford factory was another hotbed of Volunteer activity throughout the whole revolution.[54]

Even Liam Lynch's highly individual conversion must be put into this social context. Fermoy, where he worked as a clerk, lived up to its reputation as a loyal garrison town. It had no Volunteer company before July 1917 and most of those who joined subsequently were not native to the town but were, like Lynch, young apprentices and assistants from the country.[55] 'There was a big crowd at Barry's',[56] the business where Lynch was employed, and when he became a Volunteer he did so in company with George Power, his best friend and fellow shop assistant (Power had previously also joined, and left, the National Volunteers and the Hibernians with Lynch[57]), and Tommy Barry, a colleague at Barry's. Liam's brother James also joined the I.R.A. and served until the end of the Civil War.[58] Both Power and Barry went on to become I.R.A. officers and guerrilla leaders. Lynch's personal commitment cannot be doubted but the fact that his brother, friends, and workmates, his 'crowd', were fellow-travellers had much to do with shaping his revolutionary career.

Football and hurling teams were another important source of recruits. These were often the primary focus of young men's sense of territory and identity and provided their main source of recreation and prestige. It was a small leap from playing together to marching or drilling together. The two activities were often combined, Sunday after mass being the favourite time for both, with hurleys doubling as mock rifles.

In the strong hurling and football country around Bandon, several teams joined the Volunteers *en bloc* in 1917 and 1918, their captains and organizers, Dick Barrett and the Deasy and Hales brothers, becoming leading officers. Liam Deasy was responsible for bringing in the Valley Rovers:

[50] Admiralty Sec. to Under-Sec., 6 Aug. 1918, in the file on 'Sinn Feiners Employed at Haulbowline' (CO 904/23). See also Queenstown (Cobh) DI Reports of 9 Sept. 1916, 28 Jan. 1917, and 15 Jan. 1920 (Cork Co. Museum, Michael Leahy Papers, L412); Kieran McCarthy and Maj-Britt Christensen, *Cobh's Contribution to the Fight for Irish Freedom 1913–1990* (Cobh, 1992), 19.

[51] See O'Riordan, *The Price of Freedom*.

[52] See the statement on the O'Doherty family in the Muiris Meadhach Papers (CAI).

[53] Colman O'Mahony, *The Maritime Gateway to Cork* (Cork, 1986), 99.

[54] See the statement of Matt Delaney (CO 762/160) who claimed to have been hounded out of the Ford's factory, 'a large number' of whose employees 'were prominently identified with the activities of the Irish Republican Army'. These examples of republican workplaces are also based on the frequency with which their employees turn up in arrest reports or prison records.

[55] Tommy Barry, Lar Condon, and George Power (O'Malley Papers, P17b/123).

[56] Lar Condon (O'Malley Papers, P17b/123).

[57] George Power to Florence O'Donoghue, 22 June 1950 (O'Donoghue Papers, MS 31, 421 (11)).

[58] See the obituary in *An Phoblacht*, 11 Mar. 1933.

At the time I was well known in this parish [Innishannon] through G.A.A. activities that had led me and a few companions to found the Valley Rovers Hurling and Football Club there six years earlier . . . Now to see what prospects there were of founding a Company of Volunteers in the parish I sounded some of the more important members of the club, and finding that they considered the prospects favourable . . . the Company was organized, and I was duly elected its Captain.[59]

Eighty per cent of the Rovers joined the Volunteers and the company drilled on their football fields.

In Cork city, Mick Murphy, the south side battalion commander, was a championship hurler with the Blackrock club. According to Con Neenan, 'our crowd picked up all the hurley groups in the city for Mick was in 1919 a hurling man and was well known'.[60] Mick Leahy, a senior officer in East Cork, had played for the same club. Dan 'Sandow' Donovan, the north side commander, was also a medal-winning football player (and another recent convert to the GAA). His brothers were both team mates and fellow gunmen.[61]

The role of the GAA should not be overemphasized, however. The organization seems to have been highly regionalized, hurling teams being concentrated in parts of the Bandon valley, East Cork, and the city. In these areas, games and volunteering sometimes went hand in hand, but in other areas this was not necessarily the case. Even among I.R.A. men in the Bandon area, many active guerrillas never belonged to any serious club and had no idea of other officers' sporting connections.[62] Dick Barrett was the only officer of the Knockavilla football club—located in the same parish as the Valley Rovers—to become an active guerrilla.[63] Other GAA clubs show similarly tenuous I.R.A. connections. The captain of the 1918 Rosscarbery team was also captain of the town's Volunteer company, but only one of his players can be identified as a fellow member. Among their rivals for the West Cork championship, the Tullig club, no one can be identified as such.[64] In the Midleton and Blackrock (Mick Murphy's club) teams of 1917, only one player of each can be identified as a member of the I.R.A.[65] On the 1911 Bandon hurling team (winners of the West Cork Cup), three players joined the Volunteers before 1916 but none of them was prominent in later years.[66] Of those surveyed, only the 1917 Lyre (Clonakilty) football team contained a significant number of active guerrillas.[67] In fact, a great many Volunteers only joined or formed hurling or football

[59] Deasy, *Towards Ireland Free*, 18. For Knockavilla and Dick Barrett, see Walsh, *The Story of Dick Barrett*.   [60] Con Neenan (O'Malley Papers, P17b/112).

[61] Interview with AK.

[62] Three West Cork I.R.A. men interviewed by Dr John Chisholm, close colleagues of Liam Deasy, knew nothing of his family's GAA affiliations. None of the men I interviewed were active in the GAA before the revolution, although several became so later in the 1920s.

[63] See the list of Knockavilla officials, captains, and vice-captains in the *Star*, 12 May 1917.

[64] The teams are listed in the *Eagle*, 31 Aug. 1918.   [65] *Examiner*, 19 Mar. 1917.

[66] The team is named in the *Bandon Opinion*, Dec. 1980.   [67] *Star*, 13 Oct. 1917.

teams after they had volunteered, as part of the rush to embrace all things Gaelic.[68]

Local teams apart, the GAA as an organization had very little influence on the development of the I.R.A.[69] J. J. O'Connell stated that 'it was a fact that the Volunteers did not receive from the G.A.A. the help they expected'.[70] Athletes' politics were never routinely republican. Many prominent GAA players joined the British army in 1914 and 1915. Several GAA clubs—notably Redmond's in the city—remained faithful to the Irish Party.[71]

A lot of Cork guerrillas were wary of Gaelic officialdom, believing them to be talkers rather than fighters or, even worse, politicians.[72] These fears were personified by J. J. Walsh and Patrick 'Paudeen' O'Keefe, two prominent GAA organizers who made militant speeches in the early days of the revolution but wound up as Sinn Fein, and later Free State, functionaries. This distrust of the Association (which had a particularly chequered past in Cork) and its penchant for bureaucracy pre-dated the formation of the Volunteers. Many local teams never affiliated with the GAA or had broken away in the years before the revolution. Flor Crowley and his friends in Behigullane, Dunmanway, for example, viewed the Association as rule-bound and elitist, and looked upon football as a townsman's game.[73]

Football and hurling were not important to the Volunteers as an organization but as a part of local, informal youth culture. The 'hurling crowds' around Bandon were more or less the same clusters of brothers, neighbours, and 'pals' who formed the companies in Ballinadee, Kilbrittain, Kilpatrick, and Crosspound already mentioned above, the same 'boys' in a different guise.[74] Local teams were derived from these networks just as Volunteer companies were. At this level, loyalty to your pals and to your corner of the parish was indistinguishable from political and team loyalties.

Companies were usually formed on local initiative by self-nominated organizers: entrepreneurs who could count on their 'crowd' to back them up. In some cases these were men who had first joined the movement elsewhere, at work or in college or school. These men were important carriers of information and

[68] See 'Bandon History': 'practically every Company of Volunteers had a hurling or football team or both.' One company in Galway reportedly attracted recruits because it possessed the only football in the neighbourhood (CI Report, West Galway, July 1918 (CO 904/106)). Similarly, a Dublin man stated at his 1921 court martial that he had only joined the Volunteers in 1918 to play football (*Examiner*, 27 Jan. 1921).

[69] Correlating county-by-county GAA membership and I.R.A. violence over the whole of Ireland produces a coefficient of only .06 for the 1917–23 period, and of -.04 for 1917–19. See Hart, 'The Geography of Revolution in Ireland', 197, 202. See also Fitzpatrick, *Politics and Irish Life*, 134.

[70] O'Connell, 'History of the Irish Volunteers', Ch. 1, 4. See also Walsh, *Recollections of a Rebel*, 34.   [71] See, for example, *Star*, 27 Oct. 1917; *Examiner*, 19 Dec. 1918.

[72] C. S. Andrews and his south Dublin comrades also disapproved of the GAA as insufficiently concerned with the Irish language and overly influenced by priests. See Andrews, *Dublin Made Me*, 113–14.   [73] Crowley, *In West Cork Long Ago*, 25–8.

[74] The quotation is from a Bandon I.R.A. veteran interviewed by Dr John Chisholm.

organization. At the very least they could pronounce 'de Valera'. Men who returned from the British civil service acted as a catalyst for the Volunteers around Newmarket, for example. They 'brought a new dimension to the local scene'.[75] Hugh Thornton, a veteran of the Dublin rising, performed a similar function in Bandon, as did Seamus Robinson in south Tipperary.[76]

These inner circles recruited from among their relatives, co-workers, school-mates, and neighbours. One rural pioneer in West Cork told me he had joined the Volunteers along with his brother while studying in Cork city in 1917.[77] They returned home in 1918 determined to found a unit in their own neighbour-hood near Clonakilty. As was usual, they met and discussed this with 'seven or eight' of their closest friends, and made a collective decision. 'School pals came first. We started with school pals and brought in a fellow here and there, the ones we trusted.' They did not try to mobilize the whole parish. Once they had reached the limits of their like-minded friends and relatives, they stopped recruiting. In effect, their friendship group simply assumed the title of a Volunteer company.

These informal networks and bonds gave the I.R.A. a cohesion that its formal structure and drills could never have produced. On the other hand Volunteer units also inherited the local rivalries, factionalism, and territoriality that went with these loyalties. Youth groups created companies in their own image. Their subculture, and the culture of small communities in general, was antithetical to the dictates of mass organization and military hierarchy. Volunteers may have felt themselves to be soldiers in the service of the Nation but most of them still thought like—and were thought of as—'the boys'.

In any case, most companies had little contact with the rest of their organiza-tion before 1920, apart from an occasional visit from a travelling organizer sent from the battalion, brigade, or even GHQ in Dublin. These earnest young men arrived armed with drill manuals and orders of battle but they soon discovered that orders or ideas that went against the local grain were usually ignored, that most units barely distinguished between officers and men, and that the main distinction lay between the 'boys' and strangers like themselves.[78]

Official rank meant little in this milieu. Officers were drawn from the same

---

[75] Culloty, *Ballydesmond*, 237. See also O'Riordan, *Kiskeam Versus the Empire*, 6–7 and, for a parallel situation in another county, Comerford, *My Kilkenny I.R.A. Days*, 55, 71.

[76] For Thornton see 'Bandon History'; for Robinson see Breen, *My Fight for Irish Freedom*, 21, and his own 'Memoirs', 22 (NLI, Frank Gallagher papers, MS 21, 265).

[77] Interview with AB.

[78] See O'Malley, *On Another Man's Wound*, 128: 'I was on the outside. I felt it in many ways, by a diffidence, by an extra courtesy, by a silence.' Richard Mulcahy, who spent the summer of 1917 organizing for both the Gaelic League and the Volunteers (to no discernible effect), despaired of 'the whole loneliness and drudgery of the wide expanse of Cork county . . . the inspiring company contacts were scant' ('Personal Chronology', Mulcahy Papers, P7/D/3). Seamus Lankford had simi-lar experiences in North Cork: Lankford, *The Hope and the Sadness*, 115–16. Micheal O'Suilleabhain provides a picture of an organizer's visit in *Mountainy Men*, 35–9.

groups as the rank and file. Many were self-appointed like the Hales brothers. Others were the 'natural' leaders of their peers: the football or Wren Boy captains, the teachers, the fast talkers, the representatives of prominent families. In the first years of the revolution, however, companies did little beyond marching and drilling so rank was frequently given to those who would be good at giving commands and leading parades and who would look good in the eyes of the community. 'Great men to parade with a flag who lent their prestige and their money to the fight', as Tom Barry cynically put it.[79] 'The men commonly selected someone because he was popular or distinguished in some sphere or other';[80] 'He was chosen because he was from the town, a strong farmer or a neat hurler';[81] 'Sometimes these were selected if a man were good enough to play .45 or Pitch and Toss.'[82] One Tipperary man admitted, 'I know of one man who was elected on the sole grounds that he was considered to be the only man able to give an adequate word of command.'[83]

One group practically guaranteed officer status were ex-prisoners, either those who had been interned in 1916 or those who went to gaol in 1917. Another group almost guaranteed not to be chosen were former officers who were felt to have been too passive or submissive during or after the rising. These men either dropped or were pushed out, and rarely resurfaced within the movement.[84]

In practice, leadership usually flowed from a man's role in his peer group and followed the norms of youth culture. Just as friendship groups tended to be tightly knit and egalitarian in outlook ('they all sort of kept an eye on each other') so Volunteers tended to make decisions collectively and officers 'had to learn to steer as close to the unit as they could'.[85] It was the communal networks that counted, not the chain of command. Most of the men I interviewed were I.R.A. officers at one time or another but few could remember when or how they or others were elected or appointed. 'There was no formality,' said one. As far as another could recall, 'I don't think there were any officers until the Truce.'[86] What they did remember clearly were the key families and 'big fellas' who ran everything. In many units (as in Ballinadee and Bandon), rank circulated among brothers, neighbours, and friends. One activist who founded a company near Bandon with his two brothers said he had 'no particular rank. The brother was

[79] Interview with George O'Mahony.

[80] O'Connell, 'History of the Irish Volunteers', Ch. 1, 3.

[81] O'Malley, *On Another Man's Wound*, 129.

[82] Paddy MacDonnell (O'Malley Papers, P17b/130).

[83] M. J. Costello to Florence O'Donoghue, 11 Dec. 1951 (O'Donoghue Papers, MS 31, 423).

[84] In a sample of twenty-six pre-rising companies, less than one-third of the original officers remained as company, battalion, or brigade officers in the new Cork brigades (twenty-three out of seventy-four men, or 31%). This figure is based on a comparison of 1916 unit lists located in the Terence MacSwiney (Cork Co. Museum, Brigade Council Returns, L233) and Florence O'Donoghue Papers (MS 31, 437) with relevant Bureau of Military History records.

[85] Paddy O'Brien (O'Malley Papers, P17b/124).

[86] Interviews with AD and AL, 23 June 1988. In Ballyvourney, Pat O'Sullivan (whose brothers and uncle were also officers) 'fell into place' as the battalion commander: Twohig, *Green Tears*, 17.

Captain but of course I was the leader.'[87] These links continued to be important throughout the revolution. In 1922, for example, Tom Barry objected to Ted O'Sullivan becoming the commander of the 5th (south-west) Cork Brigade. O'Sullivan arranged for Gibbs Ross, his cousin and close comrade, to be appointed instead and the same Bantry families remained in effective control.[88]

The irrelevance of rank was demonstrated every time an outsider or superior tried to remove or replace an established local officer. 'The boys' almost invariably stuck together, obeyed whomever they pleased and often seceded from the organization altogether. Sean and Tom Hales struggled for a whole year to put their own men in charge of Bandon area units, faced mutinies and mass desertions, and still did not entirely succeed. When T. J. Golden was court-martialled and removed as commandant of the Donoughmore Battalion, the men of his home company in Courtbrack threatened to withdraw from the brigade. Golden persuaded them to stay and continued as an unofficial leader in the area.[89] In a nearly identical incident, Sean Moylan, commander of the Newmarket Battalion, dismissed Jeremiah Scannell as captain of the Kiskeam Company for disobeying orders, claiming that 'he was never officially appointed anyway'. However, 'many of the rank-and-file members of the Company wanted Scannell, and rather than submit to the new O/C they formed an organization of their own behind his back'.[90] Moylan wisely backed down after an angry confrontation and Scannell was re-elected. Thereafter he remained careful of local sensibilities. When he sought to discipline wayward Millstreet officers in 1921 he refused to reduce them in rank as 'it might have a bad effect on the Rank and File'.[91] Loyalties to 'the boys' almost always proved stronger than loyalty to the organization.

Similar confrontations took place in every I.R.A. brigade. A typical case was that of a company in north Kerry whose members refused to parade in November 1921 after their captain was replaced by 'an obnoxious man . . . the head of the village clique. The rank and file will follow any other man outside that clique who number only four or five.'[92] Earlier that year the whole brigade had effectively renounced GHQ control when their commander, Paddy Cahill, was dismissed—or rather, what remained of the brigade. Several units were already operating independently of Cahill and Dublin by this time, so real authority had already been lost.[93]

The intensity of these parochial (or sub-parochial) loyalties meant that much of the organizers' time was taken up with factional firefighting. Sean Moylan

[87] Chisholm interview. [88] Ted O'Sullivan (O'Malley Papers, P17b/108).

[89] Duggan (ed.), *Grenagh and Courtbrack*, 16.

[90] O'Riordan, *Kiskeam Versus the Empire*, 13.

[91] O/C Cork 2 to C/S, 13 Jan. 1921 (Liddell Hart Centre, Charles Howard Foulkes Papers, Epitome of Seized Documents No. 53/3649).

[92] Letter from J.K.W., 11 Nov. 1921 (Mulcahy Papers, P7/A/37).

[93] See the testimonies of Con Casey, Johnny Connors, Tadg Kennedy (O'Malley Papers, P17b/38), Tom MacEllistrum, Denis Quill, and Bertie Scully (P17b/102).

had to 'constantly watch ancient quarrels and local grievances'.[94] Across the border in Kerry, John Joe Rice 'spent all my time tramping from one company area to another fixing disputes and squabbles'.[95] Ernie O'Malley had to fight to overcome 'the clan spirit' and the 'distrust and jealousy' which he encountered everywhere.[96]

The rapid growth of the republican movement in 1917 and 1918 created fierce disputes between competing cliques over leadership, territory, and the right to official status as Volunteers. Few units could contain more than one strong personality, family, or faction and the usual result was for one group to leave and form their own unit—officially or unofficially—or simply quit the movement altogether. Many companies split in this way. The first faction fights were between pre-rising Volunteers and militant newcomers, as in Bandon or in the Berrings Company.[97] Later, the town of Macroom was divided between its rival east and west sides (between Chapel Hill and Masseytown).[98] The men of Clondulane derided and eventually left the Fermoy Company.[99] Derrynacaheragh Company broke away from Togher,[100] Behagh from Dunmanway (see below), and Kilbrittain from Ballinadee. One parish near Kanturk produced two overlapping companies because, according to one veteran, 'one crowd would always be against the other'. In the North Cork I.R.A. as a whole, he added, 'there were a lot of internal feuds between fellas'.[101]

Not all of these divisions were acrimonious but most represented strong groups—families, neighbours, and workmates—asserting local autonomy. These same groups also guarded their turf jealously and deeply resented any intrusions by neighbouring units. 'Between them there was a certain rivalry, the same rivalry that spurred the youth of one parish to excel in hurling or other games against the neighbouring parishes.'[102] Thus, raids for arms, collections for company funds, or even ambushes which crossed unit boundaries were a never-ending source of friction.[103] The famous ambush at Slippery Rock in August 1920 began with a fight between men of the Ballyvourney Company and their neighbours (and rivals), one of whom was Micheal O'Suilleabhain:

Now we appeared on the scene. I must say we got a very mixed reception . . . they asserted that they were quite capable of dealing with any situation without any help foreign to the parish. We mildly replied that we were born three miles away on that hill to the south, which not so long ago was part of the parish.[104]

[94] Sean Moylan Memoir, 16.   [95] John Joe Rice (O'Malley Papers, P17b/102).
[96] O'Malley, *On Another Man's Wound*, 130.
[97] For Berrings, see Duggan (ed.), *Grenagh and Courtbrack*, 14.
[98] Charlie Browne (O'Malley Papers, P17b/112).
[99] See Pat Ahern to Florence O'Donoghue, 22 Apr., 20 June 1953 (O'Donoghue Papers, MS 31, 423) and Lar Condon (O'Malley papers, P17b/96).
[100] Deasy, *Towards Ireland Free*, 128.
[101] Interview with AI.   [102] O'Suilleabhain, *Mountainy Men*, 82.
[103] See, for example, Adj., 2nd Bn. to O/C Cork 2, 19 Mar. 1920 (MA, A/0499).
[104] O'Suilleabhain, *Mountainy Men*, 83.

An uneasy truce was eventually arranged between the locals and the 'foreigners' and a temporary peace fell over the ambush site.

The same territorial disputes existed between regions, battalions, columns, and brigades. The latter, observed Sean Moylan, prosecuted the war as 'a loose confederacy' while defending their borders and independence.[105] Such tensions were evident within Moylan's own brigade—North Cork—from the moment of its formation on 6 January 1919. The leaders of the three Duhallow battalions, Kanturk, Newmarket, and Millstreet, were not even notified of this meeting, which was organized and dominated by Liam Lynch and the Fermoy Battalion (Lynch was elected O/C).[106] This west–east (and highland–lowland) split continued for well over a year, during which the Duhallow I.R.A. was left to its own devices. They were not told of the critical ambush of British soldiers in Fermoy in September 1919.[107] According to Moylan, then the commander of the Newmarket Battalion, he had 'never heard of Liam or of the Cork 2nd Brigade' before February 1920.[108] In fact Moylan and Lynch, the two regional chiefs, did not even meet until May of that year 'and even then [Lynch] only secured his co-operation after a fashion'.[109] A joint column was formed that summer but was disbanded into its constituent parts in November. Moylan explained that 'the men did best in their own districts and always wished to be there'.[110] To which George Power of Fermoy replied, 'In those days Moylan himself had only a narrow local outlook and could only think in terms of the Newmarket Battalion. In fact after his appointment as Brigade O/C [in 1921] he made no attempt to act up to his appointment but remained put in the Newmarket area until his arrest.'[111]

This split was formalized in July 1921 with the creation of the 4th Cork Brigade, leaving only the eastern rump of the Fermoy, Castletownroche, and Glanworth Battalions in the 2nd Brigade. Even within these two areas, Moylan clashed with other column leaders[112] while the Fermoy Battalion (and the town's company) was divided in two to accommodate local differences.[113]

The West Cork Brigade followed a somewhat similar path. It was dominated by the Bandon Battalion in the same way that Fermoy led North Cork, and the Hales family were as reluctant to leave their area as Moylan or Lynch. Consequently, as the origins of those present at Kilmichael and Crossbarry show (Chapter 6), the West Cork flying column was drawn heavily from the Bandon valley, to the exclusion of units to the south and west. This localism was greatly resented, especially as the column also commandeered most of the latter's

[105] Moylan Memoir, 21.   [106] See O'Donoghue, *No Other Law*, 36.
[107] Moylan Memoir, 68.
[108] Sean Moylan to Florence O'Donoghue, 20 Aug. 1952 (O'Donoghue Papers, MS 31, 421).
[109] George Power to Florence O'Donoghue, 11 Sept. 1952. See also Moylan to O'Donoghue, 26 Aug. 1952 (O'Donoghue Papers, MS 31, 421).
[110] Moylan to O'Donoghue, 20 Aug. 1952.
[111] Power to O'Donoghue, 11 Sept. 1953 (O'Donoghue Papers, MS 31, 421).
[112] Interview with AI.
[113] George Power to Florence O'Donoghue, 7 Dec. 1953 (O'Donoghue Papers, MS 31, 421).

rifles.[114] Finally, just as in the north of the county, West Cork was split so that a 5th Brigade could be formed around the Bantry, Beara, Schull, and Skibbereen Battalions.

The most notoriously territorial of all Cork I.R.A. leaders was Sean O'Hegarty, the O/C of the 1st Cork Brigade after August 1920. The Dublin GHQ wanted to divide Cork 1 along with the other brigades but O'Hegarty put up a fierce—and successful—resistance. Chief of Staff Richard Mulcahy found O'Hegarty to be 'a snarly gob. If they were taking an inch off his Brigade Area you had reams of correspondence about it.'[115] When Mulcahy came in person during the Truce he was browbeaten into giving up his scheme and was ever after a figure of fun to the Corkmen.[116] O'Hegarty also suspected the West Cork Brigade of conspiring to lure the Kinsale area away (or, as he put it, of attempting 'to seduce some of his neighbour's officers'[117]). Once again, blistering letters and accusations flew over this 'mean intrigue' until the idea was dropped.[118]

Within its sacrosanct borders, however, O'Hegarty's brigade was as divided as the others. Both the western and eastern battalions did as they liked and resented any outside interference. Mick O'Suilleabhain of the Ballyvourney Battalion said of the headquarters men in the city: 'Musha they were no good. The Brigade was no good. All the time they just put a brake on us.'[119] Dan Corkery, the Macroom commander, felt that 'we should have been a brigade in ourselves'.[120] Relations were little different at the other end of the brigade. At one point, in the middle of a dispute between the two, Diarmuid Hurley, the headstrong commandant of the Midleton Battalion, reportedly held Sean O'Hegarty captive for several days. After this, 'Hurley ignored Hegarty . . . and so the 4th [Midleton] Battalion was out on its own.'[121] Here as well a rivalry developed between 'the Midleton group' of officers and those based in Cobh who 'could be said to have acted as an independent unit', resulting in the creation of a new battalion separating the two.[122]

The Cork I.R.A. was riddled with such feuds although they never reached the epic proportions of faction fights elsewhere, most notably in Clare and parts of Limerick and Kerry.[123] In east Limerick, for example, the brigade was riven from top to bottom between the followers of Donnacha Hannigan and Liam Manahan.

---

[114]   Liam O'Dwyer, *Beara in Irish History*, 122.

[115]   Richard Mulcahy, 'Talk with M. J. Costello', 23 May 1963 (Mulcahy Papers, P7/D/3).

[116]   See Mick Leahy (O'Malley Papers, P17b/108).

[117]   O/C Cork 1 to C/S, n.d. (Mulcahy Papers, P7/A/24).

[118]   O/C Cork 1 to 1st South. Div., 29 Oct. 1921 (Mulcahy Papers, P7/A/24).

[119]   Mick O'Sullivan (O'Malley Papers, P17b/111).

[120]   Dan Corkery (O'Malley Papers, P17b/111).

[121]   Mick Leahy (O'Malley Papers, P17b/108).

[122]   Seamus Fitzgerald (O'Malley Papers, P17b/111); Michael Burke statement (CAI, Seamus Fitzgerald Papers, PR/6/39).

[123]   For examples of such factions, see Gloria Maguire, 'The Political and Military Causes of the Division in the Irish Nationalist Movement, January 1921 to August 1922', D.Phil. thesis (Oxford, 1985), 267–303.

'There were units there but they were either Hannigan or Manahan units. Bill and Mick L—— [two brothers] had two rival companies . . . to show you how far this rot had gone.'[124] In Clare west of Kilkee:

A 'Free' Republic on the best Central American lines functioned here from the end of 1920. The inhabitants revelled in an orgy of disputes, principally agrarian, viz. 'Halloran's Bog' . . . a right of way to a quarry . . . Burton's demesne . . . and Willie Studdert's land . . . one Volunteer named Shea had shot another named Blake dead in February 1920 over a disputed farm. The Lieutenant of Doonaha Company . . . had taken sides in the Halloran's Bog dispute. He was promptly betrayed to the enemy.[125]

And when J. J. O'Connell, the I.R.A.'s deputy chief of staff, toured the 1st Western Division in 1921 his reports spoke repeatedly of mutinies, 'shocking indiscipline', 'private spleens and family hates', and the 'necessity of developing a national rather than a narrow local outlook'.[126]

The same tensions existed within Cumann na mBan, Fianna Eireann, and Sinn Fein.[127] Like Volunteer companies, Sinn Fein clubs could come into being wherever some local group decided to call themselves Sinn Feiners. As a result, party headquarters in Dublin was flooded with demands that competing would-be clubs not be recognized and complaints that neighbouring clubs were trespassing or poaching members.[128] And, like the Volunteers, many clubs were divided internally and split along factional lines.

Even republican courts, set up in 1920 to supplant the British judicial system, fell prey to the same 'clan spirit'. As with the rest of the movement, courts were organized on local initiative, parish by parish, and judges were usually elected. In many cases parishes had to be divided between two courts to take local prejudices into account. When it was proposed that these be merged in North Cork in 1921, the protests were emphatic and explicit. In Dromina and Newtownshandrum, 'the two parts of the parish are entirely opposed to one another and would not work together';[129] 'the people here [Dromina] are a different kind of people altogether to the other side—and don't get on with them'.[130] The same was true in two or three other neighbouring parishes according to the district registrar. On the border with Tipperary, 'there were petty spites etc. and a refusal on the part of the justices of Burncourt to have anything to do with Clogheen'.[131]

---

[124] Bill Carty (O'Malley Papers, P17b/129).
[125] Liam Haugh, 'History of the West Clare Brigade' (MA, A/0180). See also Fitzpatrick, *Politics and Irish Life*, 227–8.   [126] Deputy C/S to A/G, 25 Oct. 1921 (MA, A/0726).
[127] For Cumann na mBan disputes in Cork city, see Sean O'Hegarty to the Cork Bde. Council, 26 Nov. 1918 (O'Donoghue Papers, MS 31, 198) and Florence O'Donoghue to Moiron Chavasse, 30 Dec. 1954 (UCD, Mary MacSwiney Papers, P48C/159). There is no mention of the split in Conlan, *Cumann na mBan*.
[128] See the R.I.C. Précis of Seized Documents—Sinn Fein Correspondence, especially for Connaught and Limerick (NLI, MS 10, 494 (1)–(6)). Unfortunately, the précis of Cork correspondence does not describe the letters' contents.
[129] Min. for Home Affairs to Registrar, North Cork, 30 Nov. 1921 (PRO, DE 10/7).
[130] Father Carroll to Min. for Home Affairs, 21 Nov. 1921 (DE 10/7).
[131] Court Org. to Min. for Home Affairs, 19 Dec. 1921 (DE 11/220).

This strong sense of place and of local identity could also determine whether or not a Volunteer company was formed at all. As the local government inspector for Cork observed (quoted on page 41), and as both I.R.A. activists and their enemies found, political attitudes could change abruptly with a parish boundary. One community might produce a strong company but their neighbours over the hill or down the road could be apathetic or actively hostile.[132] To return to the example of the Valley Rovers and Knockavilla GAA clubs, it may well be that the officials of the latter did not join the I.R.A. because the former, their long-standing rivals, did.[133] Micheal O'Suilleabhain's home village of Kilnamartyra was a Volunteer stronghold but a mile south was Ballyvoig, a 'lost valley' where 'all the inhabitants, including my uncle Patsy, were honest, peaceful and law-abiding':

none of the young men of the valley was even a nominal Volunteer . . . I knew them all. Most of them had gone to school with me. Not a Volunteer among them. All physically fit. A few good athletes among them. No good or harm in them, excepting some who covertly sneered at us.[134]

One Kanturk I.R.A. man told me that popular support for the I.R.A. in his area 'changed from place to place. You had to be careful where you went.'[135] Every guerrilla carried a similar mental map of 'good' and 'bad' communities and policemen and soldiers soon learned to do the same. In the hill country north-west of Fermoy, a British army column encountered their own 'lost valley': while 'Araglin valley was a centre of Sinn Fein activity' where 'every house contained letters from the U.S.A. urging on the fight for the Republic', over the hills 'all farmers here [were] very fed-up with events' and were very hospitable to the troops.[136] This array of—often conflicting—local loyalties turned every part of Cork into a political patchwork.

For most I.R.A. men, joining the movement in its early days required little deliberate choice or effort. If you had the right connections or belonged to a certain family or circle of friends you became a Volunteer along with the rest of your crowd. If not, you probably stayed outside or on the fringes.[137] A committed or ambitious man like Tom Barry might still eventually work his way in, but such men were exceptional. The uninvited or unwelcome were easily kept out.

Figure 2 charts the geography of volunteering within one company between

---

[132] O'Malley (*On Another Man's Wound*, 129): 'Sometimes I came to a townland where there was a company of twenty or thirty men and boys. Tall, well set up or lanky, eager, lithe, willing to learn and anxious to take risks. Six miles away across the barony the people were cowed; the men had no initiative. They were irresolute . . . Areas of country had a habit of going to sleep.'

[133] The rivalry is described in Walsh, *The Story of Dick Barrett*; the speculation is mine.

[134] O'Suilleabhain, *Mountainy Men*, 88, 91.

[135] Interview with AI.

[136] Patrol Report around Clogheen, 4–7 June 1921 in *6th Division History*, 118–22 (Strickland Papers).

[137] As the man quoted at the beginning of this chapter told me when I asked why he did not join: 'they weren't my crowd.'

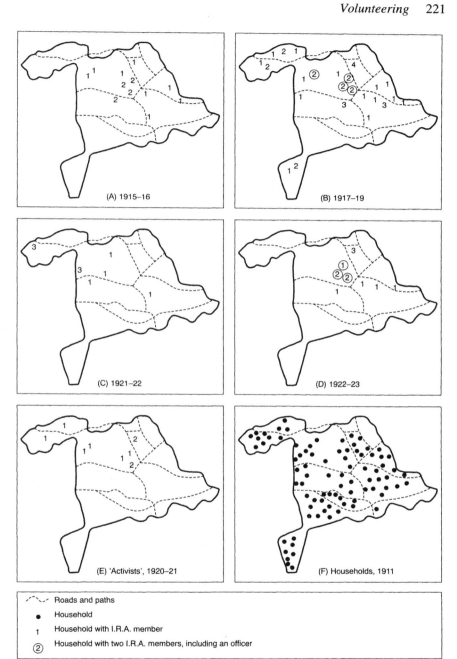

(A) 1915–16

(B) 1917–19

(C) 1921–22

(D) 1922–23

(E) 'Activists', 1920–21

(F) Households, 1911

Roads and paths
● Household
1 Household with I.R.A. member
② Household with two I.R.A. members, including an officer

FIG. 2. Behagh Company, 1915–1923

1915 and 1923.[138] The Behagh Company covered eleven townlands within the district of Manch, an area of approximately 8 square miles mostly located on the north bank of the Bandon river. Its main landmark was Manch Bridge. Three-quarters of the members were farmers' sons living on comfortable family farms.[139] Their average age in 1921 was 27. The Volunteers were first organized locally in the nearby town of Dunmanway, and the men of Manch originally belonged to this unit. They established their own company in 1917, which then became part of the Dunmanway Battalion. Here, as so often elsewhere, the movement spread from town to countryside.

These maps illustrate the importance of family and neighbourhood in determining who joined and who stayed. At every point in the company's history, the number of members with brothers in the unit was never less than half the total. It may be assumed that an even larger percentage belonged to the same extended families.

The size of the company rose and fell with the tide of revolution. The unit's official roll lists sixty-eight members: roughly 40 per cent of the men in the same age group in the district.[140] However, while this many Volunteers did pass through the organization between 1915 and 1923 they were never all together at the same time, and a significant number were purely nominal members. Eighteen men from Manch, including all four officers, joined the Dunmanway Company before the rising and several of them were forced to go on the run afterwards. All of these stayed on to form their own unit and were joined by twenty-seven others in 1917 and eight more in 1918, bringing the official membership up to fifty-four. The mystique of 1916 proved as powerful a recruiting agent here as elsewhere:

Among the newly formed members were youths who had only lately left school, drawn by the glamour of the strife to cast their lots side by side with the men whom they had learned to admire and whose previous activities had fired their imaginations and whetted their patriotic instincts.[141]

---

[138]   Information for these maps was drawn from Thomas O'Donovan, 'Behagh Company I.R.A.' (O'Donoghue Papers, MS 31, 332) and from manuscript census returns for 1911 and the records and Ordnance Survey maps of the Irish Valuation Office. Additional details were gleaned from O'Donoghue, 'History of the Irish Volunteers', from an article on the Fanlobus and Newcestown ambushes (O'Donoghue Papers, MS 31, 301), and from interviews with AA, a veteran of the Dunmanway Company.

[139]   See Table 25, Ch. 7.

[140]   This official roll number, given in O'Donovan, is confirmed by Bureau of Military History records. The estimate of the size of the age group in Manch is based on an estimate of the number of men between the ages of 15 and 34 in the district. As the ages of the Behagh Volunteers in 1921 ranged from 17 to 48, with the average age being 27, this is approximately correct. The male population of Manch (404) can be found in the 1911 census (Cork Report, table XXXIII); the proportion of men between the ages of 15 and 34 in rural West Cork in 1926 is given in the 1926 census, v. 1, table 4c.

[141]   O'Donovan, 'Behagh Company I.R.A.'

As the guerrilla war gathered steam in 1920, four men dropped out (two of the original eighteen and two new members).[142] One Volunteer was arrested at the scene of an ambush in September of that year. Six more were caught in a military round-up and interned in June 1921. After the Truce was declared the company quickly gained fourteen new members; all of them left again after the Treaty was signed in December 1921, along with about half the remaining men, leaving twenty-one anti-Treaty Volunteers to face the Free State and Civil War.

The company was physically tightly knit. Most of the Volunteers were immediate neighbours, clustered together around several crossroads in the heart of the district. Three of the four officers, Captain Tom O'Donovan, First Lieutenant Tim Crowley, and Second Lieutenant Pat Corcoran, lived side by side, forming, with their brothers, a kind of organizational nucleus. In fact, the company was named after the townland of Behagh where most of the officers and activists were concentrated. As numbers increased, the unit expanded somewhat to more distant townlands, but in 1922–3 its boundaries shrank back to its core area (Map D).[143]

Consciously or unconsciously, the company's self-defined perimeter followed a natural frontier of rivers, marshes, and woods, and excluded the three nearby 'big houses'. This line very likely marked the horizon of everyday life for the local community: 'our native valley' as Tom O'Donovan proudly called it. The main link with the outside world, the market town of Dunmanway, was also the company's link with their superiors and the rest of the organization. The ties and boundaries that defined the community also determined the shape of the I.R.A.

Those who were the least committed, the four who left in 1920 and the fourteen who waited to join until the time of the Truce—the so-called 'trucileers'—tended to be outsiders of one sort or another. Two were the sons of labourers, three had only moved to the area in 1921, and all but one of the other thirteen cannot be located in either the census returns or the land valuation records, meaning that they were probably transient labourers. As can be seen from Map C, most of the 1921 Volunteers also lived more towards the fringes of the company. These men were strangers. Without a sense of community or strong ties to local families, they remained on the outer fringes of the revolution.

Map E reveals less obvious boundaries between the Behagh Volunteers and raises further questions about the geography of activism. There was no police station in Manch (although the nearby Dunmanway workhouse became an Auxiliary barracks in December 1920) and no battles were fought there. One local man, Mick Hurley, took part in the battle of Crossbarry in March 1921

---

[142]   In other words, the official membership of the company during the Tan War (fifty) amounted to approximately 29% of their age group in Manch.

[143]   This distribution of members does not simply follow that of the general population, as Map F demonstrates. Households were fairly evenly spread over the company area; if anything, Volunteers were concentrated in slightly less populous townlands (with slightly larger farms).

while three others joined a flying column in 1922. Aside from this, some company members took part in three abortive ambushes in 1920. From this record we can assemble a list of ten 'activists': men who participated in more than one armed operation in the Tan War. Of these ten, nine had a brother or brothers in the I.R.A., seven had been Volunteers since 1915, and six of these (along with a seventh man who joined in 1917) went on to fight in the Civil War. All four officers were 'activists', as were the two Irish Republican Police officers. These men were heavily concentrated in the centre of the company. Six lived on adjacent homesteads, seven lived around the two main crossroads, and four lived in the townland of Behagh itself.

It was this small minority of guerrillas (one-fifth of the Volunteers who remained in 1920–1; one-third of those who remained in 1922–3) who did the fighting and suffered the consequences. All six of the Behagh men arrested in June 1921 were 'activists'. At least three of them were later rearrested by the National Army. Contrasted with this inner circle was the fluctuating outer fringe of eighteen nominal Volunteers who did not take part in the Tan War (27 per cent of the official unit roll) and the forty-seven who stayed out of the Civil War (70 per cent of the total).

Between these two extremes lay the majority of ordinary members who, with varying degrees of enthusiasm, marched and drilled, canvassed during elections, collected money (an impressive £403 for the Dail Loan and £176 for the arms fund), acted as policemen, carried messages, stood guard, and gave up their beds when the flying column passed through, but who never left home, never carried a rifle, and never fired a shot. We can estimate their number at about twenty, although they were almost certainly fewer at the height of the rebellion.[144]

Thus, beneath the official membership roll and hierarchy, an informal but enduring substructure can be discerned. One's place in this order depended on one's personal connections and level of activity (which often amounted to the same thing). At the centre were the fighting men who called upon a wider, shifting, network of friends and relatives—the 'small fry'[145]—when needed. And beyond these inner and outer circles was the even more transitory fringe of fair-weather comrades and assorted 'hangers-on'.

The history of the Behagh Company (which itself operated rather on the fringes of the Tan War, the Dunmanway Battalion being something of a revolutionary backwater in Cork) exemplifies the difficulty of defining what it meant to be a Volunteer beyond the mere fact of joining. Those outside the organization may have lumped them together as 'the boys' or 'Shinners'. However, the

---

[144] According to Liam Deasy's figures, thirty (or 56%) of the fifty-four Behagh Volunteers in July 1919 were 'active' (by which he meant 'reliable'), the rest inactive; if we subtract the ten 'activists' of the following year, we arrive at the number twenty. See Deasy, *Towards Ireland Free*, 317.

[145] A favourite phrase within the I.R.A., used to describe the non-fighting men: see the following chapter.

meaning of volunteering changed over time, from person to person, and from group to group. The sense of identity of Behagh's closely bound core of insiders was obviously different from that of the other Volunteers, just as those who joined or departed at different points had quite different experiences. The following chapter will explore the varieties of commitment and participation within the I.R.A.

11

Guerrillas

In my six years as a rank-and-filer of the I.R.A. I shot nobody and I was briefly under fire once. I have no war memories to record except to say: 'Were those the Troubles? And if so was it a revolution?'

(Sean O'Faolain, *Vive Moi!*)

A war in any shape or form, it grows on you . . . The decisions aren't always your own.

(John L. O'Sullivan)[1]

In July 1921, just after the Truce had been declared, Dorothy and Edie Stopford drove from Dublin to Kilbrittain where Dorothy had been appointed district medical officer:

It was an amazing journey [Edie later recorded] . . . Owing to the police interdict on cars, there were few to be seen, and since the Truce the police themselves had been confined to barracks. But occasionally we would see a Ford car with a number of trench-coated young men inside who were obviously members of the I.R.A. They were beginning to emerge from their long periods of anonymity and secrecy and to visit their friends . . . One evening we were invited to a 'celebration' *ceili* in a large but remote farm house . . . As honoured guests, we were not immediately taken to the dance-room, but were asked if we could care to come and have supper with 'some of the lads' who were resting in another room. We entered a large, rather dark room, lit by oil lamps, where we could just make out the figures of five or six young men, all apparently asleep, two stretched on sofas, the rest in armchairs. These were the I.R.A. Headquarters Staff for that area of Co. Cork [the West Cork Brigade], anonymous men who had been hunted from pillar to post with prices on their heads and liable to meet death around any corner. Their identity was completely unknown in the countryside, and they were making their first appearance among their neighbours. They were young, sober-minded, responsible and serious, and their Brigadier especially [Liam Deasy] was a fine-looking young man full of earnestness and purpose. They were, I presume, still tired from their pre-Truce life of vigil, raids, ambushes, and hair-breadth escapes, and so far as I remember they took no part in the subsequent *ceili*, being still shy of publicity. They did not stay long, but soon after supper slipped off from the farm house in their Ford car, silently and mysteriously. Dorothy and I felt that we had been privileged spectators of a very anonymous bit of history.[2]

---

[1] O'Sullivan, a member of the West Cork I.R.A., was quoted in Griffith and O'Grady, *Curious Journey*, 189.

[2] Leon O Broin, *Protestant Nationalists in Revolutionary Ireland: the Stopford Connection* (Dublin, 1985), 183–4.

The summer of 1921 was a wonderful time to be a young man if you had anything to do with the I.R.A. 'That perfect summer' Frank O'Connor called it.[3] You were saluted and cheered in the streets, work could be put to one side, dances were held in your honour, and your word held apparently undisputed sway in your part of the world. 'All things were possible.'[4] The imagined republic was practically a reality, established and run by the small band of young comrades who had the will and the ability to impose it and fight for it. A few dedicated men had indeed changed history.[5]

To outside observers like Edie Stopford, every young man in a trench coat was a rebel. Even Patrick Kavanagh, rejected by the I.R.A. for being too young, could play this role, 'and if I did I wasn't the only bluffer in town . . . as every man with a stiff lip was suspected of being an I.R.A. man'.[6] But to I.R.A. insiders like the 'lads' in the back room in Kilbrittain, most of the summer joyriders and dancers had, during the previous two years of struggle, been conspicuous only by their absence.

They had only to look around them. Out of the over 1,000 men who claimed to belong to the Bandon Battalion in July 1921, fewer than 500 had been on the rolls in July 1919, of whom fewer than 300 (or 61%) were considered 'active'.[7] By the spring of 1921 the number of reliable members had fallen to about 230.[8] In other words, only one in five (21%) of those who called themselves Volunteers in the Bandon area after the Truce had been available for duty in the months before it. The same figures hold true for the whole of the West Cork Brigade, the Behagh Company being a typical example.[9] Even in the ultra-militant Kilbrittain Company, twenty-five out of seventy nominal I.R.A. members had been listed as inactive in July 1919. Of the remainder, 'there were ten men whom [Tom] Barry could always draw on'.[10]

---

[3] O'Connor, *An Only Child*, 209.

[4] J.W.G., review of Simone Tery, *En Irlande*, in *Irish Statesman*, 29 Sept. 1923: 'In that brief hour of exaltation even the worst of our pessimists believed that all things were possible.'

[5] For accounts similar to that of Edie Stopford's or Frank O'Connor's, see Simone Tery, 'French Reporter Visits Volunteers' Training Camp, "Somewhere" in Western Ireland, August 15, 1921' (trans. Marilyn Gaddis Rose), in Dennis Jackson (ed.), *Irish Renaissance Annual III* (Newark, NJ, 1982), 124–40; O'Suilleabhain, *Mountainy Men*, 170–3; Ernie O'Malley, *The Singing Flame* (Dublin, 1978), 15–17. Florence O'Donoghue, at that time the adjutant of the 1st Southern Division, wrote on 13 July that 'the whole countryside is gone mad, cheering, shouting and so forth'. Letter to 'Dhilis', 13 July 1921 (O'Donoghue Papers, MS 31, 176). ' "Victory dances" now became the fashion', the British intelligence officer in Kanturk reported: 'Almost every little village had one or more of these shows' (Grazebrook Diary, 64, (Royal Gloucestershire Regiment Archives)).

[6] Kavanagh, *The Green Fool*, 113.

[7] The figure for the battalion's total membership comes from the Bureau of Military History rolls, which are almost identical to those given in Deasy, *Towards Ireland Free*, 318. The figures as of July 1919 are given in Deasy, *Towards Ireland Free*, 62, 317–18.

[8] Organizer's report, 1st Bn., Cork 3, 7 Sept. 1922 (MA, A/0991/2).

[9] See previous chapter. According to Deasy's figures (*Towards Ireland Free*, 62, 317–18), 62% of brigade members were considered 'active' in July 1919.

[10] Flor Begley (O'Malley Papers, P17b/111). The figures come from the Bureau of Military History rolls and Deasy, *Towards Ireland Free*, 317.

TABLE 32. North Cork company strengths, 1921

Battalion	July 1921	Spring 1921		
	Roll	Roll	Reliable	Active
Fermoy	76	42	27	10
Millstreet	75	63	42	7
Mitchelstown	75	36	23	5
Mallow	68	46	25	4
Average	74	47	29	7

Notes: The figures in the first column are derived from the Bureau of Military History Company Rolls; the others from company rolls in the Florence O'Donoghue Papers (MS 31, 223). The other North Cork units—the Kanturk, Newmarket and Charleville Battalions—were not included in these rolls.

These distinctions between nominal, reliable, and active Volunteers were recognized in every I.R.A. unit in Cork. In the Macroom Battalion in September 1919, reliable members made up only half of the total official membership.[11] For one south side company in Cork city the figure (in 1920–1) was 43 per cent, while another company on the north side was described as being 15 per cent 'active'.[12] The North Cork Brigade records assembled in Table 32 reveal the same patterns of selective commitment and participation. In the typical North Cork company, two-thirds of the men calling themselves Volunteers at the time of the Truce had done so in the spring of 1921, 62 per cent of whom had been willing to volunteer their services and 15 per cent of whom actually participated in I.R.A. operations. Or, to put it another way, fewer than one in ten of the July Volunteers had been active in April: a pattern that was equally clear to their enemies. That month, the British intelligence officer in Kanturk noted that, while a company might have eighty members on paper, 'only about half a dozen (including the officers) would be really active members'.[13]

Cork was no different from any other county in this respect. David Fitzpatrick has found that, in May 1921, less than half of the Mid-Clare Brigade's Volunteers were considered reliable and an even smaller fraction actually attended company parades.[14] The records of the 2nd Battalion of the Dublin Brigade for the same period list 59 per cent of its members as reliable; the same figure for the Fingal Brigade in April was 65 per cent.[15] J. E. Nolan found that

[11] This figure results from a comparison of Bureau of Military History Rolls with a notebook captured with Dan Corkery (the O/C of the Macroom Battalion) in September 1919 (CAI, U104).

[12] For the former, see J. O'Dwyer Statement (MA, A/0246) and Sean Daly (O'Malley Papers, P17b/112); for the latter see Sean Collins Powell, 'Details of the Anglo-Irish Conflict, 1916–1921' (MA, A/0735).   [13] Grazebrook Diary, 18.

[14] Fitzpatrick, *Politics and Irish Life*, 219.

[15] Fingal Bde. Monthly Report, Apr. 1921 (Mulcahy Papers, P7/A/17). The joke in the Dublin Brigade was that 'the Fingal Brigade was mobilized and he turned up' (NLI, Jack Plunkett Statement, MS 11, 981).

half his Dublin company existed only on paper.[16] In Sligo as of June 1921, most companies had fewer than ten reliable members apiece.[17]

Thus, the backroom boys of the West Cork Brigade who gathered that night in Kilbrittain knew themselves to be a minority, their elite status symbolized by their avoidance of the dancers and by their rather self-conscious air of secrecy and purpose. One or more of these men had been present at every major ambush in West Cork (with the exception of Kilmichael); all had been local pioneers in 1917 or earlier and all had spent time with the column. Several had lost their homes, others had lost brothers or cousins, most had been imprisoned at least once, all had been on the run for years. For these men and their fellow activists, revolution had become a vocation. Its success had been due almost entirely to their own efforts.

The guerrillas' scorn extended well beyond the inert mass of Volunteers—the 'hangers-on', 'flag-waggers', 'spare parts', 'public house I.R.A.', 'pub republicans', and 'trucileers'—to include much of the wider republican movement as well. During the Truce Liam Lynch bitterly declared:

We must admit that all civil organizations, Co. Councils, District Councils, Corporations, Urban Councils, Sinn Fein Clubs and all other organized bodies were an absolute failure during the last phase of hostilities, if anything they were a burden on the Army.[18]

Sinn Fein suffered a more precipitate decline than the Volunteers in 1920—and enjoyed an even more spectacular revival in the summer of 1921. Under the pressure of British proscription and harassment most clubs simply ceased to exist during the Tan War. While the number of official branches of Sinn Fein in Ireland stood at a record 1,485 on 31 December, 1921, only eighty-nine of these *cumann* had sent in their affiliation fee before 11 July.[19] As a result of this organizational collapse, many column men had to double as commissars. I.R.A. activists were likely to be policemen, judges, district, town and county councillors and poor law guardians, election and Belfast boycott organizers, collectors for the Dail Loan, and even TDs. To return to the example of the West Cork Brigade staff, at least five were also I.R.B. centres, at least three were justices on republican courts, two were county councillors, and two were presidents of their local Sinn Fein constituency committees.[20] In fact, in the two electoral districts in the brigade area, West and South-East Cork, over half of Sinn Fein's branch officers at the time of the Truce were also I.R.A. officers (most of them

[16] 'Figures for Companies Working' in 2nd Bn., Dublin Brigade Documents (NLI, MS 901); J. E. Nolan Statement (MA, A/0327).

[17] Sligo Bde. Returns, June 1921 (Mulcahy Papers, P7/A/22).

[18] O/C 1st South. Div. Memo re: Civil Population in War Time, 24 Nov. 1921 (Mulcahy Papers, P7/A/30).

[19] Secretary's Report, Sinn Fein *Ard Comhairle*, 12 Jan. 1922 (NA, DE/2/486).

[20] For I.R.B. positions as of November 1921, see the Florence O'Donoghue Papers (MS 31, 237); for the County Council, see the *Star*, 7 Jan. 1922; for the republican judicial system, see the court correspondence in DE/9/8, 10, 12 (NA); for Sinn Fein see the list of *cumann* officers (as of late 1921) in the Irish Military Archives (MA, A/1147).

company captains).[21] Even a full-time gunman like Frank Busteed also saw service as a parish court judge.[22]

In June 1921 a Mid-Cork Brigade organizer felt it necessary to inform his officious Dublin superiors of the realities of republican organization in rural Cork:

It must be remembered that in the country districts and the small towns the burden of all national activities frequently falls upon one or two willing individuals who are consequently called upon to discharge multifarious duties and to act in many different capacities.[23]

Another I.R.A. organizer in the North Cork Brigade found that each parish or neighbourhood had its 'local man' who effectively ran the movement in his area, and any question or suggestion of his would be met with the standard phrase: 'ask the local man.'[24]

The 'reliable' rank and file had a very different experience. Sean O'Faolain was an enthusiastic but lowly member of the Cork city I.R.A.:

The great majority of us rank-and-filers were given such undemanding if essential jobs as the gathering of more or less useful information, watching over the billets of the fighters, scouting, carrying dispatches, doing police work, helping to trench roads or fell trees . . . marching in the streets to defy some military order against it, perhaps standing guard at the public lying-in-state of some patriot . . . Otherwise we hung around, drilled, waited, felt nervy, groused, and were supremely proud and happy whenever even the most modest task made us feel we were doing something positive in the struggle for independence.[25]

Frank O'Connor was in much the same position:

I was put on Volunteer work . . . dirty, rather useless work it was too, but for me full of thrills. Lounging around street corners, cap pulled over my eyes, hands in pockets, being smacked or kicked about by sundry spiteful old policemen, reporting at night . . . and the thrill of pleasure with which one was allowed, so very rarely, to handle a revolver.[26]

These young rebels were very much aware of their place on the periphery of the organization. O'Faolain reported that 'in my six years as a rank-and-filer of the I.R.A. I shot nobody and I was briefly under fire once' while Frank O'Connor's only contact with the 'declared rebels' in his neighbourhood was to hang about in the churchyard on Sundays 'hoping for a nod or a smile from one of them'.[27] They were called—and called themselves—'only rank-and-filers' or

---

[21] This figure is based on a comparison of Sinn Fein *cumann* officers (MA, A/1147) with officer lists in Bureau of Military History records and Deasy, *Towards Ireland Free*, 326–30.

[22] Blarney Parish Court Records (DE/15/27).

[23] Report re: boycott of W. J. O'Sullivan (NA, DE/2/509).

[24] Moylan Memoir, 164–5.   [25] O'Faolain, *Vive Moi!*, 175.

[26] O'Connor, 'The Patriarch', in *Guests of the Nation*, 154–5. This autobiographical story should be compared to his memoirs, *An Only Child*, 202.

[27] O'Faolain, *Vive Moi!*, 174; O'Connor, *An Only Child*, 186. O'Faolain added that 'our regular fighters or guerrillas, few in number . . . carried the full strain of the fight, day in and day out.' (*Vive Moi!*, 180).

'small fry'.[28] 'If you were asked to do a thing, you went and did it' was how one summed it up.[29] The exploits of such men were the stuff of altogether more modest legends, as can be seen by comparing 'the Boys of Kilmichael' with 'the Boys of Aghinagh':[30]

> The sun in the west it was sinking,
> Twas the eve of a bright April's day,
> When Con Moynihan and Tim Coakley came and told us,
> To bring out crowbars right away.
>
> Then here's to the boys of Aghinagh,
> Who feared not long journeys to go,
> To tear up the roads and the bridges,
> To baffle and conquer the foe.
>
> Then over the hills went the echo,
> The sound of the crowbar and picks,
> And other wild sounds of commotion,
> Proclaimed that the boys they were bricks.
>
> Dan Buckley was there with his rifle,
> Very important was he,
> If the Black and Tans came he would shoot them,
> And shout that Aghinagh was free.

To understand this division of labour and attitudes we must ask not only why they joined the I.R.A. but also what they joined. What did it mean to be a Volunteer and how did this change as the revolution progressed?

What the men of 1917 and 1918 were not joining was the sort of 'Irish Republican Army' later embodied by the guerrillas of the West Cork Brigade. The Volunteers were initially neither armed nor illegal and, however attractive its aura of secrecy and rebellion, there was very little that was revolutionary about the organization. Some Cork companies even announced their formation in the *Cork Examiner*.[31] Publicity rather than anonymity was the aim of their early campaigns against British authority, and their usual target was the regulation of public display and association. Illegal flags were prominently flown, seditious songs were loudly sung, and banned meetings were defiantly held. When drilling was outlawed, Volunteer companies paraded *en masse* and after they were gaoled, they protested against the prison regulations. Volunteer activists

---

[28] 'I wasn't in the column then. I was only small fry.' Leo Skinner (O'Malley Papers, P17b/124). Two of my informants also used the expression about themselves: interviews with AE and AI.   [29] Interview with AD.

[30] Dept. of Irish Folklore, Schools MS 343 [Inchalea], 65. 'The Boys of Aghinagh' were apparently the men of 'B' Company in the 3rd Battalion, Cork 1. The only identifiable name in the song is that of Tim Coakley, the company's second lieutenant. Comparable verses of 'The Boys of Kilmichael' are quoted at the beginning of Chs. 2 and 6.

[31] See, for example, the *Examiner*, 15 Mar. 1918.

sought public recognition and openly courted arrest. Liam Lynch, for one, was keenly disappointed when the police felt he was not worth arresting.[32] The accompanying violence was equally public, the result of mutual provocation rather than clandestine intrigue.

Typical of such demonstrations was one which took place in Kanturk on 19 November 1917:

They were in fours and went towards Banteer. 16 boy scouts headed the procession followed by 64 girls and 120 men and boys. A Sinn Fein flag was carried in front and about 80 of the men carried pikes, having what appeared to be turf on the top of each pike [while another 22 men formed a drill party] . . . Most of the houses were illuminated with lighted candles. The streets along the route were lined with a crowd of men, women and children, who raised cheers several times.[33]

The event was held to celebrate both the release of two I.R.A. hunger strikers and a hard-won victory for Sinn Fein on the Kanturk District Council.[34] The question thus arises as to how to identify the participants. The R.I.C. district inspector labelled the march 'Sinn Fein' and the marchers 'Sinn Feiners'. Who among them were actual Volunteers? Was it all 120 men and boys who marched and formed fours, the 80 who carried pikes, or the 22 who made up the drill party? Where did the women marchers fit in?

In fact, it would be impossible to disentangle these people's organizational allegiances. In such activities, and in much of their membership, the Volunteers were nearly indistinguishable from Sinn Fein just as Sinn Fein merged into the revitalized Gaelic League. Most republicans joined them all—or rather, it was 'the movement' they joined, an amalgam of different groups defined more by a common sense of energy, youth, and direction than by strict party loyalties.

Old Volunteer companies—as in Ballinadee—sprouted Sinn Fein clubs and Irish classes as they reorganized. New companies and clubs were often formed one after the other by the same pioneers. 'In most districts' in the Bandon Battalion 'every Volunteer was a member of the Sinn Fein club and every member of the Sinn Fein club was a Volunteer'.[35] In Dunmanway 'the member- ship of these clubs consisted mainly of Volunteers and the members of their families'.[36] When George Power and Liam Lynch joined the Fermoy Volunteers, 'it was a small company . . . consisting of all the members of the Sinn Fein club which had already been in existence a short time'.[37] In Midleton, according to Edmond Desmond, a branch of Sinn Fein was set up in early 1917, 'then the young people were recruited' as both Sinn Feiners and Volunteers, whereupon a parallel company was formed.[38] In Blackpool, in Cork city, the company and

[32] O'Donoghue, *No Other Law*, 18.
[33] DI Report, Newmarket, 20 Nov. 1917 (CO 904/122).   [34] *Examiner*, 19 Nov. 1917.
[35] 'Bandon History' (Price Papers).
[36] Edward Young statement (in the possession of Edward Young).
[37] George Power statement (O'Donoghue Papers, MS 31, 335).
[38] Edmond Desmond (O'Malley Papers, P17b/112).

club were formed simultaneously, in what was formerly the Brewery Workers' Club: 'these premises literally became a Volunteer Hall under the guise of the Tomas O'Cleirigh [Tom Clarke] Sinn Fein Club, and all its members, except those precluded by reason of age, were members of "E" company.'[39] Similarly, the Mallow Volunteers met and drilled after Sinn Fein meetings in the Town Hall.[40] In the 'Thomas Ashe Sinn Fein Club and Volunteer Corps' in Glenville, and in Inchigeela, Lisgoold, and Castlemartyr, the two organizations formed a single unit with a common secretary.[41] 'There was often a common war chest. The Sinn Fein Treasurer was frequently the Quartermaster of the Volunteer company.'[42]

To the Cork R.I.C., there was 'little or no difference' between Sinn Fein and the Irish Volunteers.[43] 'When a Sinn Fein club has been established in their locality the Irish Volunteers join it in large numbers and the connection between the two is very close';[44] 'In most cases there is little to distinguish Irish Volunteer from Sinn Fein branches.'[45] Policemen were saying the same thing all over Ireland. In Donegal there was 'no practical difference between this organization [the Volunteers] and the Sinn Fein clubs'.[46] In Kerry they were 'practically synonymous'.[47] The inspector general declared in February 1918 that 'many Sinn Fein clubs (or at least a percentage of their members) must be regarded as branches of the Volunteers'.[48]

To the police—as, perhaps, to most of their own members—the insurgent organizations were simply 'Sinn Fein', an undifferentiated movement of 'a very undefined sort', marked by incessant socializing and the constant display of flags, colours, and badges.[49] 'Sinn Fein', reported the county inspector for West Cork in January 1917, 'has so far taken the form of attendance, in more or less large and organized parties, at Sinn Fein functions, concerts, dances, conferences.'[50] The following month's report gives some sense of the new republicans' jumbled enthusiasm:

They lose no opportunity of associating and meeting together at dances, Irish classes, Gaelic League concerts, G.A.A. football matches, etc., e.g. a Sinn Fein dance, attended by fifty couples, was held at Macroom on the 10th. A Gaelic League concert, organized by the Bandon Gaelic League, was held on the 11th, all the local Irish Volunteers and

[39]   Tom Daly statement (Co. Cork Museum, G1091).

[40]   Lankford, *The Hope and the Sadness*, 158.

[41]   *Examiner*, 26 Oct., 2 Jan. 1918, 3 Jan. 1919; letter from P. J. Gumbleton, 26 Mar. 1918 (Précis of Sinn Fein Correspondence, MS 10, 494(4)).

[42]   Moylan Memoir, 41–2.

[43]   CI Monthly Report, West Cork, Sept. 1917 (CO 904/104).

[44]   CI Monthly Report, West Cork, July 1917 (CO 904/103).

[45]   CI Monthly Report, West Cork, Mar. 1918 (CO 904/105).

[46]   CI Monthly Report, Donegal, Mar. 1918 (CO 904/105).

[47]   CI Monthly Report, Kerry, Oct. 1918 (CO 904/107).

[48]   IG Monthly Report, Feb. 1918 (CO 904/105). See also the I.G. Report for Apr. 1918.

[49]   CI Monthly Report, West Cork, June 1917 (CO 904/103).

[50]   CI Monthly Report, Jan. 1917 (CO 904/102).

Sinn Feiners belong to and attend these Gaelic classes regularly. Two football clubs have been formed during the month in Bandon district . . . The members include all the local Irish Volunteers with some others.

When the result of the Roscommon election was announced the band at Bantry turned out with a procession of 200–300 sympathizers and paraded the town.[51]

Within this omnibus movement, organizational boundaries and roles were indistinct. Sinn Fein members marched in formation, drilled, fought with police, and went to prison while Volunteers collected money, signatures, and votes.[52] 'Most of the young Sinn Feiners consider themselves Irish Volunteers though not actually enrolled as such.'[53] Organizational labels were largely irrelevant so long as everyone was doing much the same thing and travelling in the same direction, with a broadly shared sense of identity and purpose.

The fact that these activities and this identity were shared by both men and women was one of the movement's most novel features. More than just organizational boundaries had been blurred. Traditional gender roles, usually rigidly observed by Irish politicians of all stripes, were swept aside by young republicans caught up in the first wave of patriotic excitement. Youthful idealism seized as many girls as it did boys, particularly those who were educated and working outside the home: 'sentimentally seditious shopgirls' Edith Somerville disdainfully called them.[54] As many young women as men attended the formative requiem masses and demonstrations held in 1916 and 1917.[55]

Cumann na mBan, the women's counterpart to the Irish Volunteers, grew along with the other republican organizations, its members often being drawn from the same pool of families as the Volunteers. The head of Cumann na mBan in Macroom was Mary Corkery, wife of Dan Corkery, the battalion commander.[56] Bella O'Connell, the leader of the Beara organization, was the sister of Christy O'Connell, the captain of Eyeries Company.[57] Mary MacSwiney and Mrs Sean O'Hegarty were in charge of one of the city factions. In Kilmeen Company, again, it was the Volunteer officers' sisters who founded the local Cumann na mBan branch.[58] Over half the Courtbrack Cumann na mBan were sisters (all of whom had brothers in the I.R.A), while the Shandon branch in

---

[51] CI Monthly Report, Feb. 1917 (CO 904/103).

[52] The Précis of Sinn Fein Correspondence (MS 10, 494) contains numerous letters from all over Ireland concerning clubs drilling and arming. The MI5 Censorship Summary and Précis includes similar letters, such as the following from Nenagh, 26 June 1918: 'We have nothing here but Sinn Fein marching and drilling' (CO 904/164). See also Fitzpatrick, *Politics and Irish Life*, 209–10.

[53] CI Monthly Report, Co. Dublin, June 1918 (CO 904/106).

[54] Edith Somerville, 'Ourselves Alone' (Somerville and Ross Papers). See also Lankford, *The Hope and the Sadness*, 103–7; Aideen Sheehan, 'Cumann na mBan: Policies and Activities', in David Fitzpatrick (ed.), *Revolution? Ireland 1917–1923* (Dublin, 1990), 89.

[55] See Dalton, *With the Dublin Brigade*, 42–3.

[56] Browne, *The Story of the 7th*, 12.   [57] O'Dwyer, *Beara in Irish History*, 114.

[58] O'Leary, *Kilmeen and Castleventry Parish*, 96.

Cork city was formed and run by the Conlon and Crowley sisters.[59] For women as well as men, republicanism seemed to run in families.

As with the all-male Volunteers, Cumann na mBan members circulated freely within the movement, adding tremendously to its social momentum.[60] Many Sinn Fein clubs and nearly all Gaelic League branches had women members: the Courtbrack Sinn Fein *cumann*, for example, was one-third female, two-thirds of whom belonged to Cumann na mBan.[61] The party thereby acquired an occasionally strong (and usually suburban) feminist fringe.[62]

The British and Irish public had read with fascinated disapproval of Constance Markievicz's supposed exploits in the Dublin rising. In 1917, a host of tough young Markieviczes—dubbed by Edith Somerville 'the order of Flapper'[63]—appeared at the vanguard of republicanism, to the alarm of policemen and priests alike: 'the Flappers flaunt like banners in the forefront of the battle.'[64] Some clerics issued lurid warnings (as they had done with the Gaelic League) about 'the dangers of sex immorality in Sinn Fein clubs'[65] but female republicans took as much pleasure as their male comrades in defying such opinions and authority figures.

Republican women played a prominent role in the new street politics of urban Cork. As in the Kanturk demonstration described above, nearly every march and protest meeting included large numbers of women, marching in formation (and in uniform) along with the men.[66] One witness to a city procession in 1917 remarked that 'they certainly are drilled as methodically as the scouts'.[67] And when protests turned violent, women were again at the forefront and were present in force at nearly every riot. Indeed, confrontations between female Sinn Feiners and 'separation women' (who had husbands or sons in the armed forces) often provided the flashpoints for mass violence.[68] One of the first people in Cork to be gaoled for refusing to pay a fine was Teresa

---

[59] Duggan, *Grenagh and Courtbrack*, 64–5; Conlon, *Cumann na mBan*, 61. Billy Mullins reported the same family connections in Kerry (*The Memoirs of Billy Mullins: Veteran of the War of Independence* (Tralee, 1983), 17).

[60] In the month of June 1918 alone, six concerts, two picnics, and one sports day were organized by Cumann na mBan for Sinn Fein in the city and suburbs. Conlon, *Cumann na mBan*, 63.

[61] Duggan, *Grenagh and Courtbrack*, 64–5, 71.

[62] Mary MacSwiney and other Cork republicans had been members of the Munster Women's Franchise League before the Great War (Charlotte Fallon, *Soul of Fire: A Biography of Mary MacSwiney* (Cork, 1986), 21–3). The Bray *cumann* passed a resolution that 'Sinn Fein stands for equal rights between men and women' (*Irish Times*, 30 July 1917). The activities of suffragists in another south Dublin club are described in Andrews, *Dublin Made Me*, 100. In the 1920 local elections, four republican suffragists from Rathmines were elected (Leah Levenson and Jerry H. Natterstad, *Hanna Sheehy-Skeffington: Irish Feminist* (Syracuse, NY, 1986), 133).

[63] Somerville, 'Ourselves Alone'.

[64] John Murphy's anti-I.R.A. song 'The Farmer's Union Ball' also called republican women 'flappers' (Dept. of Irish Folklore, SMS 388, 187–93).

[65] Liam de Roiste Diary, 4 Dec. 1917 (O'Donoghue Papers, MS 31, 146).

[66] See *Examiner*, 10, 16 Apr., 15, 23 May, 4 July, 13 Aug., 19 Nov. 1917.

[67] Quoted in Conlon, *Cumann na mBan*, 52.

[68] See *Examiner*, 25, 26, 28 June, 12 July 1917.

O'Donovan, of the city Cumann na mBan, who broke her umbrella over a policeman's head.[69]

Essentially, women did just about everything men did. Women fought, drilled, organized, canvassed, collected, and were willing to go to gaol for it. In Cork city in particular, Cumann na mBan formed a vital—and often over-looked—component of the Sinn Fein electoral machine by registering first-time women voters far in advance of their opponents.[70] Most of the activists them-selves still could not vote however, as the franchise was restricted to women over 30.

The issue of equality and the status of women in the independence movement seems rarely to have surfaced. Relations between Cumann na mBan and the Volunteers were occasionally fractious but complaints went both ways.[71] On the other hand, no Cork Sinn Fein clubs had female presidents and only a few had female secretaries. Mary MacSwiney may have wielded as much power in republican back rooms as her brothers but she was the exception. The main power struggle within Cumann na mBan in late 1917 seemed to be over who would get to serve tea to de Valera.[72]

What does not seem to have been typical among women militants was the following sort of sentiment:[73]

> Harra for the Sinn Fein, the Sinn Fein are men,
> and if I were a boy I would go Sinn Fein with them.
> But as I am a girl I must lead a girl's life.
> But I'll do all in my power to be a Sinn Fein wife.

In 1917 and 1918 the movement was being made up as it went along, the prod-uct of a myriad of local entrepreneurs and initiatives. At this grassroots level, both women and men were relatively free to invent their own roles.

Thus, what most people were joining was an open mass movement in which dances, classes, meetings, committees, and paramilitary display all flowed together into a broad republican front, usually described in all its manifestations simply as 'Sinn Fein'. However, for the 'declared rebels', the men who met after the meetings and classes were over, Sinn Fein was a 'front' in a different sense. Conventions and elections were fixed to push a radical agenda, money was collected to buy guns, petitions were canvassed to know and intimidate their enemies, demonstrations were held to fight the 'peelers', and being a Volunteer meant being above politics and 'noise'.

---

[69]   Conlon, *Cumann na mBan*, 45. The incident occurred in April 1917.

[70]   See *Examiner*, 11 June 1918.

[71]   See the exchange of letters in the O'Donoghue Papers, MS 31, 198.

[72]   De Roiste Diary, 10 Dec. 1917 (O'Donoghue Papers, MS 31, 146). This was not a uniquely female preoccupation, however. Male Sinn Feiners also fought a bitter battle over access to de Valera during his Cork tour (de Roiste Diary, 25 Nov. 1918).

[73]   Anonymous (O'Donoghue Papers, MS 31, 225).

Sinn Fein, however much its officials might protest otherwise, was irredeemably tainted with 'politics' in the eyes of some Volunteers, with all of its connotations of parties, venality, and compromise. In August 1917 Liam de Roiste insisted to his diary that 'I, as a Sinn Feiner, was never a politician, and am not now' but he was soon made uncomfortably aware that some of his fellow republicans saw him as exactly that.[74] 'Some of the Oglaigh [Volunteers]', he admitted in September, 'think Sinn Fein is too tame, too moderate.'[75] At that year's national convention, Cork delegates (most of whom, ironically, were Volunteers) were told by Michael Collins that 'the Volunteers did not want politicians interfering with their military matters'.[76] In November de Roiste reported that 'our relations with Oglaigh are altogether better now' but that same month Sinn Fein was kept off the Manchester Martyrs Parade committee and by January relations had returned to normal: 'there is yet trouble with some of the Oglaigh whose attitude is that Sinn Fein is a mere political and talking machine, fit for old men only, to be despised by the young men.'[77] This absence of fraternalism was felt on both sides. During the conscription crisis the Cork Volunteers did not even consult the Sinn Fein leadership. Once this had passed it was the turn of I.R.A. officers to complain of neglect. 'Sinn Fein pay little attention now to those on the run', Tomas MacCurtain wrote in his own diary in December 1918: 'Maybe they will do something when we and our families are in the workhouse.'[78]

The city's Sinn Fein clubs and committees were the scene for fierce battles over delegate and candidate selection between militant Volunteers and less 'advanced' factions. De Roiste—a veteran of years of similar struggles—was well aware in 1917 that:

the Volunteer organization is working quite independently and is capturing, or endeavouring to capture and completely control Sinn Fein as such . . . Every man who is not a Volunteer or in the good graces of the chiefs of the Volunteers is to be pushed aside.[79]

This committee *Kampf* was revived in the run-up to the 1918 convention. Militants organized 'a temporary mass influx of members of the I.R.A., with the result that mainly I.R.A. officers were sent as delegates'.[80] Volunteer leaders also sought a veto over Sinn Fein candidates in the 1918 elections, and again in 1920 and 1921—although never with complete success, as de Roiste's political survival showed.[81]

These 'advanced' Volunteers came increasingly to define themselves against

[74] De Roiste Diary, 10 Aug. 1917.   [75] Ibid. 27 Sept. 1917.
[76] Ibid. 27 Oct. 1917.   [77] Ibid. 13 Jan. 1918.
[78] MacCurtain Diary, 31 Dec. 1918 (Co. Cork Museum, L330).
[79] De Roiste Diary, 18 Oct. 1917.
[80] Roibeard Langford, 'Personal Record' (Langford Papers, U155).
[81] See de Roiste Diary, 2 Dec. 1918, 10 May 1921 (CAI, de Roiste Papers, U271); O/C Cork 2 to A/G, 30 Mar. 1920 and A/G's response, 10 Apr. 1920 (MA, A/0499); Con Neenan (O'Malley Papers, P17b/111).

Sinn Fein. Sinn Feiners were 'older men . . . not involved in the fight for freedom'; 'the older fellas', 'the settled down people, the crowd above' or just 'no
good'.[82] One of the worst things one Volunteer activist could say about another
was that he was really only 'the Sinn Fein type'.[83] With one exception, all the
veterans I interviewed had belonged to Sinn Fein clubs and worked in elections—two had been elected to local councils—but all emphatically (even
angrily) denied having anything to do with politics or parties. Yes, they had
done all that but they had done it as Volunteers. This adamantly anti-political
stance was a core part of the guerrilla's sense of identity. When Sean Moylan
declared, 'I am not a politician; I am a soldier,'[84] he was perfectly sincere, even
though he was a sitting TD, a member of his constituency Sinn Fein executive,
and a Dail court judge.

This 'spirit of rivalry'[85] and outright contempt for the 'civil side' of the movement could be found in every unit of the I.R.A. One Sinn Fein organizer in
Meath complained that:

prominent Volunteers seem to encourage amongst their own men a feeling of contempt
for the political side of the movement, and put it down as constitutionalism. One
Volunteer officer . . . proves himself to be a good worker for Sinn Fein but spoils it all by
sneering at workers who concern themselves with club work alone.[86]

C. S. Andrews's company in Dublin 'did not take the debates of the Sinn Fein
club seriously but recognised its utility as a means of collecting money . . .
and as a cover for Volunteer activities'.[87] In Ernie O'Malley's unit, 'the men
had little use for anyone who was not of the physical force belief. Gaelic
Leaguers and members of Sinn Fein clubs who did not belong to the
Volunteers were sneered at.'[88] When the leader of the Glasgow Volunteers
complained to Michael Collins that Sinn Fein were 'no good only for singing
and dancing', Collins replied that he was hearing the same thing from all
round the country.[89] And when peace returned in the Truce, I.R.A. headquarters was still receiving complaints that its men were 'standing aloof' from
political work.[90]

It was not just Sinn Fein the organization that the guerrillas held in contempt,
but 'Sinn Fein' the mass movement with its endless socializing, posturing, and
patriotic ephemera: the 'noise', the 'blowing', 'the dances and all that carry on'.[91]
This applied equally to those in their own ranks who were merely 'passengers':

[82] Interviews with AB, AD, and AI.
[83] See Sean Breen and Sean Daly (O'Malley Papers, P17b/83, 112).
[84] *Examiner*, 19 Sept. 1921.
[85] Election Report, South Meath, May 1921 (Mulcahy Papers, P7/A/36).
[86] Organizer's Report, Meath, 9 Aug. 1919 (MA, A/0326).
[87] Andrews, *Dublin Made Me*, 101.
[88] O'Malley, *On Another Man's Wound*, 57.
[89] Joe Vize to Michael Collins, 6 June 1919 (Mulcahy Papers, P7/A/7).
[90] GHQ Weekly Memo No. 17, 21 Oct. 1921 (O'Malley Papers, P17a/2).
[91] Interviews with AH and AI.

the 'flag-waggers', 'public house I.R.A.', and 'G.A.A. hangers-on' who were 'only fit for dancing and for style'.[92]

Sean Moylan became terribly frustrated by the amount of money spent in North Cork on postcards, belts, banners and the like and declared that 'the desire for music and noise was the chief obstacle to serious organization'.[93] For many members, however, volunteering and music went hand in hand. Several companies were even formed around bands. In Moylan's territory around Newmarket, 'every Sinn Fein club and Volunteer unit desired to have a band . . . There seemed to be one in every townland.' Despite his best efforts, company funds collected for arms and uniforms would all be spent on instruments. On one occasion he went to see a unit—the Rockchapel Company—whom he had already lectured on the subject. They met in the captain's kitchen, which was soon lined 'three deep' with shy countrymen who said little but kept him under 'a constant if covert survey'. All was solemnly quiet until the mother of the house looked in and asked the boys: 'Wouldn't ye play the band for the organizer?' Like magic, their brand new instruments appeared and the real business of the evening got under way.[94]

Worst of all were the 'would-be warriors' who flooded into Volunteer companies in the spring of 1918 under the threat of conscription.[95] Most doubled in size almost overnight. The Clonakilty Company, for example, went from 40 to 150.[96] In Ballydesmond, 'we had 11 members drilling . . . the Sunday before conscription and we had 100 the following Sunday'.[97] These new recruits gave the cause sudden—albeit temporary—respectability but they were often not welcome. It was felt they would dilute the 'military character and unselfish spirit' of the Volunteers.[98] 'We knew they would not last.'[99] Many were allowed to march and drill but were never officially enrolled. The Blackpool Company formed a separate unit for the 'conscription heroes', which was disbanded after 1918.[100] C. S. Andrews's company told most newcomers to join the Sinn Fein club instead.[101]

These attitudes defined a movement within a movement, a militant tendency composed of Volunteers who saw the protest campaigns of 1917 and 1918 as a kind of phoney war. Marches, dances, and committees described who they were not. 'Their' I.R.A. was exclusive, secretive, and revolutionary. They were a small minority even within the Volunteers but they probably formed a majority of the activists, and they could count on a hard core of like-minded friends and relatives to back them up.

[92] O'Suilleabhain, *Mountainy Men*, 55; interview with AB; Bill Hammond, *Soldier of the Rearguard: The Story of Matt Flood and the Active Service Column* (Fermoy, 1977), 8; Mick Leahy and Dan Browne (O'Malley Papers, P17b/108, 112).   [93] Moylan Memoir, 42.
[94] Ibid. 45–6.   [95] Tom Daly statement (Co. Cork Museum).
[96] Deasy, *Towards Ireland Free*, 55.   [97] Culloty, *Ballydesmond*, 237.
[98] O'Donoghue, *No Other Law*, 21.
[99] Con Neenan in MacEoin, *Survivors*, 236. See also O'Suilleabhain, *Mountainy Men*, 55.
[100] Tom Daly statement. The quotation is from Con Neenan in MacEoin, *Survivors*, 236.
[101] Andrews, *Dublin Made Me*, 103.

Many militants were also I.R.B. members but theirs was more a collective mentality than a conspiracy, united by a desire for guns and for direct action in the tradition of 1916. They took pride in being the men who 'meant business'. They were fighting men and they were willing to take matters into their own hands. 'We wanted to get something going'; 'there were a number of men from every company busting to do things'; 'the whole atmosphere was depressing and called for a burst up, and we decided . . . to start this burst up on our own'; 'there were only a couple of dozen of us in the fight for freedom to begin with but we . . . had a determination to free our country'.[102]

These 'freedom fighters' first appeared on the streets of Cork city in 1917, using marches and demonstrations as a cover to provoke and attack the police. Most used hurleys and stones but, after darkness and police batons had thinned the crowds, they gave way to gunfire.[103] Three policemen were shot while on riot duty in the last six months of the year. In these early years, the militants would act suddenly and disappear quickly, but their public gestures were ominously unequivocal. When a city Volunteer died in May 1918—at the height of the conscription crisis—the funeral became a paramilitary show of strength, climaxing in a graveside salute fired by four uniformed men with service rifles. The men in uniform were sending a message of massed defiance but, for the silent men behind them, the guns held the promise of a future war:

The rifles, which were wrapped in canvas, were in charge of two men in civilian dress who had the rifles concealed under their overcoats. After the firing the rifles were again wrapped in canvas and handed to the same two men who then left the cemetery. There is nothing known as to the identity of either of these men.[104]

The anonymous gunmen belonged to a shadowy underground inside the Volunteers, loosely organized around a few extremist cells: the 'I.R.B. unit of Cork 1 Brigade'.[105] Among them were Mick Murphy, Joe Murphy, Tadg O'Sullivan, Donnchadha MacNeilus, Roibeard Langford, Dan Donovan, and Martin Donovan. Their leader was Sean O'Hegarty, the arch-Fenian and archetypal rebel.[106] These men (several dozen at most), who called themselves the 'irregulars', the 'active squad', or 'Hegarty's crowd', were responsible for the

[102] Sean Daly and Frank Busteed (O'Malley Papers, P17b/112); O'Dwyer, *Beara in Irish History*, 114; interview with AB.

[103] See *Examiner*, 24, 25 June, 27 Sept. 1917; CI Monthly Report, East Cork, Mar. 1918 (CO 904/106).

[104] Report by Sgt. A. Young, Cork South, 16 May 1918 (WO 35/99). The witness was a police informant.   [105] Michael Crowley statement (NLI, Crowley family papers).

[106] For information on this group, see Seamus O Maoileoin, *B'Fhiu An Braon Fola* (Dublin, 1958), 117–19 (kindly translated for me by Peter Smith); Seamus Malone, Dan Corkery, Moss Twomey, and Sean Daly (O'Malley papers, P17b/103, 107, 111, 112); Roibeard Langford, 'Statement of Service' (Langford Papers, U156); O'Donoghue, *Tomas MacCurtain*, 152–4. See also Con Neenan, 'Some Rapid Observations' (CAI, U129), which takes issue with some of Seamus Malone's account. Sean O'Hegarty proved his ability at intrigue when he used the I.R.B. to outmanœuvre the Ancient Order of Hibernians and get himself elected as storekeeper for the city workhouse. See *Examiner*, 12, 13 Sept. 1917.

great majority of I.R.A. shootings in the city between 1917 and mid-1920 and continued as key figures in the Tan War. They were 'a tough crowd' and acted on their own, in defiance of orders and courts martial to the contrary.[107]

The militants distrusted the Volunteers' official leadership, whom they felt were over-cautious and too political, and whom they blamed for the bloodless surrender of 1916. They were determined this should never happen again, however much 'the people in authority . . . didn't want anything done'.[108] Nor were they interested in martyrdom or heroic prison sentences. Many of their early exploits occurred while resisting arrest or escaping from gaol. They also smuggled in or stole their own arms and refused to place them under the brigade's control.[109] Moreover, they were perfectly prepared to mount their own independent rebellion if necessary—as Tomas MacCurtain, the brigade commander, only discovered in May 1919 when a secret bomb factory blew up, killing two militants and revealing a huge arsenal of explosives.[110]

This accident exacerbated tensions between the 'underground' and the 'official' I.R.A. Sean O'Hegarty was forced out of his position as vice-commandant and several 'irregulars' were court-martialled.[111] MacCurtain had already tried to stop the 'irresponsible' and 'disorderly' street violence (a sympathetic Inspector Swanzy told him, 'it is not your meetings I mind, it is the youngsters'[112]). Many of his senior officers (the 'Sinn Fein types'[113]) quit for good and MacCurtain himself temporarily resigned in exasperation but he was a gentleman among players.[114] The dissidents kept their guns and kept on using them, impervious to authority. MacCurtain's last official act on the night of 19 March 1920 was to issue an apology for the unauthorized killing of an off-duty constable. 'Whoever did it will pay the piper,' he declared. 'We can't have men roaming around armed shooting police on their own.'[115] A few hours later he was dead.[116]

All over the county—in Eyeries, Bantry, Macroom, Ballyvourney, Donoughmore, Kiskeam, Mourneabbey—similarly placed groups were 'forcing the pace' and seizing every opportunity to acquire arms and mount reprisal attacks. Nearly five times as many shootings occurred in 1919 as in 1918, while the number of Volunteer casualties more than doubled. Almost all of these were unauthorized operations. In Kilbrittain, for example, both the pivotal Rathclarin ambush of June 1919 and the shooting of Constable Bolger in

---

[107]   Moss Twomey (O'Malley Papers, P17b/107).

[108]   Seamus Malone (O'Malley Papers, P17b/103).

[109]   O'Donoghue, *Tomas MacCurtain*, 153–4; Cork 1916 Men's Association, 'Comments on Florence O'Donoghue's Life of Tomas MacCurtain' (Boston Public Library).

[110]   Moss Twomey (O'Malley Papers, P17b/107); *Examiner*, 29 Apr., 5 May 1919.

[111]   See *Examiner*, 25, 28 June, 2, 5 Oct. 1917, 19 Jan. 1918.

[112]   De Roiste Diary, 18 Apr. 1918 (O'Donoghue Papers).

[113]   Sean Breen (O'Malley Papers, P17b/124).

[114]   Tomas MacCurtain to A/G, 19 Feb. 1919 (Foulkes Papers, Epitome No. 53/2567, 2772).

[115]   Con Kelleher to Florence O'Donoghue, 2 July 1958 (O'Donoghue Papers, MS 31, 430).

[116]   Ironically, it was the insubordinate gunmen who assassinated his suspected killer, none other than Inspector Swanzy.

December were carried out by the same band of pioneer guerrillas in direct contravention of official orders.[117] The same was true of the Berrings ambush in September.

In many cases these activists were, like the Hales brothers, I.R.B. members. As in the city, this was more a badge of militancy than a well-defined organization. I.R.B. officials from Dublin or Cork had little contact or influence with the county circles. They were often distrusted or disliked and their orders were ignored as often as those of I.R.A. superiors.[118] As Dan Corkery, the I.R.B. centre and I.R.A. commandant of Macroom, put it: 'we were on our own.'[119]

The rise in uncontrolled violence, and the common perception that 'hidden forces' were behind it, alienated many Volunteers and pushed the divisions between the militants and the wider movement to the breaking point.[120] The men of 1917 and 1918 had joined for all sorts of reasons, for 'glamour' and excitement, to march and drill with their family and friends, to fight the Irish Party and conscription, to help make a new Ireland. What they had not joined to do, most of them, was to shoot neighbours and policemen.

Now, in 1919, the organization was changing around them, a change symbolized by the adoption of the title 'Irish Republican Army'. As the year wore on, there were fewer and fewer dances and meetings and the only marching done was at funerals. Men who had vaguely given their allegiance to the movement were suddenly given guns and told to fight. One such was John Gilligan of Ballyquirke, Tipperary, who also provides us with a vivid portrait of a small-town militant on the edge of revolution—in this case his nephew, James Carroll:

In March [Carroll] was talking about using the gun, saying he would soon need it, and mentioned about revolutions, and that the men of Ireland would soon need the guns. Shortly after D.I. Hunt was shot in Thurles I asked what was the object of shooting the police as they were the only protection. [Carroll] said 'forget that idea; they are the only enemies Ireland has'. I asked him if they were going to gain anything by shooting the police, and he replied that England would have to give them what they were looking for, and otherwise Ireland would be a scene of blood. He said the Sinn Feiners were well prepared for revolution and would stop at nothing.[121]

On 1 September 1919, Carroll and two comrades, John Joe Madden and Mick Hogan, set up an ambush for a police patrol and brought Gilligan with them:

---

[117] For Rathclarin, see Deasy, *Towards Ireland Free*, 66–7. For Bolger's killing, see Ch. 3.

[118] See, for example, Mick Leahy's comments about Sean O'Muirthuile (O'Malley Papers, P17b/108)—the I.R.B. organizer for Munster and perhaps the most reviled man in the republican movement. See also Mullins, *Memoirs*, 43, 78–93; 'Comments on Florence O'Donoghue's Life of Tomas MacCurtain'.   [119] Dan Corkery (O'Malley Papers, P17b/111).

[120] O/C Sligo Bde. to A/G, 4 Apr. 1920 (MA, A/0512). See also Adj. Leitrim Bde. to D/O, 25 May 1920 (MA, A/0510), who complained that 'they seem to have power over us'.

[121] *Irish Times*, 3 Apr. 1920.

They ordered me to get inside the wall then. When I was inside the wall [Carroll] opened the parcel which contained four guns. The three men started to load the guns. As soon as they were loaded Carroll passed a gun on to me. I asked them what they were going to do. One of them said 'I do not know which—we are going to hunt'. James Carroll told me not to ask any more questions and I did not.

Carroll, Madden, and Hogan shot two policemen but they and Gilligan were soon caught, whereupon Gilligan told all.

In Ballyclough, near Mallow, Jim Croke found himself included in a series of raids on houses: 'I had to do it or I would be shot . . . The men made me go . . . Another raider confided that "he was caught in the same as myself." '[122] Another apparently reluctant group were the men of the Carrig Irish class, who were roped into raiding houses for arms on 22 October 1919:

On the evening before that [Tim Heffernan later testified] . . . I met the defendant, William Herbert, who gave me a message to do something the next day. Other boys in the class got the same message. Herbert told us all to be down at Anna Minnitt's gate . . . Before the night of the raid I was speaking to Tim Kelly and Denis Cleary. They said they did not want to go on the raid at all. William Herbert was the man giving directions about everything.[123]

The same scenario was played out in The Ballagh Sinn Fein Club in Wexford in February 1920. The first witness is John Lacey:

I met Thomas Leary of Kilcotty, at Kilcotty. He asked me would I go to a meeting tonight, and I said I didn't know, and what kind of a meeting it was to be. He said a man from town [Enniscorthy] was going to give a lecture . . . We arrived at John Sinnott's barn at The Ballagh about 7 p.m . . . When we went in Bill Murray put us into line. Then [William] Dwyer stood in front and said—'There is a fault in this branch of the Sinn Fein club. The first fault is it is not supporting itself. Secondly, there were raids in every part of this county but here, and they would have to have four raids here on the same night, as every club must support itself . . .' Murray then said, 'Ye will all have to attend at Ballymacanaque lane at 8 p.m. on Saturday.'[124]

James Denby, who was also at the meeting, later said, 'I knew I was doing wrong, but I was afraid not to go.' In the ensuing raid on a local home, Lacey, who had never before handled a gun, shot a woman dead. Outside, Denby 'heard Laurence Connolly say that Mrs Morris was shot'. Bill Murray, the club leader, then handed his revolver to Dwyer and said, 'I am done with your crowd now.'

When the shooting began in earnest, large numbers of Volunteers sided with Murray and left: men like Pat Casey of Kildorrery who 'had volunteered during elections to keep order, but since then . . . did not belong to the Volunteers or take part in politics'; Steve Morley of Evergreen Street who 'marched with the Sinn Fein Volunteers some time ago' but who 'altogether ceased his connection with Sinn Fein in 1919'; or Pat Higgins of Rostellan who 'had been a member of the old Volunteers up to' 1919 but who then resigned upon his mother's advice.[125]

[122] *Examiner*, 8 Mar. 1920.
[124] *Irish Times*, 27 Feb. 1920.
[123] Ibid. 17 Nov. 1919.
[125] *Examiner*, 3 May 1921, 20 May 1919, 22 June 1921.

The mass movement peaked in 1918 with the twin victories over conscription and the Irish Party. These events mobilized huge numbers of young enthusiasts but decay set in almost immediately thereafter. The first to go were the 'conscriptioneers' who 'practically all . . . dwindled away and were not heard from again'.[126] The I.R.A. was losing far more than unwanted opportunists, however. Companies all over Cork and Ireland found their memberships melting away. In the Hales family stronghold of Ballinadee, only 35 reliable Volunteers remained in July 1919 out of 60 present at the beginning of 1918 and 100 at the height of the conscription scare.[127] In the West Cork Brigade as a whole, even with the contraction of unit rolls, nearly 40 per cent of the remaining members were inactive. As Liam Deasy diplomatically put it: 'A view of the role of the Volunteer movement at the time which had considerable support even in the ranks was that it would be most effective as a threat, and that any attempt at fighting in its almost unarmed condition could lead only to defeat.'[128]

When Michael Brennan returned home to Clare in January 1919 he discovered that 'on paper we had large numbers, but it was unusual if more than twenty five per cent of those reported for any parade. In many places no organized unit remained and all I could contact were two or three individuals.'[129] The commander of the South Roscommon Brigade encountered the same apathy: 'In one instance I visited a company—there were 103 members present. I told them that any man that was not prepared to fight for a Republic was not wanted in the Army, whereupon 89 left the meeting.'[130]

The South Tipperary Brigade discovered the depth of this resistance after the (unauthorized) Soloheadbeg ambush in January 1919 killed two policemen. This famous incident began with the familiar resolve to force the pace. The ambushers were afraid that 'the Volunteers were in great danger of becoming merely a political adjunct to the Sinn Fein organization' and that 'nothing would be done by a large body of Volunteers until a lead was given by a few'.[131] In Sean Treacy's words: 'It was a high time we did a bit of the pushing.'[132]

These sentiments found little support beyond the narrow circles of Munster militants. Local brigade officers and national Sinn Fein, I.R.A., and I.R.B. leaders all condemned the killings and those responsible found themselves isolated from their neighbours and from the movement as a whole:

---

[126] Tom Daly statement. See also Deasy, *Towards Ireland Free*, 24, 66; O'Donoghue, *No Other Law*, 21; Duggan, *Grenagh and Courtbrack* , 34; and O'Suilleabhain, *Mountainy Men*, 47.
[127] The first figure is from Deasy, *Towards Ireland Free*, 317; the latter two from Flynn, 'My Part in Irish Independence', 57.   [128] Deasy, *Towards Ireland Free*, 66.
[129] Brennan, *The War in Clare*, 36.
[130] South Roscommon Bde. Report, Oct. 1921 (MA, A/0761).
[131] Breen, *My Fight for Irish Freedom*, 30; Seamus Robinson Memoir, 68 (Gallagher Papers, MS 21, 265). The first edition of Breen's memoirs were more blunt. Blaming the general election, Breen wrote: 'There was a danger of disintegration, a danger which had been growing since the threat of conscription disappeared a few months earlier' (1924 edn. as quoted in Townshend, *British Campaign*, 16).   [132] Quoted in Breen, *My Fight for Irish Freedom*, 30.

Our former friends shunned us. They preferred the drawing-room as a battlefield, the political resolution rather than the gun as their offensive weapon . . . Even from the Irish Volunteers we got no support . . . We had to tramp from parish to parish without a penny in our pockets.[133]

By early 1920, such was the unpopularity of the lead given by the 'amateur tacticians'[134] of Soloheadbeg, three South Tipperary battalions were 'near collapse', one of which was deemed by Sean Treacy to be 'non-existent'. He added that 'the other battalions require a lot of smartening up or they'll begin to rot also'.[135]

The Cork brigades were in similar straits. When Richard Mulcahy, the chief of staff, suggested to Tomas MacCurtain in October 1919 that his brigade put their best men under GHQ control, MacCurtain replied with a frank description of organizational atrophy:

the selecting out of these men would have a bad effect on the remainder, and the result would more than likely be that the particular unit would fizzle out. It is indeed difficult enough to keep the organization going at the present time . . . To keep things going some action must be taken which would give *all* the men a chance of doing something, otherwise the men will fall away and the Companies die out.

Slackness and slowness have crept in everywhere in spite of our best efforts and a general shaking up is required to put the men in anything like order for the work.[136]

When the brigade did finally launch the sort of large-scale operation that MacCurtain wished for—the massive destruction of R.I.C. barracks at Easter 1920—it still provoked protests from within the movement itself.[137]

Some guerrillas later tried to put the best face on the situation. Micheal O'Suilleabhain argued that 'it needed a little taste of war to separate the chaff from the grain and to reduce further mere numbers to a fighting unit of quality'.[138] Liam Deasy also explained the decline in numbers as a blessing in disguise:

At such an early date [July 1919], the Volunteers were still in the process of consolidating their movement after the not-unexpected defection of many of those brought into the ranks merely because of the conscription scare. The Volunteers who remained formed a smaller but more steadfast and determined body of young men for whom the accepted duty of fighting for national freedom was a hard reality.[139]

---

[133] Ibid. 40–1.

[134] Circular letter from Eamon O'Dwyer, Bde. Quartermaster (Foulkes Papers, Epitome No. 53/3649, 137). For O'Dwyer's court-martial proceedings, see p. 150. See also Seamus Robinson Memoir, 53.

[135] This letter to Michael Collins was captured and printed in the *Irish Times*, 19 May 1921 (where it was misdated; the correction was printed on 9 June).

[136] O/C Cork 1 to C/S (O'Donoghue Papers, MS 31, 197). See also O'Donoghue, *Tomas MacCurtain*, 157 (which quotes a carefully edited version of the letter).

[137] De Roiste Diary, 12 July 1920 (de Roiste Papers).

[138] O'Suilleabhain, *Mountainy Men*, 55.   [139] Deasy, *Towards Ireland Free*, 66.

By the spring of 1920, however, Sean Buckley, a fellow West Cork Brigade staff officer, was reporting that in Bandon:

the National Organizations—civil and military—have ceased to function in the district, and that even our own people—Volunteers, Sinn Feiners, etc.—are now afraid to be seen speaking publicly to those whom the R.I.C. and military consider prominent Sinn Feiners or Volunteers. As far as I can tell, a similar state of things holds good in other districts.[140]

While many Volunteers dropped out after 1918, others were being drawn further in by conviction and circumstance. As the examples of the Ballinadee and Behagh Companies show, family and neighbourhood remained key determinants of activism. Of the fourteen Kilbrittain men who carried out the critical Rathclarin ambush in June 1919, ten were brothers, and nearly all of these went on to active service in 1920–1.[141] These networks were far from static, however. The revolution forged many new bonds and broke others. The shared experience of struggle and the comradeship among the activists was itself a force in shaping the I.R.A. Or, to put it another way, revolutionaries were as much creations of revolution as creators. Every person had a different experience, of course, but if we examine a sample of individual careers, we can recognize some common patterns amidst the diversity.

Sean (Jack) Breen first joined the Volunteers in 1916, along with many of his fellow medical students at University College Cork,[142] but did not become active until he met some returned prisoners that Christmas, just home from a British internment camp.[143] With them he went to work for de Valera in the East Clare by-election in July 1917. Breen later accompanied Cork contingents to elections in Waterford, south Armagh, and Donegal and also helped organize and drill a company in his home village of Lombardstown. His public activities were matched by his growing involvement with '[Sean] Hegarty's crowd': the city's I.R.B.-led underground movement. He took part in arms raids and smuggling and, after an arrest warrant was issued for him for his overground activities, he went on the run. In Newmarket he was given his first gun.

Breen returned to the city after the 1918 general election, took a job as a chemist, and renewed contact with the 'active squad', where his comrades included the O'Brien brothers of Broad Lane and Dick Murphy, later one of District Inspector Swanzy's assassins.[144] Among other operations, they were

---

[140]   Quoted in a letter to A/G (author and exact date unknown) (MA, A/0771).

[141]   Deasy, *Towards Ireland Free*, 66.

[142]   'It is well known in this City that nearly all medical students here were staunch republicans and at least 90 per cent of them were members of the Irish Republican Army.' Denis Cronin statement (Irish Grants Committee, CO 762/170). According to one list, twenty of the thirty-five members of the UCC company were medical students (O'Donoghue Papers, MS 31, 455 (2)).

[143]   Unless otherwise specified, this account is based on Breen's own statements in the O'Malley Papers, P17b/83, 124.

[144]   Charlie O'Brien described Breen as 'very active': interview with O'Brien in Marie O'Donoghue Diary, 13 Feb. 1970 (Marie O'Donoghue Papers). Dick Murphy also took part in the execution of Din-Din O'Riordan, as detailed in the Introduction (O'Callaghan, *Execution*, 60–2).

responsible for the failed attack on General Strickland, the commander of the 6th Division, in September 1920. Breen gave up his job soon after this and he, Murphy, and others formed their own squad, cruising the streets in a stolen car 'to draw blood'. 'We were hanging around doing city jobs for some time.' When things got too hot, Breen and Murphy joined the Cork 1 flying column and participated in the near-disastrous ambush at Coolavokig in February 1921. Breen returned to the city, but at 'a very bitter time' as British intelligence officers and death squads had made the underground a very dangerous place to be. Breen was himself a target so 'there was no time to organize any jobs or get new orders'. He returned to Lombardstown and spent the rest of the war with Dick Murphy and the local column.

Another member of 'Hegarty's crowd' was Roibeard Langford, an ardent Gaelic Leaguer and founder member of the city Volunteers.[145] A company lieutenant, he was among those junior officers who was in favour of rebellion in 1916. Disappointed by MacCurtain and MacSwiney's actions, and fired from his job as a printer at the Redmondite *Examiner*, he went to Dublin. There he attended I.R.B. revival meetings and acquired a rifle. When he returned to Cork city in mid-1917 he naturally fell in with Sean O'Hegarty, Donnchadha MacNeilus (both of whom had belonged to Langford's branch of the Gaelic League), and other disgruntled militants, eager to start anew.

Langford was appointed a company captain and an I.R.B. centre, putting him in a key position to push the radicals' agenda within both Sinn Fein and the I.R.A. In September 1917 he organized a raid on the Cork Grammar School armoury which netted forty-seven rifles. This was the dissidents' first unauthorized coup; the participants were a who's who of future guerrilla leaders, including MacNeilus, Dan and Martin Donovan, Tom Crofts, and Paddy Healy.[146] Langford was subsequently court-martialled but, as with most attempts to curb the 'irregulars', the charge did not stick.[147] His organizing work brought him into the north of the county, where he was arrested for drilling in November. He went on hunger strike and was released in December.

Langford continued to organize on behalf of the Volunteers and I.R.B. and to raid for arms with the 'active squad'. Like Sean Breen and the O'Brien family, he was part of the Brotherhood's early smuggling network, and also operated a clandestine printing press. As his now well-armed comrades moved into open warfare, Langford moved with them. He took part in several ambushes and in two of the most notorious executions of 1920: those of Divisional Commissioner Smyth and of three British court-martial officers at

[145] This account is primarily based on Langford's personal record and statement (CAI, Langford Papers, U155).

[146] See Robert Langford to Florence O'Donoghue, 11 Jan. 1953 (O'Donoghue Papers, MS 31, 423); O'Donoghue, *Tomas MacCurtain*, 133.

[147] The court martial is mentioned in a captured letter quoted in Epitome 53/2567, 230 (Foulkes Papers).

Waterfall. At the end of the year he was able to gain his revenge on the *Examiner* by leading the destruction of its plant. On the run for well over a year, he was finally captured in May 1921 and interned on Spike Island until after the signing of the Treaty.

Frank Busteed, a Blarney mill worker, joined the Fianna Eireann—the republican boy scouts—in 1910, under the influence of his ultranationalist mother.[148] He moved up to join the Volunteers in 1917, after brawling with policemen who were trying to remove a tricolour from Blarney Castle. Two close friends who joined in this fight also went on to become active guerrillas.

Busteed was soon elected as captain of the Blarney company and was also invited to join the I.R.B. but was (he says) turned down because of local prejudice over his 'Protestant' name.[149] This did nothing to alter his militancy, however, and he was soon in touch with the city underground to get arms and advice, and came to know the ubiquitous Donnchadha MacNeilus, Dick Murphy, and William and Charlie O'Brien among others.

After a brief stint in prison for collecting money without a permit, Busteed was soon 'in the soup' again after a raid on a loyalist house led to a gun battle with police. He and an old friend from the Blarney Fianna went on the run but 'there were few people to depend on so a month later I went home for I was full of lice'.[150] He was immediately rearrested and spent several months in gaol, part of it on hunger strike and in solitary confinement. Acquitted in late 1919 (witnesses having been threatened), Busteed vowed never to go to prison again, quit his job, and took up arms full-time in his new capacity as vice O/C of the Donoughmore Battalion.

From January 1920 on, Busteed took part in nearly every ambush or barracks attack between Cork and Macroom, as well as numerous operations and executions with the city gunmen. When a battalion column was formed in November 1920 he was the obvious choice as commander, and he held the post until the Truce. His mother's death after a British raid only increased his passion for revenge, which he took out on a considerable number of suspected 'spies' and 'informers', both before and after the Truce.[151] It was he who planned the Dripsey ambush in January 1921 ('a bit of a debacle'[152]) and the consequent kidnapping and killing of Mrs Lindsay and her chauffeur.

The career of Mick Fitzgerald, a mill worker in Clondulane, was virtually inseparable from that of Liam Lynch and his circle, apart from its tragic

---

[148] This account is largely derived from Busteed's interviews with Ernie O'Malley (O'Malley Papers, P17b/112); O'Callaghan, *Execution*, 43–7; and a National Army Intelligence Report, 30 May, 1924 (MA, A/0825).

[149] Busteed's deceased father had been Protestant although Busteed himself was raised a Catholic and later became an outspoken atheist.

[150] Frank Busteed (O'Malley Papers, P17b/112). National Army intelligence officers later recalled that 'finding he was not wanted [he] returned home and took up his work in the Mills' (MA, A/0825). For the police manhunt, see DI Report, Ballincollig, 12 Sept. 1919 (WO 35/108).

[151] See Ch. 13.   [152] Frank Busteed (O'Malley Papers, P17b/112).

outcome.[153] Like these men he joined the Volunteers in mid-1917 after being deeply affected by the events of 1916. Like them he was quickly elected as an officer and quickly rose through the ranks to become O/C of the Fermoy Battalion in 1919. He was also secretary of the ITGWU branch at the mill, an I.R.A. stronghold.

When conscription was announced, Fitzgerald went on the run with the other Fermoy area leaders and spent months on his bicycle organizing the neighbouring units. He and others also travelled to Waterford for its violent 1918 by-election. In April 1919 he led the successful assault on the Araglen R.I.C. barracks. Ammunition was discovered in his home in a subsequent search and he spent two months in prison. Upon release he took a leading role in the ambush of a British church party in Fermoy in September.[154] This and the Araglen attack provided the battalion's main armament for the approaching fight. Unfortunately—or perhaps on principle—he did not take the precaution of going into hiding and he was arrested soon afterwards.

The remainder of his life was spent on remand in a series of prisons around Ireland. In August 1920, still untried, he and several others went on hunger strike to demand their release. They were soon joined by Terence MacSwiney but they met an unyielding Irish administration, determined not to repeat the mass releases of prisoners that occurred in the spring. For Fitzgerald, as for MacSwiney, self-sacrifice was a vital part of revolution. 'Suffering seemed to be a joy to him.'[155] His protest lasted sixty-seven days before he died.

Sean Moylan had established himself as a builder in Newmarket by the time he became active in the republican movement in 1916.[156] Already a language enthusiast, he joined the Volunteers and Sinn Fein, and became the principal organizer for both in Duhallow (north-west Cork). Like many other local leaders, he was a delegate to both national conventions in 1917. By May 1918 he had left much of his old life behind and had gone on the run as O/C of the Newmarket Battalion. In his capacity as a military leader he led several ambushes of army and police patrols. As a Sinn Fein activist he worked not only in Cork but also in Donegal.

Exhausted and ill with influenza, Moylan went to Dublin and Waterford to recuperate. When he returned home in April 1919 he was quickly arrested and imprisoned. He was able to engineer his own escape and returned to Newmarket to pull off an equally daring coup by capturing the local R.I.C. barracks without firing a shot.[157] This gave his men the arms necessary to launch their own guerrilla campaign.

---

[153] For accounts of Fitzgerald's life, see Thomas O'Riordan, *The Price of Freedom* and *Where Martyred Heroes Rest: The Story of the Republican Plot Kilcrumper, Fermoy* (Cork, 1987); Florence O'Donoghue, 'Michael Fitzgerald of Fermoy', in *Rebel Cork's Fighting Story*, 45–9.

[154] For these episodes, see O'Donoghue, *No Other Law*, 45–56.

[155] Con Leddy to Florence O'Donoghue, 29 Dec. 1950 (O'Donoghue Papers, MS 31, 421).

[156] Moylan's revolutionary career up to 1921 is described in his own memoir. Further information was provided in interviews with Richard Moylan.

[157] Moylan's prison file can be found in GPB Records, Carton 3 (NA).

Moylan participated in several more attacks in the course of 1920, including the kidnapping of General Lucas in June.[158] He was also responsible for collecting the Dail Loan and setting up a Dail court system. After September, however, he spent most of his time in flying columns, first with the brigade and then with his battalion. From the Ballydrocane ambush in October 1920 to Toureengarriffe in January 1921 and Clonbannin in March, 'Moylan's Black and Tans' killed or wounded twenty of the enemy and captured dozens of rifles without suffering a single casualty.[159] In April he was appointed brigade O/C upon Liam Lynch's election to the new 1st Southern Division. Nevertheless, the winter campaign had taken a heavy toll on his still-fragile health. He was stalked and captured in May, again suffering from exhaustion. 'Very little could be got out of Moylan, he looked decidedly ill and frightened', the British intelligence officer responsible for his arrest remembered.[160] He soon recovered enough to impress his captors, however: 'there was no doubt he was a very quick-witted and clever customer to deal with.' Only his election—unopposed—to the second Dail and his 'chivalrous' record in dealing with prisoners saved him from the firing squad.[161] He spent the remainder of the war on Spike Island.

Denis (Sonny) Murray was a founding member of the Courtbrack Company, one of the best armed and organized units of the pre-rising Volunteers.[162] With their uniforms and Mauser rifles they were often the star attraction at parades in Cork, Limerick, and Killarney. Their *esprit de corps* only intensified Courtbrack's frustration with the events of 1916 and in 1917 they reorganized to such good effect that Murray was a wanted man by July 1917. He was arrested after an illegal march in August and carried on the fight from within Mountjoy prison. These cells became the front lines of the revolution when Murray and scores of other Volunteers went on hunger strike that autumn. He was transferred to Dundalk, fought the same battle for political status over again, and was released along with the others in November. Upon returning home he discovered that he was a hero and was unanimously elected captain of the company.

Conscription forced Murray underground again in 1918, and he spent most of the year organizing resistance and collecting arms. Like Moylan and many others in their position, his health suffered terribly. In the general election he led a Courtbrack contingent to 'keep order' on the north side of Cork city.[163] They were stationed on Blarney Lane and faced a stiff fight at the hands of the battle-hardened 'Mollies'.

---

[158]   See O'Donoghue, *No Other Law*, 75–9.

[159]   Tom Crofts (O'Malley Papers, P17b/53). The best guide to Moylan's campaign is O'Riordan, *Kiskeam Versus the Empire*. See also P. D. Mehigan, 'Across Duhallow Border: Reminiscences of the Anglo-Irish War', *Carbery's Annual* (Christmas 1940).

[160]   Grazebrook Diary, 40. The diary was written on Moylan's captured typewriter.

[161]   His chivalry was attested to at his trial: see *Examiner*, 31 May, 6 June 1921.

[162]   The main source for this account is Murray's own statement, along with those of his comrades, in Duggan, *Grenagh and Courtbrack*.

[163]   Denis Murray, ibid. 25.

In 1919 Murray and his men carried out numerous arms raids and several abortive ambushes, but it was not until July 1920 that they saw action at the siege of Blarney barracks. Murray soldiered on through a variety of other encounters, including the ambushes at Inniscarra in September 1920 and at Dripsey, both led by Frank Busteed. His record was well known to the authorities, with the result that his family home became a frequent target of raids and eventually arson. In 1921 Murray was made quartermaster for the Donoughmore Battalion, and thereafter concerned himself with the everyday tasks of destroying roads, raiding mails, and similar support work up until 11 July.

From their beginnings in scattered companies and early confrontations with policemen and warders, through internment camps, prisons, and flight and on to election campaigns, raids, and ambushes, then to life on the run and on the column, what these stories (like those of the O'Brien and Hales brothers) have in common is a sense of movement, of moving, radicalizing experiences and of expanding horizons. Street fights, police raids, reprisals, prison sentences, hunger strikes—these were the rites of passage which transformed students, carpenters, and printers into revolutionaries.

For many Volunteers, their first encounters with the police and prisons ineradicably defined the British state as violent, repressive, and, crucially, beatable. Riots, however started, brought young men and women face to face with R.I.C. batons and bayonets, usually wielded in anger to frighten and punish ('it is very essential that such parties be roughly handled'[164]). Broken bones and stab wounds were commonplace.[165] While this victimization surely deterred some would-be rebels, it confirmed others. When the Hardwick Street Sinn Fein club was attacked in November 1917, for example, and many of its members bayoneted and hospitalized, local republicans demanded 'reprisals': 'the affair has created a very determined feeling among those who were assaulted.'[166] Equally shocking were police raids on private homes. Always invasive, occasionally brutal, these became a constant feature of life as a republican activist but they never lost their power to enrage. One thing that the I.R.A. veterans I interviewed never forgot was how it felt to have their houses searched and their families harassed.

Prison turned these similar experiences into a common experience. From 1916 on, successive waves of arrested Volunteers turned British cells and camps into training and battle grounds. Here Volunteers and Sinn Feiners from all over Ireland were able to meet one another, become friends and comrades, and feel part of a truly national movement. Moreover, as the I.R.A. invariably assumed control and were frequently able to run their own affairs as *de facto* prisoners of war, prison was the closest most Volunteers came to a regular

---

[164] Circular from Staff, Midland and Connaught District to CIs, n.d. [May 1918] (NLI, MS 10, 472). 'Roughly handled' was later changed to 'firmly dealt with' (IG Circular, 24 May 1918).

[165] See *Examiner*, 25, 26 June, 28 Sept. 1917; Lankford, *The Hope and the Sadness*, 97–8.

[166] De Roiste Diary, 22, 25 Nov. 1917 (O'Donoghue Papers); *Examiner*, 23 Nov. 1917.

military environment.[167] Where the authorities resisted these demands, the prisoners rallied to Michael Collins's dictum that 'every restriction relaxed and every rule broken is a step nearer deliverance'.[168] These victorious protest campaigns were an unfailing source of fellowship, energy, and militancy, to be injected back into the movement as each wave of ex-prisoners returned home. All but one of the guerrillas profiled above spent time in prison and all but one of these took part in a hunger strike.

The first of the 'Sinn Fein universities' were Richmond Barracks and Frongoch Camp, where captured rebels and hundreds of their suspected accomplices were gathered after the 1916 rising.[169] For the first time, isolated provincial republicans who had endured hostility and derision ('Here comes the Kaiser and his country boys'[170]) and whose most rebellious act had been to wear a tricoloured tie to Easter mass,[171] found themselves thrown together with battle-hardened republican fighters. They were dangerous—and important—after all.[172]

The keenest Cork graduates of Frongoch and Richmond came from the Bandon and Macroom Battalions and the Cobh Company. Men like the Haleses, Begleys, Mannings, and Walshes, Dan Corkery, Charlie Browne, and Mick Leahy and Seamus Fitzgerald moved immediately to reorganize the I.R.A. and I.R.B. and to infuse it with their new spirit of defiance. This localized trickle of prison veterans became a county-wide flood in late 1917 with the mass arrest of over sixty Cork activists for drilling.[173] The subsequent quick release of these 'Mountjoy men' turned them into instant heroes and persons of influence within the movement.[174] Denis Murray was not the only one to be made an officer on the strength of his gaol sentence. Among the class of 1917 were Lar Condon of Fermoy, Denis Lyons of Kanturk, Jim Brislane of Charleville, Pa Twomey of Grenagh, Maurice Ahern of Dungourney, and Ed Hegarty of Riverstown, all of whom were key organizers of the resistance against conscription the following year.

The next identifiable cohort of guerrillas came out of the British crackdown and subsequent hunger strikes of early 1920. Nearly one hundred Cork I.R.A.

[167] See Louis J. Walsh, *'On my Keeping' and in Theirs* (Dublin, 1921); Darrell Figgis, *Recollections of the Irish War* (London, 1927), 168–70; Andrews, *Dublin Made Me*, 172–80.

[168] Michael Collins to D/Propaganda, 5 Jan. 1921, quoted in C. H. Foulkes to 'Marsh', 10 Oct. 1921 (Foulkes Papers).

[169] This term was first used by Tim Healy in a speech in the House of Commons.

[170] *Clonakilty and District, 1916* (Cork, 1966). See also O'Donoghue, 'History of the Irish Volunteers', 68–9; Browne, *The Story of the 7th*, 3–4.

[171] Lionel Fleming, *Head or Harp* (London, 1965), 58.

[172] See Seamus Fitzgerald, 'In English Prisons 1916–1917', *Capuchin Annual* (1967), 353. Figgis, *Recollections of the Irish War*, 168–9; John Brennan, 'Frongoch University—and After', in *Dublin's Fighting Story 1916–21* (Tralee, 1945), 112–24; Sean O Mahony, *Frongoch: University of Revolution* (Dublin, 1987).

[173] For accounts of the protests, see Brennan, *The War in Clare*, 27–35; Lochlinn MacGlynn, 'Padraic Fleming's Personal Fight for Political Rights' and Fionan Lynch, 'Recollections of Jail Riots and Hunger Strikes', in *Sworn to be Free*, 53–75.

[174] See de Roiste Diary, 25 Nov. 1917 (O'Donoghue Papers).

men took part and were released, including Richard Browne of Macroom, Steve O'Neill of Clonakilty, Mick O'Neill of Kilbrittain, Denis Galvin of Newmarket, John and Ed Stack of Cobh, Ralph Keyes of Bantry, and James O'Driscoll of Eyeries. However, while earlier protests had often been exhilarating ('I never spent such a good Hallows Eve as I did this time in jail'[175]), the great hunger strike of 1920 was harrowing for everyone concerned. One of the strikers was John J. O'Mahony of Cloundreen, Kilbrittain:

I was taken by two warders to another very filthy cell and put on a chair. I . . . got only one very dirty blanket, a dirty pillow without a slip and a criminal's dirty mattress. I expect these clothes hadn't been used for a very long time as the clothes were so dirty I had to tie a handkerchief round my face to keep the dirt off . . . the one warder said that the dog could die there now. On the following night, someone came outside my door either a soldier or a warder and asked several times in a mocking manner if the old cat was dying. On one occasion the cold drinking water was supplied in one of the cell tin vessels which was not even rinsed and was black with dirt. I was left in that cell in solitary confinement [for three days].[176]

The strike lasted twenty three days. Such an ordeal imbued the national struggle with tremendous personal suffering and triumph. Those who went through it returned home determined that their sacrifice would mean something, that the revolution would go forward.[177] Over the next year they would form the backbone of the guerrilla effort in many areas, as at the Kilmichael ambush.[178]

The elections of 1917 and 1918 provided the other great proving ground for activists. Scores of Cork Volunteers (including four of the six men profiled above, as well as the Haleses) travelled to constituencies all over Ireland to immerse themselves in the work of the movement. Each campaign was a miniature crucible of revolution, galvanizing local units and fusing the disparate visiting militants into a single force.[179] These were formative experiences for many future guerrillas, away from homes and jobs—often for the first time—and surrounded by fellow republicans. Sean Moylan was 'deeply influenced' by his work in Donegal; it was a turning point in his life.[180] The East Clare by-election had the same effect on Sean Breen. 'I met everyone who was then active, almost . . . that was fine at the time to meet the lads from different counties.'[181] The often fierce Redmondite opposition only made them 'pull together' all the more.

---

[175] J. W. Reid to Miss Hawkins, 1 Nov. 1917 (GPB Papers).

[176] Letter from John J. O'Mahony, n.d. [April 1920] (Art O'Brien Papers, MS 8443). See also Con Neenan in MacEoin, *Survivors*, 237–8.

[177] See Deasy, *Towards Ireland Free*, 107–8; O'Dwyer, *Beara in Irish History*, 113–14.

[178] In Sean Moylan's area: 'Releases after a hunger strike at Wormwood Scrubs prison . . . had brought a number of us, pioneer Volunteers, together again [and] made available for swift and decisive action the necessary force.' Moylan Memoir, 80–1.

[179] See Brennan, *The War in Clare*, 24–5; Richard Mulcahy, 'The Irish Volunteer Convention 27 October, 1917', *Capuchin Annual* (1967), 403–4. The excitement and camaraderie of these campaigns is captured in Frank Gallagher's letters to Celia Saunders (TCD, Gallagher Papers, MS 10050).   [180] Moylan Memoir, 57.

[181] Sean Breen (O'Malley Papers, P17b/124).

The same dynamic was present in the Waterford, Armagh, and Donegal campaigns:

The elections had a considerable influence on the lads who travelled from the outside areas. First they met men who had served in Easter Week, then they met senior officers from practically every County in Ireland. They learned songs and they were accustomed to meet men whom they admired and who afterwards became famous. But they also learned an esprit de corps, a handling of men and talk[ed] with many who were trying to solve similar problems as in their own area. Also they began to realize that the Irish Volunteers though deep in politics were not politicians. When they returned home they had often a new judgement on the local officers.[182]

Going on the run had much the same radicalizing impact. As they travelled the circuit of prisons, by-elections, safe houses, 'barracks', and headquarters, the fugitives formed new networks and loyalties around one another and perforce devoted themselves full time to the cause. 'From being on the run we kept together . . . the fellows were nearly always together.'[183] The intimacy of this small world can be seen in our sample of revolutionary careers. Sean Breen and Roibeard Langford travelled in the same militant circles in the city and both knew and worked with Sean Moylan and Sean Hales in organizing drives, arms smuggling, and elections. Breen was a friend of William and Charlie O'Brien. Frank Busteed was in close contact with the urban underground, took part in at least one operation with Langford and the O'Briens, and several with Denis Murray. Mick Fitzgerald worked with Breen and Sean Hales in the Waterford by-election of 1918.

Nor were these networks confined to Cork alone. Michael Brennan of east Clare knew the Haleses and Sean Treacy and the men of south Tipperary, who were familiar in turn with Liam Lynch, Mick Fitzgerald, and the Fermoy men as well as with Liam Manahan and Donnacha Hannigan of east Limerick and Pax Whelan of west Waterford.[184] Everyone knew practically everyone else and this small group of activists were to be found on the front lines of nearly every battle.

Another thing which set the guerrillas apart from the ordinary Volunteers was their possession of arms. Drilling and marching were all very well, but guns were the 'real business', the badge of the revolutionary.[185] 'Everybody wanted a gun', and for most Volunteers, a gun meant a rifle.[186] 'Nobody wanted to carry a shotgun'; 'It was amazing the change rifles made to the men—and how keenly they held on to them.'[187] A rifle gave its owner power, prestige, and military

---

[182]   Sean Breen (O'Malley Papers, P17b/124).
[183]   Mick O'Sullivan (O'Malley Papers, P17b/111).
[184]   See Brennan, *The War in Clare*, 36, 39–40; O'Donoghue, *No Other Law*, 52–4; Liam Manahan (O'Malley Papers, P17b/106), Con Leddy (P17b/123), and George Power (P17b/132).
[185]   Comerford, *My Kilkenny I.R.A. Days*, 71.
[186]   Interview with AB.
[187]   Ned Murphy (O'Malley Papers, P17b/123); Moylan Memoir.

legitimacy. It was the most potent of symbols even if revolvers and shotguns did more actual killing. As one veteran told me: 'Everybody wanted a rifle—to be a man if you like.'[188]

The psychological importance of modern arms was noted as early as 1915 by Ernest Blythe. On his visit to the Mitchelstown Company he attributed their confidence to their arsenal of forty rifles:

Here as almost everywhere else possession of arms was vitally important in relation to the National attitude of both the Volunteers and the people round them . . . they could not have kept the Company as strong and enthusiastic as it was if it had not the rifles, which made even those who were among the flabbiest, nationally speaking, of their neighbours regard it as entitled to respect.[189]

By the middle of 1919, each of the men profiled above had stolen, bought, or captured arms. On the other hand most ordinary Volunteers, like Sean O'Faolain and Frank O'Connor, did not even know how to use one.

The guerrillas drew a sometimes sharp dividing line between themselves and outsiders. Theirs was not just an intimate world but an exclusive one as well—'just the fellows'[190]—increasingly removed from local companies and their homes and families. Stan Barry described one independent squad of gunmen as 'a tough bunch. Jim [Grey] would not allow anyone into his particular group until you stood out on the road and said "F—— you, God." That was a sign that you were fit to [be one] of their company.'[191] Insider status was marked by such things as having and knowing nicknames.[192] Many guerrillas were known to their comrades by their *nom de guerre*: 'Spud' Murphy, 'Flyer' Nyhan, 'Nudge' Callanan, 'Buckshot' Hales, 'Sandow' Donovan, 'Congo' Condon, 'Calder' Corkery, and 'Hegga' O'Hegarty being but a few. One woman whose home was the headquarters of the West Cork Brigade for months never knew the men's real names until after the Truce.[193]

If you were not a column man, you were 'small fry'. From the column man's point of view, while the rank and file were 'a good help', 'the inactive men stayed at home and the rest of the men were with the columns'.[194] This attitude created many problems between columns and companies. Activists in Bandon, Fermoy, and Kanturk recruited ex-soldiers for their military skills over strenuous

---

[188] Interview with AI. This attitude is also demonstrated in the song 'The Boys of Aghinagh': 'Dan Buckley was there with his rifle | Very important was he'.

[189] Blythe, 'Kerry Better Than Cork in 1915', 3–4. J. J. O'Connell found the same thing on his inspection tours: 'The rifle was regarded by many people since the Boer War almost with superstition . . . it heartened our own men and improved the neighbours opinion of us.' 'History of the Irish Volunteers', Ch. 1, 4–6 (Bulmer Hobson Papers).

[190] Jim Bromagh (O'Malley Papers, P17b/123).

[191] Stan Barry (O'Malley Papers, P17b/111). See also Mick O'Sullivan (P17b/111).

[192] Giving nicknames—to enemies as well as to friends and comrades—was a common Cork habit in any case, especially in the city.

[193] Chisholm interview (tape in the possession of Dr John Chisholm).

[194] Paddy O'Brien and Ned Murphy (O'Malley Papers, P17b/124, 123).

local objections.[195] Some units resented having outsiders operate in their territory, demanding food and shelter, commandeering the available arms, and preempting their own plans. They frequently came to look upon the guerrillas as itinerant troublemakers who stirred things up and left the local men to take the brunt of the reprisals.[196]

The Drishanebeg train ambush in February 1921 revealed a number of these conflicts in microcosm. The Doonen and Coole Cross Companies of the Millstreet Battalion concocted a clever scheme to divert a train carrying British soldiers onto an isolated siding in order to ambush them. When the battalion column heard of it, however, they took over, refused to let the company men use their rifles, and effectively reduced them to auxiliaries in their own plan. The ambush was a great success but the enraged companies saw none of the fourteen captured rifles.[197] The Active Service Section commander admitted that 'Owing to all arms being kept with the A.S.S. temporarily, the local Company O/Cs are none too pleased' but then sanctimoniously declared that while 'I only admire them for their spirit to fight . . . we must make the best use of arms.'[198] By the spring of 1921 most companies had been stripped of their precious rifles and carbines.

Guns, nicknames, and swearing-in rituals delineated an exclusively masculine world: the world of the Wren Boy as much as of the revolutionary. Whereas Irish classes, protest committees, marches, and election campaigns had been open to women—at least at the bottom—the guerrillas drew much of their strength from communal youth culture and its informal network of loyalties among 'the boys'. Underground activity depended on these sorts of tightly knit groups and this process of male bonding actively excluded women.

As violence rose and the revolution fell into the hands of 'the boys', women's roles in the struggle also changed. Female activists had been no less militant than men in the heyday of the mass movement and no less suspicious of Sinn Fein 'politics'.[199] Cumann na mBan's 'irregulars' had been equally given to 'unauthorized' and 'irresponsible' violence, and earned the same official censure

[195] For the case of Tom Barry in Bandon, see Ch. 2; for Matt Flood in Fermoy, see Hammond, *Soldier of the Rearguard*, 8; for the notorious Dan Shields in Kanturk, see Con Meaney and Dan Browne (O'Malley Papers, P17b/112).

[196] See Con Meaney (O'Malley Papers, P17b/112).

[197] For an account of the ambush see Patrick Lynch, 'Drishanebeg Train Ambush Yielded Fourteen Rifles to Millstreet Column', in *With the I.R.A. in the Fight for Freedom: 1919 to the Truce* (Tralee, n.d.), 160–4.

[198] ASS Report, 7th Bn., 21 Feb. 1921 (Mulcahy Papers, P7/A/38). For similar disputes, see O/C Rathmore Coy. to O/C Kerry 2, 24 May 1921 (Mulcahy Papers, P7/A/18)—who complains about a North Cork column; Paddy O'Brien and Jack Bolster (O'Malley Papers, P17b/111, 112); O'Dwyer, *Beara in Irish History*, 122–4; O'Malley, *On Another Man's Wound*, 196; O/C ASS, 3rd Bn., Cork 2 to O/C A. Coy. and O/C Intell., 22 Jan. 1921 (CI Monthly Report, East Cork, Jan. 1921 (CO 904/114)).

[199] See Margaret Ward, *Unmanageable Revolutionaries* (London, 1983), 132–3; Sheehan, 'Cumann na mBan', 88.

as their male counterparts.[200] As gunmen eclipsed protesters, however, and the common ground of Sinn Fein and the Gaelic League collapsed, the militants became segregated by gender. Women were less and less involved in direct action and increasingly relegated to supporting roles within Cumann na mBan.

The conscription crisis marked the turning point in this process. Cumann na mBan branches were placed—theoretically at least—under the command of Volunteer company officers.[201] Route marches and drill were largely forgotten. Their military work would now be entirely subordinate to that of the I.R.A. and essentially domestic in nature.[202] Some women acted as organizers, couriers, or typists, but most were occupied with cooking, sewing, collecting money, and helping prisoners and their families. The Blackpool branch made kit-bags for their company.[203] The captain of the Clonakilty branch remembers providing clothing, sending parcels to prisoners, and carrying I.R.A. dispatches.[204] One West Cork republican who had stopped doing British war work after the Easter Rising found herself performing the exact same tasks for the I.R.A. a few years later.[205]

Cumann na mBan members, it must be stated, did not apparently feel belittled or marginalized. For them, as for the Volunteers, the revolution was a personally liberating experience, fostering an intense spirit of camaraderie in the face of parents and priests and much of 'respectable' society. Many branches were determined to maintain a measure of independence, and they seem to have succeeded for the most part.[206] Some resisted I.R.A. control and refused to affiliate themselves with their local company.[207] Leslie Price, a Cumann na mBan organizer in Cork (who later married Tom Barry), found that men and women treated each other as equals and 'talked out their views openly'.[208]

How Cumann na mBan members thought of themselves nevertheless did little to alter the general I.R.A. view of them as mere auxiliaries. 'Not that that movement matters a terrible lot' was Seamus Lankford's comment.[209] When

---

[200] 'Miss Cummins' Cork branch still gives great trouble. The share-holders meeting in Dublin [the Cumann na mBan executive] condemned their work and suspended the rioters, but they take no notice.' Mrs Wyse-Power to Countess Markievicz, 25 Nov. 1918 (CO 904/164).

[201] Conlon, *Cumann na mBan*, 60.

[202] This subordination is reflected in the dearth of Cumann na mBan rolls or records. Indeed, when military pensions committees were sitting in the 1930s, they were unable to establish the organization's officers or strength in at least five brigade areas (Dept. of Taoiseach, S9243).

[203] Conlon, *Cumann na mBan*, 67.

[204] Chisholm interview. See also Duggan, *Grenagh and Courtbrack*, 65.

[205] Interview with AH.

[206] See Liam Murphy to Sean O'Hegarty, 25 Nov. 1918 and O'Hegarty to Bde. Council, 26 Nov. 1918 (O'Donoghue Papers, MS 31, 198).

[207] See Florence O'Donoghue to Sec., Cork District Council, Cumann na mBan, 14 Feb. 1919 (O'Donoghue Papers, MS 31, 181); Ward, *Unmanageable Revolutionaries*, 131–3.

[208] Leslie Bean de Barra interview on RTE Radio, 1980 (tape in the possession of Donal O'Donovan). See also the interview with her published in Donncha O Dulaing, *Voices of Ireland* (Dublin, 1984); O'Faolain, *Vive Moi!*, 133–41 and Oonagh Walsh, 'Testimony from Imprisoned Women', in Fitzpatrick (ed.), *Revolution? Ireland 1917–1923*, 84–5.

[209] Seamus Lankford to Florence O'Donoghue, n.d. (O'Donoghue Papers, MS 31, 275).

Tomas MacCurtain established a Volunteer 'barracks' in the city for the 1918 election, it was the women's job 'to cater to the men in the building. They will want to start in time (to-morrow) to put the place in order, secure tablets etc . . . They may hire a woman or two to do the rough work but that will be a matter for themselves.'[210] This attitude was also revealed in retrospect in I.R.A. memoirs, which offer only token recognition of Cumann na mBan. Although Liam Deasy declared that 'it would be impossible to extol sufficiently the contribution made by this heroic body of women', this and two other references to the organization in his own book apparently proved sufficient.[211]

Women's contribution to the revolution also differed fundamentally from men's in that many women were active outside of any organization. Behind the guerrillas was an essential cadre of mothers, sisters, wives, and other domestic revolutionaries, some affiliated to Cumann na mBan but most not, who ran their homes as safe houses. Typical of these was Mrs Hickey of Badger's Hill, Glenville, whose house was a way station and headquarters for the North Cork Brigade from the conscription crisis onwards. Liam Lynch, George Power, Lar Condon, and others spent months living there and the brigade flying column was formed there.[212] Without Mrs Hickey and others like her, there would have been no column. Every brigade had its network of 'Mrs So-and-sos': vital but invisible.[213] Like the members of Cumann na mBan and Sinn Fein and stay-at-home Volunteers, they were rarely privy to the guerrilla world.

While the guerrillas went abroad in flying columns, monopolized the best weapons, and did most of the organizing and fighting, the company men mostly stayed at home, did scout duty, wrecked bridges, and robbed postmen. 'There was the fighting gang and the gang that went around raiding houses,' remembers one whose home was the object of many raids.[214] As companies shrank and reliable Volunteers became scarce, many nominal members were unwilling to do even this much. In December 1920, Seamus Robinson, the O/C of the South Tipperary Brigade, fumed at the rampant 'desertions and neglect of duty and downright cowardice' and declared that 'something in the nature of a crisis is upon us'.[215] The same month, the O/C of West Clare reported that:

I find of late in a great many companies, that the Volunteers themselves are rather inclined to fall in with the views of the old people to remain quiet. For instance, in one

---

[210] Tomas MacCurtain to Liam Murphy, n.d. [Nov. 1918] (O'Donoghue Papers, MS 31, 198).

[211] Deasy, *Towards Ireland Free*, 65. Men outnumber women in the book's index by 257 to 6. Comparable figures for similar works: O'Donoghue, *No Other Law*, 398 to 15; Michael Brennan, *The War in Clare*, 211 to 8; Desmond Ryan, *Sean Treacy and the 3rd Tipperary Brigade* (London, 1945), 284 to 42.

[212] George Power (O'Malley Papers, P17b/123); O'Donoghue, *No Other Law*, 97.

[213] See Hammond, *Soldier of the Rearguard*, 30–1; O'Dwyer, *Beara in Irish History*, 128; O'Connor, *An Only Child*, 241.   [214] Interview with BG.

[215] O/C Tipperary 3 to C/S, 3 Dec. 1920 (Foulkes Papers, Epitome No. 53/3649, 79).

particular place where an ambush was planned, the Volunteers in the vicinity refused to take any part whatever in it.[216]

By March 1921 the Skibbereen Battalion's men were not only not showing up for parades, many of the trainee column men had deserted as well.[217] In a not untypical case in the Bantry Battalion, the company detailed to act as scouts for the column simply went home, leaving the guerrillas to be surprised by the police.[218] As we move outwards from the hard core of active guerrillas to the reluctant fringes of the I.R.A., the question arises: how voluntary were the Volunteers?

It was not uncommon in 1921 for inactive Volunteers to be called up and forced into action—more or less against their will—as scouts, couriers, and road-wreckers. These were not hard men, ready to face battle, gaol, or worse. When they were captured they talked, and often repudiated the I.R.A. These incidents became so frequent that Austin Stack complained that 'of late this is being done indiscriminately by almost every man tried in Cork'.[219] Liam Lynch was forced to admit that 'most areas leave scouting to unreliable men—especially men that are not used to fighting'.[220] The case Lynch probably had in mind when he wrote this was that of Pat Casey of Kildorrery:

he volunteered during the elections to keep order, but since then did not belong to the Volunteers or take any part in politics. His home was searched by police and he went to Dublin and returned three weeks ago. He was looking for work, and at Kilfinane he met some men, they were Volunteers, who took him to a house and gave him tea. He was told to be at a place at the butt of the hill at one o'clock . . . He did not want to go but the other men said he should.[221]

Casey was caught up in a disastrous ambush (two I.R.A. men were killed and two wounded), captured, tried at a drumhead court martial, and executed. His dilemma was shared by a good number of involuntary Volunteers.[222]

Some units even felt it necessary forcibly to enrol new members. In Kanturk, for example, a 'calling up notice' was posted in May 1921. 'They pulled in all the able-bodied fellas around. They conscripted them if you like.'[223] Those who refused to join were viewed with great suspicion and became the targets of

[216] O/C West Clare Bde. to C/S, 30 Dec. 1920, quoted in *6th Division History*, 72 (Strickland Papers). For similar accounts, see Organizer's Report, Cavan Bde., 22 Feb. 1921 and O/C Donegal West Bde., 7 Mar. 1921 (Mulcahy Papers, P7/A/16, 17).

[217] 7th Bn., Cork 3 Report, 3 Mar. 1921 in 'The Irish Republican Army' [Irish Command, June 1921] (Strickland Papers).

[218] 1st South. Div. Memo, 11 June 1921 (Mulcahy Papers, P7/A/19).

[219] Austin Stack to M/D, 9 May 1921 (Mulcahy Papers, P7/A/18).

[220] HQ 1st South. Div. Report, 11 June 1921 (Mulcahy Papers, P7/A/19). For similar cases, see O/C Cork 2 to C/S, 4 Mar. 1921 and O/C Cork 1 to C/S, 25 Feb. 1921 (P7/A/38).

[221] *Examiner*, 3 May 1921.

[222] Ibid. 12 Aug. 1920, 9, 10 Mar., 18 June, 1, 2, 7 July 1921.

[223] Interview with AI. See Grazebrook Diary, 45, and Dublin Castle Press Statements (CO 904/168).

boycotts and harassment.[224] Jeremiah O'Callaghan of Aghabullogue was approached at Christmas 1920 to join but refused. A few weeks later:

He was ordered to come along with a party of men, one of whom produced a revolver, and said that if he did not go with them he would get the contents of it . . . He was told to step over the fence and ordered to watch for any soldiers coming along from Coachford to Peake . . . Later the soldiers were seen advancing and they were told to run away . . . A bullet struck him in the toe and he threw himself on the ground as he was afraid.[225]

The I.R.A. did not just want manpower, they also wanted a politically closed shop. Conscription was a way of enforcing silence and acquiescence, the equivalent of the Whiteboys' forcible administration of oaths or the Wren Boys' punishment of the uncooperative.[226] 'In the Millstreet Battalion 90 per cent of the able-bodied men were in the I.R.A. It was a way of keeping people's mouths shut.'[227] Indeed, there were cases in Munster of I.R.A. groups administering oaths in exactly the same manner as the agrarian rebels of previous centuries.[228] 'They had to have you under their thumbs.'[229]

In a few cases, conscription became a method of extortion. Sam Kingston was taken from his home near Dunmanway one night in 1921: 'they ordered me to fall in the ranks this I refused to do, then they threatened shooting me to which I replied they could and eventually they let me off on the condition I gave them money.'[230]

In 1921, non-Volunteers were regularly called upon to block or wreck roads and bridges, often at night-time and with no warning. This too could be a form of punishment or intimidation and was widely resented. William Daly of Shannonvale was wounded and arrested at the site of a road-trenching in June 1921:

He was ordered to the place where he was found. He was commandeered, and he was afraid to refuse. He knew that people had been commandeered to dig trenches . . . He had been a demobilised soldier, and had been threatened by the Republican Army a couple of times. He got a note to be there or get the full penalty.[231]

The same men were often commandeered the next day by Crown forces to repair the work they had done the night before.

---

[224]   For examples, see O/C 5th Bn. to O/C Cork 1, 29 Oct. 1921 (Mulcahy Papers, P7/A/37); O/C 1st Bn. to O/C Kerry Bde. (no. unknown); and the following statements from the Irish Grants Committee files: Julia Neligan (CO 762/32), Joseph Northridge (/37), Patrick Collins (/45), Alexander Stevens (/46), George Sullivan (/68), James Donnelly (/91), Julia Crowley (/108), Maurice O'Connor (/119), Pat Curran (/130), William Leahy (/155), William McCarthy (/157), Sam Kingston (/167), Denis Cronin (/170) and, Sam Trinder (/206).

[225]   *Examiner*, 10 Feb. 1921.

[226]   For the Whiteboys, see Michael Beames, *Peasants and Power: The Whiteboy Movements and their Control in Pre-Famine Ireland* (Brighton, 1983), 64–5; George Cornewell Lewis, *Local Disturbances in Ireland* (Cork, 1977), 158–64.

[227]   Con Meaney (O'Malley Papers, P17b/112).

[228]   See *Examiner*, 26 Sept., 12 Dec. 1919, 8 Jan. 1920.   [229] Interview with AE.

[230]   Sam Kingston statement (CO 762/167).

[231]   *Examiner*, 14 June 1921. See also Catherine Murphy to M/D, 30 Nov. 1921 (MA, A/0668).

The lawyer for one Cork youth facing execution proclaimed that 'there is a reign of terror in the country at the present time. Juveniles are drilled and get orders from H.Q., and their terror is beyond description.'[232] This was courtroom hyperbole designed to appeal to British propaganda. Nevertheless there was some truth to it. Most Volunteers were willing participants (only one of my thirteen interviewees was conscripted) but it is impossible to distinguish the willing from the unwilling when those called upon so often had very little choice. Violence bred coercion. As one increased, so did the other. By the spring of 1921 the demands of guerrilla war and the decline in I.R.A. strength had turned many columns and units into part-time press gangs.

Was the I.R.A. on the verge of internal collapse as British officers so often insisted after the Truce? The answer is no. The I.R.A. was in organizational retreat, but it was very far from turning into a rout. The Bandon Battalion may have been reduced to 200 men but there were twenty-three other battalions in the county as well. Most companies could field fewer than ten active members but there were 213 companies in all. These numbers add up. After hundreds of comrades had been killed, wounded, imprisoned, or interned, there were still perhaps 600 guerrillas at large and at work in Cork in July 1921, supported by about twice as many ready Volunteers. Nor is there any evidence that morale among these men was anything but solid—including among the prisoners. They were committed and determined. They were willing and able to fight and kill effectively. When caught, as at Dripsey, Clonmult, and Crossbarry, they fought hard against overwhelming odds. Such encounters showed the temper of the men at the heart of the movement. They did not feel defeated. They would have continued to fight.

The Anglo-Irish Treaty found the I.R.A. larger and better armed and trained than ever before, buoyed up by its experience of power during the Truce and by the expectation of inevitable victory. The ceasefire itself had been taken as proof of military success and the period that followed recalled the headiest days of 1918. Inactive members suddenly reappeared and new recruits poured into republican organizations (if only to go to the innumerable 'victory dances'). Even the Gaelic League benefited from the enthusiasm.[233] Training camps, the work of reorganization, the open re-establishment of republican courts and police, all contributed to a feeling of forward movement. The consolidation of some army and R.I.C. detachments in late 1921 meant that more areas had been left to unchallenged republican control. The guerrillas grew cocky and aggressive and confrontations with policemen or soldiers became more common. It seemed to many Volunteers as if 'the people' were united behind them and the republic was imminent.

---

[232] *Irish Times*, 3 May 1921.
[233] See Lankford, *The Hope and the Sadness*, 124–5.

TABLE 33. North Cork company strengths, 1921–1922

| Battalion | July 1921 | February 1922 | |
	Roll	Roll	Reliable
Fermoy	76	53	40
Millstreet	75	47	35
Castletownroche	75	69	49
Mallow	68	—	35
Average	74	55	40

Sources: Figures for battalions other than Mallow from Report, 29 Feb. 1922 (O'Malley Papers, P17a/87); figures for Mallow from 5th Bn. Weekly Company Reports (Lankford Papers, U169).

The Treaty changed all that. 'That perfect summer' had not prepared the new heroes for a settlement incommensurate with their sense of sacrifice and achievement. The same was true of the last wave of returning prisoners, freed from gaols and camps in time for Christmas. They too had fought hard—in the battles for Spike Island and Cork gaol—and had maintained their resolve. The response, from every Cork brigade, the 1st Southern Division, and from the South Munster I.R.B., was immediate, uniform, and visceral: no. It was clear even before Dail ratification that a solid majority of voters supported the Treaty, and that Sinn Fein was badly split, but what outsiders thought was largely irrelevant to the leaders of the Cork I.R.A.

Just as in the aftermath of the conscription crisis, however, the rank and file were quietly making their own decisions. The new recruits—the 'trucileers'—just drifted away, taking with them a good number of old hands. The speed of this decline can be seen in Table 33, which picks up where Table 32 left off. By February 1922 the North Cork I.R.A. had returned to its wartime strength of a year before. By late June, the companies of the Mallow Battalion were down to an average of twenty-four members apiece.[234] In the Millstreet Battalion, the average as of August was twenty, less than half that of the Tan War.[235] Table 34 reveals a similar picture in the West and South-West Cork Brigades. By the beginning of the Civil War the West Cork I.R.A. had lost four-fifths of its paper strength.

The Civil War shattered what was left of this fragile structure. The republican call to arms in July 1922 did briefly stiffen some units, but the immediate and overwhelming success of the Free State invasion in August returned the Cork I.R.A. to its downward course. There would be no return to ranks and precious few new recruits. By October, the Midleton Battalion had fallen to an average of seven men per company from a high of eighty-two the year before.[236] By that

---

[234]   5th Bn. Report, 12 July 1922 (Lankford Papers, U169c/42).

[235]   O/C Org. to O/C 1st Southern Div., 19 Sept. 1922 (O'Malley Papers, P17a/87).

[236]   The Truce figure is from Bureau of Military History Company Rolls; that for Oct. 1922 from Report on 4th Bn., Cork 1 (MA, A/1142).

TABLE 34. West Cork company strengths, 1921–1922

Battalion	July 1921	January 1922	June 1922
	Roll	Roll	Roll
Bandon	83	39	26
Schull	66	34	12
Skibbereen	67	82	17
Drimoleague	62	43	5
Bantry	100	55	17
Castletownbere	48	48	19
Average	71	50	16

Sources: The figures for Bandon come from Organizer's Report, 1st Bn., 3rd Cork Bde., 7 Aug. 1922; those for the other battalions from Report on 5th Cork Bde., Aug. 1922 (MA, A/0991/2).

date there were only 1,300 men left on brigade rolls in the whole of Cork, a loss of almost 90 per cent of the county's pre-Treaty strength. Of these, 518 were on 'active service'.[237] This figure probably represented the hard core of committed Volunteers at large: a year and a half later the total membership still stood at 1,204 men.[238]

How many lapsed Volunteers 'went Free State'? An exact answer would be impossible to give. National Army records did not register previous service and, in any case, some ex-I.R.A. men served the Free State without officially joining the National Army. Nevertheless, available evidence strongly suggests that only a small fraction of active Volunteers were willing to take up arms against their old comrades. The two main pro-Treaty strongholds were in the south-west, in the Schull, Skibbereen, and Drimoleague Battalions (where Michael Collins and Gearoid O'Sullivan had family and personal followers) and in the Midleton Battalion. These were also the only regions which saw fighting before the invasion of August 1922. Elsewhere, support for the Treaty within the I.R.A. was confined to isolated companies and officers acting on their own.

The great majority of former Volunteers did nothing and 'kept their mouths shut'.[239] When an anti-Treaty divisional organizer toured the West Cork brigades in August he was told in nearly every unit that most of the drop-outs were 'merely conscientious objectors and are late arrivals in the Volunteers'[240] or else 'truce Volunteers who were glad to have a way out'.[241] In Bandon only three men had joined the National Army and those 'who have fallen away are either Truce Volunteers or men who were never active'.[242] In the Beara Battalion there

[237] Brigade strengths as of the Truce in the O'Donoghue Papers, MS 31, 216; as of Oct. 1922 in the O'Malley Papers, P17a/89. [238] Bde. Reports, mid-1924 (MA, A/1204/2).

[239] O'Leary, *Kilmeen and Castleventry Parish*, 95.

[240] Organizer's Report, 1st Bn., Cork 5, 4 Aug. 1922 (MA, A/0991/2).

[241] Organizer's Report, 5th Bn., Cork 5, 5 Aug. 1922 (A/091/2).

[242] Organizer's Report, 1st Bn., Cork 3, 7 Aug. 1922 (A/0991/2).

were fewer than thirty Free State recruits.[243] Mallow Battalion records show the same pattern. Of 290 Volunteers who joined during the Truce, twenty stayed for the Civil War. Seven officers resigned but none of them—and only twelve former Volunteers in all—went Free State. Most National Army recruits were either ex-soldiers or other civilians, many of them unemployed labourers.[244]

Among those who left were Sean O'Hegarty and Florence O'Donoghue, commander of Cork 1 and adjutant of the 1st Southern Division respectively. Both had been elected to the anti-Treaty I.R.A. executive in March 1922 and had been among the moderates attempting to avoid confrontation and advocating republican unity above all else. Unlike Tom Hales, Sean Moylan, Liam Lynch, and others of the same mind, however, they were willing to break ranks rather than fight. O'Hegarty had held a parade after the March convention to announce a policy of defensive neutrality. 'We'll hold Cork', he said, 'We'll let nobody into Cork but we won't fight.'[245] His staff did not agree, and mutinied on the night of the Four Courts attack. O'Hegarty and O'Donoghue resigned, along with two battalion commanders and an unknown number of company officers. They were replaced but one senior officer admitted that 'the absence of Sean O'Hegarty in the Civil War had a very bad effect'.[246] Later in the year, appalled by the violence of the struggle, they helped found the Neutral I.R.A. Association in order to promote peace. The former Cork leaders played a dominant role in this group through 1923, but few of their own men joined, and O'Hegarty's behind-the-scenes negotiations (using his I.R.B. contacts) failed to achieve their objective.[247]

The small minorities of the I.R.A. who were positively pro- or anti-Treaty may have been resolute in their convictions but their decisions, and the motives behind them, are as elusive as when they first joined. Twelve of the thirteen veterans I interviewed had fought on the republican side. None could remember making a specific choice to do so. 'I hadn't a clue'; 'It was very confused altogether.'[248] Judging by the recollections of Cork veterans, the Treaty itself and republican ideology were rarely debated within their ranks: 'The politics of it was second place at times.'[249]

Most couched their decisions in the same collective terms they used to describe their joining the organization. 'A good 90 percent of us stayed republican'; 'the whole place [company] were against it [the Treaty]'.[250] When asked why he and his brother wound up on opposite sides of the struggle, one West Corkman explained that he had been a column man and that 'all of Barry's men

---

[243] O'Dwyer, *Beara in Irish History*, 129; Organizer's Report, 5 Bn., Cork 5, 5 Aug. 1922.
[244] 5th Bn. Report, 1 May 1923 (Lankford Papers).
[245] Tom Crofts (O'Malley Papers, P17b/108).
[246] Ibid.
[247] O'Donoghue, *No Other Law*, 288, 299; O'Donoghue Diary, 1923 (O'Donoghue Papers, MS 31, 189); D/I to President [de Valera], 11 May 1923 (NA, Sinn Fein Papers, 1094/6).
[248] Interviews with AI and AD.   [249] Interview with AD.
[250] Interviews with AI and AE.

stuck together'.[251] For the lone Free Stater among my interviewees, his choice (made in concert with his brother) was dictated by his personal loyalty to Michael Collins.[252]

These decisions were shaped, as always, by group loyalties and rivalries. Factional divisions became political battle lines. 'It was partly officers, partly jealousies and disputes.'[253] Macroom's rival east and west side companies went their separate ways[254] just as the staff of the new Fermoy Battalion went Free State while the old officers went republican.[255] Family and neighbourhood still played a role, as the example of the Behagh Company shows. Indeed, one National Army survey of West Cork concluded that the I.R.A. had survived best 'where the Irregulars had strong family connections'.[256] There were some well-known cases of brothers falling out—Sean and Tom Hales or Gearoid and Tadg O'Sullivan—but these appear to have been exceptions (in both these examples, one brother had become a member of Michael Collins's circle in Dublin). More representative perhaps was the Volunteer who went republican because 'my brother half-asked, half-ordered me'.[257]

'You went by your officer.'[258] Officers usually took their personal networks with them, even in cases where they had been court-martialled or replaced. In fact, this sort of grievance often caused the split in the first place. In Donal Barrett's Cork Harbour Company, 'it was the question of the appointment of an unpopular Captain which made all his men go Free State'.[259] The one pro-Treaty company in the city—'C' Company on the north side—did so because of 'bad feeling as the wrong men were officers'.[260] The original officers had been released from prison after the Treaty but had not been given their old ranks. They went Free State in revenge and took their men with them. A similar problem prompted Jack Lynch, the former vice O/C of the Macroom Battalion, to secede (along with his home company) when he was not given his position back: 'Jim Murphy had been V/C and had seen more fighting, but local sympathy favoured Lynch.'[261] In another company near Schull, the men went Free State because their republican captain had been 'knocking them about'.[262] Finally, in my pro-Treaty informant's company, he and his brother retained the support of 'the faithful' despite being isolated within the battalion.[263]

The most complex of these disputes took place in East Cork. Here the political realignment was driven by a combination of local loyalties, territoriality, and personal grievances. In the 4th Battalion (which encompassed Cobh and

[251] Interview with AA. [252] Interview with AB.
[253] Interview with AJ. [254] Charlie Browne (O'Malley Papers, P17b/111).
[255] George Power to Florence O'Donoghue, 7 Dec. 1953 (O'Donoghue Papers, MS 31, 421).
[256] General Situation Report, 20 Sept. 1923 (MA, A/0875).
[257] Interview with AI. [258] Interview with AD.
[259] Donal Barrett (O'Malley Papers, P17b/111).
[260] Stan Barry (O'Malley Papers, P17b/95). See also Collins Powell, 'Details of the Anglo-Irish Conflict 1916–1921' (MA, A/0735). [261] Charlie Browne (O'Malley Papers, P17b/111).
[262] Interview with AM. [263] Interview with AB.

TABLE 35. Resignation rates in West Cork battalions, 1922 (%)

Battalion	Officers Jan.–June	Men Jan.–June
Drimoleague	60	88
Skibbereen	59	79
Schull	39	65
Beara	25	60
Bantry	20	69
Bandon	15	33

Sources: The figures for rank and file strengths are from the Organizer's Report, 1st Bn., Cork 3, 7 Aug. 1922 and Report on Cork 5, Aug. 1922 (MA, A/0991/2); officer losses were calculated by comparing the lists in these reports with the Bureau of Military History Rolls.

Midleton) the leading Midleton guerrillas were cashiered by Mick Leahy, a Cobh officer, for drinking and extortion.[264] One of them, Josie Aherne (whose brothers were also activists), had previously been passed over for command of the battalion and this furore had led to the creation of a separate unit to appease the Ahernes and their friends.[265] By Leahy's own admission these men had been 'bloody good fighters'.[266] Now, to a man, they became his ardent opponents and turned much of the East Cork I.R.A. outside Cobh against the republicans.[267] Seven of the nine Midleton companies went pro-Treaty, becoming 'the backbone of the Free State in Munster'.[268]

Family and faction dictated the course of the I.R.A. split in units all over Ireland, often in highly predictable fashion. Once again, it was the Brennans against the Barretts in Clare, the Hanniganites against the Manahanites in east Limerick, and the Sweeneys versus the O'Donnells in Donegal as all the old feuds were reignited.[269] In Kerry, Dinny Daly remembered, 'When the officers went one way the men followed them'.[270]

The importance of officers in determining which side their men took can be tested in the case of the West Cork battalions. Table 35 compares the percentage of company and battalion officers who left the I.R.A. (both pro-Treaty and neutral) to the decline in overall unit strengths. With the exception of the Bantry Battalion, the trend is clear. The more officers who resigned, the more men they took with them. We can examine this pattern in greater detail in two of the most divided battalions, Schull and Skibbereen. Table 36 tracks the movement of officers and men within individual companies.

---

[264] See Mick Leahy, Mick Burke (O'Malley Papers, P17b/108), and Edmond Desmond (/112).

[265] Seamus Fitzgerald (O'Malley Papers, P17b/111).   [266] Mick Leahy (/108).

[267] Memo to C/S, 27 May 1922 (Mulcahy Papers, P7/B/191). See also O/C Cork 1 to M/D, 29, 31 May 1922.   [268] Mick Burke (/108).

[269] See Maguire, 'The Political and Military Causes', 291–3; E. Rumpf and A.C. Hepburn, *Nationalism and Socialism in Twentieth-Century Ireland* (Liverpool, 1977), 62.

[270] Dinny Daly (O'Malley Papers, P17b/102).

TABLE 36. Resignation rates in West Cork companies, 1922

Officers resigned per company (out of 3)	Average percentage men resigned per company	
	Schull	Skibbereen
0	60	67
1	66	74
2	—	82
3	89	92

Sources: These numbers were derived from the Report on Cork 5, Aug. 1922 (A/0991/2). According to these documents, all resigned officers were Free Staters.

Again the trend is unmistakable. If a unit's officers all stayed in the I.R.A. they were able to hold on to their core constituency—the 'reliable' one-third of the company (as happened in the Behagh Company). If the officers went over to the other side, however, these friends and comrades went with them and the company collapsed. The two Schull companies which lost all their officers were left with three men between them. In the Drimoleague Battalion, where over half of the officers 'deserted', the 1st Southern Division's inspector of organization reported in August 1922 that 'there are only about enough men in each area to form a Company staff, and it would be a case of all officers and no soldiers'.[271]

On the other hand, these figures also confirm the limitations of ideology and leadership where the silent majority of Volunteers were concerned. Both tables show that between one- and two-thirds of I.R.A. members dropped out of their own accord and could not be mobilized by either side. And since these statistics do not include resignations before January 1922 they actually understate the level of apathy within the organization. If we look at former guerrillas alone, a very different picture emerges. Just as most ordinary Volunteers may not have cared what their leaders—local or national—did or said, so most activists thought that the departing 'small fry' and 'Truce Volunteers' were irrelevant. As Sean Moylan declared: 'it was the plain fighting men that won the last war and we will win again.'[272] With few exceptions (and probably fewer additions), the men who fought the British in the Tan War went on to fight the Free State. Tom Barry's column—'the boys of Kilmichael'—mostly went republican, along with those led by Sean Moylan (who had one man go Free State), Paddy O'Brien and Con Liddy in North Cork, and Frank Busteed in Donoughmore. In the Fermoy area 'the majority of the *Old Stock* that were on the move . . . in the Past . . . are all still in the Republican Army'.[273] In Ballyvourney, '45 men of the old column' continued the fight: 'the same men all the time. 80 percent of the old Brigade

[271] Inspector of Org. to O/C Org., 1st South. Div., 3 Aug. 1922 (O'Malley Papers, P17a/87).
[272] *Weekly Examiner*, 8 Apr. 1922.
[273] 'Babe' to David Bernard, 8 Nov. 1922 (MA, A/1142).

Column was in our column.'[274] In the city, Con Neenan, the Murphy, Donovan, Grey, and O'Brien brothers, and almost all the gunmen of the 'active squad' stayed republican despite Sean O'Hegarty's resignation. Four of the five surviving guerrillas profiled earlier in this chapter remained committed to the struggle.

Midleton was the only place where the local column went Free State but this was a special case in that a large number of the original fighters had been killed (most at Clonmult). The south-western battalions had had no active columns and very few of the Free Staters there had fought in the Tan War. Even my pro-Treaty informant agreed that 'the best of the fighting men were against us'.[275]

This enduring gap between column and company men can also be seen in the differences between officers and men in West Cork revealed in Table 35, and particularly in the Bandon Battalion where almost all officers had spent time on the column. While the battalion lost a third of its men between January and June—and over two-thirds of its full Trucetime strength—only one in seven of its pre-Treaty officers had resigned. The same differences can be detected in the Mallow and Millstreet Battalions. If we put these numbers together with the anecdotal estimates of how many column men in Ballyvourney and Newmarket resigned (along with the four of our sample of five guerrillas who were republicans), we can estimate that, while 80 per cent of the rank and file dropped out, 80 per cent of the active guerrillas stayed the course through the autumn of 1922: perhaps 600 men in Cork as a whole.[276]

Defying the Free State was, in a sense, an assertion of identity for the 'plain fighting men': 'the young men, the fighting men, the men who count and who are ready to make sacrifices'.[277] The same attitudes and bonds which sustained them through the Tan War kept them together and active in the Civil War. These veteran guerrillas identified totally with the armed revolution. Their militant elitism and general contempt for 'politics' in any form had already set them apart as an increasingly separate caste within the movement. Their republican convictions were now inseparable from their experience of (and belief in) violence and self-sacrifice.

In the Dail Sean Moylan referred to himself as part of 'a third side . . . the fighting men of the South', ultimately responsible only to themselves.[278] Seamus Fitzgerald, the I.R.A. leader and TD from Cobh, gave a speech in a similar vein: 'the men in my area who count will never accept the Treaty.'[279] Sean MacSwiney (I.R.A. officer and brother of Terence) said 'I can answer for the Army of Munster, and I have been empowered to answer for them . . . If I cannot, I will probably be directed in the morning by officers in a position to

---

[274]   Mick O'Sullivan (O'Malley Papers, P17b/108).
[275]   Interview with AB.
[276]   1st Southern Division figures show 518 men on 'active service' in October 1922; Stan Barry of Cork city estimated that there were 500 to 600 'good men' on the republican side (O'Malley Papers, P17b/95).
[277]   Cathal Brugha, speaking of I.R.A. leaders in Kerry. *Debate on the Treaty*, 329.
[278]   Ibid. 145.   [279]   Ibid. 240.

direct me.'[280] As Moylan, MacSwiney, and Sean O'Hegarty made plain, the Cork guerrillas thought of themselves not only as republicans and fighting men but also as 'men of the South' (as distinct from those 'portions of Ireland where a shot was never fired'[281]). Dan Corkery, Macroom I.R.A. commander and member for Mid-Cork, was even more explicit:

I believe the first lorry was attacked in Mid-Cork; the people have been with us all the time up to the Truce and they never flinched though they often heard the angry crack of the rifle and machine gun. The people down there do not want war, but they are not half as much afraid of war as the people from other counties who have not fired a shot yet.[282]

In effect, the guerrillas formed their own political constituency, one adamantly distinct from fellow republicans as well as from their mutual opponents. Sean Moylan's insistence that 'I am not a party politician and I am not a follower of Arthur Griffith or of De Valera—I am a republican' was typical of the I.R.A. response to the Treaty.[283] Rory O'Connor, the leader of the extremist Four Courts garrison, declared that 'We have nothing whatever to do with politics. We are plain men who stand by the Republic.'[284] Seamus Robinson of the South Tipperary Brigade demanded that the I.R.A. (except for Truce Volunteers) be given a veto: 'we are not a national army in the ordinary sense; we are not a machine pure and simple; we have political views as soldiers.'[285]

The guerrillas thought of themselves as sovereign. They had organized and armed themselves and paid their own way. They had brought the republic into being and nobody else had a right to give it away. Moreover, they were not just defending the national republic declared in 1916 and launched in 1919, they were also defending the 'Cork republic' and the innumerable little parish 'republics' (the 'republic of Ballyvourney'; the 'republic of the Nia', the 'Free republic' of Schull[286]) proclaimed during the Tan War wherever the I.R.A. writ ran unimpeded. From the moment of the Truce onwards, each unit was in effectively undisputed control of its territory and the reality of local power was as difficult to surrender as the ideal of a purified and untrammelled Ireland.

---

[280] Ibid. 48–9.

[281] Sean O'Hegarty, 3 May 1922: *Official Report: Dail Eireann*, (1921–2), 358.

[282] *Debate on the Treaty*, 320. Just as republicans took their stand on their fighting record, so they attempted to discredit their opponents—specifically Michael Collins—on the same basis. See ibid. 291, 325.

[283] *Weekly Examiner*, 8 Apr. 1922. See also the exchange between Seamus Robinson and Eamon de Valera in *Debate on the Treaty*, 289–90.

[284] *Examiner*, 15 Apr. 1922. See also Seamus Robinson in *Debate on the Treaty*, 288.

[285] *Debate on the Treaty*, 290.

[286] Browne, *The Story of the 7th*, 45; E. M. Ussher, 'The True Story of a Revolution', 143 (Representative Church Body Library); Finbarr Barry, 'Geography of I.R.A. Activities in West Cork 1919–1921', BA thesis (Cork, 1991), 40. For other examples, see Liam Haugh, 'History of the West Clare Brigade' and I/O Cork 4 to O/C Communications, 5 Feb. 1923 (Lankford Papers, U169c).

With the exception of a handful of pioneers such as the Haleses or Sean O'Hegarty, there was almost nothing in the pre-revolutionary lives of future guerrillas that distinguished them from their contemporaries. Once immersed in the revolution however—once 'deep in the movement' or 'deep in the know'— they emerged different men. We can trace some of the common threads in these revolutionary careers—the family or factional connections, the early encounters with police, prisons, and guns—but 'the spirit of the times' remains, for those who experienced it, inexplicable to outsiders, to following generations, or to historians. 'You couldn't understand it now' is a standard answer given to the standard questions about I.R.A. motives: 'the comradeship of people who never knew each other before couldn't be understood now.'[287]

In that moment life became one with the emotion of Ireland. In that moment I am sure every one of us ceased to be single or individual and became part of one another, in union . . . It was a supreme experience . . . when in our generous youth we lived and were ready to die for one of the most wild, beautiful and inexhaustible faiths possible to man—faith in one's fellows.

The guerrilla war would have been unimaginable without this extraordinary alchemy of youthful fellowship and fervent patriotism.

As violence developed its own momentum it created new actors, new identities, and new agendas, and gave previously unknown and marginal people the power to make their own history. For those on the periphery of the movement, pulled in whether they wanted it or not, the revolution wore a different mask, often intrusive or bullying. For those people whom the 'spirit of the movement' transformed into enemies and victims, the revolution appeared as a terrifying and uncontrollable force, leaving them vulnerable and powerless. The I.R.A. was defined as much by its victims as by its activists, and it is to the victims of the revolution that we next turn.

---

[287] Interview with John L. O'Sullivan (RTE Archives, A2790). I was told the same thing in several interviews. The quotation following is from O'Faolain, *Vive Moi!*, 172–3.

PART IV

Neighbours and Enemies

12

Taking it out on the Protestants

We never killed a man or interfered with a man because of his religion . . .
but we had to face up to facts.

(Tom Barry)[1]

Remember Belfast and West Cork . . .

(Anonymous letter, 2 May, 1922)[2]

At one o'clock in the morning of 27 April 1922, James and Clarina Buttimer of
Dunmanway were awakened by shouting and banging at their front door. When
James, a retired draper, opened the door he was confronted by a group of
agitated and armed men. 'What do you want, boys?' he asked. 'We want you,
we want to talk to you.' 'Sure, you would not take an old man like him',
responded Clarina, his wife. 'Go to bed, we don't want you!' And again, to
James: 'Come out or we'll make you.' He refused. 'Surely, boys, you would not
harm an old man like me?' The boys shot James Buttimer in the face as he stood
in his doorway. He died at once, 'his brains and teeth blown out'.[3]

These anonymous men had already killed twice that night elsewhere along
Main Street. Alice Gray, a neighbour of the Buttimers, was woken up at about
the same time:

There was knocking, thumping and shouting at the door. The door was burst in. Her
husband [David, a chemist] went down and said 'Who is there? What do you want?' She
then heard a shot and her husband falling.

More shots were then fired, and she heard voices saying, 'Take that, you Free Stater',
several times. She did not come down, as she stayed with the children. When she went
down later, her husband was dead. The body was lying on the doorstep, partly out.[4]

Further down the road, Francis Fitzmaurice, an elderly solicitor and land
agent, was riddled with bullets on his doorstep as his wife Elizabeth watched.[5]
His brother William barely escaped the same fate, as did William Jagoe, another

---

[1] RTE interview (tape in the possession of Donal O'Donovan).

[2] 'Warner' to Mrs Williamson, 2 May 1922: an anonymous letter (Lankford Papers, U169).

[3] Accounts of the murder by Clarina Buttimer can be found in the *Belfast News-Letter*, 1 May
1922, the *Eagle*, 6 May 1922, and in her statement to the Irish Grants Committee (CO 762/142). See
also *Constitution*, 28 Apr. 1922.

[4] *Belfast News-Letter*, 1 May 1922.

[5] *Constitution*, 29 Apr. 1922, *Eagle*, 6 May 1922, *Belfast News-Letter*, 1 May 1922; Elizabeth
Fitzmaurice statement (CO 762/46). Fitzmaurice was shot twelve times.

draper, who had his windows shot out. 'We'll get Jagoe yet', said one of the attackers.[6] George Appelbe ('Appy') Bryan, a shopkeeper, was confronted by two men in his home and told to prepare to die. One pointed a revolver at him and pulled the trigger but his gun jammed. Bryan fled into his garden and escaped in the darkness. His house was searched and ransacked.[7] At least one other man was sought for, a teacher named William Morrison who also managed to evade his pursuers.[8] The home of James McCarthy, yet another Main Street merchant, was fired upon, as was the local branch of the Bank of Ireland.[9]

Tom Sullivan, a retired policeman, was one of many others in the town who feared for their lives:

I was in bed at the time of the shooting. I heard voices outside and my wife begged me to get up and go out. I got up in my night attire and went out the back way, taking refuge in the local cemetery one hundred yards distant until broad daylight. I could hear the weeping and crying of the relatives of those who had been shot and heard the shooting which continued for a long time.[10]

The killings continued the next night. First to be visited was the parish of Kinneigh, which lay to the east of Dunmanway along the Bandon valley. At 10.30, two men appeared at Robert Howe's door in Ballaghanure and demanded he harness a horse for them. When he refused, they followed him into his room and shot him twice.[11] Next came his neighbour and fellow farmer, John Chinnery, who was ordered to harness a horse to a cart in the shed. While he was doing this, he was shot in the back.[12] Both men were killed.

Several hours later Alexander McKinley, a youth of 16, was shot dead in the nearby village of Ballineen. His aunt, Frances Peyton, was a witness:

On Thursday night she heard shots down the street, and shortly after there was a knock at the front door. It was about half past one o'clock. Her nephew had been unwell during the evening. There was a second knock, and she went upstairs to where her nephew was in bed, and told him that there was a knock at the door, and he said to open it. She said that she would not, and she asked him to dress himself. She came downstairs and went out by the back door, and said to him to come on quickly. There was a man outside, who asked her where she was going, and she was not sure whether she answered. He ordered her back and told her to open the front door. She returned and opened the door, and asked a man who was standing outside was he going to shoot her. He said, 'No, I don't shoot

[6]   William Fitzmaurice and William Jagoe statements (CO 762/12, 4).

[7]   George Appelbe Bryan statement (PRONI, Southern Irish Loyalist Relief Fund (SILRA) Papers, D989B/2/11); Interview with BP, 21 Apr. 1993.

[8]   Interview with BO, 21 Apr. 1993.

[9]   James McCarthy statement (CO 762/13); Bank of Ireland compensation claim in NA, Dept. of Finance Records, FIN 383/102.   [10]   Thomas Sullivan statement (CO 762/175).

[11]   The witness was Catherine Howe, Robert's wife. *Irish Times*, 2 May 1922 and her statement (CO 762/31).

[12]   The witness in this case was Rebecca Chinnery, the victim's mother. See *The Times*, 29 Apr. 1922 and her statement (CO 762/31), and also George Chinnery to Miss Murray, 12 June 1928 (D989B/3/8).

women'. She came in and went upstairs. Her nephew had not stirred, and she called him again. She then came down again and went out into the yard, and after some time went away to her sister's house.[13]

McKinley was shot three times in the back of the head as he lay in bed. Elsewhere in the town William Daunt, a farmer and cattle dealer, had a pony stolen and his house shot up. 'He was a young fella at the time and he was pretty sharp. He saw a rifle or revolver and as he did he ducked and there was a chest of drawers inside the window and [his attacker] fired and he hit the chest of drawers.'[14] Further down the Bandon river, the Murragh rectory was also visited and the son of the rector, Ralph Harbord (himself a curate), was shot while standing on the rectory steps.[15]

At two o'clock another farmhouse was attacked in Caher, a townland to the west of Ballineen. Frances Buttimer was the only surviving witness:

I heard some noise and shots and next heard the smashing of windows. My son jumped out and said we're attacked. My husband [John] got out of bed and I got a weakness in the room. I got alright in a short time and came out on the landing. I met my husband and said 'For God's sake get out' and he said 'Sure I can't'. [Jim] Greenfield, was calling on me to stay with him. I went into his room and then came downstairs. I met a man at the bottom. I said 'Where are you going?' and he replied 'Where are the men?' I said 'I do not know. What do you want them for?' He said 'Only for very little'. I asked him to take my house and money and myself and spare the men. I put my two hands to his chest to keep him back and he called my husband in a most blasphemous manner to come down. He then went upstairs and another man threw me into the dining room. I then went into the kitchen. Another man put me out in the yard and I went to a neighbour's field. I came back in a very short time and I met a man, and I said 'You have killed them, but you cannot kill their souls'. When I came into the house I got a light and went through rooms. I found my husband dead in a sitting position in the boy's room, that is Greenfield's, and I found Greenfield dead in bed.[16]

Jim Greenfield, a farm servant described as 'feeble-minded', had been shot once in the back of the head as he hid his face from his attackers. John Buttimer, the owner of the house and farm, was shot twice in the face and stomach. His son escaped a determined pursuit and survived.[17]

That same night, Robert Nagle was shot dead at his home on MacCurtain Hill in Clonakilty (about 10 miles to the south) in the presence of his mother:

She said that after eleven o'clock on Thursday night there was a knock at the door. She asked out of a window who was there, and a man replied, 'Open for a few minutes'. When she did not do so the hall door was burst in, and two men, one of whom was

---

[13] *Irish Times*, 1 May 1922. McKinley's name was reported in some newspapers as Peyton, and his first name is given as Gerald in their 1911 census return.

[14] Interview with BG, 18 Apr. 1993; William Daunt statement (CO 762/100).

[15] *Church of Ireland Gazette*, 5 May 1922; Revd Ralph Harbord compensation claims (CO 762/58; NA, F/20/8/24). [16] *Weekly Examiner*, 6 May 1922.

[17] The story of his escape is well known—even celebrated—among West Cork Protestants: interviews with BP and BH, 20 Apr. 1993.

masked, entered. They said that they came to search for arms and ammunition. They proceeded to search the house, and asked where was the man of the house, meaning her husband. She said that he was away. A conversation took place in the room upstairs, where her son was in bed. Prior to this she had told the intruders that she had two children who were going to school. They asked Robert was he going to school and where he was employed. He said that he was going to a night school and was employed at the Post Office. They then told him that they had a warrant for his arrest and to get up and dress and come with them immediately. They put out the light that the witness had in her hand, and one of the men fired a revolver shot at her son as he lay in the bed and left.[18]

Robert had been hit in the chest and killed. His father Thomas, a greengrocer and sheriff's officer, was searched for but could not be found. The gunmen appeared to Mrs Nagle to be drunk.

Another near-victim in Clonakilty was Richard Helen, the owner of a cartage, dairy, and grocery business. He was taken out of his hotel by two armed men who 'asked me to come with them to the end of the town'. Helen managed to get away from his captors and took refuge in the fields.[19] Outside the town, armed men raided William Perrot's farmhouse but he was already gone.[20]

The following night it was the turn of John Bradfield, a farmer in Killowen, several miles east of Murragh. Two men broke into his house through a window calling for a horse and cart and for John's brother William. The latter had already left home in fear of just such a visit. John would probably have gone with him but he was stricken with rheumatism and could not walk without the aid of sticks. He was taken out of bed, told to stand up, and shot in the back of the neck. The men then came into his sister Elizabeth's room. One raised his gun and pointed it at her as she lay in bed. 'Surely you wouldn't shoot me?' she asked. The other man told him to 'put that down' and they left.[21]

Henry Bradfield, a Killowen neighbour and cousin of John, William, and Elizabeth, was sought for but he too had escaped. His would-be executioners had to satisfy themselves with vandalizing his house and stealing his watch and clothes. One remarked to his family that 'they would soon have the —— English out of the country'.[22]

Ten men had been shot dead, and another wounded. All were Protestant. Scores of Cork Protestants had been killed as 'spies' or 'informers' in the previous two years, but never so many at once or so (apparently) randomly.[23] The spectre of mass murder had long haunted the unionist political imagination;

---

[18]   *Irish Times*, 1 May 1922. See also Thomas Nagle's statement (CO 762/3) and *Constitution*, 29 Apr. 1922.   [19]   Richard Helen statement (CO 762/33).
[20]   William Perrot statement (CO 762/121).
[21]   Elizabeth's account can be found in the *Eagle*, 6 May 1922. For their servant's testimony see *Constitution*, 2 May 1922. See also *Irish Times*, 2 May 1922, although here, as in other places, their names were given incorrectly as Shorten.
[22]   Henry Bradfield statement (CO 762/185).
[23]   The following chapter deals with the subject of 'informers', Protestant and otherwise.

when it arrived, the reality struck with the force of a nightmare.[24] Hundreds went into hiding or fled their homes as a wave of panic, fanned by threats and rumours, raced through West Cork. Farms and shops were abandoned and in many households only women and children, or those too sick or old to travel, remained (among them Alexander McKinley and John Bradfield).

Some of these people stopped in Cork city but most continued on to Belfast and England. 'For two weeks there wasn't standing room on any of the boats or mail trains leaving Cork for England. All Loyalist refugees, who were either fleeing in terror or had been ordered out of the country.'[25] One Cork correspondent who saw the trainloads of refugees go through the city reported that 'so hurried was their flight that some of them had neither a handbag nor an overcoat'.[26] Most of these people returned within a few months but many did so only to settle their affairs, sell their land, and leave for good.

This unprecedented massacre received extensive coverage in the British press. British officials in Ireland and MPs in London expressed great shock and concern,[27] unionist organizations in England and Northern Ireland exerted themselves to aid the refugees, and destroyers were dispatched to patrol the coast of West Cork and discreetly provide what assistance they could.[28] The Provisional Government and the Dail condemned the killings and promised to 'bring the culprits to justice', but did nothing.[29] At the time, with only a small nascent army in Dublin and with the dissident I.R.A. in control of nearly the whole of Cork and Munster, there was little they could do. Irish observers, like the British, were bewildered and shocked by the killings, which seemed to come out of nowhere. Most assumed that they were a sectarian reprisal for recent attacks on Catholics in Belfast, which had been dominating southern newspapers for weeks.[30]

Nationalist outrage over northern atrocities did undoubtedly give the massacre some of its emotional impetus. Cork republicans participated enthusiastically in

[24] In the midst of the Home Rule crisis of 1914 the resident magistrate in Bandon reported that 'on the part of the minority there is a widespread fear of possible outrages against their lives and property' (CO 904/227). Francis Hackett quoted an American whose hunting friends in Cork declared in 1913 that they would fight with Ulster: 'They say they don't want to be stabbed in their beds.' *Ireland: A Study in Nationalism* (New York, 1918), 248. See also Edith Somerville to Col. John Somerville, 21 Mar., 28 May 1914 (Somerville and Ross Papers, Lot 877) and 'Sassenach', *Arms and the Irishman*, 77.

[25] Letter from Alice Hodder, Crosshaven, 28 May 1922 (CO 739/16).

[26] *Irish Times*, 1 May 1922. See also *Constitution*, 1 May 1922.

[27] As did the King, apparently. See the 4 May 1922 memorandum from Lord Stamfordham in Gilbert, *Winston S. Churchill*, companion volume iv, part 3, 1900–1.

[28] See Edith Somerville's Diary, 11, 19 Aug.; 12, 28 Sept. 1922 (Somerville and Ross Papers). Orange lodges and churches in Belfast and elsewhere took in some of these refugees: see *Irish Times*, 2 May 1922 and *Church of Ireland Gazette*, 16 June 1922.

[29] The quotation is from a joint statement of the Provisional Government and the cabinet of Dail Eireann. *Belfast News-Letter*, 29 Apr. 1922.

[30] See *Belfast News-Letter*, 1 May 1922 and *The Times*, 29 Apr. 1922 and Edith Somerville to Ethel Smyth, 2 May 1922: 'In Skibbereen they believe it is in honour of Belfast' (Somerville and Ross Papers, Lot 878).

the renewed Belfast boycott of 1922 (largely directed at Protestant-owned businesses),[31] the city I.R.A. was running guns to the north, and a West Cork flying column was in action along the border. Moreover, it was widely—and wrongly—believed (and not just by republicans) that southern Protestants had remained silent on the matter and thus tacitly supported the 'pogroms'.[32] The consequent logic of reprisal was laid out with remarkable clarity in a letter sent to many southern loyalists in April and May 1922:

> I am authorised to take over your house and all property contained therein, and you are hereby given notice to hand over to me within one hour from the receipt of this notice the above land and property. The following are reasons for this action:
>
> (1) The campaign of murder in Belfast is financed by the British Government.
>
> (2) As a reprisal for the murder of innocent men, women and children in Belfast.
>
> (3) You, by supporting the union between England and Ireland, are in sympathy with their murder.
>
> (4) In order to support and maintain the Belfast refugees.[33]

To understand the origins of the massacre, however, we must go back to the early hours of 26 April (the night before the first killings in Dunmanway), when another Protestant household was broken into in Ballygroman, about half-way between Bandon and Cork. The owner was Thomas Hornibrook and the intruders were I.R.A. officers from the Bandon Battalion led by Michael O'Neill, the acting commandant. His brother Stephen later described what happened:

> We knocked at the door, a person came to the window, and a man's voice asked 'Who is there?' [Michael], who was in charge of our party said 'Please open the door as I want to see Mr. Hornibrook on business'. The window was shut and we waited to have the door opened for about a quarter of an hour, and as it was not opened Michael knocked again. One of the Hornibrooks opened the window, and we again asked him to open the door as we wanted to see him on business, and we further added that if he would not open the door we would force the door. We heard the party above call out 'Sam'. As the door was not opened, after waiting about another quarter of an hour, Michael lifted up the left hand window of the dwelling house, which seemed to be unfastened. Michael then got in through the window and I and Charles O'Donoghue got in after him.
>
> We found ourselves in a dining room; there was no light but Michael had an electric torch. Michael went into the hall from the dining room and proceeded to go upstairs. We all followed. A shot then rang out. Michael turned and came downstairs making for the dining room again, where he fell on the floor, having exclaimed 'I am

---

[31] One Cork businessman, for example, was told by a former customer that 'they could not deal with Byfords on account of the way Roman Catholics were treated in the North of Ireland' (Samuel Byford statement, CO 762/86).

[32] See *Star*, 25 Mar., 29 Apr. 1922. In fact, there were frequent Protestant meetings and letters to newspapers condemning the northern pogroms and testifying to southern harmony in the months before the massacre. See *Church of Ireland Gazette*, 31 Mar., 7, 13 Apr., 26 May 1922; *Examiner*, 13 Apr. 1922.

[33] Proceedings of the House of Lords, vol. 51, col. 889 (31 May 1922). An almost identical letter can be found in the Lloyd George Papers (F/20/1/21). See also Adj., West Mayo Bde. to Maj. Browne, 29 Apr. 1922 (Dept. of Taoiseach, S565).

shot', immediately after the shot rang out. I and Charlie O'Donoghue took out Michael through the window; he was quite unconscious. Though Michael had a torch I did not see who fired the shot.[34]

Michael O'Neill was dead, shot in the chest.

Revenge was swift and complete. Charlie O'Donoghue drove back to Bandon and returned with reinforcements—and rope.[35] This force surrounded and laid siege to the house until eight o'clock the next morning. When Hornibrook, his son Samuel, and son-in-law Captain Herbert Woods gave themselves up—on condition their lives would be spared—they were confronted by two of O'Neill's brothers and O'Donoghue: 'I addressed the three together and asked "Which of you fired the shot last night?" Woods spoke up immediately and said "I fired it." '[36] He was beaten unconscious and all three were taken away by car.

The prisoners were driven south into hill country known for being 'a very risky area, a bad area' for Protestants.[37] There 'they were sentenced and no more to it'.[38] The sentence was death. 'They tried them at their kangaroo court. They tried them and they shot them.' Woods was shot that day and, according to local Protestant folklore, tied to the back of a car (in revenge for the same being done to local I.R.A. 'bad boy' Walter Leo Murphy by British officers the year before).[39] 'They dragged him a couple of miles up the road and that was the end of him.'[40] The Hornibrooks were executed the following day. They were said to have been made to dig their own graves. By one report, Thomas Hornibrook looked into his grave, threw his stick in, drew himself up to face his executioners, and told them to 'go ahead'.[41] All three were secretly buried. Ballygroman House was burned to the ground, the fences were broken, the plantation was cut down, and the land was seized. No Irish newspaper reported these events. To the outside world, the Hornibrooks and Woods had disappeared without a trace.[42]

---

[34] *Star*, 29 Apr. 1922. A brief portrait of the O'Neill family of Kilbrittain can be found in Liam Deasy, 'Sidelights on Ireland's Fight for Freedom: A Personal Narrative' (Mulcahy papers, P7/D/45). Michael O'Neill had been both wounded and interned during the Tan War. At the inquest into his death it was said 'he had no address for the last six years; only gaols and ditches'. *Constitution*, 28 Apr. 1922. Several of his letters from prison can be found in the Crowley family papers (NLI, Acc.4767), along with a detailed 'History of Kilbrittain Company'.

[35] Interview with BW and BX, 15 Nov. 1994.   [36] *Eagle*, 6 May 1922.

[37] Interview with BG, 19 Apr. 1993. Rumours and reports vary as to the fate of the three men. The following account is based on interviews conducted with I.R.A. veterans and former neighbours (only some of whom are quoted), many of whose accounts agree in key respects. The exact location of their bodies is unknown. A partially reliable account of these executions, presumably based on local reports, was published in the *Morning Post* (the only English paper to follow the story), 1 June 1922. The statement by Matilda Woods (Thomas's daughter and Herbert's wife, who was not present) is also useful, but her description of her family's deaths must be read with caution: 'Herbert Woods it was ascertained afterwards was hung drawn and quartered in the presence of my father and brother. Then my father and brother had to make their own graves and were shot and buried' (CO 762/133).

[38] Interview with AG.   [39] See Ch. 4.

[40] Interview with BG.   [41] Interview with AG.

[42] Free State investigators made a cursory attempt to find out what happened but could do little more than confirm the deaths (MA, A/0908–9 and DOD A/8274). The fate of Hornibrook's land is described in a Report on Land Seizures, 19 Apr. 1923 (DOD A/8506).

Why were O'Neill and his comrades breaking into Hornibrook's house at 2.30 in the morning? The raiders were experienced fighters and the raid was a deter- mined one, timed to catch the residents at home and off guard. By O'Donoghue's account, they did not even identify themselves as members of the I.R.A. By other accounts they said nothing at all and refused to halt on Herbert Woods's chal- lenge. No public explanation was ever offered. One story, that they had run out of petrol, seems disallowed by the fact that Charlie O'Donoghue was able to drive back to Bandon immediately afterwards.[43] Another is that they were there to seize Thomas Hornibrook's motor car (a common enough occurrence at that time).[44] Tadg O'Sullivan, a brigade staff officer, claimed at O'Neill's inquest that the raiders were acting under official orders but these were never disclosed.[45]

The real reason for the break-in, according to several veterans of the Bandon and Dunmanway I.R.A., was that the Hornibrooks were believed to be part of a loyalist conspiracy opposed to the republic.[46] This belief was nothing new. The West Cork guerrillas were convinced that 'the loyalists had a group called the Protestant Action Group', a counter-revolutionary underground, and that this organization had assassinated a number of Volunteers in 1920 and 1921, most notably the Coffey brothers of Enniskeane.[47]

Such conspiracy theories were flourishing in southern Ireland at this time, fed by political uncertainty, paranoia, and the continuing fear of renewed war with Britain. On the same day that O'Neill was shot, for example, another republican was killed in a raid in Wexford after receiving 'information that certain Orangemen possessed firearms'[48] and three British intelligence officers and their driver were kidnapped—and later shot as 'spies'—in Macroom.[49]

The Hornibrooks had long been the object of threats, raids, and robbery. Thomas, 'the old sinner',[50] was known as a hard man: 'very stern, would never give an inch' about politics, religion, 'about anything'.[51] The son, Sam, had a similar reputation on his own account.[52] Both were dedicated Church of Ireland

---

    [43] Interview with AE.

    [44] Interview with AG; O Broin, *Protestant Nationalists*, 177.

    [45] *Eagle*, 29 Apr. 1922. Free State investigators were similarly baffled and could only state that the raid occurred 'for some obscure reason'. Report by Sec., Exec. Council, 9 Mar. 1923 (DOD A/8274).   [46] Interviews with AE and AG.

    [47] Interview with AG. See also O Broin, *Protestant Nationalists*, 177. For the murder of the Coffeys, see *Examiner*, 15 Feb. 1921.

    [48] *Irish Times*, 29 Apr. 1922. A similar incident took place in Blackrock in June—see *Examiner*, 19 June 1922. For further examples of alarmism, see (3rd) Meath Bde. I/O Report, Sept. 1921 and 4th North. Div. I/O Report, July 1921 (Mulcahy Papers, P7/A/6, 13).

    [49] Three British officers were also released on 30 April, having been kidnapped a week before on their way from Cork to Bantry. See *Irish Times*, 1 May 1922.

    [50] The name given to him by one I.R.A. veteran. Interview with AG.

    [51] Interview with BB, 17 Apr. 1993.

    [52] 'He started the greyhound coursing around here. Canon O'Connell was over there one time and they were coursing and, you know, they were pushing in on the track where the hares would be running and [Sam] Hornibrook came along and he gave them all a tip of the whip, including Canon O'Connell and the lads of course didn't take to that.' Interview with BG. However exaggerated, it was on such stories that the family's reputation was built.

parishioners, serving regularly as select vestrymen and churchwardens.[53] Thomas had been a JP and had served regularly on the Ballincollig bench.[54] 'They weren't too popular', and, when the troubles came, swiftly stood out among their neighbours as 'outspoken' loyalists.[55] 'If you were any way stern, that would set the kettle boiling.'[56] Their unrelenting unionism made them 'enemies of the Republic', and their extensive farm and land holdings attracted covetous attention. 'There was some trouble over a piece of land, some old story of grabbing.'[57] The family had been raided for arms and money in 1918 and subsequently, and their cattle were driven and stolen, even after Thomas resigned as a justice of the peace.[58] The arrest of a local man just days before the Truce, for cutting off one of their horses's tails with a saw, may also have labelled them as informers.[59] Sam told a neighbour 'we never go to bed without a revolver under our heads'.[60] The boycott and threatening letters continued into 1922, and it was these threats which brought Captain Woods to stay at Ballygroman.[61]

Like a great many other Protestants in Cork, the political situation and the hostility of the I.R.A. made the Hornibrooks 'fair game' for robbers, extortionists, vandals, and the land-hungry.[62] In early 1922, however, even the limited protection offered by the police and army had gone. Households such as theirs were more or less at the mercy of any group of young men with guns and demands, whether or not they were Volunteers (which was often unclear). Most paid or gave something to avoid trouble. This time, someone decided to resist. Captain Woods ('a bit of a ne'er-do-well and a bit mad but he'd done splendid work in the war'[63]) challenged the anonymous intruders and killed Michael O'Neill, almost certainly unaware of his identity.[64] Local Protestants, horrified at the family's fate, were equally appalled by the 'utter foolishness' of the act which brought it on. 'He done a foolish thing. He was stupid!'[65] To the Volunteers, on the other hand, it must have confirmed their worst suspicions: they had indeed uncovered a nest of armed enemies.

[53] See Athnowen Parish Vestry Minute Book, 1899–1951 (Carrigrohane Union records).
[54] Interview with BY. Thomas's journeys to court were memorable for being driven in a sidecar on his son's motorbike.   [55] Interview with BG.
[56] Interview with BB.   [57] Interview with BB; also interview with BY, 17 Nov. 1994.
[58] CI Reports, East Cork, July 1919, June 1921 (CO 904/109, 115). Although it was said that Thomas had refused to resign his magistracy (and thus angered the I.R.A.), compare the lists of justices of the peace for Co. Cork in *Thom's Directory* (Dublin) for 1920 with those of 1921. Hornibrook appears in the former (as he had done for over a decade) but not the latter.
[59] Manchester Regiment Record of Arrests, 1921 (Manchester Regiment Collection).
[60] Interview with BY.   [61] Alice Hodder letter.
[62] The phrase 'fair game' was frequently used by Protestants to describe their situation. See, for example, W. B. Hosford's statement (CO 762/4) and the leader in the *Church of Ireland Gazette*, 23 June 1922. For its use in reverse, see Kathleen Keyes McDonnell as quoted below.
[63] Alice Hodder letter. A neighbour described him as 'a very active kind of fella, a great boxer and all that kind of thing and a fine looking young man'. Interview with BG.
[64] See H. Kingsmill Moore, *Reminiscences and Reflections* (London, 1930), 312–13, who reports hearing this version of events from 'one who was there that night'.
[65] Interviews with BV and BY.

It was undoubtedly O'Neill's death that sparked the following three nights of raids and murders.[66] Beyond this, however, we know very little for certain. No faction or member of the I.R.A. ever claimed responsibility. The Hornibrooks and Woods were presumably shot by the same members of the Kilbrittain and Ballinadee I.R.A. who captured them, possibly aided by men of the 1st Cork Brigade, whose territory bordered this area.[67] The killings of Buttimer, Gray, and Fitzmaurice were probably also carried out by a single group familiar with Dunmanway and following the same pattern in each case (all three men were shot at their front doors). Several sources have identified these killers as locals, 'right prominent I.R.A. men', and members of the 'fighting gang'.[68] One in particular was known as a 'black I.R.A. man' who 'shot people for miles around'.[69] William Jagoe claimed that the killers were 'well-known' and Clarina Buttimer seems to have recognized at least one of her husband's attackers.[70]

The next night (27–8 April) another cluster of killings is evident. John Buttimer, Greenfield, McKinley, Howe, Chinnery, and Reverend Harbord all lived in and around Ballineen and Enniskeane, along the same stretch of the Bandon valley. Howe and Chinnery, close neighbours who were both shot by two men using the pretext of wanting a horse, may possibly have been shot by a separate group. John Bradfield's killers also match this description. Frances Peyton likewise saw only two men but Frances Buttimer saw at least three.

The other victims, in and around Clonakilty, lived south of the Bandon river and were clearly attacked by a different party—or parties—altogether. No one group could have carried out all of the night's attacks in view of the distances involved and the state of the roads at that time. Both Mrs Nagle and Richard Helen reported seeing only two men but we do not know if they were the same in each case.

It is possible that a single gang was responsible for most of these deaths, travelling down the Bandon river from Dunmanway on the night of the 27th to Killowen on the 29th.[71] Even so, it seems unlikely that these were the same men who wiped out the Hornibrook household, and it would have been difficult for them to have also been in Clonakilty on the same night as the killings around Ballineen. The most plausible explanation is that there were at least two, and possibly as many as five, separate groups involved, centred around Dunmanway

---

[66] This has occasionally been denied: interview with AG. Several Cork county councillors attacked any such 'insinuations' in a 4 May meeting. *Cork Constitution*, 5 May 1922.

[67] Kevin Myers has identified two key officers of the Dunmanway and Bandon Battalions as participants in the attacks: 'An Irishman's Diary', *Irish Times*, 19 Dec. 1989, 9 Jan. 1990. I have not included the names cited by Myers or my own informants as some of this information is contradictory and the identifications are second hand and unproven. The identity of these killers remains a hugely sensitive topic in West Cork.

[68] Interview with BP.

[69] Interview with BM, 20 Apr. 1993.

[70] Jagoe statement. He does not name names.

[71] Dunmanway, Ballineen, Enniskeane, and Murragh were all on the same main road, and all except Enniskeane were stops on the Cork, Bandon, and South Coast Railway.

and Kilbrittain, but probably including members of the Ballineen, Clonakilty, and Ballincollig Volunteers. The fact that the murders stretched over three nights and encompassed so many different districts argues against the massacre being an organized effort, and for it being a series of copy-cat killings carried out by a dozen or so gunmen, probably motivated by similar fears and a common desire for revenge.

Despite a few brave attempts to blame the murders on British *agents provocateurs*,[72] the killers were clearly active members of the anti-Treaty I.R.A. Denis Lordan and other republican guerrillas have admitted it was 'our fellows'.[73] All of the men identified as participants were committed republicans—veterans of the Tan War who went on to fight in the Civil War. The original raiders at Ballygroman were such, as were the men who captured the Hornibrooks and Woods the next morning. The shouts of 'Take that, you Free Stater' further indicate the allegiance of the Dunmanway killers.

These men probably acted on their own initiative—but with the connivance or acquiescence of local units. This is demonstrated by the non-intervention of the I.R.A. garrisons in Dunmanway and elsewhere, even though they must have known what was happening. In Dunmanway the gunmen 'moved about openly' and there was so much gunfire that townspeople assumed the barracks were under attack.[74] The same was true on a smaller scale in Ballineen. The killers were free to do what they liked and no serious attempt was made to investigate or punish the culprits after they had finished.

Tom Hales, the commander of the West Cork Brigade, and other leaders condemned the attacks and promised their protection, but these statements were not issued until it was all over and had little practical significance.[75] Some of these statements even had an oddly belligerent tone, like the one issued by the O/C of the South-West (5th) Cork Brigade in Bantry:

He and his colleagues in command look upon the exodus [of Protestants] from the town and district as implying a reflection on these officers' ability to secure protection from such eruptive violence . . . These officers . . . rather resent the steps taken by the refugees.[76]

Hales also called for all arms to be handed in to I.R.A. barracks but this was aimed at loyalists as much as Volunteers and was as likely to induce raids as prevent them. In any case he was widely ignored. The killings stopped but

---

[72] See Mary MacSwiney's statement in the *Freeman's Journal*, 3 May 1922 ('I know the type of men who compose the army of the south') and that of Mr Ahern, an East Cork county councillor, who·'believed that the enemy had something to do with the shootings . . . and that it was part of the old game'. *Constitution*, 5 May 1922.   [73] O Broin, *Protestant Nationalists*, 177.
    [74] The quotation is from William Jagoe's statement. See also Thomas Sullivan's statement and *Irish Times* and *The Times*, 28 Apr. 1922.
    [75] For the declarations by Hales and Con Connolly, the Skibbereen commander, see *Eagle*, 6 May 1922. One of Mick O'Neill's brothers told the Bandon Rural District Council, 'I think it is up to us to deplore recent shootings . . . and to tender to the relatives of the victims our deepest sympathy.' *Constitution*, 9 May 1922.   [76] *Constitution*, 5 May 1922.

Protestants continued to be boycotted, harassed, threatened, and dispossessed just as before, and the flow of refugees continued.

In Kilbrittain, for example, John Bolster Barrett spent most of June on the run, sleeping in his fields and travelling in secret. 'At this time I was subjected to several threats of death by shooting, and my house threatened with destruction by fire.' In July, William Bateman of Kilronan, south of Dunmanway, 'slept out under hedges and in outhouses, with my two sons' after a series of raids by gunmen. His sons left the district soon thereafter as 'feeling ran so high that I felt [they] would never be safe in this locality'.[77] In Castletownshend, Edith Somerville recorded the following attack on her cousin, days after the (pro-Treaty) I.R.A. commandant declared 'we have no sympathy with any pogrom' along with his intention of protecting all citizens:

> She said that three nights ago their house was attacked by a gang of young blackguards who shouted for 'The Boss'. She is a plucky woman, and while she parleyed with them out of a window, 'the boss' slipped out by a side door and got away . . . They then demanded money and said if she wouldn't let them in they would break down the door. So she opened it, and they rushed in, and putting a gun to her head, said she must give them 'all the money she had in the house' . . . They were odious and insolent, but did no harm. The next morning she hunted her husband off to England and she will follow.[78]

The Skibbereen garrison did send guards to watch the house after the owners had decamped. Around Bandon and Dunmanway, not even this much was done.

To ask why the massacre took place is to move from the relatively straightforward problem of identifying the killers to the more complex question of the identity of the victims as perceived by their attackers. Who did they *think* they were killing?

Herbert Woods was responsible for O'Neill's death and Thomas and Samuel Hornibrook—although innocent in this respect—were presumably done in as accomplices and co-conspirators. Were the others also believed to be part of the conspiracy or were they just swept up randomly in the general desire for revenge?

If the victims were supposed to be plotters, then it was a most unlikely plot: unarmed (apart from Herbert Woods) and largely composed of old men and teenagers. Alexander McKinley and Robert Nagle were both 16; John Chinnery, 31; David Gray, 37; John Buttimer, 59; Robert Howe, 60; John Bradfield, 69 and bedridden; Francis Fitzmaurice, 70; James Buttimer, 82 and nearly blind. The families of Robert Nagle and Alexander McKinley seem to have believed that these boys' youthfulness would protect them when their father and uncle

---

[77] John Bolster Barrett and William Bateman statements (D989B/3/8).
[78] Edith Somerville to Ethel Smyth, 6 May 1922 (Somerville and Ross Papers). She also reported the following story: 'I heard that a most decent, prosperous, popular farmer (a great hunting friend of mine) was threatened, and had to bolt, his only possible offence being that he is a Protestant. His wife and children stayed to mind the farm, and then they also were ordered to leave. No doubt some blackguard wanted the place for himself.'

went into hiding. Their basic assumption may have been right. Nagle's killers did question him closely on his school and job, but apparently he was not young enough. At the other extreme, James Buttimer's protestation of old age was met with a bullet in the head.

Nor were the killers very scrupulous about who they shot. In some cases they did ask for people by name—Tom Nagle and William Bradfield—but in both these instances they simply shot someone else when their initial targets could not be found. In other cases they seemed intent on killing all the men in the house. 'Where are the men?' was the first question asked of Frances Buttimer.

There is no evidence whatsoever that any such conspiracy existed.[79] The Protestant community in Bandon and elsewhere in Cork had, with very few exceptions, been notably reticent during the Tan War and provided far more frustration than support to the Crown forces.[80] In fact, the murders of the Coffeys and others in 1921, for which local loyalists were blamed, appear to have been the work of an R.I.C. 'special squad' who worked undercover 'all dressed like old farmers'.[81]

The belief in the existence of a loyalist plot was real but it seems to have acted more as a spur to rage and hysteria than as the blueprint for the massacre. This does not mean that the victims were chosen entirely at random. All but one were members of the Church of Ireland.[82] Several, at least, were active in church affairs.[83] All were men—indeed, emphatically so. 'They always came for the men.'[84] The Dunmanway raiders told Clarina Buttimer that 'We don't want you'. 'I don't shoot women' said another to Frances Peyton in Ballineen. In most cases (as with Hannah O'Brien of Broad Lane), women—wives, sisters, aunts, and mothers—were the only ones to challenge the attackers and the ones left to hold the fort once the men had fled.

Apart from being uniformly Protestant and male, there was little to distinguish the victims from their neighbours, Protestant or Catholic. Almost all were natives of West Cork, where Buttimer, Bradfield, Jagoe, and Hornibrook were familiar names of long standing.[85] They came from a variety of stations

[79] That is to say, no evidence in British army, R.I.C., or I.R.A. records or memoirs, or in local memories, republican or Protestant. Furthermore, if the victims had been active in opposing the I.R.A. they or their relatives would almost certainly have mentioned it in their applications to the Irish Grants Committee or to the Southern Irish Loyalist Relief Fund.

[80] For an analysis of this point see the following chapter.

[81] Brewer, *The Royal Irish Constabulary*, 115. For further details of this Bandon constable's testimony, see Ch. 4.

[82] James Buttimer was a Methodist. James McCarthy of Dunmanway, whose house was fired upon, was Catholic but his life and livelihood were never threatened.

[83] Both Francis Fitzmaurice and David Gray were on the Fanlobbus parish (Dunmanway) select vestry, and Fitzmaurice was also a Synodsman and a Parochial Nominator (Fanlobbus Union Records, Vestry Minute Books, 1890–1965). Alice Gray managed the church choir (*Eagle*, 16 Dec. 1916). Unfortunately, the vestry books for the other relevant parishes have not survived.

[84] Interview with BF, 17 Apr. 1993.

[85] The exception was David Gray, originally from Cavan. Census returns show the others to have been born in Cork.

in life: businessmen, farmers, a lawyer, a curate, a post office clerk, a farm servant. None were poor save James Greenfield, and a few were quite prosperous. Most of the families concerned lived somewhere in between, in middling circumstances.[86]

Like the Hornibrooks, however, many of these men had been marked out as enemies long before April 1922. William Jagoe had previously been told by an I.R.A. officer that 'Truce or no truce, seven persons in Dunmanway were to be shot'. He believed that the shootings were a delayed reprisal for the notorious murder of a local priest, Canon Magner, by an Auxiliary policeman in December 1920, although this had shocked Protestants as much as Catholics. The town's Church of Ireland select vestry had (most unusually) publicly condemned the killing.[87] Jagoe himself had helped the police and it was also said that he had been 'getting too much trade' and had aroused commercial jealousy.[88] The Fitzmaurice brothers had been friendly with the Auxiliaries and were suspected of passing them information.[89] David Gray and William Morrison 'went out drinking with Black and Tans'.[90] Appy Bryan had been an ardent recruiter for the British army in the Great War, albeit one who was rather anxiously 'patriotic in every sense of the word, not a "shoneen"'.[91] James Buttimer, the only Methodist, was the only one to have departed from unionist orthodoxy. He had been a dedicated supporter of the Land League and of Home Rule.[92] Like most other long-time Redmondites, however, he had opposed the rise of Sinn Fein. He, Gray, and Fitzmaurice had also reportedly been 'very foolish' in not giving money to the I.R.A. arms fund.[93]

In Clonakilty, Tom Nagle was on a list of suspected informers (presumably by virtue of his court work), and was the caretaker and secretary of the Freemason's Lodge, a damning position in republican eyes.[94] He had, in fact, spent the day of his son's death hiding Masonic valuables before going on the run.[95] Richard Helen had been active in the voluntary recruitment effort, had been on good terms with the police, and helped them in February 1922 when their barracks was under threat of attack.[96] William Perrot had refused I.R.A. demands for money.[97]

---

[86] Most of these people lived in 'second class' houses (as categorized in the 1911 census) and most of the farmers had less than 100 acres of land (land valuation records).

[87] Jagoe statement; Fanlobbus Parish Vestry Minute Book, 17 Dec. 1920.

[88] Interview with BF.

[89] William Fitzmaurice statement. It should be noted that their names do not appear as such in either Auxiliary or I.R.A. intelligence documents. See Peadar O'Donovan, 'Why West Cork's Major Role was so Successful', *Southern Star Centenary Supplement*, 47, and 1st South. Div. list of suspected informers (MA, A/0897).　　　　　　　　　　　[90] Interviews with BF and BO.

[91] *Eagle*, 26 Feb. 1916. See also the same paper, 18 Dec. 1915, 28 Oct. 1916.

[92] *Freeman's Journal*, 28 Apr. 1922.

[93] Interview with AE.

[94] MA, A/0897. See also *Eagle*, 30 Dec. 1916. Among the victims, only William Fitzmaurice was a Freemason. Francis Fitzmaurice had been a member, but he resigned in 1913 (Grand Lodge of Freemasons Archives, Grand Lodge Register, 4th Series).　　　　　　　[95] Nagle statement.

[96] Helen statement.　　　　　　　　　　　　　　　　　　[97] Perrot statement.

Alex McKinley of Ballineen was another perceived 'friend' of the police. One local republican remembers him as being a 'precocious' loyalist.[98] Robert Howe was no stranger to political controversy, having been accused of slander in the 1914 county council election.[99] John and Henry Bradfield had a 'bad name' as members of a blacklisted family, two other Bradfield cousins having been shot in West Cork the previous year.[100] Captain Herbert Woods, himself a native of Bandon, belonged to a family as recalcitrant as the one he married into, which had received threats on its own account.[101] His being a retired officer was another strike against him. In fact, most of the victims had relatives in uniform, either army, navy, or police, making them additionally suspect.

Another connecting thread was land. Many Protestant farmers believed that this was the root cause of the attacks.[102] None of the victims was a landlord and most worked unremarkable family farms, but together they held much valuable property. Both Thomas Hornibrook and William Perrot were engaged in disputes with self-proclaimed evicted tenants, who emerged in great numbers throughout Ireland with the disappearance of the old police and courts.[103] Fitzmaurice's land agency was also the source of a great deal of friction, and not a few threats.[104] Most of this property was seized or sold under duress after the massacre.

David Gray, alone among those attacked, was called a 'Free Stater'. Opponents of the Treaty applied the term to any and all non-republicans in 1922, from unionists to pro-Treaty Volunteers.[105] It quickly became, like 'informer', a generic term of abuse; only a month after the treaty was signed the Skibbereen Town Tenants League were referring to one of their (Protestant) opponents as 'an Orange Free Stater'.[106] All of the victims were undoubtedly 'staters' in this sense. Cork Protestants generally felt betrayed by the British withdrawal but they certainly supported the Treaty settlement over the alternative. In Dunmanway, though, this passive acceptance of change may have been giving way to a more active involvement in the new politics. According to one neighbour:

What was happening was all these Protestants around town they were getting up a party between themselves and I suppose they would be talking about the way the country was and all this kind of thing . . . and they all had servants working and the servants used to be taking out the information to the I.R.A.[107]

---

[98] Interview with AH.   [99] *Eagle*, 1 Aug. 1914.

[100] Interview with BG.

[101] Edward Woods statement (CO 762/133); Report of Sec., Exec. Council, 9 Mar. 1923 (DOD A/8274).

[102] See Jack White (himself a Cork-born Congregationalist), *Minority Report: The Protestant Community in the Irish Republic* (Dublin, 1975), 85.

[103] A police report of a 3 May 1920 incident involving Perrot can be found in SPO, Crime Special Branch Records (Carton 5), Returns of Agrarian Outrages.

[104] *Morning Post*, 28 Apr. 1922.

[105] *Plain People* (9 Apr. 1922), for example, defined Free Staters as 'the Unionists, the ex-R.I.C., the retired British Army Colonels and Majors, the seonini, the time-servers, the place-hunters, the whole British officialdom that was behind the war against you'.

[106] *Star*, 14 Jan. 1922.   [107] Interview with BP.

Whether they did anything beyond talk we shall never know. Perhaps they were contemplating running or supporting an independent candidate on a pro-Treaty platform in the imminent 1922 general election. Whatever the case, no doubt the meetings once again raised the spectre of loyalist conspiracy.

Behind the killings lay a jumble of individual histories and possible motives. In the end, however, the fact of the victims' religion is inescapable. These men were shot because they were Protestant. No Catholic Free Staters, landlords, or 'spies' were shot or even shot at. The sectarian antagonism which drove this massacre was interwoven with political hysteria and local vendettas, but it was sectarian none the less. 'Our fellas took it out on the Protestants.'[108]

The gunmen, it may be inferred, did not seek merely to punish Protestants but to drive them out altogether. This was the message delivered to Henry Bradfield ('they would soon have the —— English out of the country') and to dozens of other Cork families in the days after the killings. These threatening letters and visitors all echoed the same refrain. Richard Godsil of Bandon was told 'you will be hunted out of the country, and all other Orange dogs with you'; the Ross brothers of Dunmanway were warned 'to run as other Protestant loyalists had run'; Samuel Baker of Timoleague heard that 'all Protestants would be shot and if I ever returned he or someone would do for me'; Arthur Andrews of Ballyhooly left after it was declared that 'we do not want an English dog here'.[109]

Within this rhetoric of ethnic intolerance can be detected the quasi-millenarian idea of a final reckoning of the ancient conflict between settlers and natives. To some republicans, revolution meant righting old wrongs, no matter how old, and establishing the republic entailed the reversal of the old order. The chief superintendent of the newly established Bandon Garda (Free State police) later blamed sectarian violence on the fact that 'the pre-Truce Volunteers who are now anti-Government are incensed at seeing their former enemies occupying the best farms'.[110] In an ominous speech given several weeks before the massacre, Sean Moylan, the North Cork Brigade commander and TD, declared that 'they would give a call to the fine fat Unionists with fine fat cows. The domestic enemy was most dangerous, and they would have to start fighting him now.'[111] During the Treaty debate he had declared that 'if there is a war of extermination on us . . . by God, no loyalist in North Cork will see its finish'.[112]

This vision of a world turned upside down was frequently implied and sometimes explicit. Joe Tanner, an assistant to Francis Fitzmaurice, was forced out of his house in Dunmanway by his next-door neighbour, who declared: 'as there is no law

---

[108]   Denis Lordan, quoted in O Broin, *Protestant Nationalists*, 177.
[109]   Statements by Richard Godsil (CO 762/34); William, John and Walter Ross (CO 762/180); Samuel Baker (CO 762/109) and Arthur Andrews (CO 904/104).
[110]   Chief Supt. to Comm., n.d. (Dept. of Justice, H5/1240).
[111]   *Weekly Examiner*, 8 Apr. 1922.
[112]   *Debate on the Treaty*, 146. In fairness, it should be noted that Moylan, despite his rhetoric, had nothing to do with the massacre and had the best record of any I.R.A. brigade commander in treating the Protestant minority.

in the country now I will have to get back what belonged to my forefathers.'[113] One Protestant businessman in Youghal reported that 'one of my employees actually informed me that his day was coming and that his name would yet be placed over the door of the business in place of my name'.[114] Many, like Mrs Stratford of Schull, were found 'unworthy of a place in the citizenship of the Irish Republic'.[115]

Such sentiments were by no means confined to Cork. Land disputes and sectarianism could be found anywhere, and the violence in Belfast cast a long shadow. In parts of north Tipperary: 'there is scarcely a Protestant family in the district which has escaped molestation . . . families have been warned to leave the neighbourhood. Altogether a state of terrorism exists.'[116] In Queen's County in late April, the Protestant tenants on one estate 'have been told "it is time they and their sort were out of the country." They were also told that they intended to take their Church for a Recreation Room and their School-house for their own children.'[117] The following report from Ballinasloe was written a month after the events of this chapter:

If the campaign against Protestants which has been carried on there since the end of last month is continued in similar intensity for a few weeks more, there will not be a Protestant left in the place. Presbyterians and members of the Church of Ireland, poor and well-to-do, old and young, widows and children, all alike have suffered in intimidation, persecution, and expulsion.

The campaign is carried out in the nighttime, by unnamed persons, who give no reason for their action. The system which usually is followed is, first, the despatch of an anonymous letter giving the recipient so many days, or hours, to clear out. If this notice is disregarded, bullets are fired at night through his windows, bombs are thrown at his house, or his house is burned down. In one case, an old man who had not left when ordered to do so was visited by a gang, who smashed everything in his cottage—every cup and every saucer, and then compelled him to leave the town, with his crippled son, the two of them destitute . . . The list of those proscribed is added to constantly, and every Protestant is simply waiting for his turn to come.[118]

The rise of religious antagonism had particular resonance in and around the Bandon valley, where the Protestant minority was comparatively large (16 per cent of the Bandon rural district was non-Catholic in 1911[119]) and where memories and myths were particularly acute. Castletown, Enniskeane, and Bandon itself were plantation settlements whose twentieth-century inhabitants—Catholic and Protestant—still shared a kind of frontier mentality. Kathleen Keyes

---

[113]   Joseph Tanner statement (CO 762/183).   [114]   John Brookes statement (CO 762/50).
[115]   O/C Cork 5 to Mrs Stratford, 20 Sept. 1921, in Mrs Stratford's statement (CO 762/97).
[116]   Revd Berrym to M.H.A., 10 June 1922 (H5/372).
[117]   'Land Agitation in the Queen's County', memo, 1922 (S566). See also *Morning Post*, 1 May 1922.
[118]   *Church of Ireland Gazette*, 16 June 1922. See also Hart, 'The Protestant Experience of Revolution in Southern Ireland'.
[119]   By comparison, Clonakilty's non-Catholic population was 10% and Dunmanway's 16%. For Cork as a whole, the figure was 8.5%, including British military personnel.

McDonnell, a republican activist, wrote of the 'notorious bigots' and 'traditional arrogance of the Bandon settlement' to whom 'a Bandon papist was fair game'. To McDonnell, a West Cork Protestant represented 'the foreigner'.[120] From the Protestant side, Tom, Nora and Lennox Robinson and Lionel Fleming (who grew up in Ballineen and Timoleague, respectively) have testified to the unbridgeable gap between the two communities and to the often anti-Catholic and militantly Low Church tone of West Cork congregations.[121]

Pre-revolutionary relations were amicable enough but beneath this surface ran deep undercurrents of hostility. The Home Rule crisis tapped into these, and by 1914 the Bandon resident magistrate was reporting that 'old sores have been re-opened during recent years and religious bigotry has been revived'.[122] The terrible bloodshed of 1920 and 1921 added incalculably to this burden of suspicion and tension. It is perhaps not surprising, therefore, that the reaction of the Catholic majority to the April massacre was so muted. Most I.R.A. members themselves disapproved of the killings (or at least did not approve of all of them) but did nothing. Some may have intervened to save men in their own areas but the organization as a whole utterly failed in its role as a police force. Coroners' juries occasionally expressed their sympathy with the relatives of the deceased, but they did not condemn the murders or mention the I.R.A.[123] Without exception, local councils each voted two resolutions of sympathy or condemnation, one for 'our Protestant fellow-countrymen', the other for the O'Neill family. The County Council specifically 'deplored' only O'Neill's death.[124] No one came to help the victims or their families when they were attacked or afterwards, and almost no one attended the funerals apart from local priests. In Dunmanway, only one undertaker was willing to help and he was boycotted and shot at.[125]

O'Neill's death, on the other hand, was greeted with highly vocal outrage. The jury at his inquest declared that he had been 'brutally murdered' by Woods 'in company with the two Hornibrooks, Thomas and Samuel'—in the circumstances, a clear incitement to reprisal.[126] Businesses in Bandon were closed in his honour, dances and the like were cancelled, and his funeral was largely attended. And, when it was all over, the same veil of silence was drawn over the continuing persecution and dispossession of the Protestants of West Cork. This atmosphere of fear and polarization provided the communal context for the massacre. One could not have taken place without the other. Protestants had become 'fair game' because they were seen as outsiders and enemies, not just by the I.R.A. but by a large segment of the Catholic population as well.

[120] McDonnell, *There is a Bridge*, 27, 39, 65, 66. My copy of this book contains an author's dedication which refers to 'Orange Bandon—the Derry of the South'.

[121] Robinson, Robinson, and Dorman, *Three Homes* and Fleming, *Head or Harp*. Also revealing is George Bennett's highly popular *History of Bandon*.

[122] Bandon RM Report, 1914 (CO 904/227). See also *Constitution*, 9 June 1914; *Eagle*, 20 June 1914.   [123] *Irish Times*, 1, 2 May 1922.

[124] *Constitution*, 29 Apr., 5 May 1922.   [125] John Nyhan statement (CO 762/192).

[126] *Eagle*, 6 May 1922.

These were revenge killings on many levels. Michael O'Neill's death provided the spark, inflamed by anger over the Belfast pogroms, but the desire for vengeance went further back—years, in the case of Walter Leo Murphy, the Coffeys, Canon Magner, or other unrequited betrayals and murders, a generation or more in the case of evicted or disgruntled tenants or those who resented the 'notorious bigotry' of the Bandon settlement. Some or all of these grievances were undoubtedly brought into play on those late April nights.

The shooting at Ballygroman also crystallized republican fears of Orange and British (and possibly Free State) intrigue. The minority population of West Cork were seen not only as past enemies and current undesirables but also as a future fifth column in the struggle which many I.R.A. men saw coming. Perhaps they agreed with Sean Moylan that the 'domestic enemy' had to be dealt with first.

Without further information it is not possible to sort all these possible motives into a coherent geneaology of the massacre. And indeed, it may be doubted whether such a clear rationale ever existed. These were angry and frightened young men acting on impulse and, in some cases at least, alcohol.[127] In their view Protestant unionists were traitors. Their status was codified in the political language—or mythology—of the day in terms such as: landlord, land-grabber, loyalist, imperialist, Orangeman, Freemason, Free Stater, spy, and informer.[128] These blanket categories made the victims' individual identities—their ages and helplessness—irrelevant. All were enemies. All were guilty. If the suspected informer or conspirator could not be found, his son, brother, or work-man was killed. Where possible, all the men were killed. We cannot reach a final answer to the question of who the killers thought they were killing, but the answer surely lies among this deadly collection of labels and stereotypes.

In the course of an interview with an I.R.A. veteran in West Cork, I asked him about the events of April 1922, some of which had taken place in his neighbour-hood. He astonished me by saying that one of the killings had occurred in that very house, and pointed to the spot where the man had been shot (the person I spoke to had bought the house a few years later, after it had fallen into disre-pair). He assured me that he had nothing to do with the murders and had no idea of who was responsible. 'Twas a terrible thing,' he agreed, 'but those were the times we were living in.' He insisted that the I.R.A. had not persecuted

---

[127] Robert Nagle's attackers were apparently drunk. One I.R.A. informant, AE, felt that the indiscipline and wildness (including heavy drinking) of much of the post-Truce I.R.A. were partly to blame for the massacre. The fact that the killings took place so late and were accompanied—in Ballineen, Clonakilty, and Dunmanway—by gunfire in the streets is also suggestive.

[128] The following speech, reported in *Ireland Over All*, 7 Apr. 1922 (a Cork journal which lasted one issue), is a good example of this code. The speaker is a republican complaining that the revised electoral register left out many I.R.A. names: 'If the election for Cork City and County be fought on such a register, it means that from 15,000 to 20,000 of the best Irish of Cork won't be able to record a vote, whereas every Unionist, Freemason, Orangeman, spy and informer is on the Register and will go to the polls and kill the Republic for which Cork and its people have suffered so much.' He never directly mentions Protestants, but few of his listeners could have mistaken his meaning.

Protestants—'we had nothing against them'—and that the massacre was the product of anarchy, not republicanism.

I was struck by the symbolic reversal involved in the former guerrilla living in the grand old *ancien régime* home, and by his denial of what this suggested: that the nationalist revolution had also been a sectarian one. In fact, he showed uncommon candour. Most of my Cork interviewees refused to admit, or remember, that *any* such killings had taken place.

The April massacre is as unknown as the Kilmichael ambush is celebrated, yet one is as important as the other to an understanding of the Cork I.R.A. Nor can the murders be relegated to the fringes of the revolution or described as an isolated event. They were as much a part of the reality of violence as the killings at Kilmichael. The patterns of perception and victimization they reveal are of a piece with the whole revolution. These deaths can be seen as the culmination of a long process of social definition which produced both the heroes of Kilmichael and the victims of the April massacre. The identity of the former cannot be fully understood without the latter. How the Volunteers defined their enemies—in the shape of 'spies' and 'informers'—is the subject of the concluding chapter.

13

Spies and Informers

> And now my song is ended
> I have one word to say
> To hell with every traitor
> Who gives the show away
> May every son of Cromwell
> Be banished from our shore
> And may God preserve our rebel boys
> To make Ireland free once more.
> ('Where the Dripsey River Flow')[1]

Revenge
(Written on the house of a dead 'spy', Mar. 1921)[2]

The Irish Civil War, as defined by historical and common usage, began in June 1922 and was fought between the I.R.A. and the Free State. The actual record of violence invites us to question this singular definition.[3] Even excluding policemen, the Cork I.R.A. killed nearly twice as many Irish men and women before July 1922 than after and burned three times as many homes. These were the victims of a second, unacknowledged civil war: the war against spies and informers.

In the mythology of the Irish revolution, the heroic figure of 'the rebel' had as his archetypal enemy—and polar opposite—the informer (a symbol of evil since the days of penal laws and priest-hunters). Where the young men of the I.R.A. were 'sober, clean-living [and] self-respecting', informers were typically assumed to be degraded, drunken, even misshapen. Such was their portrayal in fiction, reminiscence, and history. Liam O'Flaherty's Gypo Nolan and Frank O'Connor's Jumbo Geany[4] had their real-life counterpart in 'Monkey Mac', a Cork city informer so notorious he became a sort of folk anti-hero. Every self-respecting city guerrilla had his own story about this 'well-known ne'er-do-well' who earned his nickname from being 'small, low sized and a bit hunched', and

---

[1] UCD, Dept. of Folklore, Schools MS 345, 203. The song commemorates the disastrous I.R.A. ambush at Dripsey in January 1921. The author is unknown.

[2] The victim was John Cathcart of Youghal. *Irish Times*, 26 May 1921.

[3] See the statistics presented in Chs. 3, 4, and 5.

[4] See Liam O'Flaherty, *The Informer* (London, 1925) and Frank O'Connor, 'Jumbo's Wife' in *Guests of the Nation*. On the latter, see also Lankford, *The Hope and the Sadness*, 261.

from his reputation as a petty thief.[5] As the stories multiplied, he acquired a supernatural aura: 'Who, or what, he was I never knew . . . but when he fired, left or right, he never missed his mark. None of the city businessmen would ever look at him, because legend had it that if you did he . . . would have plugged you.'[6]

Nowhere is this opposition of images clearer than in accounts of 'the heroic fight at Clonmult' in 1921. The East Cork flying column was the embodiment of the Volunteer ideal: 'strong, healthy, clean-living boys, they revelled in the martial exercises and lectures.'[7] Their 'Judas-like' betrayer, on the other hand, a 'degenerate' and a 'tramp', 'held out a grimy hand for blood money'.[8] The conflict described is not merely one of differing loyalties, but of moral absolutes.

Previous chapters have examined how I.R.A. men viewed themselves and the social attitudes and realities that lay behind these perceptions. Yet this sense of identity was reflected as much in their enemies, real and imagined, as in their comrades. What did it mean to call someone an informer? Who was suspected, who actually informed, and who paid the price?

I interviewed over a dozen I.R.A. men but I only ever met one 'informer', and that by chance. I was in a pub in North Cork when one of my companions pointed to a middle-aged man and announced, with considerable if surreptitious venom: 'here comes the informer now.' I was introduced to a pleasant man who agreed that there was 'a lot of history' in the town to be studied but who was far too young to have even been alive in the 1920s. Oh yes, I was told afterwards, it was his father who had been the informer. They were not sure what he had done to warrant the charge, but 'the informer' was what he had been called behind his back ever after, and 'the informer' his son remained.[9] If rumour and reputation proved so virulent after seventy years, what must it have been like in the midst of guerrilla war?

To be branded a spy or informer in revolutionary Cork was to be threatened with the loss of one's home, livelihood, and life. Accused informers were subject not only to the attentions of the I.R.A. but also to those of their neighbours. Condemned informers could become outcasts within their own communities, even within their own families: 'I am sorry to say or think I had a spy belong to me if I only knew he was one I would have shot him myself'; 'As his mother I would be one of the first to banish him out of the way.'[10]

---

    [5] Con Neenan (O'Malley Papers, P17b/112). See also Con Neenan's anonymous account in the O'Donoghue Papers (MS 31, 337); Eamon Enright (O'Malley Papers, P17b/103), Sean Culhane (P17b/108) and Sean Hendrick (P17b/111). For an example of his public notoriety, see O'Rahilly to Barry Egan, 13 Oct. 1921 (CAI, Egan Papers, U404).
    [6] Clarke, *She Came of Decent People*, 46.
    [7] Padraig O Ciosain, 'The Heroic Fight at Clonmult', in *Rebel Cork's Fighting Story*, 191.
    [8] Ibid. 190; Marjorie M. Aherne, MS Account of Clonmult (Co. Cork Museum, G106).
    [9] In another town in West Cork I had a house pointed out to me as 'the informer's house', despite the fact that 'the informer' had left it to his children decades before.
    [10] Mrs Murphy to M/D, 11 Apr. 1922 (MA, A/0535); Mrs O'Brien to Michael Collins, 19 June 1922 (A/0649).

Henry Ginn of Castlelyons was 'openly and frequently accused . . . of being a British government spy'. He was boycotted, lost his business, and was forced to leave the county. In Toormore, Sam Baylie was 'hooted and hunted when met on the road and men gathered round my house night after night and hooted me, and when going to Church myself and my wife were repeatedly hooted'. He lost his dog (poisoned), his barn (burned), his windows (smashed), and most of his crops. Daniel Donoghue of Leap abandoned his home and went into hiding in 1921 after having a poster with the word 'Traitor' nailed to his gate. James Noonan of Cork city was booed by neighbours going to and from work and received threatening letters. Rita Curran, also of the city, was 'persistently insulted and taunted by my former friends and . . . had been stopped in the street by a man who held a revolver to my head and told me to leave the country at once'. She and her family left in 1922. Jeremy Kingston of Clonakilty had signs 'put on my land to the effect that no spy or traitor would live here' and was boycotted and repeatedly robbed. James Hogan of Killeagh had his store picketed by Volunteers who harassed his customers, cut the axles on his carts, and forced his daughter (a reputed spy) to leave the country. William Brady of Cobh lost his job and saw his family 'hooted and shouted' in the streets. Sam Beamish of Drimoleague was kidnapped and boycotted, and 'called a spy and an Orangeman and told I should clear out dead or alive and go to the Orangemen or over to England'. Michael Condon of Youghal was taunted and stoned by schoolboys and was also forced to go on the run from the I.R.A. In the same town, Pat Lynass 'was boycotted by everybody concerned with the I.R.A., employers were afraid to give me work; I was spat at in the streets and treated worse than a dog.'[11] Once acquired, this reputation usually proved unshakeable. One 'informer' returned to his West Cork home after the Treaty 'but no one would ever speak to him, not even the children of the place'.[12]

For hundreds of 'spies' and 'informers', however, the matter was resolved much sooner—by flight, expulsion, or, as in the case of Christy O'Sullivan of Blarney Street, by death: 'Very few of his neighbours would speak to him. The children in the street were often heard shouting "spy" after him as he passed on his way to work, and he was haunted by the conviction that he would be murdered.'[13] He was found shot to death on 27 May 1921.

O'Sullivan's death was one among many. Scores of bodies were dumped in fields, lanes, or ditches tagged with messages like 'Spies and informers beware' or 'Convicted spy'. Scores of others simply disappeared; kidnapped, shot, and secretly buried in some bog or graveyard.[14] At least 204 civilians were deliberately

---

[11] Statements of Henry Ginn (CO 762/145); Samuel Baylie (/185); Daniel Donoghue (/30); James Noonan (/158); Rita Curran (/120); Jeremy Kingston (/133); James Hogan (/166); William Brady (/174); Samuel Beamish (/193); Michael Condon (/164); Pat Lynass (/73).

[12] Flor Begley (O'Malley Papers, P17b/111).   [13] *Irish Times*, 6 June 1921.

[14] Most areas had their own clandestine burial grounds. One such site in Rylane parish was known as 'the death chamber' or 'the cottage'. ' "He's for the cottage", we'd say among ourselves, and this meant that he was for execution.' Frank Busteed (O'Malley Papers, P17b/112).

shot by the I.R.A. in Cork in the course of the revolution, the vast majority of whom were alleged to be spies or informers.[15]

It was a matter of life and death to the guerrillas as well. Their survival and the success of their ambushes depended upon their opponents not knowing who or where they were, and therefore upon the support and silence of their communities. The men who died at Broad Lane, Clogheen, and Clonmult, and many more besides, had all been given away by informers. In the midst of this pervasive fear of betrayal any suspicion could have deadly consequences.

To understand where these suspicions led, we must turn first to the term 'informer' itself. Calling someone an informer was in fact a standard rhetorical weapon in all manner of disputes—factional,[16] agrarian,[17] labour,[18] domestic,[19] or political[20]—regardless of revolution. It was one among many nationalist terms of abuse and was used interchangeably with similar fighting words like 'grabber', 'shoneen', 'souper', 'tyrant', or 'emergency man'. In 1913, for example, the priest at Farelton (near Macroom) tried to stop night dances in his parish. In response, 'bands of young men and women . . . began parading at night the public roads, shouting "informers" and "soupers" outside any houses of persons supposed to be sympathizers of the Priests'.[21] In a 1921 court case in Union Hall, a woman referred to one of her opponents in a dispute over a licensed premises as a 'tyrant' and another as a 'grabber', 'a Belfast Orange Protestant' and an 'informer'.[22]

The Cork I.R.A. inherited this vocabulary with all its variety of meanings and used it in the same spirit, to cover a multitude of counter-revolutionary sins. When Robert Beamish of Brade took his neighbour to court over a disputed shotgun in 1918, he was denounced as an informer and had his horse stabbed.[23] In Macroom district in 1919 a man who let his threshing machine to the boycotted Bowen-Colthurst family was called 'an English spy in our midst', while a group of farmers who claimed exemption from a compensation judgment were labelled 'self-confessed spies and informers'.[24] Another large category of sinners were those people who refused I.R.A. demands for money or who refused to sign anti-conscription or pro-republican petitions.[25]

---

[15]   This does not include a 'spy' shot by Cork gunmen in New York city in 1922, a (reported) suicide in I.R.A. custody in Cobh, or a man who was stabbed to death in Cork city. For the sources of this figure, see the Appendix. I have counted about twelve further unconfirmed disappearances.
    [16]   See CI Monthly Report, East Galway, May 1918 (CO 904/106).
[17]   See *Irish Times*, 3 May 1920; 16 Apr., 26 May 1921.   [18]   See ibid. 29 May 1920.
[19]   See *Examiner*, 8 Dec. 1919, 31 May 1921; *Irish Times*, 14 Apr. 1921.
[20]   See *Irish Times*, 1 July 1920.
[21]   CI Monthly Report, West Cork, Jan. 1913 (CO 904/89).
[22]   Hannah Kingston to Registrar, 27 Dec. 1921 (Dail Eireann Courts Commission, DE 14/5). See also *Eagle*, 20 July 1918.   [23]   *Eagle*, 20 July 1918.
[24]   *Examiner*, 29 Sept. 1919.
[25]   See the statements of Walter Hailes (CO 762/7), Dan Donoghue (/30), John Coleman (/77), Jeremy Kingston (/133), Michael Condon (/164), and Samuel Baylie (/185), and the *Eagle*, 8, 29 Jan. 1921.

Any contact with the police—and later the army—could be grounds for the darkest suspicions. As early as December 1918, notices were being posted in Ballyvourney warning that 'Anyone talking to the police will be shot dead on the spot' (in this case signed 'Mike O'Leary, V.C.', a triumph of local pride over ideological purity).[26] Such warnings reappeared frequently thereafter.[27] This proscription was rapidly extended to include police and army recruits[28] and anyone who served, supplied, or worked for the constabulary or the army, to anyone who entertained them socially and even, by 1921, to those who wrote letters to friends or relatives in the police or armed forces.[29] As the mails had to run the gauntlet of I.R.A. censors, all correspondence was liable to be opened and any political or personal comments could be risky.[30] Those who were caught making derogatory comments about the I.R.A.—a not infrequent occurrence— could be severely punished. Sam Beamish wrote such a letter in April 1922 and had its contents 'thrown in my face' when it was intercepted. 'From that onwards I was called a Spy and an Orangeman.'[31] Mrs Williamson of Mallow was told that 'it is you and your equals can write about other people but remember Belfast and West Cork it wont be tolerated much longer'.[32] Mrs Stratford of Schull received the following in June 1921:

As a result of a statement made by you in a letter written to a friend of yours in England, and captured by us in the mails, some time ago, we deem it necessary for us to order you to leave the country. We find you unworthy of a place in the citizenship of the Irish Republic.[33]

Mrs Stratford and her husband duly left two days later.

In January 1922 the brigades of the 1st Southern Division were ordered to compile lists of 'all persons guilty of offenses against the Nation and the Army during hostilities and to date, and of all persons suspected of having assisted the enemy during the same period'.[34] Although many battalions did not respond,[35] this extraordinary document provides a systematic index of offenders.

Of the 157 Cork suspects named, only 56 (or 36 per cent) were directly charged with giving information to the authorities. Of the remainder, 45 (29 per

---

[26] *Examiner*, 19 Dec. 1918. O'Leary, a local man, was a British war hero and recruiting campaigner.

[27] See Liam Lynch to O/C 2nd Bn., Cork 2, 9 Apr. 1921 (Lankford Papers).

[28] In February 1920, for example, a Mallow R.I.C. recruit and the sexton of his church were sent letters accusing them of being spies. CI Monthly Report, East Cork, Feb. 1920 (CO 904/116).

[29] See the statements of Dan Donoghue and John Long (CO 762/30, 187).

[30] With typical literary ingenuity, Edith Somerville and her family wrote in a code of their own devising or else wrote in French. See Edith Somerville to Col. John Somerville, 17 July 1922 (Somerville and Ross Papers, Lot 877). See also Lot 889.

[31] Samuel Beamish statement (CO 762/193).

[32] 'Warner' to Mrs Williamson, 2 May 1922 (Lankford Papers, U169).

[33] Edward Wingfield-Stratford statement (CO 762/97). For further cases, see HQ 1st South. Div. to O/C Cork 5, 13 Sept. 1922 and Adj. Cork 5 to I/O 1st South. Div., 15 Nov. 1922 (MA, A/0991/4).   [34] I/O Cork 4 to O/C 5th Bn., 31 Jan. 1922 (Lankford Papers, U169).

[35] Including those of Cork city, Bandon, Macroom, Ballyvourney, Kanturk, and Newmarket.

cent) had simply been 'friendly' with the enemy in one way or another, including many girls who were keeping company with policemen or soldiers. Here can be detected both moral outrage—such women were 'fast', 'more or less a prostitute' or a 'bad influence on other girls'—and jealousy. A Miss Sullivan of Castletownbere, who declared that the men of the I.R.A. could not compare with those of the Auxiliaries, was described as 'Good looking. Dreamy eyes.'[36]

The rest were guilty of a wide variety of supposed crimes. Some had refused to give up their guns or subscribe to the Dail Loan or the I.R.A. arms fund. Some were related to, or seen in the company of, other suspects and some had relatives in the R.I.C. Others had been given curfew passes by the army or had worked for the police or army. Yet others had insulted the I.R.A. Two had done 'immense damage' to the I.R.A.'s standing in their communities because of their public opposition to the revolution. One had cheered British troops; another had shouted 'Up the King'. A few had been named by other 'informers' in their confessions. Some suspects were simply described as 'hostile' or 'suspect'.

The real 'offences against the Nation and the Army' in most of these cases, it may be suggested, were non-cooperation and nonconformity.[37] Many suspects were guilty only by association. These were people, as one anonymous letter writer to the *Cork Examiner* put it, 'whose only crime is that they do not see eye to eye with Sinn Fein on everything'.[38]

I.R.A. shootings followed the same pattern. Almost all victims were officially described as spies or informers but in practice this could mean anything.[39] Being friendly or being seen with a policeman got a great many people killed. More than one body was found with a note attached saying 'This is the penalty for all those who associate with the Auxies, Black and Tans, and the R.I.C.'[40] William Vanston of Douglas and William Nolan of the city were shot after applying to join the R.I.C., as were Mick Sullivan of High Street and Thomas Walsh of Glashabee after enlisting in the army.[41] John Hawkes of Crowley's Lane, Dan McCarthy of Midleton, and Robert Eady had been seen entering police or military barracks.[42] John O'Leary of Beacock Lane, John Good of Barrackton, Edward Hawkins of Broad Street, and Christy O'Sullivan of Blarney Street were all employed in Victoria barracks.[43] Leo McMahon of St Luke's worked in the War Pensions Office.[44] In Youghal, Tom Collins and Pat Lynass were members

---

[36] MA, A/0897. See also O/C 1st Bn. to Adj. Cork 4, 9 Dec. 1921 on the case of a 'peeler-hunter' (A/0668).

[37] 'It was as much as a man's life was worth to utter a discordant note, let alone give information to the enemy.' Seamus O'Connor, *Tomorrow Was Another Day* (Dun Laoire, 1970, 1987), 38.

[38] *Examiner*, 14 Feb. 1919.

[39] The Cork Republican Police (in effect an extension of the I.R.A.) were told in 1922 that 'those shot during the war [are] not to be inquired into as they are all *Spies*'. O/C Cork 1 IRP memo, n.d. (MA, A/0649).   [40] *Examiner*, 18 Mar. 1921.

[41] Military Inquiry (WO 35/160); *Examiner*, 23 Feb. 1921.

[42] *Examiner* and *Irish Times*, 14 Oct. 1920; *Eagle*, 16 Apr. 1921. Hawkes described his experiences in a fascinating statement (CO 904/168).   [43] *Examiner*, 14 Feb., 11 Mar. 1921.

[44] Ibid. 20 May 1921.

of the Comrades of the Great War band and played at military dances.[45] Several victims had worked for accused spies and two others were killed because they had spent so long in I.R.A. captivity they 'knew too much'.[46] Cork units also borrowed the two favourite excuses of police and military killers. Leo Corby of Castletownroche was killed because he 'failed to halt' and Michael O'Keefe of Carrigtwohill was shot while trying to escape.[47]

Open loyalty to Britain or opposition to the I.R.A. could carry the death penalty. Major J. B. O'Connor and Alfred Reilly, both resident in city suburbs, appear to have been shot because they refused to resign as justices of the peace.[48] Reilly's murder seemed particularly puzzling in light of his efforts to free Terence MacSwiney.[49] Three members of the *Cork Examiner* staff were gunned down after their paper had refused various I.R.A. demands.[50] Joseph Bolster of Banteer died for his refusal to subscribe to the railway strikers' fund.[51] Sam Shannon of Lissaclarig was executed for helping his father resist an arms raid.[52] Other political opponents who suffered the 'extreme penalty' included Tom Downing, the head of an ex-servicemen's organization in the city,[53] and Francis Sullivan of Rosscarbery, the president of a stubbornly anti-republican branch of the Irish Land and Labour Association.[54] David Fitzgibbon of Liscarroll 'was the only member of his family who refused to have anything to do with the I.R.A. and for that reason alone he was considered "in the way". He was never a spy but just a man who minded his own business.'[55]

The pursuit of informers led to vendettas against whole families like the Goods, Bradfields, Cotters, Sweetnams, Hornibrooks, Beales, Blemins, and Woods. These were 'bad names'. 'They had their knife in those Goods' in West Cork, and anyone by that name was in danger.[56] A Bradfield who paid for some cattle by cheque was told (half-jokingly) 'your name isn't very good anyway', meaning that he might be dead before it was cashed.[57] One killing easily led to another and one suspected informer could condemn the rest of his or her family. Wives and children were often ordered out of the country after a husband or father was shot.

Many I.R.A. and other witnesses have reported cases of people being falsely accused of informing out of 'local spite', because of some feud or grievance.[58] A

[45] Military Inquiry (WO 35/147A); Pat Lynass statement.
[46] See Mick Leahy (O'Malley Papers, P17b/108); O'Riordan, *Kiskeam Versus the Empire*, 102.
[47] Military Inquiry (WO 35/148); Mick Leahy (O'Malley Papers, P17b/108).
[48] *Examiner*, 10 Feb., 12 July 1921; Clarke, *She Came of Decent People*, 53.
[49] *Christian Advocate*, 11, 18 Feb. 1921.   [50] *Examiner*, 24 May 1921.
[51] CI Monthly Report, East Cork, Aug. 1920 (CO 904/112).
[52] *Examiner*, 13 Sept. 1920.   [53] Ibid. 27 Nov. 1920.
[54] See the *Star*, 26 Apr. 1918.
[55] Testimony of Lt. F. C. Sherwood, Kerry Bde. Intell. Officer (Military Court of Inquiry, WO 35/150): 'it is a favourite thing for the I.R.A. at present to murder innocent people, so as to advertise their "Intelligence" regarding spies.'   [56] Interview with BG.
[57] Interview with BY.
[58] See Ryan, *Tom Barry Story*, 53; George Power (O'Malley Papers, P17b/100); Frank Busteed (P17b/112); Jim Bromagh (P17b/123).

large number of killings seem to have had an agrarian subtext.[59] Among those shot were two reputed 'grabbers', three land agents, two bailiffs, and two solicitors and a law clerk involved in land claims. Almost all accused landowners had their property confiscated.

Cork I.R.A. officers routinely insisted that those executed were proven, convicted traitors. 'We were careful that before a spy was shot it had to be a definite case of spying.'[60] Some were indeed 'guilty', if only by I.R.A. standards. Tom Connell and Matthew Sweetnam did identify I.R.A. arms fund collectors in court. Mary Lindsay did help give away the Dripsey ambush. The two Tom Bradfields (cousins) were 'guilty of attempting' or 'intending'[61] to help the army (although they were tricked into doing it). Such 'definite cases' were still exceptional.[62] In reality, on the run and afraid for their lives, the guerrillas usually acted on their own suspicions and 'in a panic', just as in the massacre of April 1922.[63] In the early months of 1921, for example, a series of British intelligence successes under martial law prompted a wave of I.R.A. reprisals against suspected spies. However, according to the Irish Command, 'in every case but one the person murdered had given no information'.[64] British authorities agreed that the guerrillas' war on informers was effective, but because of its 'sheer brutality', not its accuracy. 'There were very many cases where persons were shot simply because they might have given information.'[65] Not for nothing did the Cork brigades acquire a reputation within the I.R.A. for shooting first and asking questions later.[66]

The summaries of evidence given for some of the suspects on the January 1922 list are telling: 'From personal observation, I consider this person guilty in the first degree'; 'Any Volunteer called on could verify this'; 'I am perfectly confident of this woman's guilt, although I have no direct evidence against her other than suspicion'; 'Although it has been hard to trace any information given

[59]   See White, *Minority Report*, 85.
[60]   Sean Culhane (O'Malley Papers, P17b/108). See also Deasy, *Towards Ireland Free*, 200 and Barry, *Guerilla Days*, 106–7. The I.R.A.'s General Order No. 20 (20 Apr. 1921) stated that 'a convicted spy shall not be executed until his conviction and sentence have been ratified by the Brigade Commandant concerned' and that inconclusive evidence 'shall, before the arrest of the suspected person, be placed before a Court of Inquiry'. I.R.A. General Orders [New Series] (Boston Public Library).
[61]   These were the words used by the I.R.A., as quoted in the *Belfast News-Letter*, 26 Jan., 3 Feb. 1921.
[62]   For Sweetnam and Connell, see the *Eagle*, 8 Jan., 26 Feb., 9 Apr. 1921; *Examiner*, 3 Jan. 1921. For Mrs Lindsay, see below.
[63]   Con Leddy (O'Malley papers, P17b/123). See also Mick Leahy (/108), Jack Clifford, and Sean Carroll (/130).
[64]   'In that one case the murdered man was an agent known to be untrustworthy.' *Record of the Rebellion*, ii. 12 (IWM, Sir Hugh Jeudwine Papers).
[65]   Ibid. ii. 25; i. 33, 38. See also *6th Division History*, 97 (Strickland Papers). Among those whom the British authorities declared to be innocent were David Fitzgibbon, Stephen O'Callaghan (CI Monthly Report, East Cork, Apr. 1921 (CO 904/115)), Pat Sheehan, and John Sullivan (CI Monthly Report, East Cork, June 1921).
[66]   I/O 1st South. Div. to C/S, 1 June 1921 (Mulcahy Papers, P7/A/20).

by him, I have no hesitation in stating . . . '. The equation of suspicion with guilt is evident even from the composition of such lists. The 1st Southern Division document combined 'all persons guilty of offenses [and] all persons suspected'. Another, drawn up by the West Cork Brigade in July 1921, referred to 'enemy agents and other suspects'.[67] Once these lists were assembled and circulated, they acquired a permanence and authority of their own.

Two examples serve to illustrate how easily suspicion became 'guilt'. In the case of James Fehilly of Bandon, an ex-soldier threatened, expelled, and nearly shot, the I.R.A. officer responsible explained that: 'My policy was that those who were not for us at the time were against us, and as I had been informed Fehilly was in touch with the enemy, I naturally presumed he was hostile, and even suspected him of giving information to the enemy.'[68]

'I had been informed . . . I naturally presumed . . . and even suspected.' The absence of any real evidence is clear. The adjutant of the West Cork Brigade added that Fehilly and his wife 'both seem to be of the type that proved a constant menace to the National movement'. Kate Fehilly responded that 'there is no such thing as a direct charge and trial to give him an opportunity to defend himself'.[69]

A similar line of reasoning was followed in the case of Henry Forde, also of Bandon, also threatened and expelled: 'It is believed that he was a member of the Anti-Sinn Fein gang which was undoubtedly an off-shoot of the Orange Society of which he is a member . . . I think he is one of those better out of the Country for the Country's good.'[70]

In other words, as a member of the Orange lodge, Forde was automatically guilty of conspiring against the republic. In fact the only evidence the brigade intelligence officer could come up with was that Forde was 'very loyal'. Both Forde and Fehilly were condemned by virtue of being the wrong 'type'.

This idea that their enemies belonged to certain recognizable types was common throughout the I.R.A., just as it was within the Crown forces. Tom Barry said that 'we knew that men were being sold, and we knew that there were several types of spies and informers'.[71] Informers 'were generally big landlords, gombeen men and all these types . . . quite a number of what was called the Ascendency were informers'. A large number of these were Protestants although, Barry hastened to add, 'there were, of course, an equal number of Catholics'. Spies, on the other hand, 'were generally paid

[67]   I/O Cork 3 report, July 1921 (Mulcahy Papers, P7/A/7).
[68]   Vice O/C 2nd Bn., Cork 3 Report (MA, A/0659).
[69]   Kate Fehilly to Michael Collins, 20 Jan. 1922 (A/0649).
[70]   Cork 3 Report, 4 Mar. 1922 (MA, A/0960). For Forde's career as an officer of the order, see the county Grand Lodge returns in the Report of the Proceedings of the Grand Orange Lodge of Ireland at the General Half-Yearly Meeting, 1891–1909 (Grand Orange Lodge of Ireland Archives). According to these and other records, the Cork lodges in Bandon and the city appear to have lost contact with the Grand Lodge by 1920.
[71]   O'Mahony interview (tape in possession of George O'Mahony).

scoundrels', 'invariably the most vicious and degraded of the population'[72] (meaning ex-soldiers in particular[73]). Former army or navy officers constituted yet another dangerous 'type'.

The case of Henry Forde also demonstrates the unfailing I.R.A. belief in conspiracy theories. Opposition implied intrigue. Wherever the guerrillas looked they saw loyalist subversion and secret societies: in the Bandon valley, Fermoy, Skibbereen, Schull, Youghal, and Cork city, in Masonic and Orange lodges, the Post Office, the YMCA,[74] county clubs, and even some Church of Ireland congregations.[75] By extension, all members of these organizations (like Forde) became suspect. The Freemasons, those perennial objects of Catholic and nationalist paranoia, were especially feared.[76] One Volunteer involved in wrecking a lodge in West Cork still vividly remembers the sense of transgression and curiosity with which they entered the building. 'It had the queerest things in it.'[77] Identifying and suppressing masonic conspirators became a near-obsession for guerrillas all over Ireland. Intelligence officers compiled membership lists, lodges were attacked and burned, and members were threatened and killed.[78]

Nearly every executed 'spy' was believed, either before or after the fact, to be connected to one or another of these purported 'Anti-Sinn Fein Societies'.[79] The title did exist, but as a cover for Black and Tan reprisal squads, not for any counter-revolutionary underground. The Bandon valley 'Anti-Sinn Fein Society', for example, was the work of an undercover police squad.[80] The belief in a Cork city society, headed by a cabal of Protestant and Masonic businessmen, can be traced in part to two extraordinary newspaper interviews given by General Strickland in January 1921, in which he described the improvement in intelligence under martial law and openly discussed his attempts to recruit 'leading people' for a 'Citizens Committee' to assist in intelligence work. These

---

[72] RTE interview, 1980 (tape in possession of Donal O'Donovan).

[73] See Barry, *Guerilla Days*, 107–8.

[74] Martin Corry, Mick Murphy, and Con Neenan (O'Malley Papers, P17b/112); Cork YMCA general committee minute book, 22 June 1921 (Cork YMCA Records). See also Louth No. 2 Bn. Intell. Report, July 1921 (Mulcahy Papers, P7/A/13).

[75] See Flor Begley (O'Malley Papers, P17b/111); Barry, *Guerilla Days*, 111; Somerville-Large, *Cappaghglass*, 343.

[76] On the Masonic peril, see Florence O'Donoghue (O'Malley Papers, P17b/96); O/C 1st South. Div. to C/S, 4 May 1921 (Mulcahy Papers, P7/A/20); 1st South. Div. Intell. Report, 15 Nov. 1921 (O'Donoghue Papers, MS 31, 207); D/I Cork 2 to O/C 2nd Bn., 11 Apr. 1921 (Lankford Papers, U169). One of many lists of Masons compiled by the I.R.A. can be found in the O'Donoghue Papers, MS 31,200.   [77] Interview with AG.

[78] Interview with AK. See also the Annual Reports of the Grand Lodge of Freemasons of Ireland, 1920–3 (Grand Lodge Archives) and *History and Dedication Ceremony of Bandon Masonic Lodge 84* (Cork, 1926).

[79] See Stan Barry (O'Malley Papers, P17b/95); George Power (/100); Eamon Enright (/103); P. O'Reilly (/107); Mick Murphy, Con Neenan, Jamie Minihan (/112); Jim Bromagh (/124).

[80] For the I.R.A. version, see Deasy, *Towards Ireland Free*, 200 and O Broin, *Protestant Nationalists*, 177. For police operations, see Brewer, *The Royal Irish Constabulary*, 115; *Eagle*, 16 Apr. 1921.

appeals were usually rebuffed, but even this much contact put the recipients at risk.[81]

'Informers' can thus be broken down into three categories: those the I.R.A. suspected were 'guilty of offenses against the Nation and the Army'; those they punished for these alleged activities; and those who actually did give information to the authorities. What the evidence shows is that these were three quite distinct groups, with little overlap in membership. That is, the great majority of actual informants were never suspected or punished; most of those shot (or denounced, expelled, or burned out of their homes) never informed; and those blacklisted were also usually innocent—but were *not* usually attacked.

What else distinguishes these groups? Table 37 compares the backgrounds of people shot by the Cork I.R.A. with those listed as enemies in the January 1922 intelligence reports, and those identified as informants in police and military records.

Suspicion and punishment were visited upon town and country and upon all ages and all walks of life. Nevertheless, it would appear that revolutionary justice was far from blind. As Part I shows, people with property (farmers and merchants) were nearly ten times as likely as those without (unskilled and unemployed labourers) to be informants, but they were only twice as likely to be suspects, and only half as likely to be shot. Clergymen could give information without suspicion or punishment. In Part II, it is worth noting that over half of the actual informants were under the age of 30: almost double the proportion of those suspected.

Part III further elucidates some of these differences.[82] First of all, women were frequent suspects but rarely victims or informants. As for the other four categories: on the one hand, Protestants, ex-soldiers, and those described as 'tinkers' or 'tramps' made up 14 per cent of informants, 27 per cent of suspects, and fully 67 per cent of those shot.[83] On the other hand, Volunteers or their relatives do not appear on their own lists, accounted for 1 per cent of their comrades' shooting victims, but were 41 per cent of those who can be identified as giving information.

Independent confirmation of some of these statistics comes from another list

---

[81] *Irish Times*, 23 Jan. 1921; *Evening Standard*, 25 Jan. 1921. The usual response by Protestant businessmen to his approaches is described in Clarke, *She Came of Decent People*, 51–2. See also Strickland Diary, 5 Feb., 1 Sept. 1920 (Strickland Papers). The R.I.C. divisional commissioner for Cork told Mark Sturgis that the 'Anti-Sinn Fein League' did exist and was not simply a police cover but it would appear he was simply defending his men in the wake of the burning of Cork. Sturgis Diary, 14 Dec. 1920 (PRO 30/59).

[82] It should also be noted that most ex-servicemen were members of the unskilled working class, women account for most of those suspects listed in 'other' occupations, and vagrants made up a large proportion of unemployed victims.

[83] If the numbers in Part III are added, they total 73% but this includes a number of victims who fell into more than one category, here counted only once: 36% were Protestants, 25% were Catholic ex-servicemen (including several tramps), and 6% were simply tinkers or tramps.

TABLE 37. Spies and informers in Cork, 1919–1923

	Suspected by the I.R.A.	Shot by the I.R.A.	Informed on the I.R.A.
I. *Occupations*			
Sample	124	122	38
Farmer/son (%)	14	17	42
Un/semi-skilled (%)	13	25	5
Skilled (%)	6	7	16
Shop asst./clerk (%)	8	6	0
Merchant (%)	22	9	24
Professional (%)	3	3	3
Priest/minister (%)	0	0	8
Unemployed (male) (%)	7	23	0
Other (%)	27	9	3
II. *Ages*			
Sample	114	49	31
Under 20 (%)	8	12	6
20–9 (%)	26	31	48
30–9 (%)	17	6	16
40–9 (%)	14	14	6
50–9 (%)	21	16	12
60–9 (%)	9	12	10
70+ (%)	5	8	0
III. *Other*			
Sample	157	204	52
Female (%)	23	3	4
Protestant (%)	17	36	10
Ex-serviceman (%)	9	29	4
Tinker/tramp (%)	0	8	0
Volunteer/brother (%)	0	1	41

Notes: The figures for Protestants represent the number of people whose religion I have confirmed (using census and other records): the actual numbers may be slightly higher. The 'tinker/tramp' category includes only those people described as such in newspaper or police reports, or in I.R.A. sources. Again, therefore, this number is a minimum: I have collected four further accounts of 'tramps' being killed but I have been unable to confirm them, and they are not included here. The figures for those who informed are small and partial, and therefore not definitive. The list of suspects can be found in MA, A/0897. For the sources of my statistics on I.R.A. victims, see the Appendix.

of 'Enemy agents and other suspects' compiled by the West Cork Brigade in July 1921.[84] Only one of these twenty names is repeated in the January 1922 list. Comparing these people with those shot in the brigade area, women made up 25 per cent of the suspects and 4 per cent of the victims. For merchants and their sons, the figures were 25 per cent and 9 per cent respectively; for ex-servicemen, 5 per cent and 15 per cent. Protestants made up 25 per cent of the suspects and a startling 64 per cent of the victims.

In fact, the assumption that the supposedly loyal Protestant minority were the

[84]   I/O Cork 3 Report, July 1921 (Mulcahy Papers, P7/A/7).

most likely collaborators and informers, while plausible, was quite wrong. The R.I.C. and the British army found the supposed 'loyalists' to be utterly unforthcoming. When the Irish Command surveyed martial law area commanders in the spring of 1921, opinions in this regard were unanimous. 'Personally I have no very high opinion of the politic value of the loyalist'; 'Few in these counties are reliable'; 'I can see no sign of any effort to actively help the government'; 'I would say that their action is very passive . . . Whether they know things or not, I cannot say, but I do not think any try to be of any assistance in the way of intelligence.'[85]

Those who did proclaim or act on their loyalty did so knowing they were on their own. James McDougall, a Scottish businessman who had to flee Cork, stated bitterly that he 'wasn't like the spineless so-called "loyalists" I knew there'.[86] Tom Bradfield, another fervent imperial patriot (and supposed member of the Bandon valley Anti-Sinn Fein Society) who paid the extreme penalty, declared that he was 'not like the rest of them round here'.[87] Even among Irish Grants Committee claimants, who had to demonstrate their loyalty to the Crown to receive compensation, only 15 out of approximately 700 Cork applicants (or 2 per cent) said that they had provided information to the authorities, none mentioned any sort of clandestine organization, and only one had actually been an agent for British intelligence.[88]

The same was apparently true everywhere outside Ulster. A 5th Division situation report from December 1921 spoke only of 'loyalists in name' and concluded that 'active loyalists' were 'an inconsiderable class'.[89] One constable stationed in the west remembered that 'we wouldn't be a bit better in with Protestants than Republicans. We'd be less better in with them . . . because they were afraid to be accused of giving us news . . . they kept away from us altogether.'[90] The Irish Command's official history states flatly that although 'a considerable number of Unionists were murdered on wholly groundless suspicion . . . at no time did this class make an united movement towards supporting the forces of law and order'.[91]

The truth was that, as British intelligence officers recognized, 'in the south

---

[85] Extracts from reports quoted in Gen. Macready to Miss Stevenson, 20 June 1921 (Lloyd George Papers, F/36/2/19). Another Cork battalion commander wrote of the local loyalists that 'practically none take any action and nearly all hide their sentiments'. 'Appreciation of the situation in Ireland', May 1921 (Cockerill Papers, MS 10, 606). Major Percival felt that the 'old landlords' of West Cork 'had English sympathy but avoided active participation' while, of 'the Protestant element' (chiefly farmers and shopkeepers), 'a few, but not many, were brave enough to assist the Crown Forces with information'. 'Guerrilla Warfare', part 1 (Percival Papers). See also Sir Ormonde Winter, *Winter's Tale* (London, 1955), 299–300.

[86] James McDougall statement (CO 762/112).

[87] O Broin, *Protestant Nationalists*, 177. There are numerous and varied accounts of Tom Bradfield's discovery and confession: see *Eagle*, 29 Jan. 1921; Flor Begley (O'Malley Papers, P17b/111); Deasy, *Towards Ireland Free*, 200; Barry, *Guerilla Days*, 109–10, and (for a different version) Ryan, *Tom Barry Story*, 53.　　　　[88] Bride McKay statement (CO 762/181).

[89] *5th Division History*, Appendix XIV (Jeudwine Papers).

[90] Brewer, *The Royal Irish Constabulary*, 82.　　　　[91] *Record of the Rebellion*, ii. 31.

the Protestants and those who supported the Government rarely gave much information because, except by chance, they had not got it to give'.[92] Protestants, ex-servicemen, and vagrants did not have access to the right social and political circles to know anything very damaging to the I.R.A.

The typical informer was not someone with a cause but rather someone with a grudge, a grievance, or with people or property to protect.[93] Others saw an opportunity for gain or to settle old scores. 'Monkey Mac', for example, supposedly 'had a flair for going out of his way to hurt innocent men whom he disliked or with whom he had some personal rows.'[94] People were often denounced by informers for the same sorts of personal reasons for which people were denounced as informers. Much of what passed for 'intelligence' in Cork was little more than 'fear or malice'.[95]

British intelligence officers took their information wherever they could get it and from a wide variety of (usually anonymous, untimely, and unreliable) sources. Kenneth Strong, who saw service around Tullamore, found that 'my agents were not of a very high calibre. Sometimes a railway porter who noted suspicious train travellers; sometimes a shopkeeper who might report unusual purchases of food or medical supplies; a bartender who noted the arrival of strangers in the neighbourhood.'[96]

By far the best intelligence, however, came from inside the I.R.A. itself.[97] The killings on Broad Street and Broad Lane, the massacre at Clogheen, the ambushes at Nadd and Mourneabbey, the round-up at Crossbarry, and many

---

[92]   Ibid. ii. Florence O'Donoghue, the Cork city intelligence officer for most of the Tan War, wrote that 'the creatures employed [by Crown forces] were not of the calibre that could touch more than the outer fringe of the organisation'. 'Military Intelligence in the Black and Tan Days', 24 (O'Donoghue Papers, MS 31, 443).

[93]   A typical grievance was the commandeering by the I.R.A. of cars or bicycles. This was widely resented: see, for example, the Jimmy Hodnett statement, 20 July 1965 (O'Donoghue Papers, MS 31, 307(7)). One example of a protective informer was the anonymous tipster who wrote to the Lismore detachment of the Buffs Regiment to say that Joe, not John, Collins was in the I.R.A. Another informed on the men who kidnapped two policemen in Dromahane in order to establish that the cars and homes involved were commandeered—and therefore innocent. This letter is included in I/O 5th Bn. to I/O Cork 4, 26 Oct. 1921 (Lankford Papers, U169).

[94]   Anonymous [Con Neenan] memoir (O'Donoghue Papers, MS 31, 337). Neenan told Ernie O'Malley of another spy who 'was really only a nuisance to people he disliked' (O'Malley Papers, P17b/112). Yet another informer reportedly gave the names of I.R.A. men but also of 'the neighbours he did not like'. Jamie Minihan (P17b/112).

[95]   *Record of the Rebellion*, ii. 24. Catherine Murphy felt her family's persecutors were motivated by 'jealousy and spite'. Murphy to M/D, 30 Nov. 1921 (MA, A/0668). For another such example, see Edith Somerville to Ethel Smyth, 17 Apr. 1921 (Somerville and Ross Papers, Lot 878) and Somerville Diary, 13, 15 Apr. 1921.

[96]   Maj.-Gen. Sir Kenneth Strong, *Intelligence at the Top: the Recollections of an Intelligence Officer* (London, 1968), 1–5. According to the *Record of the Rebellion*, ii. 25: 'classes which could be tapped were, the clergy, bank managers, shop owners and employees, military contractors, farmers and civilians employed by the military or police'—or in other words, almost anyone. Notably included were merchants; not included were ex-soldiers.

[97]   Pat Margetts, a soldier who passed information to the I.R.A. in Cork city, said that a number of Volunteers were informers but that no one would believe him and that '[Sean] Hegarty was blind to it'. Pat Margetts (O'Malley Papers, P17b/111).

seizures of arms were caused by Volunteers who fell out with their comrades or were turned or intimidated by British intelligence. By my count there were at least thirteen I.R.A. informers in Cork during the Tan War and at least four in the Civil War.[98] Several others were brothers of Volunteers.[99] The intelligence diary of the Dunmanway Auxiliary Company records the names of four informants: one loyalist, one man who acted for money and out of 'petty jealousy', and two members of the I.R.A.[100]

When Sean Moylan was captured in May 1921, he was amazed to discover that the British officer who had hunted him down, Lt. R. M. Grazebrook, 'seemed to have the names of every member of the Active Service Unit and also had the names of some of the most prominent under-cover men'.[101] Who told on Moylan and his men? From Grazebrook's diary, kept while he was the intelligence officer in the Kanturk area, we can assemble a picture of his informants. Three were in the I.R.A., and another was a brother of a company captain. One was a newsagent (who tried to play both sides), another a successful businessman, and a number of others were farmers. Only one was described as 'a loyalist who could be trusted'. The local Church of Ireland rector once gave him some information, but most of his congregation were untrustworthy and 'seemed Protestant only in name'. Similarly, while two ex-soldiers were 'specially enlisted for intelligence work', in general they were 'one big nuisance'. There were also a large number of anonymous informers. So, there was a kind of underground resistance to the republican movement, but a totally unorganized one.

Why did these people give information? For the most part, because the rebels had harmed them or their family in some way, by taking cars or bicycles, levying taxes, trenching roads, or by kidnapping or bullying them. Although fear of the I.R.A. clearly worked to silence people, their actions also prompted a few to turn against them.[102] Perhaps most striking is the fact that none of the people accused or attacked as informers in Grazebrook's district were in fact guilty as charged—not the Protestant stationmaster 'told to clear out', nor the drunken tinker and his family whom the battalion took in, nor the others who were killed.

The general feeling among most of the Volunteers I interviewed was that

[98] For I.R.A. informers in Limerick and Kerry, see Tom MacEllistrum (O'Malley Papers, P17b/102); Sean Connell (P17b/114); Jack Clifford and Sean Carroll (P17b/130). One I.R.A. intelligence officer in east Clare reported that intercepted letters to the authorities 'usually contained information of Volunteer activity from a local spy or, sometimes, a disgruntled Volunteer'. P. A. Mulcahy statement (MA, A/0408). See also *Record of the Rebellion*, ii. 26.

[99] See, for example, the confession of 'Saunders' (one of the few detailed and semi-reliable accounts by an actual informer) in I/O 1st South. Div. to C/S, 1 June 1921 (Mulcahy Papers, P7/A/20).

[100] 'Raymond' [Flor Crowley], 'Black and Tan Diary', *Star*, 27 Nov. 1971. After examining the diary, Crowley wrote that 'it seems to me that there must have been an informer in almost every townland, so detailed and accurate was the knowledge acquired by the "Tans" '. *Star*, 23 Oct. 1971. See also O'Donovan, 'Why West Cork's Major Role was so Successful', 47.

[101] Moylan Memoir, 244.   [102] A running theme in the Grazebrook Diary.

informers were both numerous and close at hand. In the Bandon valley there were 'a terrible lot' of spies and the British troops seemed 'well informed'.[103] In Clonakilty they were 'all around . . . in the Army behind my shoulders . . . They were from respectable families often, after drink, money or else they were jealous.'[104] Around Schull there were 'all kinds'.[105] In Kanturk 'the police would know where we were'. There were a lot of collaborators including 'some big people. 'Twas barefaced. There were a lot of cute fellas.' One North Corkman who turned out to be an informer was related to several I.R.A. families. In the case of another in West Cork, 'I knew him as well as I knew my brother.'[106]

It was not these friends, relatives, and respected neighbours who bore the brunt of the I.R.A. terror. Almost anyone could be an informer. Almost anyone could be suspected of informing. Whether one was shot (or burned out or expelled), however, depended on one's position within the community. The verse quoted at the beginning of this chapter illustrates this point. The song—'Where the Dripsey River Flow'—refers to the betrayal of the Donoughmore Battalion column on 28 January 1921, which resulted in the death of one Volunteer and the execution of three others. The only 'son of Cromwell' involved was a woman, Mrs Mary Lindsay, and the man who originally 'gave the show away' was the parish priest, Father Shinnick. They had arranged that both sides would be warned in order to prevent any bloodshed, but the I.R.A. (led by Frank Busteed) disregarded the warning and so got caught. The priest was questioned and told the enraged guerrillas of Mrs Lindsay's involvement. She was kidnapped, held in miserable captivity, and secretly shot in revenge for the British executions.[107] With her died James Clarke, her chauffeur, who had nothing to do with the ambush but who was an Ulster Protestant. His death was purely a revenge killing. Father Shinnick was left unharmed.[108]

The disappearance of Mrs Lindsay was a *cause célèbre*, her fate a subject for newspaper headlines, questions in the House of Commons, and even Virginia Woolf's diary.[109] By comparison, the killing of Mick O'Sullivan, a street-singer and cattle drover of uncertain but advanced age, went almost unnoticed.[110] He was

---

[103] Interview with AE.   [104] Interview with AB.

[105] Interview with AD.

[106] Interview with AI. Dr John Chisholm recorded similar opinions in his research in West Cork (Chisholm interviews).

[107] Her house was also burned down and her land confiscated.

[108] See HQ 6th Bn. to O/C Cork 1, 30 Jan. 1921 in 'The Irish Republican Army' (Strickland Papers); O'Callaghan, *Execution*; Sheehan, *Lady Hostage (Mrs. Lindsay)*; Feeney, *Glory O, Glory O, Ye Bold Fenian Men*; Frank Busteed (O'Malley Papers, P17b/112); Terence de Vere White, 'The Shooting of Mrs. Lindsay', *Irish Times*, 17 Oct. 1978. A similar case was that of Matthew Sweetnam and Tom Connell, two Protestant farmers who were killed for giving evidence while four other Catholics who lived in the same area and went to court at about the same time went unharmed. See the *Eagle*, 5, 26 Feb. 1921.

[109] Anne Olivier Bell, *The Diary of Virginia Woolf* (New York, 1978), ii. 127.

[110] O'Sullivan was also an ex-soldier.

shot as a suspected spy and his body used as bait to ambush an R.I.C. patrol on the Cork/Kerry border in May 1921.[111] Here is one Volunteer's account of his death:

He was a very raggedy individual, a kind of tinker and hard nail. We were up early in the morning and there were hail stones at 7 o'clock. They brought on the spy, but I heard one shot only. A placard was pinned to him ['Spies and Informers Beware']. A shower came then. We were looking over the bleak black pine bog road. We could see the village [Rathmore] a mile away. Now when the shower was over and I looked out and sure enough the spy was gone. Holy God says I what's wrong with the spy. We searched around for him and we found him over across the ditch and his coat was pulled up as if he was trying to ward off the shower. I jumped out on the road then. Then he was properly finished off. It was 7 o'clock in the morning and there wasn't a soul around and you could see for miles everywhere around you.[112]

This is a remarkably vivid set of images, but the story is just as remarkable for what is left out. O'Sullivan is described as raggedy, a tinker, a hard nail and, finally, as 'the spy'. He has no name, no voice. With a dead body lying in front of him, the ambusher's eyes are drawn to the horizon, the sky, and the emptiness of the long black road: 'there wasn't a soul around.' We do not even see him killed. In most newspaper and police reports O'Sullivan was referred to as an unnamed 'old man', 'a 70 year-old man', and 'a dead body'. In some accounts of the subsequently successful ambush he was not mentioned at all.[113]

Mrs. Lindsay was separated from her Catholic neighbours by class, creed, loyalty, and a whole battery of myths and prejudices (including her own) which combined to form an insurmountable ethnic barrier. Frank Busteed revealed some of these when he told her: 'Listen you old bitch, you think you are dealing with a bunch of farm labourers, the men who will touch their caps to you and say "Yes, Madam", and "No Madam". Well, we're no bunch of down-trodden tame Catholics.'[114]

Mr O'Sullivan was a homeless, down-trodden old labourer so far on the wrong side of respectability that he had become a non-person. Mary Lindsay and Mick O'Sullivan occupied opposite ends of the social spectrum, but they were both outsiders and 'strangers' in the eyes of their executioners.[115] Both of them fell outside the moral boundaries of respectable Catholic society: one of 'them' rather than one of 'us'. They were fair game.

---

[111] For O'Sullivan's trial and death, see O'Riordan, *Kiskeam Versus the Empire*, 83–6; 'Troubled Times . . . A First Hand Account of Bog Road Ambush', *Sliabh Luacra* (June 1982), 15–20 (which identifies O'Sullivan as 'Old Tom'); O/C Rathmore Bn. to O/C Kerry 2, 24 May 1921 (Mulcahy Papers, P7/A/18). By all accounts, O'Sullivan maintained his innocence to the end. Dan Browne's commander thought he was innocent, as did the local police (Brewer, *The Royal Irish Constabulary*, 77–8).   [112] Dan Browne (O'Malley Papers, P17b/111, 112).
[113] See the *Belfast News-Letter*, *Irish Times*, *Examiner*, 5 May 1921; CI Monthly Report, Kerry, May 1921 (CO 904/115).   [114] O'Callaghan, *Execution*, 133.
[115] For a study of how Protestants and Catholics could be both neighbours and 'strangers', see Rosemary Harris, *Prejudice and Tolerance in Ulster* (Manchester, 1972).

Priests and shopkeepers, on the other hand, were generally out of bounds for the gunmen, protected as they were by their position and influence. Friends and relatives of I.R.A. men were also usually safe, as was anyone else with respectability and neighbours on their side. Not always, but usually. Women, of whatever class or denomination, were generally protected by their sex. Most guerrillas and most Irish people thought it simply unacceptable to kill women, Mary Lindsay being a rare exception to this rule.[116] Suspected female informers might be ordered out of the country or burned out but direct violence against them was conventionally limited to cutting off their hair. In all these cases, potential victims were protected by the communal sense of propriety.

Where some were reprieved by this standard, others were damned. It is indeed striking how often condemned 'spies' and 'informers' were described in terms of outraged respectability. They were not just traitors, they were 'low', 'cheap and low living', 'degenerate', 'a bad character', 'a low type', 'the tinker type', 'a bum', a 'desperado', a 'guttie', and so on.[117] Those shot included four drunks, four thieves, and six men described as sexual deviants of one sort or another. One executed spy in Limerick was officially charged not only with passing information but also with 'living up to the date of his arrest with a woman to whom he was not married'.[118] An ex-soldier who was tarred and feathered near Tralee was labelled 'a fly-boy, a blackguard and a spy'.[119]

A large number of female suspects were reputed prostitutes or at least considered 'fast'. Women who were seen with soldiers were almost automatically put in this category. One such who barely escaped with her life was Mrs Marshall, a soldier's wife in Cork city. Kidnapped by the I.R.A. in August 1920 and convicted of 'having given information to the military which led to the arrest of the late Lord Mayor of Cork [MacSwiney]', she was rescued from the female lunatic asylum by an army patrol before sentence could be carried out. Her home was also wrecked. In reality, she had nothing to do with MacSwiney's capture—that can be attributed to I.R.A. incompetence. Nor, according to British army intelligence, had 'she . . . given any information of value'. Her real crime, it would appear, was to have been a garrison seamstress and 'a woman of easy virtue'.[120]

Anonymous letters denouncing suspected informers were often catalogues of social and moral transgressions.[121] Typical of these was a letter received by Roibeard Langford's wife in November 1922 from 'National Troop':

[116]   There is no doubt that informers were often women (*Record of the Rebellion*, ii. 25) but their punishment was always controversial. See Sean Carroll (O'Malley Papers, P17a/130); Liam Deasy to Florence O'Donoghue, 27 July 1965 (O'Donoghue Papers, MS 31, 301 (7)); O/C East Clare Bde. to C/S, 12 Apr. 1921 (Mulcahy Papers, P7/A/17). General Order No. 13 (1920) declared that 'only consideration of her sex prevents the infliction of the statutory punishment of death' on a female spy.

[117]   See Jack Buttimer, Ned Murphy (O'Malley Papers, P17b/111); Con Meaney, Dan Browne, Mick Murphy, Con Neenan, Edmond Desmond (P17b/112).

[118]   O/C 2nd Bn. to O/C East Limerick Bde., 22 Mar. 1921 in 'The Irish Republican Army', 16–17 (Strickland Papers).   [119]   *Examiner*, 3 Aug. 1920.

[120]   See the March 1921 letters from J. O. C. Kelly and C. J. Pickering (O'Donoghue Papers, MS 31, 223).   [121]   See the letters to Sam Hunter (CO 762/101) and Henry Wood (/119).

Your house was raided and the works on Saturday night on information sent to the National Troops by a man and his wife who are resident . . . 9 doors from the works. The wife and daughter and that man are friendly with Jews who live opposite the works at No. 4 and from that house they are spying . . . His house No. 30 was at one time a disorderly establishment. From 1918 to 1921 he ran it as a Spy HQ for the [British]. His wife is like a demon dragged out of Hell. The daughter and her are doing the spy while he and the sons are up spying about Miss McSweeneys . . . I don't forget I fought under Mr. R. Langford and I can at any rate make it known to him who is doing the spy behind his back and a few other things.[122]

Another set of victims who can be classed as social misfits of a different sort were those deemed 'half-witted', 'feeble-minded', or 'simple'. Seven men of this description were killed as spies.[123] Again, these were marginal 'types' who often had no one to speak for or protect them.

Not all executed 'spies' and 'informers' were strangers or deviants and some of those who were, were in fact guilty of helping the authorities. Nevertheless, these were exceptions. The great majority of suspects—and, it seems, most informers—were respectable Catholics but the great majority of victims were not. They were killed not for what they did but for who they were: Protestants, ex-soldiers, tramps, and so on down the communal blacklist. Their deaths were not just a consequence of political heresy but of a persecution that went far beyond the immediate hunt for informers. Guerrilla war transformed them from the unwanted to the enemy within.

The 'tramp class' had been under pressure from the Munster I.R.A. and Sinn Fein local councils for months before they began to 'disappear' in the winter of 1920. I.R.A. units did not just want to silence loose tongues, they wanted to eliminate the 'tramp nuisance' altogether. In early 1921, for example, the North Cork Brigade ordered all vagrants to 'leave the county Cork immediately':[124] 'Most of them got off the roads, some to the workhouses, others to God knows where. The carefree life of the Irish tramp was over for the time being.'[125]

Demobilized servicemen and their families became targets for nationalist abuse soon after the Easter Rising. Already by July, ex-soldiers and their wives (the so-called 'separation women') were fighting Sinn Feiners in the streets of Cork city and other towns. After one free-for-all in Charleville, an ex-soldier—beaten and derided as 'another rejected soldier who sold his country for a Saxon shilling'—told a reporter: 'it is just because I am a soldier. I am in dread of living in my own town.' Another woman declared that 'a soldier's wife would be murdered in the town by these people'.[126] The first months of 1919 brought the first wave of returning veterans and an accompanying rise in harassment and

[122]   'National Troop' to Mrs Langford, 29 Nov. 1922 (MA, A/1119).
[123]   See Lankford, *The Hope and the Sadness*, 143, who quotes Liam Lynch as saying 'these people can cause a lot of trouble with talk'.
[124]   Pat O'Connor, 'The Capture of Lt. Vincent' (O'Donoghue Papers, MS 31, 421 (11)).
[125]   Lankford, *The Hope and the Sadness*, 183. See also the discussion of 'tinkers' and 'tramps' in Ch. 7.   [126]   *Irish Times*, 5 Aug. 1916. See also 20 July 1916.

violence. Typical of the dozens of cases which ended up in the city's police court was the complaint by the O'Driscoll boys of Evergreen Street. Upon returning home, they were met by the jeering O'Flahertys, one of whom tore the ribbons from their uniforms while 'Mrs. O'Flaherty belaboured both the O'Driscolls with a banjo'.[127]

The long-established stereotype of the old soldier as corner boy and idle drunk, and the reality of mass unemployment and petty crime[128] among the veterans of the Great War, also told against them. Forty-six per cent of Irish ex-servicemen were drawing the new out-of-work donations in November 1919, as opposed to 10 per cent in Great Britain—and since the rate was almost certainly lower in Ulster, it was probably even higher in Munster. In early May 1919, for example, there were 244 ex-soldiers and 50 civilians on the dole in Fermoy. By the end of the month the number of veterans had risen to 274 while the number of civilians had fallen to 35. This probably accounted for a large majority of ex-soldiers as the local Demobilized Soldier's and Seaman's Federation only had 260 members in April.[129] Many of those victims described as 'dirty' or 'low', or as drunks, thieves, and half-wits were former soldiers. Local councils and Poor Law Boards all over Munster passed resolutions not to employ ex-soldiers, and local post offices and railway companies were pressured to do the same. Many of these men found they had only two roles to play: 'tramp' or 'corner boy'. In the summer of 1920 they became the targets of threats and kidnappings as the I.R.A. police sought to remove suspected or potential criminals and troublemakers from their towns.[130] As the guerrilla war escalated, these assaults turned into death threats and shootings and many were forced to leave altogether.[131] In an event which summed up the plight of many, one man was stabbed to death in the city simply because he gave the wrong answer. When asked who he was he replied 'an ex-soldier'.[132]

Over the same period, Cork Protestants watched with growing apprehension as many of their nationalist neighbours turned away from or against them. Lionel Fleming, then growing up in Timoleague, recalled that 'During this time

---

[127] *Examiner*, 21 Jan. 1921. See also 17 June, 28 July 1919, 12 Jan. 1920. Bridget Sliney of Ballycotton, the wife and sister of servicemen, declared that 'I had a dog's life from the Sinn Feiners' (CO 762/21).

[128] The ex-soldier as drunk, petty thief, wife-beater and deserter became a fixture in police and magistrates' courts all over Cork: see the *Examiner*, 7, 18 June 11, 13, 16, 21, 23 Aug., 4, 10, 27 Nov., 30 Dec. 1919, 15, 20 Jan. 1920. See also the discussion of ex-soldiers in Ch. 7.

[129] *Irish Times*, 11 Nov. 1919; *Examiner*, 14 Apr., 3, 24 May 1919. See also *Irish Times*, 21 Feb. 1921.

[130] See *Irish Times*, 3 July 1920; *Examiner*, 8, 18 June; 6 July 1920; Comerford, *My Kilkenny I.R.A. Days*, 82, 243, 523–36.

[131] See, for example, Staunton, 'Royal Munster Fusiliers', 403, Jane Leonard, 'Getting Them at Last: The I.R.A. and Ex-Servicemen', in Fitzpatrick (ed.), *Revolution? Ireland 1917–1923*, 118–29 and Fitzpatrick, *Politics and Irish Life*, 162–3.

[132] *Irish Times*, 29 Mar. 1921. See also an evocative letter from an ex-soldier's mother in Cork city, 3 Apr. 1921 (PRONI, D989A/8/23).

[the Great War] the gap between Us and Them had been steadily widening, until in the end it seemed to be quite unbridgeable. They became not only different from us, they were against us.'[133] 'After the war people turned very black and bigoted . . . and we were only a daisy in a bull's mouth compared to them.'[134]

I.R.A. shootings only begin to measure the toll taken of the Protestant community during the revolution. Of 113 private homes burned by the guerrillas, 96 (or 85 per cent) belonged to Protestants. None of the more than two dozen farms seized from 'spies' in 1921 and 1922 was owned by a Catholic.[135] Protestants who wished to sell up and leave were presumed to have 'guilty consciences.'[136] Their sales were often boycotted, fined, or stopped altogether.[137] A typical case was that of Mr Ringwood, the manager of the Munster and Leinster bank in Bantry. A suspected informer, he had almost been kidnapped just prior to the Truce in July 1921 but was saved by a priest. Harassment continued, and he decided to leave the area. During the resulting auction:

a number of young men mounted the gallery and caused a disturbance which interrupted the sale. The disturbance, which at first had the appearance of a mere humorous demonstration, soon became an uproar, whereupon Mr J. J. Roycroft [the auctioneer] remonstrated with the offenders and asked them to desist, as it was a great injustice to him. One of the demonstrators, answering from the gallery, regretted they could not comply, as they had no blame to Mr Roycroft. He made certain allegations against Mr Ringwood, on hearing which those attending the auction withdrew, the result being the sale had to be abandoned.[138]

Hundreds were forced to seek refuge in Dublin, Belfast, or England. Thousands more went on the run, sleeping in barns or fields, or staying with friends or relatives. Thousands more left permanently in 1921 and 1922, rapidly reducing the Protestant minority in Cork to nearly half its pre-revolutionary size.[139] Those who stayed were frequently subjected to a regime of boycotts, vandalism, and theft. Many had their property commandeered by neighbours or

---

[133] Fleming, *Head or Harp*, 52. See also 'Letters from a Cork Farmer', 15 Mar., 5 Apr., 1921 (PRONI, D989A/8/23) and Patrick Buckland, *Irish Unionism*, i: *The Anglo-Irish and the New Ireland 1885–1922* (Dublin, 1972), 213–16.

[134] Somerville-Large, *Cappaghglass*, 343–4.

[135] See the Report on Land Seizures to Min. of Agriculture, 19 Apr. 1923 (MA, A/8506); O/C 3rd Bn. Special Infantry Corps [SIC] to Comdt. J. J. Coughlan, n.d. [May 1923?] (MA, SIC/2); 'Spy Farms' File (DOD A/613). [136] O'Mahony interview with Tom Barry.

[137] See the following statements to the Irish Grants Committee: Joseph Hosford (CO 762/7); Thomas Beamish Cooke (/14); John St. Leger Gilliman (/33); Robert McGivern (/33); Henry McGivern (/35); Anne Appelbe (/37); William Hosford Bryan (/45); Robert Warren Farran (/61); William Good Wood (/64); Robert Ginn (/71); George Tyner (/80); John Macbeth (/92); James Lambe (/117); Spencer Travers (/119); John Hosford (/133); John Kingston (/150); William Good (/184); Edmond Murnane (/191); William Conner (/198); William Bateman (/205).

[138] *Star*, 16 July, 24 Sept., 1 Oct. 1921.

[139] For the scale, timing, and context of the Protestant flight, see Hart, 'The Protestant Experience of Revolution in Southern Ireland'.

Volunteers and nearly all those who lived in rural areas had to put up with I.R.A. squatters. Some indication of the severity of the terror is given by the scores of Protestant men and women who suffered nervous breakdowns, even to the point of insanity and suicide.[140]

Moreover, the persecution of Protestants, ex-soldiers, and ex-policemen continued long after the Treaty had made old loyalties irrelevant. The I.R.A. pursued the same 'types' in 1922 and 1923 as they had in the Tan War: 44 per cent of civilians shot by the rebels after July 1921 were Protestant and 20 per cent were ex-soldiers.[141] Over three-quarters of the houses burned in the same period were Protestant-owned. Looking over the whole span of the revolution, we can see that the main themes of the West Cork massacre—conspiracy theories, land, and sectarian vengeance—were prefigured in the executions of 'informers' carried out in the previous two years.

Like the events of April 1922, the war on informers must be seen as part of the tit-for-tat dynamics of violence, driven by fear and the desire for revenge. It was not, however, merely (or even mainly) a matter of espionage, of spies and spy-hunters. It was a civil war within and between communities, with the battle lines drawn by a whole range of social bonds and boundaries.

As used by the men of the Cork I.R.A., the term 'informer' meant simply 'enemy' and enemies were defined by their religion, class, connections, respectability—in fact, by the same communal standards by which the Volunteers defined themselves. The myth of 'the Informer' thus went hand in hand with the myth of 'the People' united behind the I.R.A., so crucial to the Volunteers' corporate sense of identity and legitimacy. Traitors, by definition, had to be outsiders and monsters, the obverse of the Volunteers' embodiment of communal virtues. Alienation and solidarity were two sides of the same coin.

Beneath the welter of pretexts and suspicions, beneath its official rhetoric of courts martial and convictions, the I.R.A. were tapping a deep vein of communal prejudice and gossip: about grabbers, black Protestants and Masonic conspiracies, dirty tinkers and corner boys, fly-boys and fast women, the Jews at No. 4 and the disorderly house at No. 30. This sort of talk was normally confined to pubs, kitchens, and crossroads. What the revolution did was to take it from behind closed doors and squinting.

---

[140] The most sensational suicide was that of George Tilson: see the *Examiner*, 21, 25 Feb. 1921. For examples of mental or physical breakdowns, see the following statements to the Irish Grants Committee (usually supported by medical testimony): W. B. Hosford (CO 762/5); Thomas Gardner Wallis (/13); Harry Muggleworth (/14); Richard Baker (/19); Robert Meara (/33); Joseph Northridge (/37); Henry Smyth (/69); John Good (/86); James Thomas (/96); Eleanor Penrose (/104); Thomas Wood (/125); Mary Unkles (/140); Richard Kingston (/176); Henry Chamney (/191); John Kehilly (/199).

[141] This victimization continued well after the I.R.A.'s 1923 ceasefire: see Ministry of Home Affairs Confidential Report, Feb. 1924 (UCD, Ernest Blythe Papers, P24/323).

windows into the streets, where 'spies' and 'informers' were 'hooted and hunted', 'insulted and taunted', 'spat at in the streets and treated worse than a dog'. Silence and indifference were equally destructive, allowing gunmen and arsonists to do as they pleased. Revolution had turned these people and their families into strangers, and their neighbours into enemies.

Appendix
Sources and Definitions:
I.R.A. Membership and Violence

> We are closed in, and the key is turned
> On our uncertainty; somewhere
> A man is killed, or a house burned,
> Yet no clear fact can be discerned.
> (W. B. Yeats, 'Meditations in Time of Civil War')

I.R.A. MEMBERSHIP SAMPLE

The data on the social composition of the I.R.A. in Cork presented here were collected from a wide variety of sources:

1. *Newspapers.* A complete daily or weekly survey was done of the *Irish Times*, the *Freeman's Journal*, the *Cork County Eagle*, the *Southern Star*, and the *Cork Examiner* from May 1916 to June 1923. The *Examiner* (along with the companion *Weekly Examiner*) is the best single record of events in Cork (and of Munster as a whole). Although it maintained a steadily Redmondite and anti-republican editorial stance (and was vandalized and had several employees shot as a result), it maintained an admirably high standard of independent reporting and was attacked, censored, and suppressed by all sides in both wars. The paper was often at odds with both the British authorities and the I.R.A. It not infrequently contradicted official accounts and also published government refutations of its stories. The latter were very rare, however.

Of the other Cork newspapers consulted, the *Eagle* was staunchly anti-republican, and the *Star* was Sinn Fein-controlled from 1918 to 1922. Both of these give detailed coverage for West Cork. Neither was published during the Civil War.

These papers all contain reports of arrests, convictions, and killings, often with biographical details. Unfortunately, while civil court reports frequently gave defendants' ages and occupations, court-martial reports rarely did so, and details are scantier after mid-1920. Civil War stories were worse again, due to Free State censorship.

2. *Police Reports.* The monthly reports of the inspector general and county inspectors of the R.I.C. for all counties were surveyed from 1916 to 1921 (PRO, CO 904/102–16). These give the same range of information as newspapers, although more erratically, as individual inspectors had different styles of reportage. Some reports are missing, especially from the spring of 1920—although the parallel newspaper survey fills many of the gaps. The reports of illegal drilling in 1917–18 (CO 904/122) are particularly useful as they give the ages and occupations of a large number of Volunteers, mostly from Munster and Connaught.

3. *Military Reports.* The files of the Military Courts of Inquiry on deaths from late 1920 to early 1922 (WO 35/146A–160) usually give the ages and occupations of those killed, and the circumstances of their deaths. War Office records also include useful files

on Defence of the Realm Act (DORA) prosecutions in 1917–18 and 1920 (WO 35/99, 112). Occasional details of I.R.A. members can be gleaned from reports and mug books in the Strickland Papers (IWM), in captured documents in the Ernie O'Malley Papers (UCD, P17a), and in the A/ series of the Irish Military Archives (sometimes referred to as the Michael Collins Papers). The following National Army records in the Military Archives contain information on I.R.A. men captured or killed: Cork Command Operations Reports, Dec. 1922–May 1923 (CW/OPS/13), General Weekly Surveys, Jan.–May 1923 (CW/OPS/14D), General Weekly Returns [Irregular], Jan.–May 1923 (CW/OPS/14E), Intelligence and Raid Reports, Dec. 1922–May 1923 (CW/OPS/14F).

4. *Prison Records.* The General Prison Board records (NA) list many—but not all—of those persons committed for offences under the Defence of the Realm Act between late 1917 and early 1920. These files give prisoners' ages and charges, but unfortunately only rarely mention their occupations. The Art O'Brien Papers (NLI, MS 8443-5) contain lists with similar information on prisoners in English gaols in 1920–1. The 6th Division Internees Register (WO 35/144) provides addresses and ages for those interned in 1921. The Register of Prisoners in Military Prisons (WO 35/143) includes ages, occupations, charges, and sentences. For the Civil War period, Prisoners' Location Books, Charge Records, and Prison Ledgers for Cork Command and elsewhere (MA, P/1-6 and miscellaneous) provided background information on some I.R.A. prisoners.

5. *I.R.A. Records.* A few unit roll books have survived. Several of these, drawn up by Civil War prisoners, give occupations, ages, and marital status (MA, A/1135, A/1137, A/1138, A/1185). Also useful are lists of men who required aid from the White Cross or the Prisoners' Dependants Fund. These can be found in the Siobhan Lankford Papers (CAI, U169), in the Art O'Brien Papers, and in the A/ series documents in the Military Archives.

Finally, the task of locating individuals, their homes, and their families—especially when dealing with the townland census returns—was greatly aided by the Cork County Council's indispensable *Directory of Townlands and District Electoral Divisions* (Cork, 1985).

Most of these sources provide the home addresses of those observed, arrested, interned, or killed. These men and their families were, wherever possible, traced through the manuscript returns for the 1911 census (NA) and the records of the Irish Valuation Office, providing much additional data on ages, occupations, housing conditions, and familial property.

The sample includes only those engaged in activities specific to the Volunteers—such as drilling—or in possession of arms or a membership card, or those identified in I.R.A. records as members. This eliminates a lot of Volunteers who were arrested for collecting money, driving cattle, or making seditious speeches. As for those men killed in 1920–21, only those definitely identified as Volunteers are included, as some were shot mistakenly or arbitrarily. I have left out all uncertain cases.

Distinguishing officers from their men sometimes presented a problem. Those who led drilling or marching parties in 1917–19 are assumed to have been officers. The problem of identification is worst in 1920–1, when drillers no longer provided such grist for the judicial mill, and without the detailed and accurate Free State intelligence records to provide enlightenment. Here I was largely dependent on other records to tell who was who. I.R.A. memoirs and unit rolls are very helpful in this respect. Again, only those who were clearly identified as officers are classed as such, so that some have inevitably been included in the 'rank and file' sample.

The same person may appear in samples for different periods. The ages given are for the standard years of 1917, 1920, and 1922.

The division of the occupational sample into the various categories generally followed Guy Routh's analysis in his *Occupations and Pay in Great Britain 1906–79* (London, 1980). A few of the I.R.A. members had more than one occupation, and were listed under the presumed principal source of income. Descriptions of Volunteer occupations came from many sources, and a few are probably false, but not enough to move significant numbers from one category to another.

Farmer/son: consists largely of sons working on their family farms, although some of these probably also worked on other farms as well. Thus, there was often a fine line between farmers' sons and labourers.

Farm labourer: includes 70 per cent of those described simply as 'labourer' or 'general labourer', in line with the *General Report* of the 1911 census, which advised that 'the majority of persons in rural districts returned as "labourers" may be assumed to be Agricultural labourers' (p. xxvii). I have extended this to include town labourers outside Cork city. In fact, general labourers make up the bulk of this category.

Un/semi-skilled: covers a wide variety of occupations and social distinctions, from salaried railway employees to casual dock labourers, and 30 per cent of the 'generals'. Many I.R.A. men in this category were drivers, messengers, porters, mill or creamery workers, or builders' labourers. Most had steady jobs (although some of these became unemployed during the depression of the early 1920s) and a few were self-employed. Only a minority were casual labourers.

Skilled: includes all trades and crafts, including mechanics. Many of the tradesmen in the I.R.A. were apprentices, a large number of whom worked for their fathers. Almost none were masters or builders.

Shop assistant/clerk: covers all kinds of clerks and shop assistants, including those who worked in pubs and other licensed premises. Many of these were also apprentices or working for their fathers (although where this was specified they are included under 'merchant/son'). This category masks a great many differences in status, as bank or solicitor's clerks would have ranked far above shop apprentices in town society. The problem in differentiating these various groups is that shopkeepers' sons were frequently described as shop assistants, and shop assistants were frequently described as clerks. However, it can be safely concluded that the great majority of the men in these samples were rather junior shop assistants, most of whom worked for drapers and grocers.

Professional: Volunteers in this category were almost all teachers or assistant teachers in elementary or secondary schools. There were a number of assistant surveyors and government agricultural inspectors, and a tiny number of solicitors.

Merchant/son: covers shopkeepers, publicans, and traders of all sorts, and their sons who worked for them.

Student: includes all those in post-secondary institutions or simply described as 'student'.

Other: includes ex-policemen, fishermen, gamekeepers, commercial travellers, and insurance agents. They are almost entirely urban-oriented occupations, and there are no manual labourers (skilled or unskilled) in this category.

The census data are taken from the Census of Ireland of 1911, and from the Irish Free

State Census of 1926. The tabulation of the 1911 occupational figures was more difficult to translate into my categories, with resulting gaps in the numbers. The percentages were calculated from a base population of occupied or productive males.

It must be remembered that the 1911 and 1926 censuses lie at either end of the revolutionary period, and do not reflect the year-by-year effects of the Great War, or the economic depression which followed it in the early 1920s. The years 1911 and 1926 were ones of considerable social stability compared to most of those in between. Among other things, the war kept tens of thousands of younger men at home in the Irish countryside, and increased the area under tillage, and thus the demand for agricultural labour. It also removed tens of thousands of—disproportionately urban—young men to European battlefields, killing many thousands of them in the process. The net result is hard to gauge, but it may tentatively be stated that there were more young men and agricultural labourers in rural areas, and a comparative drop in the numbers of men of military age in urban areas.

Because of the nature of my sources, there is an undoubted bias in the samples towards I.R.A. members who attracted attention from the police, army, or newspapers. These were the movement's activists and leaders, the men most likely to be arrested, imprisoned, or shot. Volunteers who rarely participated in operations or drill exercises, or who were only nominal members, are much less likely to appear in the data. Thus, the samples may be more representative of the active or reliable membership than of the organization as a whole. It is impossible to say what impact this bias has on the statistics, but a few guesses are discussed in Chapter 7.

STATISTICS ON VIOLENCE

Violence, I believe, is best measured in terms of its victims. In addition, I have focused my statistical analysis on those categories where one can arrive at a reasonable estimate of what happened, when, and where. My human statistics are limited to deaths and to those seriously injured by guns and explosives because these are reliable and comparable. Such incidents were nearly always reported in one way or another. The use of guns indicates a certain threshold of violence below which it is very difficult to judge the effect of an incident. A bullet almost always produces a serious wound but how do we judge the severity of an assault?[1] As detailed in Chapter 9, Tom Hales and Pat Harte, the commander and quartermaster of the West Cork Brigade, were tortured to such an extent in 1920 that Hales's mouth and hands were crippled and Harte became deranged. Two R.I.C. constables who were kidnapped near Macroom in February 1922 were flogged nearly to death with wire whips.[2] These were serious injuries by any standard but what are we to make of the I.R.A.'s attack on Con O'Driscoll of Drinagh in December 1920 in which he was forcibly shaved?[3] This was a painful, fearful, and humiliating episode but O'Driscoll was not badly hurt. O'Driscoll's willingness to bring his case to court was also rare; most such events remained hidden and so cannot be counted or classified.[4]

---

[1] See also the discussion of violence in Ch. 3.   [2] *Examiner*, 11 Feb. 1922.
[3] See Ch. 4.
[4] The files of the Irish Grants Committee (CO 904/762) give some indication of the number of unreported attacks. The Committee received nearly 800 compensation claims from declared Cork loyalists (mostly Protestants) who suffered injury after the Truce of July 1921. Even within this limited—albeit significant—sample, there were thousands of violent incidents which were never mentioned in police or newspaper reports.

Tables 1 and 2 in Chapter 3 also raise the question of motive. Which acts are to be considered 'revolutionary' and which are not? Most of the I.R.A. veterans I interviewed defined their actions in strictly military terms and drew a strong distinction between 'real' I.R.A. operations and actions they disapproved of, particularly attacks on civilians.[5] Often when I asked about a specific incident I was told 'that wasn't the real I.R.A.' or 'that wasn't official'. The 'real war' was the war against the British. As one veteran put it (in an argument I encountered many times): 'there'll always be people to take advantage or do the wrong thing, but that had nothing to do with us.'[6] The same person saw murder and looting as typical of British forces.[7] The accounts of Kilmichael discussed in Chapter 2 are a good illustration of this exclusive definition of the revolution.

The same selective arguments were used in reverse by British forces and their apologists and historians. The British army's official histories of the guerrilla war, like the contemporary police reports, ignored the systematic use of illegal violence by their own soldiers while highlighting the I.R.A.'s reign of terror.[8] Similarly, published police statistics were usually limited to 'Sinn Fein outrages'.[9]

So where did 'the revolution' end and other forms of violence begin? These rival narratives of the revolution were not simply cynical propaganda; they genuinely reflected the attitudes of those involved. Nevertheless, while this polarization of perceptions was important in itself, any such distinctions are misleading. Motives and outcomes were so often mixed or indecipherable that many incidents can be assigned more than one meaning. Was Kilmichael an ambush or a massacre? How should we describe the death of Cadet Guthrie that same night, shot and buried in a bog? Can we differentiate between the shootings of Sergeant O'Donoghue and Charlie O'Brien, for example? If a Protestant farmer was attacked, was it because of his religion, his politics, or his land, or all three? Was personal spite involved?

Because of this uncertainty I have not attempted to define 'political' or 'revolutionary' violence or to divide incidents into detailed categories. The politics of an event depended on the observer's point of view. It must again be stated, however, that these incidents represent only a minority of those activities which may be termed 'violent'.

The statistical categories I use are defined as follows:

1. *Killed and Wounded.* Violent deaths and serious wounds from bullets or bombs always attract attention and are almost always mentioned in some report or other where they are known to have occurred. Even so, some deaths were hidden or went unnoticed by both newspapers and police reports, and only come to the historian's attention through personal letters or reminiscences. No one source gives a full or unbiased account.

I have included in my figures only those deaths to which there was more than one reference or witness. Because of this, over a dozen uncorroborated killings of 'spies' and

---

[5]   Many condemned the contemporary Provisional I.R.A. on this ground.

[6]   Interview with AJ.

[7]   Compare, for example, the following entries in the index of Dorothy Macardle's *The Irish Republic* (London, 1937): 'Lindsay, Mrs., Coachford, Co. Cork, executed, 1921'; 'MacCurtain, Tomas, murder of, March 20th, 1920'.

[8]   This is true of GHQ Ireland, *Record of the Rebellion in Ireland in 1920–21*, i (Operations) (IWM, Sir Hugh Jeudwine Papers) and *6th Division History* (Strickland Papers).

[9]   See, for example, *Fatalities in Irish Outrages (Murders) 1st Jan. 1919–31st March 1921*, HC 1921, 140, cols. 463–4.

'informers' mentioned in I.R.A. memoirs or interviews have not been included. The only exceptions were deaths or injuries mentioned in an official report as having happened to a member of that force. This was the case with quite a few self-inflicted I.R.A. deaths, for example.

Where two different numbers were given for the casualties of an ambush or attack (which was very common), I used the lower unless the other number was clearly more plausible. For example, republican writers have claimed that over thirty British troops died at the battle of Crossbarry on 19 March 1921 whereas the British government reported only ten soldiers and police killed and four wounded. I chose the latter figure because it was given in internal police and military documents and verified at the inquest. On the other hand, unsubstantiated government (British and Free State) claims that Volunteers were killed or wounded in encounters or in accidents (the usual formulations were 'several men were seen to fall' or 'much blood was found at the scene') were ignored unless verified by I.R.A. reports or Rolls of Honour, or unless bodies were produced. As in all wars, both sides exaggerated their claims.

The largest class of under-reported deaths is that of 'spies' and 'informers': civilian victims of the I.R.A.[10] Many of these simply disappeared and were secretly buried. Unless a relative came forward whose correspondence survives, the British government listed them as missing, or an I.R.A. man remembered the killing in print or in an interview, these deaths remained hidden. As the I.R.A. often killed tinkers, tramps, and other loners and outsiders who might never be missed, some of these killings will surely never come to light.

I have only described an incident as an I.R.A. or government shooting where this is certain or extremely likely, as in the case of Tomas MacCurtain's death in March 1920—almost certainly at the hands of policemen. Cases in which the identity of the killers is uncertain are placed in the 'Unknown' category along with civilians who were caught in the crossfire during an attack.

It should be noted that non-fatal wounds were less likely to be reported than deaths, especially if they were relatively minor. They did not require inquests or funerals and do not appear in Rolls of Honour. Consequently, the number of people wounded was probably slightly greater than the statistics show.

A few final notes about these statistics. Royal Marine casualties are included under the 'Army' heading. Members of Sinn Fein who were shot are counted as 'civilian' rather than as I.R.A. casualties.

2. *Destruction of Property*. The next most important and reliably reported category of violence is that of attacks on buildings and bridges. The statistics on the destruction of property follow the same logic as those for shootings and bombings. Burning down a house or blowing up a bridge will always be considered a serious act, and will almost always attract attention. Acts of vandalism, sabotage, or arson on a lesser scale—of roads, telephone or rail lines, hayricks, sheds, cars, crops, and so on—were far more numerous but they too were usually ignored or unreported. Broken windows must have numbered in the thousands in Cork alone. Some activities were so numerous that they were simply lumped together in descriptions like: 'last night many roads were trenched around Timoleague' or 'raiders visited a large number of homes in Riverstown searching for arms'.

---

[10] See Ch. 13.

I have only included here the burning or blowing up of buildings where significant damage was done. The destruction of houses, shops, or public buildings was usually considered important enough to warrant notice in newspapers or official reports. In the few cases where the identity of the arsonists is unclear, I have placed the attack in the 'Unknown' category.

The numbers refer to buildings burned rather than to separate arson attacks. Thus, the burning of St Patrick Street in Cork city in December 1920 began with only three or four fires but ended by destroying nearly a hundred individual houses or shops. My statistics refer to the latter.

Bridge-wrecking bears the same relation to road-trenching or blocking or rail-line destruction as the burning of houses does to lesser forms of arson—it is much easier to count and much more likely to be reported. Individual road or rail bridges can usually be identified and were small enough in number not to be lumped together in a report.

3. *Raids on Mails.* Unlike the myriad other forms of armed robbery, these raids were all directed at the same government department and were thus much more likely to be reported. The loss of mail, parcels, and pensions from even one office or route was immediately known. Here we can rely on newspapers and police reports to provide reasonably accurate information.

4. *Riots.* I have defined these events as the violent action of at least one unorganized crowd of ten or more people. This category includes food rioters and party brawlers, but not cattle drivers (unless they fought with police).

The main sources for the incidence and outcomes of revolutionary and counter-revolutionary violence were as follows:

1. *Newspapers.* In Cork, the *Examiner* was alone in consistently publishing both sides' atrocities, a policy aided by the pro-Sinn Fein bias of many of its local reporters. Fortunately, it suffered very little censorship until the I.R.A. took over Cork in early 1922. Under this and the succeeding Free State regime the news was tightly controlled and the newspaper's value to the historian is correspondingly reduced.

The *Irish Times* and *Freeman's Journal* provided the basic newspaper record for national-level statistics on violence and also served as a useful addition to the *Examiner*, particularly when the latter was censored by the I.R.A. in mid-1922. One key document that appeared in the *Irish Times* on 22 August 1921 was the British list of missing persons which lists several dozen soldiers, police, and civilians who were kidnapped and shot by the I.R.A.

2. *Police Reports.* The monthly reports of the county inspectors (CO 904/–) are reasonably comprehensive and are crucial in establishing accurate police casualties. Their main blind spot was their failure to report many killings by Crown forces (acknowledged or otherwise); for this, the newspapers are far more reliable. The police also frequently underestimated military casualties, probably because the army was reluctant to provide the information.

Other series of R.I.C. reports used were the national Weekly Summaries of Outrages for 1920–21 (CO 904/148–50), Returns of Agrarian Outrages for 1920 and 1921 (CO 904/121–121/3), and Reports on Breaches of the Truce (CO 904/152). These can be used to cross-check the regular monthly reports.

3. *Military Reports.* A very useful précis of British army reports for 1920 can be found in the Military Archives (A/0434). This, along with the Weekly Surveys of the

State of Ireland submitted to the British cabinet in 1920 and 1921 (PRO, CAB 24/), lists casualties not given in police reports or newspapers. Together these are the most authoritative sources for military engagements and losses. The Weekly Survey also provides a useful official record of events during the Truce and after the Treaty—the only one available after the police were disbanded.

The reports of the Military Courts of Inquiry (WO 35/146A–161A), although not comprehensive, give the names and details of death of the subjects. They must be used with care, however, as the real facts of Crown force killings were often covered up, ignored, or falsified.

For the period of the Civil War, the Cork Command Operations Reports (CW/OPS/14) are the principal official source for incidents and casualties. Like the British equivalents, they are not necessarily accurate with regard to National Army activities but they do contain many details not reported in newspapers.

4. *I.R.A. Reports.* The Mulcahy Papers contain monthly reports from brigades and other units, as well as reports of individual engagements (P7/A/17–39), which provide I.R.A. casualty statistics not otherwise available. The O'Malley Papers (P17a/-) and captured documents in the Military Archives (see especially A/0991–2) contain scattered similar reports from the Civil War. Lists of I.R.A. casualties can also be found in the Military Archives (A/0436).

Also useful in determining I.R.A. deaths were the official Rolls of Honour of the 1st and 3rd Cork Brigades from 1916 to 1923. These include the date, and sometimes the place, of death. These can be supplemented with *The Last Post* (National Graves Association, 1986) which lists I.R.A. dead throughout Ireland, along with personal details and the time and place of death. Neither the Rolls nor *The Last Post* are complete; the latter also often fails to distinguish between Volunteers and unaffiliated reprisal victims. None of these lists non-fatal casualties.

Killings of suspected spies, informers, or other 'enemies' are by far the most difficult to discover or verify and thus form a special statistical case. Nevertheless, a wide variety of documents beyond those listed above contain solid information about these shootings. Correspondence from relatives of missing persons to I.R.A. leaders, and the subsequent internal investigations, can be found in the Military Archives (A/0535, 0622, 0649, 0659, 0668, 0909). The *Examiner* of 14 January 1922 reports the findings of a Dublin court in several of these cases. Also important are the statements by victims and their families to the Irish Grants Committee (CO 762/–) and the testimony of I.R.A. members to Ernie O'Malley (O'Malley Papers, P17b/–). Some incidents could only be confirmed or denied by reference to memoirs, local histories, and interviews.

Once again, I found the Cork County Council's *Directory of Townlands and District Electoral Divisions* to be an invaluable aid in locating and mapping these incidents within Cork.

Bibliography

MANUSCRIPT COLLECTIONS

Dublin

University College, Dublin

Archives

Ernest Blythe Papers.
Desmond Fitzgerald Papers.
Sean MacEntee Papers.
Mary MacSwiney Papers.
Richard Mulcahy Papers.
Ernie O'Malley Papers.

Department of Irish Folklore

Schools Manuscripts, Co. Cork.

National Library of Ireland

G. A. Cockerill Papers.
Crowley family Papers.
Frank Gallagher Papers (Seamus Robinson Documents).
Bulmer Hobson Papers.
Diarmuid Lynch Papers.
Maurice Moore Papers.
Sean Moylan Papers.
Art O'Brien Papers.
Leon O Broin Papers.
Florence O'Donoghue Papers.
Dr Dorothy Price Papers.
Maire Nic Shiubhlaigh Papers.
Sinn Fein Comhairle Ceanntair Rolls.
R.I.C. Précis of Seized Documents—Sinn Fein Correspondence.
2nd Southern Division Documents.
2nd Battalion, Dublin Brigade Documents.

Irish Military Archives

I.R.A. Papers (A/ series or Collins Papers).
Cork Command Operations and Intelligence Reports.
Prison Ledgers, Prisoners' Location Books, and Charge Records.
National Army Census.
National Army Enlistment and Discharge Register.
Liaison Papers.
Special Infantry Corps Papers.
Department of Defence Miscellaneous Papers (DOD A/ series).

National Archives

Chief Secretary's Office Registered Papers.
General Prisons Board Records.
Manuscript Census Returns, 1901 and 1911.
Dail Eireann Courts (Winding Up) Commission Records.
Dail Eireann Records (DE/2).
Dail Eireann Local Government Records.
Department of Finance Records.
Department of Justice Records.
Department of Taoiseach General Files.
Sinn Fein Papers.
Sinn Fein Funds Case Files.

Irish Valuation Office

Land Valuation and Ownership Records and Maps.

Trinity College

Erskine Childers Papers.
Frank Gallagher Papers.

Representative Church Body Library

Ballyvourney Preacher's Book.
Macroom Preacher's Book.
E. H. Ussher Papers.

Grand Lodge of Freemasons Archive

Grand Lodge Register of Members.
Annual Reports.

London

Public Record Office

Colonial Office

Sir John Anderson Papers.
Censorship (Summaries and Précis) Reports.
Irish Free State Correspondence.
Irish Grants Committee Papers.
Irish Office Press Statements.
R.I.C. Inspector General and County Inspectors' Monthly Reports.
R.I.C. Illegal Drilling Reports.
R.I.C. Breaches of the Truce Reports.
R.I.C. Weekly Summaries, 1920–1.
R.I.C. Inquiries into Police Attacks.

War Office

Files on Sinn Fein Activists.
Military Courts of Inquiry Reports.
Registers of Military Prisoners and Internees.
Register and Prosecution Records of Civilians Tried by Courts-Martial.
Register of Courts of Inquiry in lieu of Inquests.
Report on the Intelligence Branch of the Chief of Police.
Dublin District Raid and Search Reports.
Dublin District and 5th Division War Diaries.

Cabinet Office

Weekly Surveys of the State of Ireland.
Cabinet Papers (miscellaneous).

Home Office

R.I.C. General Register.

Other

Midleton Papers.
Mark Sturgis Diaries.
William Evelyn Wylie MS Memoirs.

Imperial War Museum

Manuscripts

J. E. P. Brass MS 'Diary of a War Cadet 1914–1921'.
E. Craig-Brown Papers.
Sir John French Papers.
H . . ., D.F. MS 'A Side Show in Southern Ireland 1920'.
L. A. Hawes MS 'Kwab-O-Kayal: The Memories and Dreams of an Ordinary Soldier'.
Sir Hugh Jeudwine Papers.
Lord Loch Papers.
A. E. Percival Papers.
Cecil Plumb Papers.
Sir Peter Strickland Papers.
Private J. Swindlehurst Diary.
Douglas Wimberly MS 'Scottish Soldier'.

Department of Sound Recordings (Interviews)

Albert H. Bradshaw.
Bertram Neyland.

Liddell Hart Centre for Military Archives

Frederick Arthur Stanley Clarke MS 'The Memoirs of a Professional Soldier in Peace and War'.
Charles Howard Foulkes Papers.

National Army Museum
E. N. Evelegh Papers.

House of Lords Record Department
David Lloyd George Papers.

Cork

Cork Archives Institute
Daniel Corkery Papers (Seized by R.I.C.).
Ferris Papers.
Seamus Fitzgerald Papers.
Donal Hales Papers.
Roibeard Langford Papers.
Siobhan Lankford Papers.
Terence MacSwiney Papers.
Muiris Meadhach Papers.
Con Neenan MS 'Some Rapid Observations' (on Seamus O Maoileoin, *B'Fhiu An Braon Fola*).
Liam de Roiste Papers.
Cork Industrial Development Association Reports.
Malicious Injury Claims Reports.

Cork County Museum
Tom Daly MS Memoirs.
Michael Leahy Papers.
Tomas MacCurtain Papers.
Terence MacSwiney Papers.

County Cork Library
Bartholomew Walsh MS Memoirs.
Douglas Community School. The Rank and File Response: Cork City Corps, Irish Volunteers, 14 Dec. 1913–30 Aug. 1914. Unpublished essay, 1988.

YMCA Records
General Committee minute book, 1904–42.

Belfast

Queen's University Special Collections
Somerville and Ross Papers.

Public Record Office of Northern Ireland
John Kerr Papers.
John Regan MS Memoirs.

Irish Unionist Alliance Papers.
Southern Irish Loyalist Relief Association Papers.

Grand Orange Lodge of Ireland Archives
Reports of the Proceedings of the Grand Orange Lodge of Ireland at the General Half-
    Yearly Meeting.

Other

Abbeystrewrey Parish Union
Centenary File.

Boston Public Library
Cork 1916 Men's Association MS 'Comments on Florence O'Donoghue's Life of Tomas
    MacCurtain'.
I.R.A. General Orders (New Series).

Buffs Regiment Museum, Canterbury City Museum
1st Battalion, War Diary, 1920–1921.
—— Detachment Logs and Diaries, 1920–1.
—— Historical Records, 1920–2.

Carrigrohane Parish Union
Vestry Minute Books.

Fanlobbus Parish Union
Vestry Minute Books.

*King's (Liverpool) Regiment Collection, Regional History Department, National
Museums and Galleries on Merseyside*
1st Battalion Digest of Service, 1919–22.

Manchester Regiment Archives, Tameside Local Studies Library
Lt. Col. Dorling Papers.
1st Battalion, Record of Service, 1919–22.
—— Digest of Service, 1910–40.
—— Record of Arrests in Ireland 1921.

Peter Liddle Collection, Leeds University Library
John Barry Arnold MS Memoirs.
Malcolm E. Bickle Papers.
N. M. Hughes-Hallett MS 'With 2/KSLI in Ireland 1919–22'.

Queen's Lancashire Regiment Museum
2nd Battalion Loyal (North Lancashire), CO's Diary, 1921.
—— Digest of Service, 1919–22.
2nd Battalion East Lancashire Digest of Service, 1919–22.

Royal Gloucestershire Regiment Archives

1st Battalion Intelligence Officer's Diary, 1920–2.
Regimental Records, Twentieth Century, Vol. 1: 1900–39.

Staffordshire Regiment Museum

Lt. Col. M. B. Savage MS 'Looking Back: The Story of my Life'.
2nd Battalion South Staffordshire Digest of Service, 1919–22.
Major H. Billings Answers to Questionnaire.

West Cork Regional Museum, Clonakilty

I.R.A. Unit Rolls.
Minute Book of the Lord Carbery Branch, Irish National Volunteers.

In Private Possession

Bureau of Military History Company Rolls (officer lists and unit strengths).
Marie O'Donoghue Papers.
Bill Hales Papers.

Contemporary Newspapers and Periodicals

An tOglach.
Belfast News-Letter.
Christian Advocate.
Church of Ireland Gazette.
Cork Constitution.
Cork County Eagle.
Cork Examiner.
Cork Free Press.
Cork Weekly Examiner.
Essex Regiment Gazette.
Freeman's Journal.
Hampshire Regimental Journal.
Irish Farmer.
Irish Statesman.
Irish Times.
Lilywhites' Gazette. (Journal of the East Lancashire Regiment)
Manchester Regimental Gazette.
Morning Post.
Mungret Annual.
Notes from Ireland.
Plain People.
The 79th News. (Journal of the Cameron Highlanders Regiment)
Southern Star.
The Times.

GOVERNMENT PUBLICATIONS

Great Britain

Report of the Royal Commission on Congestion in Ireland, HC 1907 (Cd. 3786).
—— 1908 (Cd. 3839).
Census of Ireland, 1911: Province of Munster, HC 1912–13 (Cd. 6050).
—— *General Report* (Cd. 6663).
Appendix to the Report of the Committee of Inquiry into the Royal Irish Constabulary and the Dublin Metropolitan Police, HC 1914, xliv (Cd. 7637).
Emigration Statistics (Ireland) 1914, HC 1914 (Cd. 7883).
Report and Minutes of the Royal Commission on the Rebellion in Ireland, HC 1916 (Cd. 8311).
Judicial Statistics, Ireland, HC 1917/18 (Cd. 8636).
—— 1918 (Cd. 9066).
—— 1919 (Cd. 43, 438).
—— 1921 (Cd. 1431).
Documents Relative to the Sinn Fein Movement, HC 1921, xxix (Cd. 1108).

Ireland

Official Report: Debate on the Treaty between Great Britain and Ireland (Dublin, n.d.).
Saorstat Eireann, Census of Population 1926.

INTERVIEWS

Between 1988 and 1994 I interviewed thirteen Cork I.R.A. veterans, two women activists (one of whom had been a member of Cumann na mBan), and approximately the same number of contemporaries and relatives. In 1993, 1994, and 1996 (as part of a forthcoming study) I talked to thirty members of Protestant churches about their experiences of the revolution, a portion of which material is used here. As a large number of these interviewees requested that part or all of their testimony be quoted anonymously, I refer to them using initials only. The republican activists' initials begin with 'A'; Protestant men and women begin with 'B'. I was also kindly given permission to hear and quote interviews taped by Adrian Lewis (of an East Lancashire Regiment veteran), George O'Mahony, Donal O'Donovan, and Dr John Chisholm (the last also under condition of anonymity), as well as tapes held by the Ballineen/Enniskeane Area Heritage Group. A further set of useful taped interviews can be found in the RTE Archives, Dublin. The dates of individual interviews are given in relevant footnotes.

UNPUBLISHED THESES

BARRY, FINBARR, 'Geography of I.R.A. Activities in West Cork 1919–1921', BA thesis (Cork, 1991).
CROWLEY, JOHN, 'Cork's Jewish Community', BA thesis (Cork, 1987).

D'ALTON, IAN G., 'Southern Irish Unionism: A Study of Cork City and County Unionists, 1885–1914', MA thesis (Cork, 1972).

GRIFFIN, ANTHONY, 'The Origins, Growth and Influence of the G.A.A. in Cork City', BA thesis (Cork, 1988).

GRIFFIN, BRIAN, 'The Irish Police, 1836–1914: A Social History', Ph.D. thesis (Loyola University of Chicago, 1991).

LINEHAN, THOMAS ANTHONY, 'The Development of Cork's Economy and Business Attitudes 1910–1939', MA thesis (Cork, 1985).

LUCEY, DERMOT J., 'Cork Public Opinion and the First World War', MA thesis (Cork, 1972).

MAGNER, EILEEN, 'Sean Moylan: Some Aspect of his Parliamentary Career 1937–1948', MA thesis (Cork, 1982).

MAGUIRE, GLORIA, 'The Political and Military Causes of the Division in the Irish Nationalist Movement, January 1921 to August 1922', D.Phil. thesis (Oxford, 1985).

MURPHY, MAURA J. B., 'The Role of Organized Labour in the Political and Economic Life of Cork City, 1820–1899', Ph.D. thesis (Leicester, 1979).

REDDICK, STEPHEN McQUAY, 'Political and Industrial Labour in Cork 1899–1914', MA thesis (Cork, 1984).

STAUNTON, MARTIN, 'The Royal Munster Fusiliers in the Great War, 1914–1919', MA thesis (Dublin, 1986).

PUBLISHED WORKS: CORK

This section includes those books and articles which deal specifically with events in Cork, or those which include Cork material in an otherwise non-Irish context. Thus, for example, it includes regimental histories of units which served in the county between 1916 and 1922, even where this service might occupy only a small portion of the book. The second section lists works referred to in this book which deal with the rest of Ireland or Ireland in general.

AHERN, MADGE, *Inniscarra Looks Back* (Carrigrohane, 1995).

ALLEN, ALFRED, *A Mist in Moonlight* (Cork, 1992).

BARRY, TOM, 'The Story of the Kilmichael Ambush', *Irish Press* (26 Nov. 1932).

—— 'Auxiliaries Wiped out at Kilmichael in their First Clash with the I.R.A.', in *With the I.R.A. in the Fight for Freedom* (Tralee, n.d).

—— *Guerilla Days in Ireland* (Dublin, 1949, 1981).

—— *The Reality of the Anglo-Irish War 1920–21 in West Cork: Refutations, Corrections and Comments on Liam Deasy's Towards Ireland Free* (Dublin, 1974).

BEECHER, SEAN, *The Story of Cork* (Cork, 1971).

—— *A Dictionary of Cork Slang* (Cork, 1983).

BELL, ANNE OLIVIER, *The Diary of Virginia Woolf* (New York, 1978).

BENNETT, GEORGE, *The History of Bandon and the Principal Towns in the West Riding of County Cork* (Cork, 1869).

BIELENBERG, ANDY, *Cork's Industrial Revolution 1780–1880: Development or Decline?* (Cork, 1991).

BLYTHE, ERNEST, 'Kerry Better Than Cork in 1915', *An tÓglach* (Christmas 1962).

BOWEN, ELIZABETH, *Bowen's Court* (London, 1942).

BRADLEY, DAN, *Farm Labourers: Irish Struggle 1900–1976* (Belfast, 1988).

BROWNE, CHARLIE, *The Story of the 7th* (Macroom, n.d.).

BURKE-GAFFNEY, Lt. Col. J. J., *The Story of the King's Regiment 1914–1948* (Liverpool, 1954).

BURROWS, JOHN WILLIAM, *Essex Units in the War, 1914–1919*, i (Southend-on-Sea, 1923).

BUTLER, EWAN, *Barry's Flying Column* (London, 1971).

CANNIFFE, PAT, 'The Eviction at Knocknacurra', *Bandon Historical Journal* (1989).

CHAVASSE, MOIRON, *Terence MacSwiney* (Dublin, 1961).

Christians: The First Hundred Years. A Celebration of 100 Years of Christian Brothers College Cork (Cork, 1989).

CLARKE, OLGA PYNE, *She Came of Decent People* (London, 1985).

CLIFFORD, BRENDAN (ed.), *Reprints from the 'Cork Free Press': An Account of Ireland's Only Democratic Anti-Partition Movement* (Cork, 1984).

—— *Duhallow: Notes toward a History* (Cork, 1986).

—— and LANE, JACK (eds.), *A North Cork Miscellany* (Cork, 1987).

—— —— (eds.), *Ned Buckley's Poems* (Cork, 1987).

Clonakilty and District, 1916 (Cork, 1966).

COAKLEY, D. J. (ed.), *Cork: Its Trade and Commerce. Official Handbook of the Cork Inc. Chamber of Commerce and Shipping* (Cork, 1919).

CONLAN, LIL, *Cumann na mBan and the Women of Ireland 1913–25* (Kilkenny, 1969).

COOGAN, TIM PAT, *Michael Collins* (London, 1990).

COOKE, RICHARD T., *Cork's Barrack Street Band: Ireland's Oldest Amateur Musical Institution* (Cork, 1992).

CORKERY, DANIEL, 'Of Visions National and International', *Irish Statesman*, 2 Mar. 1924.

COSTELLO, FRANCIS J., *Enduring the Most: The Life and Death of Terence MacSwiney* (Dingle, 1995).

CRONIN, MAURA, 'Work and Workers in Cork City and County 1800–1900', in P. O'Flanagan and C. G. Buttimer (eds.), *Cork: History and Society* (Dublin, 1993).

—— *County, Class or Craft? The Politicisation of the Skilled Artisan in Nineteenth-Century Cork* (Cork, 1994).

CROWLEY, FLOR ['Raymond'], 'Black and Tan Diary', *Southern Star* (23 Oct.–27 Nov. 1971).

—— *In West Cork Long Ago* (Cork, 1979).

CROZIER, F. P., *Ireland for Ever* (London, 1932).

CULLOTY, A. T., *Ballydesmond: A Rural Parish in its Historical Setting* (Dublin, 1986).

D'ALTON, IAN, 'Southern Irish Unionism: A Study of Cork Unionists, 1884–1914', *Transactions of the Royal Historical Society* (1973).

—— 'Cork Unionism: Its Role in Parliamentary and Local Elections, 1885–1914', *Studia Hibernica* (1975).

—— 'Keeping Faith: An Evocation of the Cork Protestant Character, 1820–1920' in P. O'Flanagan and C. G. Buttimer (eds.), *Cork: History and Society* (Dublin, 1993).

DEASY, LIAM, 'The Beara Peninsula Campaign', *Eire-Ireland* (Fall 1966).

—— 'The Schull Peninsula in the War of Independence', *Eire-Ireland* (Summer 1967).

—— 'The Brave Men of Kilbrittain', *Star* (10 Apr. 1971).

—— 'The Gallant Volunteers of Kilbrittain', *An tOglach* (Summer 1971).

—— *Towards Ireland Free* (Cork, 1973).

—— *Brother against Brother* (Cork, 1982).

DE ROISTE, LIAM, 'Mar Is Cuimin Liom', *Evening Echo* (19 Aug.–6 Nov. 1954).

DONNELLY, JAMES, Jr., *The Land and People of Nineteenth Century Cork* (London, 1975).

DUGGAN, JOHN J., *Grenagh and Courtbrack during the Struggle for Independence 1914–1924* (Cork, 1973).

DUNNE, SEAN (ed.), *The Cork Anthology* (Cork, 1993).

EVERETT, KATHERINE, *Bricks and Flowers* (London, 1949).

Evidence on Conditions in Ireland Presented before the American Commission on Conditions in Ireland (Washington, 1921).

FAHY, A. M., 'Place and Class in Cork', in P. O'Flanagan and C. G. Buttimer (eds.), *Cork: History and Society* (Dublin, 1993).

FALLON, CHARLOTTE H., *Soul of Fire: A Biography of Mary MacSwiney* (Cork, 1986).

FEENEY, P. J., *Glory O, Glory O, Ye Bold Fenian Men: A History of the Sixth Battalion Cork First Brigade 1913–1921* (Dripsey, 1996).

FERRAR, Major M. L., *Officers of the Green Howards 1688–1931* (Belfast, 1931).

FITZGERALD, SEAMUS, 'In English Prisons 1916–17', *Capuchin Annual* (1967).

—— 'East Cork Activities—1920', *Capuchin Annual* (1970).

FLEMING, LIONEL, *Head or Harp* (London, 1965).

FLYNN, CORNELIUS, 'My Part in Irish Independence', *Bandon Historical Journal* (1988).

FOLEY, CON, *A History of Douglas* (Cork, 1991).

Ford in Ireland: The First Sixty Years, 1917–1977 (Dublin, 1977)

GALVIN, MICHAEL, *Kilmurry Volunters 1915–1921* (Cork, 1994).

GLENFLESK, DENIS SPILLANE, 'Rathmore: E Company, 5th Battalion: Kerry No 2 Brigade', *Sliabh Luachra* (Nov. 1983).

GOLDEN, PETER, *Impressions of Ireland* (New York, 1923).

GRIFFITH, KENNETH, and O'GRADY, TIMOTHY, *Curious Journey: An Oral History of Ireland's Unfinished Revolution* (London, 1982).

HAMILTON, NIGEL, *Monty: The Making of a General 1887–1942* (London, 1981).

HAMMOND, BILL, *Soldier of the Rearguard: The Story of Matt Flood and the Active Service Column* (Fermoy, 1977).

HART, PETER, 'Youth Culture and the Cork I.R.A.', in David Fitzpatrick (ed.), *Revolution? Ireland 1917–1923* (Dublin, 1990).

—— 'Class, Community and the Irish Republican Army in Cork, 1917–23', in P. O'Flanagan and C. G. Buttimer (eds.), *Cork: History and Society* (Dublin, 1993).

History and Dedication Ceremony of Bandon Masonic Lodge 84 (Cork, 1926).

HOARE, M. JESSE, *The Road to Glenanore* (London, 1975).

HOGAN, DAVID [Frank Gallagher], *The Four Glorious Years* (Dublin, 1953).

HORGAN, JOHN J., *Parnell to Pearse: Some Recollections and Reflections* (Dublin, 1948).

HURWITZ, CECIL, *From Synagogue to Church* (Cork, 1991).

JACKSON, JOHN, *Report on Skibbereen Social Survey* (Dublin, 1967).

JACOBSON, D. S., 'The Political Economy of Industrial Location: The Ford Motor Company at Cork 1912–26', *Irish Economic and Social History* (1977).

KEANE, BARRY, 'The Church of Ireland Population in County Cork (1911–1926)', *Chimera* (May 1986).

KELLEHER, JAMES, *Memories of Macroom* (Blarney, 1995).

KEOHANE, JOHNNY, and BILLING, KAREN, *Neath the Blackthorn: An Anecdotal History of Drinagh, West Cork* (Cork, 1990).

KNIGHT, Col. C. R. B., *Historical Records of the Buffs (Royal East Kent Regiment) 3rd Foot 1919–1948* (London, 1951).

LANKFORD, SIOBHAN, *The Hope and the Sadness* (Cork, 1980).

LEWIN, RONALD, *Man of Armour: A Study of Lieut-General Vyvyan Pope* (London, 1976).

LOWE, Brevet Major T. A., 'Some Reflections of a Junior Commander upon "The Campaign" in Ireland 1920 and 1921', *Army Quarterly* (Oct. 1922).

LYNCH, DENIS, 'The Years of Ambushes and Round-ups', *Sliabh Luacra* (1989).

LYNCH, PATRICK, 'Drishanebeg Train Ambush Yielded Fourteen Rifles to Millstreet Column', in *With the I.R.A. in the Fight for Freedom: 1919 to the Truce* (Tralee, n.d.).

MCAULIFFE, JOHN, 'The Troubled Times in Cloyne', *The Book of Cloyne* (Cork, 1977).

MCCANN, JOHN, *War by the Irish* (Tralee, 1946).

MCCARTHY, KIERAN, and CHRISTENSEN, MAJ-BRITT, *Cobh's Contribution to the Fight for Irish Freedom 1913–1990* (Cobh, 1992).

MCDONNELL, KATHLEEN KEYES, *There is a Bridge at Bandon* (Cork, 1972).

MACSWEENEY, A. M., *Poverty in Cork* (Cork, 1917).

MAUME, PATRICK, *'Life That is Exile': Daniel Corkery and the Search for Irish Ireland* (Belfast, 1993).

MEHIGAN, P. D., 'Across Duhallow Border: Reminiscences of the Anglo-Irish War', *Carbery's Annual* (Christmas 1940).

—— 'When I was Young', *Carbery's Annual* (1945–6).

Memories of Dromleigh, a Country School: 1840–1990 (1990).

MEMORY, F. W., *'Memory's': Being the Adventures of a Newspaperman* (London, 1932).

MEWS, STUART, 'The Hunger-Strike of the Lord Mayor of Cork, 1920: Irish, English and Vatican Attitudes', in W. J. Sheils and Diana Wood (eds.), *The Churches, Ireland and the Irish* (Oxford, 1989).

MITCHELL, MAUD, *The Man with the Long Hair: The Spirit of Freedom in a Woman's Story* (Glenwood, 1993).

MOORE, H. KINGSMILL, *Reminiscences and Reflections* (London, 1930).

MURPHY, DONIE, *'The Men of the South' in the War of Independence* (Inchintotane, 1991).

MURPHY, JOHN A., 'Cork: Anatomy and Essence', in P. O'Flanagan and C. G. Buttimer (eds.), *Cork: History and Society* (Dublin, 1993).

MURPHY, M., 'Financial Results on Mixed Dairy Farms in 1937–'38', *Journal of the Statistical Society of Ireland* (1938–9).

—— 'Financial Results on Sixty-One West Cork Farms in 1940–'41', *Journal of the Statistical Society of Ireland* (1941–2).

MURPHY, MAURA, 'The Economic and Social Structure of Nineteenth Century Cork', in David Harkness and Mary O'Dowd (eds.), *The Town in Ireland* (Belfast, 1981).

MURPHY, NED, *Newcestown: Echoes of the Past* (Midleton, 1995).

MURPHY, SEAMUS, *Stone Mad* (London, 1966).

O'BRIEN, BARRY, *A History of the Macroom G.A.A. Club 1886–1987* (n.d.).

O'BRIEN, JOHN, 'Population, Politics and Society in Cork, 1780–1900', in P. O'Flanagan and C. G. Buttimer (eds.), *Cork: History and Society* (Dublin, 1993).

O'BRIEN, JOSEPH V., *William O'Brien and the Course of Irish Politics 1881–1918* (Berkeley, 1976).

O'BRIEN, Mrs WILLIAM [Sophie], *In Mallow* (London, 1920).

O'CALLAGHAN, SEAN, *Execution* (London, 1974).

—— *Down by the Glenside: Memoirs of an Irish Boyhood* (Cork, 1992).

O'CONNELL, Comdt., DENIS, 'Paddy O'Brien and North Cork's Fight for Freedom', *Seanchas Duthalla* (1991).

O'CONNELL, MICHAEL, 'The Craft of the Cooper in Clonakilty', *Seanchas Chairbre* (Dec. 1982).

O'CONNOR, FRANK, *An Only Child* (London, 1961).

O'DONOGHUE, FLORENCE, 'The Irish Volunteers in Cork 1913–1916', *Journal of the Cork Historical and Archaeological Society* (Jan.–Dec. 1966).

—— 'Rescue of Donnchadha MacNeilus from Cork Jail', in *Sworn to be Free: The Complete Book of I.R.A. Jailbreaks 1918–1921* (Tralee, 1971).

—— *Tomas MacCurtain: Soldier and Patriot* (Tralee, 1971).

—— *No Other Law* (Dublin, 1986).

O'DONOVAN, PEADAR, 'Why West Cork's Major Role was so Successful', in *Southern Star Centenary Supplement* (Skibbereen, 1989).

O'DWYER, LIAM, *Beara in Irish History* (New York, 1977).

O'FAOLAIN, SEAN, *An Irish Journey* (New York, 1943).

—— 'The Plain People of Ireland', *Bell* (Oct. 1943).

—— *Vive Moi!* (Boston, 1963).

O'FLANAGAN, PATRICK, and BUTTIMER, CORNELIUS G. (eds.), *Cork: History and Society* (Dublin, 1993).

O'HEGARTY, P. S., 'The Wren Boys', *Bealoideas* (1943–4).

O'LEARY, CON, *Wayfarer in Ireland* (London, 1935).

O'LEARY, DANIEL, *Kilmeen and Castleventry Parish* (Jerry Beechinor, 1975).

O'MAHONY, COLMAN, *The Maritime Gateway to Cork* (Cork, 1986).

O'MAHONY, EDWARD, 'The Death of Michael Collins', *Magill* (May 1989).

O'MAHONY, JEREMIAH, *West Cork and its Story* (Cork, 1961, 1975).

O'MAHONY, SEAN, *The History and Folklore of Carrigaline* (Carrigaline, 1993).

O MAOILEOIN, SEAMUS, *B'Fhiu An Braon Fola* (Dublin, 1958).

O'NEILL, STEPHEN, 'The Ambush at Kilmichael', *Kerryman Christmas Number* (Dec. 1937).

O'REGAN, MAURICE, 'When the I.R.A. Split on Class Issues', *Labour News* (21 Aug. 1937).

O'RIORDAN, JOHN J., *Kiskeam and That Way Back* (Limerick, 1969).

—— *Kiskeam Versus the Empire* (Tralee, 1985).

—— *Where Araglen So Gently Flows* (Tralee, 1989).

O'RIORDAN, TOMAS, *The Price of Freedom* (Cork, 1971).

—— *Where the Owenacurra Flows: A History of the Parish of Lisgoold* (Cork, n.d.).

—— *Where Martyred Heroes Rest: The Story of the Republican Plot Kilcrumper, Fermoy* (Cork, 1987).

O'SUILLEABHAIN, MICHEAL, *Where Mountainy Men Have Sown* (Tralee, 1965).

O'SULLIVAN, JOHN L., *By Carrigdonn and Owenabue* (Ballinhassig, 1990).

Oxford and Buckinghamshire Light Infantry Chronicle, 1919–1920 (London, 1921).

Oxford and Buckinghamshire Light Infantry Chronicle, 1921 (London, 1922).

Oxford and Buckinghamshire Light Infantry Chronicle, 1922 (London, 1923).

Rebel Cork's Fighting Story (Tralee, n.d.).

Record of Activities: 7th Battalion, Cork No. 1 Brigade (Macroom, n.d.).

RING, DENIS PAUL, *Macroom through the Mists of Time: An Historical Geography of Macroom c.500–1995* (Carrigadrohid, 1995).

ROBINSON, LENNOX, ROBINSON, TOM, and DORMAN, NORA, *Three Homes* (London, 1938).

ROCHE, CHRISTY (ed.), *The Ford of the Apples: A History of Ballyhooly* (Fermoy, 1988).

RUISEAL, LIAM, *Liam Ruiseal Remembers* (Cork, 1978).

RUSSELL of Liverpool, Lord, *That Reminds Me* (London, 1959).

RYAN, MEDA, *The Tom Barry Story* (Cork, 1982).

—— *The Real Chief: The Story of Liam Lynch* (Cork, 1986).

—— *The Day Michael Collins Was Shot* (Swords, 1989).

'SASSENACH', *Arms and the Irishman* (London, 1932).

SHEEHAN, Cpt. D. D., *Ireland since Parnell* (London, 1921).

SHEEHAN, TIM, *Lady Hostage (Mrs. Lindsay)* (Dripsey, 1990).

—— *Execute Hostage Compton-Smith* (Dripsey, 1993).

SMYTH, WILLIAM J., 'Explorations of Space', in Joseph Lee (ed.), *Ireland: Towards a Sense of Place* (Cork, 1985).

—— 'The Personality of West Cork', *Chimera*, Parts 1 and 2 (1989–90).

SOMERVILLE-LARGE, PETER, *Cappaghglass* (Dublin, 1984).

Southern Star Centenary Supplement 1889–1989 (Skibbereen, 1989).

The Spirit of Freedom; Prize Winning Entries in the Bobby Sands Commemoration School Essay Competition (Dublin: 1983).

'Troubled Times . . . A First Hand Account of Bog Road Ambush', *Sliabh Luacra* (June 1982).

'The Troubles of 1920–1921', *Stafford Knot* (Oct. 1971).

TWOHIG, P. J., *Green Tears for Hecuba* (Dublin, 1979).

—— *The Dark Secret of Bealnablath* (Cork, 1991).

TWOMEY, MAURICE, 'The Story of Liam Lynch', *An Phoblacht* (23 Apr. 1932).

VERDON, MICHAEL, *Shawlies, Echo Boys, the Marsh and the Lanes: Old Cork Remembered* (Dublin, 1993).

WALSH, J. J., *Recollections of a Rebel* (Tralee, 1949).

WALSH, JOE, *The Story of Dick Barrett* (Cork, 1972).

WHELDON, HEW (ed.), *Monitor: An Anthology* (London, 1962).

WHITE, JACK, *Minority Report: The Protestant Community in the Irish Republic* (Dublin, 1975).

WHITE, TERENCE DE VERE, 'The Shooting of Mrs. Lindsay', *Irish Times* (17 Oct. 1978).

The Wild Heather Glen: The Kilmichael Story of Grief and Glory (Ballineen/Enniskeane, 1995).

'Working for Farmers', *Sliabh Luacra* (June 1987).

OTHER PUBLISHED WORKS

ANDERSON, MICHAEL, 'The Social Implications of Demographic Change', in F. M. L. Thompson (ed.), *The Cambridge Social History of Britain 1750–1950*, ii (Cambridge, 1990).

ANDREWS, C. S., *Dublin Made Me* (Dublin, 1979).

'Are Villages Less National Than Country Districts?', *An Phoblacht* (31 Dec. 1926).

ARENSBERG, CONRAD M., *The Irish Countryman* (Garden City, NY, 1968).

—— and Kimball, Solon T., *Family and Community in Ireland* (Cambridge, Mass., 1968).

AUGUSTEIJN, JOOST, *From Public Defiance to Guerrilla Warfare: The Experience of Ordinary Volunteers in the Irish War of Independence, 1916–1921* (Dublin, 1996).

'Bad Influence in our Townland', *An Phoblacht* (7 Jan. 1927).

BAGENAL, PHILIP, 'The Royal Irish Constabulary; and Sinn Fein', *Nineteenth Century and After* (July 1922).

BEAMES, MICHAEL, *Peasants and Power: The Whiteboy Movements and their Control in Pre-Famine Ireland* (Brighton, 1983).

BENNETT, RICHARD, 'Portrait of a Killer', *New Statesman* (24 Mar. 1961).

BEW, PAUL, *Conflict and Conciliation in Ireland 1890–1910: Parnellites and Radical Agrarians* (Oxford, 1987).

BIRMINGHAM, GEORGE, *Irishmen All* (London, 1913).

—— *An Irishman Looks at his World* (London, 1919).

BOYCE, D. G. and HAZLEHURST, CAMERON, 'The Unknown Chief Secretary: H. E. Duke and Ireland, 1916–18', *Irish Historical Studies* (Mar. 1977).

BREEN, DAN, *My Fight for Irish Freedom* (Tralee, 1964).

BRENNAN, JOHN, 'Frongoch University—and After', in *Dublin's Fighting Story 1916–21* (Tralee, 1945).

BRENNAN, MICHAEL, *The War in Clare 1911–1921: Personal Memoirs of the War of Independence* (Dublin, 1980).

BRETHERTON, C. H., 'Irish Backgrounds', *Atlantic Monthly* (Dec. 1922).

—— *The Real Ireland* (London, 1925).

BREWER, JOHN D., *The Royal Irish Constabulary: An Oral History* (Belfast, 1990).

BUCKLAND, PATRICK, *Irish Unionism*, i: The *Anglo-Irish and the New Ireland 1885–1922* (Dublin, 1972).

CAMPBELL, COLM, *Emergency Law in Ireland 1918–1925* (Oxford, 1994).

COLUM, PADRAIC, *Arthur Griffith* (Dublin, 1959).

COMERFORD, JAMES J., *My Kilkenny I.R.A. Days 1916–22* (Kilkenny, 1978).

COOGAN, OLIVER, *Politics and War in Meath 1913–23* (Dublin, 1983).

DALTON, CHARLES, *With the Dublin Brigade (1917–1921)* (London, 1929).

DUFF, DOUGLAS V., *Sword for Hire* (London, 1934).

FIGGIS, DARRELL, *Recollections of the Irish War* (London, 1927).

FITZPATRICK, DAVID, *Politics and Irish Life 1913–1921: Provincial Experience of War and Revolution* (Dublin, 1977).

—— 'The Geography of Irish Nationalism 1910–1921', *Past and Present* (Feb. 1978).

—— 'The Logic of Collective Sacrifice: Ireland and the British Army, 1914–1918', *Historical Journal* (1995).

FLACKES, W. D., *Northern Ireland: A Political Directory* (London, 1983).

GAILEY, ALAN, *Irish Folk Drama* (Cork, 1969).

GARVIN, TOM, *The Evolution of Irish Nationalist Politics* (Dublin, 1981).

—— *Nationalist Revolutionaries in Ireland, 1858–1928* (Oxford, 1987).

GAUGHAN, J. ANTHONY, *Austin Stack: Portrait of a Separatist* (Mount Merrion, 1977).

GILBERT, MARTIN, *Winston S. Churchill*, companion volume iv, part 2 (Boston, 1978).

GLASSIE, HENRY, *All Silver and No Brass* (Dublin, 1975).

GLEESON, JAMES, *Bloody Sunday* (London, 1962).

GODLEY, Gen. Sir ALEXANDER, *Life of an Irish Soldier* (London, 1939).

HACKETT, FRANCIS, *Ireland: A Study in Nationalism* (New York, 1918).

HADDEN, Dr GEORGE, 'The War on the Railways in Wexford 1922–23', *Journal of the Irish Railway Record Society* (Autumn 1953).

HANNAN, DAMIEN, 'Kinship, Neighbourhood and Social Change in Irish Rural Communities', *Economic and Social Review* (Jan. 1972).

HARRIS, ROSEMARY, *Prejudice and Tolerance in Ulster* (Manchester, 1972).

HART, PETER, 'The Thompson Submachine Gun in Ireland, Revisited', *Irish Sword* (Summer 1995).

—— 'The Protestant Experience of Revolution in Southern Ireland, 1911–1926', in Richard English and Graham Walker (eds.), *Unionism in Modern Ireland: New Perspectives on Politics and Culture* (London, 1996).

—— 'The Geography of Revolution in Ireland, 1917–1923', *Past and Present* (May 1997).

—— 'The Social Structure of the Irish Republican Army, 1916–1923', *Historical Journal* (March 1999).

HARVEY, A. D., 'Who Were the Auxiliaries?', *Historical Journal* (Sept. 1992).

HAWKINS, RICHARD, 'Dublin Castle and the R.I.C. (1916–1922)', in T. Desmond Williams (ed.), *The Irish Struggle 1916–1926* (London, 1966).

HEADLAM, MAURICE, *Irish Reminiscences* (London, 1947).

HOPKINSON, MICHAEL, *Green against Green: A History of the Irish Civil War* (Dublin, 1988).

HYMAN, LOUIS, *The Jews of Ireland from Earliest Times to the Year 1910* (Shannon, 1972).

'I.O.' [C. J. C. Street], *The Administration of Ireland 1920* (London, 1921).

KANE, EILEEN, 'Man and Kin in Donegal', *Ethnology* (1968).

KAVANAGH, PATRICK, *The Green Fool* (Harmondsworth, 1975).

KENNEDY, ROBERT E., *The Irish: Emigration, Marriage, and Fertility* (Berkeley, Calif. 1973).

KEVIN, NEIL, *I Remember Karrigeen* (London, 1944).

KOTSONOURIS, MARY, *Retreat from Revolution: The Dail Courts, 1920–24* (Dublin, 1994).

LARKIN, EMMET, *James Larkin: Irish Labour Leader 1876–1947* (London, 1965).

LAVERTY, MAURA, *Never No More* (London, 1942).

LEONARD, JANE, 'Getting Them at Last: The I.R.A. and Ex-servicemen', in D. Fitzpatrick (ed.), *Revolution? Ireland 1917–1923* (Dublin, 1999).

LEVENSON, LEAH and NATTERSTAD, JERRY H., *Hanna Sheehy-Skeffington: Irish Feminist* (Syracuse, NY, 1986).

LEWIS, GEORGE CORNEWELL, *Local Disturbances in Ireland* (Cork, 1977).

LYNCH, FIONAN, 'Recollections of Jail Riots and Hunger Strikes—Grim Times in Mountjoy, Dundalk and Belfast Jails', in *Sworn to be Free: The Complete Book of I.R.A. Jailbreaks 1918–1921* (Tralee, 1971).

MACEOIN, UINSEANN, *Survivors* (Dublin, 1980).

MCKEOWN, MICHAEL, *Two Seven Six Three: An Analysis of Fatalities Attributable to Civil Disturbances in Northern Ireland in the Twenty Years between July 13, 1969 and July 12, 1989* (Lucan, 1989).

McNabb, Patrick, 'Social Structure', in Jeremiah Newman (ed.), *The Limerick Rural Survey 1958–1964*, iv (Tipperary, 1964).

Macready, General Sir Nevil, *Annals of an Active Life* (London, 1924).

Martin, F. X. (ed.), *The Irish Volunteers 1913–1915: Recollections and Documents* (Dublin, 1963).

—— 'MacNeill and the Foundation of the Irish Volunteers', in F. X. Martin and F. J. Byrne (eds.), *The Scholar Revolutionary: Eoin MacNeill, 1867–1945, and the Making of a New Ireland* (Dublin, 1973).

Montmorency, Hervey de, *Sword and Stirrup* (London, 1936).

Mulcahy, Richard, 'The Irish Volunteer Convention 27 October, 1917', *Capuchin Annual* (1967).

Mullins, Billy, *The Memoirs of Billy Mullins: Veteran of the War of Independence* (Tralee, 1983).

Neeson, Eoin, *The Civil War 1922–23* (Swords, 1989).

O'Brien, George, *Village of Longing* (London, 1990).

O Broin, Leon, *Protestant Nationalists in Revolutionary Ireland: The Stopford Connection* (Dublin, 1985).

O'Callaghan, Miceal, *For Ireland and Freedom: Roscommon's Contribution to the Fight for Independence* (Boyle, n.d.).

O'Connor, Sir James, *A History of Ireland 1798–1924*, ii (London, 1925).

O'Connor, Seamus, *Tomorrow Was Another Day* (Dun Laoire, 1970, 1987).

O'Donnell, Peadar, *Not Yet Emmet* (Dublin, n.d.).

O'Donoghue, John, *In Kerry Long Ago* (London, 1960).

O Dulaing, Donncha, *Voices of Ireland* (Dublin, 1984).

O'Halpin, Eunan, 'H. E. Duke and the Irish Administration, 1916–18', *Irish Historical Studies* (Sept. 1981).

—— *The Decline of the Union: British Government in Ireland 1892–1920* (Dublin, 1987).

O'Hegarty, P. S., *The Victory of Sinn Fein* (Dublin, 1924).

O Mahony, Sean, *Frongoch: University of Revolution* (Killiney, 1987).

O'Malley, Cormac K. H. (ed.), 'Ernie O'Malley Autobiographical Letter', *Cathair na Mart*, 9, 1 (1989).

O'Malley, Ernie, *On Another Man's Wound* (Dublin, 1936).

—— *The Singing Flame* (Dublin, 1978).

O'Shea, Patrick, *Voices and the Sound of Drums* (Belfast, 1981).

Phillips, W. Alison, *The Revolution in Ireland* (London, 1923).

Quill, Shirley, *Mike Quill—Himself: A Memoir* (Greenwich, 1985).

Rumpf, E., and Hepburn, A. C., *Nationalism and Socialism in Twentieth-Century Ireland* (Liverpool, 1977).

Ryan, Desmond, *The Rising: The Complete Story of Easter Week* (Dublin, 1949).

—— *Sean Treacy and the 3rd Tipperary Brigade* (London, 1945).

Sheehan, Aideen, 'Cumann na mBan: Policies and Activities', in David Fitzpatrick (ed.), *Revolution? Ireland 1917–1923* (Dublin, 1990).

Shutes, Mark, 'Production and Social Change in a Rural Irish Parish', *Social Studies* (1987).

Silverman, Marilyn and Gulliver, P. H. (eds.), *Approaching the Past: Historical Anthropology through Irish Case Studies* (New York, 1992).

STRONG, Maj.-Gen. Sir KENNETH, *Intelligence at the Top: The Recollections of an Intelligence Officer* (London, 1968).

SUTTON, MALCOLM, *An Index of Deaths from the Conflict in Ireland 1969–1993* (Belfast, 1994).

TERY, SIMONE, 'French Reporter Visits Volunteers' Training Camp, "Somewhere" in Western Ireland, August 15, 1921' (trans. Marilyn Gaddis Rose), in Dennis Jackson (ed.) *Irish Renaissance Annual III* (Newark, NJ, 1982).

'Through an Ulsterman's Eyes: The Birth of the Irish Free State', *Atlantic Monthly* (Oct. 1922).

TOWNSHEND, CHARLES, *The British Campaign in Ireland 1919–1921* (Oxford, 1975).

—— 'The Irish Republican Army and the Development of Guerrilla Warfare, 1916–1921', *English Historical Review* (Apr. 1979).

VALIULIS, MARYANN GIALANELLA, *Portrait of a Revolutionary: General Richard Mulcahy and the Founding of the Irish Free State* (Dublin, 1992).

WALSH, LOUIS J., *'On my Keeping' and in Theirs* (Dublin, 1921).

WALSH, OONAGH, 'Testimony from Imprisoned Women', in David Fitzpatrick (ed.), *Revolution? Ireland 1917–1923* (Dublin, 1990).

WARD, MARGARET, *Unmanageable Revolutionaries* (London, 1983).

WILSON, THOMAS M., 'Culture and Class among the "Large" Farmers of Eastern Ireland', *American Ethnologist* (Nov. 1988).

WINTER, Sir ORMONDE, *Winter's Tale* (London, 1955).

Index

Printed in Great Britain
by Amazon

69806462R00210